Developing and Administering

A CHILD
CARE CENTER

THIRD EDITION

NOTICE TO THE READER

Cover Background: Jennifer McGlaughlin
Cover Design: Douglas Hyldelund

Delmar Staff

Acquisitions Editor: Jay Whitney
Developmental Editor: Christopher Anzalone
Project Editor: Theresa M. Bobear

Production Coordinator: Jennifer Gaines
Art & Design Coordinator: Douglas Hyldelund

COPYRIGHT © 1995
By Delmar Publishers Inc.
an International Thomson Publishing Company

The ITP Logo is a trademark under license

Printed in the United States of America

For more information, contact:

Delmar Publishers Inc.
3 Columbia Circle Drive, Box 15015
Albany, New York 12212

International Thomson Publishing
Bershire House
168-173 High Holborn
London, WC1V7AA
England

Thomas Nelson Australia
.102 Dodds Stret
South Melbourne 3205
Victoria, Australia

Nelson Canada
1120 Birchmont Road
Scarborough, Ontario
M1K5G4, Canada

International Thomson Publishing GmbH
Konigswinterer Str. 418
53227 Bonn
Germany

International Thomson Publishing Asia
221 Henderson Bldg. #05-10
Singapore 0315

International Thomson Publishing Japan
Kyowa Building, 3F
2-2-1 Hirakawa-cho
Chiyoda-ku, Tokyo 102
Japan

2 3 4 5 6 7 8 9 10 XXX 01 00 99 98 97 96 95

Library of Congress Cataloging-in Publication Data
Sciarra, Dorothy June.
    Developing and administering a child care center / Dorothy June
Sciarra, Anne G. Dorsey. — 3rd ed.
        p.   cm.
    Includes bibliographical references and index.
    ISBN 0-8273-5873-3
    1. Day care centers—United States—Administration. I. Dorsey,
Anne G.
HQ778.63.S35   1995
362.7'12'0973—dc20   94-30040
                                                                CIP

CONTENTS

Chapter 3   Licensing and Certifying   29

Chapter 4   Establishing and Working with a Board   47

PREFACE

This third edition was written primarily for students of early childhood education; but like the previous editions, it is also a rich source of updated information for practicing directors. The authors are early childhood education specialists with many years of experience in teaching both at the preschool and college levels. Both authors have administered programs, and Professor Dorsey has taught graduate and undergraduate courses in child care administration for the past two decades. Since the book covers the director's responsibilities for starting a new center and for maintaining an ongoing program, readers are introduced to the total range of administrative demands in different types of early childhood education centers.

A unique feature of this book is its focus on interpersonal relationships, combined with emphasis on developing sound fiscal and program management skills. Funding and budgeting skills, evaluating, hiring, collecting fees, and writing reports are essential for program survival; however, we are convinced that these skills are not sufficient for effective program operation unless they are combined with good interpersonal communication skills. Therefore, the book presents administration information in an interpersonal framework.

Director's Resources and Director's Library are again featured in this edition. The Director's Resources includes sample letters, job descriptions, personnel policies, parent handbook, and many other forms directors may need. An annotated bibliography of resource books supplementing this comprehensive administration text can be found in the Director's Library. The Working Papers at the end of each chapter include suggested assignments and classroom activities for college level students.

Material for the Director's Corner came from interviews with experienced practicing child care directors and/or special educators. We gratefully acknowledge the directors who participated in these informative interviews. They are: Debbie Gleason, Sandy Hoover, Chris Kelly, Pam Mitchell, Barbara Pearson, Annette Quallen, Eila Roark, Diane Rocketenetz, Tracey Rowe, Sally Wehby and others we interviewed for the previous edition. These interviews gave us insight into the "real world" of the working director, and inspired us to make a special place in the book for sharing their words and comments with our readers.

Photos, unless otherwise marked, are by Lisa Souders. Thanks to Diane Blackburn who agreed to serve as the director in all the photos which required someone in that role. We also appreciate the cooperation of the staff, parents and children at Arlitt Child Development who participated in the photographing. We thank Emily von Allman for coordinating that effort for us. We are indebted to Barton Canfield, Managing Accountant, and Patricia Gleason, Program Administrator for Roark Learning Centers, Inc. for their helpful suggestions relative to center budgets and handling financial matters (covered in Chapters 5 and 6). We would also like to thank the reviewers whose thoughtful comments have made this a better revision.

This updated edition addresses a number of timely issues for the 1990s. Among these are: 1) meeting guidelines for the Americans with Disabilities Act, 2) increased interest in inclusive classrooms and the consequent interdisciplinary teams, 3) suggestions for fiscal management including use of computers, and 4) following NAEYC Developmentally Appropriate Practice Guidelines to achieve quality programming and accreditation. Rather than devote separate chapters to new and timely topics, we again elected to incorporate this information at appropriate places throughout the text.

We hope we have been successful not only in presenting the technical information needed to operate a viable program, but also in conveying the challenge and personal satisfaction derived from creating and implementing an excellent educational program for young children and their families.

D.J.S. and A.G.D.

DIRECTOR'S CORNER

To Do

— Call plumber 555-1234

— Talk to building inspector ✓ left message

— ~~Call Red Cross — 1st Aid Training dates~~

— ~~Need detergent~~

— Do statistics for YMCA committee

— Send bills to parents who haven't paid tuition

— Rewrite snack menu

— Check coverage for classroom for Monday — teachers have parent conference ✓ OK—Susie will do

— Meet with Toddler teachers 1:45

— Appointment 5:00 — parents to see center

— Call job applicant for interview for part-time

— Place ad for full-time job — deadline Friday for Sunday paper

— Order supplies

    tissues

    paper plates

    plasic gloves

John
555-2345

"Making a 'To Do List' is the only way I can come close to keeping track of the many things I must do each day. I recommend it to your readers who hope to become directors. By the way, I also recommend they learn something about plumbing!"

Director, community agency center

CHAPTER 1

Developing Interpersonal Relationships

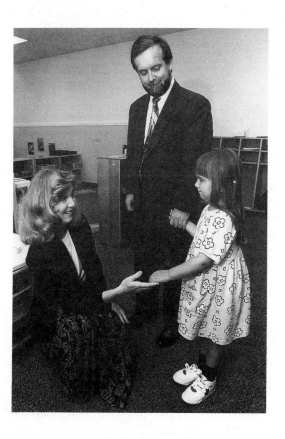

Photo above   The emotional tone at the center is set by the way the director feels about others and by the success with which those feelings are communicated to others in the setting. (Photo by Lisa Souders)

The following quote is from the director of a community nonprofit child care center: "In order to be successful as a director of a child care center, I think, above all else, you have to be a *people person*. You have to realize that this job goes far beyond administrative policy and doing paperwork; that being *the boss* here is not really being a *boss* in the traditional sense. Being the boss here has to do with forming trusting relationships with your staff, respecting their individuality, being firm when you need to be firm and being gentle when they need a gentle hand. It's important to remember that you won't get respect if you don't show respect. Also, remember that others can do the paperwork, but you are the one who must build the relationships with your staff."

Clearly, the interpersonal issues and the time it takes to work them out are at the very core of every management position. Much of what follows in this text deals with budgets, boards, licensing, and record keeping, but the *real* task of the director as a manager[1] is to work effectively with, and provide support to, those who will implement the program. The manager must relate to these people and motivate them to do the tasks delegated to them. Members of the staff implement the total program, but the director, acting in the capacity of leader and motivator, orchestrates.

The student may then legitimately ask, "Why learn about boards and budgets? Why not focus on interpersonal skills?" These questions are, indeed, legitimate, but books about interpersonal skills and management strategies have been written by others with particular expertise in both management and communication. The Director's Library includes helpful suggested readings in the section entitled, "Leading People." Familiarize yourself with some of those books so that as you learn about budgeting and buying equipment, developing personnel policies or planning a facility you will be able to use that information in concert with effective interpersonal strategies.

The discussion in this chapter focuses on the importance of first developing good management skills and then using these skills, coupled with good communication skills, as the basis for functioning as an administrator of a child care center or any other type of child care program. Obviously, the person in charge must have knowledge of how to draw up a budget, write policy and job descriptions, decide about equipment, and so forth. However, writing policy, hiring staff, making budgets, and ordering equipment will all be wasted efforts unless the manager has those special interpersonal and communication skills necessary to select, motivate, and relate to the people who are to carry

out the program within the framework set by the program philosophy, the budget, and the personnel policies.

Once the policies are established, the members are hired, and the children are enrolled, the function of the administrator parallels that of a classroom teacher. The administrator or director makes the total center program "go," much as the teacher makes the classroom "go" after the learning environment has been set up. Evans suggests, "It is like leaping from one to another of a dozen different merry-go-rounds, each traveling at a different speed, each playing a different tune, and each blaring a separate cadence. Yet the administrator (*teacher*) must land gracefully, never missing a beat, always in perfect time with the music" (italics added).[2] Once the program is going, the function of the director becomes catalytic or facilitative. The total task of the director is then accomplished by creating an environment in which others may grow. Through the growth and development of staff members, the program is implemented and the program goals are reached; the process unfolds in much the same way as in the classroom, where the teacher attains the program goals through the growth and development of the children and their families.

CREATING A POSITIVE CLIMATE

As a leader, the director has the major responsibility for creating a climate of care, trust, and respect. This climate can best be achieved by demonstrating caring behavior, by taking steps to build a feeling of community or partnership, and by creating a climate for good communication among and between all members of the center community. The goal is to optimize the developmental potential of children, families and staff.

---

1 The terms *manager*, *director*, and *administrator* will be used interchangeably. All these terms refer to the person who is in charge of, and responsible for, the total program.
2 E. Belle Evans, *Day Care Administration*, Educational Day Care Services Association, Cambridge, MA, n.d., p. 2.

Modeling

The emotional tone at the center is set by the way the director feels about others and by the success with which those feelings are communicated to others in the setting. The director creates a climate of warmth, caring, and acceptance by relating to staff members, parents, and children with honesty and openness. Mutual trust and respect will grow in an environment in which respect is earned, and the best way to earn respect is to show respect for others.

Emotional stability, maturity, and a positive sense of self are the basic characteristics of a leader who has the potential for assuming responsibility and leading people in a caring manner. This leadership style creates a climate that, in turn, motivates others to imitate the pattern of acceptance and warmth in their interactions; the caring behaviors become contagious. Most of you have read about and observed "modeling" in young children. One child who is perceived as the leader displays a pattern of behavior, and others imitate it. Johnny says, "Yuk! Spinach!" and soon everyone at the table is saying such things as "Yuk, spinach!" "Slimy spinach!" "Yucky B. M. spinach!" However, if Johnny says, "Yummm, spinach!" other children are more likely to respond positively to the vegetable being served. Although this example is clearly an oversimplification of what typically happens in a group, behavior *is* contagious, and there is evidence that a leader who serves as the model does indeed control the behavioral climate of the setting.

Modeling begins with the very first encounter the director has with the new staff members as they come into the center for interviews, or when a newly hired director is introduced to the staff for the first time. The basic trust and mutual respect that are communicated and felt during this initial meeting are the building blocks for the relationships that will develop among the people in the center. The pattern established during these first meetings will set the stage for future meetings and will influence the ways in which staff members will interact with one another and with the families and children who come to the center.

Although warmth, acceptance, and mutual respect are clearly fundamental to creating a favorable environment for the growth and development of the people involved in the center program, other behaviors demonstrated by successful directors also facilitate personal and professional growth and lead to more favorable environments for children. The director who shows intellectual curiosity and is always seeking more information to do a better job can inspire others to do the same. A leader who does not serve as a model of professional commitment and enthusiasm for learning more about children, families, human relationships, and trends and issues in early childhood cannot expect staff members to invest energy in these areas. The leader's responsibility is to show interest and enthusiasm for what is going on in the program and in the profession, and to serve as a resource for staff members and parents. They, in turn, will be stimulated to improve themselves as people and as caregivers[3] of children.

Community Building

The director is responsible for developing and maintaining a sense of community among staff, parents, and children. Morale will be higher and the environment more conducive to growth for all involved if there is a "we" feeling—a feeling of belonging. As the feeling of belonging increases, anxiety, self-doubt, hostility, and feelings of rejection decrease.

Staff members who feel that it is *their* center and *their* program, who feel a sense of ownership about the program, will be more self-assured and more enthusiastic about assuming responsibility. They will not only perform the tasks they are competent to perform, but they will also be willing to invest energy into learning more so they can extend their area of responsibility. The total task of serving children and families becomes *our* task, and *we* provide the richest and

3 *Caregiver* is defined as "one who is responsive to the needs of children."

best service we can, given our human and material resources.

The "we" feeling radiates beyond staff to families and children. It becomes *our* center or *our* program, and children begin to talk about "my" school. The feeling of community permeates the entire environment; all who participate in the many aspects of the center program feel they play an important part in the total program. All participants feel that they *own* a piece of the program and contribute to its success or failure. Parents and children alike recognize that they are valued and that their contribution to the program is important. They come to understand that they are the very reason for the center's existence; there would be no reason for the center to continue if there were no families and children to serve.

All the discussion about a feeling of community or partnership in a child care environment surely produces questions about what a director can do to create and maintain that atmosphere. Some of it will grow out of the trust and mutual respect that result from the modeling behavior described previously. Community feeling also stems from good interpersonal communication.

REFLECTIONS

Take a moment to reflect on your own practicum experiences. Think through whether or not there was a sense of community in the center in which you gained experience. Consider whether or not you were made to feel that you were an important member of the community. If you recall feeling positive about the experience, who was most instrumental in creating that accepting environment for you? Did you sense the children also felt this was *their* place? Who was responsible for creating the "we" feeling in the classroom?

DIRECTOR'S CORNER

"I often think back on my own experiences in the classroom when I was there eight hours a day. I remember that I was expected to be nurturing and giving of myself *all* day long—it helps me remember how much I, in turn, needed to be nurtured. That's why I have an "open door" policy for my staff—I take time to actively listen, to problem-solve with them, to listen to them. I often have to put my paperwork aside because I know that a staff person needs to talk *right now*! This job goes beyond, 'I'm the boss and you're the staff person' relationship."

Director, independent not-for-profit center

Communicating

Every director will do a certain amount of written communication. When there is a need to communicate in writing, the first question to ask is, Who needs to know? Interpersonal relationships are often damaged inadvertently because some members of the group do not receive information that they feel should be relayed to them. For example, although a change in next week's menu may, on the surface, affect only the cook in a child care center, a teacher who has planned a special science experiment around one of the foods to be served on a given day may be very annoyed to learn about the change in menu *after* implementing the special lesson. The message itself, including the exact wording, can be more easily drafted once the audience for the message has been determined. Thus the audience receiving the message will determine both the content and the wording.

Although some communication will be in writing, much of it will be face-to-face communication, verbal or nonverbal. To be an effective leader, the director must be a competent communicator and must take responsibility for helping the entire staff develop communication skills.

Verbal communication skills can be learned. The director can learn to send effective messages, to become a good listener, and to engage in effective problem solving. It is possible to define specific behaviors, both verbal and nonverbal, that block communication. It is possible to improve communication skills and, as a result, enhance interpersonal relationships. Note that we have said this is *possible,* but it is not easy. Unless directors believe wholeheartedly in the importance of open communication for good interpersonal relationships, they are unlikely to invest the energy necessary to develop the skills and to practice the skills until they become totally integrated into a personal communication style. However, once this integration has come about, the director's communication style will inevitably serve as a model for others. The model will set the pattern for all the other people in the center and will create an atmosphere more conducive to open communication.

It is important that verbal and nonverbal messages be congruent. Sensitive leaders will take care to convey the *real* message with both their words and their body postures. "Some communications researchers believe that fully 60 percent of all communication between people is based on body language."[4] Words that convey approval or acceptance but are accompanied by a frown and a closed body posture conveying rejection and hostility send a "mixed message" that is confusing to the receiver. Supportive, positive words and actions will help build trusting relationships among the people in the center. In a trusting relationship, criticism or negative reactions can be handled without destroying the relationship, provided that they are given discretely and are carefully timed. For the director to criticize a teacher in front of the receptionist when the teacher is on the way to the classroom to help a crying child is the epitome of poor communication, and it will have a negative impact on future attempts at open communication. Other, more subtle blocks to communication that will set the stage for a defensive response, hostility, or feelings of inadequacy include demanding and controlling messages, put-downs, use of

sarcasm or threats, or flip, humorous responses to serious concerns. It is important to consider what needs to be said, how to say it, *and* when to say it.

A sensitive leader is well advised to consider carefully whether a situation calls for *telling* or *listening.* Telling often comes more easily than listening; however, in many situations, listening is a better vehicle for maintaining open communication and strengthening a relationship. Dealing with the personal problems of families or staff members often requires listening rather than telling. Such communication is energy draining and time consuming, but when done well, it has a powerful and positive influence on the entire network of interpersonal relationships. It is time and energy well spent.

In spite of all the caring and planning that go into creating a supportive atmosphere, conflict will arise. This is human and does not necessarily mean poor management; nor does it imply weakness in the network. It does, however, require attention, and there are communication skills that can be learned by the director and the staff to facilitate conflict resolution. It is beyond the scope of this book to train students in basic communication and problem-solving skills, but there are a number of excellent resources that provide both basic information about effective communication and training exercises for practice purposes. Several suggested readings are included in the Director's Library.

MOTIVATING THE STAFF

The director does the orchestrating, but programs are effected through the efforts of other people. The staff of a center must be motivated to plan and implement the total program. Just as communication skills can be learned, so the skills for guiding mental and physical energies toward defined goals can be learned. Without training in how to guide and to motivate human energy toward shared goals, the director will follow some rules of thumb that may leave the role of director-as-motivator to chance. This practice may be compared to designing a program for young children based on knowledge gained from having been a child, having parented a child, or having been through a public school system. Although these experiences may be useful, they cannot substitute for theoretical knowledge and sound educational background in the field.

As directors begin to think about ways to motivate employees, they usually think about salary increases, a better building, new equipment, more help in the center, and a number of other items that are related to money and budget. Certainly, low salaries and poor working conditions can lead to dissatisfaction, but the promise of more money, or the threat of less, will probably not have far-reaching or long-lasting effects on individual or group performance levels. In addition, if a leader is using dollars to control and motivate performance, it becomes increasingly more difficult to find the necessary supply to meet the demand.

What, then, is a director to do? There are a number of useful strategies for motivating people to commit themselves to a task and to actualize their potential. Two of the strategies that seem particularly applicable to the child care setting are use of encouragement and provision of job enrichment.

Use of Encouragement

Encouragement is a positive acknowledgment focused on a specific attribute of some action or piece of work completed.[5] Rewards or reinforcements may motivate the staff, but as with teaching they tend to increase dependency on the one who controls the source of the rewards and they also heighten competition, thus defeating the overarching goal of developing a sense of a cooperative community. Encouragement, on the other hand, tends to build self-confidence and a sense of intrinsic job satisfaction.

Just as the classroom teacher makes sure that encouragement is specific, focused on process, usually given in private and is neither judgmental nor evaluative, so the director keeps these

---

DIRECTOR'S CORNER

"Encouraging staff is *so* important. The little words of praise, "good job" or "how nice" do not mean the same as when you take ten minutes of conversation with a staff person to say, 'Look at the changes in your room! What happened that made you think about changing the dramatic play area to a ballet studio? The aesthetics of the area and the detailed thought you've given to the choice of props is surely a delight for the children.' "

Director, independent not-for-profit center

---

same principles in mind when working with staff. To encourage a teacher who has just helped a screaming toddler, you might say, "I noticed how calm you managed to be with Tommy while he was having such a hard time in the bathroom. It worked out well." These words of encouragement are both more specific and process-oriented than, "I like the way you work with toddlers." Telling the teacher of four-year-olds, "You must have done some detailed planning for the graphing activity you did today to make it go so smoothly. It's surely fun for you to watch their progress" is more specific and less evaluative than, "That was a nice graphing activity."

Job Enrichment

Job enrichment is a management strategy that enhances job satisfaction by presenting more challenges and increasing responsibility which, in turn, produce a sense of personal achievement and on-the-job satisfaction.

It is possible to design a job enrichment program for a child care center so that staff members

---

5 Randy Hitz and Amy Driscoll, "Praise or Encouragement? New Insights Into Praise: Implications for Early Childhood Teachers," *Young Children*, Vol. 43, No 5, July 1988. Although the focus of the article is on teacher–child interactions, the principles also apply to director–staff relationships.

are motivated to higher levels of commitment; as a result, they will experience greater intrinsic rewards. The job enrichment principles particularly applicable to child care centers are as follows:

1. Give new and added responsibilities to staff members so they are constantly challenged and empowered to control aspects of their work setting.
2. Provide opportunities for ongoing training that will contribute to quality of performance and to personal and professional growth.
3. Give staff members special assignments, including occasional delegation of coworkers' or supervisor's jobs, to broaden each person's understanding of the total operation of the organization. This procedure can bring more recognition from other staff members and open up greater opportunities for advancement.

Obviously, there is some overlap among the three stated principles, both in terms of the method used and the outcome expected. There are also other ways to enrich staff members' jobs that will broaden their experience and bring them both intrinsic and extrinsic rewards. The many possibilities are limited solely by the creativity and imagination of the person in charge.

At first glance, it may seem that added responsibility will lead to dissatisfaction and demands for more money or other material rewards. However, there is evidence to suggest that, more often than not, the person who is challenged and who "stretches" to assume more responsibility will feel a sense of pride and achievement. For example, the classroom aide who, at midyear, is given the added responsibility of meeting and greeting parents and children at arrival time will probably find that job intrinsically satisfying. The aide will develop better skills for helping children make that first daily break from a trusted caregiver, and acquire new skills for accomplishing the added responsibility. Assigning added duties can best be accomplished in an atmosphere of mutual trust, and it must be done through the use of positive communication skills.

The training needed to develop the skills necessary for managing a new task effectively can often be offered informally by other members of the staff and by exposure to resources such as books, pamphlets, videos, or opportunities to observe. Ongoing training can be expanded to include more formalized in-service sessions on curriculum, child abuse, communication skills, working with children with disabilities and their families, or other topics selected to serve a specific need within the center program. Release time or financial support for workshops, seminars, and additional course work are still other ways to provide job enrichment opportunities for the personal and professional growth of staff members.

Delegating special assignments to staff members usually evokes a sense of achievement and recognition even though it means extra work. A cook who is consulted about menu planning and buying, and who is later asked to help evaluate the total food service program when the center is undergoing a self-study for accreditation, not only gains an understanding of what is involved in the total food planning and preparation program but is also developing a greater potential for advancement whether in the present job or in another work setting.

SUMMARY

In this first chapter the intent is to point out the importance of good interpersonal relationships and trust within a center. Only through a feeling of community and a spirit of cooperation can a director create a supportive environment where both adults and children can grow to their fullest potential. There must be a strong element of acceptance and positive regard in the surrounding climate to establish a mutually helping relationship for staff, families, and children. It is the responsibility of the director, as a leader, to serve as a model of caring and respect for others in order to build a strong sense of community among all the people involved in the center program. Effective interpersonal communication among the staff members, children, and families is also an important basic element in creating a supportive, comfortable environment at a center, and it is up to the director to be the model of good communication in order to create an atmosphere of openness, warmth, and acceptance.

The director uses encouragement and job enrichment to motivate staff members. Neither of these motivational means requires money; however, both require special interpersonal skills a director can acquire. Effective use of these support tools will not only facilitate personal growth and a feeling of positive self-worth but will also help move the center program forward.

Class Assignments

1. Read one of the books from Director's Library, Leading People section, and write a short paper on the book, including an analysis of how the material covered would be useful to you as a director of a child care center.
2. Write a brief essay on the "we" feeling or sense of community which prevailed (or was absent) in a center where you worked with children. Consider the following:

   - Who set the prevailing emotional tone of the setting?
   - What elements or daily happenings contributed to your feeling of belonging to the center staff?
   - How did the emotional tone effect your feelings about yourself, your peers, the children and so forth?

Class Exercises

1. Think of yourself as a center director and, in small groups with other class members, discuss the motivating factors that you as a director can control or change.

   a. List five effective motivating factors directors can control.
   b. Compare the lists produced by the small groups and develop a final list of strategies to encourage staff and enrich jobs that do not cost money.

2. Think about yourself as the director of a center where you have observed or taught. Using Working Papers 1-1, write appropriately phrased acknowledgments and create the job enrichment strategies requested.

Working Paper 1-1

Job Enrichment Strategies

1. Based on your understanding of the use of encouragement as a motivator, write an appropriately phrased positive acknowlegment for:

   the secretary

   the cook

   the custodian

2. Describe a way you could use the job enrichment strategy with:

   the assistant infant teacher

   the van driver

   the student teacher

CHAPTER 2

Assessing Community Need and Establishing a Program

Creating a new institution is an exciting challenge that requires abundant creativity and energy and is overwhelmingly complex. The amount of activity inevitably taking place simultaneously during the early thinking and planning stages for establishing a center makes it impossible to outline a set pattern of sequential steps to be followed in these stages. Clearly, there must be a need for the program, and there must be some driving force in the community, whether an individual or a group, that will generate the creative energy to (1) examine the need, (2) develop the program philosophy, and (3) decide about the type of program that will fit the need and the resources. These three

Photo above Holding small group discussions with parents who express interest in having their children participate is a good way to obtain information about need. (Photo by Lisa Souders)

major activities will be taking place simultaneously, and each will influence the type of program as well as the program philosophy. On the other hand, the type of program that is realistic to offer will influence the question of the ability to respond to the need.

The driving force might be an early childhood educator with a desire to open a center, or a group of parents who have an interest in providing child care services for their children. Sometimes community agencies choose to expand their services to include child care, and there is also an expansion of both employer- and public-school-sponsored child care programs.

The nucleus of the driving force, whether it be an individual, an agency or a corporation, must be prepared to carry out all preliminary tasks until a director is hired. They may have to deal with funding issues, undertake public relations campaigns, and carry out the needs assessment.

Program sponsors must examine what services can be delivered realistically without diluting the quality of the program. Usually, it is unrealistic to try to set up a program that will be responsive to every demand and meet all needs. It is also unrealistic to expect to start a new program and have it fully enrolled immediately. It can take several years to bring a new program up to full enrollment. It is better to begin on a small scale, carefully weighing the assured need against the services that can be delivered under the existing financial and resource constraints. It is dangerous to overextend by trying to meet everyone's need *or* by providing a large-scale operation that overtaxes the resources. Problems also arise when the need is overestimated and a program is set up that is underenrolled. In either case, program quality diminishes and children become the victims of impoverished environments. Then families do not trust the program to deliver the promised services and it is doomed to failure.

DIRECTOR'S CORNER

"I projected it would take us three years to reach capacity in this new center which is licensed for 115 children. We are now at the beginning of the third year of operation and we are about two-thirds full—so my prediction was on target."

Director/Owner, franchised center

ASSESSING THE NEED

To ensure that the planned program is properly scaled to meet both the size and the nature of the community need, it is important to do a needs assessment during the preliminary planning period. The needs assessment can begin before or after a director is designated or hired, but it must be completed before any financial or program planning begins. The purpose of the needs assessment is to determine the number of families and children that will use a child care service and the type of service desired by those who will use it.

What Must You Know about Need?

The first step in the needs assessment process is to determine what you need to know. Once that has been decided, procedures for collecting the data can be worked out.

Number of Families and Children. First, you must find out how many families are interested in having their children participate in an early childhood education program and the number of eligible children in each family. It is useless to go beyond the earliest thinking or planning stage unless there are families available who will use the service. Simply assessing the *number* of children is not sufficient because number alone does *not* determine interest or need. If you currently are running a program for preschool children but get many calls for infant/toddler or school-aged-child care, you are alerted to a need to expand your program offerings. However, between the time you assemble your waiting lists and accomplish the program expansion, many of those families on your list will have made other child care arrangements. One quick and informal way to decide whether or not to proceed with a needs assessment is to find out if other centers in the vicinity have waiting lists.

Not only do planners overestimate the number of families who need child care, but they fail to consider how many of those families will *use* or pay for center-based care if it is provided. Although the numbers of preschoolers in child care whose mothers work outside the home has increased threefold since the 1970s, almost half of preschoolers from working families are cared for by family members.[1]

Socioeconomic Level of Families. Many families may be interested in child care services but are unable to pay enough to cover the cost of the services they choose or need. When families are unable to pay the high cost of quality child care outside the home, operators cannot depend on tuition but must seek outside sources of funding if planned programs are to succeed. When families are able to pay, it is important to determine what they are willing to pay for center-based or home-based care. It is reasonable to expect that most families can afford to pay up to 10 percent of their total income for child care. However, low-income families may pay as much as 25 percent of their income for child care, while this figure may be as low as 5 percent for those in higher-income brackets.[2]

Ages of Children to Be Served. The ages of participating children affect all the program planning considerations and can make a considerable difference in the cost of delivering the service. Determine the number of families who expect to have infants or toddlers participate in the group care program outside the home. Although early childhood education programs traditionally served three- and four-year-old children, the increase in the number of one-parent families and the number of working mothers has increased the demand for care before and after school, as well as the need for year-round programs for school-aged children. Therefore, when doing the needs assessment, inquire not only about three- and four-year-olds who may need care, but also about older children as well as those under age three.

Type of Service the Families Prefer. In assessing the need for a program, one of the first things you must find out is whether families prefer full-day child care or a half-day program. Working families must have full-day care, and they will often need full-day care for children ranging in age from birth through school-age.

Families that choose half-day programs may use a program for toddlers and three- and four-year-olds (sometimes called preschoolers), but may prefer to keep infants at home. These families might select a five-day program for preschoolers but often prefer a two-day or three-day program for toddlers. Parents who wish to become very involved in the program may choose to place their children in a cooperative child care program. Other parents may not have the time or the interest in becoming directly involved in the school program.

In some situations family child care homes may be more suitable than a center-based program because they can serve a broad range of needs, they can be available for emergency care, and they can provide evening and weekend care. The family child care home involves parents taking their children to someone else's home and paying for child care on an hourly, daily, or weekly basis. These arrangements are usually made individually, although there is often some regulation of the number of children for whom care can be provided in a given home. In a few cases, satellite programs are set up involving the coordination of family child care homes by a child care center staff or an employer. Parents make arrangements through the child care center or the employer referral service for placement of their children in an affiliated family child care home, and make payments to the center or make use of this employer benefit. The center or employer, in turn, pays the caregiver and provides the parents with some assurance that the home and the caregiver have been evaluated and that placement for the child will be found if the caregiver becomes unable to provide the service due to illness or for other reasons. When the need for care is immediate and critical, it may be useful to locate and organize a few child care homes while the planning and financing of a center-based program is underway.

How Do You Find Out about Need?

Once you have determined the kind of data necessary to substantiate the need for a program,

---

1 *Good Housekeeping,* September 1992, p. 174.
2 *Wall Street Journal,* "Work & Family," December 1, 1992.

you are ready to decide how to collect the data. Some information for long range planning can be obtained from census figures, Chambers of Commerce, or data on births from the Health Department. However, detailed information needed for decision making is best obtained through other means. The data must be collected, recorded, compiled, and analyzed so that the need for the program can be explained to anyone who is involved in initial planning, including members of a sponsoring group or funding agency. The data-collection process might be formal and wide in scope to cover a broad potential population, or it can be informal and confined to a very small group of parents and community representatives. Mailed questionnaires, telephone surveys, or informal small-group meetings are possible methods of collecting needs assessment data.

Use of Questionnaires. When a large group of potential clients must be sampled, it is wise to develop a questionnaire that can be returned in an enclosed, addressed, and stamped envelope. Returned questionnaires provide specific data that can be recorded, compiled, and analyzed. These data are usually quite accurate; however, it is possible that some families will indicate interest in child care and then no longer need it or decide not to use it when it becomes available.

The major problems encountered with questionnaires used for data collection are the low percentage of returns and the task of developing a good questionnaire. Enclosing an addressed, stamped envelope increases the number of returns, but it does not eliminate the problem of lack of response. Unreturned questionnaires create more questions because it isn't clear whether those families are not interested in the service, or whether they are interested but have neglected to return the questionnaire.

Good questionnaires are very difficult to develop. Not only must the questionnaire be brief and understandable by the recipient, but the items included also must be carefully selected to provide precisely the data that are important to the needs assessment for any given program. Therefore, if you are involved in drafting a questionnaire, it is imperative to analyze the potential audience first so that items are covered in terms that the audience understands; then you must be sure to include inquiries about

all the information you need while keeping the form brief.

Review the sample needs assessment questionnaire in Director's Resources to see what types of questions are asked for assessing need. Before planning location, type and size of program, and ages of children to be served, it is helpful to ask about the following:

- number of adults in the household
- number of those adults employed
- number and ages of all children in the household
- number of children currently cared for outside the home
- number and ages of children with special needs
- estimate of family income
- estimate of how much is or could be spent on child care
- days and hours child care is needed
- preferred location of child care
- will the family use the proposed child care center when it becomes available?

Use of Telephone Surveys. Since the percentage of returns on mailed questionnaires is unpredictable, a telephone survey of potential users of a program may be a more accurate procedure for collecting needs assessment data. Telephone surveys are time consuming and costly if you expect to survey a large number of families. However, you can sample a large potential population and obtain fairly accurate information about the total group without calling each family. If you are involved in an extensive needs assessment program, you should consult a marketing specialist about appropriate sampling techniques. On the other hand, if you have access to a group of volunteers who can do some telephone calling and if the population to be contacted is small, telephoning prospective families may yield accurate data, provided that the questioning is conducted uniformly and that the data collected are what you need to know.

To ensure uniformity, telephone surveys must also utilize a questionnaire. The survey caller verbally asks the questions and fills in the questionnaire. The same considerations that apply to mailed questionnaires apply to those used in telephone surveys, namely, (1) understandable wording, (2) complete coverage of data, and (3) brevity.

Small Group Meetings. Holding informal group discussions with parents who express interest in having their children participate in a program is a good way to obtain information about need. It is practical where the potential client population is defined (for example, church members, apartment complex dwellers, employees of a particular company) or where the size of the community or neighborhood limits the number of families who might use the center. Informal meetings have the advantage of establishing a basis of trust and open communication between the providers of the service and the families who will use it. Without the constraints of a specific questionnaire, parents are free to discuss their values and goals for their children, their unique needs and desires in terms of their family situation, and their feelings about different types of programs that might become available. However, this informal data collection process yields information that is often less valid and reliable as well as more difficult to tabulate and analyze than questionnaire data. You may find that it is beneficial to work out a combination of the informal discussion and formal questionnaire procedures by holding a series of small-group meetings in which parents fill out a brief questionnaire at the close of the meeting. Needs

REFLECTIONS

Think, for a moment, about being called by someone doing a telephone survey. What was your reaction to the call? Was the call at a convenient time, or did it interrupt your study time or dinner? Did the caller get to the point quickly or waste your time inquiring about your health or if you were having a good day? What led you to agree to participate in the survey, or decline and hang up? Recalling your reaction to a phone survey can help you gain insights into how parents might respond to a needs assessment phone survey.

assessment data that are collected through both formal and informal channels not only provide the basis for the decision about whether or not to have a program, but also furnish information about family values and goals that will enter into formulating the program philosophy. Of course, the values and the educational interests of the program planners and the director will also have a significant impact on the philosophy.

PROGRAM PHILOSOPHY

The characteristics of an early childhood education program are based on the philosophy of the program. The program goals that determine what the curriculum and teaching strategies will be are based on the program philosophy. If, for example, the program philosophy is based on the theoretical assumption that it is through the process of inventing ideas and developing hypotheses that children come to understand about things and people in their world, then the overarching program goal would be to have children become autonomous problem-solvers. Therefore, in the child care classroom, rather than planned activities set up to teach letters or numbers, the adult would provide a print-rich environment which would include many books, charts and a writing center, and children would enjoy the use of math games, measuring tools and simple machines such as pulleys and pendulums. The two major questions to be answered in connection with the program philosophy are: Who decides about the philosophy? and What is the basis for deciding what the philosophy should be?

Who Decides about Philosophy?

During the early planning stages, the individuals who make up the nucleus of the driving force must discuss and finally formulate a program philosophy. Occasionally this discussion is delayed until a director is hired because it is important that the director feel comfortable with the adopted philosophy. However, when the planners have very specific ideas about program philosophy or a new director is hired for an ongoing program, the philosophy is written and a director is hired who can operate within the adopted philosophical frame-work. Frustrations over incompatible philoso-phies can create unworkable teaching situations for dedicated staff who need the support of the new director.[3] If the adopted position is based on the assump-tion that the child is born *a tabula rasa* (meaning the mind at birth is a blank tablet to be written upon by experience, and the stated goal of education is to fill that tablet with experiences), it is imperative that the program director be com-mitted to that same philosophy. A director with a cognitive–developmental or constructivist point of view who does not accept the *tabula rasa* premise could not develop or direct an educa-tional program that would reflect the stated pro-gram philosophy.[4]

The program philosophy must reflect the values, beliefs and training of the director, as well as the wishes and interests of the program planners and families who will participate in the program. "An identifiable philosophy is the key to any successful early childhood program."[5] When administrators carry out programs for which they are unable to state a philosophy and substantiate that the curriculum and accompa-nying pedagogical strategies can be explained in terms of that philosophy, they risk internal con-fusion, lack of unity and loss of teamwork, plus an inability to help parents understand their true purpose.

What Is the Basis for Choosing a Philosophy?

When programs are planned and imple-mented, the curriculum content and teaching strategies either consciously or unconsciously reflect a philosophy that is based on (1) assump-tions about how children learn, (2) values of the program planners and the families involved, and (3) views of the planners regarding basic issues in education. Although the three areas that influ-ence the philosophy of the program can be dis-cussed separately, they interact with one another and, in reality, are almost impossible to identify and delineate.

Assumptions about How Children Learn. In the very broadest sense and in the most simplistic terms, assumptions about how children learn fall into three major categories; namely, environ-mental, maturational, and interactional. The environmental position assumes that the child's learning is dependent on extrinsic motivators in the form of tokens, compliments, smiles, gold stars, and so forth. What the child is to learn is decided by the adult, who then plans lessons designed to teach content and skills. One of the basic assumptions of this position is that any-thing worth teaching is also observable and mea-surable. Attempts to relate this particular assumption about learning to some theoretical base usually lead to the mention of people like Thorndike, Watson, and Skinner.

The maturational position assumes that there is an internal driving force that leads to the emergence of cognitive and affective systems, which, in turn, determine the child's readiness for mastery of developmental tasks. Mastery of the task is itself rewarding, so the reinforcement is based on intrinsic satisfactions derived from accomplishment and task mastery. Learning is controlled by an internal growth force, and the child selects from various offerings, thus learn-ing what he or she is ready to learn. The theorists who are associated with the extreme matura-tional position are Freud and Gesell.

The interactional position assumes that learning results from the dynamic interaction between the emerging cognitive and affective systems, and the environment. The interaction with both the material and the human environ-ment is not driven solely by an internal force but

3 Jo Kuykendall, "Child Development: Directors Shouldn't Leave Home Without It," *Young Children*, NAEYC, July 1990, p. 49.
4 Rheta DeVries and Lawrence Kohlberg, *Programs of Early Education: The Constructivist View*, Longman, 1988 has a good discussion of constructivism and a comparison of programs sharing the cognitive–developmental orientation.
5 Celia A. Decker and John R. Decker, *Planning and Administering Early Childhood Programs* (5th edition), Merrill, 1988, p. 23.

is also nurtured, facilitated, and intensified by the timely intervention of significant adults in the environment. The child is intrinsically motivated to select appropriately from the environment, but the adult is responsible for preparing the environment and for timely and appropriate questions and ideas to alert the child to the learning opportunities in each situation. The adult facilitates the development of intellectual competence. The impetus for the interactional approach came from Piaget's work. Rheta DeVries says, "... (the) theory of Piaget is ... the most advanced theory we have of mental development."[6]

Values of the Program Planners and the Parents. The program philosophy is influenced by the priorities parents and planners set for the children. When questioned, most administrators would state that they value the optimum development of the whole child—the social, emotional, physical, and cognitive development of the child. However, when the philosophy or the ongoing program is analyzed, it may become

---

REFLECTIONS

Think about a program in which you have taught or have observed. Carefully analyze the time and energy the children and the adults invested in different activities offered in the daily program. Would you judge that cognitive development was valued over social/emotional development or *vice versa*? What evidence could you present to support your judgment? Think about activities you may have planned for children or behaviors you encourage and try to determine the area of development you most value.

---

clear that priorities do, indeed, exist. Concern for the development of the whole child is the stated position, but careful analysis reveals that cognitive outcomes are given priority over social/emotional goals or *vice versa.*

Views on Basic Issues in Education. A number of basic issues in education are implied, if not directly addressed, in the philosophy. One of these issues is the content versus process issue, which is sometimes interpreted as school orientation versus human orientation. Those who subscribe to the content orientation support the notion that the goal of education is to provide children with content that enables them to succeed in school as it exists. Their focus is on preparation for the next step in schooling, and achievement is evaluated by relating each child's progress to norms or to grade level. The goal of education for those who support human orientation is the upward movement of the child as an independent learner to higher levels of intellectual competence. The process of learning and the development of problem-solving skills are more important than content mastery. Autonomy, collaboration, and cooperation are valued, and the years in school are considered an integral part of life itself. The major goal is for children to become autonomous problem-solvers.[7] Schooling is not viewed as either preparation for later school or preparation for life. Achievement is not dependent on reaching a norm or the next grade level, but on the ability to cope with the here and now.

The philosophy dictates what the role of the teacher will be. If the focus is on content, the adult is expected to "teach" the children letters, numbers, shoe tying, manners, etc. On the other hand, in a process oriented environment, the adult, as an interacter, is a questioner, role model, reflector, observer and evaluator.

At first glance, this discussion about program philosophy may seem unrelated to the problems of starting a center, or to taking over as director of an ongoing program. However, it is impossible to make program decisions without a

---

6 R. DeVries and L. Kohlberg, l988, p. ix (Preface).

7 Constance Kamii, "Number in Preschool and Kindergarten: Educational Implications of Piaget's Theory," National Association for Education of Young Children, 1982, pp. 73–86.

commitment to an agreed-upon philosophy. Once that is in place, subsequent program decisions can be checked against the philosophy to ensure consistency with the stated position. The sample philosophies in Figure 2-1 will serve as a guide for writing a program philosophy.

The third major item to be determined, after the need has been assessed and the program philosophy written, is the type of program to be offered. After deciding on the type of program in terms of sponsoring agency and funding, the decision about ages of children to be served must be made before making arrangements for site-selection, licensing, budgeting, staffing and equipping the center, and enrolling the children.

TYPES OF PROGRAMS

The type of program that will be set up is certainly related to the assessed need and to the stated philosophy, but it also depends on the sources of available funds and the origin of the impetus for the program. Not-for-profit programs receive financial support through government funding or subsidies from sponsoring agencies, while proprietary programs are supported by capital investments of individuals or corporations. A wide range of program philosophies, including Waldorf and those based on Montessori's teachings, can operate under any of the program types discussed in the following section.

Not-for-Profit Programs

There are public and private not-for-profit programs (sometimes called non-profit) that range in size and scope from the small cooperative nursery school to the large complex agency-sponsored child care center. Although not-for-profit and non-profit may be differentiated for

Figure 2-1   Program Philosophies

Program Philosophy #1
The program is based on the philosophy that most children can learn the skills necessary to succeed in school, that each child learns at his own rate, and that success in learning will develop the child's self-image.

Program Philosophy #2
The educational philosophy of the Child Development Center is based on meeting the developmental needs of children. The work of Erikson and Piaget provides the theoretical framework around which programs are planned to meet each child's emotional, social, cognitive, and physical needs.

This developmental program is based on the assumption that growth is a sequential and orderly process and that children do indeed pass through stages of development which occur in a predictable sequence in their physical, emotional/social, and cognitive growth. The adult's responsibility in a developmental program is to assist the child in growing to his or her fullest potential by recognizing each stage of development and

fashioning a curriculum that will nurture and facilitate growth during that stage.

Program Philosophy #3
The program is designed to meet the developmental needs of young children (3-5 years). It provides experiences that enrich and enhance each child's cognitive, language, social, emotional physical, and creative development. Within the center's daily schedule, each child has opportunities to create, explore the environment, learn problem solving and personal interaction skills, and learn concepts through first-hand experiences. Children develop a positive self-concept through a balance of self- and teacher-directed activities. Opportunities for solitary play as well as group activities are provided. Staff serve as positive role models and provide care that is supportive, nurturing, warm and responsive to each child's individual needs. We respect parents as the primary and most important provider of care and nurturing, and we believe parents and teachers are partners in children's care and education.

legal reasons in some states, in most places the terms are used interchangeably.

Individual Cooperative Programs. Cooperative programs, often called *parent co-ops*, are owned and operated by a group. Since parents are expected to help in the classroom, the small co-op usually functions with one or two paid staff members, one of whom is usually a teacher/director. Costs are kept at a minimum and tuition is lower than in other centers. Most co-ops are half-day programs because they require parent participation; however, there are co-ops organized as child care centers.

Agency-Sponsored Programs. Many not-for-profit early childhood education programs are sponsored by community agencies, such as church groups, labor unions, service agencies, neighborhood houses, and United Way organizations. These programs may be set up as full-day care centers for working families or as half-day enrichment programs. Such programs are found in both rural and urban areas and can serve both lower-income and middle-income families, depending on how much support is provided by the sponsoring agency. Agency-sponsored programs sometimes receive partial support from a sponsor, such as United Way, and obtain the remaining support from tuition, government funds, and/or grants.

Government-Sponsored Programs. Head Start is perhaps the best known of the federal government-sponsored, early childhood education programs. Head Start is a comprehensive *compensatory* program that serves children of low-income families. That is, it is a program intended to compensate for experiences the children from impoverished families may have missed. In addition to preschool education, Head Start provides health and nutrition services for children, social services for the whole family, and opportunities for parent involvement and support.[8] The funding for Head Start programs is allocated by the federal government from the U.S. Department of Health and Human Services,

Administration for Children, Youth and Families (ACYF), Head Start Bureau (HSB). These funds are usually distributed through and monitored by the local Community Action Agency. Funding for Head Start programs may go to public school systems, universities, and public or private not-for-profit agencies. The programs may be center-based or home-based, may provide child care on a full-time or half-time basis, and usually serve four-year-olds. Those who receive funds from Head Start (grantees), are mandated to serve children with disabilities (10% of enrollment opportunities) who must be mainstreamed and receive a total care package through direct services from the grantee or from other resources in the community. Innovative programs for younger children are funded through special Head Start grants. The Department of Defense and the Veteran's Administration also sponsor child care programs in some regions of the country.

Public-School-Sponsored Programs. More states are mandating that local school boards provide preschool programs. These programs are usually funded through local or state tax monies, or other public funds. Full-day or half-day public school programs are staffed by people hired through public school personnel offices, and the programs are housed in public school buildings. Local school boards, public school administrators and teacher unions typically have a voice in making policy as well as in both teacher and program evaluation. The building principal is the appointed instructional leader, and at the state level these programs fall under the jurisdiction of the superintendent of public instruction or the commissioner of education.

Practices in public preschools still tend to focus on academic success, school readiness and standardized testing; but advocates for developmentally appropriate practice in preschools are challenging this academic readiness position of some public school instructional leaders. These philosophical differences are at the forefront of educational reform.[9] The 1988 report of a task force of the National Association of State Boards

---

8 "The State of America's Children 1992," Children's Defense Fund, 1992, p. 15.
9 Delores A. Stegelin, "Kindergarten Education: Current Policy and Practice," in *Changing Kindergartens*, Stacie G. Goffin and Dolores A. Stegelin (eds.), National Association for the Education of Young Children (NAEYC), 1992, p. 5.

of Education (NASBE), which advocates early childhood units in public schools, will affect how young children are served in public schools in the next decade.[10]

Before-and-after school programs for school-aged children are often housed in public schools, and some are also public-school-sponsored while others are run by community agencies or service groups such as the Salvation Army and YMCA. The public-school-sponsored programs may be staffed by teachers in the building or by high school or college students who are free during early morning and late afternoon hours. Often, the person in the school system responsible for the preschool programs also oversees these before-and-after-school programs, and the building principal is the on-site administrator-in-charge.

Campus Child Care Programs. Laboratory schools and child care programs for children of students, faculty, and staff are two types of programs that can be found on college campuses. The programs may be sponsored and subsidized by the college or university, or by government funds. These programs often provide facilities for research, observation, and teacher training. They may be full-day or half-day and may charge full, or in some cases, partial, tuition for those affiliated with the university. In some places where student groups as well as the university itself offer support for the care of students' children, the students pay minimum tuition for their children, and the program hours are flexible to accommodate the students' course schedules.

Privately-Sponsored Not-for-Profit Programs. Many large industries, hospitals, and apartment complexes are including child care centers in their facilities and are offering services for the children of their employees and residents. These not-for-profit centers are set up for the comfort and convenience of the employees and residents. The hours are often flexible and, in some cases, fees are on a sliding scale to encourage full use of the available facilities. In the case of hospital- and industry-operated programs, fees may be part of an employee benefit package implemented through the use of vouchers, direct payment to the caregivers, or a child care allowance to the employee.

Some employers offer a Dependent Care Assistance Program (DCAP) which allows employees to set aside a certain amount of their yearly pre-tax salary for child care expenses, thus providing a substantial tax savings to the employee.

Employers are realizing they cannot meet the challenge of fulfilling employees' child care needs on their own and are reaching out to the child care community for help in managing on-site centers. Some contract with centers for a reduced fee or funded slots for employees, while others prefer to contract for information and referral services in the area, but are not involved in service delivery.[11]

Profit-Making Programs (Proprietary)

Although much is written about not-for-profit programs such as Head Start, United Way centers, and public school programs, a large majority of the early childhood education programs in the United States are proprietary. These programs are set up to provide a service which will make a profit.

Independent Owner. Many full- and half-day child care programs are owned and operated by an individual or a small group (partnerships or small corporations). In the case of the proprietary center, tuition is the only source of income and the operators frequently have budgeting and financial problems. The proprietary operators may be able to draw a salary from the tuition that is paid by families using the service, but the operators rarely make a profit over and above that because of the high cost of operating a quality program. Sometimes proprietors open more than one center in a community or region and begin a small chain operation. Although it is difficult to make a profit from the small chain,

---

10 Report of NASBE Task Force on Early Childhood Education, *Right From the Start*, 1988. Available from: NASBE, 1012 Cameron Street, Alexandria, VA 22314 ($5.00).
11 *Child Care Information Exchange* #87, 9/92, p. 22.

quantity buying and shared service costs can sometimes reduce the cost per child and increase the possibility of making a profit over and above operating expenses.

Corporate Systems. Large child care chains are operated by a parent company that develops a prototype and sets up a number of centers throughout a state or region, or across the nation and into Canada. Some of these corporations have gone public and their stock is traded on the New York Stock Exchange. These national child care chains operate under a central administration that furnishes the financial backing and is usually very powerful in setting the policy and controlling the program. There is often a prototype building and program, which are publicized by identifiable slogans, logos, brochures, and advertisements. Some corporate systems operate all centers carrying the chain name, while others work on a franchised basis. In the latter case, an individual purchases a franchise from the parent company for a basic purchase price and then pays the company a percentage of gross intake for the ongoing use of the name and the program. In addition, the parent company supplies guidelines for fees, sample documents, brochures, advertising materials, etc. Some of these sample documents must be changed by center operators in order to meet local regulations and/or be in line with local practice. The parent corporation often monitors the franchised centers to maintain the company standard of quality control. Since company policy often controls the program, directors are usually expected to adopt the program as outlined by the corporate body, but can also adjust some practices based on their own philosophy. A list of the nation's largest for-profit child care organizations, "The Exchange Top 50," can be found in Director's Resources.

Family Child Care Homes

Family child care is reminiscent of an extended family where a small group of children is cared for in the home of a child care provider.[12] Although this type of child care service is most popular for infants and toddlers, these home providers also care for preschool children and offer before-and-after-school care. The provider may be an employee of a system but most often operates independently, contracting directly with families who choose home care over center-based care. In some states family child care homes must be licensed, while in other places they are certified by a community agency authorized to pay for children of low-income families who are in the home. Many providers join employer or community agency Information and Referral Registries which take calls from parents seeking child care. Registered family child care homes may or may not be subject to inspection by a responsible community agency. In some places, inspections are made only after a complaint has been filed.

Military Programs

The Department of Defense (DOD) operates child care programs at military installations across the country. Financed by a combination of government appropriations and sliding scale parent tuition fees, the programs may be full-day center-based care, part-day nursery schools, drop-in care, and, in some places, evening and weekend care.

Each of the military services (Air Force, Army, Marines and Navy) operates its own child care service, but all must follow the mandates in the Military Child Care Act of 1989. The Act addresses program funding, required training for staff, competitive pay rates for staff and an internal inspection system. In order to meet the demand for child care services, the DOD is expanding preschool and school-aged-child care options by increasing the number of programs on military installations, by using existing Resource and Referral Programs to help families locate available child care, and by contracting with off-installation centers to guarantee spaces for DOD children.

12 Anne Gordon and K. W. Browne, *Beginnings and Beyond* (3rd edition), Delmar, 1993, p. 44.

SUMMARY

Starting a center is a challenging and exhausting undertaking. During the early planning stages, a number of concurrent activities interact with one another. The individual or group forming the nucleus of the driving force which gets a center started must assess the need for a program while developing a program philosophy and determining the type of program that will meet the expressed need. Many decisions must be made concerning how needs should be assessed, what philosophy will be most representative of the thinking of the planners and the prospective director, what type of program is feasible in terms of financing, and so forth. The people who are interested in starting a center must recognize that a great deal of time and energy must be invested prior to the time when financial support is available and before a program can begin to deliver service to children and families.

Class Assignment

1. Review the sample needs assessment questionnaire in the Director's Resources (p. 26) and adjust it so you could use it for a telephone survey.

   a. Include exactly what you would say to open the conversation.
   b. What incentive would you offer to encourage participation in the survey?
   c. What questions would you ask (or not ask) on the basis of answers you receive?
   d. How would you close the conversation?

Class Exercises

1. Using Working Paper 2-1, discuss and record the thinking of the group about the items listed.
2. Using Working Paper 2-2, write your own program philosophy based on your thinking about the items listed in Class Exercise 1 on Working Paper 2-1.
3. Reread Sample Philosophy #1 (p. 18) and, using Working Paper 2-3, rewrite it to make it more comprehensive and congruent with your own thinking.

Working Paper 2-1

Discussion Form

In groups of four, discuss and record the thinking of the group about the following items:

1. What are your assumptions about growth and development?

2. How does learning or the development of knowledge come about?

3. During the early years of the child's life, what is the adult's role relative to:
Physical development?

   Social development?

   Emotional development?

   Cognitive development?

   Language development?

   Moral development?

4. What goals do you have for the children in your care?

Working Paper 2-2

Assume you have been hired as a director of a new center. Based on your own thinking about the items listed on Working Paper 2-1 (p. 23), write a program philosophy for your new center.

Working Paper 2-3

Assume you have been hired as the director of a center which has been in operation for a number of years. The Program Philosophy they pass along to you to rewrite is as follows:

> The program is based on the philosophy that most children can learn the skills necessary to succeed in school, that each child learns at his own rate, and the success in learning will develop the child's self-image. (Program Philosophy #1, p. 18)

You are to expand this stated philosophy and include your own ideas based on your training and the theoretical base upon which you make program decisions.

Director's Resource 2-1

Sample Needs Assessment

1. How many adults are there in this household?_____
2. Is there a husband in this household?   Yes____ No___
3. Is there a wife in this household? Yes____ No___
4. If there is a wife, does she work? Yes____ No___
   (a) If yes, part time____full time____
5. Are there other adults in the household? Yes____ No___
6. What is the total number of children under the age of sixteen?_____
7. What is the number of children under six?____
      Check ages of children under six.
      Under one___
      Between 1–2____
      Between 2–3____
      Between 3–4____
      Between 4–5____
      Between 5–6____
      Between 6–12____
   Note: If you have no children younger than five, skip to #12.
8. Does any child in this family, younger than school age, regularly spend time away from home? Yes____ No___
   If yes, does this child have any special disabling condition?   Yes____ No___
   If yes, does the condition require attendance at a special school or program?   Yes____ No___
9. How many children younger than school age regularly spend time away from home?_____
10. If any child regularly spends time away from home, how many hours does he or she spend?_____
11. Is/Are your child/children regularly cared for every day in your home by someone who does not live with you? Yes____ No___
12. How many children over five regularly spend time away from home before or after school?____
13. What are the ages of the children over five who spend time away from home before and after school?___;____;____
14. For statistical purposes only, please give the total family income in this household. $_____
15. If the mother is employed, what is her income? $____
16. Approximately how much do you pay every week for the care of all of your children? Give that figure in column A. In column B mark how much you would be willing to pay for quality care for all of your children? Mark with X.

A	B
$0____	____
$5 or less____	____
$6–10____	____
$11–15____	____
$16–20____	____
$21–25____	____
$26–30____	____
over $30____	____

17. Many parents have a difficult time arranging for the care of their children. Indicate what has been your experience.
    Easy time_____
    Not very difficult____
    Difficult time_____
    Extremely difficult_____
    No opinion____

Director's Resource 2-1 (*continued*)

18. If you had a choice of arrangements of the care of your child, what would be your first choice?
Care in child care center for four hours or less_____
Care in child care center for more than four hours_____
Care by another mother or someone in her own home_____
Care by a sitter in your own home_____
Care in a center before and after school_____
19. If you could have the type of arrangement you prefer, how many days would you want your child/children to spend there?_____
20. Would you prefer to have your child/children cared for
Near where you work_____
Near where you live_____
Other location_____
21. Generally speaking, in selecting an ideal child care arrangement, which is more important to you? (Assume that quality is equal)
Cost more important_____
Closeness to home more important_____
Closeness to work more important_____
No opinion_____
22. If a day care center opens across the street from your office (insert home, church, factory, as appropriate), will you be likely to use it
For your infant?_____
For your toddler?_____
For your preschooler?_____
For your school-aged child/children?_____

Director's Resource 2-2

The Exchange Top 50—
The Nation's Largest For-Profit Child Care Organizations

Organization	Headquarters	CEO	Capacity*	Centers*
KinderCare Learning Centers	Montgomery, AL	Tull Gerreald	144,545	1,235
La Petite Academy, Inc.	Kansas City, MO	Jack L. Brozman	90,000	780
Children's World Learning Centers	Golden, CO	Duane Larson	63,000	485
Childtime Childcare, Inc.	Brighton, MI	Harold Lewis	13,256	120
Children's Discovery Centers	San Rafael, CA	Richard Niglio	8,100	92
Tutor Time Learning Centers	Ft. Lauderdale, FL	Michael Weissman	7,800	39
Pinecrest Schools	Sherman Oaks, CA	Donald Dye	5,250	21
Creative World Schools, Inc.	Raytown, MO	Billie J. McCabe	5,000	48
New Horizons Child Care	Plymouth, MN	Susan Dunkley	3,900	43
Bright Horizons Children's Centers	Cambridge, MA	Roger Brown	3,440	42
Sunrise Preschools, Inc.	Scottsdale, AZ	James Evans	3,361	16
Rocking Horse Child Care Centers	Cherry Hill, NJ	Douglas Carneal	3,306	87
Children's Friend, Inc.	Warner Robins, GA	Dewayne Foskey	3,210	26
Discovery Learning Centers	Grosse Pointe Park, MI	C. Thompson Wells, Jr.	3,026	20
Phoenix Preschool Education Centers	Greensboro, NC	Bob Greear	2,900	21
Young World, Inc.	Greensboro, NC	Robert Lennon	2,800	16
American Child Care Centers	Tempe, AZ	Geoff Jennings	2,471	24
Primrose Schools	Marietta, GA	Paul Erwin	2,400	18
ECLC Learning Centers, Inc.	Providence, RI	Ronald Bates	2,132	12
Corporate Child Care Management Services	Nashville, TN	Marguerite Sallee	2,130	19
Youthland Academy	Corral Springs, FL	Jan Schmidt	2,000	16
Minnieland Private Day Schools	Woodbridge, VA	Jackie Leopold	1,900	24
Storytime Learning Centers	Dublin, OH	Jeffrey Roby	1,800	18
American Family Service Corporation	King of Prussia, PA	Judith Walsh	1,625	12
The Sunshine House	Greenwood, SC	Roseann & Dennis Drew	1,550	11
Kiddie Korner Day School	Charlotte, NC	Sylvia Eagle	1,471	12
Little People Day School Associates	Norristown, PA	Robert Sprague/Harold Wood	1,390	10
Kiddie Kare Schools, Inc.	Fresno, CA	Patricia Fisher	1,368	9
Next Generation Child Development Centers	Carrollton, TX	Dr. Layton Revel	1,310	10
Educo, Inc.	Reston, VA	Richard McCool	1,282	9
Prodigy Child Development Centers	Atlanta, GA	Yuri Eidelman	1,260	8
Hester's Creative Schools, Inc.	Greensboro, NC	Henrietta Hester Harris	1,243	9
Country Home Learning Centers	San Antonio, TX	Sharon Reinhart	1,232	6
Tender Care Learning Centers	Pittsburgh, PA	Frank Reabe	1,230	16
Enrichment Preschools, Inc.	Nashville, TN	Dorsey Tynes	1,200	10
Children's Wonderland	Agoura, CA	Debby Berthiaume	1,200	6
Creative Child Care, Inc.	Hurst, TX	Gene Little	1,194	11
Creative Day Schools	Greensboro, NC	Belvin Smith	1,194	7
Chappell Child Development Centers	Jacksonville, FL	Katheryne Chappell Drennon	1,157	3
Mulberry Child Care Centers	Boston, MA	D. Jarrett Collins	1,109	12
Playcare Child Care Centers	Rochester, NY	Sandra Alexander	1,073	11
Apple Tree Children's Centers	Urbandale, IA	Lynn Meservey	1,067	7
Goddard Early Learning Centers	King of Prussia, PA	Joseph Scandone	1,050	10
Resources for Child Care Management	Morristown, NJ	Robert Lurie	1,050	6
Do Re Mi Learning Centers, Inc.	Oak Park, MI	Lecester Allen	1,020	12
The Peanut Gallery	Carrollton, TX	Pat Burgesser	964	5
Future Generation	Elizabeth, NJ	Janna Gaughan	952	12
Children's Social and Learning Centers	Las Vegas, NV	Gary Mohler	921	7
Bright Beginnings Preschools	Fontana, CA	Robert Orsi	869	7
Child Care Consultant Services	Christiansburg, VA	Donna Thornton	800	8

* Total licensed capacity and total centers in operation providing primarily child care services on a full day basis. If you believe your organization should be on this list the next time it is presented, call Exchange at (800) 221-2864.

* From: Child Care Information Exchange: The Directors' Magazine, 3/92, p. 59.

CHAPTER 3

Licensing and Certifying

Child care center directors are responsible for understanding licensing, certification and other regulations pertaining to provision of services for young children. Each type of regulation is developed by a governmental body and each has specific purposes. Directors must understand which regulations apply to their programs and must ensure that all requirements are fulfilled in a timely manner. In the future, people who assume responsible roles in children's programs will probably have to deal with more and more regulatory functions. This increase in regulation is related to both the expanded use of public funds and the broader acceptance of the fact that programs for young children must not only provide care and protection for children, but must also be educationally sound. Educa-tional accountability points to greater focus on the need for certifying the people responsible for

Photo above The primary function of the licensing agent is to ascertain whether a program is in compliance with minimum requirements. (Photo by Lisa Souders)

children's programs, while protection of children's health and safety requires licensing of centers.

After programs are in compliance with the minimum standards required for local or state licensing, they can move toward model standards and gain some form of professional recognition. Accreditation awarded by the National Academy of Early Childhood Programs of the National Association for the Education of Young Children (NAEYC) is the most widely recognized system. Betty Caldwell is quoted in the foreword to the NAEYC Position Statement:

Our aim has been to formulate criteria which are general enough to cover different types of settings, yet specific enough to be objectively observable. . . .

The foreword continues:

Accreditation of early childhood programs helps teachers and directors evaluate and improve their practice and helps parents make informed decisions, but most of all, it helps the children.[1]

On-site directors and boards are responsible for providing the necessary inspiration and the leadership to improve the center. They work to move a program from compliance with minimum licensing requirements to meeting quality performance standards. Even beyond these standards lies the goal of dynamic development that continues to produce a quality educational program. Model program directors are always working to refine their programs as they move toward the goal of excellence. Since the knowledge base in child development and early childhood education is constantly growing, no program can afford to rest on its laurels.

LICENSING

Licensing of centers is required in most states, and coverage varies from state to state. For example, in some states only full-day child care programs are required to obtain a license, while in other states all full-day care, half-day, and home-based programs must be licensed. Depending on the type of program being planned and the geographical location of the center, it is possible that both local and state requirements will need to be met and where federal funding is involved, there will be additional requirements. In some states, program sponsorship determines program licensing. For example, programs affiliated with public schools may be licensed by the state department of education. Your licensing agent can provide updated licensing information. Director's Resources contains a list of sources of information on licensing in each state.

The licensing function is a result of legislation, and its thrust is accountability for the health and safety of children. Licensing requirements are usually minimal and measurable, but they do not guarantee either quality of care or protection for the children. Licensing requirements usually include minimal educational qualifications for staff members but rarely address the educational quality of the program. The licensing function is essential and valuable but it is often misunderstood. A license gives permission to operate rather than indicating quality.

In most localities the building department will review the plans and the fire, building, and sanitation departments will send individual representatives to inspect the proposed space where the services for children will be offered. After initial inspection and approval, inspections and license renewals will be required on a regular basis. Directors are responsible not only for making certain that their programs are in compliance with regulations, but also for being familiar with appeal and grievance procedures should conflicts regarding compliance with the regulations arise.

Licensing Regulations

Local and state licensing regulations typically cover building safety and requirements for physical space, and establish base teacher–child ratios. Although licensing regulations vary greatly from state to state, most licensing regulations include:

1. *Building safety.* Licensing regulations always include at least the minimum fire, sanitation, and building safety standards that apply to all private and public services. Fire regulations usually cover the type of building construction, ease of evacuation from the building in the event

---

1 National Association for the Education of Young Children, *Accreditation Criteria & Procedures of the National Academy of Early Childhood Programs,* Washington, D.C., 1991, p. x.

of fire, alarm systems, smoke detectors, sprinkler systems, availability of fire extinguisher, and methods of storing combustible materials. Building codes usually cover wiring, plumbing, and building construction including building materials. Sanitation regulations cover conditions in all areas of the building, with particular attention to the bathrooms and food service operations.

When infants and/or children who are non-ambulatory are to be enrolled in the program, the director must be sure to meet licensing requirements for those groups. Typically these requirements focus on egress in case of emergency. Usually housing these programs on the first (ground) floor is required.

2. *Physical space.* Licensing regulations usually specify the amount of space necessary for programs for infants, toddlers, and preschool children. The requirement for three- to five-year-old children is typically a minimum of 35 square feet per child of indoor space and 60 to 75 square feet of space per child outdoors. Since programs for infants and toddlers require cribs, feeding tables, and diaper changing areas, such programs require more space per child than do programs for three- to five-year-olds. Levels and sources of light, levels of heat, sources of fresh air, fencing of outdoor areas, protection of radiators and low windows, and numbers of toilets are also included in regulations covering physical space. These standards are minimal and good programs usually exceed them. Providing more than minimal space, particularly for children who will be at the center all day is likely to make both children and staff more comfortable.

3. *Teacher-child ratios.* Some licensing regulations include minimum teacher–child ratios. These state or local ratios vary, but they are in the range of three to eight infants to one adult, four to twelve toddlers to one adult, and six to twenty preschoolers to one adult. The baseline licensing standards for child/staff ratios in child care centers in some states already meet the standards used by NAEYC, but most states are still below these significant ratios. Most regulations require that two responsible adults be on the premises at all times. The ratios are established

to furnish a baseline standard for protecting the safety of children; however, group size is even more important and is also regulated by some states.

According to the NAEYC Accreditation Criteria, "An important determinant of the quality of a program is the way in which it is staffed. Well-organized staffing patterns facilitate individualized care. Research strongly suggests that smaller group sizes and larger numbers of staff to children are related to positive outcomes for children such as increased interaction among adults, and less aggression, more cooperation among children."[2]

4. *Staff qualifications.* The teacher's training in child development and her interactions with the children are key factors in creating a quality program. In fact, NAEYC points out that "The quality of the staff is the most important determinant of the quality of an early childhood program. Research has found that staff training in child development and/or early childhood education is related to positive outcomes for children such as increased social interaction with adults, development of prosocial behaviors, and improved language and cognitive development."[3]

Although licensing regulations sometimes address staff qualifications, requirements are often minimal. Some states require that caregivers be able to read and write, while others require at least a high school diploma for anyone who is hired as a teacher or teacher assistant and/or aide. Most states require a director to have at least a high school diploma, while a few states require some college training, which may or may not be in child development or early childhood education. Others, however, require specific training in early childhood education or attainment of the Child Development Associate credential. Professional organizations are working to upgrade the criteria for early childhood staff as one component of the effort to improve staff salaries. As this process evolves, we can expect licensing standards to continue to improve. Psychologists, nurses, doctors-on-call, and other professionals must meet the appropriate credential requirements of their respective professions.

2 Ibid., p. 39.
3 Ibid., p. 30.

5. *Transportation.* In centers where transportation service is provided, the service must usually meet the state motor vehicle department standards for school bus service. These standards regulate numbers of children, type of vehicle, types of lights on vehicles, proper identification on the vehicle, use of car seats and seat belts, and appropriate licensing and insurance coverage for the vehicle and the driver. Even when it is not required, it is wise to provide drivers with training in child development and management so that time spent on the bus will be positive as well as safe for both children and drivers.

6. *Other standards.* In centers serving infants, licensing usually requires detailed plans for diapering, including the surface on which the baby is to be placed, a plan for disposing of soiled and wet diapers, and hand-washing by staff after each diaper change. Additional requirements for storing food and feeding babies and for washing toys are also included.

As you review this section on licensing regulations, it should become clear that, depending on the size, the location, and the scope of the program for which you are responsible, you could find yourself working with local, state, and federal regulatory agencies. At times the regulations from the various bodies are not totally compatible, and they may even be contradictory in some cases. It is your task to deal with all these regulatory agents so that your program is in compliance. If your program is not in compliance, you run the risk of having a fine imposed or of being unable to take full advantage of available funds and community resources. There is also the risk of having to delay the opening of a new program or having to close down an ongoing program because of failure to meet minimum licensing requirements.

The Licensing Process

Directors who are seeking initial licensing should allow plenty of time for the on-site visits and for conferences with inspectors from all the departments involved, because the process is lengthy. It is wise to allow *at least* ninety days to complete the initial licensing process. All departments must provide clearance before the license is issued. On rare occasions programs are permitted to continue operation when they are out of compliance, because licensing specialists are trying to help provide sufficient child care in the community; but the regulatory agencies constantly monitor the work being done to bring the program into compliance with the minimum requirements. The burden is on the operator, who must present data to show that the program qualifies for a license or is working toward that goal within a well-defined limited time line.

Since total compliance with all regulations may be very expensive, it is important to have a clear understanding about the changes that are essential before a program can operate, and those changes which can be made as money becomes available. For example, the fire inspector may not allow children in the building until all required fire extinguishers are purchased, mounted appropriately, and made accessible. The sanitation department might allow a child care program to begin before a separate sink for hand-washing is available in the food preparation area, provided that adequate hand-washing facilities are available elsewhere in the building and that there is a double sink in the kitchen. Monies must be budgeted to move toward compliance in any areas that require further work. Therefore, the director and any board members who are involved in budget preparation should be well informed about any aspects of the program and the physical environment that might need modification to be in compliance with licensing standards. The time allowed for total compliance with all the licensing regulations will vary greatly and may be negotiable.

The steps involved in the licensing process are as follows:

1. Request a copy of licensing requirements from the appropriate regulatory agency.

2. Ensure that the zoning authorities in the area have approved the land use; that is, does zoning allow child care at the site you have chosen? Present the zoning permit from the zoning department to the department responsible for licensing.

3. Obtain information from the licensing agent about contacting the sanitation inspector, the fire inspector, the building inspector, and the public health office.

4. Arrange for conferences with, and on-site visits from, representatives of all necessary departments.

After programs are in compliance with minimum standards required for local or state licensing, they can move toward model standards which may lead to accreditation. (Photo by Lisa Souders)

5. When all inspections have been completed and the inspectors have provided evidence of approval, complete the application for the license and send it, with the required fee, to the appropriate licensing agent. You may be required to submit a detailed plan for operating the center, including number of staff, daily schedule, equipment list and center policies and procedures. You may also have to show copies of forms you will use for gathering required information such as health and emergency data.

6. On receipt of the license, post it in a conspicuous place in the child care center so that it is visible to parents.

7. Check the expiration date and establish a procedure to ensure that the renewal process will be set in motion in time to eliminate the possibility of having to interrupt the provision of services to the children or having to pay a fine.

The director, or in special cases a designated member of the board, is responsible for obtaining a license for the child care center. Renewals, although less time consuming for both the director and the licensing agents, must be taken care of on a regular basis. The cost of a state or local license itself is minimal when it is considered in light of a total budget, but it is an item that must be included in the budget. Although some states do not charge a fee, others charge varying amounts and some states base their rates on the number of children served. Some states have additional fees for special services, such as review of a particular building prior to a decision to obtain that building.

The Licensing Specialist

The primary function of the licensing specialist is to ascertain whether or not a program is in compliance with the licensing regulation and to issue, or recommend issuing, a license to those programs that meet the minimum requirements.

When programs do not meet minimum requirements, the function of the licensing specialist is to provide support and to suggest resources that will help bring the programs into compliance rather than to close them. The specialist's goal is to *improve* services for children and families. Licensing specialists are being viewed more and more as people who provide services rather than as people who just issue licenses or close centers. In one Midwestern community, a licensing specialist noted that she actually issues licenses for the equivalent of only two months of the year, but that she is available to directors to provide resource information and support throughout the year.

Knowledge of the community combined with a thorough knowledge of the licensing regulations makes the licensing specialist a valuable resource for directors who are seeking training for staff, looking for educational program consultants, and exploring the best and least expensive ways to meet the fire, health, or building regulations. The licensing specialist may also be available as a consultant when a director is petitioning to have an unusual or unrealistic restriction varied or adjusted. In situations where licensing regulations are inappropriate for children's programs, licensing specialists are available to support community efforts to have the regulations changed. Often specialists are not in a position to initiate an action to change a very restrictive regulation. However, they may

provide support and information to a group of lay or professional people who organize to bring about changes that will allow for quality service to children and, at the same time, free the programs from unrealistic restrictions. Should you find yourself confronted with a local or state regulation that seems impractical or unworkable, you may want to enlist your licensing specialist's help in making contact with other directors who feel as you do about the regulation, and form a task force to investigate the process necessary to have the regulation changed. In one locality where *all* staff people were required to hold first aid certificates, center operators and licensing specialists worked together to adjust the requirement and make it more realistic, without jeopardizing the health or safety of the children. An unreasonable or outdated requirement may be included in licensing and may need to be changed, but the regulation will remain until some very pragmatic, energetic director comes along who is willing to organize the forces necessary to create change. You may find yourself interested in doing just that, with the help of other directors, related agencies, and your licensing specialist.

The licensing specialist can also help you work through a grievance process if you encounter a unique problem with licensing. For example, one specialist explained a situation in which the fire inspector was holding to the letter of the law by requiring that an expensive special type of glass be installed in the windows of a center building that was not the required 30 feet from an adjacent building. The regulation requiring 30 feet is appropriate and necessary for adequate fire protection, but, in this case, the center windows were 28 feet away from an all brick, fire-resistant building separated from the center by a grassy area. There was no real hazard to the children in this particular center. The licensing specialist provided special help to the director to expedite the grievance process, and the requirement was waived for the center.

In another situation, a new all-day program was to begin for a one-year period on an experimental basis. The kitchen facility was totally inappropriate for cooking lunches for children who were to stay all day. The director, with the help of the licensing specialist, was able to obtain a temporary permit to operate the experimental program for one year by having the

DIRECTOR'S CORNER

"I spend a lot of time keeping track of paperwork. I know that I have to have all the staff and child medical records as soon as a new child or staff member comes to the center. That's one of the first things I do. I also make a calendar each year that reminds me when to apply to renew our license, to get our fire inspection, and our kitchen inspection."

Director, private not-for-profit center

children bring brown bag lunches. Bag lunches are strictly forbidden in this particular locality under the center licensing regulations and so this particular experimental program could not have been implemented without the understanding support of the licensing specialist. It was understood, of course, that the conditions in the center's food service area would have to meet minimum standards if the program were to be extended beyond the first experimental year, and that the bag lunches would have to be appropriately stored each day during the experimental year. The center provided information to parents about appropriate nutritional content of sack lunches.

Licensing specialists are well acquainted with many directors and teachers in the community, so they can serve as a communication bridge between centers by taking ideas and news from one center to another. For example, sharing the news about how a director in a neighboring community solved a budget problem or a staffing problem (without breaking confidentiality) can be very helpful to the director who is dealing with what seem like unsolvable problems and who is isolated from contact with colleagues facing similar problems. The specialist can assist directors who are trying to effect budget adjustments or staffing changes but are meeting resistance from board members or influential community groups. Occasionally, for economic reasons, some board members will pressure the director to over-enroll a group to increase revenue. Over-enrolling is a risk because there are days when all the enrollees appear, which means that the classroom is overcrowded and understaffed on those days. It may be difficult to convince some board members that overcrowding or understaffing for a few days a month can be demoralizing for staff members and disruptive for children. In some states, over-enrolling is illegal.

ACCREDITATION

While licensing implies meeting minimum standards, *accreditation* implies performing at a high degree of excellence and meeting model standards. Directors of accredited programs volunteer to be reviewed by an accrediting agency, and those programs that are accredited are worthy of the trust and confidence of both the private and professional community.

Groups such as the American Montessori Society, the Association Montessori Internationale, The Child Welfare League of America, and the YMCA have various programs to assure that their centers provide quality child care. However, the most far-reaching effort is that of the National Academy of Early Childhood Programs, a division of the National Association for the Education of Young Children (NAEYC). One facet of this professional organization's attempt to improve the quality of life for young children and their families is the accreditation system based on criteria developed over several years with input from a wide range of early childhood educators. (Further information about this process appears in Chapter 13. Accreditation materials may be obtained by writing to NAEYC. The address is included in Appendix B.)

Since licensing is intended merely to assure that a center meets minimum standards, engaging in the accreditation process is productive for the director, staff, parents, and ultimately for children. The self study process may be revealing to the director since it requires reviewing all facets of the center's operation. The process can also provide opportunities for the director and staff to work together in achieving the quality they desire.

DIRECTOR'S CORNER

"We were a little bit leery of going for NAEYC accreditation. It was a lot of work but the staff and parents really got interested. And when we got the letter saying we were accredited, I felt like we'd accomplished something as a team."

Director, agency center

CREDENTIALING

Individuals who work in a profession may be awarded a credential indicating that they have demonstrated the capabilities necessary for successful participation in that profession. While licensing is required for an agency to operate a program, credentials are related to the educational preparation of individual staff members. Credentials may or may not be required by licensing but they are an indication that the individual has had appropriate preparation for the early childhood profession. There are several types of credentials in the field of early childhood education.

State Certification

Certification of early childhood personnel has been under discussion in many states for a number of years and more and more states are creating prekindergarten or early childhood teaching certificates. The certificate is usually issued by the State Department of Education. In some cases the state provides enabling legislation; that is, the certification is available but the state does not require that everyone who teaches preschool children be certified. (Note that although about half the states offer early childhood certificates, there are up to nine different configurations—birth to five years, birth to eight years, three to five years, etc.) Individual center policies may require that teachers be certified, but often directors find that they are unable to find certified teachers willing to work in child care centers at the salaries offered. Directors who require certification as a qualification for their teachers must be aware that there are many kinds of teaching certificates. Preparation for elementary or secondary teaching certificates, for example, does not include attention to most of the knowledge, skills, and attitudes necessary for those working with younger children. Therefore, these certificates are usually not good

criteria for early childhood teachers. (An added confusion is that some states refer to teaching certificates as licenses to teach.)

Child Development Associate Credential[4]

In 1971 a group of child development and early childhood education professionals shared a vision that would bring a more unified consistent approach to training child care providers. . . . Out of this vision came a concept . . . to develop an innovative, comprehensive plan for training, assessing, and credentialing child care staff.[5] Thus the national Child Development Associate (CDA) program was born.

> The CDA Competency Standards became the foundation for staff training and evaluation. . . . The Council for Early Childhood Professional Recognition (the Council) was established specifically to administer the CDA Program. The Council sets the policies and standards and awards the Credential. These standards define the skills needed by caregivers to serve children and families.[6]

The six core competency areas for the Child Development Associate credential are:

1. Set up a safe and healthy learning environment for young children.
2. Advance their physical and intellectual competence.
3. Build their positive self-concept and individual strength.
4. Organize and sustain the positive functioning of children and adults in a group learning environment.
5. Bring about optimum coordination of home and center child-rearing practices and expectations.
6. Carry out supplementary responsibilities related to the children's program.

---

4 The information in this section is taken from *Competence,* a publication of the Council for Early Childhood Professional Recognition. For further information, write to CDA National Credentialing Program, 1341 G Street, N.W., Suite 400, Washington, D.C. 20005-3105.
5 Reprinted from *Competence* (10) 2, p. 1.
6 Ibid.

Caregivers can earn the CDA in the following endorsements: center-based preschool, center-based infant/toddler, family child care, and home visitor. Some colleges provide credit-based CDA courses. The CDA credential is granted after a candidate has been assessed following procedures established by the CDA National Credentialing Program. The assessment is based on teaching behavior with a group of children in the classroom rather than on the number of hours of course work in various subject matter areas. The assessors also review the portfolio or resource file prepared by the candidate to demonstrate knowledge in each functional area. A parent representative may be asked to provide a summary of evaluations gathered from all parents of children with whom the candidate works.

The Council has designed a relatively new program, CDA Professional Preparation Program (CDA P_3). Candidates complete about six months of field work, monitored by a Field Adviser. These advisers are early childhood professionals who must meet specific requirements and are then listed on a registry. Their role is supervision of field experiences and provision of candidate support. Individuals interested in being Field Advisers or in obtaining a list of available advisers may contact the Council. The address is listed in Appendix B.

Candidates then participate in 120 clock hours of seminars and complete a final evaluation guided by their field advisers who conduct a formal observation, oversee the development of professional resource files and gather data from parents using a Parent Opinion Questionnaire.

Upon completion of training and preparation of materials, a Council representative visits the candidate's site, conducts an oral interview, and verifies that the candidate demonstrates competence in working with children and families. Results of the verification visit are sent to the Council Office where determination regarding credentialing is made.[7]

Although there are fees associated with participating in this credentialing process, there are also scholarships available and some agencies pay all or part of the fees. Contact the Council for application materials and a list of fees.

SUMMARY

The director of a child care program is responsible for initiating licensing procedures and carrying through with on-site visits from building, fire, and health inspectors. If program adjustments or building changes are necessary to bring a center into compliance with local, state, or federal regulations, the director must take steps to bring about the changes or risk a delayed opening date or a denial of a license renewal. The licensing specialist is a good source of information and advice through the initial licensing process, as well as the renewal process.

Accreditation, particularly through the NAEYC National Academy of Early Childhood Programs, is an important approach to improving quality in child care centers and to involving staff in the process. Since licensing is designed to assure that minimal standards are met, centers that have participated in the accreditation process demonstrate to parents that they are interested in exceeding minimum requirements and that they are attempting to provide high quality care for their children.

Although licensing of child care programs is mandated in most localities, few states require certification of prekindergarten teachers, a college-degree-based credential. Through special training programs and after special assessment procedures, some caregivers are qualified to receive the Child Development Associate credential.

7 *CDA Professional Preparation Program,* a brochure of the Council for Early Childhood Professional Recognition, April 1993.

Class Assignments

1. Use the address list in Director's Resources and write for a copy of state licensing regulations. (Your professor may assign you a specific state.) Request a copy of the state licensing requirements and ask for copies of the forms needed to apply for a license to operate a program for young children in the state. After you receive this information, answer the following questions:

   a. What is the allowable adult–child ratio in the state?
   b. What qualifications are staff required to meet?
   c. Were the materials you received understandable and easy to read? Was it easy to find the information you needed?

   Write your answers on Working Paper 3-1.

2. Write to the appropriate state department to establish the status of early childhood certification in that state (your professor may assign you a specific state). Ask for the following information and record it on Working Paper 3-2:

   a. Does the state provide certification for prekindergarten teachers?
   b. What are the requirements for obtaining this certificate?
   c. Does the state require that prekindergarten teachers have this certificate?

3. Interview a child care center operator and write the responses to the following questions on Working Paper 3-3:

   a. Have you asked your licensing specialist for help?
   b. Has the licensing specialist been helpful? In what way?
   c. What kinds of experiences have you had with the fire inspectors? health and/or sanitation inspectors? building inspectors?

Class Exercises

1. Invite the licensing specialist from the community to come to a class session to discuss all the services provided by the licensing agency. Request copies of the local licensing regulation for class members.

   a. As a group, review the licensing regulations and determine which sections of the code would help you do a more effective job as a center director.
   b. Evaluate the regulations and determine which sections (if any) should be revised so that more effective service could be delivered to children.

2. Divide the class into small groups to consider the pros and cons of certification for prekindergarten teachers.

    a. Can you think of any individuals or groups that provide services for young children who would be opposed to certification? Why would they be opposed?

    b. Does certification guarantee quality service to young children? Discuss the reasons for your conclusion.

    c. What are the best ways to guarantee quality service to children?

Report your conclusions to the class.

Working Paper 3-1

State Licensing Requirement Form

Name of state _____
1. Staff–child ratios:

    a. The staff–child ratio for infants is _____.
    b. The staff–child ratio for toddlers is _____.
    c. The staff–child ratio for three-year-olds is _____.
    d. The staff–child ratio for four-year-olds is _____.
    e. The staff–child ratio for five-year-olds is _____.
    f. The staff–child ratio for school-age children is _____.

2. Staff qualifications are:

3. Were materials understandable and easy to read? If not, give an example.

Working Paper 3-2

Early Childhood Certification

1. To whom did you write regarding state early childhood teacher certification?

   Name:

   Address:

2. Does the state provide certification for prekindergarten teachers?

3. What are the requirements for obtaining this certificate?

4. Does the state require that prekindergarten teachers have this certificate?

Working Paper 3-3

Director Interview Form

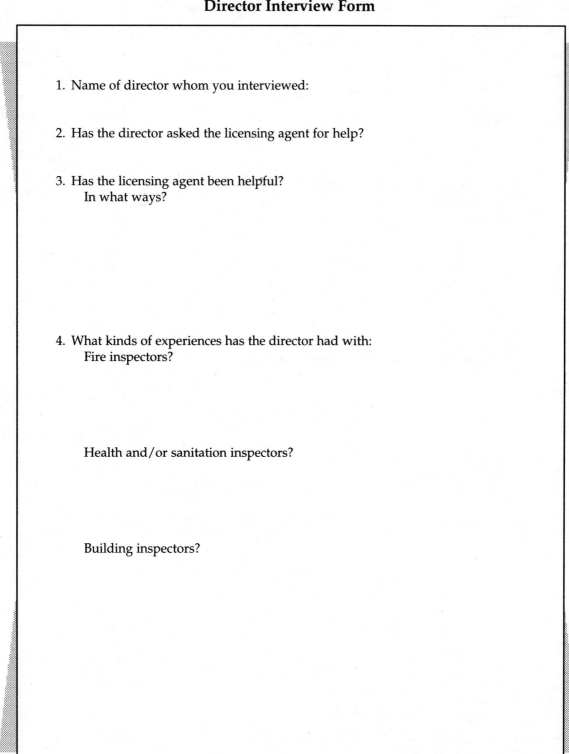

1. Name of director whom you interviewed:

2. Has the director asked the licensing agent for help?

3. Has the licensing agent been helpful?
   In what ways?

4. What kinds of experiences has the director had with:
   Fire inspectors?

   Health and/or sanitation inspectors?

   Building inspectors?

Director's Resources 3-1

State Child Care Licensing Agencies

ALABAMA
State Department of Human Resources
Office of Day Care and Child Development
50 Ripley Street
Montgomery, AL 36130-1801

ALASKA
Division of Family & Youth Services
Department of Health & Social Services
Box 110630
Juneau, AK 99811-0630

ARIZONA
Arizona Department of Health Services
Office of Child Care Licensure
1647 E. Morten Avenue, Ste. 230
Phoenix, AZ 85020

ARKANSAS
Department of Human Services
Division of Child Care Licensing
626 Donaghey Plaza South
7th & Main Streets, P.O. Box 1437 Slot 720
Little Rock, AR 72203-1437

CALIFORNIA
Department of Social Services
Community Care Licensing Division
Children's Programs Unit
744 P Street, Mail Station 19-50
Sacramento, CA 95814

COLORADO
Department of Social Services
1575 Sherman Street
Attention: Licensing
Denver, CO 80203

CONNECTICUT
Day Care Licensing Supervisor
Department of Health Services
Day Care Licensing Unit
150 Washington Street
Hartford, CT 06106

DELAWARE
Department of Administrative Services
Townsend Building
P.O. Box 1401
Dover, DE 19903

DISTRICT OF COLUMBIA
Department of Human Services
1905 E. Street, SE, 5th Floor
Washington, DC 20003

FLORIDA
Department of Health & Rehabilitative Services
Children and Families Program Office
2811-A Industrial Plaza Drive
Tallahassee, FL 32301

GEORGIA
Department of Human Resources
Child Care Licensing Section
2 Peachtree Street, NW, Suite 20-102
Atlanta, GA 30303-3167

GUAM
Department of Public Health and Social Services
Bureau of Social Services Administration
P.O. Box 2816
Agana, GU 96910

HAWAII
Department of Social Services & Housing
P.O. Box 339
Honolulu, HI 96809

IDAHO
Department of Health and Welfare
Division of Family & Community Services
450 West State Street
Boise, ID 83720

ILLINOIS
Department of Children and Family Services
Office of Licensing, Station #60
406 East Monroe Street
Springfield, IL 62701-1498

Director's Resources 3-1 (*continued*)

INDIANA
Family and Social Services Administration
Bureau of Family Protection and Preservation
Child Care Licensing
402 W. Washington Street, Room W-364
Indianapolis, IN 46204

IOWA
Department of Human Services
Hoover State Office Building
Des Moines, IA 50319

KANSAS
Department of Health and Environment
Bureau of Adult and Child Care
Suite 400-C, Mills Building
109 S.W. 9th Street
Topeka, KS 66612-2217

KENTUCKY
Cabinet of Human Resources
275 East Main Street, 4th Floor East
Frankfort, KY 40621

LOUISIANA
Department of Social Services
Bureau of Licensing
P.O. Box 3078
Baton Rouge, LA 70821

MAINE
Department of Human Services
Bureau of Child and Family Services
Augusta, ME 04333

MARYLAND
Department of Human Resources
Child Care Administration
2701 N. Charles Street, 5th Floor
Baltimore, MD 21218

MASSACHUSETTS
Director of Licensing
Office for Children
One Ashburton Place
Boston, MA 02108

MICHIGAN
Child Day Care Licensing Division
Department of Social Services
2355 Grand, P.O. Box 30037
Lansing, MI 48909

MINNESOTA
Division of Licensing
Department of Human Services
Human Services Building
444 Lafayette
St. Paul, MN 55155-3842

MISSISSIPPI
Mississippi State Department of Health
P.O. Box 1700
Jackson, MS 39215-1700

MISSOURI
Division of Health
Child Care Unit
P.O. Box 570
Jefferson City, MO 65102-0570

MONTANA
Montana Department of Family Services
P.O. Box 8005
Helena, MT 59604-8005

NEBRASKA
State of Nebraska Department of Social Services
P.O. Box 95026
Lincoln, NE 68509-5026

NEVADA
Department of Human Resources
Bureau of Services for Child Care
711 E. Fifth Street
Carson City, NV 89710

NEW HAMPSHIRE
Division of Public Health Services
Bureau of Child Care and Licensing
Health and Welfare Building
6 Hazen Drive
Concord, NH 03301

Director's Resources 3-1 (*continued*)

NEW JERSEY
Division of Youth and Family Services
Bureau of Licensing
CN-717
Trenton, NJ 08625-0717

NEW MEXICO
Children, Youth and Families Department
Child Care Licensing Bureau
P.O. Box 5160, Pera Building
Santa Fe, NM 87502-5160

NEW YORK
Bureau of Child Care
New York State Department of Social
Services
40 North Pearl Street, 11-B
Albany, NY 12243-0001

NORTH CAROLINA
North Carolina Department of Human
Resources
Division of Child Development
P.O. Box 29553
Raleigh, NC 27626-0553

NORTH DAKOTA
Early Childhood Services
Department of Human Services/Children
& Families Division
State Capitol-600 East Boulevard Avenue
Bismark, ND 58505

OHIO
Child Day Care Licensing
Ohio Department of Human Services
65 E. State Street, 5th Floor
Columbus, OH 43215

OKLAHOMA
Programs Administrator
Office of Child Care
Department of Human Services
P.O. Box 24352
Oklahoma City, OK 73125

OREGON
Child Day Care Regulation
Child Care Division
875 Union Street
Salem OR 97311

PENNSYLVANIA
Pennsylvania Department of Public Welfare
Office of Children, Youth and Families
Bureau of Child Day Care Services
P.O. Box 2675
Harrisburg, PA 17105-2675

PUERTO RICO
Department of Social Services
Licensing Office
P.O. Box 11398
San Juan, PR 00910

RHODE ISLAND
Department of Children, Youth and Their Families
Day Care Licensing Unit
610 Mount Pleasant Avenue
Providence, RI 02908

SOUTH CAROLINA
South Carolina Department of Social Services
P.O. Box 1520
Columbia, SC 29202-1520

SOUTH DAKOTA
Department of Social Services
Child Care Services
700 Governors Drive
Pierre, SD 57501-2291

TENNESSEE
Department of Human Services
400 Deaderick Street
Citizens Plaza Building
Nashville, TN 37248-9800

TEXAS
Texas Department of Protective & Regulatory
Services
Licensing Department (MC-E550)
P.O. Box 149030
Austin, TX 78714-9030

Director's Resources 3-1 (*continued*)

UTAH
Utah Department of Social Services
120 N. 200 West, P.O. Box 45500
Salt Lake City, UT 84145-0500

VERMONT
Division of Licensing and Regulation
Children's Day Care Licensing Unit
103 South Main Street
Waterbury, VT 05671-2401

VIRGIN ISLANDS
Department of Human Services
Division of Volunteer & Special Programs
Knud Hansen Complex, Building A
1303 Hospital Ground
Charlotte Amalie, VI 00802

VIRGINIA
Department of Social Services, Division of
Licensing Programs
Theater Row Building
73 D East Broad Street
Richmond, VA 23219-1849

WASHINGTON
The Department of Social &
Health Services
State Office Building 2
Mail Stop 440
Olympia, WA 98504

WEST VIRGINIA
Bureau of Social Services, Licensing Unit
State Capitol Complex
Building 6, Room 850
Charleston, WV 25305

WISCONSIN
Office of Regulation and Licensing
P.O. Box 7851
Madison, WI 53707

WYOMING
Department of Family Services
Self Sufficiency Division
Hathway Building
Cheyenne, WY 82002

CHAPTER 4

Establishing and Working with a Board

Most child care centers have a governing body that is *ultimately* responsible for the total program. This group is usually constituted as a policy-making body, which is called a *board of directors* or a *board of trustees*. The center director, who is responsible to this policy-making body, implements the center program as mandated by the board. In practice, board involvement runs the gamut from heavy involvement with the center to leaving *all* the work to the director. In the former situation, the board carries out all the functions described in this chapter and then charges the director with full responsibility to act on decisions that the board has reached. In the latter case, the board does not question the rationale or the philosophical basis for the rec-

Photo above The board carries out some functions related to personnel, finance, facilities, and program, and keeps in touch with the director who is also working on fiscal and program matters. (Photo by Lisa Souders)

ommendations presented by the director for board review, and gives carte blanche approval. Ideally, a board should function somewhere between these two extremes by carrying out some functions related to personnel, finance, facility, and program, and by keeping in close contact with the director who also is working on fiscal and program matters. Although some proprietary centers operate without the guidance of a governing group, the organizational structure of most agency sponsored and public-funded programs includes a board of directors.

When the center is an arm of another agency, for example, a church-sponsored child care program, the agency board may serve as the governing board, sometimes with representation from the center. In other cases, an advisory committee for the center is formed. As the name implies, the role of the advisory committee is much less structured and the committee has less authority than a board. When child care is part of a public school system, often the principal assumes many of the director's responsibilities and a lead teacher assumes others. The actual board then would be the elected boardof education.

When a center is to be operated as a corporation, it is a board responsibility to initiate the incorporation process. Because laws vary from state to state, an attorney should be consulted. The laws do not require that child care centers incorporate, but incorporation is desirable. The liability of the corporation is limited to the assets of the corporation; thus individuals holding positions within the corporation are generally protected from personal liability for acts or debts of the corporation. Many centers incorporate in order to qualify for tax-exempt status under the Internal Revenue Code. Contributions made to the center are then deductible by the donor.

To form a corporation, (1) Articles of Incorporation must be filed with the state (usually with the Secretary of State), (2) bylaws, which are also referred to as regulations or a constitution, must be adopted, and (3) a governing body, which is usually called a Board of Trustees, must be formed to set policy and assume overall responsibility for the operation of the corporation. A sample form for filing Articles of Incorporation appears in Working Paper 4-4 and sample bylaws appear in Director's Resources.

A corporation is owned by one or more shareholders. The shareholders elect directors to manage the affairs of the corporation, and the directors, in turn, elect officers to handle the day to day business of the corporation. Both federal and state laws regulate registration of stock issued to shareholders.

In the case of a not-for-profit corporation, the corporate structure is different. For example, there are no shareholders in a nonprofit corporation. Rather there are members who in turn elect trustees to manage the affairs of the corporation. The required number of trustees and officers varies from state to state. Once incorporated, the corporation must function in accordance with the state laws, the Articles of Incorporation, and the bylaws.

Not-for-profit corporation status does not automatically result in tax-exempt status. Based on Internal Revenue Code 501, it is still necessary for the corporation to apply to the Internal Revenue Service (IRS) for tax-exempt status and to demonstrate that the organization's purpose is educational or falls under one of the other IRS exempt categories. Department of the Treasury form 1023 must be accurately completed. This form requires a statement of the organization's sources of financial support, fund-raising program, purpose, activities (past, present, and future), relationship to other organizations, and policies (such as non-discrimination). This lengthy form also requires a statement of revenue and expenses and a list of governing board members. Exemption from state and local taxes, including sales tax, is often tied to exemption from federal income tax, but application for exemption must be made to each taxing body.

Because tax law is subject to change, the director and board must keep abreast of new requirements. New directors, moving in to existing centers, must check to see that the documents are in order and that proper procedures are being followed.

DIRECTOR'S CORNER

"The board treasurer keeps track of all the tax forms and other reports that are due. Once when we changed treasurers, we forgot to file a particular form and wound up with a big fine even though we hadn't owed any money. The board needed a lawyer on that one!"

Director, not-for-profit incorporated center

Board membership, board duties, committee structure, and board operations vary, depending on the size and type of center and on the relationship of the center to a sponsoring or funding agency. In spite of the inevitable variation in the structure and function of center boards, you will be better equipped to assist in establishing a board or to work with an existing board if you have some basic information about governing boards and how they operate.

BOARD MEMBERSHIP

Most well-planned boards consist of from ten to twenty members who are either elected or appointed to board positions. A board operates most efficiently when its size is small enough for members to know each other and feel comfortable about speaking out when issues are being discussed, yet large enough for members to cover all the committee assignments that are required to conduct business without overworking any board members. Tenure for board members is specified in the bylaws. Requirements for board membership are based not only on program philosophy and needs but also on state laws and sponsoring agency mandate.

Selection of Board Members

At the outset, boards may be made up entirely of appointed members, but after the bylaws are developed and incorporation is accomplished, ensuing boards are usually elected through a regulated process that is required by law and stated in the bylaws. When a director, a board, or a nominating committee chooses persons to be appointed or elected to a child care center board, the background and personality of the candidates and the current board composition must be considered.

Professionals from the fields of health, education, finance, and law are often asked to serve on child care center boards. These professionals can provide expertise in decision making in their areas and often volunteer time and expertise to help solve problems. For example, the physician who is a board member may direct the board to accurate information about health practices in

the center, or the accountant may help draw up the budget and prepare for an audit. A board member who can write effective proposals and who has contacts with various funding sources can be a real asset. Some boards reserve a percentage of slots for parents and a teacher may also be a member, though usually non-voting.

Before people join the board, they should receive information about the center and its philosophy. If they are not in general agreement with the goals and philosophy of the center, it may be more productive for everyone if they volunteer their services elsewhere. However, openness to new ideas is critical if the center is to move ahead. Prospective board members should also be informed of their responsibilities because being a board member is both a rewarding and a demanding experience.

Large agencies usually provide liability coverage for board members, but smaller organizations may be unable to afford this coverage. Nonetheless, board members are usually legally liable for center operation. Prospective board members should be informed that they will need to provide their own liability coverage if that is the case. Director liability is controlled by state law and additional information on this important topic can be obtained from your insurance agent or attorney.

Terms for Board Membership

Continuity in board membership is important. Therefore, many boards elect members for a three-year term, with one-third of the members being new each year. To achieve this ratio, the initial board members draw lots to determine who will hold three-, two-, and one-year terms. This time frame may not be workable for parent members who may not feel comfortable about joining the board until their child has been at the center for a while but who may no longer be interested if they are still board members once their child has left the center.

Although continuity is valuable, stagnation may occur when board members serve too long. Consequently, bylaws should contain a provision for a limited number of terms of board service. Provision should also be made for replacing members whose attendance is poor. When a board member resigns, an exit interview may provide insight regarding possible changes in board operation. Members who feel overworked or undervalued may choose not to complete a full term.

BOARD DUTIES

Initially, the board is responsible for drawing up the bylaws for the center's operation. Subsequently, the board makes policy decisions and provisions for the operation of the center.

Drawing Up Bylaws

Bylaws for operation of the center are written by the board and should contain:

1. name and purpose of the organization
2. composition of the board of directors, including information about when and by whom its members are elected or appointed
3. officers to be elected, their duties and terms of office, and description of the procedure for elections
4. method of replacing a board member or officer when necessary
5. frequency of meetings or minimum number of meetings to be held annually
6. standing committees—their composition and duties
7. relationship of staff to board
8. rules governing the conduct of meetings
9. procedures for amending the bylaws.

Other items may be added to meet the needs of a particular board.

Along with the establishment of bylaws, the board works on developing the philosophy for the center unless the philosophy has already been set by the organizers of the center. The process involved in developing a philosophy is discussed in Chapter 2.

Making Policy

After the philosophy has been established, the board sets goals for the program which are based on the philosophy. (If goals have already been established prior to the formation of the board, the board formally adopts them.) The board then informs the director and staff about the philosophy and goals, which form the basis for establishing the objectives for the daily program. In some cases, a knowledgeable director can take a leadership role in guiding the board's decision making about philosophy and goals which reflect sound theories. In any case, the board establishes policies and the director uses these policies as the basis for formulation of procedures. A *policy* is a course of action that guides future decisions. A *procedure* is a series of steps to be followed, usually in a specific order, to implement policies. It is important to have written policies for the center's major components, such as personnel policies, policies relating to the children's program, and policies about parent involvement. Ensuing decisions will then be consistent because they will be based on established policy. Since the policies should not be changed without serious consideration, the board should make them general enough and flexible enough so that the director is able to implement them without disregarding the goals of the center and without being required to request policy changes every time a new circumstance arises. Procedures are more detailed than the policies. Their purpose is to provide an implementation plan that is clear and uniform. Fire drill procedures or procedures for checking out material from the storeroom are good examples. Procedures may also be written for using the building after the children leave, for using equipment in the multipurpose room, or for filling a staff vacancy.

Policy decisions regarding personnel and program are ultimately subject to board approval; but in practice, they are often made by the director with official board approval becoming a mere formality. Occasionally, a very involved, knowledgeable board will carefully scrutinize policies presented by a director, often asking for the rationale to support each policy. In some instances staff and program policies are actually written by board members.

The type of program offered and the population served are both program policies subject to board approval. Decisions about the number and age span of children, the method of selection, and the population served are all board decisions. Examples include decisions about enrollment of children with disabilities, the question of ethnic balance, and the setting up of the program schedule to include after-school care or care for children on a part-time basis. Although these policy decisions are usually based on the director's recommendations, the board makes the final determination.

Operating the Center

The board is responsible for making provisions for the operation of the center. Major decisions in this category are:

1. Selecting a director
2. Providing for appropriate staff members and for their suitable in-service training opportunities
3. Providing facilities and equipment
4. Preparing or approving the budget and managing the finances of the center
5. Writing proposals and obtaining funding, including setting rates of tuition
6. Complying with local, state, and federal laws
7. Evaluating the operation of the program and the work of the director, and assisting the director in the evaluation of other staff
8. Arranging for an annual audit of financial records
9. Arbitrating problems between the staff and the director that cannot be resolved by the director

After provisions are made for operating the program, it becomes the director's responsibility to implement the program, at which point the director becomes accountable to the board for the total program operation.

BOARD COMMITTEES

Board work is usually done by committees. Each standing committee has a charge that is spelled out in the bylaws; when all the standing committees are in place and working, the basic board functions are carried out. As special needs arise, ad hoc board committees are appointed by the board chairperson to perform specific,

short-term tasks and report to the board. When the task has been completed, the committee is dissolved.

The board chairperson appoints members to each standing committee based on their interest and expertise and makes an attempt to balance the membership on committees by sex, race, age, point of view, and type of skill. Some boards have special requirements for committee membership. For example, the bylaws may state that each committee must have a parent member or a community representative.

Board committees convene at intervals that correspond to meeting the demands of their workload. When a center is being formed, most committees are extremely active; however, in an ongoing program, some committees have activity peaks. For example, the building committee deals with building maintenance, which is fairly routine; but if a decision is made to remodel, relocate, or build a new facility, the building committee would become very active.

Decisions about the number and the types of standing committees needed to carry out the board functions are made when the bylaws are written. Some of the typical standing committees are: executive, personnel, finance, building, program, and nominating.

DIRECTOR'S CORNER

"We work with a church committee of nine members and they report to the church board because the center is part of the church's mission. I'm responsible for running the program and they handle the finances. Recently we built a major addition to the building. Then I met with the building subcommittee almost every week."

Director, not-for-profit church-sponsored center

Executive Committee

The executive committee is composed of the board's officers, with the center director often serving as an ex officio member. The executive committee advises the chairperson on actions to be taken, on changes to be made, and on committee assignments. This committee conducts board business between meetings and acts in place of the total board in emergency situations. However, it is critical that the executive committee plan far enough in advance to avoid as many "emergency" situations as possible, lest the way be opened for making important decisions without total board participation. Board members will become disgruntled and fail to contribute time or energy to board business if they find that crucial decisions are being made outside official board meetings. Whenever possible, board decisions should be made by the total board.

Personnel Committee

The personnel committee is responsible for hiring a director who will adhere to the philosophy of the center and implement the policies established by the board. To accomplish this task, the committee advertises the position, conducts the interviews, and prepares the director's contract. The personnel committee is also responsible for firing the director, should that become necessary.

Personnel committee members usually assist the director in writing job descriptions, interviewing job candidates, and discussing the merits of each applicant. After these steps are completed, the hiring recommendations are made to the total board for final approval.

In small centers where there is no evaluation committee, personnel committee members may be asked to conduct the evaluation process. In this capacity the committee determines the method of evaluation, carries out the evaluation of the director, and monitors the director's evaluation of the center staff and program.

Finance Committee

Because they prepare the budget and appropriate the funds, finance committee members must have an understanding of the program's overall operation and of the way in which the operation relates to the program philosophy. In situations where the director prepares the budget and secures the funds, the finance committee approves the budget, monitors the record keeping, and arranges for the annual audit. In some centers the finance committee sets salary schedules and reviews bids for major purchases.

Building Committee

The responsibility for finding and maintaining a facility that is suitable for the type of program being offered rests with the building (or facility) committee. Prior to starting a center or establishing a new facility, the committee spends an extraordinary amount of time making decisions about purchasing, constructing, or leasing a building. The committee is responsible for locating the new facility or the construction site. Building committee members work closely with the architect when the construction or remodeling is in process and must remember to involve the director who presumably has the most knowledge of what the center needs.

It is the building committee's responsibility to see that the building and grounds are clean, safe, and attractive. Preventive maintenance as well as emergency repairs are authorized by this committee. Although directors usually manage the details of applying for a license and arranging for necessary changes at the center to keep the program and facility in compliance with licensing standards, the building committee is the group designated by the board to monitor licensing.

Many boards also assign the building committee responsibility for the center's equipment. The director must obtain the approval of the committee on major equipment orders and the committee sanctions orders after considering whether or not the suggested purchases are suitable, in both type and quantity, and are within the budget. The committee members also ascertain whether the equipment is properly stored, maintained, and inventoried.

The building committee makes long-range plans by considering such questions as the center's future building needs. It projects the type and amount of space that will be needed and plans for ways to meet those needs. Equipment needs are considered in a similar way. Long-range planning prevents the board from suddenly finding that a major addition or repair is needed when no funds are available. Long-range planning also enables the center to stagger the purchase of equipment so that the quality and quantity are constantly maintained at a high level, and so that the budget is not suddenly unbalanced by the need to replace large quantities of worn-out equipment.

Program Committee

The responsibility for all center programs ultimately rests with the program committee; however, in practice, any work on the program is handled completely by the director and the staff. The children's program, the parent program, and the in-service program for staff may all be under the auspices of the program committee. The committee recommends policies to the board, focusing on the enrollment and grouping of children, the hours and days of operation, and the offering of ancillary services, such as health, nutrition, and social services. Some boards set up separate committees for medical services and social services if these are major components of the center's program. These separate committees are responsible for determining what services are needed, where, and at what cost they can be obtained. The committees may also help with transportation arrangements to the medical center if required and with recruitment of volunteers to assist children and families needing special social or educational services.

Nominating Committee

Potential members of the board are screened by the nominating committee. The committee's function is twofold. Its members handle board nominations and they also prepare the slate of board officers for election by the board. The process should be open and the committee should check with prospective members for permission to nominate them.

A separate committee may be set up for the orientation of new board members, or the nominating committee may serve in this capacity.

Continuing the process begun at nomination, the committee makes sure that new board members understand their duties and the operating procedures of the board. New members may receive a manual containing a brief history of the center, copies of the bylaws, and explanations of all the policies and procedures applicable to the center. A binder is convenient for storing this material because additional and replacement items, such as board minutes, committee reports, and changed bylaws, can be added. The binder should also contain a list of all current board and staff members' names and addresses, and the expiration date of each person's term. When a board member leaves, the manual should be updated as necessary and passed along to the new member.

From the committee descriptions, it should be obvious that the functions of the committees are interrelated, and therefore, that communication among committees is essential. For example, the building committee must know what kind of plans the program committee is making in order to provide an appropriate facility. However, the building committee cannot choose a facility without an understanding of how much the finance committee plans to allocate for physical space. To avoid duplication of efforts, each committee's task must be clearly delineated. Sometimes a board member may be assigned to two closely related committees to facilitate communication between the committees. Care must be taken to divide the work of the board equitably among its members and to see that every board member is involved in and aware of the operations of the board and of the center.

BOARD COMMUNICATION

The board shares responsibility with the director not only for maintaining open communication within the board itself but also for maintaining open communication among the staff, the board, the sponsoring agency, and the families who use the center's services. The most successful boards are those that communicate effectively with the center's director and with each other. Both the board and the director have responsibilities here, and it may be worthwhile to provide training in interpersonal communication for all concerned. If staff and board

Board members may be invited when a special activity is planned at the center, and they are always welcome to visit. (Photo by Bobbie Boudreau)

members both attend the training sessions, communication skills are improved, staff and board members become better acquainted with each other's values, and the outcome is a greater sense of community among those people who are responsible for the center's operation. An obvious place to start is to make sure that new board members are introduced and that continuing board members also introduce themselves. Perhaps taking new board members on a tour of the facility and introducing them and the staff to one another could also be planned. When board members and staff members have developed effective communication skills, all will be expected to use the skills. Ideas will be expressed and considered openly; likewise, disagreements will be stated specifically and objectively. Board and staff members lacking these skills may be less willing to address problems directly, with the result that disagreements may not be resolved and that factions may develop within the organization.

As with all good communication, communication between the board and the staff is two-way. The board informs the director of policies that have been formulated because the director is responsible for seeing that the policies are executed. The board also explains the reasons for its decisions and approaches any necessary changes in a positive way, rather than in a dictatorial manner. The director, in turn, communicates to the board any difficulties that the staff is having with the existing policies or suggests policy changes, providing reasons for these changes. For example, if the director finds that there are a number of parents asking for a program for their two-year-olds, the suggestion is presented to the board and is supported with arguments for or against the admission of two-year-olds. Facts concerning the type of services that could be provided, the facilities available, the cost of such a program, and the advisability from an educational standpoint should also be presented to the board. Considering the data and the recommendation of the director, the board makes the final decision about the admission of two-year-olds.

It is the responsibility of the board to use the director's recommendations and all other pertinent data in formulating policy. Policy decisions must be based on sound data so that they are fiscally responsible, educationally sound, and realistic. For example, a policy requiring the director to be on duty whenever the center is open may be educationally sound but will be unrealistic in practice in a child care center that operates for ten hours a day. Similarly, a board policy requiring the director to hire only well-qualified, trained teachers would make the hiring task nearly impossible if available salaries are held at the minimum wage level. Since the director is mandated to carry out board policy, the board ideally gives careful consideration to his or her recommendations to ensure that final policy is not only mutually agreeable but also feasible.

The board serves as the communications liaison between the center program and the sponsoring agency. The director keeps the board informed about the center's functioning by sending the board members copies of newsletters, special bulletins, and meeting notices, by reporting at board meetings, and by presenting a written report to the board at least annually. Board members may be invited when a special activity is planned at the center, and they are always welcome to visit. The board, in turn, communicates to the sponsoring agency by reporting regularly to the agency board. This type of communication is two-way in that the board also receives information from the sponsoring agency concerning the expectations of the sponsoring group. For example, a community group may provide partial funding for the center with the stipulation that it be used to provide training for a staff member or for a parent program, or a church sponsor may expect preferential admissions for members' families. As long as these stipulations and expectations are compatible with the center's philosophy, they should be fulfilled.

BOARD OPERATION

When a new center is starting, the board must meet frequently, even daily, during very busy planning periods; however, in ensuing years, boards may meet monthly, quarterly, or in some cases annually. When the board is working closely with the director and is intimately involved in policy making, monthly meetings are essential. On the other hand, the board that assigns most of the decision making to the director may meet only annually to receive the director's report, approve the budget for the ensuing year, and make any adjustments in goals, policies, or procedures that seem necessary. Note how unrewarding service on such a board might be.

The board that meets frequently contributes to the operation of the center by working closely with the director and by utilizing fully the skills of all board members. The board that meets annually provides the director with maximum freedom to operate on day-to-day matters, although within definite guidelines. Each board must decide which alternative procedure seems to be more appropriate for the type of center being planned, and the director is chosen to fit into the selected method of operation.

Although each board has its own style, board meetings must be conducted according to recognized parliamentary procedures, which may be covered in the bylaws. In large, formal organizations, a parliamentarian who is appointed or elected makes sure that business meetings are conducted according to the procedures adopted. Although too much formality may be uncomfort-

DIRECTOR'S CORNER

"I know that our board members are really interested in our program but they aren't early childhood educators. So I have to make sure they understand the needs of the center and of our staff. I put a lot of effort into making sure key persons are well informed. Maybe I'll have lunch with the board chairperson or talk about an idea I have over coffee. You definitely don't want to surprise your chairperson with a new idea during a meeting."

Director, agency-sponsored
child care center

REFLECTIONS

Consider how you might work most effectively as a director. Would you prefer a board that left the decision making to you and expected an annual report about what you had done? Or would you prefer to be in a situation where you had to check back with people in authority on a regular basis to get the benefit of their thinking, after which you would follow their lead as you continued your work? You may be able to relate this idea to college classes in which you operated independently and received feedback from your instructor only on the final exam, compared with classes in which you regularly submitted written work throughout the course and regularly received information from your instructor about your work. It would be wise to give careful consideration to your own needs and your administrative style before accepting a directorship.

able for some board members, total informality leads to loose practices, with disputes arising over decisions that are based on improper voting procedures or other points of order.

The board of an incorporated center is obligated, by law, to conduct its business in an organized manner and to keep accurate records of all transactions. In situations where record keeping is not required by law, it is just sensible business practice to operate an agency in an orderly manner. Therefore, minutes of all board meetings, committee reports, and financial records should be kept. Copies of contracts and agreements, job descriptions, and correspondence should also be in the files.

SUMMARY

Not every center has a board of directors, but such a group must be formed as the governing body of an early childhood education center that is incorporated. When members are chosen carefully in terms of the contribution they are capable of making and willing to make, the director can receive excellent guidance from them. A well-organized board operates with a group of committees whose functions relate to the major components of the center's operation. Records of ongoing operations keep information about the functioning of the board open to everyone involved, and good communication between the board and the director produces a well-run organization. The board creates policies and the director implements those policies, but it is the ultimate responsibility of the board to see that its plans are brought to fruition.

Class Assignments

1. Find out how many people are on the board of directors of your college or local public school district.

   a. How did they become board members?
   b. What are their duties?
   c. How often do they meet?

   If possible, talk with a board member or attend a board meeting. Write your findings on Working Paper 4-1.

2. Arrange to talk to the director of an early childhood education center and ask whether or not there is a board of trustees.

    a. How are members chosen?
    b. How long is a member's term?
    c. What are the duties of board members?
    d. How often does the board meet?
    e. Are minutes of each meeting kept?
    f. What is the relationship of the director and the board?
    g. Is the director a voting member of the board?

    Report your findings on Working Paper 4-2.

3. Obtain a copy of the bylaws of an organization with which you are associated or of any type of community agency. (Consider your sorority or fraternity, your church group, PTA, a 4-H group, and so forth.) Compare the bylaws of the group you select with the bylaws in Director's Resources.

    a. How are they similar in structure?
    b. What are the substantive differences?
    c. How do the differences in the documents reflect the differences in the purposes of the organizations?

    Write your answers on Working Paper 4-3.

4. Using Working Papers 4-4, 4-5, and 4-6, fill out the Articles of Incorporation form, the Original Appointment of Statutory Agent form, and the Report of Use of Fictitious Name form. You may obtain information from a center with which you are familiar or create a hypothetical center.

Class Exercise

1. Involve the whole class in role playing a meeting of the board of directors of a center that provides full-day child care for three- to five-year-olds. (If your class is large, two simultaneous meetings may be held.) Appoint a president, a secretary, a treasurer, and a director of the early childhood education center. Assign other class members to be early childhood education specialists, doctors, lawyers, accountants, parents, and community members at large, and include members of any other group that you feel should be represented.

    The agenda for the meeting is to consider whether to apply for funding to renovate and equip the outdoor area, which is blacktopped and surrounded by a rusty fence. There is no permanent equipment. Think about what board members would need to know in order to make an informed decision and from where that information should come.

Working Paper 4-1

Board Members Form

How many people are on the board of directors of your college or local public school district?

How did they become board members?

What are their duties?

How often do they meet?

Working Paper 4-2

Board of Trustees Form

Is there a board of trustees for this center?

How are members chosen?

How long is a member's term?

What are the duties of board members?

How often does the board meet?

Are minutes of each meeting kept?

What is the relationship of the director and the board?

Is the director a voting member of the board?

Working Paper 4-3

Bylaws Form

1. For which organization did you obtain bylaws?

2. Compared with the bylaws in the Director's Resources:

   How are they similar in structure?

   What are the substantive differences?

   How do the differences in the documents reflect the differences in the purposes of the organizations?

Working Paper 4-4

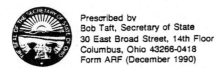

Prescribed by
Bob Taft, Secretary of State
30 East Broad Street, 14th Floor
Columbus, Ohio 43266-0418
Form ARF (December 1990)

Approved_____
Date _____
Fee _____

ARTICLES OF INCORPORATION

(Under Chapter 1701 of the Ohio Revised Code)
Profit Corporation

The undersigned, desiring to form a corporation, for profit, under Sections 1701.01 et seq. of the Ohio Revised Code, do hereby state the following:

FIRST.   The name of said corporation shall be _____

_____ .

SECOND.   The place in Ohio where its principal office is to be located is_____

_____ , _____ County, Ohio.
       (city, village or township)

THIRD.   The purpose(s) for which this corporation is formed is:

Working Paper 4-4 (*continued*)

FOURTH. The number of shares which the corporation is authorized to have outstanding is:
(Please state whether shares are common or preferred, and their par value, if any. Shares will be recorded as common with no par value unless otherwise indicated.)

IN WITNESS WHEREOF, we have hereunto subscribed our names, this _____ day of
_____, 19 _____.

By:_____, Incorporator

By:_____, Incorporator

By:_____, Incorporator

Print or type incorporators' names below their signatures.

INSTRUCTIONS

1. The minimum fee for filing Articles of Incorporation for a profit corporation is $75.00. If Article Fourth indicates more than 750 shares of stock authorized, please see Section 111.16 (A) of the Ohio Revised Code or contact the Secretary of State's office (614-466-3910) to determine the correct fee.

2. Articles will be returned unless accompanied by an Original Appointment of Statutory Agent. Please see Section 1701.07 of the Ohio Revised Code.

Working Paper 4-5

Prescribed by
Bob Taft, Secretary of State
30 East Broad Street, 14th Floor
Columbus, Ohio 43266-0418
Form AGO (August 1992)

ORIGINAL APPOINTMENT OF STATUTORY AGENT

The undersigned, being at least a majority of the incorporators of _____

_____, hereby appoint
(name of corporation)

_____ to be statutory agent upon whom any
(name of agent)

process, notice or demand required or permitted by statute to be served upon the corporation may
be served. The complete address of the agent is:

_____
(street address)

_____, Ohio _____.
(city)   (zip code)

NOTE: P.O. Box addresses are not acceptable.

_____
(Incorporator)

_____
(Incorporator)

_____
(Incorporator)

ACCEPTANCE OF APPOINTMENT

The undersigned, _____, named herein as the statutory agent for

_____, hereby acknowledges and accepts the
(name of corporation)

appointment of statutory agent for said corporation.

_____
Statutory Agent

INSTRUCTIONS

1)   Profit and non-profit articles of incorporation must be accompanied by an original appointment of agent. R.C.
1701.07(B), 1702.06(B).

2)   The statutory agent for a corporation may be (a) a natural person who is a resident of Ohio, or (b) an Ohio corporation or a foreign profit corporation licensed in Ohio which has a business address in this state and is explicitly
authorized by its articles of incorporation to act as a statutory agent. R.C. 1701.07(A), 1702.06(A).

3)   An original appointment of agent form must be signed by at least a majority of the incorporators of the corporation.
R.C. 1701.07(B), 1702.06(B). These signatures must be the same as the signatures on the articles of incorporation.

* As of October 8, 1992, R.C. 1701.07(B) will be amended to require acknowledgement and acceptance by the appointed
statutory agent.

Working Paper 4-6

Prescribed by
Bob Taft, Secretary of State
30 East Broad St., 14th Floor
Columbus, Ohio 43266-0418
Form NFO (September 1992)

Approved_____
Date_____
Fee $10.00

REPORT OF USE OF FICTITIOUS NAME

1. The exact fictitious name being reported is: _____

_____

(SEE INSTRUCTION # 1 ON REVERSE)

2. The user of the above name is: (check appropriate box)
   ☐ an individual
   ☐ a General Partnership
   ☐ a Limited Partnership; County in **Ohio**
      where certificate or application of
      limited partnership is filed is_____

   ☐ an Ohio corporation, charter no._____
   ☐ a foreign corporation incorporated in
      the state of _____
      holding Ohio license no._____
   ☐ an unincorporated association
   (NOTE: Ohio has no provision for limited liability companies; if user is a limited liability company, please check this box.)

3. The name of the user designated in item 2 is:_____

_____

NOTE: Where the user is a partnership, the name of the partnership must appear on this line. If the registrant is a foreign corporation licensed in Ohio under an assumed name, both the assumed name and actual corporate title of such foreign corporation must appear on this line.

4. The business address of the user is:_____
                                                                  (street address)

_____, _____ County, _____ _____
(City, Village or Township)   (State)   (Zip Code)

NOTE: P.O. Box addresses are not acceptable.

5. Complete only if user is a partnership:

NAMES OF ALL GENERAL PARTNERS	COMPLETE RESIDENCE ADDRESSES
_____	_____
_____	_____
_____	_____
_____	_____

(NOTE: Pursuant to OAG 89-081, if a general partner is a foreign (out-of-state) corporation, it must be licensed to transact business in Ohio; if a general partner is a foreign corporation licensed in Ohio under an assumed name, please note both the assumed name and the actual corporate title of such general partner.)

6. The nature of business conducted by the user under the fictitious name is:

_____

This document is signed by a corporate officer, general partner, or association member or officer, or the individual applicant.

By: _____

Title: _____

Working Paper 4-6 (*continued*)

INSTRUCTIONS

Section 1329.01 of the Ohio Revised Code defines a fictitious name as "a name used in business or trade that is fictitious and that the user has not registered or is not entitled to register as a trade name."

1. The **EXACT NAME** to be reported must be provided on line 1. Words or phrases which are not part of the name being reported must **NOT** be included on this line. For example, if the user is a Delaware limited partnership, the words "a Delaware limited partnership" should be included in line 1 **ONLY** if those words are part of the name being reported and not merely descriptive of the type of business.

2. The filing fee for a fictitious name report is $10.00. Please make checks payable to the Secretary of State.

3. A fictitious name report must be renewed every five years. In addition, if the user is a partnership, the report must be renewed whenever there is a change in the listing of the general partners. The fee for renewal is $10.00.

---

30 East Broad Street, 14th Floor   **Columbus, Ohio 43266-0418**   **(614)466-3910**

Director's Resource 4-1

The Apple Tree, Inc. Bylaws
(Reprinted with permission of the Apple Tree, Inc.

DEFINITION AND OBJECTIVE

The Apple Tree, Inc.

(A) Provides quality day care for the children of key personnel in the medical fields for the benefit of patients and the public in general.

(B) Provides day care of a racially-non-discriminatory nature. It does not discriminate against staff or students on the basis of race, color, religion, or ethnic origin.

(C) Provides education for 18-month through five-year old children, employing accredited teachers and meeting all preschool standards of the Cincinnati Board of Health (City License), Ohio Department of Human Services (State License), and United States Department of Agriculture (Food License).

By-laws of The Apple Tree, Inc.
ARTICLE I

NAME
The name shall be The Apple Tree, Inc., founded by The Auxiliary to the Academy of Medicine of Cincinnati, Inc., hereinafter referred to as The Apple Tree.

ARTICLE II

BOARD
The Apple Tree shall be governed by a board to provide leadership and administration for The Apple Tree.

ARTICLE III

OBJECT
To carry out such activities as are deemed advisable to promote the objectives of The Apple Tree.

ARTICLE IV

MEMBERS

Section 1—
The majority of The Apple Tree Board shall be elected from members of The Auxiliary to The Academy of Medicine of Cincinnati, Inc. The remainder elected from the community-at-large.

Section 2—
There shall not be more than fifteen (15) members of whom five (5) shall be elected each year to serve for a term of three years without compensation.

ARTICLE V

OFFICERS

Section 1—
The Officers shall be Chairman, Vice-Chairman, Recording Secretary, Corresponding Secretary, and Treasurer, which shall comprise the Executive Committee.

Section 2—
The Officers shall perform the duties prescribed for them in the parliamentary authority adopted by this Board.

Section 3—
The Officers shall hold office for one year, or until their successors are elected.

ARTICLE VI

NOMINATIONS AND ELECTIONS

Section 1—
A nominating committee of three shall be elected in January from the membership of The Apple Tree Board.

Director's Resource 4-1 (*continued*)

Section 2—	The nominating committee shall recommend candidates for election to the membership of The Apple Tree Board at least one month prior to the Annual Meeting in May.
Section 3—	The nominating committee shall prepare a slate containing the names of one or more members for each office to be filled.
Section 4—	Nominations may be made from the floor. No names may be placed in nomination without the consent of the nominee.
Section 5—	At the Annual Meeting in May, the election shall be by ballot, and a plurality shall elect. When there is no contest, the election may be by oral vote. New Board Members and Officers will assume their responsibilities in June.
Section 6—	Any vacancy which may occur shall be filled for the unexpired term by a majority vote of the remaining members.
Section 7—	Any officer or member of the Board may be removed therefrom by written petition of a simple majority of the Board for non-performance of duty. The petition must be presented to the Executive Committee and then acted upon by ballot by the majority of the Board.

ARTICLE VII

MEETINGS

Section 1—	Meetings during the fiscal year may be held at any time or place; the number and day to be designated by the Executive Committee.
Section 2—	There shall be an Annual Meeting in May.
Section 3—	A majority of the members of The Apple Tree Board shall constitute a quorum at any meeting.

ARTICLE VIII

COMMITTEES

Section 1—	The Executive Committee shall meet at the discretion of the Chairman for the purpose of making recommendations to The Apple Tree Board.
Section 2—	The Executive Committee, immediately following the election, shall appoint the Standing Committee chairmen who will assume their responsibilities in June.
Section 3—	Each Standing Committee chairman shall perform duties for one year or until a successor is appointed.
Section 4—	The Standing Committees shall be—Admissions, By-Laws and Parliamentarian, Finance, Food, House and Grounds, Long-Range Planning, Personnel, and Ways and Means.
Section 5—	Special Committees may be appointed by the Executive Committee.

ARTICLE IX

PARLIAMENTARY AUTHORITY The rules contained in "Robert's Rules of Order Newly Revised" shall govern this organization in all cases to which they are applicable and in which they are not inconsistent with these By-Laws.

ARTICLE X

AMENDMENT These By-Laws shall be amended at any regular meeting of the organization by a two-thirds vote of those present, provided written notice of the proposed revision shall have been given each member at least ten days in advance.

ARTICLE XI

DISSOLUTION If deemed advisable by members of The Apple Tree Board, the organization may be dissolved pursuant to the applicable provisions of the corporation laws

Director's Resource 4-1 (*continued*)

of the State of Ohio, and in event of dissolution all of its remaining assets and property of any nature and description shall be paid over and transferred to one or more corporations, trusts, community chests, funds or foundations, preferably to one whose objectives are the same or similar to the purpose of the organization as described in its Articles of Incorporation.

Director's Resource 4-2

Bylaws of the Lytle Park Child Development Center, Inc.
(Reprinted with permission of the Lytle Park Child Development Center, Inc.

Article I.   Name.
The name of this Corporation shall be Lytle Park Child Development Center, Inc.

Article II.   Not-For-Profit-Corporation.
The Corporation is a corporation as defined in Sections 1702.01 et seq., Revised Code of Ohio.

Article III.   Purposes.
  1. The purposes for which this Corporation is formed are:
      A. The establishment and operation of a child development center; including but not limited to: purchasing and leasing of real and personal property; hiring and firing of teaching and other personnel; and, all acts, steps, and procedures necessary, proper and incidental to the furtherance of the afore-stated purposes.
      B. The establishment of an educational environment for children ages 3 months through 5 years that promotes learning experiences which enhance cognitive and affective development.
  2. No substantial part of the activities of this Corporation shall be for the purpose of carrying on propaganda, or otherwise attempting to influence legislation. None of the activities of this Corporation shall consist of participating in, or intervening in (including the publishing or distributing of statements), any political campaign on behalf of any candidate for public office.
  3. No part of the net earnings of this Corporation shall inure to the benefit of any private shareholder or any individual. The property of this Corporation is irrevocably dedicated to charitable purposes and upon liquidation, dissolution or abandonment of the owner, after providing for the debts and obligation thereof, the remaining assets will not inure to the benefit of any private person but will be distributed to a non-profit fund, foundation, or corporation which is organized and operated exclusively for charitable purposes in which has established its tax-exempt status under Section 501(c)(3) and 509(a)(1), (2) or (3) of the Internal Revenue Code of 1954.

Article IV.   Duration
The period during which this Corporation is to continue as a corporation is perpetual.

Article V.   Address.
The area to be served by this Corporation shall be the Cincinnati, Ohio metropolitan area.

The post office address of its principle office is 300 Lytle Street, Cincinnati, Ohio 45202.

The name and address of its registered agent is *, a natural person resident in the county in which the undersigned has its principle office, as its statutory agent upon whom any process, notice or demand required or permitted by statute to be served upon the undersigned may be served. The complete address of said statutory agent is *, Cincinnati, Hamilton County, Ohio 45202.

Article VI.   Members.
1. Definition
      The members of this Corporation shall be the Board of Trustees and the parents of the children who are enrolled in the child development center.
2. The Classes of Members and Voting
      The Corporation shall have one class of members. Each member shall be entitled to one vote on each matter submitted to a vote of the members except as otherwise provided by law.

Article VII.   Board of Trustees.
  1. The affairs of this Corporation shall be under the control of a Board of Trustees consisting of no less than nine, but no more than twelve persons, all of whom shall be volunteers and neither

Director's Resource 4-2 (*continued*)

   paid personnel of this corporation nor of any organization receiving financial support from this corporation, all of whom shall be of full age and at least one of whom shall be a citizen of the United States and a resident of the State of Ohio.

2. The Board of Trustees shall be comprised of five to seven parents whose children are enrolled in the child development center, one representative from Cincinnati Union Bethel, one representative from *, and two community members selected by the rest of the Board for their expertise in child care. Additional members might be selected for expertise in such areas as pediatric medicine, early childhood education, financial affairs, fundraising, or marketing.

3. The members shall elect the parent representatives on the Board of Trustees for overlapping two-year terms. No person may serve more than two consecutive terms except after the absence from the Board of Trustees of one year.

4. The duties of the Board of Trustees shall be to establish the general policies of the Corporation and to manage the business and affairs of the Corporation.

5. Procedure for election of parent board members.
   Annually, the members of the Corporation will be solicited for interest in serving on the Board of Trustees by the Nominating Committee. The Nominating Committee shall present to members of the Corporation for a vote a slate of candidates from which new Board members shall be elected.

Article VIII. Meetings, Notices, Quorum.

1. The Annual meeting of the members of this Corporation shall be held in the Spring at such place and on such day and hour as the Board of Trustees may determine.

2. Special meetings of the members for any purpose or purposes may be called pursuant to a resolution of the Board of Trustees, and shall be called by the President or Vice President/Treasurer at the request of one-third of the trustees in office, or at the written request of one-third of the members of the Corporation. Such request shall in any case state the purpose or purposes of the proposed meeting. Business transacted at all special meetings shall be confined to the subjects stated in the call and matters germane thereto.

3. Notice of any meeting of the members, annual or special, stating the time when and the place where it is to be held shall be served personally or by mail, upon each member entitled to vote at such meeting, not less than 10 or more than 30 days before the meeting.

4. The presence in person of not less than 20 members entitled to vote is requisite and shall constitute a quorum at all meetings of members for the election of trustees or for the transaction of other business except as otherwise provided by law or by these bylaws.

5. Any action by a majority of members where a quorum is present shall be the action of the membership of this Corporation.

Article IX. Meetings of Board.

1. Meetings of the Board of Trustees of this Corporation shall be held at least six times per year and additional meetings may be held on the call of the President or, if s/he is absent or unable or refuses to act, by any officer, or by any 4 trustees.

2. Notice of any meeting of the trustees, regular or special, stating the time when and the place where it is to be held shall be served personally, by telephone, or by mail, upon each trustee not less than 5 days before the meeting. Business transacted at all special meetings shall be confined to the subjects stated in the call and matters germane thereto.

3. The presence in person of not less than 5 trustees is requisite and shall constitute action by a majority of trustees where a quorum is present shall be the action of the trustees of this Corporation

4. In addition to the powers by these bylaws expressly conferred upon them, the Board of Trustees of this Corporation may exercise such powers and do such lawful acts and things as are not by statute or by these bylaws required to be exercised by the members or officers.

Article X. Officers.

1. The officers of this Corporation who shall be elected by the Board of Trustees shall be a President and a Vice President/Treasurer, each of whom shall be members of the Board of Trustees. All officers shall hold office for one year and until their successors are elected and qualify.

Director's Resource 4-2 (*continued*)

2. The President, or in his/her absence, a Vice President/Treasurer selected by the Board of Trustees, shall preside at all meetings of members and of the Board of Trustees and shall perform the duties usually devolving upon a presiding officer.

3. The Vice President/Treasurer shall have the custody of all funds and securities of the Corporation and shall keep full and accurate accounts of receipts and disbursements in books belonging to the Corporation and shall deposit all moneys and other valuable effects in the name and to the credit of the Corporation in such depositories as may be designated by the Board of Trustees. S/He shall disburse the funds of the Corporation as may be ordered by the Board of Trustees, taking proper vouchers for such disbursements, and shall render to the Board of Trustees at the regular meetings of the board, or whenever they may require it, an account of all transactions and of all financial condition of the corporation.

4. The Board of Trustees may require the Vice President/Treasurer and, may at its discretion, require any other officer of this corporation, or employee of the Management Contractor, to give a bond in a sum and with one or more sureties satisfactory to the Board of Trustees, conditioned upon the faithful performance of the duties of his/her office and for the restoration to the Corporation in case of death, resignation, retirement or removal from office of all papers, vouchers, money and other property of whatever kind in his/her possession or under his/her control belonging to the Corporation.

5. The President shall ensure that minutes of meetings are taken and that records of activities are maintained in a permanent record, as legally required.

6. The Board of Trustees shall cause the financial records to be audited annually by a public accountant.

7. The Board of Trustees may authorize any officer(s) or agent(s) of the Corporation, in addition to the officers authorized by these by-laws, to enter into any contract or execute and deliver any instrument in the name of and on behalf of the Corporation, and such authority may be general or confined to specific instances.

Article XI. Committees.

1. There may be an *Executive Committee* consisting of the officers and one other member of the Board of Trustees elected by the board. The Executive Committee shall have and exercise all the powers of the Board of Trustees subject to such limitation as the laws of the State of Ohio or resolutions of the Board of Trustees may impose.

2. The President shall serve as chairperson of the Executive Committee. The Executive Committee shall have power to make rules and regulations for the conduct of its business. A majority thereof shall constitute a quorum.

3. The Executive Committee shall keep regular minutes of its proceedings and report same to the Board of Trustees.

4. The President shall appoint a *Nominating Committee* of not fewer than 3 members of this Corporation to make nominations for the election of parent members and trustees. The Nominating Committee shall also nominate persons to serve as officers and as members of the Executive Committee.

5. There shall be a *Finance Committee* composed of the Vice President/Treasurer, as chairperson, and at least one other member of the board, to be appointed by the President with approval of the board and shall have power to invest and reinvest any funds of the Corporation. Their policies of investment, however, shall be subject to review by the board. The Treasurer is authorized and empowered to execute on behalf of the Corporation, when so directed by the Finance Committee, such documents as may be necessary to effectuate the sale, exchange, or transfer of securities. The Finance Committee should report to the board at regular intervals, and a complete auditor's report on the Corporation's finances should be sent annually to all officers of the board and made available to all board members. The committee shall consider the details of the budget which is prepared by the Management Contractor and presented to the board, along with the committee's recommendation, by the Vice President/Treasurer or the executive. The board, voting in official meeting, shall determine the budget for the Corporation.

6. There shall be a *Scholarship Committee* appointed by the President and approved by the board whose responsibility is to establish policies for granting reduced fees to parents. The committee

Director's Resource 4-2 (*continued*)

also establishes procedures and reviews individual applications for such reduced fees. The Scholarship Committee should report to the board all actions at regular intervals.

7. All committee appointments shall be made as soon as possible after the election of officers or vacancies occur. Committee members shall serve for such terms as may be provided by the board.

8. The President shall from time to time appoint such standing or special committees as are authorized by the Board of Trustees. Each committee shall consist of such number of persons as the Board of Trustees deems advisable. All acts of such committees shall be subject to approval of the Board of Trustees.

9. The chairpersons of standing committees who are not already serving on the Board of Trustees shall be eligible to attend and advise at all meetings of the Board of Trustees.

Article XII. Vacancies.

1. All vacancies in the Board of Trustees, whether caused by failure to elect, resignation, death or otherwise, may be filled by the remaining trustees, even though less than a quorum, at any stated or special meeting, or by the members at any regular or special meeting.

2. All vacancies in the Executive Committee whether caused by failure to elect, resignation, death or otherwise may be filled by the Board of Trustees at any stated or special meeting.

3. In case there is a vacancy in any office of the Corporation, whether caused by failure to elect, death, resignation or otherwise, such vacancy may be filled by the Board of Trustees at any regular or special meeting. Such officers so elected to fill vacancies shall serve until the next annual meeting of members and until their successors are elected and qualify.

Article XIII. Management Contract.

The Board of Trustees shall enter into a contract with an agency or individual who shall serve as the general manager of the child development center. Terms of the contract shall include responsibilities in the following areas: general, fiscal, space and equipment, staff, evaluation, enrollment, parent involvement, health, safety, children's program and community relations. Also included are provisions for insurance, term, compensation and termination.

Article XIV. Fiscal Year.

The fiscal year of this Corporation shall be the calendar year.

Article XV. Nondiscrimination.

The members, officers, trustees, committee members, contractors, and persons served by this Corporation shall be selected entirely on a nondiscriminatory basis with respect to age, sex, race, religion, sexual preference, and national origin.

Article XVI. Miscellaneous Provisions.

1. Depositories. All funds of the Corporation, not otherwise, employed, shall be deposited from time to time to the credit of the Corporation in such banks, savings and loan associations, trust companies, or other depositories as the Board of Trustees may elect.

2. Checks, Drafts, Etc. All checks, drafts, or orders for the payment of money, notes, or other evidence of indebtedness issued in the name of the Corporation shall be signed by such persons and in such manner as shall from time to time be determined by resolution of the Board of Trustees. In the absence of such determination by the Board of Trustees, such instrument shall be signed by the Vice-President/Treasurer or by the President of the Corporation.

3. Investment. Any funds of the Corporation which are not needed currently for the activities of the Corporation may be invested at the discretion of the Board of Trustees.

4. Books and Records. The Corporation shall keep correct and complete books and records of accounts and shall also keep minutes of the proceedings of its members, Board of Trustees and committees having any of the authority of the Board of Trustees, and shall keep a record giving the name and addresses of the members entitled to vote. All books and records of the Corporation may be inspected by any member, or his/her agent or attorney or the general public, for any proper purpose at any reasonable time.

Director's Resource 4-2 (*continued*)

5. **Parliamentary Procedure.** All Board of Trustees and membership meetings shall be governed by *Roberts' Rules of Order* (current edition), unless contrary procedure is established by the Articles of Incorporation, these bylaws, standing rules, or by resolution of the Board of Trustees.

Article XVII.   Amendments.
The bylaws may be altered, amended, or repealed and new bylaws may be adopted by a two-thirds (2/3) majority vote of the Board of Trustees, or a majority of the voting members of the Corporation present at an Annual meeting or a duly summoned special meeting of the Trustees or members of the Corporation.

*Names and addresses deleted by author to protect the privacy of those named.

CHAPTER 5

Handling Financial Matters

Photo above Often the director is responsible for the center's financial management, but when an additional staff member assumes this role, the director must still be involved in decision making. (Photo by Lisa Souders)

The director's role as one who sets the tone for the center has already been established, but he or she must also be a pragmatist who is capable of dealing with all the financial obligations of running a center. The financial operation of a center should be as smooth as possible to ensure that the director can maintain control of the finances. Poor financial management leads to constant lack of funds and continuously hinders personnel as they work to achieve program goals.

75

The two major components of the financial plan are developing a system for managing financial resources and obtaining adequate funding. The latter will be discussed in Chapter 6.

Every center needs a long range financial plan and a plan for the upcoming year. A money management system including both policies and procedures is essential. Although many aspects of a good early childhood education program cannot be purchased at any price, high-quality care for young children is expensive and funds must be allocated properly to provide a developmentally sound program on which children and parents can depend. No matter how good the intentions of the staff may be, a program cannot continue to operate for long without a balanced budget.

In a new center, or one that is reorganizing, a decision must be made regarding who will be responsible for the center's financial management. Usually, the director is selected for this job, although sometimes a board member, parent (particularly in a parent co-op), or an assistant director carries all or part of the load. If there is a board with a finance committee, the staff member responsible for financial management works closely with this committee. A corporate system may have a regional or national finance director who oversees the financial operation of all the system's centers, and in a public school system the finances are usually handled through the central office.

BALANCING INCOME AND EXPENSES

A major task of the director or finance committee is the preparation of a budget. The director's goal is to balance income and expenses and, in some cases, to show a profit. However, the cost of the desired early childhood education program is often higher than the total income available. The director prepares a budget by:

1. estimating how much the program will cost (based on the center's goals)
2. determining how much income will be available (see Chapter 6)

3. seeking more income to equal expenditures, adjusting expenditures to equal income, or doing both

Estimating Costs

The financial director's first task is to figure program cost. This task requires an overall understanding of the early childhood education program, its goals, and its objectives. The director determines what is needed for children in the particular community and program and then analyzes the cost of meeting these needs. If other people are preparing the budget, the director works with them in interpreting the program needs. In this planning model some objectives may have to be postponed or omitted because of a lack of funds. Priorities should be established on the basis of the program goals, while the cost and the availability of funds determine the scope of the program. For example, a center may select improving salaries as a primary goal. If new playground equipment is also desirable, the decision about providing equipment in addition to improving salaries will be made based on the availability of funds.

Another question that has an impact on both program and finances is, What is the population to be served? Does the program serve children from three to five years of age, for example? If so, the director might arrange to have all children in one group; if this does not appear to be workable or is in conflict with licensing rules, the children may be placed in two or more groups. Immediately, this decision affects the budget in terms of the space allocations, the number of teachers, duplicate equipment, and so forth. Other questions might be: How many teachers will be needed and for what hours? Will it be necessary to have aides? a cook? a janitor? a secretary? a bus driver? Answers to these and dozens of additional questions should be available from the people that are responsible for designing the program. By using this method, the director keeps the goals and the philosophy of the center paramount.

Some directors have difficulty with the initial phase of budgeting. Instead of starting with the goals and objectives, they start with the dollars available and attempt to determine what can be done with those dollars. Such a center is truly ruled by the budget (or by the finance director), and maintaining an educationally and financially sound program under these conditions is extremely difficult.

Although program and financial decisions may be made at the national or regional level, in a corporate system the director of each center is responsible for implementing these decisions. The national or regional financial officer provides information about how much money is budgeted for each category; each local director then orders equipment and supplies through the main or regional office and is responsible for generating the required tuition.

Determining the dollar amount of a budget is a major part of the overall financial plan. This figure is arrived at by listing the items needed to operate the program for a year in categories, such as salaries, rent, and equipment. Next the budget director determines with as much accuracy as possible how much each of these categories will cost. The sum of the costs for each category is the amount of income needed for a year. A sample budget in Director's Resources provides an idea of the costs of each category and of the costs of the total program for a hypothetical center. This sample budget is not meant to be utilized in the form presented here but may be used as a guide to budget preparation. Center directors and other professional groups and organizations in each community, such as gas and electric companies, kitchen equipment suppliers, toy suppliers, and business associations, can furnish more specific and more relevant cost information for individual centers.

Factors that will influence the total amount spent by a center and the ways in which that amount is allocated are:

1. number, ages, and special needs of children enrolled
2. teacher–child ratio
3. staff training
4. type and location of building
5. amount of equipment already owned or available
6. type of program and services provided
7. section of the country in which the center is located
8. general economic conditions
9. amount and type of in-kind contributions

The sum of the costs for each category is the cost of running the center for one year. Dividing this figure by the number of children to be served establishes the cost per child, a figure that can be further examined on a monthly, weekly, daily, or hourly basis. The cost of various program components, such as infant or school-age programs, can be figured this way also.

It is important to consider whether the center is a nonprofit organization or whether one of the goals is to make a profit. This question is sometimes a hotly debated issue among early childhood educators, many of whom feel that early childhood education centers should not

REFLECTIONS

Think about the tuition that is paid by parents, particularly in regard to its relationship to the salaries that are paid by a center. Consider a situation in which a teacher's annual salary is $14,000 and the assistant teacher's annual salary is $10,000. With a total of $24,000 a year for salaries, 15 families would each pay $1,600 a year to cover these salaries alone. Unless the center has other sources of income, tuition costs must also cover costs of equipment, supplies, food, facilities, utilities, benefits, administration, and so forth. Since the last child will leave the center from ten to twelve hours after the first child has arrived, staff members will have to be present on a staggered schedule and additional help will be needed, all of which will increase salary costs. What would tuition have to be to produce a profit for the program sponsors?

Think about how much you will probably earn as a teacher in a child care center. If you were to earn minimum wage as a child care center teacher, working eight hours a day, five days for fifty-two weeks, what would your total salary be? If you were a parent earning minimum wage, how much could you afford to pay for child care?

be operated for profit because someone then makes money at the expense of the children. Admittedly, early childhood education costs are high and it is difficult to make a profit. Nonetheless, if a person or group can provide a good program, meeting the needs of both children and staff while showing a profit, there is no reason to discourage such a financial plan. It is the director's responsibility to ensure that children are not short-changed in the interest of profit making. This ethical issue may become even more challenging if the director's salary is tied to the amount of profit.

Adjusting Budget Figures

While it is relatively easy to change the budget figures on paper, chronic budgetary problems will drain staff energy from the daily operation and will remain unless the center can actually pare costs to the level of income earned.

Each expense must be analyzed with an eye toward its relative importance in the overall program. Can the equipment budget be lowered by substituting some free or inexpensive materials? Can food costs be lowered by cooperative buying? Can the consumable supply budget be reduced without a major effect on program quality?

When no cost reductions are feasible, both new and current funding sources can be

approached with clear documentation of the need in relation to goals. When a center's financial management is poor, the director may continue operating past this point without becoming aware that the inevitable outcome will be a poor quality program or bankruptcy.

PREPARING THE BUDGET

Types of Budgets

Budgets are classified in several ways. They may be based on the stage of development of the center, or they may be categorized according to the stage to which the budget itself has been carried. The creation of a new center demands one kind of budget, while the ongoing operation of a center requires a budget of a different type. Budgets may also reflect the center's accountability mechanism.

Start-Up Budgets. When a center is beginning operation, the director prepares two budgets: the start-up budget and the operating budget. The *start-up budget* consists of all the expenses incurred in starting the center. These expenses include initial building expenses (downpayment on the purchase of the building, the cost of building renovation, or rent deposit), the purchase of major equipment, the cost of publicizing the center, the director's salary for several months prior to the children's attendance, the deposit on telephone service, and the utility charges during the start-up period. Salaries for any additional personnel needed to assist the director of a large center must also be provided. Total start-up costs vary widely, and when these costs are incurred the usual sources of revenue have ordinarily not become available; in these cases a special grant may be needed or the organizers of the center may arrange for a loan or invest their own funds. When a loan is obtained, the cost of the interest must be recognized as constituting a very real budgetary item.

Occasionally, suppliers will permit purchasers to defer payment for ninety days, and the center can schedule purchases so that the first tuition is received before the ninety-day period ends. However, the first receipts will

---

REFLECTIONS

It may be easier to think about the financial aspects of an educational program by looking at your own educational finances. Think about the following questions: How is your college coursework being financed? If you are paying tuition, what percentage of the actual cost of your education do you pay? Who finances the balance? Taxpayers? Endowments? How are other school expenses (high school and elementary school) financed?

certainly not cover all the expenses. If receipts are due from agency or government funds, those first payments are usually made after the services have been provided. In the meantime, suppliers may charge interest on unpaid bills. Therefore, it is important to obtain as much assurance as possible that funds for start-up will be available when needed.

The United States General Accounting Office report on child care costs found start-up costs of $8,000 to $900,000 with a median of $48,500. These costs included, in descending order of amount spent, costs for space, supplies and equipment, planning and administration, and teacher training.[1]

Operating Budget. The *operating budget* consists of an income and expense plan for one year and is used when centers enroll children and begin the program. The center may operate on a calendar year (from January 1 to December 31) or on a fiscal year, which is a twelve-month period chosen for ease of relating financial matters to other operations of the center. Centers funded by agencies that operate on a fiscal year running from July 1 to June 30 find it easier to work on the same schedule as the funding agency, but many early childhood education centers choose September 1 to August 31 for their fiscal year, since those dates are closely related to the start of their school year. Once a center has selected its fiscal year, no change should be made without serious reason. Planning one year's budget from January 1 to December 31 and then changing to a September-August fiscal year in the following year not only causes confusion but may need to be justified for tax purposes.

Before hiring or purchasing can begin, the budget must be approved by the board and the funding source. At this point conflict may arise among the board, the funding agency, and the director; each group may have varying interpretations of the center's goals and of the means for reaching these goals. Once a consensus has been reached and the budget has been approved, the budget becomes the working financial plan, and the director must see that it is followed.

Analyzing Budget Categories

Most boards of directors have a finance committee that oversees the preparation and implementation of the budget. However, even when this committee assumes major responsibility, the director is still responsible for understanding and articulating what is needed to operate the program successfully. Many board members have limited knowledge of the actual cost of child care.

Some centers budget by function, rather than simply by category; that is, administrative costs and the costs of each aspect of the program are budgeted separately. For example, if 20 percent of the director's time is spent working directly with the children and 80 percent is spent on administration, then 20 percent of the director's salary would be allocated to the children's program *salaries* category and 80 percent would fall under *administration*. A complex center may provide and budget several separate functions, such as infant program, preschool program, and after-school program. This budgeting method clearly delineates the actual cost of the children's program, and when coupled with a description of the services offered it provides a mechanism for

DIRECTOR'S CORNER

"Our needs assessment indicated that over 100 children would use our center. Two major corporations in the neighborhood worked with us. Many of their employees expressed interest in enrolling their children. We were shocked when we spent the whole first year with only nine children enrolled. Luckily we had strong financial backing and we have now reached capacity enrollment."

Director, private not-for-profit center

1 United States General Accounting Office, *Early Childhood Education: What Are the Costs of High-quality Programs?* (January, 1990). Briefing report to the chairman, Committee on Labor and Human Resources, U.S. Senate.

comparing costs with other programs and for including the value of the services provided in relation to the costs incurred. This method also provides information used in determining tuition.

The following budget categories will provide a rough idea of the costs of early childhood education and the formats used for presenting a budget.

Salaries. In any early childhood education budget, the major component is salaries—a center can expect to spend up to 80 percent of its operating costs for personnel. This figure includes salaries and wages for full- and part-time staff members (director, teachers, cooks, janitor) and for substitutes; it also includes fringe benefits for the full-time staff. In determining the budget for salaries, the personnel policies should be consulted in regard to pay rates and fringe benefits. The salary policies may address issues such as staff member's education level, previous experience, or meritorious service. The director must also comply with the minimum wage laws, tax laws, and laws regarding employee responsibility. Other factors which may influence salaries are public school affiliation, union membership, and salary standards of the sponsoring agency.

Personnel costs to the center, over and above the salaries and wages paid to employees, consist of the percentages of these wages that are imposed as taxes by various governmental agencies and that the employer may be required to pay. For example, the employer pays percentages of the employee's salary for social security, workers' compensation, and unemployment compensation. The center also incurs the bookkeeping costs that are involved with keeping accurate records for each employee and filing reports with a variety of government agencies. Benefits, such as health insurance, are included in personnel costs and provision must be made for substitute staff who work during employees' sick and vacation leave. Although benefit costs may seem expendable, they often mean the difference between a stable and a transient staff. Keep in mind that high staff turnover means additional costs for advertising, additional training time, and perhaps loss of clients. More importantly, high staff turnover has a negative effect on the quality of child care.

In addition to the benefits described above, the agency is also required to withhold certain taxes from each employee's paycheck, to accrue these funds, and to submit them to the appropriate governmental body in a timely manner with accurate records. Although these taxes are not paid by the employer, here again the cost of record keeping does contribute to the overall cost of operating the center.

Consultants. A second component of a center budget that is closely related to salaries is contract services or consultant fees. This category covers payments to people who agree to perform specified services for the center or its clients, such as accountants, lawyers, doctors, dentists, social workers, psychologists, nutritionists, and educational consultants. These types of professionals could be employees of a large center or system. However, they usually serve as consultants by agreeing, for example, to give dental examinations to all children enrolled in the center or to provide workshops for teachers one day per month. When the center's staff is not well trained or when a broad range of services is provided for children, many consultants are needed. Although some centers do not hire consultants and most will hire only a limited number, the overall quality of the program may be increased by the services they provide.

When consultants come from out of town, their transportation, meals, and lodging may be additional costs. Sometimes consultants are paid a per diem rate to cover meals and lodging. The current per diem rate of the federal government might be used in budgeting. Both the center and the consultant should agree in writing on all financial arrangements in advance of any services rendered. Under no circumstances should the director attempt to classify a staff position as a consultancy. Serious legal ramifications may be the result.

Plant and Equipment. The largest cost in the physical plant category is rental or mortgage payments on the facility. The costs for the maintenance of, and the repairs to, the building and grounds are also part of this budget item. When maintenance work is done on a regular basis, the costs will usually be lower in the long run. However, since it is impossible to predict all maintenance and repair needs in advance, a lump sum for this purpose should be allocated each year. A preliminary assessment of the main components of a building (roof, plumbing, wiring, heating system, termite damage, and so forth) will provide a rough idea of when major repairs may be expected.

Also included in *physical plant* in the operating budget are utilities (heat, electricity, and water). In some cases, one or more of the utility charges may be covered in the rental fee, a point that should be fully understood before an agreement to rent is made. Some centers may also have to pay for garbage removal. When utilities are not included in the rent payments, an approximate budget figure can be obtained by checking with previous tenants or with the utility companies.

In budgeting for a new center, equipment for the office, for the kitchen, and for the children is a major part of the start-up budget. For a continuing center, the operating budget includes supplementary pieces, as well as repair and replacement where needed. Leasing charges for equipment are included here. For example, a center may lease a floor sander for a day or two or a copy machine for a year. The continuing equipment budget will be about 10 percent of the start-up equipment budget; so if the start-up equipment budget is $500 per child, the continuing equipment budget would be $50 per child per year.

Supplies. Three types of supplies must be purchased: office and general supplies, classroom supplies, and food supplies. The first category, office and general supplies, includes items such as pencils, stationery, toilet paper, paper towels, cleansers, and brooms. Construction paper, paint, crayons, pet food, and doll clothes are included in classroom supplies. Food supplies encompass all items available for human consumption. Usually, two meals and two snacks per child per day are served in full-day centers, with one snack offered in a half-day program. In any case, sufficient food should be provided so that teachers can eat with the children. Food costs vary depending both on the availability of federal food subsidies and on factors in the economy. A nutritionist engaged as a consultant can aid the director in setting up a nutritionally and financially sound food plan.

All consumable supplies should be ordered in large quantities when that is more economical, assuming that the supplies will be used while they are still in top condition (for example, paint dries out when it is stored too long) and there is sufficient storage space. The cost of providing storage space and the possibility that plentiful supplies will be used more freely by the staff must be weighed against the savings accrued from purchasing in quantity.

Transportation. This category may include the purchase or lease of several vans for transporting children to and from school and on field trips. In such cases, insurance, gas, maintenance, and license fees must be budgeted. Some centers contract with a company to provide transportation for children and some may rent a bus for special occasions. Vehicles must be equipped with child safety seats or seat belts, depending on the size of the child, and other governmental regulations regarding vehicles must be followed. Your state may require that you transport children in vehicles meeting special school bus regulations and that drivers have special licenses. The many financial, safety, and liability issues involved lead many centers to require parents to provide the child's transportation to and from school.

Costs for staff members to travel to professional meetings, to other centers for observation, and to homes for home visits are included in the transportation category. The mileage rate for automobile travel reimbursement is usually based on the current federal government mileage rate.

Telephone. Telephone costs can be determined by checking with the telephone company. In deciding on the number of phones to order, consider the center's staffing pattern. For example, if a classroom staffed by one adult is located on another floor away from other classrooms, an extension phone is needed to allow that teacher to get help when necessary. Licensing requirements in some states specify where a phone is required. In any case, enough lines should be provided to enable parents and other callers to reach the center without undue delays. Call waiting is often less costly than a second line, and improves accessibility for outside callers. Getting emergency messages through immediately is a priority item and providing staffers with access to a phone for personal calls during breaks is a benefit that recognizes their needs and helps them feel that they are respected members of the organization.

Insurance. Insurance agents can quote rates and provide information about appropriate kinds of insurance. A center usually needs at least fire, theft, and liability insurance. A child accident policy is valuable and inexpensive. Be sure to read each policy carefully and ask questions about any items which you do not understand.

Postage. Postage covers the cost of mailing payments, bills, and information to parents and prospective client families. Postage costs can be held down to some extent if information is distributed by sending notes home with the children, but keep in mind that these items may not always reach the parent. Some centers establish the policy that payment is due on a particular date each month and no bills are sent.

Marketing. Marketing includes newspaper and phone book advertisements, brochures and fliers, and radio or TV announcements. Some agencies design a logo and use it on various products such as tee shirts, stationery, business cards, and beverage mugs. Once a center is well established, the marketing budget may be minimal, but in the initial stages, and in highly transient neighborhoods, it is an income-producing expense. All centers are wise to maintain a good public relations plan so that the community knows about and supports their work; but perhaps the best marketing tool is a satisfied customer.

Licensing. Information about licensing costs can be obtained from the licensing agent; these costs will vary according to the center's location. Other professional fees, such as those for NAEYC accreditation, also belong in this category.

Audit. Yearly audits are essential. They assure the board and funders that the center's financial matters are being handled properly. You should ask your accountant for a cost estimate and build that into the budget.

Miscellaneous. This category includes funds for small items that do not fall under any of the previously mentioned categories. However, attributing expenditures to a particular category provides a more accurate picture of the center's financial status and eliminates slippage in expenditures. For example, if postage and advertising were both included under *miscellaneous*, postage expenditures could skyrocket and not be recognized as a budgetary problem.

In-Kind Contributions. Some budget items are not received in cash, nor are they paid for in cash. These are called *in-kind contributions* and should be shown in the budget so that the true cost of operating the center is known. For example, a center may rent two 600-square-foot rooms in a church building for $100 per month per room, which would cost the center $2,000 for a ten-month program. If the fair rental cost is at the rate of $5.00 per square foot (a total of $6,000), then the church is, in effect, contributing $4,000 to the center program.

Consultants may volunteer their services, and such services should also be shown as in-kind contributions. For example, assume that a child development specialist conducts a one half-day workshop without charging the center. The specialist's contribution is valued at $200, which is the hypothetical per diem rate for professional services.

Budgeting for Second and Subsequent Years

Several months prior to the end of the year, the director and members of the finance committee meet to review the budget the director has prepared for the ensuing year. For the second and subsequent budgets, the previous year's figures can serve as a guide, but the new budget figures, which are based on experience and on program changes, will differ from those of the previous year. Still, the income and expenses must balance.

OTHER FINANCIAL RESPONSIBILITIES

The budget is the major tool used by the financial director for management of center finances, but balancing income and expenses is only one aspect of an overall ongoing financial system. The director has a number of continuing financial responsibilities, all of which relate ultimately to the budget.

Designing Budget Systems

Once the sources and amounts of income have been determined, these facts must be written down along with the plan for spending discussed earlier in this chapter. This written plan must be prepared in such a way that the people who need to read it will be able to understand it.

Small centers can use a very simple format. Centers that are publicly funded may be required to use whatever system is designated by the funding agency. Many centers use budget codes or account numbers, assigning a code number to each budget category and using separate numbers for each item within that category.

For example, if the budget item *equipment* is coded as 110, then the subcategories might be:

111 office equipment
112 classroom equipment
113 kitchen equipment

Similarly, personnel might be coded as 510, with

511 salaries
512 social security
513 worker's compensation

Such a system enables the financial director to record transactions according to appropriate budget categories and to ascertain quickly how much has been spent and how much remains in a given category.

In order to have an accurate picture of the center's current financial position, accrual, rather

Whenever a financial transaction occurs, it should be recorded promptly in a specific form. Access to a personal computer and appropriate software makes this task relatively easy and provides clear, readily available reports which show the financial position of the center on a monthly, weekly and even daily basis. (Photo by Lisa Souders)

than cash, accounting is essential. This means that revenues are recorded as they are received and expenses are recorded as they are incurred. By using this system, the director avoids the inaccurate picture presented when expenses are recorded only when they are paid rather than when the money is encumbered. This information is reported on a monthly cash flow report, an estimate of how much you expect to receive and spend each month. The director estimates receipts and disbursements for the year, month by month. The amount of cash expected to be on hand at the end of one month of course becomes the amount of cash expected to be on hand at the beginning of the following month. As actual figures become available, these are entered in the "actual" column so that monthly comparisons can be made between anticipated and actual expenses for the month and for the year-to-date.[2] (A sample cash flow report appears in Director's Resources.)

DIRECTOR'S CORNER

"I thought we were in good financial shape. We were showing a solid bank balance and we had full enrollment. What our cash accounting system didn't show was that we had several thousand dollars in bills which the bookkeeper hadn't paid yet. I learned that checking the cash on hand and even looking at how much we had budgeted for a category weren't necessarily appropriate ways to make decisions about what I could spend."

Director, for-profit proprietary center

Ordering Goods and Services

With an approved budget in hand, the director or purchasing agent (or someone assigned to this role) can begin to order supplies, equipment, and services. The first step is to consult the person or people who will use the item or services. The janitor may be consulted about a waxing machine, while the teachers should be involved in decisions about tables and chairs for the children. Both janitor and teachers could participate in selecting carpeting for the classrooms. However, when it comes to the actual ordering of the goods and services, as few people as possible—one is preferable—should be involved.

Several methods of ordering goods and services are utilized, depending on the nature of the purchase. Major purchases are usually approved by the director, the board, or a committee. If outside funding has been received, the center's contract may require that bids be submitted for large items or for large quantities of items (such as food or paper goods). The purchaser writes out required specifications for the item and either submits these specifications to suppliers or advertises for bids in the case of a large order. Then the purchaser examines the bids and contracts that each supplier offers. The lowest bid must be accepted unless the bidder does not meet the specifications. Specifications can refer to a description of the item in question (that is, a commercial dishwasher), to the performance of the item (with water temperature of 180 degrees), or to its delivery date (to be delivered by September 1, l9xx).

Smaller purchases, or those that are routine (such as art supplies), may be ordered from a wholesaler. However, some centers require that price information on such items be obtained and that the item of appropriate quality having the lowest price be purchased. Sometimes purchases are made with particular outlets because they allow credit, but this choice may be false economy.

2 Keith Stephens, CPA, *Confronting Your Bottom Line: Financial Guide for Child Care Centers*, Redmond, WA: Exchange Press Inc., 1991.

In some large cities several centers may band together to purchase large quantities of items at reduced prices in a plan called *cooperative buying*. Each center may contribute to the buyer's salary and must usually transport items from a central location to their own centers.

Making Payments

The director (or someone so designated) is responsible for making all payments. When shipments arrive, they are checked and then paid for as soon as possible within the terms of agreement; for example, if the vendor gives 30 days to pay, the center should use the money until the payment is due, but should carefully monitor bill payment so that unnecessary interest is not incurred. In cases where a discount is offered for prompt payment, that may be a wise course to follow. Before paying for any item, it is important to verify that the items received are proper in quantity and quality and that the price on the invoice is correct.

A center should immediately establish a checking account so that payment for goods and services can be made promptly and safely. If the center is small, there may be the temptation to pay expenses directly from cash income. This practice is a major mistake because under such a plan, money can easily be lost or stolen, and errors or misunderstandings are more likely to occur. Furthermore, no audit trail of these items is available. Most centers use checking accounts and some centers require two signatures on each check—perhaps the signatures of the board treasurer and the director. In small centers or in proprietary centers, the director signs all checks. However, even more important is that there be a person other than the bookkeeper assigned to reconcile the bank balance.

When specific procedures for money management are in place, fewer errors are likely to occur. There must be a specific place to store bills and a specific time set aside for paying them. In small co-ops a parent may work at home recording transactions. In large, complex organizations all finances may be handled through a central administrative office that may be in another city or state.

Recording Transactions

Whenever a financial transaction occurs, it should be recorded promptly in a specific form. Access to a personal computer and appropriate software makes this task relatively easy and provides clear, readily available reports which show the financial position of the center on a monthly, weekly, or even daily basis. Of course, whether a center uses computerized records or handwritten reports, these will be timely and accurate only when timely, accurate information is recorded.

Regular Financial Statements are discussed in Chapter 6.

Auditing

In most businesses, including early childhood education centers, an auditor reviews the books annually. The director makes available to the auditor the financial records, whether on computer or in a ledger, the checkbook, canceled checks, receipts, and invoices. The director or bookkeeper must keep these documents in an organized manner and they must be regularly updated. Shoe boxes or laundry baskets full of invoices are totally unacceptable and are certainly unprofessional. At the very least, such lack of organization leaves the impression that the financial transactions of the center are not accurately maintained.

"The primary purpose of an audit is to enable an independent auditor to express an opinion on the fairness of the financial statements, their compliance with *generally accepted accounting principles,* and the consistency of the application"[3] rather than to examine every transaction or to establish that each entry is valid. An annual audit not only protects the financial personnel of the center by making sure their job is being done according to procedures, but also protects the entire operation by ensuring that the use of funds is being recorded as planned.

3 Teresa P. Gordon, CPA, "When You Think You Need an Audit: Points to Consider," *Child Care Information Exchange,* October 1984, pp. 22–24.

Handling Petty Cash

The director also regulates the petty cash fund, setting the procedures for its use and maintaining sufficient cash to keep the system working effectively. This fund is usually small because serious losses by theft or carelessness may occur when large amounts are kept on hand.

There are several ways to operate the petty cash fund. Each teacher may receive a specified sum of money to spend for the classroom, or the director may allocate a certain sum per staff member, paying cash when the staff member presents an appropriate receipt. Some centers use petty cash for all unexpected small needs. The director keeps a sum of cash on hand and gives it to staff members who present legitimate requests. For example, if the cook has run out of bread, petty cash may be used to purchase a loaf or two. Petty cash should be used as little as possible to avoid obscuring substantial program expenditures under the heading *petty cash*. If $20 worth of food is purchased weekly with petty cash, then the item *food* in the budget is under-represented. All expenditures should be recorded (or allocated) to the correct account. This can be accomplished by the bookkeeper when the user presents receipt documentation.

Handling Salaries Category

Once the budget is approved, the financial director informs the personnel committee of the allocation for salaries. In a new center, the committee may then begin the employment process in accordance with the personnel policies. In continuing centers, raises should be considered.

The director keeps additional records relating to the budget category *salaries*. Professional staff may be paid monthly, biweekly, or weekly, but their salaries are a fixed expense regardless of the number of hours worked as long as that individual remains on the payroll. Other staff receive wages based on number of hours worked during the pay period. Employees who are paid hourly must have some way to record the amount of time spent on the job if that is the basis on which they are paid. Some centers have employees record their working time on weekly time cards which are referred to when paychecks are prepared. Large centers may have time clocks. The director keeps a record of the sick days and the professional days used for all employees, including those who are salaried. Payments are made to each individual employee on the basis agreed on in the employment contract. In small centers where staff have the same schedule daily, time sheets may not be kept. In any event, the director is responsible for keeping track of hours worked, sick leave and vacation time. Here again, entering this information into a computer data base enables the fiscal officer to prepare up-to-date reports and facilitates preparation of the payroll.

Before the employee is paid, the employer must make the appropriate deductions from the amount earned. These deductions may include federal, state, and local income taxes, Social Security tax, retirement, and medical insurance. Some centers, at the employee's request, deduct union dues, parking fees, or contributions to the United Way and other fund-raising groups. When these categories are part of a computer program, changes in percentages or dollar amounts can be made simply and accurately. An explanation of each deduction must be provided to each employee with each pay check. The employer must obtain a federal taxpayer identification number from the IRS.

Information is available from the Internal Revenue Service regarding federal income tax. Each employee is required to file a W-4 form with the center upon employment and to update it as needed. These forms, available from the Internal Revenue Service, enable the employer to determine how much tax must be withheld from each paycheck, based on that employee's income and exemptions. The employer also must check with state and local governments about income taxes that may have to be withheld. The person in charge of preparing the payroll is responsible for learning what the deductions are and for seeing that they are made correctly. Your accountant can list the taxes for which your business is liable.

The director must give each employee a W-2 form by January 31 of each year, showing how much the employee earned during the previous year and how much was paid in taxes. Many employers also provide an annual summary of benefits, including in-kind benefits such as meals provided by the center.

The employer serves as a collection agent, turning over to the appropriate agency the deducted money. Tax dollars are sent to the nearest Internal Revenue Service Center, to the state treasury, and to the local government treasury. For Social Security, the employer contributes an amount equal to the amount that is deducted from the employee's pay; this amount is based on a rate determined by the federal government and both the employer's and the employee's portions are sent by the employer to the Internal Revenue Service. Workmen's compensation is paid entirely by the employer. This program covers payments to the employee for job-related injuries, and diseases and disabilities that occur as a result of working conditions.

The director must check with each taxing body to determine the amount of taxes to be withheld and the time at which they must be reported and paid. Penalties and interest are charged if payments are late or inadequate, and these costs are paid by the center, not the employee. If the center provides benefits such as medical insurance or collects fees for these benefits from employees' pay, the director is responsible for making the payments at the appropriate time.

Payroll checks must be delivered to the employees at the agreed-upon time. Staff morale is lowered considerably when paychecks are not ready on the appointed day. Accuracy is essential.

SUMMARY

To provide a good program for young children, a center must delegate the responsibility for developing and carrying out a financial plan to a competent financial director or committee. The overall plan must be carried out by a person who has knowledge of basic accounting and budgeting procedures and an understanding of the requirements of a good program for young children.

The plan must be based on the priorities for meeting children's needs and on the available funds. The major tool used by the financial director is the budget, which is a plan for balancing income and expenses. The director is responsible for all other financial matters including designing budget systems, ordering goods and services, making payments, recording transactions, and preparing the new budget. An appropriate computer program can save time and money, and, if used correctly, can provide timely, accurate data in a readily accessible format.

Class Assignments

1. Prepare a start-up budget for a center designed to serve 40 preschoolers. Decide where your center will be housed, whether it will be for-profit or not-for-profit, and who will be implementing the start-up plan. Record your answers on Working Paper 5-1.
2. Using Working Paper 5-2, list the facilities, goods, and services you will need to purchase for a year of operating of a child care program for sixty children and provide the cost of each category. Assume that the start-up equipment is already in place and include in your plan only replacement and supplementary equipment. Provide for classroom, general, and office supplies, and for food for one year. List also the number and type of personnel needed for one year and include benefits and other items that will cost money. If you feel that some items could be donated, list those as in-kind contributions. Then total all the costs. How much will your year's budget cost per child?

3. Ask an insurance agent about the types and the cost of insurance that is recommended for an early childhood education center in your area. Report your findings on Working Paper 5-3.

4. Check with several early childhood education directors in your community about the cost per child per week for their centers. Find out what services are provided for this amount of money. Record your findings on Working Paper 5-4.

5. Survey four centers to determine the salary ranges for various positions, such as teacher, assistant teacher, and director. Is there much difference among these salary ranges? To what do you attribute the differences or similarities? Report your findings on Working Paper 5-5.

Class Exercises

1. Using the budget provided in Working Paper 5-6, answer the following questions:

   a. What is the overhead cost per child per week?
   b. What are the weekly expenses for the infant program on a per child basis?
   c. What are the weekly expenses for the toddler program on a per child basis?
   d. What are the weekly expenses for the preschool program on a per child basis?
   e. Consider the overhead cost per child plus the infant expenses per child. What is the total cost to provide care for an infant? What is the difference between that cost and the amount received in tuition from one infant for a year?
   f. Consider the overhead cost per child plus the toddler expenses per child. What is the total cost to provide care for a toddler? What is the difference between that cost and the amount received in tuition from one toddler for a year?
   g. Consider the overhead cost per child plus the preschool expenses per child. What is the total cost to provide care for a preschooler? What is the difference between that cost and the amount received in tuition for one preschooler for a year?
   h. How do you think the difference is accounted for? How does this director balance the budget?

2. Using the Sample Cash Flow Statement (Director's Resource 5-2) as a guide, complete Working Paper 5-7. Assume these January estimates: Cash at beginning of period $1,600. Total cash available $30,000, Total cash paid out $29,000. Fill in the rest of the chart with hypothetical figures to show cash at end of March. Explain what the figures mean.

Working Paper 5-1

List the items you will include in a start-up budget for a center preparing to serve 40 preschoolers. Indicate whether your center will be for-profit or not-for-profit, where it will be housed, and who will be responsible for implementing the start-up phase.

Working Paper 5-2

Facilities, Goods, and Services Form

List the facilities, goods, and services you will need for one year of full-day child care for 60 children. Assume that start-up equipment is already in place. List the cost of each category.

Working Paper 5-3

1. What types of insurance are recommended for an early childhood center in your area?

2. What is the approximate cost of this coverage?

Working Paper 5-4

Cost Versus Servce

1. Center A:
     Cost per child per week is $_____
     Services provided:

2. Center B:
     Cost per child per week is $_____
     Services provided:

3. Center C:
     Cost per child per week is $_____
     Services provided:

Working Paper 5-5

Salary Range Form

Salary	Center A	Center B	Center C	Center D
Director:				
Teacher:				
Assistant Teacher:				

Working Paper 5-6

Sample Budget by Program

Director	$28,000	
FICA, FUTA, WC	2,800	
Health Insurance	2,400	
Cook	9,360	
FICA, FUTA, WC	900	
Management Services Fee	15,000	
Maintenance and Repair	7,000	
Cleaning Service	9,100	
Custodial Supplies	700	
Insurance (Liability and Building)	3,200	
Bookkeeping / Audit	11,100	
Rent	16,000	
Food	20,000	
Education Supplies	3,500	
Utilities / Phone	11,500	
Office and Paper Supplies	3,000	
Training / Consultants	4,000	
Licenses	600	
Garbage Removal	550	
Payroll Service	1,440	
Travel / Field Trips	1,500	
Advertising	300	
TOTAL		$151,950
Overhead Charge per Child ($151,950 / 73)		$2,082

INFANT EXPENSES (BASED ON A 3:1 RATIO):

Infant Primary Caregivers (3)	49,000	
Infant Aides (2)	10,600	
FICA, FUTA, WC	5,960	
Health Insurance	4,680	
Substitutes	3,170	
Vacancy (8%)	5,878	
TOTAL	$79,288	
Overhead (9 x $2082)	18,738	
TOTAL INFANT EXPENSES		$98,026
TOTAL INFANT INCOME (9 X $157 X 52)		73,476
TOTAL INFANT PROFIT / <LOSS>		($24,550)

Working Paper 5-6 (*continued*)

TODDLER EXPENSES (BASED ON A 5:1 RATIO):

Toddler Head Teacher	17,500	
Toddler Assistant Teacher	13,000	
Todder Aide	7,480	
FICA, FUTA, WC	3,700	
Health Insurance	3,120	
Substitutes	2,120	
Vacancy (8%)	5,574	

TOTAL	$52,494		
Overhead (10 x $2065)	20,650		
TOTAL TODDLER EXPENSES		$73,144	
TOTAL TODDLER INCOME (10 x $134 x 52)		69,680	
TODDLER PROFIT / <LOSS>			($3,464)

PRESCHOOL EXPENSES (BASED ON A 9:1 RATIO):

Head Teachers (3)	60,000
Assistant Teachers (3)	39,600
Preschool Aides (3)	18,900
FICA, FUTA, WC	9,360
Health Insurance	9,360
Substitutes	6,340
Vacancy (8%)	24,690

TOTAL	$168,250	
Overhead (54 x $2065)	111,510	
TOTAL PRESCHOOL EXPENSES		$279,760
PRESCHOOL INCOME (44 x $115 x 52)	263,120	
PRESCHOOL INCOME (SUBSIDIZED) (10 x $87.50 x 52)	45,500	
TOTAL PRESCHOOL INCOME		$308,620
PRESCHOOL PROFIT / <LOSS>		$28,860

TOTAL CENTER PROFIT / <LOSS> $846

Working Paper 5-7

Cash Flow Tracking

Period	January		February		March		Total	
	Estimate	Actual	Estimate	Actual	Estimate	Actual	Estimate	Actual
1. Cash at Beginning of Period								
2. Add: Cash Received from:								
Tuition-Parents								
Dept. Human Services								
USDA								
Donations								
Community Chest								
Other sources								
Total Cash Received								
Total Cash Available								
3. Subtract: Cash Paid out:								
Payroll								
Supplies								
food								
educational								
office								
miscellaneous								
Insurance								
Taxes								
Employee benefits								
Other expenses								
Equipment								
Total Cash paid out								
Cash at End of Period								

Director's Resource 5-1

Sample Child Care Center Budget

INCOME

TUITION

Infants (8 x $145 x 51)	59,160	
Toddlers (12 x $125 x 51)	76,500	
Preschooler's (51 x $100 x 51)	260,100	
Total Gross Tuition		395,760

DISCOUNTS

Second child (6 x $10 x 51)	<3,060>	
Vacancy (3%)	<11,873>	
Total Discounts		<14,933>

OTHER INCOME

Application Fees (30 x $20)	600	
Interest on account	600	
Fund raisers	1,000	
Grant award (literacy program)	2,500	
Total Other Income		4,700

TOTAL INCOME		385,527

EXPENSES

PERSONNEL

Director	20,800	
Head Teachers (5)	83,200	
Teachers (5)	67,600	
Assistants (10 part time)	46,800	
Substitutes	2,000	
Secretary	10,400	
Custodian	6,500	
Cook	10,400	
FICA, Workers' Comp., Unemploy.	35,941	
Health Insurance (13 x $1,200)	15,600	
Total Personnel		299,241

RENT	28,800	
UTILITIES AND PHONE	15,169	
ADVERTISING	1,200	
FOOD	31,027	
OFFICE SUPPLIES	710	
CUSTODIAL SUPPLIES	780	
CLASSROOM EQUIPMENT & SUPPLIES	4,200	
C.P.A. FEES	500	
INSURANCE	3,000	
LICENSES	100	
STAFF DEVELOPMENT/TRAINING	300	
TEACHERS' PETTY CASH	500	
Total Non-personnel		86,286

TOTAL		385,527

Director's Resource 5-2

Sample Projected Cash Flow Statement

Period	January Estimated	January Actual	February Estimated	February Actual	March Estimated	March Actual	Total Estimated	Total Actual
1. Cash at Beginning of Period	$1,430	$1,500	$1,071	$1,074	-$983	-$730	$1,518	$1,844
2. Add: Cash received from:								
Tuition-Parents	28,595	28,395	26,600	26,800	30,590	30,400	85,785	85,595
Dept. Human Services	520	507	520	520	520	494	1,560	1,521
USDA								
Donations			100				100	
Community Chest								
Other Sources								
Total Cash Received	$29,115	$28,902	$27,220	$27,320	$31,110	$30,894	$87,445	$87,116
Total Cash Available	30,545	30,402	28,291	28,394	30,127	30,164	88,963	88,960
3. Subtract: Cash Paid out:								
Payroll	20,400	20,400	20,400	20,400	20,400	20,400	61,200	61,200
Supplies								
food	2,800	2,753	2,600	2,614	2,800	2,817	8,200	8,184
educational	100	102	100	79	100	94	300	275
office	50	—	50	84	50	27	150	111
miscellaneous	100	20	100	123	100	131	300	274
Insurance	500	500	500	500	500	500	1,500	1,500
Taxes	—	—	—	—	—	—	—	—
Employee benefits	3,060	3,060	3,060	3,060	3,060	3,060	9,180	9,180
Other expenses								
rent	1,000	1,000	1,000	1,000	1,000	1,000	3,000	3,000
utilities	1,264	1,264	1,264	1,264	1,264	1,264	3,792	3,792
Equipment	200	229	200	—	200	305	600	534
Total Cash paid out	$29,474	$29,328	$29,274	$29,124	$29,474	$29,598	$88,222	$88,050
Cash at End of Period	$1,071	$1,074	-$983	-$730	$653	$566	$741	$910

CHAPTER 6

Funding the Program

Photo above The director is responsible for assuring that funds are available, but board members often assist in securing needed loans or grants. (Photo by Lisa Souders)

Securing funds to start and maintain an early childhood education program is a challenging task. Directors may find themselves carrying the full responsibility for fundraising or figuring out ways to meet the budget established for the program. But, in many situations, board members, prospective parents, or members of sponsoring agencies are willing to help find funding sources. Obtaining initial capital or start-up money is often as difficult as funding the program operation. When tuition is the only source of income, initial capital must be obtained through loans, donations, or grants. In some centers tuition ensures coverage of operating expenses, but many program directors must seek other sources of funding for operating expenses, as well as for initial capital expenses, since quality care is costly and many parents are

unable to pay for the actual cost of care. Outside funding from foundations or government agencies is most available when low-income groups are served or when plans include the development of an innovative addition to an ongoing program. The greatest difficulty in obtaining outside funding is in locating the appropriate sources and writing a persuasive proposal.

In writing proposals for start-up or operating grants, directors must first check available sources. Next they must be able to state clearly what their needs are and relate those to the funder's goals. Finally, they must follow the proposal guidelines carefully and must prepare an easy to understand, professional document. (See Director's Library for books on proposal writing. A sample grant appears in Director's Resources.)

START-UP CAPITAL

Start-up capital includes the money that must be available before the program begins and the money that is needed to support the initial program operation until the flow of tuition and other funds is sufficient to support the ongoing program. Once a director is hired, it takes two to three months to complete the necessary preliminary planning before the program begins. Money for space, equipment, office supplies, and some staff salaries must be available during these early months before the center opens. Since programs are often under-enrolled during the first few months of operation, and since checks from funding sources are sometimes delayed until the program operation is well underway, it is also wise to have sufficient capital on hand at the outset to operate the program for at least six months. These operating monies to cover costs for three months of planning and six months of operation are in addition to the capital needed to finance the purchasing or remodeling of a site and to purchase equipment and supplies for the children's program. In other words, it takes a considerable amount of money to start a program, and it is important to make very careful calculations to ensure that the start-up money is adequate to cover the costs until regular operating funds become available.

Most agency-sponsored centers are nonprofit and many are eligible to receive funding from other community or governmental agencies once there is an established, ongoing program to fund. Operators of proprietary centers that are established for profit or that have no sponsoring agency must invest personal capital, seek donations or one-time grants from a foundation, or arrange for a loan in order to get started. Foundation money is rarely offered to proprietary centers, but rather is reserved for serving particular populations chosen by the

DIRECTOR'S CORNER

"The bank wouldn't lend me the money to start a center. They said it would take too long to show a profit. Finally we put our house up as collateral and we got the loan. But I didn't get any salary for three whole years. We're in good shape now after five years and we're expanding."

Director, private for-profit center

foundation and meeting specific foundation-determined goals.

When the community expresses great interest in getting a program started, it may be possible to promote a successful fund-raising program. However, only relatively small amounts of money can be obtained through raffles, bake sales, or paper drives. Established philanthropic groups such as Kiwanis, Lions, various community groups, and fraternal organizations are sometimes willing to donate money to cover start-up costs such as equipment, or to support a capital improvements fund-raising campaign; but like other funders, they seldom provide operating expenses.

A company may provide start-up funding for a center for its employees' children with the understanding that the director will need to secure adequate funding for operating costs, largely tuition, from other sources. Centers in public schools are usually funded through special government grants and the central administration may manage the budget. In the case of large chains of centers, the corporate office secures investors and funds the start-up of new centers based on their market research.

Programs that start without a sufficient funding base are in fiscal trouble from the outset. Since it is very difficult to maintain a balanced budget for an early childhood education program, it is paramount to keep a balanced budget at the outset by finding enough capital to cover start-up costs.

SOURCES OF OPERATING FUNDS

Once the facility is established and the basic equipment has been purchased, income must be adequate to ensure daily program operation. Operating funds can come from tuition, from community resources such as United Way, from private foundations, or through various state and federal governmental programs.

Tuition

When the center is largely dependent on tuition for operating funds, it will be necessary to balance the number of children to be enrolled, the amount of tuition their families can reasonably be expected to pay, and the amount of money needed to operate the program. The program will not always be fully enrolled; therefore, the budget should have at least a 3 to 8 percent vacancy rate built in. Programs just beginning may enroll only a few children for many months, necessitating close management of the initial budget and reduction of variable costs to the lowest possible level. Even some fixed costs can be reduced. For example, a director may employ only one or two salaried teachers until the tuition receipts warrant the addition of more staff.

Since the salaries of most preschool teachers are unreasonably low, and since salaries comprise the biggest expenditure by far in an education budget, it is sensible to charge an amount that will provide the fairest possible salary to the staff. Thus, the tuition rate should be based on a number of facts, including:

1. the amount needed to meet professional commitments to staff
2. the amount that is reasonable in terms of the type of program offered to families
3. the amount charged by comparable centers in the area

In determining the amount of funds needed, a break-even chart is useful. You and your accountant can prepare such a chart by first determining the fixed costs of operating the center, such as rent, utilities, director's salary—costs that will remain at the same level regardless of enrollment.

Next, variable costs are calculated. These are the costs for operating the program that change as children are added or subtracted. For example, when four or five children are added, the cook probably orders more food, more art materials are needed, and so forth.

Based on licensing requirements, and also on center policies, when a certain enrollment is reached, an additional teacher must be employed. A simple example would be to think of a center with thirty children in which a 1:10 ratio is required. When the thirty-first child is added, the center must provide an additional teacher even though the additional tuition generated by one child will surely not pay a teacher's salary. However, if six new children are added, it may be financially feasible to have four groups of nine children. Of course, if tuition from ten children is required to pay the expenses then the director should not add children until she can insure a class of ten or realize that money will be lost on that class.

Using the break-even chart, the director projects the income based on the enrollment. She then looks for the points at which the total costs meet the income and checks to see at what enrollment levels that occurs.[1]

To assist parents or to attract clients, centers may decide to offer lower tuition when two children from the same family attend, or they may choose to offer one or more weeks' tuition free for vacation or illness. The director must balance this loss of income against the potential loss of two children or else must make the initial tuition rate high enough to cover such factors. However, since these costs are quite variable, depending on how many two-child families are enrolled in the center at a given time, they may add to budget instability. Holding a space for an expected

---

1 Keith Stephens, CPA, *Confronting Your Bottom Line: Financial Guide for Child Care Centers*, Redmond, WA: Exchange Press Inc., 1991.

infant for partial tuition has a similar budgetary effect. Giving a free vacation week may negatively affect cash flow if most parents decide to take advantage of this plan during the same week, thus severely curtailing income. This event would be particularly damaging in a center which used the cash, rather than accrual, method of accounting.

Some centers charge tuition on a sliding scale based on the parents' ability to pay. Often these centers receive government or agency funds to supplement tuition income. A sliding fee scale formula is prepared that takes into account the amount of income, the number of dependents, and other circumstances such as extraordinary medical bills. However, whenever a family pays less than the actual cost of care, the difference must be covered by making the top of the scale higher than the cost (so that some families pay more than the cost of care) or by securing outside funds. (A sample sliding fee scale appears in Director's Resources.)

Tuition charges are set not only by estimating what families are willing and able to pay for services but also by considering what rates are charged by competing agencies in the community. Local professional organizations or the local or state universities may have information about the amount of tuition that can be reasonably charged in a particular community. Unless a program offers something very different from that offered by nearby centers (such as NAEYC accreditation), it may be difficult to convince parents to pay significantly higher tuition for one program over another; thus, tuition rates must be reasonably competitive. On the other hand, if tuition is lowered to attract clients, it may be difficult to cover costs and compete with other centers in offering teachers reasonable salaries and in hiring competent staff. Directors of quality centers often have to educate members of the community about the differences in program quality, and in particular, about the value of well-prepared and more costly staff.

Community Resources

Many early childhood education programs are subsidized by local charities and church groups or by United Way funds. Church groups or other charitable sponsoring agencies typically do not provide cash to help meet the operating

budget; instead, they provide in-kind contributions such as free rent, janitorial service, coverage of utility bills, volunteer help, and so forth. Should the director and the board find themselves with an unbalanced budget at the end of the year because of unforeseen problems with enrollments or unexpected expenditures, some sponsoring agencies will cover the losses. This practice is particularly prevalent in situations where one of the sponsoring agency's goals is to provide child care services to low-income members of the community. However, the director who is not managing her budget well is not likely to be "bailed out" more than once.

United Way funds, raised through a United Appeal campaign, are available for child care services in many communities. Eligibility for these community funds will vary depending on the locale, the amount of money available, and the demands placed on that source of funding.

As a director of a program that may need community support money, you should familiarize yourself with eligibility requirements in your community so that you can plan accordingly. Often a number of preliminary steps must be taken before a program can be presented for funding consideration. Also, some United Way agencies will not give either start-up money or operating funds to new programs. Eligibility requirements for funds typically include the following:

1. The agency must be an incorporated, voluntary, nonprofit, charitable organization, possessing tax-exempt status under Section 501 (c)(3) from the Internal Revenue Service. The agency must be licensed by the appropriate authority, must carry on a needed health, welfare, or social service, and must have a qualified and representative governing body that serves without compensation.

2. The agency must have, and must implement, a written policy of nondiscrimination and nonsegregation on the basis of race, ethnic origin, disabling condition, sex, or religion regarding its governing body, its employees, and the people it serves.

3. The agency must have been established and must have continued to function for a minimum of three years (number varies here) before applying for funds.

4. The agency must be willing to cooperate in the fund-raising campaign and to abide by all the policies of the United Way agency.

Once the minimum eligibility requirements have been met, the necessary steps for funding consideration must be taken by the director of the center or by a designated board member. The director is usually the only person who has all the necessary information for completing application forms and therefore is the one ultimately responsible for filing the numerous ongoing attendance and financial records most United Way agencies require. If a board member assumes this responsibility, the director must still provide the necessary data. Thus, it is important that the director be familiar with the application procedures and clearly understand the ongoing reporting requirements for funded programs *before* entering into any agreements with the funding agency.

The application for funding may seem intimidating to some directors and may hinder them from applying for available funds. The process does become easier as the director gains more experience in applying and finds that many applications require similar information. Once it has been gathered, some of the data can be re-used in subsequent proposals. Nonetheless, directors must be prepared to spend a great deal of time and energy on routine reporting if they expect to use outside funds.

FOUNDATIONS

A *foundation* is a fund administered by trustees and operated under state or federal charter. Foundation funds are sometimes made available to child care centers for major equipment purchases or for a special project. Occasionally, a foundation will provide funds for building or remodeling a facility. Foundation support for a program depends on whether or not the trustees of the foundation have declared education, or more specifically, early childhood education, as an area of interest.

Large philanthropic foundations such as Ford, Carnegie, and Rockefeller Foundations have broad-ranging programs with specific interest areas that change periodically. For example, there may be a general interest in funding innovative educational programs, but monies may be going into literacy or single-parent programs during one funding period, only to shift to programs for preschool developmentally-delayed children or innovative child care models during the next funding period. Smaller foundations may limit support to programs in a certain geographic area or to a given problem area that may change every few years, while other special interest foundations limit support efforts to very specific interest areas that do not change.

Money from corporate foundations is available in many communities. In smaller cities it is wise to solicit funds from small, local corporations that often have some funds set aside for use by local agencies. Frequently, the small corporate funds are controlled by corporate managers who are very sensitive to the public relations value of making a gift to the local agencies, which will, in turn, give due credit and recognition to the funder.

When directors plan to approach a foundation for money, they must know precisely what they expect to do with the money and how they expect to do it. Their appeal for money must be tailor-made to the foundation's interest areas, and all funding requests must move through the proper channels. However, personal contacts with foundation trustees or other people connected with the foundation are considered very helpful. Perhaps a member of the center's parent group or a board member has personal contacts with a foundation or can help find the best channels to use for personal contacts.

DIRECTOR'S CORNER

"When I write a proposal, I always try to think of something that will appeal to the proposal reader—a catchy title or an intriguing goal such as introducing preschoolers to good nutrition through 15 microwave cooking projects. In the long run, we not only meet the goal, but we still have the microwave to use for daily food preparation."

Director, agency-sponsored
not-for-profit center

Your local library will be able to provide you with lists of foundations to contact. Keep in mind that foundation funds are rarely, if ever, given to an agency just because the agency is operating at a loss. Funds tend to flow toward challenging and interesting programs in well-run organizations rather than to needy institutions which are faltering.

GOVERNMENT FUNDING

Federal, state, and local governments all have a commitment to the care of the children of working mothers, with the federal government being the forerunner of that movement as far back as the early 1940s. Although state and local government agencies have been involved in licensing and monitoring early childhood education programs for some time, the availability of state and local money for child care for working mothers is relatively recent when compared to federal monies available on a somewhat sporadic basis for about fifty years. Government monies typically are available for programs that serve low-income families or those that serve children with special needs. Currently, the Head Start program and the proliferation of programs for young children with various disabling conditions serve as evidence of the federal

government's focus on children with special needs. California was the first state to establish an extensive network of state-supported child care centers; however, New York, Ohio, and a few other states are moving to expand their state-supported systems. Although some funds are available, many children, particularly in certain areas, are underserved or receive no services.

A number of major sources of federal funding were established during the 1960s and continue to provide some basic support for child care and for children with special needs. Often legislation involving child care is controversial. As more women work outside the home and more children grow up in single parent families, child care has taken on new political importance. Center directors need to keep informed of current and pending legislation and make their views known to state and federal legislators who can provide up-to-date information. Local and national organizations such as the National Association for the Education of Young Children (NAEYC) are good sources of information on legislation related to young children. Local libraries can help you find the names of your legislators.

Directors should also become familiar with legislation enacted in other countries, such as Canada's Child Care Act of 1988 which provided $6.4 billion for start-up and operating costs for centers and for enhanced tax assistance to families with young children.[2]

REFLECTIONS

Think about a time when you needed a loan, whether from a bank or from your parents or a friend. Did you plan ahead what you would say and how you would explain your need? Did you mention the amount you needed and the purpose of the loan? How did you decide whom to approach for a loan? A director who writes a proposal must answer similar questions.

2 Ann Miles Gordon and Kathryn Williams Brown, *Beginnings & Beyond,* (2nd ed), Albany, NY: Delmar, 1989, p. 444.

The director uses the daily transaction records to prepare monthly financial reports. (Photo by Robert W. Dorsey)

DONATIONS

Directors may also encourage parents, grandparents, and friends of the center to donate funds or stock that has appreciated. The latter may provide a tax break for the donor; and although directors are not expected to know the fine points of tax law, they should be aware enough to provide general information to prospective donors. Many agencies disseminate this type of information in special brochures.

REPORTING TO FUNDERS

Whether the funders are organizations providing support to assist needy families, stockholders investing for profit, members of a parent co-op, school board members, or individuals who own and direct the center, every funder needs to know how the business is doing.

Accurate, timely, and understandable reports are essential. The director uses the daily transaction records to prepare monthly financial reports for the funders as well as for internal use in making budgetary decisions. (These reports also should be available to those staff members who choose to read them.) The director may present this information at a board meeting or may mail it to board members and other concerned persons. Either way, the information should be presented in clear, neat, and concise form. Computer-generated reports can be revised readily so that the most current information is available. The director must be prepared to answer questions regarding the month's operating budget and to justify the figures in the report.

Since the purpose of the report is to inform the reader, it is meaningless to present a highly technical report to a group with no background in reading such reports. On the other hand, large organizations may require that each center follow a particular reporting format. In any event, the income and expenses must be presented in such a way that the reader can easily grasp the financial situation of the center. If a report indicates the need for changes in the budget (for example, an unpredictable expense such as a furnace that must be replaced immediately), the person or the people who have to approve such changes can review the budget and make appropriate revisions.

The director prepares or oversees the preparation of several types of reports.

1. *Center enrollment report.* How many children are enrolled and how many are on the waiting list? If the center serves various age groups, the report should be subdivided, e.g., infants, toddlers, preschoolers, after-school care. The director may also project the number of children expected to move up to the next age group on a month by month basis. For example, if six children will no longer be eligible for the toddler group in March, based on licensing rules will there be room for them in the preschool classrooms?

2. *Accounts receivable.* The director should receive a report at least weekly of accounts receivable. In a child care center, this figure will consist primarily of tuition owed. Repeated billing on a specific schedule (usually weekly) is essential. When friendly and specific reminders are ineffective, phone the parent and state your expectation that the bill will be paid by a specific date. If the parent is experiencing problems, an installment plan may be worked out. Be sure to document all phone calls, agreements reached and so forth, but at the same time respect the parent's rights by keeping this information confidential. If you are unsuccessful in your collection efforts it may be necessary to turn past due bills over to an attorney or a collection agency.[3] Even though you have planned ahead by including a factor for bad debt in the budget, serious attempts to collect are essential to maintaining your clients' understanding that these obligations are important unless the funding precludes that approach.

3. *Budget comparison report.* Each month the director prepares or receives from the bookkeeper a report showing what was spent the preceding month in each category. The report also shows budgeted spending for that month, and actual and budgeted spending for the year to date. The director or board can then spot cash flow problems, analyze expenditures, project remaining expenses, and revise the budget if necessary.

4. *Balance sheet.* On a monthly basis a balance sheet should be prepared, showing assets (what you own) and liabilities (what you owe).

5. *Income Statement.* An income statement must be created at the end of each year. this statement reflects the total of all revenue earned and all expenses incurred during the fiscal year. The difference between revenue and expense is net income if revenues are greater than expenses, and net loss if expenses are greater than revenues. The income statement is widely considered the most important financial statement because it is a measure of how well a business is doing at the end of the year. The statement shows whether the company has generated a profit or is incurring losses. The income statement represents the actual figures for each of your previously budgeted categories. It can be used as a tool to evaluate monies allocated to specific categories on your budget. For instance, if maintenance and repair expense was actually $7,000 for the year according to the income statement but was budgeted at $2,500 on your operating budget, you would want to reevaluate your budgeted figure provided that the dollars spent for maintenance and repair were not one-time, unusual expenditures. In addition to this latter example, the income statement can be helpful for other kinds of statistical analysis.

6. *Annual report.* At the end of the fiscal year, the director presents a final report showing the amount budgeted in each category and the amount actually spent. Up-to-date cash flow statements make it relatively easy to prepare the annual report.

A computer is an invaluable tool in preparing financial and other reports. A computer with basic word processing and spreadsheet software can be utilized for budgets, enrollment reports, budget comparison reports, cash flow statements,

3 Child Care Information, *Ideas for Directors,* "Collecting Overdue Fees," March 1985, pp. 11–12.

income statements, balance sheets, annual reports and virtually any other financial statement that a child care program would ever need. Examples of word processing software are Microsoft Word® and Word Perfect®. Examples of spreadsheet software are Lotus 1-2-3® and Microsoft Excel®. Although all four of the latter examples are well known and widely used, there are many other brands of software available for word processing and spreadsheet applications. In addition to financial reporting, a computer with the aforementioned software can also be utilized for a multitude of other functions such as mailing lists, general letters to parents, class rosters, class medical instructions, bulletin board notices, grant application letters, center handouts, general signs, educational supplies inventory, and so forth. The possibilities for use are endless.

As technological advances are made and products become more widely available, the cost of the average personal computing system (computer with keyboard, monitor and printer) is going down. Investment in a personal computer is not only worthwhile, but cost effective. Careful consideration should be given to the trade-off between the purchase price of the system and the costs associated with not having the system, such as staff hours spent manually updating reports, staff hours spent revising and editing reports on a typewriter, printing costs, outside service preparation costs, inability to produce professional reports and letters in-house, and so forth. Additionally, in many cases when you purchase a personal computer, the computer comes preloaded with some type of word processing and spreadsheet software. The cost of this software is included in the purchase price of the system. Although this pre-packaged software may be simplistic as compared to the four examples above, it could be very useful for child care program needs. Additional higher level software can be purchased at a later date if necessary. Child care centers do not usually need the most powerful (and expensive) equipment available. Some software manufacturers provide software specifically designed for child care programs. These packages tend to be expensive. However, the software does provide for many of the specific needs of a child care program.

Data which many directors now have on computer includes registration information, waiting lists, prospective clients, staff information, billing and payment data, payroll, attendance, scheduling and correspondence. When this information is entered appropriately, data can be presented in a variety of ways. For example, reports on which children will need an immunization within a specified time period can be generated along with personalized letters to their parent reminding them.

The software you select should be "user friendly" or easy to operate and the vendor should provide you with opportunities to have your questions answered by phone. You'll want to know which hours this service is available and whether the consultant is three time zones away or on the same schedule as your work-time. The consulting service may be free for six months or so and thereafter users may be charged a monthly or annual fee if they choose to purchase the service. Support is even more essential if you are purchasing specialized child-care-program-specific software that is not as widely used by others in the field.

Before you buy, ask to try the software and hardware yourself rather than just watching the sales representative demonstrate. Although it will take awhile to learn the finer points, you should be able to comprehend the basics with some initial coaching. Ask whether training for your staff will be provided. Find out whether the components of the software are integrated. For example, you should be able to enter parents' names and addresses once, perhaps on the registration form, and then call up that information without re-entering it when you want to send letters to all the parents.

As with any other major purchase, checking on the vendor helps insure a satisfactory transaction. How long has the company been in business? Can they provide references from other programs similar to yours? What kinds of software upgrades do they provide, how often, and at what cost to current users?

Because both hardware and software are continually being upgraded, directors must seek the latest information when they are ready to purchase. The director should start this process by developing a listing of how the computer will be utilized in that particular child care program. Once developed, this listing will assist the director in determining software and hardware needs and requirements.

If you work with a board of directors, you should ask for the assistance of any board member with a background in computer software and hardware. Another good source of information would be other program directors who are usually glad to share information about the types of software and hardware they purchase and use. They will be able to discuss the overall performance of their system as well as any problem areas.

Professional journals often review software and relate its capabilities to the needs of child care directors. *Child Care Information Exchange* publishes an annual software review that specifically addresses child care center management. Nonetheless, each director must be sure that the package will do what is needed in a particular center and the director must be able to understand and modify the software. Checking the warranty, getting references from current users and even giving hardware and software packages trial runs may save a center hundreds of dollars as well as protect the director from purchasing a product that does not fit the center's needs or cannot be utilized easily and effectively.

SUMMARY

Tuition for child care programs is set based on cost of the program, parents' ability to pay, availability of other funds, and the marketplace. Many programs in early childhood education depend on outside funding for partial or total support. Knowledge of the sources of funding and some skill in proposal writing are both important for directors who may be forced to find funds to operate their programs when tuition is not sufficient to support a high quality program. Some programs receive funds from their sponsoring agencies, while others depend on United Way funds, grants from foundations, or government grants.

When a center operates with a board, the board makes policies about tuition, usually to balance the need to retain enrollment and the need to meet budgetary requirements. Board members also participate in securing funds and in creating the three- to five-year financial plan for the center.

The breakeven analysis, budget comparison report, and balance sheet are important financial management tools for the director and provide a clear, accurate picture for funders.

Class Assignments

1. Find out who provides money for early childhood education in your community. Are any programs funded by the federal government, state or local government, Community Chest or United Way, private individuals, chain or franchised centers, universities or colleges, businesses, or proprietors? Is anyone else funding early childhood education in your community? Write your findings on Working Paper 6-1.

2. Contact a rural or inner-city child care center director (not a Head Start center). Inquire about the funding base. Try to find answers to the following questions and write them on Working Paper 6-2.

   a. How much tuition do parents pay?
   b. How much of the total budget is covered by tuition?
   c. What outside funding sources are available to support the program and how much money is available through those sources?
   d. How were outside funds obtained?

3. Use the figures in Working Paper 6-3 to determine how many children will be in each group for the next six months. If licensing requires one adult for each four infants, one for each eight toddlers, and one for each 12 preschoolers, what effect will the changing enrollment have on your budget?

4. Read the Business Plan Questionnaire in Working Paper 6-4. Fill out the form using a hypothetical situation.

Write a paragraph about your reaction to these questions.

Class Exercises

1. Work with a group of your classmates to make the following decisions. Assume that your center serves 60 preschoolers in four classes of 15 children each. Your operating expenses are $200,000.

   a. How much will the annual tuition be? How much will the weekly tuition be?
   b. Will you take into account bad debts and a vacancy factor?
   c. Assume that ten families can pay only $1,000 a year ($20 a week) for their ten children. How much tuition will every other family have to pay to make up the difference if you don't get scholarship funds from other sources?

2. Form a small group with several of your classmates to decide a policy based on the following information. Four families at the center you direct announce they are expecting babies in about six months. They want to hold places for them and they want to keep the older siblings home for three months (without paying tuition) while the mother is on maternity leave. What will your policy be?

Working Paper 6-1

Funding Form

Who provides money for early childhood education in your community?

Federal government?

State government?

Community Chest or United Way?

Private individuals?

Chains or franchised centers?

Universities or colleges?

Businesses?

Proprietors?

Other?

Working Paper 6-2

Funding Base Form

1. Name of the center you contacted:

2. Funding base

   - How much tuition do parents pay?
   - How much of the total budget is covered by tuition?
   - What outside funding sources are available to support the program and how much money is available through those sources?
   - How were outside funds obtained?

Working Paper 6-3

Enrollment Figures

February

Enrolled

Infants	10
Toddlers	16
Preschool	24

Waiting List

Infants	12
Toddlers	3
Preschool	0

Ready to Move Up

Infants to Toddlers

March	1
April	0
May	2
June	1
July	1
August	0

Toddlers to Preschool

March	0
April	1
May	0
June	2
July	0
August	0

Working Paper 6-4

Business Plan Questionnaire

Financial Analysis

1. Will you need a loan to start or expand the center? If so, approximately how much?

2. What will the loan be used for?

3. What sources will you use to obtain the loan? (Bank, Credit Union, State, City, etc.)

4. What is(are) the item(s) to be puchased and at what cost(s)?

5. Who will be supplying these items?

6. Do you have a personal, savings, checking, or business account with a local bank? If so, which one, and who is your banker?

7. Have you approached them about your loan request? What was their response?

8. Do you own any assets or items of value? If so, what?

9. Would you be willing to use your personal assets as collateral against a loan to provide your center with a stable equity base?

10. Have you prepared a projected Profit and Loss Statement showing the potential revenues versus expenses of your center during your first three years of operation?

11. Will you need assistance in preparing such statements?

12. Can you provide personal tax returns for the past three years?

13. How will a loan make your business more profitable?

(Adapted from "Business Plan Questionnaire," The Ohio Department of Development, Small and Developing Business Division, Office of Management and Technical Services, Columbus, OH, 43216-0101)

Director's Resource 6-1

Sample Sliding Fee Schedule

Parent pays:	20%	30%	40%	50%	60%	70%	80%	90%
Infant	$20/wk	$30	$40	$50	$60	$70	$80	$90
Toddler	$18	$27	$36	$45	$54	$63	$72	$81
Preschooler	$16	$24	$32	$40	$48	$56	$64	$72

Director's Resource 6-2

Sample Income Statement
For the Year Ended December 31, 199X

Income Statement
For the Year Ended December 31, 199___

Revenues

Infant Program Income	$70,500
Toddler Program Income	64,500
Preschool Program Income	247,120
Federal Child Care Program	41,500
Donations/Contributions	500
Parent Fundraising	1,100
Other Income	50

Total Income	$425,270

Expenses

Salaries / Wages	267,100
Health Benefits	19,650
Employment Taxes and Insurance	21,840
Management Services Fee	15,000
Training / Consultant Fees	7,200
Food / Beverage Supplies	21,300
Educational Supplies	4,100
Office & Paper Supplies	3,300
Rent	16,000
Payroll Service Fees	1,420
Cleaning Service Fees	8,920
Custodial Supplies	950
Equipment Expense	2,800
Utilities / Phone Expense	11,300
Garbage Removal	650
Advertising	850
Travel / Field Trips	1,600
Bookkeeping / Audit Service Fees	11,500
Licenses	625
Maintenance & Repair Expense	5,920
Insurance Expense	3,200

Total Expense	425,225

Net Income (Net Loss)	$45

Director's Resource 6-3

Sample Balance Sheet
As of April 30, 199X

Assets

Cash-Operating	$7,000
Cash-Payroll	8,000
Accounts Receivable	11,200
Educational Supplies	900
Office Supplies	400
Property, Plant, and Equipment	42,000
Total Assets:	$69,500

Liabilities

Accounts Payable	$11,000	
Wages Payable	5,000	
Mortgage Payable	32,000	
Long Term Labilities	15,000	
Total Liabilities:		63,000

Equity

Capital	6,500
Total Liabilities and Equity	$69,500

Director's Resource 6-4

Sample Grant Application*

Doe Learning Center Inc., is a nonprofit corporation that operates four child care centers in the greater metropolitan area. The centers provide quality child care for children ages three months through five years, and also offer school-age care at two of the sites. As a United Way agency, the centers' common goal is to work toward alleviating the current crisis of child care, as outlined in the Long Range Plan for Child Care of the United Way/Community Chest in 1992. This study shows that there is an urgent need for quality programming for children identified as having special needs. Doe Learning Center Inc. has responded to this need by operating four centers whose common goal is the inclusion of all children.

STATEMENT OF AGENCY COMMITMENT

Metropolitan Learning Center (MLC) is located in the central area of the city. The program serves sixty-seven children ages three months through five years. In the summer we enroll an additional twenty children in our school-age program. Established in 1984, MLC was the first full day program in this city to be accredited by the National Association for the Education of Young Children.

Largely based on the theories of Piaget and Erikson, the center's philosophy reflects a focus on the development of the whole child and the formation of strong trusting relationships. The developmental constructivist approach holds the belief that children develop sequentially from one stage of development to another. Because of this we believe that children must be provided with opportunity that will challenge them and aid in their progression from one stage to the next. It is a necessity that learning be based on actual experience and participation. Talking without doing is largely meaningless to young children.

We believe that in order for children to grow, they must be placed in a setting that meets their basic needs. Therefore it is our utmost concern that our program provide a nurturing, comfortable environment that is specifically structured to meet the physical, emotional and cognitive needs of each individual child.

This philosophy was the foundation for the development of the agency. Due to this commitment, the question of inclusion was never discussed; only how to do it well.

In this time of severe staff shortages in the ECE field, MLC feels fortunate to have an outstanding quality of professionals.

- four preschool head teachers—M.Ed.
- one toddler head teacher—Associate in Early Education
- two infant teachers—Bachelor Education and two infant teachers—Associate Education
- Dr. John Jones professor emeritus at the Metropolitan University has been consulting with our agency for three years. This past year Dr. Jones is working strictly at MLC coordinating our educational services.

* Names of people and places are fictitious.

Director's Resource 6-4 (*continued*)

MLC has worked extensively with the Early Childhood Education Department, Metropolitan University. The program has been a training site for the past five years, and works with an average of three to four students per quarter.

According to Washington County Child Day Care: *The State of Today and Plans for 1992*, "Special needs children are still at a great disadvantage. Most child care providers feel ill-equipped to serve children with developmental problems and physical disabilities." MLC has successfully integrated approximately twenty-five children identified as having special needs. One family called over sixty child care centers before finding a placement at MLC for their child with cerebral palsy. The center has served many children with a wide variety of special needs including but not limited to: pervasive development disorder, fragile x syndrome, autism, mild mental retardation, receptive language disorder, and visual impairments, to name a few.

One of the primary goals of the organization is to meet the needs of the family, parent and child. MLC has identified its ability to meet these needs as follows:

Needs of the child—
- placement in a program meeting the standards of developmentally appropriate practice
- Master level staff capable of identifying and working with high-risk children

Needs of the parent—
- providing high quality care for their children
- providing quarterly parent education/training programs
- providing assistance in identifying (or working with existing) available services (i.e., early intervention) for their children

MLC has been identified in the community as a program which will not only serve children with special needs, but give them priority on the waiting list. Metropolitan University acknowledged the endeavors of the center by placing students from the Special Education department under the guidance of our experienced staff. We have worked with many agencies in order to provide more comprehensive services to these children.

These agencies include:

- Washington County Department of Human Services
- Special Education Regional Resource Center (SERRC)
- Cerebral Palsy Services Center
- Center for Developmental Disorders
- Speech and Hearing
- Speech Pathology
- Child Advocacy Center
- Association for the Blind
- Metropolitan University—Early Childhood/Special Education Department
- Foster Grandparent Program
- The Council on Aging
- The Single Parent Center

II   STATEMENT OF NEED

There are currently eight children enrolled in the program who have been identified as having special needs. There are several children that are integrated into the environment and are receiving

Director's Resource 6-4 (*continued*)

services from support agencies. MLC feels confident that we can meet their needs without additional services. There are two children that pose challenges to our existing program. One child is currently enrolled in our infant program. He is twenty months old and has cerebral palsy. When we enrolled Ed we assessed that we could meet his needs in the infant program. Though Ed is non-mobile, and non-verbal, he uses smiles, cries, and coos to communicate with his caregiver.

In order to continue serving Ed,

- We need to be able to meet the challenge of facilitating his growth through experiences with the toddlers.
- We need to acquire the equipment to encourage his further development.
- We need release time for his caregiver to meet with his therapist to learn how to use specialized equipment and participate in his I.E.P. meeting.

Our second child has been identified with pervasive developmental disorder and mild characteristics of autism. Communication has been the primary barrier in the progression of Ryan's development. This aspect of his disorder carries over into other areas of his growth including the development of self control. Ryan has been enrolled in our program for one year and within that period has gone from single word utterances to communicating in four to five word sentences. Because of this increased ability to communicate, the agency believes that a transition to the oldest preschool classroom is the next step. The goal of this move is to place Ryan in an environment of his same-age peers where he might benefit from the modeling of age-appropriate behaviors and participation in activities. Any changes in daily schedule and transition times are extremely difficult for Ryan and separation from his current classroom teacher will be a tremendous undertaking.

Our belief is that in order to best aid in this transition, MLC will need the assistance of an additional staff person for the following reasons:

- to meet the needs of Ryan during the period of transition so that classroom staff may continue to meet the needs of his peers
- to act as a facilitator, giving Ryan assistance with social interactions so that he might form relationships with his peers and staff
- to give the classroom staff opportunity to focus on forming trusting relationships with Ryan, without concern that the experiences of his peers are being limited.

PURPOSE OF FUNDING/BUDGET

The purpose of our funding breaks into three categories; equipment, consulting/training and additional staff to decrease ratios.

Equipment

Type	Purpose	Cost
Outdoor swing	seat enables severely challenged student to enjoy the sensation of swinging	$126.95
Floor sitter	allows non-mobile child to interact with peers but have necessary support	$150.00
Button switch toy		$42.00
Jelly Bean switch toy		$42.00
Circus Truck		$27.00

Director's Resource 6-4 (*continued*)

Bumper Car			$25.00
Brontosaurus			$29.50
Oversized Ball	easier to manipulate than typical ball	18″	$24.35
		34″	$69.50

Consulting/Training
Topic (we would like to open these to public)

"How to adapt 'typical' equipment to meet the needs of physically challenged children"	$100.00
"How to use switch toys"	$80.00
"How to write an appropriate I.E.P. and how to make the I.E.P. meeting work for the child	$100.00

Consulting

How to arrange the toddler environment to meet the needs of a physically challenged child	$100.00
How to encourage positive peer relationships with typical and atypical children	$50.00

Support Staff

Enrolling a physically challenged child into the infant program was within the abilities of our staff. Allowing time for this child to interact with peers of his own age and slowly transitioning him into the toddler room will be a challenge for us. We need time for his caregiver to visit the toddler room with him and then time for the toddler teacher to have one-on-one time for him. This cannot be done without additional staff. Any choice we make with the current staff situation will either short-change Ed or the other children enrolled. We are requesting a part-time assistant for six months.

Cost $6,656

Having children that model age appropriate behaviors has been the most vital ingredient to Ryan's development. To continue his progress it is imperative that he be surrounded by children exhibiting the behaviors that Ryan is striving for. As mentioned earlier any transition is very difficult for Ryan. In order to continue serving Ryan and meet his needs by transitioning him to be with children of his own age, we will need additional staff.

We are requesting a part-time assistant for six months.	Cost $6,656
TOTAL REQUESTED	$14,278.30

EXPECTED OUTCOME

This grant will enable us to purchase equipment that will:

- allow physically challenged children to become more accessible to the other children by being positioned near them on the floor
- provide stimulation and encourage peer interaction
- allow isolation to lessen so that relationship with peers will increase.

This grant will enable us to provide sufficient staff to:

- allow challenged children to be surrounded with children of their own age providing appropriate models
- allow staff to meet the needs of our children with special needs without denying other children the attention they need
- encourage smooth transitions that encourage success with meaningful relationships with other children
- make inclusion a successful experience that will encourage staff to include additional children.

Director's Resource 6-4 (*continued*)

This grant will provide technical assistance that will:

- give the staff and management the knowledge to include these children and additional children in the future
- encourage other early childhood programs to attend these training sessions and build support through networking with other teachers participating in inclusion.

We will be asking staff who are working with Ed and Ryan to fill out a short questionnaire before we provide additional services and again after. We would like to see if these support services change any possible insecurities or feelings of being overwhelmed that had previously occurred.

CHAPTER 7

Developing a Center Facility

Photo above It is important to work with an architect throughout the building and renovation process. (Photo by Lisa Souders)

An early childhood education program should be housed in a spacious, attractive facility that has been created or redesigned for children and that also meets the needs of staff members and parents. The director is responsible for ensuring that appropriate space is available; thus, space needs are analyzed carefully for both ongoing and new programs. This job may be done in cooperation with the board building committee or the director may assume full responsibility for analysis of space needs. These needs would then be submitted to the board for action. Corporate systems often have a prototypical design for all centers in the system, and they usually designate an employee to provide and manage the physical facilities for the system's centers. Similarly, pre-school facilities in public schools are usually planned by central administration although the principal may have a major decision-making role.

ANALYZING SPACE REQUIREMENTS

In providing a suitable facility, the first task is to analyze the space needs. When a program is already in operation, this analysis is made periodically to ensure the availability of proper facilities for both present and future needs. If the center program or the enrollment change, it may be necessary to move to a different location or add or eliminate space in the existing center. When a new center is created or when a move is proposed, the director usually assumes major responsibility for locating appropriate facilities. All renovation, relocation, or initial facilities choices should be based on the space needs analysis.

Space needs are based on consideration for the users (children, staff, and parents), program requirements, and governmental regulations. Therefore, the director must have up-to-date information in all these areas.

Users' Needs

Users of an early childhood education facility fall into three groups—children, staff, and parents. An analysis of space requirements must be based on the needs of each of these types of users. Since a child care center is planned primarily to meet the needs of children, all child care facilities should be comfortable and convenient both in terms of children's sizes and their developmental levels. School-aged programs require space for larger children and must take into account the need for active play as well as relaxation, studying, and preparing and eating snacks. Children who spend six or seven hours in a school classroom need a change of pace and should not feel they are in a school room before and after school. The building must also be comfortable and convenient for adult users if they are to work effectively with the children.

The primary needs planners must consider for each of these users are:

1. Health and safety
2. Accessibility of facilities
3. Controlled traffic flow
4. Personal space
5. Opportunities for independence and growth
6. Aesthetic character

Meeting the needs of each group of users (children, staff, and parents) has a cumulative and reciprocal effect, since when the needs of one group are met a step is taken toward meeting the needs of the other two groups. The dynamics of a human environment involve the impacting of each group on the others. In a well-run center, the three groups interact effectively because each is involved in the joint, sensitive process of child development.

Health and Safety. Center planners must be aware of the safety aspects above and beyond those stipulated in licensing regulations. A hazard-free building meets the needs of staff and parents, as well as children. Directors must keep abreast of environmental issues. For example, asbestos and lead paint, once considered appropriate building materials, are now not used in child care centers. Some sealed buildings in which air is recirculated may be found to be circulating poor quality air. Governmental regulations will usually determine the type of building and decorative materials, such as carpeting, to be used, the number and type of exits (including panic hardware and lighted exit signs), the number and location of fire extinguishers, smoke detectors, and fire alarm systems, and location of furnace and water heaters relative to the children's play area. All these regulations protect children and staff from dangers associated with fire. Children also must be protected from such hazards as tap water that is too hot, slippery floor surfaces, unsafe or unprotected electrical outlets and wiring, and poorly lighted spaces. (Covered convenience outlets or specially designed safety outlets are needed throughout the classroom for audiovisual equipment, computers, aquaria, and so forth). The director must ensure that the flooring is even, that there are no protrusions to cause falls, that stairs are provided with sturdy, low rails, and that protective screening is installed on all windows. Although the director is primarily responsible for establishing and maintaining a basic safety plan for the center, every staff member must remain alert to potential hazards and must teach children simple safety procedures such as mopping up spilled water and reshelving toys. (A Site Safety Checklist appears in Director's Resources.)

In public schools where older children use the hallways, plans for entering and exiting the building and moving about must be made so that young children experience minimal encounters with large groups of grade schoolers and so that regimentation is avoided. Although older children can move about the building independently, additional staff may be required so that small children will have escorts when they go to the library, the office, or the restroom. Ideally each classroom for young children will have its own adjoining bathroom.

In any building, many safety practices revolve around the enforcement of center safety rules such as prohibiting children from climbing on window sills; but it is preferable to adapt the building itself so that it is a safe place for children. Placing locks on the furnace room door is less disturbing to everyone and is far safer for children than telling them that they must not enter the furnace area. Be sure, however, that security devices such as locks or gates do not block an emergency exit. Guidelines for fire safety can be obtained by consulting the fire inspector.

For safety reasons, programs for children are usually housed on the ground-floor level of the building, even where licensing regulations do not require this location. In the event of a fire or other emergency that requires building evacuation, preschool children may become easily confused and may need individual guidance to reach safety. In such situations staff members caring for infants, toddlers, and non-ambulatory preschoolers will be able to remove only the one or two children they can carry. Some centers place several babies in a crib and roll the crib to safety. Therefore, stairways are dangerous obstacles to quick and safe building evacuation and it is unsafe to use elevators.

Over and above promoting the ease of evacuation, other safety considerations make ground-level facilities immediately adjacent to fenced outdoor space very advantageous. When children can go directly from their classrooms to a fenced outdoor area, the teaching staff can supervise both those children who choose outdoor play and those who remain indoors; and the outdoor space is viewed as an extension of the indoor. Fenced-in play areas prevent children from leaving the play space and prevent others from entering and damaging equipment, interfering with children's play, or leaving dangerous materials such as broken glass around the area. Some covered outdoor space provides an additional advantage because it can be used on rainy days or on very hot, sunny days.[1]

All exits from the building and the outdoor playground should be in locations where supervision of who comes and goes can be readily maintained. While the center may welcome community visitors, strangers should not be permitted to wander through the building. Similarly, children should not be able to leave unnoticed, either alone or accompanied by anyone other than authorized personnel. Panic hardware must be provided on all exit doors but they should be locked so that visitors cannot enter without being admitted. Parents and staff will probably have to be reminded that holding the door open for an arriving visitor is unwise since that person's presence in the center may go unnoticed.

Accessibility of Facilities. All users must have access to the building, its program, and its materials. Many parents do not want to subject their children to long daily trips to and from the center and they prefer a center close to home. Others will look for a center close to the workplace so that they can visit the child during the day. Location near public transportation is also desirable for staff and parents.

Access to the center is increased when people feel comfortable about entering the building; therefore, the scale of the building is another consideration. As children approach the center, they should feel that it fits them. Even a large building should have some features that indicate

---

1 For further information about playground safety see: U.S. Consumer Product Safety Commission, *A Handbook for Public Playground Safety. Volume 11: Technical Guidelines for Equipment and Surfacing,* Washington, D.C., (n.d.).

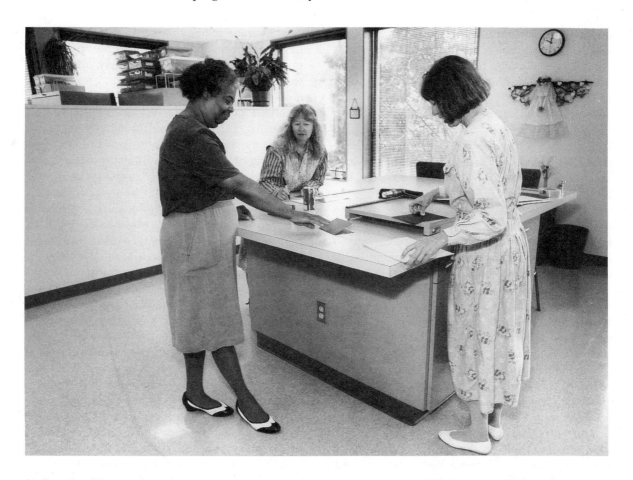

Staff work space includes space to prepare materials to use in the classroom. (Photo by Lisa Souders)

to the children that the building is theirs. Entranceways and the areas surrounding them can be scaled to the children's requirements so that the children are not overwhelmed by a huge, heavy door or a stairway wide enough for a regiment.

Since parents and visitors often form opinions about a program on the basis of external appearances, the grounds must be well maintained, and the building itself must be inviting. A building welcomes people through its scale, color, texture, and design. When the building is compatible with other buildings in the neighborhood, the center can begin to establish itself as a positive force in the community and be considered as an integral part of the total community. Understandably a contemporary building might not be welcome in a traditional residential neighborhood.

When a child care center is housed in a building shared by other users, the center should

have a separate entrance that is clearly marked so that families and visitors can find it. Entrances used by older students, agency clients or other tenants may mean heavy traffic which may intimidate children and may make supervision of their arrival and departure more difficult.

The parking area should be located near the center's entrance and should be large enough to accommodate the cars of staff, parents, and visitors. A safe walkway from parking to entry is essential since many parents will arrive with several children, diaper bag, and favorite toys.

Inside the building there should be clear indications of where to proceed. Signs, supergraphics, or pathways incorporated in the flooring (such as tile arrows) can lead the visitor to the proper place even if no receptionist or secretary is available. A pleasant greeting from a receptionist is ideal, especially when the child and parent are called by name, but many centers are unable to afford a staff member to fill that role.

When the receptionist's or secretary's office has a large glass window overlooking the entry, visual contact can be made with people as they arrive, and parents or visitors are likely to feel more comfortable about asking for assistance. In the office adjacent to the entry, the center staff can greet people and can receive payments and forms from families. If parents or visitors find no one with whom to communicate when they enter the building, they may become disgruntled and leave, feeling that no one cares about their needs. Or a visitor may search out the classrooms and begin a conversation with a busy teacher, disturbing activities there and probably inviting a cursory response that is detrimental to good public relations. The entry should also be accessible to the director's office so that the director is highly visible and readily available. Furthermore, it is imperative that all visitors be screened to ensure that everyone who enters has a legitimate purpose.

In any case, the entry itself should say "welcome." The colors used in the entry should indicate that this is a place for growth and vitality; grayness and drabness do not belong here. Entry surfaces are also important and must be designed to withstand muddy shoes or boots and dripping umbrellas. Although the entry should be large enough to accommodate several people without being crowded, it should not be too large since such space has minimum use but still costs about as much per square foot as areas that are heavily used. Furthermore, large entranceways may overwhelm a child or intimidate an unsure parent. Some children will interpret large open spaces as an invitation to run.

The required minimum number of entrances and exits is determined by fire laws, but to determine the best locations for these doors the planners should take into consideration the traffic patterns of people who come to the building. Teachers like to greet parents as they arrive with their children; therefore, locating the arrival point close to the classroom helps not only the parent and child but also the teacher. Similarly, when the children leave, the teacher can see the parents. Just as children should be able to reach their classrooms without walking through long, uninteresting, and perhaps frightening hallways, so should adults be able to get to their areas

conveniently and without disturbing children's play. For instance, deliveries to the kitchen or other service areas should be easy to make, without having to negotiate stairs and without moving through the children's space.

Accessibility carries an additional importance for those who have disabilities. The Americans with Disabilities Act (ADA) protects them by requiring that facilities be designed so that all services can be used by all clients and employees. Entrances and exits, traffic flow patterns, and facilities throughout the building and grounds should be designed for ease of use by the disabled. People (children included) in wheelchairs or on crutches should be able to move about comfortably, to use bathrooms, drinking fountains, and telephones, and to participate in all aspects of the center's program. Seemingly small items such as the type of faucet on sinks or the handles on cabinets can be designed to facilitate use by persons who otherwise would have to ask for assistance. The ADA requires this for centers that meet certain conditions, but even in situations where the accommodations are optional, concern for the comfort of all individuals necessitates that efforts be made to modify buildings. (An Adaptive Environments Center and Barrier Free Environments Checklist for existing facilities is included in Director's Resources. Some of the dimensions in this list, such as lavatory height, would, of course, need to be modified for children.)

Traffic Patterns. Planners should consider the children's daily traffic patterns between indoor and outdoor spaces, as well as within those spaces. For example, children will move from classroom to multipurpose room and back, and from classroom to outdoor area and back. They may leave from the outdoor area if they are playing there when their parents arrive. A good floor plan takes into account the fact that young children should be able to go directly outdoors, preferably from their own classroom or at least with minimal walking in hallways or in areas used for other purposes.

Coat storage should be near the door where the children enter. When coats are stored in the classroom, shelving may be used to create a coat area separate from the play space.

Well-planned children's areas are designed so that teachers can supervise all areas from almost

REFLECTIONS

Think about how the traffic pattern of a building you use frequently affects you. When you arrive at this building, which room do you go to first? Where is that room in relation to the door you use to enter the building? Think about the directions in which you move through the building during the day. Are there any places that could be rearranged to save you steps? Classrooms can be arranged for variety and ease of traffic flow if areas within the room are clearly demarcated and exits are located so that traffic does not cross through a number of areas. Block shelves are excellent room dividers that can be used to separate the block area from the housekeeping area and from the heavy traffic area, thus providing a special space for undisturbed block building. Reading and writing areas can be separated from noisy carpentry or music areas by shelves or dividers; then children can find quiet, secluded spaces for solitude and concentration. Children can work comfortably without being disturbed when traffic patterns in the classroom are taken into consideration in planning the children's space needs.

any vantage point without excessive walking. A teacher supervising in a room with an alcove may have to walk over to that area repeatedly to know what is happening there. An L-shaped outside area may be spacious, but such an area becomes impossible to supervise because as soon as children turn the corner, they are out of sight and beyond the reach of the supervising adult.

Serving meals to children further complicates the traffic flow in the center. Since preschool children usually eat in their classrooms, there is no need for a separate cafeteria. In fact, in a public school, the noise and confusion of a cafeteria is inappropriate for preschoolers and the furniture is too large to accommodate them comfortably. Preschool classrooms, therefore, must be large enough to contain tables and chairs for all the children and teachers without crowding the play space, and the kitchen should be nearby. Steps or doorways between the kitchen and the classrooms make moving food carts or carrying trays difficult, and long distances between kitchen and classrooms may mean long walks for teachers and long waits for children when something extra is needed during mealtime.

The kitchen must function primarily in relation to the classrooms and secondarily in relation to adult areas. The amount of kitchen space required varies according to the activities to be conducted. The center that uses a catering service for lunches may need very little space, while the center in which hot lunches are prepared will require additional equipment and space. In very large centers a kitchenette may be provided for staff use, for preparation of refreshments for parent meetings, and so forth.

Licensing laws regulate the number of toilets and sinks required, but the location of the bathroom is equally important. Children need bathrooms immediately adjacent to their classrooms, multipurpose room, and outdoor play areas so that they can get to them quickly. Each of these areas may not need a separate bathroom, but planning can include location of one bathroom to serve two areas as shown in Figure 7.1. Since prekindergarten boys and girls are comfortable sharing the same bathroom, doors in front of each toilet can be eliminated.

Location of adult bathroom facilities is often determined by designing a plumbing core, around which the bathrooms and kitchen are built. Although a plumbing core design is economical, it may not be practical in terms of the traffic pattern and the program needs because adult bathrooms must be placed appropriately to serve the people in classrooms, offices, meeting rooms, and kitchen. It is particularly important that classroom teachers have easy access to adult bathrooms while children's programs are in session.

In planning for traffic flow, the staff's daily traffic patterns must also be considered, with attention focused on which areas they use in what sequence on a typical day. Figure 7.2 shows the relationship of staff members' spaces to children's spaces in one center. Teachers need a conveniently located general storage room to

Figure 7-1 Portion of Hypothetical Floor Plan Showing Bathrooms Serving Two Areas

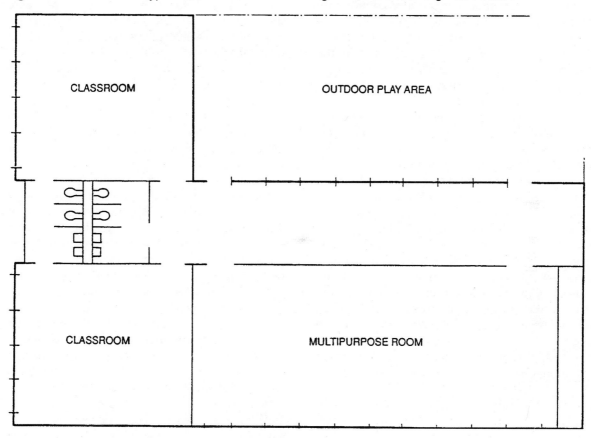

Figure 7-2 Hypothetical Center Floor Plan Showing Relation of Staff Space to Child Space

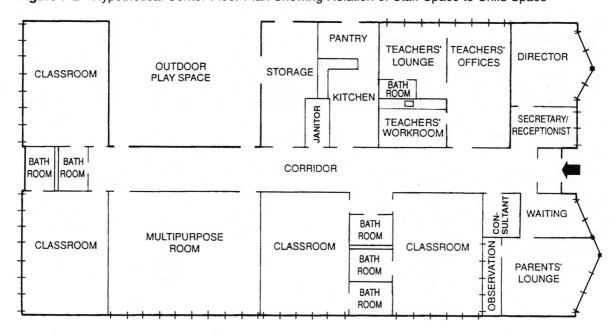

enable them to set up the day's activities efficiently. They must be able to move comfortably and quickly from the storage areas to the classroom, the outdoor area, or the multipurpose room, depending on where the equipment or the supplies are needed. Teachers also need coat storage that is readily accessible when they go outdoors with children.

Office space is sometimes placed close to the classrooms so that immediate additional supervision can be provided in an emergency situation; but planners may decide to place the offices farther away from the classrooms to eliminate distractions for the director, off-duty teachers, or other staff members. An intercom system can be installed to facilitate communication in emergency situations and to eliminate disturbances. The intercom or a telephone may be a necessity if a classroom or any other area used by children is isolated from direct contact with the rest of the center. For example, all classrooms may be located on the ground floor, while the multipurpose room is a level above them. A teacher using the multipurpose room needs a phone to reach additional help if a crisis occurs.

Personal Space. A comfortable and convenient classroom for young children includes enough space for each child to work and play without being disturbed by other activities. Thirty-five square feet per child is usually considered minimum, so a classroom for ten three-year-olds must have *at least* 350 square feet—making it measure about 18 feet by 20 feet. Fifty square feet per child is more realistic and more space should be provided whenever possible. However, extremely large classrooms are difficult to supervise and may feel overwhelming to children.

Children need cozy places where they can relax while they look at books, examine interesting objects or daydream. These spaces should be small enough to promote a sense of privacy and intimacy, yet large enough to be shared with a friend or two. Sometimes a loft can meet this need; it must be quite sturdy and have some kind of siding to prevent objects from falling to the floor and hitting anyone below. The space under the loft can be used for storage or for small group activities. In any event, the teacher must be able to supervise the area.

The classroom must also include a meeting area that is large enough for a number of children to gather for a story or special activity. Furniture can be moved for these occasions. Movable shelving and furniture facilitate such rearranging. These movable pieces will also be valued when teachers are placing cots for children's naps. Most centers do not have a separate nap room and must consider how to place cots so that children will not be too close to one another as required by many licensing rules. When cots are too close together children may find it difficult to rest. Space must also be availabe for cot storage.

Staff members have a variety of space needs. These include personal space for storing their belongings, bathroom facilities separate from those used by the children, and a lounge area in which to have refreshments during break times. Work space includes places in which they work with children, places in which they prepare materials for classrooms, and places in which they do paper work or hold conferences. Work space that meets the staff members' needs assists them in performing their duties well. Some personnel have specialized work spaces (that is, maintenance staff, the cook, or the nurse). Each work place must be of a size suitable for the activity in question. For example, full-time office staff members each need approximately 100 square feet of office space. This space should be arranged to provide for some privacy and sound control so that work can be accomplished with minimal interruption.

Parents and visitors need a comfortable lounge area in which to wait for their children or to talk with each other. Parents also need a space that is large enough for group meetings and space that is small enough for individual conferences with a teacher or the director. Even if a whole room is not available, centers can at least provide some seating in another area. Fire laws may preclude having furniture in hallways. Facilities for observing the classrooms, while going unnoticed by the children, represent both a convenience and a learning experience for parents and visitors.

Often employer-sponsored child care is provided near the work site. Parents will appreciate an area in the classroom where they can spend quiet time with their own children, sharing a book or puzzle. In infant centers, a private space for nursing offers a relaxing time for mother and baby.

Children who come to the center for before and after school care will treasure some personal space. Imagine spending 10 hours a day in a relatively small space with 30 people primarily following someone else's directions. Although many adults *do* spend eight hours in a work environment crowded with equipment and people, they at least have the opportunity to go out for lunch or take a short break. Children in schools are usually required to stay with their class for the entire day. After school, having some private space provides a welcome respite. Before and after school, elementary grade children also need spaces for organizing clubs and playing games, for informal sports and for creating and carrying out their own wonderful ideas. They need adult supervision, but at the same time they need much more independence in organizing and reorganizing the space, perhaps decorating it so it is theirs. Since these needs are quite different from those of younger children, it is clear that they need separate spaces.

Independence. The facility should be planned to promote the independence of both children and staff. An environment for children fosters independence and growth when it is arranged so they can make decisions and solve their own problems. Such a setting has child-sized appointments, including sinks, toilets, drinking fountains, and door knobs that children can reach and operate (where that is desirable), and wall decorations that are placed at the children's eye level. Planners must keep in mind that independence is equally important for children with disabilities.

A setting that encourages independence also has classroom storage that is directly accessible to children, enabling them to find and reach all the materials and equipment they use. When such storage is adequate, each piece of equipment is displayed so that the children can see it easily, can remove it from the shelf without moving other items stacked on top of it, and can return it to its proper place. Clearly marked storage space for children's personal belongings, located so that children can get to it, will also promote independence. In addition, however, storage space that is out of children's reach is also needed in each classroom so that teachers can store materials and supplies they do not want the children to obtain, such as gallon jugs of glue.

Single purpose buildings allow programming to be based on users' needs (especially those of children) rather than requiring that the program be planned based on the needs of a range of occupants. A center allows teachers to feel independent when the design of the facility enables them to plan programs for their children without constantly checking with other teachers. For example, teacher independence is curtailed when a preschool class is housed in a public elementary school where the young children must use the bathroom, lunchroom, or outdoor play space for specific time blocks because older children use these facilities at other times. Even if the children's needs suggest a deviation from this schedule, the teacher may be required to follow it. Some teachers in centers that move children from room to room for various activities find that they are not able to plan as independently if they have to direct children from the art room to the music room and then to the play room on a daily basis at a predetermined, scheduled time rather than having the children move at their own pace.

The environment that fosters independence and growth is one in which variety is apparent, offering children an *appropriate* number of choices. They are not overwhelmed with choices, nor are they bored with repetitive sameness in design of space. Variety in color, texture, floor level, and building materials, if not overdone, can give children a sense of vitality that can be stimulating. Noise level is another area in which variety can be appropriate. Some spaces may be set aside for noisy play, while others are retained for quieter activities. Although acoustical ceilings, carpeted floors, and curtains all absorb sound and contribute to the auditory comfort of everyone in the center, children can still learn to use appropriate sound levels in each space and to choose their activities accordingly. Thus the environment leads to cooperation as well as to independence.

Aesthetic Character. An environment for children should be aesthetically pleasing to them. The factors relating to other users' needs and to program requirements can be designed so that they appeal to the children's sense of beauty. For example, it is just as easy to have an interesting painting in the classroom as it is to put up a fake window with curtains over the play sink.

Both serve the purpose of making the room more attractive.

Wall surfaces can provide texture and color that contribute to the room's vitality. Garish decorations or "cute" wall coverings, emblems, or cut-outs contribute little to children's appreciation of beauty. Carpets replete with numbers and letters add "busyness" to the environment but provide neither aesthetics nor intellectual stimulation. Children and staff will probably be more inclined to take care of an attractive environment. It is easy to develop messy habits when the surroundings are poorly designed with inadequate facilities and unappealing spaces. It is equally easy and more satisfying for everyone to develop good habits and an appreciation of beauty when the facilities are well designed.

Having analyzed the facility requirements for a high quality early childhood education program and the information provided by a specific needs assessment, the director can determine the center's current facility needs and can project the building and grounds needs of the center for several years. This long-range planning is useful in enabling a center to coordinate program, facility, and financial decision making. Whether the director is analyzing need in terms of possibly rearranging or remodeling the existing center's facilities, or of leasing or constructing a new center, the users' needs are kept in the forefront in working toward a decision about the facility.

DIRECTOR'S CORNER

"Our entire staff spend hours discussing what our ideal center would look like. We listed all the criteria for each space including details such as height and depth of classroom sinks, number of feet of shelving in the toy storage room, and type of door knobs. We couldn't have everything we wanted because of the cost, but we all felt like we had helped design our new center."

Director, agency-sponsored center

Programmatic Requirements

The director and building committee members must be thoroughly familiar with the early childhood education program before they attempt to evaluate an existing or proposed facility. They must understand the types of activities planned, the program goals, and the enrollment projections. For example, in contrast to a half-day program, a full-day program must provide a place for resting and for eating meals. Many children who spend the entire day at a center also need room in which to seclude themselves from the group for short periods of time—a quiet place supervised by the teacher but free from the intrusion of other children.

The center's philosophy influences the type and arrangement of space. If the philosophy places heavy emphasis on parent involvement, space will be needed for meeting rooms and a lounge, and additional parking will have to be provided. The prevailing climate also affects the type of building. If children are able to be outdoors most days on a year-round basis, they will need more outdoor space and slightly less indoor space. On the other hand, a center located in a region with temperature extremes will put emphasis on indoor areas and will give major consideration to effective heating, ventilating, and air conditioning systems. Floor level temperature in the children's areas is critical since children frequently play on the floor.

Planning for carpeting and tiling sections of the classroom floor should be done with activities in mind. Cleaning is facilitated when art and food activities take place on hard surfaces, and teachers will be able to focus on the children's needs rather than protecting the carpeting. A sink in the classroom is a much-used and much-desired convenience and should also be on the tiled area.

Admission policies will have an impact on the facilities requirements. For example, centers that accept infants must provide space for infant cribs and a number of feeding tables, as well as safe places where infants can explore their environment freely. Spaces for infants and toddlers must be designed for them, rather than being scaled down versions of preschool classrooms. Ramps, wide doorways, and low light switches are necessities for children with disabilities. When planning a facility it is mandatory to provide for children and adults with special needs so that they can be served effectively and so that the requirements of federal and state laws can be met.[2]

Governmental Regulations

In communities that have zoning laws, an early childhood education center that is operated for profit may be limited to locating in a business or less restrictive zone, while a nonprofit educational facility may generally be located in any zone. Prior to opening a center or even signing a lease or contract to purchase, the director must check with the local zoning board to see if usage of the particular piece of property would be in compliance with the zoning code. In some cases a zoning variance may be allowed; that is, the director may petition to use the location for a center if it can be shown that the presence of the center will not have a negative effect on neighboring sites. Zoning ordinances may also include parking requirements, and off-street parking provisions may have to be made for center staff and visitors including those who are disabled.

When a new facility is built or an existing building renovated or put to a new use, current codes usually apply. For example, a building being used as a public school would be inspected based on the codes in existence when that building was put into use. However, if a child care center leases the space, the owner will be required to meet the *current* regulations. When a building is renovated or a new facility is constructed, the Americans with Disabilities Act (ADA) must be followed. Some requirements include access via ramps instead of stairs, accessible restroom facilities, doors which can be opened by a person in a wheelchair, and low drinking fountains.

Other governmental regulations pertain to licensing. These are discussed in Chapter 3 and include number of square feet of space for children's use both indoors and outdoors, fencing, exits, building materials, and toilet and handwashing facilities. Before you purchase, lease, or renovate a building, ask your licensing agent to ensure that the facility is in compliance with governmental regulations or can be renovated appropriately and at an affordable price.

PLANNING A NEW CENTER

In planning for a new center, the director, who sometimes works along with a building committee of the board, must decide on a site early in the planning stage. The decision may be to construct a building, to buy, rent, or lease an existing building, or to locate space that would be donated by the owner on a temporary or permanent basis. Planning for a new center involves the same analysis of space requirements that is done when an ongoing program facility is assessed. The one item that stands out as being conspicuously important in decisions about planning a new center is *cost.*

The director who has started facilities planning with a needs assessment has applicable information about zoning, licensing, program requirements, and clients. These data, combined with the availability of a particular amount of money, are applied as criteria in the search for appropriate facilities. Some centers assess needs, locate facilities, and then mount a fund drive, anticipating that sufficient money will be obtained. The director or building committee must realistically assess the amount of money that will be *available* for establishing and maintaining the center facility and the amount of money that will be *required* to meet the assessed need.

The building committee works closely with the budget committee to determine the amount of money needed and available for constructing, purchasing, renovating, or renting a building. Costs of real estate and construction vary widely depending on geographical location, and within a given city vary from the inner city to the suburbs. Costs must be checked for each locale. Careful planning is essential because once construction starts changes are costly.

---

2 Public Law 99-457 (amending Public Law 94-142, Education of Handicapped Act) requires free public education be available for all disabled children. Many of these children will be included in private centers as well as in public schools, making it important that all buildings be accessible to them.

Considering New Construction

Both land and building costs must be considered. The lot must be large enough for a building of the required size, for a playground of at least 75 square feet per child (groups of children may use this area at different times), and for parking for staff, parents, and visitors. The cost of the building will depend on the size of the building, on the quality and elaborateness of the materials used, and on the intricacy of the design. A major advantage of new construction is that the building looks like a place for children; and, if it is well designed, it will be a place in which the program can be delivered efficiently, effectively, and with a high level of comfort for all users.

Using Existing Buildings

Costs involved with the use of an existing building are (1) purchase price, (2) rent, and (3) renovation. A center may incur none, one, or two of these costs, depending on the owner and on the condition of the building.

Sometimes a church or community service organization will permit an early childhood education center to use its facilities at little or no charge. Available rooms may also be found in school buildings. This contribution is a major cost benefit to the program. Before agreeing to this use of the building, however, both the contributor and the center board should have a clear written understanding of the rights and responsibilities of each party. For example, both will need to know how liability insurance will be handled.

If funds are available, a down payment on the purchase of a lot or a building, or plans for extensive remodeling, may be made. The board must be certain that funds for monthly payments, including interest as well as principal, will be available. A bank or savings and loan company can provide information on interest rates, length of mortgage, and payment procedures; it can also explain penalties, foreclosures, and insurance requirements.

Renting

Since purchasing a building involves high initial costs, most centers rent or lease all or part of a building. Both renting and leasing involve periodic payments. Under a lease the leaser and the lessee agree that the space will be available and paid for during a specified length of time, usually at least a year. A longer lease is preferable since moving can be expensive and clients may be lost if the center changes locations. When a space is rented, the renter may have to pay only for the period during which the space is actually used; for a nine-month nursery school program, this savings could be important and significant. Such a situation occurs primarily when renting from a church. The school's equipment may have to be moved out during the summer months or may be used by other groups as part of the rental agreement.

A lease should spell out these conditions and should include items such as:

- beginning and ending dates of the lease
- whether or not the lease is renewable
- who is responsible for maintenance and repairs
  - what is included
  - who pays for it
  - who provides materials, supplies, and tools
  - when maintenance and repairs will be done
  - who is responsible for compliance with building code
- who pays for utilities

For example, if the Board of Health requires the addition of a hand-washing sink (a permanent fixture), will the center or the landlord pay for the sink and its installation? The center cannot operate a program without the sink because a license will not be granted; but if the center should move, the landlord will still have the sink.

If the landlord is responsible for maintenance, can an agreement be reached that the grass is not cut during children's regular playground hours? Think about securing a written agreement about spraying for insects. Will it be done when children are present, meaning that you will have to move them to another area? Will all materials to be used be safe for areas used by children?

If the facility is shared because the landlord uses part of it or rents part of it to someone else or because the center owns a building and rents or leases part of it to someone else, all the preceding items must be considered. In addition, the building committee or director will settle the matter of who has access to the building and when they may have access. For example, if a teenage group uses the building in the evenings, will they be allowed to use the playground during the late afternoon before all the children have left? Other points to be considered are:

- who may have master keys
- who may use what equipment and supplies
- who is responsible for ordering and paying for shared equipment and supplies
- who pays the phone bill

Other questions involve use of the center's space by other organizations or individuals when the children are not present, such as during the evenings or on weekends. The use of the facilities (their own and that of others) by center staff members and the parent group during evening, weekend, and holiday hours must also be considered.

It is easier to reach agreement on these issues before the building committee signs a lease and takes occupancy. If a lease has been signed, the center usually cannot be moved without financial penalty, which could mean that an uncomfortable situation exists for a number of months. When the lease clearly details the rights and responsibilities of each party, most questions can be settled amicably.

Renovating

Renovation costs also vary widely depending on the location of the building and the type of work to be done. Complex changes such as relocating plumbing, rewiring electrical circuits, or installing exits, stairways, and fire-resistant surfaces are costly. The type and amount of renovation to be done will be based on the particular licensing requirements, including fire and building codes, and on the requirements of the planned program. If the center owns the building, renovation is usually a worthwhile investment.

DIRECTOR'S CORNER

"When the renovation was initially being planned and the architects were working up the drawings, the chairperson of the committee and I went in and talked about what we would like to see happen. It seemed to break down after the initial meetings and there were some outcomes that we were not that pleased with. Everything was ordered and half way done before I realized what was happening. There wasn't any way that we could go back and ask for change."

Director, church nursery school

WORKING WITH OTHER PROFESSIONALS

A variety of professionals outside the field of early childhood education can be helpful in planning a space for young children. Usually the cost of their services is relatively high on an hourly rate, but in the long run the expertise they contribute to the center's development is often worth far more than the actual expenditure. However, checking references and credentials before you sign an agreement with the individual or company is critical. Written agreements with each service provider are essential.

Licensing Agent

Since most programs must be licensed, the first professional that the building committee contacts is the licensing agent. This specialist often provides free services and is funded through state or local taxes. Through this agent, the committee works with other professionals in the building, sanitation, and fire departments. Community planners may also be involved either at the governmental level or through community councils. Even though these professionals are not paid by the center, the licensing and inspection fees must be paid as required. (See Chapter 3.)

Architect

During the very early planning stage, retaining an architect can produce positive results. An architect can evaluate a site in terms of a center's needs or can examine an existing building and make recommendations about the renovations that are necessary for safety, efficiency, and aesthetics.

Ongoing architectural services can be contracted at an hourly rate, flat fee, or on a percentage basis. The architect should spell out clearly in a contract the services that are to be provided—survey, site selection, design, working drawings from which a building can be built or remodeled, contractor selection, construction supervision, and/or final inspection. The architect may also include in the contract the fee for services rendered and the dates that payments are due.

When selecting an architect, choose someone with whom you feel comfortable. Many architects are unfamiliar with child care center needs and you will want to choose one who is willing to listen to your concept and incorporate your ideas. Keep in mind, however, that architects have knowledge about design and construction which can help you attain a more attractive, more functional building within your budget. A few architects will want to put a great deal of emphasis on the exterior of the building using such a large portion of the budget there that little money remains for finishing and furnishing. Listen to your architect with an open mind, but be willing to insist on components essential to your program.

When the plans are complete, asking a colleague to review them with you may help uncover details you hadn't considered. Changes made at this stage are relatively easy; changes made once construction begins may be impossible. At the very least, they are usually quite expensive.

Generally the architect will oversee the job but the general contractor is responsible for scheduling subcontractors, ordering materials, and so forth. Some architects also serve as construction managers and some contractors also offer building design services.

Contractor

A contractor may plan the construction or remodeling of the center's building and carry the work through to completion. Parts of the job may be subcontracted, such as the electrical or plumbing work, but the contractor retains responsibility for the satisfactory and timely completion of that work. Nonetheless, the director must pay attention to the job as it moves along. Balancing frequent site visits with allowing the contractors to do their work is necessary, but asking questions when you aren't sure about an aspect of the construction or when the work is not as promised is essential. Sometimes directors feel intimidated because they don't understand the drawings and specifications for the work. Part of the contractor's job is making sure that the work is done to the client's specifications as determined by the written contract.

Accountant

The building committee works with an accountant to determine the amount of money that can be responsibly invested in construction, purchase, or rental. The accountant may also help locate a lending agent and may help the building committee find the best interest rate. Information about depreciation and taxes may also be provided. An accountant may charge an hourly rate or a flat fee for a particular piece of work. Some centers pay an accountant a monthly retainer in exchange for whatever services are needed including preparation for the annual audit.

Attorney

When the building committee decides to enter into a contract or sign a lease, its attorney reviews the document to ensure that the center's needs are being met and that all legal aspects have been covered. The attorney also participates in settling disputes in relation to payment, failure to perform work satisfactorily, and so forth; in a few cases, these disputes may be taken to court. In those special situations the attorney would represent the center in court.

SUMMARY

Whether it is a brand new building or one that was constructed years ago for another purpose, the ideal early childhood education center environment is created to meet the needs of the children, the staff members, the parents, and the visitors, while satisfying all licensing requirements. Health and safety, accessibility of facilities, traffic patterns, personal space, opportunities for independence, and aesthetic character are the guidelines for determining the design. Professional services from the architects and contractors, who work with building committee members, staff members, parents, children, and other professionals, provide these aspects within the framework of the budget to create a center that is best suited for carrying out the program for which it has been designed.

Class Assignments

1. If you do not know how to compute the number of square feet in an area, find out. When you determine the square footage of a room for a center, you include all of the area, except those spaces that are used for permanent fixtures. For example, if a playroom has a sink that is two feet by three feet, you would have to deduct six square feet from the size of the room. However, it is not customary to deduct square footage for movable pieces such as tables or shelves. Record your answers to the following scenarios on Working Paper 7-1.

   1. a. Assume that your center has a room 20 feet by 30 feet with a sink that is two feet by three feet. How many children could use the room? Consider first the minimum requirements in terms of square feet.
      b. Re-figure the number of children that could be accommodated in terms of 50 square feet per child.
   2. You want to have twenty children in a group at your center. What might the dimensions of the room be if you were to provide the minimum amount of space required?
   3. What dimensions might the room have if you wanted to allow 50 square feet per child? (Assume you want to have twenty children in the group.)

2. With the director's permission, visit an early childhood education center (or use your student-teaching or work site). Record information on Working Paper 7-2 about the following areas:

   • parking
   • exterior appearance of building and grounds
   • identifying sign
   • identifiable entrance
   • entry area
   • location of offices (director, teachers, secretary)
   • waiting room or lounge
   • adult bathrooms
   • classrooms (number, size, ease of supervision, arrangement of areas, attractiveness, neatness, noise level, temperature, relation to other areas used by children)
   • multipurpose room (size, arrangement of equipment, ease of supervision, attractiveness, temperature, noise level)

- outdoor play area (size, fencing, arrangement of equipment, attractiveness, ease of supervision, variety of surfaces, shelter)
- children's bathrooms in relation to classrooms, multipurpose room, and outdoor area

3. Using Working Paper 7-3, draw a floor plan of the center where you student teach or work. Include all indoor and outdoor spaces that are used in any way by children, staff, and parents. Make your drawing approximately to scale. Now draw the traffic patterns. Use red to show the children's pattern, blue for teachers, and green for parents.

Class Exercises

1. Work with a classmate to design a floor plan for a child care center for 44 children (6 infants, 8 toddlers, 14 three-year-olds, and 16 four-year-olds). Show also the spaces that are used by adults. Be prepared to explain your design to the class.
2. Work with a classmate to design a building plan for a half-day nursery school for 14 three-year-olds and 16 four-year-olds. Make your drawing approximately to scale.
3. Compare the drawings in exercise 1 and exercise 2. Are any of the differences attributable to full-day vs. half-day child care?

Working Paper 7-1

Area Form

1. Your center has a room 20 feet by 30 feet with a two-foot by three-foot sink.

   a. How many preschool children can use the room?

   b. How many children can the room accommodate if you decide to allot 50 square feet per child?

2. What might the dimensions of the room be if you were to provide the minimum square footage required for 20 children?

3. What might the dimensions of the room be if you were to provide 50 square feet per child for 20 children?

Working Paper 7-2

Facilities Visitation Form

Name of center:

Record information about the following:

- Parking

- Exterior appearance of building and grounds

- Identifying sign

- Identifiable entrance

- Entry area

- Location of offices (director, teachers, secretary)

- Waiting room or lounge

- Adult bathrooms

- Classrooms (number, size, ease of supervision, arrangement of areas, attractive-ness, neatness, noise level, temperature, relation to other areas used by children)

- Multipurpose room (size, arrangement of equipment, ease of supervision, attrac-tiveness, temperature, noise level)

- Outdoor play area (size, fencing, arrangement of equipment, attractiveness, ease of supervision, variety of surfaces, shelter)

- Children's bathrooms in relation to classrooms, multipurpose room, and outdoor area

Working Paper 7-3

Floor Plan

Director's Resource 7-1

Site Safety Checklist

Date Inspection Was Made_____

Name of Person Performing Inspection_____

Rooms and Units	Satisfactory		Corrections Needed	Date Corrections Made
Floors are smooth, clean and have a nonskid surface.	OK	Not OK		
Medicines, cleaning agents and tools are inaccessible to children. There are no aerosols in the room. Art supplies are nontoxic.	OK	Not OK		
First aid kit is present and adequately supplied. No medicines are unlocked.	OK	Not OK		
Walls, ceiling clean and in repair. No peeling paint, damaged plaster. Less than 20% of wall surface is covered by hangings.	OK	Not OK		
Children are never unattended, always supervised by enough staff to evacuate.	OK	Not OK		
Lighting and electricity: brightness is OK, outlets are covered, no dangling or covered extension cords.	OK	Not OK		
No free standing space heater.	OK	Not OK		
Heating and ventilation systems are working OK. Pipes and radiators are inaccessible or covered to prevent body contact if 110 °F or above.	OK	Not OK		
Humidity level is comfortable.	OK	Not OK		
Hand washing facility: hot water should not exceed 110 °F (43 °C), facility is easily accessible, soap and towel supplies are adequate.	OK	Not OK		

(Reprinted from *Health in Day Care. A Manual for Health Professionals*, © 1987, American Academy of Pediatrics)

Director's Resource 7-1 (*continued*)

Rooms and Units	Satisfactory		Corrections Needed	Date Corrections Made
No disease-bearing animals, vermin or poisonous plants (no turtles, hamsters, or harmful pets).	OK	Not OK		
Trash storage is covered. Sanitation adequate especially in food service areas, cots or mats, dust traps.	OK	Not OK		
Exits are clearly marked and unobstructed. Easy access to emergency phone. Emergency contact information is current.	OK	Not OK		
Locked doors to closed spaces can be opened by an adult.	OK	Not OK		
No smoking in child care area.	OK	Not OK		
No precariously placed small or sharp or otherwise hazardous objects. Plastic bags are safely used.	OK	Not OK		
Rest equipment is labeled. Linens, mats, cribs, cots, and blankets appear clean.	OK	Not OK		
Toys and furnishings are in repair and free of pinch or crush points.	OK	Not OK		
Decor is pleasant, nonflammable materials are used.	OK	Not OK		
Windows securely screened and opening limited to 6 inches.	OK	Not OK		
Fans in use have covers or guards with openings smaller than one half inch.	OK	Not OK		
Infant Toddler Programs Toys are lead-free. Mouthed toys are sanitized between different children's use.	OK	Not OK		
High chairs have wide base and safety strap.	OK	Not OK		
Diaper changing area clean, adequately supplied with changing pads and disposable sheeting. Sanitized after each use.	OK	Not OK		
Soiled diapers disposed of in securely tied plastic bag.	OK	Not OK		
No bottles in crib or infants lying down drinking.	OK	Not OK		
No toddlers walking around with bottles.	OK	Not OK		

Director's Resource 7-1 (*continued*)

Rooms and Units	Satisfactory		Corrections Needed	Date Corrections Made
Hand washing for child and caregivers practiced after each diaper change.	OK	Not OK		

Hallways and Stairs	Satisfactory		Corrections Needed	Date Corrections Made
Smoke detectors are OK	OK	Not OK		
Exits are neither obstructed nor cluttered. Clear exit routes are marked. Alarm system is working. Fire extinguishers OK. Emergency lighting is OK.	OK	Not OK		
Monitoring for entrance of strangers is consistently done. Emergency phone numbers (police, fire, rescue, poison control) are posted by phone.	OK	Not OK		
Doors open in direction of exit travel.	OK	Not OK		
Door are operational with panic hardware on emergency exits. Windows are screened	OK	Not OK		
Floors are smooth, clean and have a nonskid surface. Rugs are attached.	OK	Not OK		
Walls are painted with lead free paint. Plaster is intact. There are no loose nails or other hazards.	OK	Not OK		
There are no disease-bearing animals, vermin or poisonous plants (no turtles, hamsters, or harmful pets).	OK	Not OK		
Heating and ventilation are working OK. Pipes and radiators are inaccessible or covered to prevent body contact. Humidity level is comfortable.	OK	Not OK		
Lighting electricity: Brightness is OK. Outlets are covered. There are no dangling or covered extension cords.	OK	Not OK		
Right hand descending railing secured at child height.	OK	Not OK		

Director's Resource 7-1 (*continued*)

Hallways and Stairs	Satisfactory		Corrections Needed	Date Corrections Made
Stairs and stairways free of stored items. Stairways well lit by artificial or natural light.	OK	Not OK		
Safeguards to prevent children from entering unsupervised or hazardous areas.	OK	Not OK		
Clear glass panels used in traffic areas are safety glass or equivalent and are clearly marked to avoid accidental impact.	OK	Not OK		
Fans in use have covers or guards with openings smaller than one half inch.	OK	Not OK		

Kitchen and Storage Areas	Satisfactory		Corrections Needed	Date Corrections Made
Plumbing and water temperature: at least 170°F water or sanitizing agent is used for sanitization. Plumbing is working properly.	OK	Not OK		
Trash storage covered and litter minimum. Trash kept away from potential food storage and preparation areas. No storage near furnace or hot water heaters.	OK	Not OK		
Heating and ventilation systems are working OK. Pipes and radiators are inaccessible or covered to prevent body contact. Humidity level is comfortable.	OK	Not OK		
No animals or vermin are present. Insects are controlled by screens. No pesticides are used on food, food preparation or storage surfaces.	OK	Not OK		
No pest strips or pesticides used where possible contact with food can occur.	OK	Not OK		
Cleaning agents and tools and utensils including matches are stored away from food storage and used safely. Toxic materials are in original containers separately stored away from food.	OK	Not OK		

Director's Resource 7-1 (continued)

Kitchen and Storage Areas	Satisfactory		Corrections Needed	Date Corrections Made
Lighting and electricity: Brightness is OK. Outlets are covered, there are no dangling or covered extension cords. Fire extinguishers in safe and working order.	OK	Not OK		
Food Storage: Inventory and dated rotation methods are used. Refrigerator temperatures less than 45 °F. Frozen foods are stored at 0 °F or below. Handled leftovers are discarded.	OK	Not OK		
Food is stored on shelves; containers are labeled; made of insect resistant metal or plastic (not plastic bags).	OK	Not OK		
First aid kit is available and adequately stocked.	OK	Not OK		
Fire extinguisher is charged. Staff know how to use it.	OK	Not OK		
Personnel are healthy and perform appropriate, frequent hand washing, use hair restraints, wear clean clothing. No smoking allowed in food preparation area.	OK	Not OK		
Sanitation: Surfaces are clean, free of cracks or crevices. Wood cutting boards are not used.	OK	Not OK		
Eating utensils are free of cracks and chips.	OK	Not OK		
Pot handles on stove are turned inward where they cannot be knocked over and contents spilled.	OK	Not OK		

Outdoors	Satisfactory		Corrections Needed	Date Corrections Made
Free of litter and sharp objects.	OK	Not OK		
Play equipment is smooth, well anchored and free of rust, splinters or sharp corners. No exposed uncapped screws or bolts. Size appropriate to child users. Bars stay in place when grasped. Maximum height, 6 feet. Safe way out on all climbers.	OK	Not OK		

Director's Resource 7-1 (*continued*)

Outdoors	Satisfactory		Corrections Needed	Date Corrections Made
No "S" hooks or other open hooks. Swing seats are lightweight, flexible and noncutting. Equipment is placed in safe location (away from where other children would play).	OK	Not OK		
Slides have horizontal steps and good tread. Rim on slide to prevent falls, flat bottom to slow down. Metal beds are shaded from the sun. Steps 7 inches apart, flat (not tubular).	OK	Not OK		
Are sandboxes covered when not in use? Places for adults to sit where needed to supervise?	OK	Not OK		
Rings do not permit entry of child's head or they are large enough for whole body.	OK	Not OK		
No pinch or crush points on equipment.	OK	Not OK		
Fences or natural barriers prohibit access to hazardous areas and keep animals out.	OK	Not OK		
No stagnant pools of water.	OK	Not OK		
Playground surface is non-abrasive, and impact-absorbing (shredded tires, wood chips), free of litter and concealed debris; no animal excrement.	OK	Not OK		
Poisonous plants and stinging insect nests removed.	OK	Not OK		
Street traffic controlled. Pick-up and drop-off procedures are safe.	OK	Not OK		
Vehicles				
School bus signs are in place.	OK	Not OK		
Vehicles are mechanically in order.	OK	Not OK		
Safety restraints are adequate in number and type and are used.	OK	Not OK		
Safety locks or child door-opening restraints present.	OK	Not OK		
Driver training for school bus safety is up-to-date.	OK	Not OK		

Director's Resource 7-1 (*continued*)

Outdoors	Satisfactory		Corrections Needed	Date Corrections Made
Attendants present as required.	OK	Not OK		
First aid kit is adequately stocked.	OK	Not OK		
Current emergency contact and medical information is in vehicle when in use.	OK	Not OK		
Trips are planned with emergency management and health facilities identified beforehand.	OK	Not OK		
Children have identification including their name and emergency contacts.	OK	Not OK		

Bathroom and Laundry Room	Satisfactory		Corrections Needed	Date Corrections Made
Hand washing facility: hot water temperature is less than 120°F, facility is easily accessible, soap and towel supplies are adequate.	OK	Not OK		
Covered lids on trash in adults' bathroom. Trash storage and litter is adequately controlled.	OK	Not OK		
Cleaning agents are inaccessible to children. No other toxic products stored in area.	OK	Not OK		
Windows, doors, ceilings, walls are clean and well maintained. Floors are not slippery.	OK	Not OK		
Temperature and ventilation are adequately and safely maintained.	OK	Not OK		
Toilets and sinks are age-appropriate size or adapted. Step stools are provided where appropriate. No potty chairs.	OK	Not OK		
There is no electrical equipment near water.	OK	Not OK		
Exits are clearly marked.	OK	Not OK		
Animals and vermin are controlled.	OK	Not OK		
Towels, toilet tissues and soap (liquid, not bar) are available.	OK	Not OK		
Other	OK	Not OK		

Director's Resource 7-2

Checklist for Existing Facilities

INTRODUCTION

Title III of the Americans with Disabilities Act requires public accommodations to provide goods and services to people with disabilities on an equal basis with the rest of the general public. The goal is to afford every individual the opportunity to benefit from our country's business and services, and to afford our businesses and services the opportunity to benefit from the patronage of all Americans.

By January 26, 1992, architectural and communication barriers must be removed in public areas of existing facilities when their removal is readily achievable—in other words, easily accomplished and able to be carried out without much difficulty or expense. Public accommodations that must meet the barrier removal requirement include a broad range of establishments (both for-profit and nonprofit)—such as hotels, restaurants, theaters, museums, retail stores, private schools, banks, doctors' offices, and other places that serve the public. People who own, lease, lease out, or operate places of public accommodation in existing buildings are responsible for complying with the barrier removal requirement.

The removal of barriers can often be achieved by making simple changes to the physical environment. However, the regulations do not define exactly how much effort and expense are required for a facility to meet its obligation. This judgment must be made on a case-by-case basis, taking into consideration such factors as the size, type, and overall financial resources of the facility, and the nature and cost of the access improvements needed. These factors are described in more detail in the ADA regulations issued by the Department of Justice.

The process of determining what changes are readily achievable is not a one-time effort; access should be re-evaluated annually. Barrier removal that might be difficult to carry out now may be readily achievable later. Tax incentives are available to help absorb costs over several years.

PURPOSE OF THIS CHECKLIST

This checklist will help you identify accessibility problems and solutions in existing facilities in order to meet your obligations under the ADA.

The goal of the survey process is to plan how to make an existing facility more usable for people with disabilities. The Department of Justice recommends the development of an Implementation Plan, specifying what improvements you will make to remove barriers and when each solution will be carried out: ". . . Such a plan . . . could serve as evidence of a good faith effort to comply. . . ."

TECHNICAL REQUIREMENTS

This checklist details some of the requirements found in the ADA Accessibility Guidelines (ADAAG). However, keep in mind that full compliance with ADAAG is required only for new construction and alterations. The requirements are presented here as a guide to help you determine what may be readily achievable barrier removal for existing facilities. Whenever possible, ADAAG should be used in making readily achievable modifications. If complying with ADAAG is not readily achievable, you may undertake a modification that does not fully comply with ADAAG using less stringent standards, as long as it poses no health or safety risk.

Each state has its own regulations regarding accessibility. To ensure compliance with all codes, know your state and local codes and use

Director's Resource 7-2 (*continued*)

the more stringent technical requirement for every modification you make; that is, the requirement that provides greater access for individuals with disabilities. The barrier removal requirement for existing facilities is new under the ADA and supersedes less stringent local or state codes.

WHAT THIS CHECKLIST IS NOT

This checklist does not cover all of ADAAG's requirements; therefore, it is not for facilities undergoing new construction or alterations. In addition, it does not attempt to illustrate all possible barriers or propose all possible barrier removal solutions. ADAAG should be consulted for guidance in situations not covered here.

The checklist does not cover Title III's requirements for nondiscriminatory policies and practices and for the provision of auxiliary communication aids and services. The communication features covered are those that are structural in nature.

PRIORITIES

This checklist is based on the four priorities recommended by the Title III regulations for planning readily achievable barrier removal projects:

Priority 1: Accessible entrance into the facility
Priority 2: Access to goods and services
Priority 3: Access to rest rooms
Priority 4: Any other measures necessary

HOW TO USE THIS CHECKLIST

✔ *Get Organized:* Establish a time frame for completing the survey. Determine how many copies of the checklist you will need to survey the whole facility. Decide who will conduct the survey. It is strongly recommended that you invite two or three additional people, including people with various disabilities and accessibility expertise, to assist in identifying barriers, developing solutions for removing these barriers, and setting priorities for implementing improvements.

✔ *Obtain Floor Plans:* It is very helpful to have the building floor plans with you while you survey. If plans are not available, use graph paper to sketch the layout of all interior and exterior spaces used by your organization. Make notes on the sketch or plan while you are surveying.

✔ *Conduct the Survey:* Bring copies of this checklist, a clipboard, a pencil or pen, and a flexible steel tape measure. With three people surveying, one person numbers key items on the floor plan to match with the field notes, taken by a second person, while the third takes measurements. Think abut each space from the perspective of people with physical, hearing, visual, and cognitive disabilities, noting areas that need improvement.

✔ *Summarize Barriers and Solutions:* List barriers found and ideas for their removal. Consider the solutions listed beside each question, and add your own ideas. Consult with building contractors and equipment suppliers to estimate the costs for making the proposed modifications.

✔ *Make Decisions and Set Priorities:* Review the summary with decision makers and advisors. Decide which solutions will best eliminate barriers at a reasonable cost. Prioritize the items you decide upon and make a timeline for carrying them out. Where the removal of barriers is not readily achievable, you must consider whether there are alternative methods for providing access that are readily achievable.

✔ *Maintain Documentation:* Keep your survey, notes, summary, record of work completed, and plans for alternative methods on file.

✔ *Make Changes:* Implement changes as planned. Always refer directly to ADAAG and your state

Director's Resource 7-2 (*continued*)

and local codes for complete technical requirements before making any access improvement. References to the applicable sections of
ADAAG are listed at the beginning of each
group of questions. If you need help understanding the federal, state, or local requirements,
contact your Disability and Business Technical
Assistance Center.

✔ *Follow Up:* Review your Implementation
Plan each year to re-evaluate whether more
improvements have become readily achievable.

> To obtain a copy of the ADAAG or
> other information from the U.S. Depart-
> ment of Justice, call: (202) 514-0301
> Voice, (202) 514-0381 TDD, (202) 514-
> 0383 TDD. For technical questions,
> contact the Architectural and Trans-
> portation Barriers Compliance Board
> at (800) USA-ABLE.

QUESTIONS	POSSIBLE SOLUTIONS

PRIORITY 1:
ACCESSIBLE ENTRANCE

People with disabilities should be able to arrive on the site,
approach the building, and enter the building as freely as
everyone else. At least one path of travel should be safe and
accessible for everyone, including people with disabilities.

Yes No

Path of Travel (ADAAG 4.3, 4.4, 4.5, 4.7)
Is there a path of travel that does not require
the use of stairs?

❑ Add a ramp if the path of
travel is interrupted by stairs.
❑ Add an alternative pathway
on level ground.

Is the path of travel stable, firm and
slip-resistant?

❑ Repair uneven paving.
❑ Fill small bumps and breaks
with beveled patches.
❑ Replace gravel with hard top.

Is the path at least 36 inches wide?

❑ Change or move landscaping,
furnishings, or other features
that narrow the path of travel.
❑ Widen pathway.

Director's Resource 7-2 (*continued*)

QUESTIONS	POSSIBLE SOLUTIONS

              Yes   No

Path of Travel (*continued*)
Can all objects protruding into the path be
detected by a person with a visual disability
using a cane?

    ❏ Move or remove protruding
       objects.
    ❏ Add a cane-detectable base
       that extends to the ground.
    ❏ Place a cane-detectable object
       on the ground underneath as
       a warning barrier.

   In order to be detected using a cane, an object
   must be within 27 inches of the ground.
   Objects hanging or mounted overhead must
   be higher than 80 inches to provide clear head
   room. It is not necessary to remove objects
   that protrude less than 4 inches from the wall.

Do curbs on the pathway have
curb cuts at drives, parking, and
drop-offs?

    ❏ Install curb cut.
    ❏ Add small ramp up to curb.

Ramps (ADAAG 4.8)
Are the slopes of ramps no greater than 1:12?

    ❏ Lengthen ramp to decrease
       slope.
    ❏ Relocate ramp.
    ❏ If available space is limited,
       reconfigure ramp to include
       switchbacks.

   Slope is given as a ratio of the
   height to the length. 1:12 means
   for every 12 inches along the
   base of the ramp, the height
   increases one inch. For a 1:12
   maximum slope, at least one   **1 : 12**
   foot of ramp length is needed
   for each inch of height.

Do all ramps longer than 6 feet have railings on
both sides?

    ❏ Add railings.

Are railings sturdy, and between 34 and 38
inches high?

    ❏ Adjust height of railings.
    ❏ Secure handrails.

Is the width between railings at least 36 inches?

    ❏ Relocate the railings.
    ❏ Widen the ramp.

Are ramps non-slip?

    ❏ Add non-slip surface material.

Is there a 5-foot-long level landing at every
30-foot horizontal length of ramp, at the top and
bottom of ramps and at switchbacks?

    ❏ Remodel or relocate ramp.

   The ramp should rise no more than 30 inches
   between landings.

Director's Resource 7-2 (*continued*)

QUESTIONS	POSSIBLE SOLUTIONS

Yes   No

Parking and Drop-Off Areas (ADAAG 4.6)
Are an adequate number of accessible parking spaces available (8 feet wide for car plus 5-foot striped access aisle)? For guidance in determining the appropriate number to designate, the table below gives the ADAAG requirements for new construction and alterations (for lots with more than 100 spaces, refer to ADAAG):

Total spaces	Accessible
1 to 25	1 space
26 to 50	2 spaces
51 to 75	3 spaces
76 to 100	4 spaces

☐ Reconfigure a reasonable number of spaces by repainting stripes.

Are 16-foot-wide spaces, with 98 inches of vertical clearance, available for lift-equipped vans?

At least one of every 8 accessible spaces must be van-accessible.

☐ Reconfigure to provide a reasonable number of van-accessible spaces.

Are the accessible spaces closest to the accessible entrance?

☐ Reconfigure spaces.

Are accessible spaces marked with the International Symbol of Accessibility? Are there signs reading "Van Accessible" at van spaces?

☐ Add signs, placed so that they are not obstructed by cars.

International Symbol of Accessibility:

Is there an enforcement procedure to ensure that accessible parking is used only by those who need it?

☐ Implement a policy to check periodically for violators and report them to the proper authorities.

Entrance (ADAAG 4.13, 4.14)
If there are stairs at the main entrance, is there also a ramp or lift, or is there an alternative accessible entrance?

Do not use a service entrance as the accessible entrance unless there is no other option.

☐ If it is not possible to make the main entrance accessible, create a dignified alternate accessible entrance. Make sure there is accessible parking near accessible entrances.

Director's Resource 7-2 (*continued*)

QUESTIONS	POSSIBLE SOLUTIONS

	Yes	No	

Entrance (*continued*)
Do all inaccessible entrances have signs indicating the location of the nearest accessible entrance? ☐ ☐

☐ Install signs at or before inaccessible entrances.

Can the alternate accessible entrance be used independently? ☐ ☐

☐ Eliminate as much as possible the need for assistance—to answer a doorbell, to operate a lift, or to put down a temporary ramp, for example.

Does the entrance door have at least 32 inches clear opening (for a double door, at least one 32-inch leaf)? ☐ ☐

☐ Widen the door.
☐ Install offset (swing-clear) hinges.

Is there at least 18 inches of clear wall space on the pull side of the door, next to the handle? ☐ ☐

A person using a wheelchair needs this space to get close enough to open the door.

☐ Remove or relocate furnishings, partitions, or other obstructions.
☐ Move door.
☐ Add power-assisted door opener.

Is the threshold level (less than 1/4 inch) or beveled, up to 1/2 inch high? ☐ ☐

☐ If there is a single step with a rise of 6 inches or less, add a short ramp.
☐ If there is a high threshold, remove it or add a bevel.

Are doormats 1/2 inch high or less, and secured to the floor at all edges? ☐ ☐

☐ Replace or remove mats.
☐ Secure mats at edges.

Is the door handle no higher than 48 inches and operable with a closed fist? ☐ ☐

The "closed fist" test for handles and controls: Try opening the door or operating the control using only one hand, held in a fist. If you can do it, so can a person who has limited use of his or her hands. ☐ ☐

☐ Replace inaccessible knob with a lever or loop handle.
☐ Retrofit with an add-on lever extension.

Can doors be opened without too much force (maximum is 5 lbf)? ☐ ☐

You can use a fish scale to measure the force required to open a door. Attach the hook of the scale to the doorknob or handle. Pull on the ring end of the scale until the door opens,

☐ Adjust the door closers and oil the hinges.
☐ Install power-assisted door openers.
☐ Install lighter doors.

Director's Resource 7-2 (*continued*)

QUESTIONS	POSSIBLE SOLUTIONS

	Yes	No	

Entrance (*continued*)
and read off the amount of force required. If you do not have a fish scale, you will need to judge subjectively whether the door is easy enough to open.

If the door has a closer, does it takes at least 3 seconds to close?   ☐ ☐   ☐ Adjust door closer.

Emergency Egress (ADAAG 4.1.3 (14), 4.28)
Do all alarms have both flashing lights and audible signals?   ☐ ☐   ☐ Install visible and audible alarms.

Is there sufficient lighting in egress pathways such as stairs, corridors, and exits?   ☐ ☐   ☐ Upgrade, add, or clean bulbs or fixtures.

PRIORITY 2: ACCESS TO GOODS AND SERVICES

Ideally, the layout of the building should allow people with disabilities to obtain goods or services without special assistance. Where it is not possible to provide full accessibility, assistance or alternative service should be available upon request.

Horizontal Circulation (ADAAG 4.3)
Does the accessible entrance provide direct access to the main floor, lobby, or elevator?   ☐ ☐   ☐ Add ramps or lifts.
☐ Make another entrance accessible.

Are all public spaces on an accessible path of travel?   ☐ ☐   ☐ Provide access to all public spaces along an accessible path of travel.

Is the accessible route to all public spaces at least 36 inches wide?   ☐ ☐   ☐ Move furnishings such as tables, chairs, display racks, vending machines, and counters to make more room.

Is there a 5-foot circle or a T-shaped space for a person using a wheelchair to reverse direction?   ☐ ☐   ☐ Rearrange furnishings, displays, and equipment.

Director's Resource 7-2 (*continued*)

QUESTIONS			POSSIBLE SOLUTIONS
	Yes	No	
Doors (ADAAG 4.13) Do doors into public spaces have at least a 32-inch clear opening?	☐	☐	☐ Install offset (swing-clear) hinges. ☐ Widen doors.
On the pull side of doors, next to the handle, is there at least 18 inches of clear wall space so that a person using a wheelchair can get near to open the door?	☐	☐	☐ Reverse the door swing if it is safe to do so. ☐ Move or remove obstructing partitions.
Can doors be opened without too much force (5 lbf maximum)?	☐	☐	☐ Adjust or replace closers. ☐ Install lighter doors. ☐ Install power-assisted door openers.
Are door handles 48 inches high or less and operable with a closed fist?	☐	☐	☐ Lower handles. ☐ Replace inaccessible knobs or latches with lever or loop handles. ☐ Retrofit with add-on lever extensions. ☐ Install power-assisted door openers.
Are all thresholds level (less than 1/4 inch), or beveled, up to 1/2 inch high?	☐	☐	☐ Remove thresholds. ☐ Add bevels to both sides.
Rooms and Spaces (ADAAG 4.2, 4.4, 4.5, 4.30) Are all aisles and pathways to all goods and services at least 36 inches wide?	☐	☐	☐ Rearrange furnishings and fixtures to clear aisles.
Is there a 5-foot circle or T-shaped space for turning a wheelchair completely?	☐	☐	☐ Rearrange furnishings to clear more room.
Is carpeting low-pile, tightly woven, and securely attached along edges?	☐	☐	☐ Secure edges on all sides. ☐ Replace carpeting.
In routes through public areas, are all obstacles cane-detectable (located within 27 inches of the floor or protruding less than 4 inches from the wall), or are they higher than 80 inches?	☐	☐	☐ Remove obstacles. ☐ Install furnishings, planters, or other cane-detectable barriers underneath the obstacle.
Do signs designating permanent rooms and spaces, such as rest room signs, exit signs, and room numbers, comply with the appropriate requirements for accessible signage?	☐	☐	☐ Provide signage that has raised and brailled letters, complies with finish and contrast standards, and is mounted at the correct height and location.

Director's Resource 7-2 (*continued*)

QUESTIONS	POSSIBLE SOLUTIONS

	Yes	No	
Controls (ADAAG 4.27) Are all controls that are available for use by the public (including electrical, mechanical, window, cabinet, game, and self-service controls) located at an accessible height? Reach ranges: The maximum height for a side reach is 54 inches; for a forward reach, 48 inches. The minimum reachable height is 15 inches.	☐	☐	☐ Relocate controls.
Are they operable with a closed fist?	☐	☐	☐ Replace controls.
Seats, Tables, and Counters (ADAAG 4.2, 4.32) Are the aisles between chairs or tables at least 36 inches wide?	☐	☐	☐ Rearrange chairs or tables to provide 36-inch aisles.
Are the spaces for wheelchair seating distributed throughout?	☐	☐	☐ Rearrange tables to allow room for wheelchairs in seating areas throughout the area. ☐ Remove some fixed seating.
Are the tops of tables or counters between 28 and 34 inches high?	☐	☐	☐ Lower at least a section of high tables and counters.
Are knee spaces at accessible tables at least 27 inches high, 30 inches wide, and 19 inches deep?	☐	☐	☐ Replace or raise tables.
Vertical Circulation (ADAAG 4.3) Are there ramps or elevators to all levels?	☐	☐	☐ Install ramps or lifts. ☐ Modify a service elevator. ☐ Relocate goods or services to an accessible area.
On each level, if there are stairs between the entrance and/or elevator and essential public areas, is there an accessible alternate route?	☐	☐	☐ Post clear signs directing people along an accessible route to ramps, lifts, or elevators.
Stairs (ADAAG 4.9) Do treads have a non-slip surface?	☐	☐	☐ Add non-slip surface to treads.
Do stairs have continuous rails on both sides, with extensions beyond the top and bottom stairs?			☐ Add or replace handrails.

Director's Resource 7-2 (*continued*)

QUESTIONS	POSSIBLE SOLUTIONS

	Yes	No	

Elevators (ADAAG 4.10)
Are there both visible and verbal or audible door opening/closing and floor indicators (one tone = up, two tones = down)? ☐ ☐

☐ Install visible and verbal or audible signals.

Are the call buttons in the hallway no higher than 42 inches? ☐ ☐

☐ Lower call buttons.
☐ Provide a permanently attached reach stick.

Do the controls outside and inside the cab have raised and braille lettering? ☐ ☐

☐ Install raised lettering and braille next to buttons.

Is there a sign on the jamb at each floor identifying the floor in raised and braille letters? ☐ ☐

☐ Install tactile signs to identify floor numbers, at a height of 60 inches from floor.

Is the emergency intercom usable without voice communication? ☐ ☐

☐ Replace communication system.

Are there braille and raised-letter instructions for the communication system? ☐ ☐

☐ Add simple tactile instructions.

Lifts (ADAAG 4.2, 4.11)
Can the lift be used without assistance? If not, is a call button provided? ☐ ☐

☐ At each stopping level, post clear instructions for use of the lift.
☐ Provide a call button.

Is there at least 30 by 48 inches of clear space for a person using a wheelchair to approach to reach the controls and use the lift? ☐ ☐

☐ Rearrange furnishings and equipment to clear more space.

Are controls between 15 and 48 inches high (up to 54 inches if a side approach is possible)?

☐ Move controls.

PRIORITY 3: USABILITY OF REST ROOMS

When rest rooms are open to the public, they should be accessible to people with disabilities. Closing a rest room that is currently open to the public is not an allowable option.

Director's Resource 7-2 (*continued*)

QUESTIONS			POSSIBLE SOLUTIONS
	Yes	**No**	
Getting to the Rest Rooms (ADAAG 4.1) If rest rooms are available to the public, is at least one rest room (either one for each sex, or unisex) fully accessible?	☐	☐	☐ Reconfigure rest room. ☐ Combine rest rooms to create one unisex accessible rest room.
Are there signs at inaccessible rest rooms that give directions to accessible ones?	☐	☐	☐ Install accessible signs.
Doorways and Passages (ADAAG 4.2, 4.13) Is there tactile signage identifying rest rooms? 　Mount signs on the wall, on the latch side of the door. Avoid using ambiguous symbols in place of text to identify rest rooms.	☐	☐	☐ Add accessible signage, placed to the side of the door (not on the door itself). ☐ If symbols are used, add supplementary verbal signage.
Is the doorway at least 32 inches clear?	☐	☐	☐ Install offset (swing-clear) hinges. ☐ Widen the doorway.
Are doors equipped with accessible handles (operable with a closed fist), 48 inches high or less?	☐	☐	☐ Lower handles. ☐ Replace inaccessible knobs or latches with lever or loop handles. ☐ Add lever extensions. ☐ Install power-assisted door openers.
Can doors be opened easily (5 Ibf maximum force)?	☐	☐	☐ Adjust or replace closers. ☐ Install lighter doors. ☐ Install power-assisted door openers.
Does the entry configuration provide adequate maneuvering space for a person using a wheelchair? 　A person using a wheelchair needs 36 inches of clear width for forward movement, and a 5-foot diameter clear space or a T-shaped space to make turns. A minimum distance of 48 inches, clear of the door swing, is needed between the two doors of an entry vestibule.	☐	☐	☐ Rearrange furnishings such as chairs and trash cans. ☐ Remove inner door if there is a vestibule with two doors. ☐ Move or remove obstructing partitions.
Is there a 36-inch-wide path to all fixtures?	☐	☐	☐ Remove obstructions.

Director's Resource 7-2 (*continued*)

QUESTIONS			POSSIBLE SOLUTIONS
	Yes	**No**	
Stalls (ADAAG 4.17) Is the stall door operable with a closed fist, inside and out?	☐	☐	☐ Replace inaccessible knobs with lever or loop handles. ☐ Add lever extensions.
Is there a wheelchair-accessible stall that has an area of at least 5 feet by 5 feet, clear of the door swing, OR is there a stall that is less accessible but that provides greater access than a typical stall (either 36 by 69 inches or 48 by 69 inches)?	☐	☐	☐ Move or remove partitions. ☐ Reverse the door swing if it is safe to do so.
In the accessible stall, are there grab bars behind and on the side wall nearest to the toilet?	☐	☐	☐ Add grab bars.
Is the toilet seat 17 to 19 inches high?	☐	☐	☐ Add raised seat.
Lavatories (ADAAG 4.19, 4.24) Does one lavatory have a 30-inch-wide by 48-inch-deep clear space in front? A maximum of 19 inches of the required depth may be under the lavatory.	☐	☐	☐ Rearrange furnishings. ☐ Replace lavatory. ☐ Remove or alter cabinetry to provide space underneath. Make sure hot pipes are insulated. ☐ Move a partition or wall.
Is the lavatory rim no higher than 34 inches?	☐	☐	☐ Adjust or replace lavatory.
Is there at least 29 inches from the floor to the bottom of the lavatory apron (excluding pipes)?	☐	☐	☐ Adjust or replace lavatory.
Can the faucet be operated with one closed fist?	☐	☐	☐ Replace faucet handles with paddle type.
Are soap and other dispensers and hand dryers 48 inches high or less and usable with one closed fist?	☐	☐	☐ Lower dispensers. ☐ Replace with or provide additional accessible dispensers.
Is the mirror mounted with the bottom edge of the reflecting surface 40 inches high or lower?	☐	☐	☐ Lower or tilt down the mirror. ☐ Replace with larger mirror.

Director's Resource 7-2 (*continued*)

QUESTIONS	POSSIBLE SOLUTIONS

Yes   No

PRIORITY 4:
ADDITIONAL ACCESS

When amenities such as public telephones and drinking fountains are provided to the general public, they should also be accessible to people with disabilities.

Drinking Fountains (ADAAG 4.15)
Is there at least one fountain with clear floor space of at least 30 by 48 inches in front? ☐ ☐
☐ Clear more room by rearranging or removing furnishings.

Is there one fountain with its spout no higher than 36 inches from the ground, and another with a standard height spout (or a single "hi-lo" fountain)? ☐ ☐
☐ Provide cup dispensers for fountains with spouts that are too high.
☐ Provide an accessible water cooler.

Are controls mounted on the front or on the side near the front edge, and operable with one closed fist? ☐ ☐
☐ Replace the controls.

Does the fountain protrude no more than 4 inches into the circulation space? ☐ ☐
☐ Place a planter or other cane-detectable barrier on each side at floor level.

Telephones (ADAAG 4.30, 4.31)
If pay or public use phones are provided, is there clear floor space of at least 30 by 48 inches in front of at least one? ☐ ☐
☐ Move furnishings.
☐ Replace booth with open station.

Is the highest operable part of the phone no higher than 48 inches (up to 54 inches if a side approach is possible)? ☐ ☐
☐ Lower telephone.

Does the phone protrude no more than 4 inches into the circulation space? ☐ ☐
☐ Place a cane-detectable barrier on each side at floor level.

Does the phone have push-button controls? ☐ ☐
☐ Contact phone company to install push-buttons.

Director's Resource 7-2 (*continued*)

QUESTIONS			POSSIBLE SOLUTIONS
	Yes	**No**	
Telephones (continued)			
Is the phone hearing aid compatible?	☐	☐	☐ Contact phone company to add an induction coil (T-switch).
Is the phone adapted with volume control?	☐	☐	☐ Contact the phone company to add volume control.
Is the phone with volume control identified with appropriate signage?	☐	☐	☐ Add signage.
Is one of the phones equipped with a text telephone (TT or TDD)?	☐	☐	☐ Install a text telephone. ☐ Have a portable text telephone available.
Is the location of the text telephone identified by accessible signage bearing the International TDD Symbol?	☐	☐	☐ Add signage.

International TDD Symbol:

CHAPTER 8

Equipping the Center

It is both challenging and rewarding to equip a center. Your personality will be reflected in the physical environment you create as you strive to meet the needs of the children and as you select things that enable you to set up a program congruent with your program philosophy. Although many programs are being implemented with inadequate, unsuitable materials, supplying equipment that is appropriate contributes significantly to the success of early childhood education programs and is necessary for successful program implementation. Creating rich learning environments that are replete with abundant opportunities for children to be actively involved with age-appropriate and individually appropriate materials requires thoughtful, careful selection of classroom equipment and supplies. Also, staff members are able to do

Photo above Supplying appropriate equipment contributes significantly to the success of early childhood education programs. (Photo by Lisa Souders)

their assigned jobs more efficiently and comfortably when they work in adequately equipped environments.

Equipping a center is costly, and when mistakes are made, replacements are doubly costly. (Many companies charge about 30 percent of the cost of items which have been returned, unless of course they arrived damaged. In addition, the center pays the return shipping.) Impulse buying is irresponsible when you are in charge of purchasing equipment. Therefore, plan your purchases carefully by first assessing your needs, next developing criteria for equipment selection, and finally relating needed and desired items to your budget. After selections are made, decide on ordering procedures and develop a maintenance and storage system to reduce unnecessary repairs and losses.

ESTABLISHING NEEDS

There are three major areas to equip in a child care center, and a director must determine the type and amount of equipment needed for each of these areas. The areas are: (1) children's spaces, both indoors and outdoors, (2) adult spaces including offices, waiting rooms, conference rooms, and lounge areas, and (3) service areas. Equipment includes not only furniture and classroom materials but also consumable supplies, such as paints, paper towels, food, and stationery. The equipment and supplies budgets should provide for initial purchases, as well as for long- and short-term replacement of both basic furnishings and consumable supplies. Information about equipment and suppliers is provided in Appendix A.

Directors entering an ongoing program begin by taking inventory of what is on hand and setting up a priority system for securing new equipment, for replacing worn out items, and for replenishing supplies of consumable materials. Directors of new centers are confronted with the somewhat overwhelming task of equipping an entire center.

Children's Spaces

Program philosophy and the needs of children dictate what will be ordered for the children's spaces in the center. Most programs are set up in basic curricular areas such as art, music, science, manipulative and pretend play, plus special spaces for math games and writing materials. All of these curricular areas require special furnishings and materials. Provisions must also be made for water and sand play, carpentry, cooking, building, and large muscle activities. Furniture for working, resting, and eating is needed, including such accessories as clocks, plants, wastebaskets, and curtains.

Adult Spaces

Even a very small center requires some office space—a locked file cabinet for records at the very minimum. Since adult desks are not used in classrooms for young children, some space for teachers to use as they plan their curriculum and prepare reports is essential. Furnishings that facilitate curriculum development include shelving for a teacher resource library and a work table with paper cutter, laminator, and storage for supplies such as posterboard, scissors, and markers.

When office space is provided, the basic furnishings for each occupant include two chairs, a desk, a file cabinet, and a bookshelf. A desk and cabinet can be shared by two teachers who spend most of their time in the classroom. Teachers need access to a phone for parent contacts and for limited personal calls when they are on break. The location of the phone should allow for quiet and for privacy. At least one computer equipped with word processing and data management software is essential. Directors of larger centers find that a copy machine is a worthwhile investment in terms of the time and money saved in duplicating such items as newsletters, menus, and forms. Although these machines are initially expensive, they pay for themselves over time by saving staff time and they enable the center to produce materials of professional quality.

The staff needs a place for meetings. When staff meetings are held after children leave, the classrooms can be used. However, it is certainly more comfortable for the adults attending meetings to have a space furnished with adult-sized chairs and tables. Comfortable furniture should be provided for use by parents who come to the center for conferences and by consultants who come to meet with staff members. Bulletin boards and coat racks are convenient accessories for adult spaces. Since some adults who come to the center have disabilities, consider the seating and other furnishings and equipment in terms of their needs.

Some centers provide a separate lounge for parents and visitors. This area should have comfortable seating, lamps, tables, a bookshelf for pertinent reading materials, and perhaps facilities for coffee or other refreshments. Wall hangings or pictures, plants, a rug or carpet, and curtains all enhance the appearance of the space. A shelf of toys and books for visiting children indicates that the center is sensitive to children's needs.

Service Areas

Basic equipment in the bathrooms, the kitchen, the laundry, and the janitor's closet is usually built in and therefore is not purchased from the equipment and supplies budget. In a new facility, some appliances may be included in the equipment line. Consumables for service areas must be furnished, and of course, appliances must be replaced over time. Dishes, cutlery, cooking utensils, and serving carts must be provided in centers where lunch is served. In large centers special appliances such as commercial dishwashers, rug shampooers, heavy-duty automatic washers and dryers, and large refrigerators and freezers are needed.

USING SELECTION CRITERIA

Selection of all equipment should be based on a set of pre-established criteria. The primary consideration is usefulness; that is, will a specific piece of equipment meet the needs of this center in a safe manner? Other criteria are versatility, suitability, durability, ease of maintenance, attractiveness, and user preference. Some equipment for children should encourage and even necessitate cooperative play. All equipment should work the way it is supposed to and should be durable and economical. Although these criteria apply to all equipment purchases, this chapter covers primarily information about equipment which children will use.

The goals and objectives of a particular center will dictate some purchases. Thus, a center that emphasizes academic development with a special focus on mathematics and problem solving will purchase a wide variety of materials

The director is responsible for equipment for adult, child and service areas. (Photo by Lisa Souders)

REFLECTIONS

Think of yourself as a director who is responsible for equipment purchases. Did you realize that you would not only pore over classroom equipment and materials catalogs but would also find yourself searching through office equipment and restaurant supply catalogs? Your duties have now expanded from educator and administrator to that of purchasing agent. This responsibility probably seems like an overwhelming undertaking at the moment, since many of you have been responsible only for purchasing personal items and, in some cases, basic household equipment. You are, no doubt, beginning to realize that the role of the director has many facets and requires a wide variety of special skills.

suitable for helping children attain knowledge about math. In this case, some advanced math games will be included, with the expectation that the comprehensive program in math will enable the children to enjoy these more complex materials. On the other hand, a center that emphasizes social development may concentrate more heavily on materials for pretend play and on equipment that can be used simultaneously by a number of children. Most schools will focus on these two areas equally, and only a few, if any, will exclude either area. The focal points of a program will be based on its philosophy and will determine, in part, the types of equipment and the quantity of equipment of various types to be purchased. Suitability of specific curricular materials will not be discussed here since a number of texts include this information in the context of program development.

Usefulness

The usefulness of a piece of children's equipment is measured, first, by how well it meets the developmental needs of the children in the program and second, by whether or not the equipment can be put to multiple uses by those children.

Developmental Needs. The developmental levels, the capabilities, and the age range of the children enrolled influence what will be purchased. A center serving two-year-olds will need some pull toys and small climbers that would not be needed if the youngest child were three. Infants require special furnishings, such as cribs, changing tables, and high chairs, that are not needed by older children. (Some centers use low chairs designed for feeding older infants as a safety measure. Young infants are always held during feeding.) Infants also require washable, chewable toys, bibs, sheets, blankets, and disposable diapers. Parents may be asked to furnish some of these necessary items and to take responsibility for their infant's laundry.

Toddlers may need potty chairs instead of built-in toilets, which are unsuitable for toilet training some children. (Note that potty chairs may not be permitted by some sanitation codes.) Toddlers also need toys that provide opportunities for filling and dumping, big toys that can be carried during early walking stages, and lots of duplicates so that sharing will not be necessary.

School-aged children in after-school care programs need games and crafts that are far too complex and frustrating for younger children. They may also need well-lighted working areas for homework, larger furniture in which they can sit and work comfortably, and equipment for active semi-organized sports.

Children with disabilities may require modified equipment or equipment that has been specifically designed to meet a particular need. A director who has established contact with agencies serving people with disabilities can seek their assistance in providing modifications or special equipment. The equipment should enable the child to do as much as possible independently.

Versatility. A piece of equipment that can be used in several ways is a bonus both financially and in terms of enriching the learning environment for children. Such a piece not only saves space and money but also gives children the opportunity to use their imaginations in creating different functions for one object. An example would be the large hollow blocks that can be used to make a puppet stage or a grocery store or can serve as individual work spaces for children's small projects. A bookshelf can be both a room divider and a storage facility. Two-year-olds may find the water table to be a relaxing place for splashing while four-year-olds may be more interested in using this equipment for constructing a water maze. Many pieces of equipment may be shared by two or more classes for the same or different purposes, eliminating the purchase of duplicate materials and freeing up money for other purchases.

Some equipment can be used both indoors and outdoors—a practice that not only is economical but also provides a wider variety of learning experiences for children. Easels, water tables, and movable climbing equipment are a few items that may be moved outside if the building and play area have been planned to facilitate such indoor–outdoor movement. When the physical facility makes indoor–outdoor movement difficult for teachers, the janitor or the older children can be called on to help carry heavy items up and down the stairs or in and out of the indoor–outdoor storage spaces. In public school settings, having school-aged children assist in the preschool helps create a community feeling throughout the school building.

Safety

No matter how versatile, attractive, durable, economical, and suitable a piece of equipment may be, it must be rejected if it is not safe. A climber with protruding bolts, blocks of soft wood that splinter, and tricycles that tip over easily should not be used in the center. A kitchen appliance that requires a long extension cord is a hazard to the cook and to the children and should be avoided. All equipment used by the children must be of nontoxic material and must not have sharp or pointed edges. Safety is maintained by staff members who make a point of being constantly alert to the condition and the arrangement of the equipment that is placed in the learning environment.[1]

Suitability

Some equipment must be provided in several sizes. Specific equipment must be provided to meet the needs of each user. For example, the secretary must have a standard adult-sized chair, but chairs for children are usually 10, 12, and 14 inches high, depending on the child's age and height. Children's chairs that are so large that seated children cannot put their feet on the floor are not suitable for those users. Children's chairs should also have a wide base so they will not tip.

Stereotypes. Equipment must be chosen with the understanding that it may be used equally by all children. Staff members who plan curricula in a stereotyped way will need special guidance on this point so that boys are not relegated to playing with blocks and trucks and girls are not always expected to dress dolls and play quiet table games. People with special needs should be depicted in books, puzzles, and classroom displays and they should be shown participating in a variety of activities. Classroom materials should reflect many cultures and should depict a variety of roles being chosen by members of various cultures and of both sexes. For example, dolls of many races should be available. The play figures that are used as block accessories should include female postal workers and black doctors. Books, music, foods, and posters should be carefully selected to avoid any stereotyping and to depict the culturally pluralistic society in which the children live.

Special Needs. In determining the suitability of equipment, you must consider children with disabilities. Children who cannot walk, for example, may need easels and water tables that can be used while the children sit in a chair or a wheelchair. Sometimes such equipment is very low to enable children who are sitting on the floor to use it. In selecting the equipment, you should consider the height of the chair or wheelchair that is used and the length of the children's

1 S. C. Wortham and J. L. Frost (eds.), *Playgrounds for Young Children: American Survey and Perspectives,* Reston, VA: American Alliance for Health, Physical Education, Recreation and Dance, 1991.

REFLECTIONS

Think about your previous experiences with individuals with disabilities. Have you had enough experience to be aware of their special needs? If you have a friend or relative with a lifelong disability, imagine what his or her special needs might have been during the preschool years. Now consider yourself responsible for equipping an environment that is suitable not only for that child but also for a group of typically developing children. What special provisions would have to be made for your friend or relative with special needs to provide a suitable learning environment?

arms; in this way you can determine the optimum height of the working spaces for children with disabilities.

If children are crawling in body casts or in leg braces, they need comfortable floor surfaces. Wheeled equipment such as a sturdy wagon or a special buggy with seat belts will make it possible for children with physical disabilities to enjoy tours around the center neighborhood with the rest of the class. Other children may need an augmentative communication system so that they can interact with staff and children.

Children with hearing impairments need ample visual cues, such as pictures attached to storage areas, so that they can tell where equipment belongs even though they cannot hear the teacher's directions. Children with visual impairments need some toys that vary in terms of weight, texture, and sound. Balls with a bell inside and storage containers covered with different materials (for example, velvet on a container of beads or corduroy on a box holding small blocks) are especially appropriate for these children. When children who do not have disabilities use these same materials, they develop greater insights into the experience of children with disabilities.

In purchasing equipment for a center, the director will need to know, in general, what the lifestyles of the families are and what the learning styles and interests of individual children are. Children must be provided with enough ordinary, simple equipment so that they need not be bombarded nine hours a day with novelty. A balance of the familiar with the novel creates a learning environment that is neither overstimulating nor boring; the proper balance may be different in full-day child care centers than it is in half-day programs.

Ease of Maintenance

Ease of maintenance should also be a consideration in choosing equipment; sinks, toilets, and drinking fountains that must be cleaned daily and table tops that must be washed several times each day should be extremely simple to clean. The surfaces should be smooth and all areas should be easy to reach. Small pieces that are hard to clean around may cause problems and harbor dirt and germs. Equipment parts that are cleaned separately, such as high chair trays, should be easy to remove and replace. Some plastic chairs have surfaces that are slightly roughened or ridged, and, although the surface feels relatively smooth to the hand, there are actually shallow indentations that attract and hold dirt. It is almost impossible to wipe or even scrub these chairs so that they look clean. This type of furniture may be slightly less expensive than other furniture, but maintenance problems outweigh the possible savings.

Outdoor equipment that must be repainted frequently should be designed so that it can be sanded and painted easily. Places that are difficult to reach are a nuisance, and surfaces that catch and hold rain increase the need for maintenance. Equipment that will rust or rot easily should not be purchased for outdoor use.

Attractiveness

Child care center equipment should be well designed and aesthetically attractive. Most parents and teachers would like their children to appreciate beauty, and one of the best ways to help children acquire this appreciation is to surround them with beauty. An attractive environment also carries the subtle message that children, families, and staff who enter the setting are much appreciated and that great care is taken to make their environment beautiful. A material that is aesthetically appealing need not be expensive. In fact, often it is the ability of the director or teacher to find beauty in nature that provides the most attractive places for children. A colorful tablecloth on the housekeeping area table with a small vase of wildflowers in the center makes that classroom area attractive and inviting. A large square of interesting gift-wrapping paper or a square yard of fabric serves as an attractive and inexpensive wall hanging.

When equipment is made for the classroom, it should be prepared with special attention to its visual appeal. A math game, for example, can be made using well-designed stickers or beautiful pictures cut from duplicate copies of magazines, rather that using cartoon-like gimmicky stickers or drawings. The cardboard should be cut evenly and laminated or covered with a plastic coating instead of being presented to children with rough, crooked edges. Preparing beautiful materials takes a little longer and may require initial costs that are somewhat higher, but the product is worth the investment. It is the director's job to help staff and children value quality rather than quantity and appreciate the beauty in the objects around them.

Teacher Preference

Sometimes teacher preference determines the type of equipment ordered. One teacher may choose to buy many books, while another depends heavily on the library; one sees an autoharp as a necessity, while another finds this instrument encumbering. One teacher may choose a guinea pig as the ideal classroom pet, another prefers a fish, and still another considers all pets to require an inordinate amount of the teacher's time. As long as these teacher preferences do not mitigate against appropriate classroom practice, they are legitimate and should be honored if at all possible. When budgeting constraints or other equipment needs make it impossible to fill all teachers' requests, the director must notify teachers that their preferences are under consideration and that plans are being made to fill all requests as soon as possible. The teacher who wants an autoharp may have to wait until next year's budget provides it, but meanwhile the director can support that teacher by informing the staff of planned equipment purchases. Each teacher's preferences deserve careful consideration because each teacher will ultimately set the stage for learning through the use of the center's equipment. Of course, the director will have to intervene if a teacher chooses to order inappropriate items such as games with very small pieces for toddlers or workbooks for preschoolers.

WORKING WITHIN A BUDGET

Durability and Economy

Durability and economy often go hand in hand. The climbing apparatus that costs three times as much as a competitor's product is worth the original investment if it lasts three times as long or is safer and sturdier. When more durable items are purchased, the center is not faced with the problem of replacement so often, and considerable shipping costs are saved, particularly with large pieces of equipment. Price and durability are not always perfectly correlated, but it is safe to say that bargain basement tricycles, which may be appropriate for home use, are inappropriate for group use. When used at a center, the standard equipment that is used at home will be in the repair shop far sooner and more frequently than will the sturdier, more expensive equipment that is designed for school use. Keep this fact in mind when well-meaning Board members want to donate items their children have outgrown rather than including sufficient dollars in the equipment budget.

In child care centers many adults and children will use the kitchen equipment, leading to heavy usage and contributing to misuse because of a lack of knowledge or concern regarding proper care of the equipment. Refrigerator and freezer doors are opened frequently and are often left standing open while children take out ice cubes or put in trays of sloshing jello. Dishwashers may be improperly loaded or overloaded, and sinks are sometimes scoured with rough scouring pads or abrasive powders. It is important to provide heavy-duty kitchen equipment because equipment made for home use will require costly service calls when it is subjected to the hard use it will inevitably get in a center.

In setting up a new center, the director can expect to spend $6,000–$12,000 per classroom on equipment. The variance is due to the number of children in each classroom and the quality of the items purchased. A typical budget for manipulatives (puzzles, table toys, and small blocks) for a center of about 75 children is about $2,000, assuming that the items are centrally stored so that teachers can share them. To reduce this cost, directors often search for free materials and supplies. However, the director may then have to pick up the items or enlist a volunteer for this service.

ORDERING EQUIPMENT

Decisions about what, when, and where to buy equipment are usually left to the director. In any case, directors are consulted and they have considerable control over what is bought with the money that is budgeted for equipment and supplies.

Equipment Requisition

Directors usually develop an equipment request procedure. Staff members notify the director, in writing, of the type of equipment that is needed or desired, providing additional information such as the rationale to support the need, a possible vendor, and an estimated purchase price. All of these data are helpful when final purchase decisions are made. Some centers use purchase order or requisition forms, which are nothing more than request forms that can be sent to vendors with a duplicate retained for center records (see Working Paper 8-1). Even though this request procedure is formal and perhaps cumbersome, it puts the purchase of equipment on a businesslike basis and gives each staff member an equal opportunity to bid for the equipment dollars in the budget.

In corporate systems, requisitions are processed through a central purchasing agent and shipments are made directly to the center from the manufacturer. The central office handles all the orders and saves money through collective, quantity buying and through careful selection of suppliers. This approach cuts costs but limits the options for those staff members selecting equipment. Public school programs usually have specific purchasing procedures to follow, requisitioning their supplies through the principal or through a supervisor responsible for the preschool or after-school programs.

In centers where directors are fully responsible for receiving staff requests and placing orders, they check requests against the established selection criteria and the budget allowance before completing order forms. All order forms should include quantity, price, catalog order number (if available), and name or description of each item. When making final decisions on purchases, make certain that careful consideration is given to possible savings through bulk buying. For example, newsprint for painting can be bought from some vendors for as much as $2 less per ream when bought in 48-ream packages. Economies realized through bulk buying are practical only if adequate storage space is available for the unused materials.

Equipment costs can also be reduced in nonprofit centers by applying for tax-exempt status. When orders are sent to suppliers, the center will not be charged a sales tax if the order includes the center's tax-exempt number.

Some centers have provisions for teachers to purchase specified dollar amounts without permission and within a given time period. For example, a teacher may receive $100 to spend for the classroom each year (in addition to the center-wide purchases which the director makes). In some cases the purchase is made and the teacher is reimbursed on presentation of the receipt to the board treasurer or to the director. The practice of giving teachers some petty cash to spend for classroom materials gives them some freedom to provide for special program needs and, more importantly, communicates trust in their ability to make appropriate choices for their children.

Purchase Time Line

Equipment purchasing occurs in three different time frames: start-up, supplementary, and replacement.

REFLECTIONS

Assume that your classroom is stocked with basic equipment for your fifteen four-year-old children. You have received $100 from petty cash. Think about how you might spend your allocation.

First, there must be a major start-up equipment purchase when a center is opened so that all the basic aspects of the program can function with appropriate equipment. This phase is obviously the most expensive of the three, but extensive purchases at this point are absolutely essential because it is unfair to children and staff to operate a program without basic equipment. To save money, some secondhand, borrowed, or home-made equipment can be used, keeping in mind the criteria described earlier. There is no formula that can tell a director exactly what must be provided, but the staff will need equipment of the type, quantity, and quality that will allow them to focus on the children and their needs, rather than on the equipment or the lack thereof. Children in a classroom with inappropriate or inadequate equipment will be quite likely to engage in inappropriate behavior as they seek to create something interesting to do.

The second phase of equipment purchasing is the supplementary phase, which provides for additional equipment purchases throughout each year. When supplementary equipment purchases are spaced throughout a program year, both children and staff members enjoy greater variety and a change of pace. Furthermore, teachers can adjust equipment requests to meet the needs of particular children, such as a child with special needs who enrolls mid-year and requires a chair with particular supports, a prone board, or a walker. Although outside funding may be available for some of these larger items for an individual child's use, teachers will still need to consider books with large print, puzzles with large knobs, or writing tools that have been adapted for easier handling.

Lastly, the replacement phase not only helps maintain a constant supply of equipment that is in good repair but also allows for adjustments in available equipment and materials as program needs change or as new items come on the market. For example, a few years ago all African-American dolls had Caucasian hairstyles and facial features, but newer dolls have features that match the ethnic group being represented.

The budget should also include enough money for emergency replacements. Although careful usage, combined with a maintenance plan, minimizes the need for emergency replacements, unexpected breakage or loss is sure to occur. When a copier repair is too costly, it is sometimes more economical to buy or lease a new model than to repair the old one.

Sources of Equipment

Much equipment for early childhood education centers is purchased from catalogs. If the dealers are reliable, this arrangement is satisfactory. It is wise to check with other directors, professional organizations, or the Better Business Bureau to determine the suitability of making purchases from a particular company. Among the advantages of purchasing by catalog are the wide variety of merchandise that is often available and the lowering of costs with the bypassing of the retailer. On the other hand, shipping costs may be charged and return of unsatisfactory merchandise may be cumbersome. It is helpful to have a supply of catalogs available to the staff. Most companies will be pleased to put your center on their mailing list. (Appendix A lists equipment suppliers.)

Equipment purchased from local retail outlets can be seen and tried out, which has obvious advantages; but most retail outlets cater to home users and carry a limited stock of classroom equipment. If a local outlet has access to a manufacturer of school equipment, it may be possible to order from a catalog through a local retailer. A buying co-op is another equipment source that is worth investigating because group buying can be very economical. In this system the co-op group buys in quantity at a wholesale price and sells items to co-op members at just enough above cost to pay the co-op operating expenses.

Toy libraries are popular equipment sources in some areas. A center director or teacher may borrow anything from a puzzle to a complete set of housekeeping equipment, just as one borrows library books. Sometimes a group of center directors finds it worthwhile to help establish a toy library for their mutual benefit and it is especially helpful to have toy-lending programs which furnish materials for special needs children. Occasionally, toy-lending or toy-sharing systems are set up by community organizations to make equipment available both to centers and to parents.

Secondhand shops, discount stores, antique shops, and garage or yard sales frequently are excellent sources of equipment or raw materials for pieces needed by the center. The buyer may discover a hand grinder which can provide an interesting physical knowledge experience for children. With imagination and effort, large ice cream cans can become storage places for musical instruments or some other equipment that demands a number of relatively small, easily accessible spaces. Perhaps a used desk or file cabinet for the center office can be located. When such discoveries need to be put into finished or usable and attractive form, it is sometimes possible to enlist the help of the parent group, a high-school vocational class, or a senior citizens' organization whose members enjoy repairing and painting. In some regions, high-school woodworking or metal working classes or Junior Achievement groups make new equipment and sell it to centers at reasonable prices.

Another way to obtain equipment is to solicit the help of parents, teachers, board members, or residents of the community in equipment-making parties. This activity enhances the feeling of community in the center's program. Some parent co-ops expect each parent to make a certain number of pieces of equipment for the classroom each year in addition to the time they are asked to spend in the classroom. Child care center staff members often take advantage of the children's naptime to make classroom materials. Encouraging staff members to make some materials is important because few centers have unlimited resources and commercial equipment cannot always be suitably adapted to meet individual children's needs.

Gifts of equipment are usually welcome, but their suitability must be measured against the same criteria employed for equipment purchases. A gift, such as a toy gun, in a center where pretend gun play is discouraged, or the gift of an animal that induces allergic reactions in some children must be refused graciously.

MANAGING EQUIPMENT

Even before equipment is delivered to the center, the director must consider how it will be managed. All equipment must be checked and inventoried upon delivery and before it is stored or put into use, and a maintenance plan should be set up to minimize repair and replacement needs.

Checking and Inventorying Equipment

When equipment is received, it must be checked against the order to ascertain whether or not it corresponds with the order in terms of quantity, size, color, and so forth. It is also important to make certain that only the items actually received are listed on both the order and the packing slip, and that prices are correct. If discrepancies are found, the vendor must be notified immediately, and it is wise to keep original packing materials in case any equipment needs to be returned.

Most center directors keep a record of at least the major items purchased, and some directors keep a running account of all small items and consumables as well. An inventory of purchases can be recorded as items are unpacked by listing each item on a file card or on computer, noting the description, supplier, price, date of purchase, and location in which the item is to be used. Some directors mark equipment with the name of the center, with an inventory number, or with an identifying number so that if a center owns five identical record players, each is individually identifiable. In public schools, the usual practice is to put the room number on each piece of equipment. The labeling practice is helpful when pieces are sent out for repair, when school buildings are cleaned during vacation periods, or when items are stolen. Of course, valuable equipment should be insured. When equipment is added or removed from the center, the inventory should be updated.

An accurate record of equipment will always be available when the inventory is updated regularly. Working Paper 8-2 shows a suggested inventory form. The inventory should be kept in a safe place, in a fire-resistant file cabinet or other storage unit if possible, so that losses can be reported accurately in the event of fire or theft. Computer inventories should be backed up and discs should be safely stored. Furthermore, an ongoing, updated inventory minimizes the work of taking an annual inventory (which is usually necessary for insurance purposes), for annual reporting to the board, sponsoring, or funding agency, or for reporting to a corporate central office that must have an accurate annual inventory to determine the assets of the corporation. Updated inventories also give directors a clear picture of what is available in the center and help pinpoint center areas or types of equipment that are incurring heavy damage. This information is useful not only in determining how much and when to reorder but also in making decisions about changing vendors or brands of equipment ordered. Information about persistent damage in certain areas should lead to a careful examination of the storage and maintenance system.

After the equipment is checked in and inventoried, the director must notify the staff that the new equipment is available for use. No doubt everyone will know when a new climbing tower arrives or when a new microwave oven is available, but if twelve new puzzles are placed on the shelves or a fresh supply of felt markers is stored, it could be weeks before all teachers in a large center discover the new materials.

Maintaining and Storing Equipment

As soon as equipment is placed in the center, the job of maintenance begins. In the very act of placing equipment, maintenance decisions are made. For instance, an untreated wooden climber that is placed outdoors in a rainy area is doomed to rot. It will need immediate treatment, followed by periodic coatings of a penetrating nontoxic stain if it is to withstand weathering. Carpeting under an easel will become stained with paint unless additional floor covering such as a rubber or plastic mat is placed on top of the carpet under the easel.

Equipment used by the children must be checked daily and removed if it is in need of repair, even if immediate replacement is impossible. Children need attractive, usable equipment and should not be subjected to the frustration of trying to make sense out of broken or incomplete classroom materials. Puzzles with missing pieces, tricycles with broken pedals, or books with torn or defaced pages should not be left in the classroom.

Storage of equipment is also directly related to its maintenance. It is easy to return equipment after it has been used when each piece has a specific, clearly delineated storage space. The space, whether in a storage room or on a classroom shelf, must be large enough so that the object does not have to be jammed into place and perhaps damaged, and the space must be accessible to staff members (and in many cases, to children) to ensure that it will be used for storage purposes. When storage spaces are inconveniently located relative to the areas in which the equipment is used, items may be moved from temporary place to temporary place until eventually many parts are lost or broken, or everyone has difficulty locating the misplaced items. Each center must work out a method for storing certain equipment and supplies that are used daily and must remain in the classroom; other supplies should be designated for return to a central area. Storage must also be provided for items such as tricycles that are used daily but must be protected from weather and theft. Additional storage is needed for items that are purchased in quantity for long-range use, such as paper towels and paint.

When a large number of people have access to the central supply storage areas, there is some tendency for each person to assume that someone else will maintain order and cleanliness in the area. Therefore, many of the users feel little or no responsibility for maintaining the area. When this happens, some users return materials in a haphazard way, fail to place them on the correct shelves, or return them in poor condition. Other staff members become irritated when they try to find what they need and have to cope with a messy storage area. These frustrations lead to conflict and a breakdown in positive staff relationships. Sometimes this problem can be avoided by assigning each teacher the responsibility for maintaining a specific storage area, such as for art materials, outdoor equipment or books and records, for a given length of time. In other centers periodic work sessions are scheduled to involve the entire staff in cleaning and straightening central storage areas. Some centers institute a system for checking equipment in and out of the storage room that is similar to the practice conducted in a library. A few centers keep all the equipment in classrooms either on shelves available to the children or in closed cabinets available to the teacher, but this practice is expensive because it requires so much duplication.

In whatever way equipment is stored, its placement should be neat and easy to find so that children and teachers alike will be encouraged to maintain some degree of order in their attractive environment. The director's job is to establish and follow routines that lead to the easy accessibility of all equipment to everyone. These routines make putting things away far less burdensome for both teachers and children. Orderliness does not have to be an obsession; rather, it is an appropriate way to manage a large variety of equipment which is used in a number of ways by a wide range of people.

SUMMARY

Appropriate equipment allows the staff to focus on the essentials of their work as they provide an excellent early childhood program. Initial purchases are made when a center opens, and additional items for children's and adults' spaces and for service areas are purchased to supplement and replace this equipment. Most centers acquire equipment from a variety of sources, but all equipment should be considered in terms of its usefulness, durability, economy, ease of maintenance, attractiveness, teacher preference, and safety. Once equipment is made available, it must be properly maintained and stored. A plan for use and care of equipment must be developed for both children and staff as a component of the center's program.

Class Assignments

1. Visit a local toy store. Select two dolls for possible use in a class of four-year-old children. Compare the two dolls using the following criteria:

   - suitability
   - durability
   - economy
   - ease of maintenance
   - attractiveness
   - safety
   - your preference as a teacher

   Repeat this assignment using two tape recorders for classroom use. Make a third set of comparisons using infant rattles. Using Working Paper 8-1, prepare a purchase order for the doll or the tape recorder.

2. Visit local stores or check equipment catalogs to find the current prices for enough equipment to supply one classroom serving fifteen children. List the sources. Compute the total cost. What is the cost per child? Enter five of the major items on your list on the sample inventory form found in Working Paper 8-2.

3. Visit two centers (or draw on your previous or current experiences in two centers). Write a comparison of the equipment in general, using the information provided in this chapter.

Class Exercises

1. Work with fellow students on the following role-playing situations. Have several students role play, using different approaches to each problem. Discuss the strengths and weaknesses of each group's approach.

   a. You are a nursery school director. Mrs. Jane Jones has just given you twenty-four coloring books with an advertising message for her husband's business on the cover. You never use coloring books at the center because you know that they are not developmentally appropriate and would not meet NAEYC guidelines. How might you handle this?

   b. Suppose that the same situation as in problem (a) occurred but that the donor is Mrs. Thomas Vanderbilt. Last year she gave your center $1,000 for equipment. What might you say to Mrs. Vanderbilt?

2. Your preschool class is in the planning stage and will be held in a public school building. Discuss with your principal your four-year-olds' needs and ways in which their equipment will be different from that of older children.

Working Paper 8-1

Purchase Order Form

REQUISITION/PURCHASE ORDER
THE CHILDREN'S CENTER

To:_____

_____

_____

Catalog No.	Description	Quantity	Price	Total

Ship to:
The Children's Center
1099 Main Street
Centerville, CA 00000-0000

Account charged:_____

Approved by:_____

Date ordered:_____

Date received:_____

Working Paper 8-2

Sample Inventory Form

INVENTORY FORM					
Date Purchased	Description	Identifying Number	Source	Price	Location in Center

Director's Resource 8-1

SUGGESTED EDUCATIONAL EQUIPMENT AND MATERIALS FOR:	**A Nursery School Group** 16–20 CHILDREN — AGES 3–5	SUGGESTED ORDER OF ACQUISITION

SUGGESTED ORDER OF ACQUISITION

Essential Items
First Year — **A**
Replacements and Additions
Second Year — **B**
Replacements and Additions
Third Year — **C**
Luxury Items — **D**

Note: Items, quantities and priorities suggested on the following pages of this section are to be thought of as guides rather than inventories.

SUGGESTED ITEMS	A	B	C	D
I BASIC ENVIRONMENTAL EQUIPMENT				
Benches for outdoor use to seat 8-10 children and adults			2	
Bookcase for children's books, on casters, 1 or 2 slanted shelves on top	1			
Bookshelf, for adult books, up high	1			
Bulletin boards, portable	2			
Cabinets:				
Movable, sturdy, with adjustable shelves for storage of curriculum materials, cleaning supplies, food, etc.	4			
Movable, sturdy, with rigid shelves, child height for self-help equipment and displays	2		2	
Chairs:				
Adult size:				
Desk	1			
Folding, for meetings	10	20	20	
Rocking	1			
Child size:				
Bean bag				1
Rocking		1		
Stackable, light weight but sturdy, 1 per child, several for staff and visitors	30			
Chalkboard, portable, with chalk and erasers	1			
Clock, wall	1			

*Indicates that multicultural materials are suggested or should be included.

SUGGESTED ITEMS	A	B	C	D
Counter or shelf for preparation of craft materials and food	2			
Cubbies:				
Indoor, wood, with bottom shelf, hooks above and 1 or 2 shelves at the top, 1 per child	20			
Outdoor storage space, approx. 10" x 10" x 12", for children's belongings—useful in warmer climates		20		
Drinking fountain, child height	1			
Filing cabinet, 2-4 drawers	1			1
Laundromat (See Housekeeping Supplies—Cleaning.)				
Loft, with rugs and pillows, high enough for children to stand under and adults to supervise				1
Peg board with pegs for storage/display	1			
Pillows	4			
Refrigerator	1			
Rugs, if room not carpeted, indoor/outdoor, approx. 9' x 12'	1	1		
Shed, outdoor, with cupboards, for storage of maintenance supplies and items such as hollow blocks, vehicles, sand-box toys, art materials, etc., rain and vandal-proof	1			
Shelf unit, for blocks, so individual sizes and shapes can be easily seen, chosen and put back by children and adults	1			

Director's Resource 8-1 (*continued*)

SUGGESTED ITEMS	QUANTITIES			
	A	B	C	D
Sinks:				
Indoor, with counter space	1			
Outdoor, with counter space		1		
Sofa				1
Step-stool	1			
Stove	1			
Tables:				
Adult size:				
Seating 4, folding	1			
Seating 8-10, folding for meetings				2-5
Child size:				
Seating, 4-8, same height, so can be combined, 18" to 20" high	4			
Seating 8-10 children and adults, for outdoor use	1-2			
Serving cart	1			
Serving table				1
Toilet facilities:				
Lavatories, 28" high	3			
Toilet seats, 12" high	3			
Trash cans, with lids, large	2			
Wastebasket, large with lid	2			

II GENERAL MAINTENANCE, INDOOR/OUTDOOR

SUGGESTED ITEMS	QUANTITIES			
	A	B	C	D
Broom, push, heavy duty for outside	1			
Buckets, 1 metal, 1 plastic, flat bottom, large	2			
Carpentry tools (See Building and Construction.)				
Electrical extension cord and plug, heavy duty	1			
Hardware kit: nails, nuts, bolts, sandpaper, screws, staples, washers, etc.	1			
Iron, electric	1			
Ironing board	1			
Ladders:				
Extension			1	
Stepladder		1		
Stepstool (See Basic Environmental Equipment.)				
Lawn mower, hand or power, if needed	1			
Light bulbs	12	12	12	
Painting supplies: alcohol, brushes, paint, shellac, turpentine, varnish, (items accumulated)	X	X	X	
Plunger	1			
Power tools, set				1
Rakes:				
Garden	1			
Leaf	1			
Rope, 4' to 8'	1			
Shovel or spade	1			
Trash cans with tight-fitting lids	1		1	
Trash bins	1			
Trouble light	1			
Twine, cone	1		1	

III HOUSEKEEPING SUPPLIES

SUGGESTED ITEMS	QUANTITIES			
	A	B	C	D
Cleaning and Laundry:				
Brooms:				
Push	1		1	
Regular	1			
Brushes:				
Bottle	2	2	2	
Counter	1	1		
Toilet	1	1		
Cleansers:				
Glass cleaner, can	1	1	1	
Scouring powder, cans	12	12	12	
Cloths:				
Cleaning	6	2	2	
Dish	4	1	1	
Dishpan	2			
Drying rack, folding	1			
Fly swatter	1			
Garbage can with lid	1			
Iron (See General Maintenance, Indoor/Outdoor.)				
Ironing board (See General Maintenance, Indoor/Outdoor.)				
Mops:				
Dust	1		1	
Wet	1		1	
Pails or buckets (See General Maintenance, Indoor/Outdoor.)				
Plunger (See General Maintenance, Indoor/Outdoor.)				
Soap:				
Bar, doz.	3	3	3	
Flakes, box	3	3	3	
Liquid, qt.	3	3	3	
Powder, box	3	3	3	
Sponges, several sizes	6	6	6	
Strainer, sink	1			
Toilet paper, carton of 3,000	5	5	5	
Toilet protective tissue covers and dispenser, pkgs.				3
Towels:				
Bath, each child brings own	X	X	X	
Dish	12	12	12	
Hand	12			
Paper, case of 3,000	6	6	6	
Vacuum cleaner if floor is carpeted	1			
Vacuum cleaner bags, as needed	X	X	X	
Wastebaskets (See Basic Environmental Equipment.)				
Sewing:				
Buttons, assorted	25	15	10	
Cloth, variety of odds and ends	X	X	X	
Iron (See General Maintenance, Indoor/Outdoor.)				
Ironing board (See General Maintenance, Indoor/Outdoor.)				
Needles, assorted package	1		1	
Pins, roll	6	6	6	
Scissors and shears (See Creative Arts.)				
Sewing machine				1

Director's Resource 8-1 (*continued*)

SUGGESTED EDUCATIONAL EQUIPMENT AND MATERIALS FOR:	**A Nursery School Group** 16–20 CHILDREN — AGES 3–5

SUGGESTED ORDER OF ACQUISITION

Essential Items
First Year — **A**
Replacements and Additions
Second Year — **B**
Replacements and Additions
Third Year — **C**
Luxury Items — **D**

SUGGESTED ITEMS	A	B	C	D
Tape measure	1			
Thimbles	2			
Thread, black and white, spools	2			
String, ball	1		1	
Yarn, ball	2		2	
IV HEALTH AND SAFETY				
First Aid Supplies:				
Cotton blankets, one per child	24			
First aid cabinet stocked in accordance with individual school regulations or with the following items:				
Antiseptic soap (Phisoderm)	2		2	
Band-Aids, boxes	6	6	6	
Eye bath	1			
Gauze, sterile, boxes	4	4	4	
Gauze pads, sterile, boxes	4	4	4	
Ice pack	1		1	
Medicine glass	1			
Nonallergenic adhesive tape	2	2	2	
Red Cross First Aid Manual	1			
Rubbing alcohol, bottle	1			
Safety pins, pkg.	1		1	
Thermometer, 1 oral, 1 rectal	2			
Tweezers	1			
Flashlight	1			
Handkerchiefs, paper, small hospital size, boxes	18	18	18	
Rugs, plastic covered foam mats or cots for resting, 27" x 48", or towels from home	24			
Soap, liquid (See Housekeeping Supplies.)				
Toilet paper (See Housekeeping Supplies.)				
Towels, paper, junior size, pkg. of 150	10	10	10	
Food Preparation and Service: Food and cooking are considered part of the education program for children and adults, as well as serving nutritional needs. Health standards and regulations must be observed. Items* are suggested only for schools that serve hot meals daily.				
Blender*	1			
Bottle opener	2		2	

SUGGESTED ITEMS	A	B	C	D
Bowl scrapers, various sizes	2			
Bowls:				
Serving, unbreakable, assorted sizes	3			
Soup-cereal, plastic	30			
Soup, paper, for special foods or events			36	
Sugar	2			
Cake pans, unbreakable	4			
Canister, or other food containers, with lids	6			
Can openers:				
Electric	1			
Hand	1	1	1	
Coffee maker	1			
Colander	1			
Cookie:				
Cutter, assorted sizes, special shapes for holidays	12			
Decorator			1	
Sheets	4	1	1	
Corn popper, hand or electric	1		1	
Cups:				
Coffee, unbreakable, for adults	6			
Dispenser for paper cups			1	
Hot drink, disposable	48	48	48	
Paper, flat bottom, box of 100 5 oz.	6	6	6	
Cutlery:				
Forks:				
Heavy plastic, reusable, for special events	60			
Long handled	2			
Salad, stainless steel, for children and adults*	36			
Serving	3			
Knives:				
Bread	1			
Butcher	1			
Dinner, heavy plastic, reusable, for special events	60			
Paring	2	2		
Stainless steel, for children and adults	12-20			
Spoons:				
Coffee-dessert, heavy plastic				
Cooking, with long handles, unbreakable	3			
Serving	6			

Director's Resource 8-1 (*continued*)

SUGGESTED ITEMS	A	B	C	D
Soup, stainless steel	6			
Teaspoons, stainless steel*	36			
Deep fat fryer				1
Double boiler*	2			
Egg beater, hand	1			
Electric mixer*	1			
Extension cord (See General Maintenance, Indoor/Outdoor.)				
Flour sifter	1			
Fry pans:				
Electric	1			
Regular, 6", 8", 10", 12"	1	1		
Funnels:				
Large	1			
Small	1	1		
Glasses, unbreakable:				
Large, 10 oz.	6			
Small, 6 oz.	24-36			
Grinder*			1	
Hot pads	4	2		
Hot plate, electric—stove, if full day	1			
Ice cream freezers:				
Electric			1	
Hand	1			
Ladles	2			
Measures:				
Bowls, nesting set, unbreakable	3			
Cups, unbreakable, sets	2			
Spoons, sets	2			
Napkins, paper, buy in quantity	X	X	X	
Oven, portable, if no stove available		1		
Pepper grinder			1	
Pepper shakers	1			
Pie pans, unbreakable	6			
Pitchers, unbreakable:				
Cream	1			
Pt. size	4			
1-2 qt. size	4			
Plates:				
Dessert, paper	48		48	
Dessert, plastic, 1 per person plus several for guests*				36
Dinner, heavy plastic*	36			
Dinner, paper	36			
Serving, assorted sizes	4	2		
Pot holders	4		2	
Rolling pins, additional ones for children's use	2			
Salad bowl and servers*	1			
Salt shakers, incl. one for stove	4			
Sauce pans, 1 qt., 4 qt., 6 qt., with lids*	4			
Serving cart (See Basic Environmental Equipment.)				
Sieves:				
Large	1			
Small	1			
Spatulas, assorted sizes	3			
Storage containers:				
Freezer*	2			

SUGGESTED ITEMS	A	B	C	D
Refrigerator	4			
Tablecloths, plastic, to be used for meals or cooking activities, one for each table	X			
Table mats, plastic, if desired		24		
Teakettle	1			
Tongs	1			
Trays, assorted sizes	6			
Vegetable peeler	1			
Warming tray, electric			1	
Resting Facilities: (If desired.)				
Cots, aluminum frame, washable canvas, stackable	X	X	X	
Blankets, cotton (See Health and Safety, First Aid.)				
Resting mats	X	X	X	
Room dividers	X	X	X	
Sheets, cot size	X	X	X	

V AUDIOVISUAL EQUIPMENT

	A	B	C	D
Films (access to)				
*Filmstrips	6	2	2	
Filmstrip projector		1		
Headphones				2-4
Jack for headphones				1
Movie and sound projector, 16mm (access to)				
Record player (See Music.)				
*Records (See Music.)				
Slide projector (access to)				
*Slides (access to)				
Tape recorder	1			
*Tapes or cassettes for listening and recording	4	2	2	

VI PSYCHO-MOTOR DEVELOPMENT

	A	B	C	D
Balance beam with supports		1		
Balls, rubber, 4", 6", 8", 10", 12"	4	1	1	
Barrels	1		1	
Bean bags	20		5	
Bicycle pump	1			
Boards:				
Resilient, for jumping	2		1	
Plain, 6'-8'	3		2	
Cleated, 4'-6'	1	1		
Boxes, large, wooden	2			
Bridges, set of nesting, metal sawhorse type, set		1		
Climbing structures: old tires, empty electrical reels, concrete culvert units	2		1	
Crawl through tunnel or cubes, large	1			
Crates, packing boxes	1	1	1	
Digging hole	1			
Dollies, hand	1	1		
Fences, portable, 6' lengths		3		
Hoops, 18" to 24" in diameter	20			
Hose, length as needed	1			
Ladder, lightweight, sturdy for children, 4' to 6'	1			

Director's Resource 8-1 (*continued*)

SUGGESTED EDUCATIONAL EQUIPMENT AND MATERIALS FOR: A Nursery School Group

16–20 CHILDREN — AGES 3–5

SUGGESTED ORDER OF ACQUISITION

Essential Items
First Year — **A**
Replacements and Additions
Second Year — **B**
Replacements and Additions
Third Year — **C**
Luxury Items — **D**

SUGGESTED ITEMS	A	B	C	D
Net, cargo, for climbing		1		
Pails, assorted sizes, for outdoor play	3			
Platform with railing, ladder, sliding pole, storage or play space underneath		1		
Playhouse frame				1
Pulleys	1	1		
Recordings, suggesting gross and fine muscle activities	4			
Rope, 6' to 8' length	1		1	
Sandbox frame with sand (water faucet and hose nearby)	1			
Sawhorses, assorted sizes	2			
Shovels, small but sturdy	4			
Slide, portable or attached to climbing structure (Long board can be used for sliding.)		1		
Steering wheel, to fit on block or frame		1		
Step platforms, if steps not otherwise available		2		
Stick horses		2		
Swing set, double with canvas or rubber seats	1			
Swing, tire		1		
Tubs, metal, different sizes	1	1		
Tumbling mats		1	1	
Wands	10	10		
Wheel toys:				
Tricycles	2	1		
Tricycle trailers	1	1		
Wagons	2			
Wheelbarrow		1		

VII PERCEPTUAL DEVELOPMENT

SUGGESTED ITEMS	A	B	C	D
Beads, wooden, 1/2" cubes and assorted shapes, box of 1,000	1			
Bead counting frame, abacus (See Mathematics.)				
Bead laces	12		6	
Counting rods, sets	2			
Dressing frames	4			
Games, matching:				
Card: animals, geometric shapes, flowers, vehicles, etc.	4	1	1	
Block: attribute, design, domino, number, property, etc.	4	1	1	

SUGGESTED ITEMS	A	B	C	D
*Frame: bingo and lotto type with birds, flowers, food, clothing, zoo animals, etc.	4	1	1	
Felt board (See Language Arts.)				
*Felt board figures (See Language Arts.)				
Geometric solids, wooden (See Mathematics.)				
Magnetic board, 18" x 36"	1			
Magnetized figures, 50 items, set	1			
Mechanical board: bolts, nuts, locks, etc.	1			
Nest of rings or boxes, 6 to 8 items	1			
Olfactory materials: spices, foods, greenery, etc. in plastic bottles with perforated, tightly sealed lids	X	X	X	
Parquetry blocks (See Building and Construction.)				
Pegboards (See Mathematics.)				
Pegs (See Mathematics.)				
Puzzles (See Language Arts.)				
Shape or sorting box with interchangeable panels	1			
Sound cylinders, approx. 3" high, 2" diameter, set of 5	2			
Tactile materials: sandpaper, cloth, wood, metal, sponge, etc., in container	X	X	X	
*Taste materials: sugar, flour, salt, fruit juices, etc., in plastic containers with removable lids	X	X	X	
Weighing and measuring items (See Mathematics.)				

VIII BUILDING AND CONSTRUCTION

SUGGESTED ITEMS	A	B	C	D
Bin for lumber			1	
Blocks:				
Hollow	30		20	
Parquetry, set	2		1	
Table, choose from cube, interlocking, nesting, regular small sets in variety of materials: wood, plastic, rubber	3	2	1	
Unit, full school set (protected floor space and appropriate shelving important)	150	150	150	

Director's Resource 8-1 (*continued*)

SUGGESTED ITEMS	A	B	C	D
Boards, small flat 24"-36" long, to use with blocks	4		2	
Building sets: (Choose from such as the following in school size sets of sufficient quantities to satisfy needs.)				
Crystal Climber	1			
Giant tinker toys			2	
Lego	2			
Lincoln Logs		1		
Rig-a-jig	1			
Rising Towers	1			
Tinker toys		1	1	
Carpentry: (All tools real adult, not toy.)				
Bench	1			
Bits, ¼", ½", and ¾"	1	3		
Brace, adult size, 1½lbs.	1	1		
Coping saw, wooden handle	1		1	
Coping saw blades	1		6	
Hammers, 13 oz., 16 oz., flat head with claws	2			
Hand drill and drill sets	1			
Measuring rod, tape, ruler, one of each	3			
Nails, assorted sizes, ½" to 2", some very long, lbs	5	5	5	
Nuts and bolts, assorted, box	1		1	
Pliers	1			
Sandpaper, medium grit, pkg.	1			
Saws, crosscut, 14" blade, 18" blade, 8 teeth per inch	2			
Screwdrivers, 8", 12", regular and Phillips	2			
Screws, steel, flat head, assorted sizes, box of 50	2		1	
Washers, assorted sizes, box		1		
Cloth, yds.	2	2	2	
Corks, supply accumulated	X	X	X	
Foam rubber pieces, supply accumulated	X	X	X	
Glue, tubes	1	1	1	
Lumber:				
Assorted shapes and sizes, soft, scrounged (often available from lumber yard disposal bins and carpentry shops) 50-75 pieces	X	X	X	
Assorted sizes, rough measure footage, 30'-60', purchased	1	1	1	
Puzzle frame/holder	1			
Puzzles (See Language Arts.)				
Rope (See Psycho-Motor Development.)				
Sandbox (See Psycho-Motor Development.)				
Sand/water play materials, all unbreakable:				
Brushes, large	3		3	
Containers, wide variety	6	6	4	
Dishes, variety	4	4	4	
Dishpans	1	1		
Floating toys and objects	4		2	

SUGGESTED ITEMS	A	B	C	D
Funnels, assorted sizes	2		1	
Hose, small pieces, can be scrounged	2		1	
Measuring sets:				
Cups	2			
Spoons	2			
Molds, assorted	3	2	1	
Pails, assorted sizes (See Psycho-Motor Development.)				
Pitchers	1		1	
Scoops	4	2	2	
Sieves	2			
Soapflakes, box	2	2	2	
Sand/water table or tray	1			
Shellac, clear, qts.	1		1	
Straws, plastic, pkg.	1	1	1	
String (See Housekeeping Supplies.)				
Tongue depressors or craft sticks, pkg. of 1,000	1		1	
Toothpicks, colored box	1	1	1	
Twine (See General Maintenance, Indoor/Outdoor.)				
Vehicles:				
Construction, large, sturdy, variety	3		1	
Transportation, unbreakable, in various sizes	6	2	2	
Wheels, wooden discs	6	4	2	

IX CREATIVE ARTS

SUGGESTED ITEMS	A	B	C	D
Aprons, plastic or cloth, homemade	10	6	6	
Beads, and other objects for stringing	500	250	250	
Brushes, paint, ½"-1" thickness, handle length, 6"-9"	12	6	6	
Cans, cookie cutters, for cutting dough, assorted sizes	4	2	2	
Chalk:				
Assorted colors, large, box	2	1	1	
White, box	1	1	1	
Clay, gray and red, lbs. each	25	25	25	
Cloth:				
Like old sheeting to paint/draw on, supply accumulated	X	X	X	
Plastic drape, one for each table	X	X	X	
Burlap and/or heavy weight mesh for stitchery, yds.	2	2	2	
Clothes pins, for hanging art work	48			
Collage materials, scrounged such as pieces of cloth, paper, leather, plastic, old greeting cards, buttons, styrofoam, yarn, ribbon, sequins, glitter, beads, etc., supply accumulated	X	X	X	
Cotton balls, bags	4	4	4	
Containers:				
For clay, plastic with lid	2			

Director's Resource 8-1 (*continued*)

SUGGESTED EDUCATIONAL EQUIPMENT AND MATERIALS FOR: A Nursery School Group

16–20 CHILDREN — AGES 3–5

SUGGESTED ORDER OF ACQUISITION

Essential Items
  First Year — **A**
Replacements and Additions
  Second Year — **B**
Replacements and Additions
  Third Year — **C**
Luxury Items — **D**

SUGGESTED ITEMS	A	B	C	D
For collage materials: old boxes, baskets, jars, etc., supply accumulated	X	X	X	
For paint: small cans, cut down cartons, plastic, with lids	10	5	5	
Cookie cutter, for use with play dough	12		6	
Crayons, jumbo, assorted colors, boxes	10	5	5	
Crayon holders	2			
Drying rack for art materials, if needed	1			
Easels:				
Community, for outdoor use, if space available				1
Double adjustable	2			
Garlic presses for use with clay	2			
Glue, white, inexpensive (See Building and Construction Materials.)				
Hole puncher	1			
Kiln (access to)				
Knives, table, for use with clay and dough (can be old)	6		4	
Laces for stringing (See Perceptual Development.)				
Looms, handmade out of cardboard, paper plates, wood and nails, for simple weaving	2	2	2	
Marking pens, non-toxic	6	6	6	
Masking tape, roll	4	4	4	
Paint:				
Finger, commercial, pts.	6	6	6	
Finger (Make as needed out of starch, water, tempera and soap flakes.)	X	X	X	
Liquid tempera, assorted colors, qts.	10	10	10	
Powdered tempera, assorted colors, boxes	6	6	6	
Watercolors, boxes with brushes	2	2	2	
Paint jars, plastic with lids	16+			
Paper:				
Brown, wrapping 45 lb. roll with dispenser	1			
Construction, colored, 9" x 12", pkg. of 50 sheets	20	20	20	
Construction, colored, 12" x 18" pkg. of 50 sheets	8	8	8	

SUGGESTED ITEMS	A	B	C	D
Crepe, 20" x 7½", pkg.	2	2	2	
Frieze, one side glazed, other side rough, 24" x 180', roll	1			
Manila for drawing, 12" x 18", reams	8	8	8	
Poster, colored, 9" x 12", pkg. of 100 sheets	20		20	
Poster, colored, 12" x 18", pkg. of 100 sheets	4	4	4	
Tagboard, medium weight, 24" x 36", sheets	10		10	
Tissue, 20" x 30", pkg. of 24 sheets	4	4	4	
News, unprinted, 18" x 24", pkg.	15	15	15	
Paper brads or fasteners, boxes	2		2	
Paper bags, approx. 8" x 14"	20	20	20	
Paper clips, box of 100	4	4	4	
Paper cutter, 12" blade	1			
Paste, semi-liquid, gal.	2	2	2	
Paste jars, 2" diameter, 1½" deep, with covers	10			
Pastesticks, hardwood, pkg. of 500	1		1	
Pencils, soft, thick lead, without erasers	12	12	12	
Pencil sharpener	1			
Pie tins or other containers, for children to use in mixing paint	6		6	
Pins:				
Safety, medium size, box of 100	1	1	1	
Straight (See Housekeeping Supplies.)				
Pipe cleaners, assorted colors, pkgs.	2		2	
Plasticine, single color, lbs.	5	5	5	
Play dough, can be made or purchased, as needed	X	X	X	
Potter's wheel (access to)				
Printing materials for play dough, clay, and paint, assorted kinds: cut vegetables, spools, blocks, etc., supply accumulated	X	X	X	
Rolling pins for play dough	4	2		
Rulers (See Mathematics.)				
Rope, for hanging art work, approx. 12'			1	
Salt, for cooking and making play dough, boxes	2	2	2	

Director's Resource 8-1 (*continued*)

SUGGESTED ITEMS	QUANTITIES			
	A	**B**	**C**	**D**
Sand:				
Indoor sandbox, white, fine, lbs., or cornmeal or sawdust in comparable amounts	200			
Outdoor sandbox, coarse, lbs.	800			
For painting, lb.	2	2	2	
Scissors:				
Double handled training, child-size	2			
Rounded, one pair left-handed, child-size	8		2	
Semi-pointed, one pair, left-handed, child-size	8		2	
Shears, pair, adult-size	1			
Scotch tape, rolls	4	4	4	
Soap:				
Flakes, to whip for painting (See Housekeeping Supplies.)				
Liquid, to put in paints (See Housekeeping Supplies.)				
Sponges, to be cut into pieces approx. 1″ x 2″ x 2″ for painting	2	1	1	
Squeeze bottles, supply accumulated	X	X	X	
Staple remover	1			
Stapler	1			
Staples, box	2	2	2	
Starch for mixing finger paint, boxes	2	2	2	
String and twine, for collages, painting and weaving (See Housekeeping Supplies.)				
Thread, black and white, spools, (See Housekeeping Supplies.)				
Tape, Mystic, cloth with plastic finish, 3″ wide x 108″, roll	1		1	
Tongue depressors or craft sticks, for use with clay, collage and dough, box (See Building and Construction Materials.)				
Toothpicks, for painting and use with clay, collage and dough, (See Building and Construction Materials.)				
Water color markers, non-toxic, water soluable, pkg.	3	3	3	
Wheat paste, lbs.	1	1	1	
Wood pieces for collage and construction, scrounged, supply accumulated	X	X	X	
Yarn for collage, stitchery and weaving, scrounged and balls	4	4	4	

X DRAMATIC PLAY

SUGGESTED ITEMS	QUANTITIES			
Animal:				
Costumes, homemade or scrounged		2	2	
*Figures, small, plastic/rubber a variety in quantity for use with blocks and sand/water play	16		8	
*Puppets, assorted	6	1	1	
Stuffed animals	4		2	

SUGGESTED ITEMS	QUANTITIES			
	A	**B**	**C**	**D**
Camping:				
Backpack, from surplus store	1			
Blankets				2
Camper truck			1	
Flashlight (See Health and Safety, First Aid.)				
Lantern		1		
Pup tent		1		
Sleeping bag		1		
Stove			1	
Utensils	4		2	
Doctor/Nurse:				
Bandages/band-Aids, kit	1		1	
Hospital gown and uniform, one of each		2		
Instruments:				
Sphygmomanometer for blood pressure		1		
Stethoscope		1		
Mirrors:				
Angle				1
Head		1		
Mask		1		
Grooming-toilet articles: male and female, comb, hair brush, hair rollers, hand mirror, nail brush, manual razor without blades and/or electric razor with plug off, shaving brush, soap	X	X	X	
Home Management and Family Living:				
Bathing and cleaning:				
Aprons, plastic (See Creative Arts.)				
Bathinette		1		
Bottle brush	1			
Broom, child size	1			
Dishcloth	2			
Dishpan		1		
Drainer		1		
Dry mop	1			
Dustpan	1			
Iron, wood or plastic	1			
Ironing board		1		
Pail	1			
Soap, hand (See Housekeeping Supplies, Cleaning and Laundry.)				
Soap flakes, sample boxes	1	1	1	
Towels:				
Bath	1			
Dish	2			
Hand	2			
Washcloths	2			
Vacuum cleaner, 30″ handle				1
Washer, dryer, approx. 16″ x 16″ x 24″				1
Wet mop, 30″ handle	1			
Cooking and eating equipment, real unbreakable:				
Baby bottle		2		

Director's Resource 8-1 (continued)

SUGGESTED EDUCATIONAL EQUIPMENT AND MATERIALS FOR:

A Nursery School Group

16–20 CHILDREN — AGES 3–5

SUGGESTED ORDER OF ACQUISITION

Essential Items
First Year — **A**
Replacements and Additions
Second Year — **B**
Replacements and Additions
Third Year — **C**
Luxury Items — **D**

SUGGESTED ITEMS	A	B	C	D
Cutlery: forks, knives, spoons, place settings	4			
Dishes: bowls, cups, saucers, small glasses, plates, place settings	4			
Food containers, empty	X	X	X	
Food, pretend	6		4	
Utensils: cake pan, colander, frying pan, kettle, ladle, large spoon, measuring cups and spoons, mixing bowls, pie pan, sauce pan, sieve	8	2	2	
*Dolls, baby boy, girl, multi-ethnic, multi-cultural, unbreakable, washable				
Doll play and equipment:				
Baby bottles	2			
Bed	1			
Buggy and stroller	1	1		
*Clothes, assorted, male, female, baby, older, various fastenings	12	4	4	
Dishes, place settings	2	1		
Doll house, open on sides, top removable			1	
*Doll house dolls: families, multi-ethnic, multi-cultural, bendable preferred, to use also with blocks, vehicles, sand/water play		4	4	
House cooking utensils, for doll house				6
Doll house furniture and accessories			16	
*Dress-up properties, male and female: aprons, belts, billfolds, blouses, dresses, hats, hose, jackets, jewelry, pants, purses, scarves, shawls, shoes, skirts, suitcase, ties, watches, wigs, supply accumulated	X	X	X	
Furniture for playhouse area, sturdy, unbreakable:				
Bed and matress, big enough for child to curl up on	1			
Bed linens: blankets, pillow, sheets, spread	4	2		
Chairs:				
High chair with tray	1			
Rocking	1			

SUGGESTED ITEMS	A	B	C	D
Straight	4			
Clothes rack and hangers		1		
Curtains, as desired	X	X	X	
Dresser or chest	1			
Hat rack		1		
Mirror, full-length, child height	1			
Radio				1
Refrigerator	1			
Rug, if desired	X	X	X	
Sink	1			
Sofa				1
Stove	1			
Table, to seat four children	1			
Telephone	1			
T.V. frame, scrounged				1
Toilet training chair				1
Office and School:				
Attaché case, scrounged	1			
Chalkboard		1		
Chalkboard eraser		1		
Desk and desk chair		1		
Paper pads	2	2	2	
Pencils and erasers	2	2	2	
Telephone (See Home Management and Family Living.)				
Typewriter, scrounged		1		
Playhouse, outdoor	1			
Puppets, family, hand or finger	4	2	2	
Repair and Yard Work:				
Carpentry apron	1			
Lawn mower, 24" handle			1	
Paintbrushes				
Paint cans containing colored soapsuds	3			
Push broom		1		
Rake, 24" handle				
Sewing Materials: buttons, cloth pieces, decorations (pieces of lace, ribbon, beads), large needles, rounded scissors, thread, yarn, scrounged	X	X	X	
Toolbox			1	
Tool kit		1		
Transportation/Occupations: buy and scrounge				
Dress-up clothes: hats, uniforms, tools for a variety of occupations, such as bakers, bus drivers, carpenters, divers, en-				

Director's Resource 8-1 (*continued*)

SUGGESTED ITEMS	A	B	C	D
gineers, fire fighters, air pilots, police officers, sailors, taxi drivers, train engineers, postal workers, construction worker	X	X	X	
Model sets: airport, camper, fire station, garage, space center, etc., with proportioned buildings, figures, furnishings, tools, vehicles			4	
*People figures, proportioned plastic, rubber, wood, representing a variety of workers	6	3	3	
*Puppets, representing different workers	4	2	2	
Snap train sets			2	
Traffic signs for air terminals, highways, railroad crossings, waterways		5		
Vehicles, large, sturdy, some ridable, some that carry blocks: cars, boats, planes, rockets, trains, trucks, tractors (See Building and Construction.)				
Vehicles, metal or plastic, small, wheeled, that fit unit blocks (See Building and Construction.)				

XI MUSIC

SUGGESTED ITEMS	A	B	C	D
Autoharp	1			
Dancing clothes: scarves, skirts, streamers, supply accumulated	X	X	X	
Records: permanent collection of quality children's records and access to others (See Audiovisual Equipment.)				
Record player, good but inexpensive (See Audiovisual Equipment.)				
Rhythm Instruments:				
Bells, variety: ankle, cow, wrist, melody set, supply accumulated	X	X	X	
Castanets	2			
Cymbals:				
Finger		2		
Large		1		
Drums, variety: snare, tom-tom, etc., can be homemade	2		1	
Maracas	4			
Piano		1		
Recorder, wind instrument			1	
Sticks, rhythm	12			
Tambourines	2			
Tone blocks, set		1		
Triangles		1		
Tuning fork			1	
Wood blocks		2		

XII LANGUAGE ARTS

SUGGESTED ITEMS	A	B	C	D
Alphabet letters, moveable, sandpaper, tactile, in several sizes	300		300	

SUGGESTED ITEMS	A	B	C	D
*Books: Permanent collection of 30 or more, and circulating collection borrowed from library. Choose high quality children's books, look for multi-cultural, multi-ethnic, non-sexiest content. Topics to include: Animals, Child activities, Community, Fairy tales, Fantasies, Holiday, Mother Goose, Seasonal, Tender topics—adoption, divorce, illness	X	X	X	
*Easy to read books	X	X	X	
*Picture books, including alphabet books and dictionaries	X	X	X	
*Poetry to read aloud	X	X	X	
*Resource books on such topics as biological science, community, crafts, cultures, family, geography, holidays, physical sciences, space science	X	X	X	
Camera for snapshots of children, etc.	1			
*Cassette tapes (See Audiovisual Equipment.)				
Chalkboards, portable, with chalk and erasers	1			
Chart paper, large, for experiences	2	2	2	
Felt board	1			
Felt board pieces: alphabet, stories, animals, familiar objects, etc. pkg. of 50 items	1			
Films (See Audiovisual Equipment.)				
Filmstrips (See Audiovisual Equipment.)				
Games, simple, such as lotto and other picture games	4	2	2	
Language Master				1
Notebooks for dictated stories	3	3	3	
Perception cards, set	1	1	1	
*Pictures and posters (See topics under Books.)	12	6	6	
Puppet theater	1			
*Puppets (See Dramatic Play.)				
*Puzzles, wooden, 9 to 16 pieces	8	3	2	
*Records (See Audiovisual Equipment.)				
*Slides (See Audiovisual Equipment.)				
Talking book unit			1	
Typewriter, primary			1	
Writing materials: crayons, pencils, marking pens (See Creative Arts.)				

Director's Resource 8-1 (*continued*)

SUGGESTED EDUCATIONAL EQUIPMENT AND MATERIALS FOR:

A Nursery School Group
16–20 CHILDREN — AGES 3–5

SUGGESTED ORDER OF ACQUISITION

Essential Items
  First Year — **A**
Replacements and Additions
  Second Year — **B**
Replacements and Additions
  Third Year — **C**
Luxury Items — **D**

SUGGESTED ITEMS	A	B	C	D
XIII MATHEMATICS				
Abacus		1		
Attribute blocks, set		1		
Counters, unbreakable: animals, beads, blocks, buttons, cards, nails, napkins, etc., supply accumulated	X	X	X	
Cuisinaire rods, set			1	
Fraction manipulatives, wood or plastic, apple, candy bar, pie, etc.		3		
Food to cut and divide	X	X	X	
Geometric figures, wooden, 3" units, approx. 6 items, set	1			
Measuring equipment, English and Metric:				
Dry units	4	2		
Liquid units	4	2		
Tape	1			
Rulers	2			
String, twine, rope (See General Maintenance, Indoor/Outdoor.)				
Thermometers:				
Cooking				1
Hand manipulated model	1			
Indoor/Outdoor	1			
Money, play, homemade	X	X	X	
Nesting toys, assorted boxes, blocks, dolls, units (See Perceptual Development.)				
Number games	4	2	2	
Numerals, tactile in variety of sizes and materials	20		10	
Objects: any in environment to examine their properties, likenesses and differences	X	X	X	
Peg boards, 12" x 12"	4			
Pegs, hardwood, ⅛" diameter, 2" long, box of 1,000	1			
Shapes, basic sets, tactile, unbreakable, variety of sizes and materials, supply accumulated	X	X	X	
Sorting containers, unbreakable: baskets, boxes, cans, glasses	3	2	1	
Timers, buy or scrounge, as needed for curriculum:				
Calendars	2			

SUGGESTED ITEMS	A	B	C	D
Clocks:				
Alarm, hand wound	1			
Electric, wall	1			
Plywood, with geared, adjustable hands	1			
Egg timer		1		
Food timer	1			
Watch	1			
Weights, English and Metric:				
Standard pan balance		1		
Graduated cylinder balance			1	
Bathroom scale	1			
Kitchen scale	1			
Spring scale		1		
XIV SCIENCE				
Air Experiments: (Obtain as needed each year.)				
Balloons	6	6	6	
Bellows		1		
Bicycle pump (See Psycho-motor Development.)				
Bubble pipes	20			
Kite		2		
Squeeze bottles, supply accumulated	X	X	X	
Straws	24	24	24	
Tubing, 3' length	1		1	
Animals: Follow all public health and safety laws and regulations, provide adequate food, medical care, shelter. Choose from:				
Baby chicks		6-12		
Ducks		2		
Fish	4	4	4	
Gerbils (where permitted by law)		2+		
Guinea pigs		2+		
Hamsters	2+			
Insects, silk worms	3	3	3	
Mice		2+		
Parakeet	1			
Rabbits	2+			
Rats			2+	
Snails	5			
Snakes			2	

Director's Resource 8-1 (continued)

SUGGESTED ITEMS	A	B	C	D
Sponges, living			2	
Aquarium	1			
Animal foods that are appropriate for any of the above	X	X	X	
Eggs and incubator	4-6			
Cooking equipment (See Health and Safety.)				
Grow chart, height, weight	1			
Food and Gardening:				
Use of food in science is essential to a child's experiencing the changes of state in matter. (See also Health and Safety.)				
Aprons (See Creative Arts.)				
Children's cookbook	1			
Containers: bottles, cartons, flower boxes, flower pots, jars, etc., suply accumulated	X	X	X	
Cotton, box	1			
Dirt box or dirt plot	1			
Fertilizer, lbs.	5			
Food:				
Natural foods, fruits, nuts, vegetables	X	X	X	
Packaged mixes and processed foods, pkg.	4	2	2	
Raw ingredients: flour, salt, soda, spices, sugar, etc., in tightly covered containers, one for each item	X	X	X	
Garden tools, child size: hoe, rake, spade, set	1	1		
Plants, cultivated and wild	X	X	X	
Seeds, collected from nature and purchased, supply accumulated	X	X	X	
Stakes and string or wire fencing	X	X	X	
Terrarium	1			
Watering cans or hoses	2	1		
Light and Heat:				
Binoculars, pair				1
Camera (See Language Arts.)				
Electricity: batteries, bulbs, buzzers, simple circuits, supply accumulated	X	X	X	
Flashlights (See Health and Safety.)				
Magnifying glasses, hand	2			
Magnifying glasses on stand		1		
Microscope				1
Mirrors, unbreakable	2			
Prisms, assorted	2	1		
Liquids and Supplies:				
Liquids:				
Ice:				
Dry, bar				1
Regular	X	X	X	
Oil, ½ pt. can	1			
Other liquids	X	X	X	
Supplies:				
Containers, plastic, supply accumulated	X	X	X	

SUGGESTED ITEMS	A	B	C	D
Kettle	1			
Medicine dropper	2	1		
Paper:				
Blotting, odds and ends	X	X	X	
Filter, pkg.				1
Sponges	2	2	2	
Sprayer		1		
Squeeze bottles, supply accumulated	X	X	X	
Squirt bottles, for spraying, supply accumulated	X	X	X	
Mechanics and Physics: (See Building and Construction Materials and Mathematics.)				
Inclined planes	1	1		
Magnets, variety of shapes and sizes, and things to try to pick up	2	1	1	
Nails, nuts, bolts, screws (See Building and Construction.)				
Rubber bands, elastic (See Office Supplies and Record Keeping.)				
Siphon	1			
Take-apart equipment (donated): old clocks, typewriters, vacuum cleaners, etc., supply accumulated	X	X	X	
Wheels	4	1	1	
Minerals: rocks, stones, etc. (See also Building and Construction, Math, Music and Creative Arts.)				

XV OFFICE SUPPLIES AND RECORD KEEPING

SUGGESTED ITEMS	A	B	C	D
Manila envelopes, 2 sizes	36	36	36	
Manila folders	36	36	36	
Marking pens, several colors	4	4	4	
Microcomputer				1
Paper clips, 2 sizes, boxes	2	2	2	
Paper cutter (See Creative Arts.)				
Pencils, boxes	6	6	6	
Pencil sharpener (See Creative Arts.)				
Pins:				
Safety, box (See Creative Arts.)				
Straight, roll (See Creative Arts.)				
Rubber bands, assorted sizes, boxes	4	4	4	
Rulers (See Mathematics.)				
Staplers and staples (See Creative Arts.)				
Stationery, letterhead and plain, 2 sizes, quire of each	10	10	10	
Tapes:				
Masking, roll (See Creative Arts.)				
Mystic, roll (See Creative Arts.)				
Transparent Scotch, rolls (See Creative Arts.)				
Transparent tape dispenser	1			
Thumbtacks, boxes	8	8	8	
Typewriter		1		

Director's Resource 8-1 (*continued*)

SUGGESTED EDUCATIONAL EQUIPMENT AND MATERIALS FOR:

A Nursery School Group

16–20 CHILDREN — AGES 3–5

SUGGESTED ORDER OF ACQUISITION

Essential Items
First Year — **A**
Replacements and Additions
Second Year — **B**
Replacements and Additions
Third Year — **C**
Luxury Items — **D**

SUGGESTED ITEMS	A	B	C	D
Writing paper tablets, ruled and unruled, in several sizes	8	8	8	
Xerox copier (access to)				
Yardstick	1			
XVI TRANSPORTATION				
For field trips and emergencies. Check local/state laws regarding insurance and licensing for				

SUGGESTED ITEMS	A	B	C	D
carrying children in private car with and without school bus license.				
Private cars: (access to)				
Parent	4	4	4	
Staff	4	4	4	
Public transportation	X	X	X	
School bus, owned by school	1			
Station wagon, owned by school		1		

CHAPTER 9

Staffing the Center

The basic tools used in developing plans and procedures for hiring the child care center staff are written personnel policies and job descriptions. On the surface, these documents and procedures appear to be easily drawn and delineated; at a more subtle level, they reflect the philosophy of the overall program as it focuses on individuals and their worth as human beings. As policies and procedures are adjusted and changed, they will reflect the ability of responsible administrators in the organization to make optimum use of available human resources.

An analysis of each center's purposes and manner of operating will determine the broad policy areas to be covered in the personnel policies.

Photo above   The director may take full responsibility for interviewing all job candidates for available staff positions. (Photo by Lisa Souders)

The center that employs large numbers of professional and ancillary staff may have policies with separate sections for each category of employees and other personnel, including substitutes, resource teachers, and other support staff. In all cases, every policy statement should contain an affirmative action section that verifies the center's intent to adhere strictly to acceptance of all personnel regardless of race, age, sex, creed, national origin, sexual preference, or disability.[1]

1 For information regarding employment discrimination and affirmative action issues and questions, contact: Public Information Unit, Equal Employment Opportunity Commission (EEOC), 1801 L. Street, N.W., Washington, D.C. 20507 (202-663-4700, 800-669-3362 (publications only), 800-669-4000 (connects to caller's state office).

DESIGNING PERSONNEL POLICIES

Purpose

The need of the personnel for security and confidence in their daily job performance should be balanced with the center's need to function effectively in the establishment of carefully conceived personnel policies. When staff members are unsure about their rights and their responsibilities, some of them may tend to probe and test to determine where the limits lie. The dissension among staff members that ensues drains energy from child care. On the other hand, the staff members who know what is expected of them can recognize how their assigned roles fit into the overall organizational structure, and can therefore function more comfortably in those roles. Administrators also can function more assuredly when there is little doubt about policies because questions can be handled by referring to policies, rather than by involving individual personalities. When the rights and responsibilities of each staff member are understood by the entire staff, friction is eliminated and negotiations can be conducted between members.

Inclusive personnel policies tailored to a specific child care operation, whether it is staffed by few or by many, serve two purposes. First, they reduce procedural errors and free administrators from unnecessary involvement in resolution. Second, they reduce anxiety by helping each staff member to understand expectations and move, independently *and* as part of the team, toward efficient operation of the program.

A written statement of the personnel policies and procedures should be given to each employee at the beginning of the term of employment. These policies will set the parameters within which the total staff will function. Of course, there may be situations in which a new employee may require time on the job before fully understanding all that is written in the policy statement; nonetheless, distribution of the written policy to everyone is a tacit statement on the part of administrators that communication is open and that there are no secret or hidden agreements or rules at any level in the staff hierarchy. The administrator should make a point of checking periodically with employees to ascertain whether or not the policies are understood. Although these policies must be tailored to the needs of each program, the samples in Director's Resources will serve as a guideline for their preparation.

DIRECTOR'S CORNER

"During my new staff orientation program, I sit down with each new employee and read through the Personnel Policies, leaving time for questions and discussion. I give special attention to the section on holidays, sick days, personal days and vacation time. It helps me feel comfortable that this new staff person has at least looked at the Personnel Policies once, and not just put the document in a file or on her night table to read later when she has more time."

Director, private not-for-profit center

Source

Since the task of writing personnel policies is complex and the sphere of their influence is extensive, the decision about who writes them requires careful consideration. Not only must they be precise, well written, and inclusive, but also the best interests of staff, children, and families must be considered. The interest of the sponsoring group, whether it be to make a profit or not, deserves consideration as well. For example, a one-year probationary period for a new teacher may be agreeable to a sponsoring agency and may provide good protection for a new staff member, but it could turn out to be devastating for the children if a newly-hired individual clearly demonstrates a lack of skills in the classroom. In turn, the reputation and the income of the sponsoring group could suffer. Therefore, those who are responsible for writing the policies must have both an understanding of the scope of the program and insight into the vested interests of all involved.

Depending on the size and the organizational structure of a center, the personnel policies might be prepared by the hired director of a community-sponsored center, an owner of a proprietary center, a personnel director of a center sponsored by an industry, or of a national child care chain. Existing public school personnel policies for teachers or, in some cases, for civil service employees, will often be applicable in public-school-sponsored programs.

The more usual practice in child care settings is to have policies drawn by a subcommittee or a standing personnel committee of the policy-making board. The bylaws, as drawn up by the policy board, should contain the mechanism for creating a personnel committee and should detail the manner in which the membership of that committee will be selected. The center director should serve on the committee and represent the staff's interest. Other members of the committee might be parents, people from the community, and representatives of licensing and/or certifying groups who would, in each case, represent a special-interest group. (See Chapter 4 for the establishment of a policy board, standing committees, and so on.)

Inclusions

In general, personnel policies cover all matters relating to employment and include job responsibilities, tables of organization, schedules of reimbursement for services, evaluation and grievance procedures, and description of the steps necessary to change the policies themselves. They must conform to union requirements, where applicable, and to all regulations which apply to employment practices. For example, as of

July, 1992, employers with 25 (this number is 15 as of July, 1994) employees or more, must comply with the Americans with Disabilities Act (ADA) which covers nondiscrimination practices related to recruitment, advertising, tenure, layoff, leave, fringe benefits, and all other employment related activities.[2] Since many of these elements are included in the personnel policies, it is important to understand the implications of the ADA for you and your staff to insure compliance with these regulations, as well as protection for your program. Personnel policies spell out specifically the rights of employees and what they may expect from the employer; therefore, they should include the following items.

Career Ladder. Developing the career ladder for a center is a challenge to the director and/or the Board. Each center must develop its own version of a career ladder after reviewing the roles and responsibilities of each staff position, budget limitations and the professional goals of the center. The career ladder clearly defines education and experience plus corresponding salaries and benefits for every step in the hierarchy.[3]

Contract. The contract is usually a bilateral agreement signed by both parties, that mutually binds the employee and the employer to acquire certain rights from each other. In this case, the employee agrees to provide a service (as defined by the appropriate job description) and the employer agrees to reimburse the employee for the service at a given rate for a specific length of time. The samples shown in Figures 9-1 and 9-2 show alternative forms which include some of the alternative features of a contract.

Employment at Will. "Employment at Will" is operative in most states *unless* you have contracted with an employee and your contract says something other than that the employee is an employee at will. When the personnel policies state that employees are employees at will, it

---

2 *The Americans with Disabilities Act: Questions and Answers,* U.S. Equal Employment Opportunity Commission, July 1991, p. 1.
3 Paula Jorde Bloom, M. Sheerer, and J. Butz, *Blueprint for Action,* distributed by Gryphon House, Inc., 1991, pp. 135–142 for a detailed discussion of career ladders.

Figure 9-1 Mountview Child Development Center Employment Contract

Employee's Name _____

Employee's Position _____

From _____ to _____
        (appropriate date)   (appropriate date)

The Mountview Child Development Center Board agrees to the following:
(1) Salary $ _____ per _____
(2) Proportional benefits including Blue Cross/Blue Shield, retirement benefits as described in Personnel Policies for this position, sick leave as described in Personnel Policies, provide up to $75.00 per year for additional training and/or education (at the discretion of the Director).

The Employee agrees to the following:
(1) Fulfill the responsibilities of the job based on the Job Description for this position.
(2) Give at least two weeks notice if a change in employment is anticipated.

_____
Director - Mountview Child Development Center

_____
Board Chairman - Mountview Child Development Center

_____
Employee's Signature

Date _____

Figure 9-2 Park Lutheran Church Nursery School Employment Contract

12 Park Place -- telephone 231-7642

Date _____

Dear Ms. Smith,

    After interviewing several candidates for the teacher position at our nursery school, it is the decision of the Personnel Committee that you meet the qualifications for the position. Therefore, you are invited to become a staff member at the Park Lutheran Church Nursery School for the year beginning September, _____, and ending _____.

    Your beginning salary has been set at $_____, subject to annual increases in accordance with the Personnel Policy. Your working hours will be from _____ to _____ Monday through Friday, subject to exceptions in accordance with the Personnel Policies.

    If these terms are to your satisfaction, and if you have read the Personnel Policies and agree to abide by the terms therein, please sign and date both copies of this agreement and return them to us. One copy will be sent back to you after our signature has been added.

                                        Sincerely,

                                        Albert J. Jones, Chairperson
                                        Personnel Committee

Accepted _____   Date _____
              Director

         _____   Date _____
         Chairperson - Personnel Committee

Approved _____   Date _____
         Ms. Jeanne Smith - Teacher

means either the employer or the employee may terminate the employment relationship for any reason or without reason. The sample Personnel Policies in Director's Resources provide exact wording for those who choose to use the employment at will provision; but, that being the case, it is important to use caution in wording the Staff Handbook so nothing in that document can be viewed by the court as a contract. Since employment law is changing all over the country, it is wise to consult an attorney on these employment related questions and issues.

Job Description. The job description is a detailed outline of what is expected from the person who fills a specific job opening, including director, head teacher, teacher assistant, cook, custodian, and so on. Job descriptions are discussed in greater detail later in this chapter.

Salary Ranges. Salary range for each position on the career ladder should be indicated clearly. Salary will then be based on the training, experience, and years of service that the person brings to the particular position. Details about overtime pay, merit pay, raises, vacation pay, pay for holidays, sick leave or professional days should be detailed under salary and salary range.

Staff and Fringe Benefits. Staff and fringe benefits available to employees must be clearly stated in the personnel policies. Retirement plans, health insurance, educational opportunities for personal or professional staff-development, reduced tuition for family members, Social Security, Workmen's Compensation, liability coverage while working in the center with children, and any other items that might be covered under staff and fringe benefits should be included.

Health and Safety Measures. A health examination for all staff members is required in most centers. In many localities the law requires the health examination of center administrators, who are viewed as being ultimately responsible for the health and safety of the children in the center. Those who work with children should be free of any infectious disease, whether or not there is a local certifying or licensing group responsible for monitoring health regulations. It is also recommended that child care staff be advised to update their immunizations because intimate contacts with children puts them at risk for contracting a variety of infectious diseases. Furthermore, since the work is often physically demanding, the examination protects members of the staff by exploring their health limitations and by reminding them to follow basic healthful practice such as getting adequate rest and proper food.

Child abuse and other child safety issues are a major concern among child care professionals. Therefore, there is an increasing trend to seek ways to certify that employees do not use drugs and have no criminal record. Some states and/or government-funded programs require that prospective staff be screened for one or more of these. After July, 1994, employers with more than 15 employees must comply with the 1992 ADA when dealing with employment issues. Employers must avoid job related discrimination based on an employees' disability, but ". . . may prohibit use, or working under the influence of, alcohol or illegal drugs as well as smoking in the workplace."[4] The problem of AIDS is one which is causing concern as well. In some states this disease is treated as a disability, and employers may not ask candidates about it on applications or during the pre-hiring process. The sample form in Figure 9-3 which covers the criminal record issue will serve as a guide for a way of obtaining information from staff members as well as job candidates about some sensitive areas of inquiry. If there are questions about the legality of making inquiries of this nature, contact the Equal Employment Opportunity Commission (EEOC) or seek legal counsel.

Personnel policies should state clearly that professional staff must submit certified copies of credentials, and that personal and professional references furnished by all new employees will be contacted before job offers are made.

Daily Hours and Employment Period. The daily schedule and the total employment period

---

4 *Young Children*, National Association for the Education of Young Children, July 1992, p. 19.

Figure 9-3   Sample Declaration Form for Prospective Employees in Head Start Programs

For use by Head Start Agencies to comply with 45 CRF Part 1301, Subpart D, Head Start Grants Administration, Personnel Policies, Section 1301.31(c) and (d).

Name of Prospective Employee:_____

Federal policies now require that Head Start agencies require all prospective employees to sign a declaration prior to employment which lists:

1. All pending and prior criminal arrests and charges related to child sexual abuse and their disposition;
2. Convictions related to other forms of child abuse and/or neglect; and
3. All convictions of violent felonies.

The declarations may exclude:

- Any offense, other than any offense related to child abuse and/or child sexual abuse or violent felonies committed before the prospective employee's 18th birthday, which was finally adjudicated in a juvenile court or under a youth offender law;
- Any conviction for which the record has been expunged under Federal or State law; and
- Any conviction set aside under the Federal youth Corrections Act or similar State Authority.

Note that individuals who declare, through this form, that they have been arrested, charged with or convicted of any of the offenses listed above are not automatically disqualified from being hired. Head Start agencies must review each case to assess the relevance of an arrest, charge or conviction to a hiring decision.

Please provide your signature on the appropriate category below:

I *have not been* arrested, charged and/or convicted on one or more of the three types of offenses listed above.

_____   _____
Signature   Date

OR

I *have been* arrested, charged and/or convicted on one or more of the three types of offenses listed above.

If so, please attach information listing the offense(s), the date(s) of the arrest, charge and/or conviction, and other relevant information.

_____   _____
Signature   Date

IMPORTANT:
Each Head Start agency must take necessary steps to assure the confidentiality of this form.

should be stated in the personnel policies. Careful scheduling of personnel is critical for effective and efficient operation of all centers; this schedule should be stated in the personnel policies and then should be reiterated in each contract or letter of employment. Daily hours will not exactly coincide with the hours the children are present in the center, nor will they be the same for each staff member. Obviously, some staff members must arrive before children do, to prepare the learning environment. Furthermore, large child care centers will need extra staff to cover peak hours. For example, if school-aged children come to the center before and after school or for lunch, the staffing needs will be increased during those hours. A key staff member must be present late in the day to chat with people who pick up the children near closing time. When all children have gone, the center must be put in order for the early arrivals on the following day; therefore, some of the staff must stay beyond the time that all children leave.

The complexity of the staffing plan and the format used to lay out the plan in an understandable way will vary. The major consideration is to set it up so it provides sufficient coverage not only to meet the licensing requirements, where applicable, but also to guarantee safety of children and adequate staff to maintain high standards of quality throughout each day. In planning the staffing patterns, directors must keep in mind the concerns about child abuse in child care centers, and take prevention precautions. Schedule at least two caregivers to be present at all times, particularly early and late in the day and during nap and toileting routines. This will not only protect children, but also staff, should one be unjustly accused of abuse.[5] The sample staff plans in Director's Resources (pp. 257– 266) will serve as guidelines for setting up staffing patterns in single program centers (i.e. infant programs) and in multiple program centers. Use of graphing, listing by staff member, listing by room, or listing by program are a few of the ways to record a staffing pattern so it is clear to those who are interested in it, including staff, board members, licensing agents, and, especially, parents.

In addition to information on staffing plans, the policy statement should also indicate methods for obtaining tenure if that is a possibility within the system.

Relief Periods. A planned system of daily relief periods should be stated. The policy on rest periods may be very flexible or carefully scheduled; but in either case, the policy should be clearly stated and should include the designated space where staff may take breaks. Staff must know that it is acceptable to need to be away from the children for a time each day and that it is even acceptable to go the bathroom now and then, although some administrators fail to provide that option. In half-day nursery schools it is rare to find a set policy on rest periods due to the short time span of concentrated effort required by staff members. On the other hand, in child care programs in which a teacher may work an eight or nine hour day that includes having lunch with children, it is essential to provide time to rest and be away from the children. Some centers prefer to have some staff members work a split shift to provide time for rest, shopping, or study at midday. This serves to reduce costs at a time of low need.

Vacations, Holidays, and Sick Leave. A statement on vacations and holidays should appear in the personnel policies. Specific details about lead time for vacation applications, and the length and timing of vacations is advisable for larger, year-round centers, but smaller centers in session only during the typical school year may not require the same specificity in their policy. However, both large and small centers observe certain holidays. These holidays will vary depending on the religious and ethnic orientation of the staff and/or the children served, the agency with which the school is affiliated (church, public school, and so on), and the community mores. All employees should know exactly which holidays will be observed by closing the center.

Sick days and personal days, maternity leave and child rearing leave for either parent, and special leave days for jury duty or voting should

5 *Child Care Information Exchange: The Directors' Magazine,* Issue #60, March 1988, p. 11.

be included in the personnel policies. It is also wise to cover details like use of unused leave days, the necessity for documenting illness, and policies around closing due to bad weather. Some employers allow "earned time" over and above holidays and each employee decides how and when to take that time. This flexible earned time plan may make it difficult for a director who must find substitutes, and it could be detrimental to the well-being of the children. A variation on this plan is to give one Friday or Monday off each month to each staff person, thus guaranteeing one long weekend a month. Staff members decide when they want their long weekend, and in a large center, the director can hire a regular substitute to work every Monday and Friday, which gives greater continuity to the program for the children.

The center's plan for hiring substitutes for each staff position during vacation periods, for special holidays, and for sick days must be clearly spelled out. The policy should state that all health, safety and training qualifications for staff also apply to substitutes. Maintaining a substitute file which includes all the necessary personnel information and payroll paperwork on available persons will make it easier to find substitutes on short notice. A plan for hiring substitutes avoids confusion when emergencies occur and also facilitates budget planning for these special needs.

Meeting Schedules. Scheduled staff meetings, parent meetings, and board meetings should be listed in the personnel policies. Most programs, regardless of size, have a series of meetings at various levels to gather individuals together to discuss plans and mutual concerns. In some cases only selected personnel are expected to attend meetings. The personnel policies should state which meetings each employee is expected to attend and the frequency of such meetings, as well as those meetings that are open to any interested staff member. Whether or not there will be reimbursement or comp-time for attending meetings outside the working day should be made clear.

Probationary Periods. Many programs include probationary periods after initial employment to allow an adjustment period for both adults and children in the program. A director may be appointed on an "acting" basis for as long as a year. The time period must be long enough for the new employee to demonstrate competency in a given position but not so long that valuable aspects of the program can be undermined by an incompetent individual.

Teacher competency can be validated in a three- to six-month period by an experienced director who operates under a clearly defined philosophy of education and evaluates with an experienced eye. Since the teacher works directly with the children and any incompetence could have direct detrimental effects on them, the probationary period for teachers should be carefully delineated and clearly understood at the time of employment. This practice not only protects the welfare of the children but also is more equitable for the teachers in the long run, because they come into a new role with a clear understanding of the time allowed for initial review and evaluation.

Evaluation and Grievance Procedures. Evaluative review of personnel should be scheduled on a regular basis. Evaluation and grievance procedures are included in the personnel policies. (See Figure 9-4.) These procedures should be made available to all center personnel. Ideally, they will include details about who evaluates whom, when the periodic evaluation will take place, what techniques or instruments will be used in the evaluation, who makes the decision on whether or not the criteria are met, and what the consequences are of not meeting the stated criteria.

Not meeting stated criteria could mean no recommendation for a raise, no opportunity for advancing to a higher level position, or termination. When there are other actions which could cause dismissal such as use of corporal punishment, these should be in writing. In some situations there may be no recourse once a decision to deny a raise or to terminate an employee has been made. Although that may seem unfair, it is better to state it at the outset than to deal with all the negative feeling generated by the decision when an employee is unaware that there is no way to appeal it.

Evaluation Forms. Staff members are entitled to know evaluation procedures as well as evaluation criteria. Therefore, evaluation forms for all

Figure 9-4   Townville Child Development Center (a United Way Agency)   Evaluation and Grievance Procedures

EVALUATION AND GRIEVANCE PROCEDURES

1. Frequency of Evaluation
    Performance evaluations will be made twice during the probationary period
    for every new staff member -- at the midpoint and the end of the proba-
    tionary period -- and annually thereafter. It is the responsibility of
    the Personnel Committee to evaluate the work of the Director and the
    responsibility of the Director to evaluate all members of the staff. All
    evaluations will be shared with the employee and then become part of
    the employee's file.

2. Purpose of Evaluation
    The primary purpose of the annual evaluation is to create a mutual under-
    standing between the Director and each member of the staff of what is
    expected and how they both view the best way to move toward fulfilling
    those expectations.

    Annual evaluations will be used as a basis for continued employment,
    horizontal or vertical movement on the career ladder, salary increments
    in cases where the job description allows for merit raises, and demotion
    or dismissal.

3. Basis for the Evaluation
    Staff members will be evaluated on knowledge of the job as described
    in the job description, quality of skill demonstrated in fulfilling the
    job, interest and initiative, dependability, personal and professional
    growth, attendance and punctuality, and ability to work effectively in ·
    cooperation with other staff members.

    Evaluation forms for each staff position in the Center are included
    in these Personnel Policies.

4. Evaluation Procedure
    Each staff member will be notified as to when his/her evaluation will
    take place. The evaluation will be discussed with the staff member,
    at which time the staff member will be given the opportunity to express
    his/her disagreement or agreement with the evaluation. The outcome of
    this discussion will become part of the staff member's record.

5. Review of Grievances
    The staff member who wishes to present a grievance must present it
    first to the Director. Failing to reach settlement with the Director,
    the staff member may submit to the Chairperson of the Personnel Commit-
    tee a written statement of the situation, requesting that the grievance
    be reviewed by the Personnel Committee. The Personnel Committee will
    review the grievance and report with recommendations to the Board of
    Directors for action.

staff positions should be part of personnel policies. The Sample Teacher Evaluation Forms in the Director's Resources provide a prototype for other evaluation forms needed. Although there may be some overlap in areas covered by the evaluation forms such as physical and mental health, ability to work well with other adults, and personal attributes such as enthusiasm or sense of humor, some are unique to a given position. For example, the cook must be able to manage time well in order to have meals ready for serving at a given hour while a teacher must adjust the daily schedule based on changing needs of children. Knowledge of evaluation criteria helps build a sense of trust and partnership between staff to be evaluated and the evaluator who is either the director or another staff member.

Organizational Chart. An organizational chart that is part of the personnel policies and is made available to all members of the staff can clarify lines of communication and responsibility for everyone in the center. For a newcomer, even a very simple organizational pattern may be difficult to see unless it is presented in a diagram or flow chart. (See Figure 9-5 for a Sample Organizational Chart.) An organizational chart enables an employee to determine how each position meshes with other positions in the center. This information, coupled with complete job descriptions, evaluation procedures and forms, and open staff communication, leaves little doubt about expectations, areas of responsibility, and who will be the evaluator for each position.

Amending and Changing the Policies. The personnel policies should contain a section that details the procedure for amending the policies. The amending procedure *presumably* parallels the one that was used initially for developing the policies and that is stated in the bylaws, but the policy-making body may now be expanded to include staff members or parents who were not available during the initial stages of development. As the center undergoes its regular evaluation period, the personnel policies should also be checked to determine whether or not changes are needed. The board can then follow the amendment procedures when it becomes necessary to make changes. Once a change has been

adopted, the board's duty is to inform all personnel of the changes and the director is charged with implementing the new policy.

Clearly, small private centers will not use all the preceding items in their personnel policies; however, large, complex organizations will undoubtedly include all of these and more. Policies must be drawn and shaped to the unique needs of each center, and they must be constantly evaluated and changed to meet the ever-changing and growing needs of the program for which they are written.

DRAWING UP JOB DESCRIPTIONS

One mechanism for reducing conflict and uncertainty for staff members is to provide a clear definition of the role of each member on staff. Each role requires a thorough description so that no matter who fills the role, the same basic job will be done. The description must be written to clarify expectations, and yet retain the personal freedom of all staff members to follow through in the performance of their roles according to their own unique style. Well-written job descriptions provide a framework within which an individual can function creatively while performing the tasks required for the program. Detailed descriptions of knowledge, skills, and physical abilities are important because subsequent performance evaluations are based on the job description. Sample job descriptions included in the Personnel Policies and others which are not part of the sample Personnel Policies (Director's Resources) provide guidelines for writing descriptions for various staff positions, including full-time and part-time professional and support staff for both agency-sponsored and proprietary child care centers as well as public school preschools. Job descriptions usually cover at least the following:

- job title
- person to whom responsible
- people for whom responsible
- qualifications (education, experience, personal health, physical abilities, and so forth)

Figure 9-5   Sample Organizational Charts

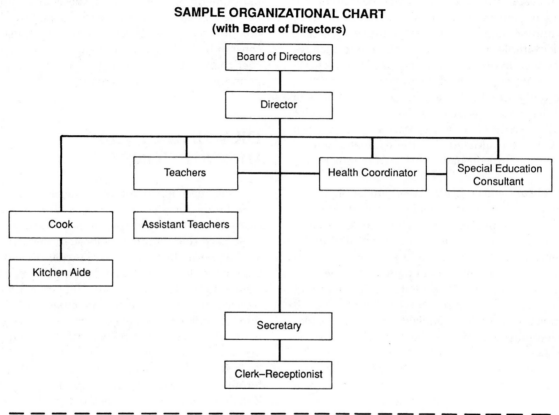

SAMPLE ORGANIZATIONAL CHART
(with Board of Directors)

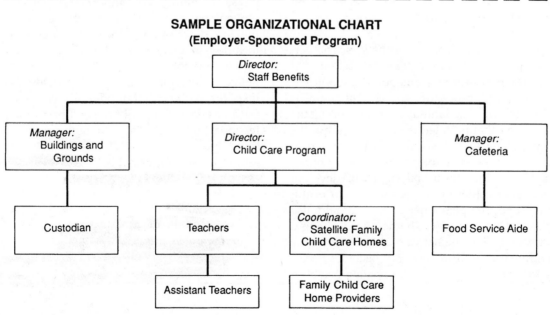

SAMPLE ORGANIZATIONAL CHART
(Employer-Sponsored Program)

- duties and responsibilities
- salary schedule
- work schedule

Job descriptions should be reviewed on a regular basis to determine whether changes are necessary. Such periodic review is useful because you not only deal with changing rules or regulations governing practices, such as the recent Americans with Disabilities Act (ADA), but you also adjust the policies as role expectations at different levels shift and change when new personnel bring changing talents and skills to a staff. For example, menu planning and shopping may be part of a director's job description, but a new cook who has been trained to plan meals may take over that function. Job descriptions for both the director and the cook can be adjusted accordingly, allowing staff members to perform at their highest creative level.

REFLECTIONS

Think about yourself as a practicum student or a new teacher and remember the uncertainty and accompanying anxiety you felt when you did not have a clear understanding of what was expected of you. How did you feel when you were unsure about who was to set up the snack or who was to straighten up the storage room? How did you manage when you were not sure about who to call when you knew you would be late because you had missed the bus? How did you react to criticism when you did not put all the blocks on the shelf while another adult had the children outside, and you had not been informed that you should do that? Can you remember how energy-draining these experiences were and how they interfered with your creative work with children? A carefully written job description for your position might have helped you have a clearer understanding of your role.

Initial writing of job descriptions is only the first step in an ongoing process. This process requires expertise in using information from the program evaluation and an ability to adjust to changing and growing strengths of personnel in order to make efficient use of available talent for a more effective program. Individual staff members might assist in updating job descriptions, and with input from the director, these might become part of the evaluation and review process.

Recruiting

Once the job descriptions have been written, the major hiring procedure begins. In fact, in many large centers or in programs with a board, the first task assigned to a new director is to initiate staff-recruitment procedures. Each center should establish and follow some general procedures regarding advertising, interviewing, and selecting employees to use during initial hiring in a new center and in filling vacant staff positions for an ongoing program.

Advertising for new staff is usually the director's responsibility. However, in some public schools and in corporate settings, the personnel office may set up school district or company advertisements which cover available positions throughout the organization. If the center program is ongoing, the director should first notify current staff members, board members, and parents about job openings as they become available. People in the organization may choose to apply for the new job, or they may know qualified individuals who would like to apply. For employees to learn of openings in their own center from an outside source is disconcerting, and it exemplifies poor communication within the center.

Affirmative action statements must be included when advertising for center personnel. Advertising should appear in a range of publications to make the information available to diverse segments of the population. Figure 9-6 shows examples of advertisements. Local professional organizations that publish classified ads in their newsletters are good places to advertise for classroom staff, as are high schools, colleges, or universities that have child care training programs. Ads may also be placed in

Figure 9-6   Sample Advertisements

Sample Classified Advertisement for the *Waynesburg Chronicle*

Teacher Assistant in a Child Care Center. Responsibilities include assisting the classroom teacher in the planning and implementation of the daily program for children, assisting in the family involvement aspect of the program and taking responsibility for some designated record keeping. Must have an Associate Degree in Early Childhood Education or equivalent. Experience preferred. Job available immediately. Send written resume to P.O. Box 320, Waynesburg, Iowa 36103. Our employees know about this opening. We are an Equal Opportunity Employer.

Sample Classified Advertisement for the Local Association for the Education of Young Children Newsletter

Director wanted for the Community Head Start Center. Responsibilities include hiring and supervision of entire staff for a program serving 75 children, record keeping, proposal writing, working with Center staff, Community Action agency, parents, and other community agencies. Applicant must have a Master's Degree in Early Childhood Education with some training in at least one of the following: social work, special education, administration. Three years administration experience required—Head Start teaching experience preferred. Send resume to Community Head Start Center, 352 Ninth St., Sioux City, Iowa. Deadline for applications, July 1. We are an Equal Opportunity Employer.

Sample Classified Advertisement for *The New York Times*

Nursery School Teacher wanted for suburban church-affiliated nursery school. Responsibilities include planning and implementing an age-appropriate developmental type nursery school program for a group of 15 three- and four-year-old children. Bachelor's Degree required—nursery school teacher experience preferred. Write for application to Ms. D. L. Jones, Director, Upper Plains Christian Church, 130 Meadows Place, Upper Plains, New York 11112, or call (713) 431-6037 Monday through Thursday from 1:00 to 3:00 P.M. We are an Equal Opportunity Employer.

Sample Classified Advertisement for the *Parkville Times*

Cook wanted for child care center at outskirts of town. Responsibilities include preparing snacks and lunch for 65 preschool children, cleaning kitchen appliances and cupboards, and making weekly shopping list. Experience preferred. Please send resume to, P.O. Box 932, Parkville, VA 23221. Equal Opportunity Employer.

national professional journals if there is sufficient time to meet publication deadlines and to wait until the circulation date. Some colleges and vocational high schools maintain placement services and some hold placement conferences so that employers can interview applicants. Notices of job openings can also be posted on community bulletin boards and in community papers that reach special segments of the population, such as the African-American or Native American community, or non-English speaking groups.

The classified section of newspapers is frequently used for advertising, but the result may be large numbers of unqualified applicants, who then must be screened before interviewing can begin. Nonetheless, when a position must be filled quickly, advertising in both small community, weekly newspapers and large city, daily newspapers is helpful because information is quickly disseminated to large numbers of people.

Personnel ads should include enough information to minimize the number of applications from completely unqualified persons but should not be so narrowly written that qualified persons fail to apply. If you are expected to write the advertising copy, you must be completely familiar with all the qualifications that are essential for performance of the job. Careful review of the job description is a good way to become familiar with the desired qualifications for potential candidates. Each advertisement should include the job title, a brief job description, the essential qualifications, the method of applying (phone, letter, application blank), and the name of the person to contact with a phone number and/or address. Starting date, working hours, starting pay, fringe benefits, and goals of the organization may also be included.

Advertisements that clearly state all non-negotiable items will eliminate practically all unqualified applicants. On the other hand, negotiable items stated equivocally tend to attract a more diverse pool of candidates from which to choose. For example, "experience necessary" is much more restrictive than "experience preferred." If experience is a non-negotiable qualification, then say, "experience necessary." However, if the position could be filled by a person with good training and a variety of life experiences that may or may not have been with children, then say "experience preferred." The latter phrase appeals to a broader population and will increase the number of applicants.

The director should be cautious about luring people into the field by presenting a glowing picture of life in a child care center; hiring staff members under false pretenses can quickly lead to job dissatisfaction. Rapid staff turnover not only disrupts program continuity but is very hard on the families and children who must constantly establish new relationships. Therefore, an advertisement that lists the required job qualifications in specific and realistic terms increases the probability of getting the best match between applicants and available positions, and reduces turnover.

Careful consideration must be given to the best method for receiving applications. If the need is urgent and immediate, it may be necessary to accept applications by phone. This option means that a new employee can be found quickly because an interview can be scheduled moments after the ad appears; but it also means that current staff members may have to spend hours on the phone, which detracts from their work with the children and puts them in the position of answering questions from people who are not seriously interested in the job.

Listing a post office box number in an ad places fewer demands on the director and the staff because potential candidates do not know the identity of the center and are unable to phone. On the other hand, qualified people may decide not to apply if they are unsure of the source of the ad. Others may feel that they could be applying to the center in which they work, which is another reason for notifying all employees of every opening. In fact, occasionally ads read, "Our employees know about this advertisement."

Allowing applicants to apply in person can be very inconvenient and is inappropriate for some positions. Unless the center has its own personnel director or one that is affiliated with a sponsoring agency such as public school, having applicants appear at the door during the hours in which children are present is awkward. However, this problem can be handled by setting specific hours during which interviews may be scheduled. In neighborhoods where many people do not have phones and where letter writing is difficult for some adults, it may be appropriate to have people apply in person. If the job does not entail making written reports, such as in the case of a cook or a housekeeper, then the ability to communicate effectively in writing may not be a criterion for selection and there is no need to see a resume or written application. On the other hand, in the case of a teacher, teacher assistant, or special education resource teacher, writing skills are important. For these positions, a written response to an advertisement provides helpful data for initial screening of applicants and should be mandatory before an interview is scheduled.

The advertiser will also have to decide whether to have the candidates request an application form or send a resume. If a secretary is available to answer requests for application blanks, the process can be speeded up. If the director will be distracted from work by recording the name and address of applicants and mailing out applications, it is wiser to have candidates mail in resumes and fill in a formal application when they are interviewed. Application forms in Figures 9-7 and 9-8 show how applications are adjusted depending upon availability of a resume from the applicant.

When all the applications have been collected, they must be screened to eliminate obviously unsuitable candidates. If no suitable candidates have applied, and attempts to recruit staff from other centers has failed, the advertising and application process is reopened. The director or the chairperson of the personnel committee usually screens the applications for those that meet the job requirements, particularly in the areas of education, health, or experience, and then interviews can be arranged. Interviewers should not be burdened with candidates who have no qualifications for the job. Therefore, the careful writing of the ads to interest qualified candidates and the initial screening process to eliminate totally unqualified candidates are both important steps in the recruiting process.

Applications that are received from people who are not subsequently called for an interview

Figure 9-7   Sample Application Form (no resume)

<u>SAMPLE APPLICATION FORM</u>

(Suggested for use when no resume is on file)

Application for Employment

Jewish Community Nursery School -- Fairmount, Pennsylvania

Name of Applicant _____
                      Last   First   Middle or Maiden

Address _____Zip _____

Telephone _____Social Security No._____

Birthdate_____

Citizenship: USA_____   Other_____

RECORD OF EDUCATION

School	Name and Address of School	Years Attended From	Years Attended To	Check Last Year Completed	List Diploma or Degree
High				1 2 3 4	
College				1 2 3 4	
Other (Specify)				1 2 3 4	

Figure 9-7 *(continued)*

List below all present and past employment, beginning with your most recent

Name and Address of Employer	From		To		Describe in detail the work you did	Weekly Starting Salary	Weekly Last Salary	Reason for Leaving	Name of Supervisor
	Mo.	Yr.	Mo.	Yr.					

List all professional and community organizations with which you are affiliated. (Indicate if you hold office in the organization)

_____

_____

Write your educational philosophy.

What do you feel most qualifies you for this position?

What are your professional goals?

List names and addresses of three references.

1.

2.

3.

Figure 9-8 Sample Application Form (resume on file)

```
                    SAMPLE APPLICATION FORM
          (Suggested for use when a resume  is available)
                    Application for Position
                    University Day Care Center
           Ogden University, Ogden City, Michigan


Name of Applicant_____
                      Last          First      Middle or Maiden
Address _____

        _____Telephone_____

Birthdate _____Social Security No._____

Title of position for which you are applying._____

What do you feel best qualifies you for this position?_____

_____


_____

Would you be willing to continue your education by taking

college courses or in-service training if recommended to do

that?

_____


_____

What satisfaction do you expect to receive from this position?

_____


_____

List three references (Preferably one former employer, one

former teacher and one community person).

1.

2.

3.
```

should be retained so that affirmative action procedures can be completed where that is a requirement. A record must be kept listing the reasons why any applicant was not interviewed, and they should receive written notification that they will *not* be interviewed. Applicants who are called for an interview should be advised to bring identification to prove citizenship. A candidate who is not a United States citizen will be required to prove eligibility to work in this country. In order to be in compliance with the Immigration Reform and Control Act of 1986, every person hired must complete Form I-9, available from the Immigration and Naturalization Service (INS). A list of local INS offices and a copy of Form I-9 can be found in Director's Resources (p. 279).

Interviewing

Interviewing is essential and should not be eliminated no matter how urgent the need for obtaining a staff member may seem. Even though a candidate can make an excellent impression during an interview and then turn out to be ineffective as a staff member, interviewing will provide insights that cannot be gleaned from written applications or resumes and will facilitate judicious hiring decisions in the majority of cases. The relative amount of time spent interviewing can be extremely profitable when compared with the amount of time that might otherwise be spent solving personnel problems because a poor candidate was hastily selected. The person or group responsible for staffing the center must decide who will interview the candidates and must develop the plan for the interview.

Interviewers. While applications are being collected and screened, decisions must be made about who will interview the viable candidates. In a very small program the director may take full responsibility for all interviewing or may do it with the help of one or more of the following:

- staff person
- member of the Board
- community person
- other professional (social worker, special educator, physician, school principal)
- people responsible to the new employee

In most programs the interviews are conducted by committees, often by the personnel committee.

The composition of the interview committee may be previously established by the board, as in the case of the personnel committee; or the committee can be set up by the director to pertain specifically to the job being filled. For example, when there is an opening for a teacher, the committee might be composed of the director, a teacher, and a parent. Community people could be included, as well as people from other professions, such as community health or special education. There might be more than one person from a given category, but if the committee is too large, its effectiveness will diminish. It can be difficult for large numbers of people to interview a given candidate at one time, and the procedure can be very threatening for the candidate. Nonetheless, it is best if the committee is representative of the center staff with whom the person will work, of the families who use the center, and of the people who represent the sponsoring agency if all who have a vested interest in the position to be filled are to be represented.

Although the committee make-up may vary, depending on the type of center and on the position to be filled, both the committee members and the candidates must be aware that the organizational structure of the center takes precedence in making hiring decisions. For example, if a janitor is being hired, it may be appropriate to have the teachers express a preference for the candidate who would be most able to meet their needs for classroom maintenance. However, if the person who becomes janitor is going to be responsible to the center director, then the director's opinion must weigh heavily in the final hiring decision.

A major exception to this hiring and interviewing procedure is in public-school-sponsored programs where hiring is based on established school district policies. Public school union contracts often dictate hiring policies and procedures. In most cases, the personnel office will handle advertising, interviewing and hiring. Involving teachers or parents in the process is unlikely. This could result in a team which will have to spend time building a workable partnership and working through possible philosophical differences.

Preparation for the Interview. Just as candidates should come to the interview prepared to express their strengths, weaknesses, goals, expectations, and past experiences, so the interviewers should be prepared for each interview. Their questions should reflect a thorough knowledge of the center, its program, its staff, and the clients served by the program. Not only should interviewers be familiar with the information in the candidate's resume, application form and reference letters, but they should also look for evidence of warmth, good-natured calmness and ease of relating to others. As Greenberg notes, it is important to select caregivers who have "the right stuff" to start with, because "you can teach people to conform to certain schedules, perform specific acts, use assorted tips and techniques—but you cannot develop an entirely different character, personality, and self-esteem in a staff person."[6] An interview is conducted most productively when all parties are well prepared and when the environment has been set up for a meaningful dialogue between interviewers and interviewee.

Interviewer Information. Each interviewer should be totally familiar with the job description for the vacant position and should have copies of the candidate's application and references. A letter or questionnaire that has been prepared in advance for submission to all listed references will provide comparable data for all candidates and make it easier for reference people to respond. If reference letters are not received promptly, the candidate may be asked to contact the reference person, and sometimes it is necessary to proceed with interviewing before information has been received from all references. Although it is important to have written information from the candidate's references, a follow-up call to discuss the written responses can provide valuable information. (See sample Reference Letter in Figure 9-9.)

Interview Plan. Interviewers must plan the type of interview they will conduct. Sometimes a predetermined list of questions is developed so that all candidates will respond to the same questions. This procedure provides uniform data but is somewhat inflexible and may not elicit the most useful data from each candidate. Sometimes questions are developed as the interview progresses. This spontaneous procedure is more likely to give rise to potentially constructive data but requires more skill on the part of the interviewers.

The person who develops the questions should keep in mind the parameters of the job description and should understand the requirements of Title VII of the 1964 Civil Rights Act and the ADA. There must be a "business necessity" for all questions asked during the interview. Questions to avoid include, ". . . date of birth or age, marital status, spouse's occupation, pregnancy issues and number of children, childcare arrangements, religious affiliation, membership in organization (except pertaining to the position) . . . union memberships and disabilities."[7] The first question should be open-ended and require more than a simple yes or no answer. Furthermore, it should focus on previous jobs, education, or hobbies, or any other subject matter with which the candidate is very familiar. This technique puts the candidate at ease and creates an environment for more focused probing later in the interview. For example, the interviewer might say, "I see in your resume that you have worked for Head Start in California. What were the aspects of that job that you liked best?" or "I see you studied at Wheelock in Boston. Tell us about that program." From these questions, it is possible to cull out material that can be examined at greater depth. "You said you enjoyed working with the Parent Policy Committee in California. What did you do with that group which you see as applicable to this job?"

Interviewers can learn a great deal about the ways in which a teacher candidate would fit into their center's program by posing hypothetical situations and asking question such as, "What would you do if a child kicked you?" or "How would you work with a toddler who is not yet talking?" This type of question can produce ideas about

6 Polly Greenberg, *Character Development: Encouraging Self-Esteem and Self-Discipline in Infants, Toddlers and Two-Year-Olds*, NAEYC 1990, p. 5.
7 Celia Anita Decker and J. R. Decker, *Planning and Administering Early Childhood Programs*, Merrill (an imprint of Macmillan), 1992, p. 117.

Figure 9-9   Sample Reference Letter

TO: Mr. L. N. Davidson
     University Court - Rm 416
     Midtown University
     Midtown, KY   35231

FROM: Mr. John Wilkins, Director
       Midtown Child Development Center
       414 Main Street
       Midtown, KY 35213

_____ has given us your name as
a reference. We are interested in having any information from you about this
applicant which will help us in hiring the best person available for an
assistant teacher position on our staff. Your cooperation is greatly appreciated.

In your opinion, what is this applicant's ability in each of the following
areas?

Working with other staff members

Working with young children

Working with families from the inner city

Capacity for personal and professional growth

Ability to evaluate self

In what capacity did you know this applicant?

How long have you known this applicant?

Comments:

                                   Signature _____

                                   Title   _____

                                   Date   _____

curriculum, classroom management, parent involvement, staff relations, and understanding of the development of young children. Of course, the questions should relate to the job for which the person is applying. For example, a prospective cook might be asked, "What would you do if sandwiches were on today's menu and the bread delivery had not been made by 10:00 A.M.?" A list of sample questions in Director's Resources (p. 256) can give you some ideas for questioning both degreed and non-degreed job candidates.

Interview Setting. Before the interview, careful thought must be given to the setting. Will the candidate be as comfortable as possible? Will everyone be able to see and hear everyone else? Is the seating arrangement comfortable and planned so that desks or large tables do not separate the candidate from the interviewers? Is the interviewing room free from distractions? Has the time of the interview been appropriately chosen so that everyone can focus on the interview rather than on the next appointment? Is the time available adequate for developing rapport and exploring details of the answers to the questions? Has provision been made to offer water or

REFLECTIONS

Can you recall your first job interview? If so, you may be able to remember some of your reactions during that interview. Were you put at ease when you entered the room? Were you introduced to everyone before the questioning began? Did you feel the interviewers had prepared for the session by reviewing your resume and credentials? Were you given time to ask questions? How did they close the interview? As you think about being interviewed and recall the stress you experienced, you will increase your sensitivity to an applicant's feelings.

some refreshments to the candidate? When the goal is to make applicants feel welcome and at ease, the interview setting becomes a matter of central concern. Indeed, the interviewers are revealing to the candidate a major part of the center philosophy as they create an accepting environment for an interview, and are more likely to obtain an accurate picture when the candidate is at ease.

The director sets the non-verbal tone for the interview by being relaxed and friendly. It is important to sit back, smile, and maintain an open posture, with arms down in the lap and body facing the candidate.

The Interview. At the beginning, candidates should be given some idea about the length of the interview and should be informed that there will be a time at the end of the interview to ask questions. Interviewers should be prepared to present information about the program's philosophy, the job, and the center and should clearly and honestly answer the applicant's questions. The interviewers should maintain eye contact and let the applicant do most of the talking. They should refer to the personnel policies to clarify thoroughly the expectations that are held regarding performance standards for the position.

Of course, the interviewers will look for an applicant who plans to stay with the center for a number of years because staff stability provides continuity for children and nurtures a sense of community at the center. Nonetheless, caution should be used about requesting any information in sensitive areas mentioned above. It is recommended that employment records be limited to that information relevant to employment decisions, and that disclosures of that information to third parties be strictly limited where not authorized by the candidate or employee. It is advisable that child care centers develop a written policy and procedures concerning this issue. Also, since federal law provides only a portion of the employment discrimination picture, and many states have their own discrimination laws, it is wise to consult an attorney regarding applicable state laws for your center.[8]

Interviewers should obtain as much information as possible during the interview, but

8 Consult an attorney or contact EEOC if you are uncertain about what may be asked in an interview.

note-taking or discussing the candidate's qualifications should be done after the interview. Some discussion about the candidate within the groups is useful, and reaching a consensus serves a worthwhile purpose. Discussion provides the opportunity for interviewers to share their impression of the candidate as they draw upon each other's perceptions. Confidentiality is a critical issue and all committee members must understand that information on candidates and any committee discussion must be kept confidential.

Teaching Interview. Observing a teacher or assistant teacher candidate in a classroom setting provides the committee with additional data on classroom presence and skills with children. Some candidates are able to give you all you want to hear in an interview, but when you observe them with children it becomes obvious that they are not comfortable with children. It is

unfair to have the regular classroom teacher leave a new person alone in the classroom because of the anxiety that would be produced in both the candidate and the children, but a great deal can be learned by observing a prospective teacher read a story to a few children or join a small group for snack. Asking to see sample lesson plans, resource files, or picture files also provides useful information to the interview committee. Some centers select candidates from the substitute list, in which case the center staff will have worked with the candidate before the interview.

SELECTING THE EMPLOYEE

When interviewing is completed, the person or committee responsible for selecting the employee uses material such as the personnel

Observing a candidate in a classroom setting provides the interview committee with data on classroom presence. (Photo by Lisa Souders)

policies and the job description, combined with all the information from the interview and the observation, to reach a final decision. All data is weighed and balanced until the best match among job description, current staff composition, and candidate qualifications is obtained. It is also important to review the non-discrimination prohibitions in this decision making process, especially if you have an applicant with a disability. An employer is not required to give preference to a qualified applicant with a disability over other applicants, but may not consider the disabled candidate unqualified if that person can perform the "essential functions" of the job.[9] It may be helpful to have a second interview with selected candidates from the pool who seem best qualified for the position in order to further narrow the choice. The procedure for making a decision should be clear to all interviewers. Will the director ultimately choose the employee? Will the director present two or three names to the board and the board will make the decision? Will the board make the decision or will the committee rule by majority vote? Generally, the director will make the decision, taking into account the recommendations of the interviewing committee. Final approval from the board is sometimes part of the hiring policy.

The selected candidate should be notified of the job offer by the director or the chairperson of the committee. On acceptance, the new employee may be asked to sign a contract stating the salary and the length of time covered by the contract, provided the Personnel Policies do not state that all employees are employees at will. (See Sample Contracts Figures 9-1 and 9-2.) The job description is usually referred to in the written contract. Both the employer and the employee retain copies of this document. Immediately after the new employee has been informed of the job and has accepted it, all other interviewees are informed of the selection, thanked for their interest, and told that their resumes will be kept on file if another vacancy should occur.

ORIENTING THE EMPLOYEE

The director is responsible for introducing the new employee to the work environment. The new person will need to know where to find work space, what storage facilities and materials are available, and what schedule is to be followed. A tour of the building and introductions to all other staff members either during the tour or at a staff meeting shortly thereafter are essential to the orientation procedure. The person who conducts the tour and makes the introductions sets the tone for the employee's future interpersonal relationships with the other staff members. Each staff member has an obligation to become involved with making the new employee's transition to the staff position as smooth and satisfying as possible.

The new employee also should be introduced to the parents at the earliest possible time. Some directors notify parents of staff additions or changes by mail; others use their bulletin boards or newsletters; and still others introduce the new member informally as the occasion arises or at a regularly scheduled meeting.

DIRECTOR'S CORNER

"We do a five day orientation for each new staff person before we finalize the hiring process. The prospective employee is paid for those hours of classroom participation, meetings with me, joint reading of some Do's and Don'ts in the classroom, etc. It's well worth the time and money, and has helped us make good hiring decisions."

Director, private not-for-profit center

---

9 Ibid. *The Americans with Disabilities Act: Questions and Answers*, pp. 2, 3.

During the initial weeks of employment it is important for the director to check with the new staff member to answer any questions and make a conscious effort to build a positive relationship. At the same time, the Director can continue to reiterate expectations and expand upon ways to follow and implement the program philosophy. A carefully planned staff orientation program can promote better staff relationships and reduce staff turnover.

Sometimes it is difficult for the director to be available to the new teacher often enough. It can be helpful to establish a mentor program or assign a staff member to watch over the new staff person. It also helps to leave a note in the teacher's box asking questions like, "What went well today?" or "What did I miss today in your room that you would like to share with me?" The director might also leave a message about being available the next day at nap time, or a plan to stop in before lunch to see how things are going. These steps help make the new teacher feel that the director really is available to give support and help.

Some directors prepare handbooks and provide a copy for each employee. In corporate centers, the parent firm may prepare a handbook for use in *all* centers, whether franchised or run by the corporation. Guidelines in this handbook may even detail how many children should be permitted in blocks or dramatic play at any given time, or exactly how the daily cleaning is to be done by the classroom teachers. However, handbooks are rarely that detailed, nor do they usually include expectations for teachers to clean the premises. More often they include items like:

- philosophy of the center
- bylaws of the board (if applicable)
- personnel policies
- policies and procedures for the children's program
- copies of forms used by the center
- information about the community the center serves
- information about the staff (job titles, home addresses, telephone numbers, and so forth)

A handbook is useful because it gives everyone a common reference point and provides new employees with materials that familiarize them with the center.

REFLECTIONS

Perhaps you can recall your first day as a new student or an employee in a child care center. How did you feel on that first day? What else do you wish you had known about the center or the program? Do you recall what it was like not to know where the extra paper towels were kept or how awkward it was when you could not find the easel paper? As you recall those feelings, consider what you would tell a new teacher in your center if you were responsible for orienting the new employees.

SUMMARY

The staffing process in a child care center is based on the personnel policies and job descriptions that define the staffing requirement to operate the center's program. Decisions about the content of advertisements, interview questions and procedures, and final hiring should be based on specific job requirements that are detailed in the job descriptions. Interviewing may be done individually or in a group and should be a time for two-way communication between the candidates and the representatives of all aspects of the center's programs. Questioning should focus on the requirements of the position and the candidate's potential for fulfilling those requirements. The purpose of the entire process is to provide the employer with the information that is necessary for selecting the best available person for each staff position.

Class Assignments

1. Write a resume of your training and experience up to this point in your education and professional career and bring it to class. Use Working Paper 9-1 to complete this assignment.
2. A job description for a cook in a Head Start center can be found in Working Paper 9-2.

    a. Write the qualifications for that position based on the job description.
    b. Write an advertisement for the position of cook in the Head Start center based on the qualifications you have written for that position plus information in this chapter on content of advertisements (pp. 203–205).

3. Fill in the application form in Working Paper 9-3. Apply for the position of assistant teacher.

Class Exercises

1. Review the job description for the infant/toddler teacher assistant (Director's Resources, p. 272) and develop a list of questions that would be appropriate to ask candidates applying for the job.
2. Select three class members to serve as interviewers of applicants for the assistant teacher's position. Select one class member as a candidate for the position.
3. After the three interviewers review the candidate's application for the position (see Assignment 3), have them role play an interview with the candidate using questions based on those developed in Exercise 1 in addition to information from the application.
4. After the interview, all class members participate in summarizing, in writing, the candidate's qualifications for the job. Use Working Paper 9-4 to complete this exercise.

Working Paper 9-1

Resume Format

Name:
Permanent Address   *Present Address*

Phone: *Phone:*
Position Objective:

Education:

Employment Experience (in chronological order):

Honors and Activities:

References (names, addresses and phone numbers of three):

Working Paper 9-2

Job Description

Cook

Schedule: Monday through Friday — 7:30 A.M. to 3:30 P.M.

Responsible to the Head Start Director.

Responsible for:

1. Safe preparation of all food (breakfast, lunch, and snacks).
2. Requisition appropriate amounts of foodstuffs based on designated menus.
3. Check food deliveries against orders.
4. Store foods appropriately, before preparation, in refrigerator, freezer, bins, cupboards, etc.
5. Prepare all foods using methods that maintain food value and freshness.
6. Follow menus, recipes, or other directives furnished by Headstart nutrition consultant.
7. Record amounts of food used daily and maintain an inventory of staples on hand.
8. Wash and sterilize dishes and all utensils according to sanitarian's directions.
9. Clean appliances and storage areas according to a designated schedule.
10. Supervise assistant cook.

Qualifications: (fill in as assigned in Class Assignments, Chapter 9, Question 2)

Working Paper 9-3

Sample Application Form

```
                    Application for Employment

        Jewish Community Nursery School -- Fairmount, Pennsylvania

        Name of Applicant _____
                            Last          First    Middle or Maiden

        Address _____Zip _____

        Telephone _____Social Security No._____

        Birthdate_____

        Citizenship:   USA_____   Other_____
```

RECORD OF EDUCATION

School	Name and Address of School	Years Attended		Check Last Year Completed	List Diploma or Degree
		From	To		
High				1 2 3 4	
College				1 2 3 4	
Other (Specify)				1 2 3 4	

Working Paper 9-3 (*continued*)

List below all present and past employment, beginning with your most recent

Name and Address of Employer	From		To		Describe in detail the work you did	Weekly Starting Salary	Weekly Last Salary	Reason for Leaving	Name of Supervisor
	Mo.	Yr.	Mo.	Yr.					

List all professional and community organizations with which you are affiliated. (Indicate if you hold office in the organization)

_____

_____

Write your educational philosophy.

What do you feel most qualifies you for this position?

What are your professional goals?

List names and addresses of three references.

1.

2.

3.

Working Paper 9-4

Interview Summary

Candidate Qualifications for Infant/Toddler Assistant Teacher

Education:

Experience with children:

Other relevant experience:

Ability to express ideas verbally:

Congruence of philosophy to that of the center:

General appearance:

Evidence of ability to work as part of the teaching team:

Other comments:

Director's Resource 9-1

Sample Personnel Policy and Procedures—Roark Learning Centers

ROARK LEARNING CENTER, INC.*
PERSONNEL POLICIES, BENEFITS,
AND JOB DESCRIPTIONS

General Policies

I.   INTRODUCTION
This employee handbook is presented for informational purposes only, and can be changed at any time by the company with or without notice. This handbook is not an employment contract, expressed or implied. Company employees are employees at will and either the employee or the company can terminate the employment relationship at any time for any reason or without reason. No supervisor or any other representative or employee of the company, other than the Executive Director, has the authority to enter into an agreement (written or oral) with an employee that is contrary to the foregoing.

II.   ADMINISTRATION OF PERSONNEL POLICIES
It is the responsibility of the Director and the Board of Roark Learning Center, Inc. to review and submit revisions of the Personnel Policies each year. Any additions to and/or deletions from the policies must be approved by the Board before going into effect.

III.   EQUAL EMPLOYMENT OPPORTUNITY
Roark Learning Center, Inc. recognizes our employees as one of our greatest assets. We are committed to providing equal employment opportunities for all, without regard to race, color, religion, national origin, age, sex, disability, and/or sexual orientation.
      These opportunities include, but are not limited to, recruitment, hiring, training and promotion, compensation, benefits and all other terms and conditions of employment.

IV.   COMPENSATION
Compensation is to be set for each employee according to agreement among the employee, Director, and the Board. Compensation will be based upon abilities, training, length of service, education, experience, and job responsibilities. Increases to compensation will be based on the performance, professional growth, responsibilities of the employee, the company's financial ability and upon agreement between the Director and the Board.
      Questions concerning your compensation or pay should be directed to your supervisor.

V.   HOURS OF WORK
Teachers' hours will be set upon hiring. Schedules will change according to enrollment and all teachers are required to sign in and out each day. *No staff member will be guaranteed a specific shift.* If a teacher should be late for any reason, he/she must call the center to notify staff as early as possible. Teachers are required to attend all staff meetings and expected to attend parents' meetings when scheduled and any activities to improve parent–teacher relations. When staff meetings are scheduled after shift hours, staff will be compensated for this time.

* Reprinted by permission of Roark Learning Center, Inc.

Director's Resource 9-1 (*continued*)

VI.   RECRUITMENT
Applications are always to be accepted and filed. The Center works with the University of Cincinnati and local vocational schools to provide placements for students in teacher training programs. When a position becomes available within the corporation, staff are notified and can be considered for the position if qualified.

VII.   RESIGNATION
If you choose to resign from the Center, it is requested that you submit a written two-week notice.

VIII.   PROFESSIONAL DEVELOPMENT
Regardless of their previous education or experience, employees will be expected to continue studies of and training in early childhood education practices in order to keep abreast of new developments in the field. This continued study and training may take place on the employee's own time outside of regular working hours, and as recommended by the Director. Methods employed may include, but are not limited to: in-service training classes at the Center, attendance at a recommended professional conference or meeting, membership in a professional organization and attendance at their monthly meetings, enrollment in pertinent courses offered by local colleges and universities.

A.   *Child Development Training*
Each non-degreed (ece) staff person must complete a minimum of 15 hours of child development training each year. Each degreed staff person must complete a total of six hours of training, four of which will be child development topics. These requirements may be waived by the Director if the staff person is taking a university credit course of one to three hours.

B.   *City and State Requirements*
Within the first three months of employment each staff person must complete first aid, communicable diseases, and child abuse training to comply with city and state standards. This training for all staff will be paid for by the Center. Staff members must attend all training for which they are registered. If a staff member misses a training session they must reimburse the Center for the cost of the training.

C.   *Inservice Training*
Two days each year, typically on Good Friday and the Friday after Thanksgiving, the Center will be closed for inservice training. The inservice days will consist of training and individual time for planning, goal setting, etc. *Every staff person must attend.* If someone misses due to illness they must make this time up on a Saturday and replacement training will be at their own expense. This inservice must be made up within 30 days of it being offered/scheduled.

IX.   SUPERVISION AND PROBLEM RESOLUTION
An Open Door philosophy is an essential part of maintaining open communications and a positive work environment. We are interested in knowing our employees' ideas, questions, suggestions, problems and concerns.

In most instances, your immediate supervisor is the person best qualified to solve a problem or answer a question and you are encouraged to communicate your concerns and suggestions to them.

However, there may be times when you wish to discuss a concern or problem with someone other than your immediate supervisor. You are encouraged to bring these matters to any other member of management.

Director's Resource 9-1 (*continued*)

Following is a listing of the reporting relationship within our organization:

- Board of Directors
- President of the Board
- Executive Director
- Director
- Assistant Director
- Educational Coordinator
- Head Teacher
- Assistant Teacher
- Teacher's Aide

X.   DRESS CODE
All staff are encouraged to wear comfortable clothing. A professional appearance must be maintained at all times. The following should be observed:

- jeans should be in good condition
- no halter or tube tops
- good hygiene (clean hair, clothes, etc.)
- hiking shorts or sun dresses are appropriate summer wear

XI.   CONFIDENTIALITY POLICY
Records of all children are confidential and only staff and referral agencies may have access. A file may not leave the Director's office without approval. A staff member may be dismissed for discussing children outside of the school, staff or referral agencies.

XII.   CHILDREN AND CLOSING
It is the closing staff's responsibility to confirm that all children have been picked up before leaving the building. Two staff members must always be present when a child is in the Center. In the event that a child is not picked up at the closing of the Center, the remaining staff will follow these guidelines:

A. If attempts to reach parent at work and home are unsuccessful, call emergency contact number.
B. If attempts to contact emergency contacts are unsuccessful, contact the director immediately.
C. YOU ARE A PROFESSIONAL: AT NO TIME MAY YOU TRANSPORT A CHILD OR LEAVE A CHILD UNATTENDED.

XIII.   CLASSROOM EXPENSES
The following conditions must be met for staff to receive reimbursement for any expenses for classroom activities:

- approval is granted by the Director or Assistant Director.
- a written receipt must be submitted.

XIV.   NO SMOKING
In an effort to provide a healthy, comfortable, smoke-free environment for all of our employees and children, smoking in all of our facilities is prohibited.

Director's Resource 9-1 (*continued*)

XV.   DRUGS AND ALCOHOL
The possession, sale, distribution or use of illegal drugs and the possession, sale, use or being under the apparent influence of alcohol or other intoxicants while on work time or on company property, is strictly prohibited.

XVI.   PERSONAL PROPERTY
The center cannot assume responsibility for any staff member's personal property. It is encouraged that staff do not bring personal belongings to the Center.

XVII.   TUITION PAYMENTS
Only management staff may accept tuition payments. No cash will remain on site.

Employee Benefits

I.   VACATION
The eligibility for paid vacation is based on the status of employment and length of continuous service.

Upon hiring, each full-time (40 hour/week) employee will receive two vacation days to be used in their first year of employment. Upon hiring, each full-time employee will accrue one vacation day for every 52 days worked to be used in the following year. After one year of employment vacation days are accrued at one for every 37 days worked, also to be used in following years. Vacation days must be used each year or be forfeited. The following chart outlines how vacation days are accrued for full-time employees:

Period	Vacation Days
0–12 months	2 days
after 1st anniversary	5 days
after 2nd anniversary and on	7 days

Part-time employees are entitled to two vacation days per year after their first full year of service. Management personnel are entitled to vacation that will accrue at a rate of one day every 26 days worked.

Requests for vacation time must be approved in advance by the director, who will take into consideration the employees' length of service. No deductions from pay will be made for vacation or holiday closings.

II.   HOLIDAYS
All employees are paid for the following holidays: New Year's Day, Memorial Day, July 4th, Labor Day, Thanksgiving, and Christmas Eve and Christmas Day, when these days fall on a regular work day (Monday through Friday).

III.   PERSONAL DAYS
After 30 days of employment, each full-time (40 hours/week) employee will receive one personal day each month. These days will be scheduled by the Director or scheduled no more than three months before, and no less than one before. The Center reserves the right under special circumstances to reschedule personal days. These days are not accrued vacation and none will be due to staff who resign or are terminated. A staff person may save up to three personal days per year to be used as vacation. They must be used within the same year.

Director's Resource 9-1 (*continued*)

IV.   SICK DAYS
      Upon hiring, each full-time (40 hours/week) staff person immediately receives two sick days, and will then start accruing sick days for their first year of employment. Sick days are accrued at a rate of one sick day for every 52 days worked, with a maximum of five sick days per year. These must be used within the calendar year as sick days or vacation days.

V.   BREAKS
      Breaks will be offered to staff if coverage of duties/responsibilities is available. Breaks may not be taken at the end of a schedule or accrued as vacation.

VI.   OVERVIEW OF TIME OFF

Benefit	Full-time	Part-time
Vacation: First year	2	0
Vacation: Second year	5	2
Vacation: 3+ years	7	2
Personal days	12	0
Sick days	5	0
Holidays	7	7

VII. INSURANCE BENEFITS
      All employees will be covered by Social Security, Workmen's Compensation, and State Unemployment. Each full-time (40 hours) employee will also receive a $35,000 life insurance policy. A single policy group health insurance program has been established that each full-time employee may take part in. After two months of employment, the Center will pay 100% of the health insurance premium for each full-time employee.

      Maternity Leave/Medical Disability
      An employee's position and benefits will remain in effect three months from the final day of work during a disability or maternity leave. Employees must have a disability statement from their physician in order to be eligible for disability leave.
      The employee is responsible for covering the full cost of insurance benefits while on a personal leave of absence.

VIII. TUITION REDUCTION
      Center employees may be granted a reduced tuition rate as follows:

      All full-time employees: 1/3 tuition reduction

      Reduced tuition slots are limited based upon available accommodations and management's discretion.

IX.   PERSONAL LEAVE
      Unpaid personal leaves may be granted at the Director's discretion based on the staffing needs of any center. Leaves in excess of 90 days during any 12-month period are not permitted. The employee is responsible for covering the full cost of insurance benefits while on a personal leave of absence.

Director's Resource 9-1 (*continued*)

JOB DESCRIPTION
DIRECTOR

PERSONNEL ADMINISTRATION
1. Insures the development and periodic review of a wage and administration program that insures similar remuneration for similar responsibility, education and experience.
2. Insures the adherence of agency personnel policies and practices.
3. Insures program compliance with federal, state and local laws and regulations covering equal opportunity employment.

SUPERVISION
1. Develops supervisory standards for the program. Insures adherence to the standards.
2. Supervises directly the teachers and educational coordinator. Makes recommendations for salary adjustments, dismissals and promotions for employees in the program.
3. Supervises the development of in-service training programs for the staff.

PUBLIC RELATIONS
1. Develops an atmosphere of support for the program within the geographic program area of the community.
2. Maintains liaison with community agencies, organization and ethnic groups.
3. Assists colleges and universities in teacher training and internship programs.
4. Acts as a resource person of other township, state and federal programs.
5. Makes speeches; writes articles; and assists in the development of brochures and news releases.

GENERAL
1. Shapes the programs; leads; coordinates; makes decisions; develops and maintains a quality early childhood program.

REPORTING RELATIONSHIP
1. Reports to the Executive Director
2. The director will build the organizational chart to reflect the professional staff and size of the program she/he administers.

LIMITS OF AUTHORITY
1. Must have prior commitments
   a. to set program policy
   b. to set fiscal policy
   c. to add/delete programs
2. May take action but must inform
   a. when re-organizing the program's administrative structure
   b. when revising wage and salaries
   c. when terminating employees
   d. when hiring employees that are not consistent with the educational requirements
3. May take action without informing
   a. when insuring preparation of procedure statements and manual
   b. when insuring the development of the programs; staffing plans; licensing requirements
   c. when developing supervisory standards, supervising staff; insuring the development of in-service training programs

Director's Resource 9-1 (*continued*)

  d. when developing a public relations image for the agency; acting as a resource person; making speeches; writing articles
  e. when leading; coordinating; making decisions; developing and maintaining a quality agency

JOB REQUIREMENTS
  1. Knowledge of children's physical, emotion and developmental patterns
  2. Knowledge of general learning theories and curriculum development with an emphasis on Jean Piaget, Erik Erikson and the constructivist approach
  3. Demonstrated ability to administer a program and budget
  4. Demonstrated professional skills in the areas of curriculum planning; in-service training; program goal setting; federal, state and city funding sources; and establishing procedures for evaluating the progress of individual children
  5. Demonstrated ability to discern when enrolled children may need special medical or psychological services
  6. Demonstrated ability in accessing outside agencies for referral and consultation
  7. Ability to delegate authority judiciously
  8. Articulate in making prepared and extemporaneous talks
  9. Evidence of emotional maturity and stability
  10. Highly demonstrated personal integrity

EDUCATIONAL REQUIREMENTS
A Master's or Bachelor's degree in Early Childhood Education; experience as a preschool teacher, preferably NAEYC accredited; experience supervising support staff and teaching assistants; knowledge in the field of budget management.

Director's Resource 9-1 (*continued*)

JOB DESCRIPTION
HEAD TEACHER—INFANTS

The person selected for this position will be responsible for the care and supervision of the three infants assigned to her/his pod. She/he is directly responsible for working closely with assistant infant teachers to ensure that continuity of care is maintained throughout the infant's entire day at the Center. However, because infant care requires that caregivers work as a team, she/he will also be responsible for aiding in the care and supervision of all the infants in the program.

QUALIFICATIONS

The person selected for this position must be at least 18 years of age and have a strong desire to work with children. This person must have a warm, nurturing and friendly personality, be sensitive to the feelings and needs of others, be able to relate well with children and be willing to fulfill her/his responsibilities in accordance with the Center's philosophy. Because infant care requires a team approach, this person must have a mature attitude that allows her/him to communicate effectively, problem solve and anticipate the needs of her/his fellow workers. An educational background in early childhood is preferred.

RESPONSIBILITIES

The head teacher is responsible for:

1. Being the communications liaison between the Center and the parents. All pertinent information about the Center should be relayed through the head teacher and/or directly through the Program Coordinator or Director.
2. Implementing the infant's schedule in accordance with the parents established schedule.
3. Ensuring that assistant infant teacher is kept informed on a daily basis of any changes in the babies' schedules.
4. Reporting daily events, changes in schedule, feeding times, food amounts, infant's health and sleeping habits to the aides so that continuity of care is maintained. (This can best be accomplished through the completion of end-of-shift report form.)
5. Completion of Daily Report Sheet during the course of her shift. This includes writing a general note about the infant's day.
6. Completion of monthly planning sheet. (This will be completed with aid of Program Coordinator.)
7. Completion of weekly anecdotal record sheet.
8. Arranging and planning for an environment that best meets the individual infant's developmental needs. This includes planning art and sensory activities along with providing variety of toys and gross motor equipment. Toys and equipment should be rotated approximately every two weeks.
9. Directly overseeing assistant infant teachers. Your role in the classroom is to act as a role model to assistants, to interject. When inappropriate behavior may cause immediate harm report to program coordinator or director inappropriate behaviors or general observations made about assistant. Your input is vital part of staff evaluation.
10. Completion of Infant Competency Profile Assessment Form. These should be completed preferably every three months but at least every six months.
11. Holding Parent Conferences. These should be held in conjunction with completion of the assessment form. These conferences are established so that you and the parents can meet together to establish goals for their infants.
12. Contributing equally in the housekeeping tasks of the infant area.

Director's Resource 9-1 (*continued*)

13. Being a competent member of the infant care team. This entails maintaining open communication between fellow team members, contributing equally in daily routine tasks, and being aware of the overall needs of the infant program and coming to lack others' aid as needed.
14. Attending all staff meetings, parent meetings and other mandatory or required in-services.
15. Maintaining confidentiality of children, parents and fellow staff members.
16. Dressing appropriately in accordance with the Center's established dress code policy.
17. Maintaining professional attitude and loyalty to the school at all times.
18. Lastly, you are responsible for knowing the policies of the program in regards to:
    a. communicable disease and exclusion of sick children
    b. first aid and medical emergency
    c. fire evacuation
    d. tornado and severe weather evacuation
    e. child abuse reporting
    f. discipline
    g. termination

Director's Resource 9-1 (*continued*)

JOB DESCRIPTION
ASSISTANT INFANT TEACHER

The person selected for this position will be responsible for the care and supervision of the three infants assigned to his/her* pod. She is directly responsible for working with the head teacher of that pod in order to insure continuity of care for the infants. However, because infant care does require the care-givers to work as a team, she will also be responsible for aiding in the care and supervision of all the infants in the program.

QUALIFICATIONS

The person selected for this position must be at least 18 years of age and have a strong desire to work with children. This person must have a warm, nurturing and friendly personality, be sensitive to the feelings and needs of others, be able to relate well with children and be willing to fulfill her responsi-bilities in accordance with the Center's philosophy. She must be willing to be a working member of the team to ensure that the children are cared for in a warm, safe and nurturing environment. Background in early childhood education or experience in working with infants is preferred.

RESPONSIBILITIES

1. You are expected to arrive at work at the scheduled time. If unable to come to work at the speci-fied time, you are expected to contact your supervisor as soon as you know so that arrangements can be made for a substitute.
2. You are responsible for knowing the policies of the program in regards to:
   a. communicable disease and exclusion of sick children
   b. first aid and medical emergency
   c. fire evacuation
   d. tornado and severe weather evacuation
   e. child abuse reporting
   f. discipline
   g. termination
3. You are expected to dress appropriately in compliance with the Center's dress code policy.
4. You are responsible for signing in and out on a daily basis. The bookkeeper will only pay you for the hours for which you have signed in.
5. Upon arrival, at the beginning of your shift, you are expected to get a report on your children from the head teacher of your assigned pod. A sample of the report is included in the orienta-tion manual.
6. You are responsible for aiding head teachers in the completion of their work so they can leave on a timely basis.
7. You are expected to keep open communication between head teacher, parents, supervisor, director and other team members.
8. You are responsible for equally aiding in the completion of the closing procedures. These include
   a. wash toys every day
   b. take out garbage from infant area and activity room
   c. vacuum activity room
   d. vacuum pods if necessary
   e. straighten pods and beds in pods
   f. mop activity room floor and infant floor if needed
   g. straighten toy shelves in activity room

Director's Resource 9-1 (*continued*)

    h. turn out lights

    i. turn off heaters/fans/air conditioner

9. Most importantly, you are accountable for your three children during the course of your shift. This includes:

    a. relaying information to parents about infant's day

    b. giving specific information to parents from head teacher and/or from the parents to the head teacher as the need arises

    c. charting on infants for all diaper changes, feeding, naps. This is very important information. To the parents, if it is not charted, then it was not done. At times, you may also be responsible for writing a general note about the infant's day. If the head teacher doesn't write this, then you should either remind them to do this or you should complete it yourself.

10. Attend all staff meetings, parent conferences and recommended required training programs.

11. Maintain professional attitude and loyalty to the school at all times.

12. Maintain confidentiality of the children and their parents. Failure to do this can result in termination of employments.

13. While you are primarily responsible for your three assigned babies, the infant teachers work as a team. This requires that you are also responsible for ensuring that each infant is well cared for in a safe and nurturing environment.

14. Several times a week, a head teacher will leave the classroom when you arrive at 2:00 P.M., so that she can work on assessment forms and planning. You are then responsible for the supervision of those children in her absence.

15. Lastly, because you are a vital member of the infant caregiving team, your input is very valuable. We expect for you to contribute any observations made during your time spent with the infants. These can be written as anecdotal records, verbally transmitted to the head teacher and/or stated during staff meetings.

Director's Resource 9-1 (*continued*)

JOB DESCRIPTION
ASSISTANT TEACHER—PRESCHOOL

QUALIFICATIONS

A person applying for this position must be at least 18 years of age, in the process of becoming professionally prepared to be a teacher of young children, and meet the requirements of the city and state licensing agencies. This person must have a warm and friendly personality, be sensitive to the feelings and needs of others and be able to relate well to children. In addition he/she must be willing to fulfill his/her responsibilities in accordance with the Center's educational philosophy.

RESPONSIBILITIES

- Assisting in planning and implementing the daily program under the direction of the head teacher
- Assisting in planning and preparing the learning environment, setting up interest centers, and preparing needed materials and supplies
- Supervising the classroom when the teacher is out of the room
- Helping with the general housekeeping tasks
- Assisting the teacher in any other appropriate way
- Maintaining professional attitudes and loyalty to the program at all times
- Treating all of the children with dignity and respect
- Attending all staff meetings and recommended training programs and conferences
- Participating in professional organizations that work toward the improvement of early childhood education

Director's Resource 9-1 (*continued*)

JOB DESCRIPTION
COOK

Responsible to the Director

Requirements: previous experience cooking for large groups and be able to demonstrate knowledge of basic math.

The person hired to prepare meals will be able to:

- work cooperatively with teaching staff and communicate with and be sensitive to children and their needs
- read and follow directions successfully
- finish projects promptly
- be able to prepare alternates in menu planning in the event of an emergency
- list food proportions
- prepare morning breakfast, lunch and afternoon snacks
- prepare all meals according to USDA requirements
- discuss any changes that might be made in menus and food purchases
- keep the kitchen clean at all times (mop floors, clean refrigerator, freezer, stove, cabinets and food storage areas)
- put dishes away neatly and keep inventory of dishes and utensils
- purchase all food from local stores and prepare food order
- encourage good health habits and nutrition with children when cooking
- answer the telephone according to the standards of the Center
- call the night before if ill

Director's Resource 9-2

Sample Personnel Policies and Job Descriptions—The Christ Child Day Nursery

THE CHRIST CHILD DAY NURSERY

PERSONNEL POLICIES

August 19__

Revised: December 19__

January 19__

August 19__

Reprinted by permission of Christ Child Day Nursery

Director's Resource 9-2 (*continued*)

INTRODUCTION

The aim of the Christ Child Day Nursery is to establish a
warm, constructive relationship with young children whose homes
are broken or unsuitable, whose parents or guardians must work,
or who lack supervision or adequate stimulation for learning.
It recognizes the necessity of trying to maintain a meaningful
relationship with those parents or guardians.

The first obligation of professional workers is to the agency,
members of the community who support the agency and the neighborhood served by the agency. A staff position in a community service
agency means for the workers at least 40 hours per week of full-time
dedication to top-level performance of their responsibilities and
a constant seeking of how those responsibilities can more effectively serve the children and parents they seek to help. Workers
must recognize that this means continuous high quality of service
and flexibility within the accepted work schedule.

A worker has the responsibility, above and beyond any listed
on a "work schedule," of establishing and maintaining good working
relationships with the interdependent parts of the agency: Board,
Administration, Clients, Volunteers, other professional and non-
professional staff, and particularly, the Children's Federation of
the Community Health and Welfare Council, the Cincinnati Association
for the Education of Young Children of the Ohio Department of Public
Welfare, the Division of Social Administration Child Welfare Service,
and other groups who are endeavoring to work toward the good of the
child and his family which is also the goal of the agency.

Professional workers are under obligation to exercise judgment
in expressing views on broad community problems and issues. At
such times as they speak on such problems and issues they should
identify clearly whether they are speaking as individual citizens
or as representatives of their agency, remembering also that they
are to speak for the agency only when generally or specifically
authorized to do so.

The board has recognized the rights of the staff and dignified the employment relationship through written personnel policies,
job classifications and pay plans. Information concerning these
matters is made available to all employees upon accepted application.

Director's Resource 9-2 (*continued*)

There is no discrimination in employment with regard to race, creed, political affiliation, marital status, sex or number of dependents. A staff which is representative of both men and women and of varied religious, racial and cultural backgrounds is to be encouraged for the good of the children, their parents, and the community, as well as that of the staff itself.

Purpose of these Personnel Policies

An effective program of service to the community requires joint participation of the Board, Staff, and appropriate community agencies in the operation of the Day Care Center. Written personnel policies help to achieve such cooperation.

The Board, representing the community, is the body with ultimate administrative authority. In practice, however, it is necessary for the good of the clients and the agency that the Board function as a policy-making and planning body. The Board delegates to a Director the responsibility for the day-to-day administration, and to the staff, through the Director, responsibility for the practices of the agency.

Administration of Personnel Policies

1.   The Personnel Committee

The Personnel Committee of the Board will have responsibility for the general administration of the personnel policies for the agency. Members of this committee and its Chairman, who must be a Board member, will be appointed by the President of the Board. The President of the Board will be a voting member of this committee. The Chairman, or a substitute appointed by the Committee, will preside at all meetings of the Committee, will have a vote, and will make all committee reports and recommendations to the Board. There will be close cooperation between the Personnel Committee and the staff.

The Committee will review the statement of personnel policies every five years or as conditions change and will suggest such changes as seem necessary to the Board for its consideration.

2.   The Director

To the Director is delegated direct responsibility for the administration of personnel policies. She (he) will see to it that the statement of personnel policies is at all times available to the staff and candidates for position on the staff. Each member of the staff shall be given a copy of the personnel policies,

Director's Resource 9-2 (*continued*)

and after reading it thoroughly, shall sign a statement that
he or she has read and understood the policies and realized
his or her obligation to carry out these policies under the
direction of the Director.

3.   Staff Positions

    (a) Full-time salaried employees are those who work 35
hours or more a week and who are paid a designated amount a
year.

    (b) Half-time employees are those who work between 20
and 35 hours a week as the job requires, and who are also paid
a designated amount a year.

    (c) Hourly-paid workers are paid a designated rate per
hour.

4.   Basis for Computing a Day's Pay

    Using the basis of 20 working days a month, not including
Saturdays, Sundays and holidays, the daily rate of pay is
computed 1/20 of the monthly salary rate regardless of the number
of days in any given month.

5.   The Employment Date

    The employment date, which determines vacation time, sick
leave, eligibility for retirement participation and compensation,
is the date on which the employee reports for duty.

6.   Salary Increases

    Salary increases will generally coincide with the beginning
of a new fiscal year, dependent on the money budgeted by the
Community Chest for this agency. The present fiscal year is
computed as January 1 to December 31. Therefore, an evaluation
of the work of each employee should be made during the month of
November by the Director, who will report her findings to the
Personnel Committee. However, evaluations may be made at any time
the Board and the Personnel Committee deem it advisable.

Policies Regulating Employment

1.   Procedure

    It shall be the responsibility of the Personnel Committee
to require and check written references for all prospective
employees. This responsibility may be delegated to the Director.

Director's Resource 9-2 (*continued*)

A.   The <u>Director</u>.   The employment of a Director, to whom
administrative responsibility is delegated by the Board of
Directors, is a function of the Board.

In the event of a vacancy in the position, the Personnel
Committee, as a committee of the Board charged with this special
responsibility, will as far as possible, utilize the service of
the Children's Federation of the Community Health and Welfare
Council, as well as other appropriate agencies, in recruiting
candidates for the position, will contact candidates, evaluate
their qualifications and make recommendations to the Board for
Board action.

Acceptance of the resignation or the dismissal of the
Director is by the Board of Directors, acting upon the recommendation of the Personnel Committee.

Appointment of a Director shall be upon the basis of
qualifications and demonstrated competence for the position.
These shall include, preferably, training in early childhood
education at an approved school, and social work orientation;
experience in a day care center or in the day care field in which
she has demonstrated ability to coordinate and integrate the
various areas of the agency program; and supervisory experience.

B.   <u>Professional and Maintenance Staff</u>.   The Director has
responsibility for the employment of staff.   In selecting candidates for recommendation for employment, the Director will use the
recognized professional consultative employment resources.   Qualifications for a staff position shall include demonstrated competence
and skill for the specific position to be filled.

A personal interview with the Director and/or the Personnel
Committee is considered part of regular employment procedure.

The Director has the responsibility for giving the prospective employee information concerning both the organization and
program of the agency, as well as defining the requirements and
conditions of employment relative to the specific position for
which he or she is applying.

The prospective employee has the responsibility for giving
the Director facts concerning training, experience, individual
interests, capacities, special skills, and at least 2 outside
references, preferably from former employees.   Also, it is expected
that any factors which might hinder effectiveness in the job will
also be presented.

Director's Resource 9-2 (*continued*)

When a staff member is hired, it is the Director's responsibility to authorize a letter to the employee and to the Community Chest to confirm the appointment and conditions of employment. A copy of this letter will be placed in the employee's file.

A probationary period of three months (90 days) will be required of all new employees in order to determine whether or not the arrangements are mutually satisfactory. During this time, either party may terminate the agreement upon written notice to the other party. At the end of the probationary period, the worker's performance shall be evaluated in writing by the Director, shared with the employee, and a copy placed in the employee's file.

Appointments to the staff are reported to the Board by the Director.

2.   Job Classification and Salary Range

A job description and salary range for each agency position is included as part of an appendix to these policies. These positions and salary ranges will be reviewed every five years or as conditions change, by the Personnel Committee.

3.   Evaluations

Annual evaluations shall be used as a basis for continued employment, promotion, salary changes, demotion or dismissal, and for references. Each employee's evaluation shall be discussed with him, and a copy placed in his file. It is the responsibility of the Personnel Committee to evaluate the work of the Director. It is the responsibility of the Director to evaluate all members of the staff and to present these evaluations to the Personnel Committee.

4.   Promotions

Promotion from one job classification to another is based upon the staff member's preparation, ability, qualifications and willingness to assume the new job. Other factors being equal, staff vacancies will be filled by the promotion of agency staff members.

The number of staff positions in each job classification at a given time shall be determined by the Personnel Committee in conference with the Director. These will be selected in terms of the extent and nature of the services required of the agency by the community.

Director's Resource 9-2 (*continued*)

5. <u>Salary</u>

Salaries and salary increases are dependent upon the money appropriated to the agency by the Community Chest and are determined by the Budget Committee in conjunction with the Personnel Committee, and the Director. Any increases are based on the annual evaluations of the staff members.

6. <u>Review of Grievances</u>

The procedure for consideration and adjustment of grievance of any member of the staff shall be as follows: The staff member will consult with the Director. Failing to reach settlement in conference with the Director, the staff member will submit a written statement of the situation to the Chairman of the Personnel Committee requesting that the grievance be reviewed by the Committee. A copy of this statement will be given by the worker to the Director also. The Personnel Committee will review the grievance and report with recommendations to the Board for action.

7. <u>Vacation Privileges at Termination of Employment</u>

When employment with this agency is terminated <u>by the employee</u> according to the terms set forth in this statement, the employee shall receive vacation pay earned up to the time of termination so long as he or she has been employed by the agency for a period of at least two years.

Suggested policy re:
1. <u>Vacations</u>

Accumulation of vacation time for salaried employees begins upon the date of employment. Vacations shall be computed to the nearest 1/2 month of employment. The employee must use all time earned for vacation each year and at one time. Sometimes this may not be convenient or even possible for the employee or the agency. Vacations may then be divided when planned in advance consultation with the Director.

If the Nursery closes for a definite period during the summer, all vacations shall be taken at that time. If the Nursery remains open all summer, vacation schedules shall be worked out by the Director who will take into consideration the smooth running of the Nursery, the seniority, and the convenience of each worker.

Only earned vacations shall be granted with pay. Vacation time for professional and maintenance personnel is computed as follows:

Director's Resource 9-2 (*continued*)

A. Professional Staff:

At least six months' service before any vacation is taken. In each year, one day is earned by each month until 10 work days (2 weeks) are accumulated.

For those who have given five full years of service: 1-1/4 work days of vacation time are accumulated up to a maximum of 15 work days (3 weeks).

After 10 full years of service, four weeks vacation will be given.

B. Non-Professional:

At least six months' service before any vacation is taken. Vacations will be computed on this basis: One work day for each month of service up to the maximum of 10 work days (two weeks).

No vacation time is provided for temporary employees.

2. Holidays

Holidays granted with pay are: New Year's Day, Memorial Day, Fourth of July, Labor Day, Thanksgiving Day and the day following, and Christmas.

3. Leaves

A. Sick Leave: The sick leave policy is a plan to protect employees from financial loss during illness. This is a privilege, not a right; consequently, unused sick leave shall not be payable upon termination of employment or at any other time and may not be used to extend vacations or for personal business. The Director shall have the privilege of contacting the employee's physician.

After three months' service, one day of sick leave is earned for each month of service until a maximum of 12 days sick leave per annum has been accumulated. Accumulated sick leave does not carry over from year to year. Actual leave will be deducted from accumulated sick leave earned.

Deductions cannot be made at any time in amounts greater than accumulation. Sick leave may not be used for any absence other than illness or accident liability of the employee. Excess sick leave may be deducted from vacation credit or from the pay period in which the absence occurred, as preferred by the employee.

Director's Resource 9-2 (*continued*)

B. Leave for Personal Business: Leaves of absence with pay in the case of death or serious illness of an immediate member of the family shall be allowed on a limited basis, to be worked out with the Director, who shall have the privilege of contacting the doctor.

Leaves of absence for personal business, other than in case of illness or death, will be planned with and approved by the Director and will be deducted from salary.

C. Maternity Leave: An employee may work during pregnancy as long as she is able to fulfill the requirements of her job as evaluated by the Director, and the employee's physician. An employee shall be given a maximum of six months maternity leave without pay.

D. Personnel Development: For professional stimulation, continued development of staff and agency programs, attendance at professional meetings, courses, conferences, and seminars, is desirable. An educational fund for career development will be made available to staff members for enrollment. All arrangements must be made with the approval of the Director.

4. Tenure

Tenure in all jobs and positions will be dependent upon satisfactory performance.

5. Termination of Employment and Demotions

A. Resignation: Notice of resignation shall be in writing, delivered in advance of the date of termination as follows:

Director:	At least 90 days (delivered to the President of the Board of Directors).
Professional Staff:	At least 30 days (delivered to Director).
Non-Professional Staff:	At least 14 days (delivered to Director).

At the time of the staff member's leaving, it is expected that the work of the staff member who is leaving be brought up to date so that his or her successor can readily take over.

Director's Resource 9-2 (*continued*)

B. Dismissals: The Board of Directors, upon the recommendation of the Personnel Committee, is responsible for the dismissal of the Director.

The Director shall have the right to dismiss employees for any of the following reasons. However, she should consult with the Personnel Committee of the Board on matters pertaining to paragraphs 1 and 3 below. In case of dismissal for any reason, the employee is entitled to a written explanation and may utilize the approved grievance procedure outlined in 6 on Page 6.   (Review of Grievances)

1. Malfeasance. Definition: Malfeasance connotes a serious behavior problem. It has broad interpretations but would indicate a major problem, such as theft, acts in the community of a totally unprofessional nature, drunkenness, a criminal offense, assault on a child at the Nursery or any member of the staff or any persons on the Nursery premises, and so forth. Misappropriation of funds or willful damage to the agency's property also warrants dismissal. Misconduct more minor in degree could warrant dismissal.

Conditions: No dismissal notice shall be required and the employee shall forfeit all privileges relating to vacation.

2. Incompetence: Definition: Incompetence shall be measured in terms of such factors as:

1) Inadequacy of the employee's personality for sound relationships with the membership, volunteers, staff, supervisors, Board.

2) Lack of growth and progress on the job.

3) Little skill in the performance of duties.

4) No understanding or acceptance of the philosophy and purpose of the agency.

5) Poor professional community relationships.

6) Absenteeism and lack of punctuality.

These factors shall be weighed in relation to the extent that each applies to the job in question.

Director's Resource 9-2 (*continued*)

Conditions: When the work of a staff member appears to be unsatisfactory, the staff member shall receive an evaluation of her performance in conference, to be followed by a reasonable opportunity for improvement. The period for improvement shall be specified and shall not exceed one month for professional employees, and two weeks for non-professional employees. If, at the end of the period, the Director finds the worker incompetent, notice of dismissal shall be given. Dismissal notice shall be one month for professional and two weeks for non-professional employees. Accrued vacation pay shall be granted.

3. Reorganization and Retrenchment: Definition: Reorganization shall be considered to include any change in the philosophy, purpose, organization, program or technique of the agency, or of one of its departments, which alters the job in question, changes job requirements, eliminates a position, or results in the creation of a newly defined position, and which provides no suitable place for the person concerned. Retrenchment shall cover the elimination or refunction in the working schedule of a position, arising from organizational or program changes in the agency necessitated by insufficiency of funds.

Conditions: It is assumed that the Board, upon recommendation of the Personnel Committee and the Director, will give as much notice as possible with a minimum of one month for professional workers dismissed on this basis and of two weeks for full-time non-professional employees. It is suggested that severance pay amount to one week's salary. In the event of dismissals for these causes, the agency shall give first consideration to the dismissed staff member in filling another position when it becomes available for which the worker is qualified, and shall make every effort to assist her in securing another position.

Any plan for retrenchment and reorganization shall be discussed thoroughly by the Board and the Personnel Committee and their decisions explained to the staff.

4. Retirement: Retirement generally is to be considered at 65 years of age, but the length of employment may be extended at the discretion of the Director and the Board.

Employee Benefit Plans

Members of the staff receive more than a bi-weekly pay check. Besides paid vacation, holiday and sick leave benefits, the Nursery has a number of other employee benefit plans as a Community Chest agency; some required, others optional.

The required plans are these:

Director's Resource 9-2 (*continued*)

National Health and Welfare Retirement Insurance

The National Health and Retirement Association is a non-profit organization established to insure benefits for personnel of non-profit health and welfare agencies throughout the country. The Retirement Plan will provide a guaranteed income for life directly related to earnings, after retirement.

An employee will become eligible and must become a member on the next month after he first meets the eligibility requirements. For information on this plan, see the brochure from the Community Chest. This brochure is available from the Director upon request.

Social Security

Participation in the Federal Old Age and Survivors Insurance program is required by law and salary deductions will be made accordingly. To cover the cost of paying benefits to an increasing number of people, the law provides for gradual increases in the Social Security rates. The Finance Department will explain the details of the present program to any interested person.

Worker's Compensation

All employees are covered by the provisions of the Ohio Workman's Compensation Law. It is the employee's responsibility to report immediately to the Director any accident or injury resulting from his employment at the Christ Child Day Nursery.

Unemployment Compensation

Unemployment compensation is governed by the agreement between the Christ Child Day Nursery and the Community Chest of the Cincinnati Area, relevant to non-profit organizations in Ohio. (Effective January 1, 19_)

The optional plans are these:

Hospital Care and Blue Shield Plans

At the time of employment, an employee will be given an opportunity to enroll in the Hospital Care and Blue Shield plans. These are non-profit insurance plans to help take care of hospital and surgical expenses for the employee and his family. To take advantage of these plans, an employee makes payments through payroll deduction. Enrollment cards will be provided by the Community Chest. If an employee does not enroll at the time of his initial employment, he must wait until the once-a-year "open period," usually in the fall.

Director's Resource 9-2 (*continued*)

Christ Child Day Nursery

Job Description

Director

Hours: 9:30 - 5:30

Responsible to the Board of Directors of Christ Child Day Nursery
for day-to-day operation of entire school.

A.   Staff - professional and non-professional

1. Hire necessary replacements when vacancies occur.
2. Supervise educational program of all classrooms.
3. Hold staff meetings.
4. Provide in-service training through this agency and
    utilizing training available through other institutions
    in the community.
5. Hold individual conferences with staff members as
    necessary.
6. Make written evaluation of all staff members once a year
    and discuss individually with each employee.
7. Maintain overall goals and objectives of agency; enforce
    personnel policies.
8. Introduce new staff members to the Board at Board Meeting.

B.   Building

1. Supervise general condition and upkeep of building.
2. Maintain license requirements for building; keep all
    licences current.
3. Supervise closing of building at end of each school day.

C.   Office

1. Pay bills through Community Chest of Cincinnati; keep
    President of Board of Directors and Treasurer informed
    of monthly financial status of the school.
2. Keep attendance records of staff, children, NYC students;
    check on reasons for absence when necessary.
3. Open and handle all mail.
4. Answer telephone whenever possible; handle all phone
    inquiries and other general school business.
5. Collect service fees from parents and deposit in appro-
    priate Community Chest account; keep records of all fee
    payments.

Director's Resource 9-2 (*continued*)

---

    6. Pick up staff paychecks at Community Chest bi-monthly and distribute.
    7. Authorize any salary increases, overtime pay, pay deductions with the Finance Department of the Community Chest.
    8. Keep up to date medical files on staff and children; comply with Board of Health regulations.
    9. Order school and building supplies.
   10. File weekly attendance report to Hamilton County Welfare Department Day Care Unit.
   11. File monthly food reimbursement forms to U.S. Dept. of Agriculture.
   12. File monthly report of purchased services to Hamilton County Welfare Department.

D. Parents

    1. Interview all parents enrolling children in school.
    2. Be available for telephone and/or personal parent conferences whenever necessary.
    3. Attend all parent meetings and assist in planning and execution of all parent functions.
    4. Supervise preparation and distribution of all children's progress reports to parents 3 times per year (Oct., Feb., June).
    5. Collect fees from parents; re-evaluate set fees when necessary.
    6. Encourage parent participation as part of classroom activities as well as parent group functions.

E. Cook and kitchen

    1. Discuss and assist in planning of meals.
    2. Authorize ordering of food and kitchen supplies.
    3. Check for cleanliness and upkeep of kitchen facility.

F. Meetings

    1. Staff.
    2. Board of Directors (monthly).
    3. Community Chest of Cincinnati.
    4. Parents group.
    5. Other.

G. General

    1. Maintain neat and clean physical appearance.
    2. Notify school in event of illness and place one teacher in charge of the agency.
    3. Work with all staff members and persons affiliated with the Christ Child Day Nursery in a cooperative manner.
    4. Follow the personnel policies of the Christ Child Day Nursery.

Director's Resource 9-2 (*continued*)

Christ Child Day Nursery

Job Description

Head Teacher

Hours: 8 hours per day

General responsibilities:

1. Maintain prompt hours; notify Director in event of illness.
2. Maintain neat and clean appearance.
3. Work with all other staff members in a cooperative manner.
4. Attend staff meetings; report problems of child or room management to the Director promptly.
5. Attend in-service training whenever possible; keep up to date on developments in the field of early childhood education.
6. Follow personnel policies of Christ Child Day Nursery.

Head teacher responsibilities:

1. Assume responsibility for operation of the agency in the absence of the Director.
2. Assume responsibility for planning and seeking out in-service training opportunities for teaching staff with the approval of the Director.
3. Maintain close contact with the Board of Directors in the event of extended absence of a Director.
4. Assist Director whenever necessary.

Classroom responsibilities:

1. Provide planning and execution of appropriate early childhood education experiences with a variety of materials in the fields of art, music, literature, science, mathematics, etc.
2. Promote and supervise activities which promote the healthly emotional, social, intellectual, and physical development of each child.
3. Provide and maintain a neat organized classroom; take responsibility for upkeep of all educational equipment and materials.
4. Eat all meals with the children and assist in development of good nutrition habits.
5. Maintain records of progress of each child's growth and development; prepare progress reports on each child three times per year (Oct., Feb., June) and discuss report with Director and each child's parent or guardian.

Director's Resource 9-2 (*continued*)

6. Work with parents whenever possible to promote understanding of growth and development of their child in
   school; encourage parent participation in school programs
   whenever possible; be available for parent conferences
   whenever necessary; attend parent group and other school
   functions whenever possible.

7. Supervise all activities to insure safety of each child
   at all times.

Director's Resource 9-2 (*continued*)

Christ Child Day Nursery

Job Description

Teacher

Hours: 8 hours per day

General responsibilities:

1. Maintain prompt hours; notify Director and school in event of illness.
2. Maintain neat and clean appearance.
3. Work with all other staff members in a cooperative manner.
4. Attend staff meetings; report problems of child or room management to the Director promptly.
5. Attend in-service training whenever possible; keep up to date on developments in field of early childhood education.
6. Follow personnel policies of Christ Child Day Nursery.

Classroom responsibilities:

1. Provide planning and execution of appropriate early childhood education experiences with a variety of materials in fields of art, music, literature, science, mathematics.
2. Promote and supervise activities which promote the healthly emotional, social, intellectual, and physical development of each child.
3. Provide and maintain a neat organized classroom; take responsibility for upkeep of all educational equipment and materials.
4. Eat all meals with children and assist in development of good nutrition habits.
5. Maintain records of progress of each child's growth and development; prepare progress reports on each child 3 times per year (Oct., Feb., June) and discuss report with Director and child's parent or guardian.
6. Work with parents whenever possible to promote understanding of growth and development of their child in school; encourage parent participation in school programs whenever possible; be available for parent conferences whenever necessary; attend parent group and other school functions whenever possible.
7. Supervise all activities to insure safety of each child at all times.

Director's Resource 9-2 (*continued*)

Christ Child Day Nursery

Job Description

Teacher Assistant

Hours: Full time - 8 hours per day; part time - 4 to 6 hours.

General responsibilities:

1. Maintain prompt hours; notify Director and school
   in event of illness.
2. Maintain neat and clean appearance.
3. Work with all other staff members in a cooperative
   manner.
4. Attend staff meetings; report problems of child or
   room management to teacher and Director, if necessary.
5. Attend in-service training when possible and work to
   increase skills in field of early childhood education.
6. Follow personnel policies of Christ Child Day Nursery.

Classroom responsibilities:

1. Assist teacher in providing appropriate early childhood
   education experiences for the children in art, music,
   literature, etc.
2. Assist in promoting and supervising the healthy
   emotional, social, intellectual, and physical development of each child.
3. Assist in arrangement and upkeep of classroom and
   all classroom equipment and materials.
4. Eat all meals with children and assist in development
   of good nutrition habits.
5. Help children establish good habits of toileting and
   personal hygiene.
6. Assist in supervising all activities to insure safety
   of each child at all times.
7. Attend parent group and other school activities whenever
   possible.

Director's Resource 9-2 (*continued*)

Christ Child Day Nursery

Job Description

Cook

Hours: 7:30 - 3:30

Daily:

1. Prepare breakfast.
2. Wash breakfast dishes.
3. Prepare morning snack.
4. Wash snack glasses.
5. Prepare lunch.
6. Clean up lunch dishes and trays.
7. Prepare afternoon snack.

General:

1. Prepare menus and food orders and check them with Director.
2. Supervise putting away of all food orders.
3. Clean kitchen cupboards and closets as necessary.
4. Clean stove and refrigerator as necessary.
5. Maintain neat and clean physical appearance.
6. Work with all other staff members in a cooperative manner.
7. Maintain prompt hours; notify Director and school in event of illness.
8. Attend staff meetings when necessary.
9. Follow personnel policies of Christ Child Day Nursery.

Director's Resource 9-2 (*continued*)

Christ Child Day Nursery

Job Description

Housekeeper

Hours: 9:00 - 5:00

Daily:

1. Wash the laundry.
2. Wash cot covers.
3. Keep laundry room neat and clean.
4. Clean bathroom toilets.
5. Clean sinks.
6. Vacuum front and back stairs.
7. Keep hallways and other public areas of building neat and clean.
8. Wash afternoon snack glasses and put on trays.

Twice a week:

1. Clean and dust office.

Once a week:

1. Clean off woodwork on stairways, around doors and windows.
2. Wash inside of kitchen windows.
3. Clean Board room.

Every three months:

1. Clean radiator covers with mild soap and water.

Other:

When necessary:
1. Assist in classrooms with children.
2. Assist in clean up of classrooms and cupboards throughout building.
3. Assist in putting away canned goods and meat orders.
4. Notify cook and/or Director when cleaning and other household supplies need to be ordered.

General:

1. Attend staff meetings when necessary.
2. Maintain prompt hours, notify Director and school in event of illness.
3. Maintain neat and clean appearance.
4. Work with all other staff members in a cooperative manner.
5. Follow personnel policies of Christ Child Day Nursery.

Director's Resource 9-2 (*continued*)

Christ Child Day Nursery

Job Description

Janitor

Hours: Part time, 6 hours per day.

Daily:

1. Wash kitchen floor thoroughly.
2. Wash bathroom floors thoroughly.
3. Empty trash cans.
4. Bring out playground toys, weather permitting.

Weekly:

1. Wash all classroom floors and rooms where children eat.
2. Sweep or hose front and back outside walks, around trash cans, and playground. (In winter, put salt down on ice.)
3. Sweep out basement and basement steps.
4. Wash out trash baskets.
5. Put out trash for trash collectors and bring in empty cans.

Monthly:

1. Wax classroom floors.
2. Sweep out third floor.
3. Clean out basement.
4. Dust - tops of light fixtures, window shades, walls and ceilings.

When necessary:

1. Replace burnt out light bulbs.
2. Move furniture within the building.
3. Small repair jobs.

Follow personnel policies of Christ Child Day Nursery.

Director's Resource 9-3

Interview Questions*

DEGREED CANDIDATE
1. Tell us about your past experiences in this field—both your previous work experience and/or your practicum placements.
2. Of all the theories and ideas you studied in school, what had the greatest impact on you with regards to discipline in the classroom?
3. How do you think children learn? Give an example of how you would set up an experience for learning about a simple machine like an inclined plane or a pulley.
4. What would you do when an irate parent approaches you about an incident (such as biting in the classroom)? How would you handle that?
5. How would you handle problem solving in the classroom? For example, if two children are arguing over a basket of Legos, each saying she had it first, what would you do?
6. Choose an area of the curriculum (ex. science, math, music, etc.). Tell us how you would set it up.
7. How do you view your role as a preschool teacher?
8. What would you strive for in a parent/caregiver relationship?
9. What do you see as strong points in our program? Weak points?
10. How do you feel about themes when planning a curriculum?
11. How do you feel separation issues should be handled? For example, a child comes in with a special toy from home and he is very reluctant to have Mom leave him. How might you handle that situation?
12. What are your long-term professional goals?
13. Since consistency is important in every program, how do you feel about committing to one year here?

NON-DEGREED CANDIDATE
1. Tell us about your experience in the field of early childhood education, as well as any other work experience you have had.
2. What do you see as your particular strengths which would apply to a position like this?
3. What are your professional goals? Would you be willing to attend some training sessions in the fall?
4. How would you handle an irate parent who approaches you at the end of the day when the teacher has gone?
5. If two children are arguing over Legos, each saying she had them first, what would you do?
6. What do you see as your role in the classroom?
7. What do you think the purpose of child care should be?
8. How would you handle a situation where a child has just knocked down another child's block building?
9. How do you think discipline is different from punishment?
10. What did you see during your tour of our center which you particularly liked? What were some of your questions as you toured the classroom?
11. What special skills and abilities do you feel you can bring to our program?

* Adapted and used by permission from Roark Learning Centers, Cincinnati, OH.

Director's Resource 9-4

Sample Staffing Plan—Infant Program

The sample staffing schedule offered here can be used to staff a small program or an individual class in a larger program. Guidelines for its use in programs with varying numbers of children follow. This schedule assumes a 1:3 adult-child ratio, for twelve infants.

Schedule for one classroom of 12 infants

B = paid rest break of 15 minutes   Lunch = unpaid lunch break of 30 minutes
. . . = 15-minute intervals (i.e., 8:15, 8:30, 8:45)

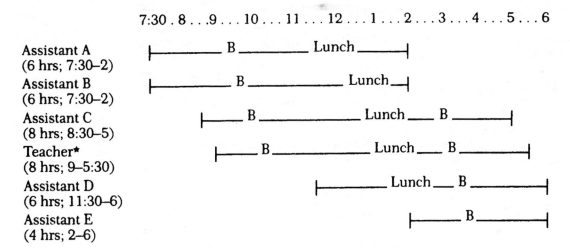

```
                    7:30 . 8 . . .9 . . . 10 . . . 11 . . . 12 . . . 1 . . . 2 . . . 3 . . . 4 . . . 5 . . . 6

Assistant A              |————————— B —————————— Lunch ——————|
(6 hrs; 7:30–2)

Assistant B              |————————— B —————————— Lunch —|
(6 hrs; 7:30–2)

Assistant C                    |——————— B ——————————— Lunch ———— B ————————|
(8 hrs; 8:30–5)

Teacher*                            |——————— B ——————————— Lunch ——— B ————————|
(8 hrs; 9–5:30)

Assistant D                                    |————————— Lunch ——— B ————————|
(6 hrs; 11:30–6)

Assistant E                                          |—————————— B —————————|
(4 hrs; 2–6)
```

* These 8 teacher hours may be covered by more than one qualified teacher.
Note: This schedule shows child care staff only. Hours for administration and housekeeper or other maintenance personnel are not included.

(Linda Gordon, "Staffing Schedules," in Annabelle Godwin and Lorraine Schrag (co-chairs), *Setting Up for Infant Care: Guidelines for Centers and Family Day Care Homes*, NAEYC, 1988, p. 50.)

Director's Resource 9-5

Sample Staffing Plan—Multiple Program A

STAFF PLAN BY GROUP

HOURS OF STAFF MEMBER

(8) INFANTS

CO-HEAD TEACHERS
1. 7:15-4:15
   15-MINUTE BREAK 9:45-10:00
   45-MINUTE PERSONAL TIME 1:30-2:15
2. 9:30-6:30
   45-MINUTE PERSONAL TIME 2:15-3:00
   15-MINUTE BREAK 4:00-4:15

PART-TIME STAFF

1. 7:15-11:00 INFANT ROOM
   15-MINUTE BREAK 11:00-11:15
   11:15-12:30 ASSISTANT TO THE COOK OR FLOATER IF NEEDED
2. 1:15-6:30 INFANT ROOM
   15-MINUTE BREAK 3:30-3:45

(10) TODDLERS

CO-HEAD TEACHERS
1. 7:15-4:15
   15-MINUTE BREAK 9:45-10:00
   45-MINUTE PERSONAL TIME 1:30-2:15

2. 9:30-6:30
   45-MINUTE PERSONAL TIME 2:15-3:00
   15-MINUTE BREAK 11:15-11:30

PART-TIME STAFF
1. 7:15-12:30
   15-MINUTE BREAK 10:15-10:30

2. 1:15-6:30
   15-MINUTE BREAK 3:30-3:45

(24) THREE-YEAR-OLDS

TWO (2) HEAD TEACHERS
1. 7:15-4:15
   15-MINUTE BREAK 10:00-10:15
   45-MINUTE PERSONAL TIME 1:15-2:00

(Reprinted by permission of Nola Jacobs, Selan Springer, and Mary Gallagher)

Director's Resource 9-5 (*continued*)

2. 9:30-6:30
    15-MINUTE BREAK 11:15-11:30
    45-MINUTE PERSONAL TIME 2:00-2:45

TWO (2) TEACHERS
1A. 9:30-6:30
    15-MINUTE BREAK 11:00-11:15
    45-MINUTE PERSONAL TIME 2:00-2:45

2B. 7:15-4:15
    15-MINUTE BREAK 10:15-10:30
    45-MINUTE PERSONAL TIME 1:15-2:00

(28) FOUR-YEAR-OLDS

TWO (2) HEAD TEACHERS
1A. 7:15-4:15
    15-MINUTE BREAK 10:00-10:15
    45-MINUTE PERSONAL TIME 1:15-2:00

2B. 9:30-6:30
    15-MINUTE BREAK 11:15-11:30
    45-MINUTE PERSONAL TIME 2:00-2:45

TWO (2) TEACHERS
1A. 9:30-6:30
    15-MINUTE BREAK 11:00-11:15
    45-MINUTE PERSONAL TIME 2:00-2:45

2B. 7:15-4:15
    15-MINUTE BREAK 10:15-10:30
    45-MINUTE PERSONAL TIME 1:15-2:00

OTHER STAFF MEMBERS

DIRECTOR
7:00-4:00
1-HOUR LUNCH 12:-1:00

ASSISTANT DIRECTOR
1:30-6:30

COOK/NUTRITIONIST
8:30-1:30
COOK HAS 15-MINUTE BREAK FOR PERSONAL TIME CAN BE TAKEN AT HER CONVENIENCE

MAINTENANCE PERSON
6:30 P.M.-9:30 P.M.
SATURDAYS-9:00 A.M.-2:00 P.M.

Director's Resource 9-5 (*continued*)

STAFF PLAN GRAPH

INFANT STAFFING HOURS GRAPH—1

==============================

	H.T.1	H.T.2	P.T.1	P.T.2
7:00				
	XXXXX		XXXXX	
	XXXXX		XXXXX	
	XXXXX		XXXXX	
8:00	XXXXX	XXXXX		
	XXXXX		XXXXX	
	XXXXX		XXXXX	
	XXXXX		XXXXX	
9:00	XXXXX		XXXXX	
	XXXXX		XXXXX	
	XXXXX	XXXXX	XXXXX	
	/////	XXXXX	XXXXX	
10:00	XXXXX	XXXXX	XXXXX	
	XXXXX	XXXXX	XXXXX	
	XXXXX	XXXXX	XXXXX	
	XXXXX	XXXXX	XXXXX	
11:00	XXXXX	XXXXX	XXXXX	
	XXXXX	XXXXX		
	XXXXX	XXXXX		
	XXXXX	XXXXX		
12:00	XXXXX	XXXXX		
	XXXXX	XXXXX		
	XXXXX	XXXXX		
	XXXXX	XXXXX		
1:00	XXXXX	XXXXX		
	XXXXX	XXXXX		XXXXX
	/////	XXXXX		XXXXX
	/////	XXXXX		XXXXX
2:00	/////	XXXXX		XXXXX
	XXXXX	/////		XXXXX
	XXXXX	/////		XXXXX
	XXXXX	/////		XXXXX
3:00	XXXXX	XXXXX		XXXXX
	XXXXX	XXXXX		XXXXX
	XXXXX	XXXXX		/////
	XXXXX	XXXXX		XXXXX
4:00	XXXXX	/////		XXXXX
	XXXXX	XXXXX		XXXXX
		XXXXX		XXXXX
		XXXXX		XXXXX
5:00		XXXXX		XXXXX
		XXXXX		XXXXX
		XXXXX		XXXXX
		XXXXX		XXXXX
6:00		XXXXX		XXXXX
		XXXXX		XXXXX
		XXXXX		XXXXX
7:00				

Director's Resource 9-5 (*continued*)

```
                    INFANT STAFFING HOURS GRAPH--2
                    ==============================

            H.T.1         H.T.2         P.T.1         P.T.2
            ========================================
 7:00  ---------------------------------------------------
            XXXXX                       XXXXX
            XXXXX                       XXXXX
            XXXXX                       XXXXX
 8:00  -----XXXXX-----------------------XXXXX-----------
            XXXXX                       XXXXX
            XXXXX                       XXXXX
            XXXXX                       XXXXX
 9:00  -----XXXXX-----------------------XXXXX-----------
            XXXXX                       XXXXX
            XXXXX         XXXXX         XXXXX
            /////         XXXXX         XXXXX
10:00-----XXXXX------XXXXX------XXXXX-----------
            XXXXX         XXXXX         /////
            XXXXX         XXXXX         XXXXX
            XXXXX         XXXXX         XXXXX
11:00-----XXXXX------XXXXX------XXXXX-----------
            XXXXX         /////         XXXXX
            XXXXX         XXXXX         XXXXX
            XXXXX         XXXXX         XXXXX
12:00-----XXXXX------XXXXX------XXXXX-------------
            XXXXX         XXXXX         XXXXX
            XXXXX         XXXXX         XXXXX
            XXXXX         XXXXX
 1:00  -----XXXXX------XXXXX--------------------
            XXXXX         XXXXX                       XXXXX
            /////         XXXXX                       XXXXX
            /////         XXXXX                       XXXXX
 2:00  -----/////------XXXXX----------------XXXXX
            XXXXX         /////                       XXXXX
            XXXXX         /////                       XXXXX
            XXXXX         /////                       XXXXX
 3:00  -----XXXXX------XXXXX----------------XXXXX
            XXXXX         XXXXX                       XXXXX
            XXXXX         XXXXX                       /////
            XXXXX         XXXXX                       XXXXX
 4:00  -----XXXXX------XXXXX----------------XXXXX
            XXXXX         XXXXX                       XXXXX
                          XXXXX                       XXXXX
                          XXXXX                       XXXXX
 5:00  -------------------XXXXX----------------XXXXX
                          XXXXX                       XXXXX
                          XXXXX                       XXXXX
                          XXXXX                       XXXXX
 6:00  -------------------XXXXX----------------XXXXX
                          XXXXX                       XXXXX
                          XXXXX                       XXXXX

 7:00  ---------------------------------------------------
```

Director's Resource 9-5 (*continued*)

```
                   THREE-YEAR-OLD STAFFING HOURS
                   =======GRAPH--3=============

               CLASS 1                  CLASS 2
            H.T.1       TEA.1       H.T.2       TEA.2
            =======================================
7:00 ---------------------------------------------
            XXXXX                               XXXXX
            XXXXX                               XXXXX
            XXXXX                               XXXXX
8:00 -----XXXXX-----------------------------XXXXX
            XXXXX                               XXXXX
            XXXXX                               XXXXX
            XXXXX                               XXXXX
9:00 -----XXXXX-----------------------------XXXXX
            XXXXX                               XXXXX
            XXXXX       XXXXX       XXXXX       XXXXX
            XXXXX       XXXXX       XXXXX       XXXXX
10:00-----/////------XXXXX------XXXXX------XXXXX
            XXXXX       XXXXX       XXXXX       /////
            XXXXX       XXXXX       XXXXX       XXXXX
            XXXXX       XXXXX       XXXXX       XXXXX
11:00-----XXXXX------/////------XXXXX------XXXXX
            XXXXX       XXXXX       /////       XXXXX
            XXXXX       XXXXX       XXXXX       XXXXX
            XXXXX       XXXXX       XXXXX       XXXXX
12:00-----XXXXX------XXXXX------XXXXX------XXXXX
            XXXXX       XXXXX       XXXXX       XXXXX
            XXXXX       XXXXX       XXXXX       XXXXX
            XXXXX       XXXXX       XXXXX       XXXXX
1:00 -----XXXXX------XXXXX------XXXXX------XXXXX
            /////       XXXXX       XXXXX       /////
            /////       XXXXX       XXXXX       /////
            /////       XXXXX       XXXXX       /////
2:00 -----XXXXX------/////------/////------XXXXX
            XXXXX       /////       /////       XXXXX
            XXXXX       /////       /////       XXXXX
            XXXXX       XXXXX       XXXXX       XXXXX
3:00 -----XXXXX------XXXXX------XXXXX------XXXXX
            XXXXX       XXXXX       XXXXX       XXXXX
            XXXXX       XXXXX       XXXXX       /////
            XXXXX       XXXXX       XXXXX       XXXXX
4:00 -----XXXXX------XXXXX------XXXXX------XXXXX
            XXXXX       XXXXX       XXXXX       XXXXX
                        XXXXX       XXXXX
                        XXXXX       XXXXX
5:00 ----------------------XXXXX------XXXXX----------
                        XXXXX       XXXXX
                        XXXXX       XXXXX
                        XXXXX       XXXXX
6:00 ----------------------XXXXX------XXXXX----------
                        XXXXX       XXXXX
                        XXXXX       XXXXX

7:00 ---------------------------------------------
```

Director's Resource 9-5 (*continued*)

```
                    FOUR-YEAR-OLD STAFFING HOURS
                    ======GRAPH--4=============

              CLASS 1                  CLASS 2
           H.T.1        TEA.1        H.T.2        TEA.2
           ==========================================
7:00  ----------------------------------------------------
           XXXXX                                   XXXXX
           XXXXX                                   XXXXX
           XXXXX                                   XXXXX
8:00  -----XXXXX-----------------------------------XXXXX
           XXXXX                                   XXXXX
           XXXXX                                   XXXXX
           XXXXX                                   XXXXX
9:00  -----XXXXX--------------------------------XXXXX
           XXXXX                                   XXXXX
           XXXXX        XXXXX        XXXXX         XXXXX
           XXXXX        XXXXX        XXXXX         XXXXX
10:00-----/////------XXXXX------XXXXX------XXXXX
           XXXXX        XXXXX        XXXXX         /////
           XXXXX        XXXXX        XXXXX         XXXXX
           XXXXX        XXXXX        XXXXX         XXXXX
11:00-----XXXXX------/////------XXXXX------XXXXX
           XXXXX        XXXXX        /////         XXXXX
           XXXXX        XXXXX        XXXXX         XXXXX
           XXXXX        XXXXX        XXXXX         XXXXX
12:00-----XXXXX------XXXXX------XXXXX------XXXXX
           XXXXX        XXXXX        XXXXX         XXXXX
           XXXXX        XXXXX        XXXXX         XXXXX
           XXXXX        XXXXX        XXXXX         XXXXX
1:00  -----XXXXX------XXXXX------XXXXX------XXXXX
           /////        XXXXX        XXXXX         /////
           /////        XXXXX        XXXXX         /////
           /////        XXXXX        XXXXX         /////
2:00  -----XXXXX------/////------/////------XXXXX
           XXXXX        /////        /////         XXXXX
           XXXXX        /////        /////         XXXXX
           XXXXX        XXXXX        XXXXX         XXXXX
3:00  -----XXXXX------XXXXX------XXXXX------XXXXX
           XXXXX        XXXXX        XXXXX         XXXXX
           XXXXX        XXXXX        XXXXX         /////
           XXXXX        XXXXX        XXXXX         XXXXX
4:00  -----XXXXX------XXXXX------XXXXX------XXXXX
           XXXXX        XXXXX        XXXXX         XXXXX
                        XXXXX        XXXXX
                        XXXXX        XXXXX
5:00  ----------------XXXXX------XXXXX----------
                        XXXXX        XXXXX
                        XXXXX        XXXXX
                        XXXXX        XXXXX
6:00  ----------------XXXXX------XXXXX----------
                        XXXXX        XXXXX
                        XXXXX        XXXXX

7:00  ----------------------------------------------------
```

Director's Resource 9-6

Sample Staffing Plan—Multiple Program B

STAFF PLAN BY STAFF MEMBER

Title	How Many	Schedule	Recommended Salary	Total Yearly
Director/Administrator	1	MWF 7:30am– TTH 12:00pm	$11.00/hr $22,880.00/yr	$22,880.00
Head Teachers	5	7:30–3:00pm 30-min. break between 12:00–1:30pm	$8.50/hr $17,680.00/yr	$88,400.00
Teachers	5	11:00–7:00pm 30-min. break between 1:00–2:30pm	$7.00/hr $14,560.00/yr	$72,800.00
Morning Assistants	5	7:30–12:30pm 15-min. break between 11:00–12:00pm	$5.00/hr $6,500.00/yr	$32,500.00
Afternoon Assistants	5	12:30–7:00pm 15-min. break between 2:30–3:00pm	$5.00/hr $8,450.00/yr	$42.250.00
Secretary/Bookkeeper	1	9:00–5:30 1-hr. lunch	$6.00/hr $10,400/yr	$12,480.00
Custodian	1	5:00–10:00pm Mon.–Thur. 5 hrs. on Sat. 15-min. break	$5.00/hr $6,500/yr	$6,500
Cook	1	7:30–3:00pm 30-min. lunch	$5.00/hr $10,400/yr	$10,400

Total Yearly Salaries: 288,210.00

(Reprinted by permission of Tara Schnicke and Brigid Nally)

Director's Resource 9-6 (*continued*)

STAFF PLAN BY CLASSROOM

Classroom	No. of Children	Staff/Child Ratio
Infants	8	required: 5:1
		maximum: 8:3
Rm:101		minimum: 8:2
Toddlers	11	required: 7:1
		max.: 11:3
Rm:201		min.: 11.2
3-Year-Olds	17	required: 12:1
		max.: 17:3
Rm:202		min.: 17.2
3-and 4-Year-Olds	17	required: 12:1
		max.: 17:3
Rm:203		min.: 17.2
4-Year-Olds	17	required: 14:1
		max.: 14:3
Rm:204		min.: 14:2

Each classroom will be staffed as follows:

1 Head Teacher	7:30– 3:00pm
1 Teacher	11:00– 7:00pm
1 Assistant	7:30–12:30pm
1 Assistant	12:30– 7:00pm

This flexible schedule allows ample time for classroom planning in the morning and evening when the ratios will be low because most children arrive at the center between 8:00–9:00am and leave between 5:00–6:00pm. Nap time is when team planning and communication takes place.

Director's Resource 9-6 (*continued*)

ADDITIONAL COMMENTS ABOUT STAFFING

— Breaks must maintain staff/child ratio at all times.

— Flexibility in scheduling breaks is necessary to meet the immediate needs of the classrooms.

— Short restroom breaks or emergency phone calls could be arranged as needed as long as ratio is maintained.

— Staff schedules designed for enhancing staff communications and for meeting the needs of the children.

— Swing scheduling for director designed to encourage and maintain communication with all staff members, family members, board, and community contacts.

— Teacher's responsibility to take care of housekeeping emergencies during the day.

— Cook is solely responsible for cleaning kitchen other than the clean-up after the afternoon snack, which is the teacher's responsibility.

— One morning snack, one afternoon snack, and one full meal will be provided each day.

— Encourage male applicants for all positions to balance male–female models.

— Parent(s)/surrogate provide transportation.

— Tuition $95/week for infants and $85/week for all others.

— 80 percent of tuition income goes for salaries.

Director's Resource 9-7

COMMUNITY DAY CARE ASSOCIATION

NAME:_____   DATE:_____

CENTER:_____   DIRECTOR_____

EVALUATION OF TEACHER

Indicate evaluation by using numbers 1 through 5: 5 meaning high, appropriate, or very good; 3 average; and 1 low, inappropriate, or poor in that particular characteristic.

PERSONAL QUALITIES

1. _____ Friendly, warm.

2. _____ Appearance: dress, posture.

3. _____ Speech and voice: Clear and well modulated.

4. _____ Tact and courtesy: Observes social conventions; tolerant and considerate of others.

5. _____ Displays a sense of humor.

6. _____ Dependable.

7. _____ Self-confident.

8. _____ Enthusiastic about teaching.

9. _____ Expresses a desire to learn

10. _____ Ability to evaluate self.

11. _____ Profits by criticism.

ASSUMING RESPONSIBILITIES

12. _____ Is independent in assuming responsibility.

13. _____ Adjusts temperature, light, and ventilation.

14. _____ Achieves efficient and satisfactory arrangement of playroom and play yard.

15. _____ Is flexible in planning program for children.

16. _____ Plans activities to enrich the lives of children according to their level of development.

17. _____ Overall planning for program activities.

18. _____ Daily preparation for program activities.

19. _____ Discusses pertinent problems with director.

Director's Resource 9-7 (*continued*)

WORKING WITH CHILDREN

20. _____   Creates a warm and accepting environment.

21. _____   Likes children, shows a real enjoyment of them.

22. _____   Recognizes when children are happy and relaxed.

23. _____   Enjoys humorous incidents with children. Seems to enjoy laughing with them.

24. _____   Understands children on their own level.

25. _____   Accepts each child as he is.

26. _____   Recognizes that each child is a sensitive, thinking individual and treats him accordingly.

27. _____   Shows awareness of progress or lack of it in a child's behavior.

28. _____   Relates easily to children.

29. _____   Impartial in dealing with children.

30. _____   Aware of differing moods of children, adjusts standards for them at times when they are fatigued, irritated, overstimulated, etc.

31. _____   Uses different, though consistent, methods in dealing with different children.

32. _____   Is imaginative and creative.

33. _____   Is resourceful in a practical way, has common sense.

34. _____   Uses positive approach.

35. _____   Helps children accept limitations.

36. _____   Makes suggestions without antagonizing.

37. _____   Does not overstimulate or cause tension in children.

38. _____   Removes distracting influences.

39. _____   Alert to total group, even when dealing with a part of it.

40. _____   Remains controlled in startling or difficult situations.

41. _____   Encourages and guides the expression of feelings.

42. _____   Assists children in gaining confidence.

43. _____   Treats the child's possessions and projects with care.

44. _____   Gives children opportunity for manipulating various kinds of creative materials.

45. _____   Explains relations between a child's individual rights and group rights.

46. _____   Guidance of children in group relationships.

47. _____   Guidance of activities according to group needs and interests.

48. _____   Guidance of children in developing motor coordination.

49. _____   Guidance in music experiences.

Director's Resource 9-7 (*continued*)

50. _____ Guidance in story and language experiences.
51. _____ Guidance in science experiences.
52. _____ Guidance in use of creative materials.
53. _____ Guidance in toileting routine.
54. _____ Guidance in resting.
55. _____ Guidance in eating experiences.

WORKING WITH ADULTS

56. _____ Is interested in people, thinks in terms of helping them rather than criticizing.
57. _____ Cooperates well with adults.
58. _____ Is considerate of activities of other adults.
59. _____ Welcomes new ideas, flexibility as shown by willingness to consider new ideas.
60. _____ Maintains high standards of professional ethics in regard to children and staff.
61. _____ Realizes that situations cannot always be handled in the home as they are at school.
62. _____ Attitude in working with parents is cooperative.

SPECIFIC STRENGTH OF TEACHER:

SPECIFIC LIMITATIONS OF TEACHER:

OTHER COMMENTS:

Director's Resource 9-8

Job Descriptions for Infant Care Program—Director, Teacher, and Assistant Teacher

DIRECTOR

When a center is small and is directed by a teacher–director, that position is defined by both the teacher and the director job descriptions.

Duties

The director is responsible for:

- All aspects of program development, supervision, budget, money management, enrollment, and facilities
- The smooth flow of the program and its adherence to the stated philosophy
- Overseeing the care, safety, and well-being of all children at the center
- Staff meetings, staff training, and encouragement of continuing education
- Enrollment, parent conferencing, parent education, and parent involvement
- All aspects of staffing, scheduling, and supervision of personnel
- Overall maintenance of a safe, clean, and appropriate environment
- Compliance with codes of all state and local governing agencies: social services, fire, and health departments
- Networking with the community

Supervision

- Supervises all personnel
- Supervised by a board of directors if the center is a nonprofit organization, by an owner if the center is owned by a nonparticipating owner, or by self if the director is the owner (in this case an advisory group is highly recommended)

Skills required

- Thorough understanding of infant growth and development
- Thorough understanding of appropriate programming
- Sound knowledge of business practices
- Ability to hire, train, and supervise adults
- Commitment, flexibility, and good problem-solving skills
- Ability to maintain positive relationships with infants, toddlers, staff, and parents
- Knowledge of community resources including health, remedial services, and child development specialists who can assess infants when there is concern about development
- Ability to represent the program within the community
- General knowledge of nutrition, health, and first aid
- Ability to provide ongoing staff training sessions and to maintain appropriate materials for staff and parent use
- Planning and evaluation skills

(From Annabelle Godwin and Lorraine Schrag, Co-Chairs San Fernando Valley Child Care Consortium, *Setting Up for Infant Care: Guidelines for Centers and Family Day Care Homes,* NAEYC, 1988, pp. 45–49.)

Director's Resource 9-8 (*continued*)

Experience and education
- B.A. degree in child development or its equivalent
- One or more courses in program administration
- Three years experience as a head teacher in an infant/toddler program or program for two-year-olds
- Preferably, some prior staff supervision experience

Additional requirements
- Good health as confirmed by a physician's statement
- Proof of being free of tuberculosis
- Fingerprint clearance

INFANT/TODDLER TEACHER

Duties

The infant/toddler teacher is responsible for:

- A small group of children, as their primary provider
- The care, safety, and well-being of all children in the group
- Planning and implementing a program geared to infants and toddlers
- Setting up the physical environment to meet the changing needs of infants and toddlers
- Demonstrating verbally and by role modeling a sound knowledge of good teaching practices and of child growth and development
- Taking the place of the director in her or his absence and dealing with any special situations that may arise
- Participating in staff meeting discussion and ongoing training regarding program, children, and parents
- Providing information to parents regarding their children as well as general child development information

Supervision
- Assists in the supervision of assistants, volunteers, and parents
- Supervised by the director

Skills required
- A good understanding of infant/toddler growth and development
- Ability to apply this understanding of infants and toddlers to appropriate activities
- Ability to instruct other adults, especially by good role modeling in interactions with infants and toddlers
- Ability to work with infants warmly, calmly, and in an unhurried way
- Ability to meet the social-emotional, physical, and developmental needs of individual infants and toddlers
- Ability to oversee both small and large groups of children at the same time
- Ability to maintain a safe, clean, and pleasant environment

Director's Resource 9-8 (*continued*)

- Ability to plan, prepare, and present appropriate nutritious food supplements geared to individual infant/toddler needs
- General knowledge of nutrition, health, and first aid
- Special ability to maintain positive relationships with children, coworkers, and parents
- Ability to move quickly, maintain visual contact with a broad area, get up and down from floor quickly

Experience and education
- A.A. degree in child development or its equivalent*
- Appropriate child development courses to meet state requirements
- Prior experience working with infants, toddlers, or two-year-olds
- Preferably a course in infant/toddler development and program development

Additional requirements
- Good health as confirmed by a physician's statement
- Proof of being free of tuberculosis
- Fingerprint clearance

INFANT/TODDLER TEACHER ASSISTANT

Duties

The infant/toddler teacher assistant is responsible for:

- A small group of children as their primary provider
- The care, safety, and well-being of all children in the group
- The physical care of children
- Carrying out activities
- Maintaining a safe, clean, and pleasant environment
- Demonstrating increasing understanding of child growth and development in working with children, in recording activities, and in talking with parents
- Participation in staff meeting discussions regarding the program and activities

Supervision
- Supervised by the teacher and the director

Skills required
- Increasing understanding of infant/toddler growth and development
- Ability to role-model for children, volunteers, and parents

* Although the title *teacher* is used here, the minimum education level required for this position corresponds to the Early Childhood Associate Teacher position as described in the NAEYC Position Statement on Nomenclature, Salaries, Benefits, and the Status of the Early Childhood Profession (1984), an entry level teacher position.

Director's Resource 9-8 (*continued*)

- Ability to apply an understanding of developmental levels to activities
- Ability to meet the social–emotional, physical, and cognitive developmental needs of infants and toddlers
- Comfortableness in holding and caring for babies
- Ability to maintain a safe, clean, appropriate environment for infants and toddlers
- General knowledge of nutrition, health, and first aid
- Ability to lift and carry babies, ability to be on floor with babies yet get up quickly in an emergency
- Willingness to accept supervision
- Special ability to maintain positive relationships with children, coworkers, and parents
- Willingness to read, learn, and increase understanding of infant development through workshops and study

Experience and education
- High school graduation or its equivalent
- Preferably one or more courses in child growth and development or infant/toddler growth and development
- Prior experience working with very young children

Additional requirements
- Good health as confirmed by a physician's statement
- Proof of being free of tuberculosis
- Fingerprint clearance

Director's Resource 9-9

Sample Job Description—Special Education Consultant

Title: Special-Education Consultant

Responsible to: Center Director

Responsibilities: The special-education consultant is responsible for assisting the director and the professional staff in identifying, evaluating, locating special services for and working with special needs children and their families who are enrolled in the program. Duties include the following:

1. Participate on the team involved in screening, selecting and placing the disabled children in this program.
2. Assist the staff in identification of disabled children during the process of screening and assessment.
3. Provide special education services when deemed appropriate after the initial information gathering process.
4. Act as case manager for each identified disabled child.
5. Participate in the I.E.P. team process: the in-house staffings, the multi-disciplinary team conferences with the parents, and the implementation of the I.E.P. when necessary.
6. Assist the Director with referral sources, connections to public and private agencies, as well as the public school system.
7. Participate in quarterly staffings on each enrolled disabled child.
8. Be available to the teaching staff on an "as needed" basis for consultation and problem-solving regarding the disabled children in the classrooms.
9. Facilitate the referral of identified disabled children, through the development of a systematic procedure for documenting services to disabled children in the area of screening, assessment, diagnosis, placement, and referral.
10. Provide or arrange for appropriate special-education-related inservices as deemed necessary after consultation with the director.

Qualifications: A Master's degree in Early Childhood Special Education or equivalent and some classroom experience with both disabled and non-disabled preschool children. Some experience using screening and assessment tools and knowledge of agencies providing special education services.

Work Schedule: Five hours per week on a schedule worked out with the director and based upon staff and family needs. Total hours not to exceed 20 hours per month.

Salary Schedule: Range $20.00 to $30.00 per hour based upon training and experience.

Director's Resource 9-10

Sample Job Description—Public School Instructor II and Instructor I

Public Schools
Civil Service Personnel Branch

Position Description

TITLE
Instructor II

PILOT PROGRAM
Constructivist Preschool Pilot Program at Social and Academic Skills Demonstration Schools.

RESPONSIBLE TO
School Principal; in collaboration with Constructivist Pilot Program Supervisor, and/or Project Coordinator

SUPERVISES
Instructor Assistant, volunteers and/or student teachers

REQUIREMENTS
1. Minimum—Bachelor in Child Development or Early Childhood Education from accredited college; some teaching experience with preschool children; ability to communicate articulate knowledge of child development with a focus on constructivist theory; must demonstrate ability to implement a constructivist's approach to teaching young children; must have good oral and written communication skills.
2. Must have the results of the annual physical and Mantoux TB test on file at the center before the first day of school for children.
3. Must have transporation available in order to make required home visits and other parent or community contacts.
4. Must be able to relate well to adults and children and work effectively with another adult in a classroom situation.
5. Must be available for evening meetings when scheduled.
6. Must have a current First Aid Certificate from the American Red Cross on file at school.

PERFORMANCE RESPONSIBILITIES
1. Be responsible for a reasonable amount of processing with Instructor Assistant on a regularly scheduled basis.
2. Plan and evaluate the ongoing classroom program with Instructor Assistant on a weekly basis.
3. Evaluate Instructor Assistant according to the method chosen by the school system.
4. Confer with Constructivist Pilot Program Supervisor and Instructor Assistant on a regularly scheduled basis.

CHILDREN
1. Plan, execute, and maintain a file of weekly educational plans for classroom activities for children. Plans are posted for parents' review. These must be based on constructivist theory.
2. Set up and maintain a safe, attractive, developmentally appropriate classroom environment for children—one which encourages autonomy, creativity, and particularly individual and group problem-solving.

(Reprinted by permission of Cincinnati Youth Collaborative)

Director's Resource 9-10 (*continued*)

3. Conduct ongoing observations of the children enrolled in the classroom and maintain anecdotal records in order to assess each child's construction of knowledge and overall developmental progress.
4. Develop and facilitate activities which will promote the healthy social, emotional, intellectual and physical development of each child, allowing the child to feel accepted and free to express feelings.
5. Maintain accurate, up-to-date records—a. Pupil folders, attendance, referrals, progress reports; b. Inventories of equipment and materials.
6. Supervise serving of breakfasts, snack, and lunch.

PUBLIC SCHOOLS
CIVIL SERVICE PERSONNEL BRANCH

Position Description

TITLE
Instructor Assistant I

PILOT PROGRAM
Constructivist Pilot Preschool Program at Social and Academic Skills Demonstration Schools.

RESPONSIBLE TO
Principal and/or designee (i.e. Preschool Instructor).

REQUIREMENTS
1. MINIMUM—Associates Degree in Child Development or Early Childhood Education from an accredited college. Some teaching experience preferred.
2. Must have the ability to communicate, articulate and demonstrate a sensitivity toward and nurturing of children.
3. Must have a current school medical form, tuberculin test results, and verification of degree/certificate on file at the school.
4. Must have or obtain a current First Aid Certificate from the American Red Cross on file at the School.
5. Must have good written and oral communication skills.
6. Must be available for occasional evening meetings/activities when scheduled.
7. Must follow directions and work independently.

RESPONSIBILITIES
1. Cooperate with and assist Instructor in implementing a constructivist approach to teaching young children.
2. Assist Instructor in setting up and maintaining an orderly, safe, healthy, nurturing environment for young children.
3. Prepare and implement, with teacher's guidance, appropriate curriculum activities (i.e. art, music, cooking, etc.) with individual children and small groups. As guided by Instructor, supervise children as they manage clothing, toileting, eating, etc.
4. Maintain a communicative relationship with young children in the expression of needs and feelings which will foster the development of positive self concepts.
5. Assist Instructor and/or assume responsibility for cleanup of activities and total classroom environment.
6. Assist Instructor in maintaining storage of classroom equipment in a safe and orderly manner.
7. Perform clerical duties relative to the classroom as directed by the Instructor to include but not be limited to such items as assisting parents with forms; documenting attendance, putting children's names on notes.
8. Make community contacts by assisting with recruitment as needed; making parent contacts as directed by Instructor.
9. Plan and discuss the ongoing classroom program with Instructor on a regular basis.
10. Confer with Constructivist Pilot Program Supervisor and Instructor on a regular basis.
11. Attend and participate in in-service to further develop a constructivist knowledge base.
12. Observe and adhere to school policies and to the Ohio Association for the Education of Young Children's Code of Ethics

Director's Resource 9-11

Local Immigration and Naturalization Service Offices

How to Obtain More Information: If you have questions after reviewing this handbook, you may obtain information from one of the following local INS offices. Direct your letter to the attention of the *Employer and Labor Relations Officer.*

ALABAMA
77 Forsyth St. S.W., Rm. G-85
Atlanta, GA 30303

ALASKA
620 East 10th Ave., Suite 102
Anchorage, AK 99501

ARIZONA
2035 N. Central Ave.
Phoenix, AZ 85004

ARKANSAS
701 Loyola Ave., Rm. T-8005
New Orleans, LA 70113

CALIFORNIA
300 N. Los Angeles St.
Los Angeles, CA 90012

880 Front St.
San Diego, CA 92188

630 Sansome St.
San Francisco, CA 94111-2280

COLORADO
4730 Paris St., Albrook Center
Denver, CO 80239-2804

CONNECTICUT
JFK Federal Building
Government Center
Boston, MA 02203

DELAWARE
1600 Callowhill St.
Philadelphia, PA 19130

DISTRICT OF COLUMBIA
4420 N. Fairfax Dr.
Arlington, VA 22203

FLORIDA
7880 Biscayne Blvd.
Miami, FL 33138

GEORGIA
77 Forsyth St. S.W., Rm. G-85
Atlanta, GA 30303

GUAM
595 Ala Moana Blvd.
Honolulu, HI 96813

HAWAII
595 Ala Moana Blvd.
Honolulu, HI 96813

IDAHO
900 N. Montana Ave.
Helena, MT 59601

ILLINOIS
10 W. Jackson Blvd., Rm. 533
Chicago, IL 60604

INDIANA
10 W. Jackson Blvd., Rm. 533
Chicago, IL 60604

IOWA
3736 S. 132nd St.
Omaha, NE 68144

KANSAS
9747 N. Conant Ave.
Kansas City, MO 64153

KENTUCKY
701 Loyola Ave., Rm. T-8005
New Orleans, LA 70113

LOUISIANA
701 Loyola Ave., Rm. T-8005
New Orleans, LA 70113

MAINE
739 Warren Ave.
Portland, ME 04103

MARYLAND
1530 Caton Center Dr., Bldg. D, Suite M
Baltimore, MD 21227

MASSACHUSETTS
JFK Federal Building
Government Center
Boston, MA 02203

MICHIGAN
Federal Building, 333 Mt. Elliott St.
Detroit, MI 48207

MINNESOTA
2901 Metro Dr., Suite 100
Bloomington, MN 55425

MISSISSIPPI
701 Loyola Ave., Rm. T-8005
New Orleans, LA 70113

MISSOURI
9747 N. Conant Ave.
Kansas City, MO 64153

MONTANA
900 N. Montana Ave.
Helena, MT 59601

NEBRASKA
3736 S. 132nd St.
Omaha, NE 68114

NEVADA
2035 N. Central Ave.
Phoenix, AZ 85004

NEW HAMPSHIRE
JFK Federal Building
Government Center
Boston, MA 02203

NEW JERSEY
Federal Building, 970 Broad St.
Newark, NJ 07102

NEW MEXICO
343 U.S. Courthouse, P.O. Box 9398
El Paso, TX 79984

NEW YORK
68 Court St.
Buffalo, NY 14202

26 Federal Plaza
New York, NY 10278

NORTH CAROLINA
77 Forsyth St. S.W., Rm. G-85
Atlanta, GA 30303

NORTH DAKOTA
2901 Metro Dr., Suite 100
Bloomington, MN 55425

OHIO
1240 E. 9th St., Room 1917
Cleveland, OH 44199

OKLAHOMA
4149 Highline Blvd., #300
Oklahoma City, OK 73108

OREGON
511 N.W. Broadway
Portland, OR 97209

PENNSYLVANIA
1600 Callowhill St.
Philadelphia, PA 19130

PUERTO RICO
P.O. Box 365068
San Juan, PR 00936

RHODE ISLAND
JFK Federal Building
Government Center
Boston, MA 02203

SOUTH CAROLINA
Room 110 Federal Building
334 Meeting St.
Charleston, SC 29403

SOUTH DAKOTA
2901 Metro Dr., Suite 100
Bloomington, MN 55425

TENNESSEE
701 Loyola Ave., Rm. T-8005
New Orleans, LA 70113

TEXAS
8101 N. Stemmons Freeway
Dallas, TX 75247

P.O. Box 9398
El Paso, TX 79984

805 No. T St.
Harlingen, TX 78550

509 N. Belt
Houston, TX 77060

727 E. Durango, Suite A301
San Antonio, TX 78206

UTAH
4730 Paris St., Albrook Center
Denver, CO 80239-2804

VERMONT
739 Warren Ave.
Portland, ME 04103

VIRGINIA
4420 N. Fairfax Dr.
Arlington, VA 22203

VIRGIN ISLANDS
PO Box 610, Charlotte Amilie
St. Thomas, VI 00801

Po Box 1270, Kingshill, Christiansted
St. Croix, VI 00850

WASHINGTON
815 Airport Way South
Seattle, WA 98134

WEST VIRGINIA
1600 Callowhill St.
Philadelphia, PA 19130

WISCONSIN
10 W. Jackson Blvd., Rm. 533
Chicago, IL 60604

WYOMING
4730 Paris St., Albrook Center
Denver, CO 80239-2804

Director's Resource 9-12

U.S. Department of Justice
Immigration and Naturalization Service

OMB No. 1115-0136
Employment Eligibility Verification

Please read instructions carefully before completing this form. The instructions must be available during completion of this form. **ANTI-DISCRIMINATION NOTICE.** It is illegal to discriminate against work eligible individuals. Employers **CANNOT** specify which document(s) they will accept from an employee. The refusal to hire an individual because of a future expiration date may also constitute illegal discrimination.

Section 1. Employee Information and Verification. To be completed and signed by employee at the time employment begins

Print Name: Last	First	Middle Initial	Maiden Name

Address (Street Name and Number)	Apt. #	Date of Birth (month/day/year)

City	State	Zip Code	Social Security #

I am aware that federal law provides for imprisonment and/or fines for false statements or use of false documents in connection with the completion of this form.	I attest, under penalty of perjury, that I am (check one of the following): ☐ A citizen or national of the United States ☐ A Lawful Permanent Resident (Alien # A _____) ☐ An alien authorized to work until ____/____/____ (Alien # or Admission # _____)

Employee's Signature	Date (month/day/year)

Preparer and/or Translator Certification. *(To be completed and signed if Section 1 is prepared by a person other than the employee.) I attest, under penalty of perjury, that I have assisted in the completion of this form and that to the best of my knowledge the information is true and correct.*

Preparer's/Translator's Signature	Print Name

Address (Street Name and Number, City, State, Zip Code)	Date (month/day/year)

Section 2. Employer Review and Verification. To be completed and signed by employer. Examine one document from List A OR examine one document from List B **and** one from List C as listed on the reverse of this form and record the title, number and expiration date, if any, of the document(s)

	List A	OR	List B	AND	List C
Document title:	_____		_____		_____
Issuing authority:	_____		_____		_____
Document #:	_____		_____		_____
Expiration Date (if any):	___/___/___		___/___/___		___/___/___
Document #:	_____				
Expiration Date (if any):	___/___/___				

CERTIFICATION - I attest, under penalty of perjury, that I have examined the document(s) presented by the above-named employee, that the above-listed document(s) appear to be genuine and to relate to the employee named, that the employee began employment on (month/day/year) ____/____/____ **and that to the best of my knowledge the employee is eligible to work in the United States. (State employment agencies may omit the date the employee began employment).**

Signature of Employer or Authorized Representative	Print Name	Title

Business or Organization Name	Address (Street Name and Number, City, State, Zip Code)	Date (month/day/year)

Section 3. Updating and Reverification. To be completed and signed by employer

New Name (if applicable)	B. Date of rehire (month/day/year) (if applicable)

If employee's previous grant of work authorization has expired, provide the information below for the document that establishes current employment eligibility.

Document Title:_____ Document #:_____ Expiration Date (if any): ___/___/___

I attest, under penalty of perjury, that to the best of my knowledge, this employee is eligible to work in the United States, and if the employee presented document(s), the document(s) I have examined appear to be genuine and to relate to the individual.

Signature of Employer or Authorized Representative	Date (month/day/year)

Form I-9 (Rev. 11-21-91) N

Director's Resource 9-12 (*continued*)

LISTS OF ACCEPTABLE DOCUMENTS

LIST A		LIST B		LIST C
Documents that Establish Both Identity and Employment Eligibility	**OR**	**Documents that Establish Identity**	**AND**	**Documents that Establish Employment Eligibility**

LIST A — Documents that Establish Both Identity and Employment Eligibility

1. U.S. Passport (unexpired or expired)

2. Certificate of U.S. Citizenship (*INS Form N-560 or N-561*)

3. Certificate of Naturalization (*INS Form N-550 or N-570*)

4. Unexpired foreign passport, with *I-551 stamp* or attached *INS Form I-94* indicating unexpired employment authorization

5. Alien Registration Receipt Card with photograph (*INS Form I-151 or I-551*)

6. Unexpired Temporary Resident Card (*INS Form I-688*)

7. Unexpired Employment Authorization Card (*INS Form I-688A*)

8. Unexpired Reentry Permit (*INS Form I-327*)

9. Unexpired Refugee Travel Document (*INS Form I-571*)

10. Unexpired Employment Authorization Document issued by the INS which contains a photograph (*INS Form I-688B*)

OR

LIST B — Documents that Establish Identity

1. Driver's license or ID card issued by a state or outlying possession of the United States provided it contains a photograph or information such as name, date of birth, sex, height, eye color, and address

2. ID card issued by federal, state, or local government agencies or entities provided it contains a photograph or information such as name, date of birth, sex, height, eye color, and address

3. School ID card with a photograph

4. Voter's registration card

5. U.S. Military card or draft record

6. Military dependent's ID card

7. U.S. Coast Guard Merchant Mariner Card

8. Native American tribal document

9. Driver's license issued by a Canadian government authority

For persons under age 18 who are unable to present a document listed above:

10. School record or report card

11. Clinic, doctor, or hospital record

12. Day-care or nursery school record

AND

LIST C — Documents that Establish Employment Eligibility

1. U.S. social security card issued by the Social Security Administration (*other than a card stating it is not valid for employment*)

2. Certification of Birth Abroad issued by the Department of State (*Form FS-545 or Form DS-1350*)

3. Original or certified copy of a birth certificate issued by a state, county, municipal authority or outlying possession of the United States bearing an official seal

4. Native American tribal document

5. U.S. Citizen ID Card (*INS Form I-197*)

6. ID Card for use of Resident Citizen in the United States (*INS Form I-179*)

7. Unexpired employment authorization document issued by the INS (*other than those listed under List A*)

Illustrations of many of these documents appear in Part 8 of the Handbook for Employers (M-274)

Form I-9 (Rev. 11-21-91) N

FPI-RBK

CHAPTER 10

Publicizing the Center and Selecting the Children

Photo above Some centers adopt a symbol to use on all brochures, ads, stationery, and newsletters. (Photo by Lisa Souders)

An important part of the director's job, in both new and ongoing programs, is publicizing the center. Decisions about the total population of children to be served by the center will determine the nature of the publicity that is written, as well as the audience to whom it is addressed. Publicity is not only related to recruitment and selection of children but is also integrally related to the center's public relations program.

PUBLICITY

Publicizing a program can be done through newspaper, magazine, or journal advertising, radio or television advertising, fliers or posters, and neighborhood papers or church bulletins. The director's first task is to decide where to direct the major thrust of the advertising.

Where and How to Publicize

The direction that the publicity takes should be based on the consideration of which families need to be reached in order to recruit children and promote the program. Obviously, young families are the first to come to mind since most programs are set up to serve children from infancy to five years of age or primary-school-aged children in before-and-after-school programs; however, there are other considerations. If program survival depends on tuition, the target population is clearly limited to those who can afford to pay for the service. On the other hand, if outside funding sources exist, it will be necessary to increase the scope of the publicity effort so that a greater portion of the potential clientele can be reached. Whether or not the program will serve families within walking distance of the center or will draw from a broader geographical area by transporting children from rural areas, surrounding suburbs or nearby businesses will affect the publicity effort. Likewise, the program sponsorship and program location will exert an influence in this regard. For example, sometimes program sponsors limit the population to be served to university families, poverty-level families, children of hospital personnel, children of families who are employed in a particular factory or office complex, children of club or church members, and so forth.

All these factors, and others that you may have thought about, will enter into the decision about where and how to publicize the center. Newspaper ads and radio announcements reach a wide audience, while a more limited population is reached through direct mailing of brochures or circulars, display of window placards, door-to-door solicitation, and advertisements in local papers, church bulletins and military newsletters.

As a director, it behooves you to take advantage of opportunities to invite reporters to the center to do newspaper or television pieces on your center. If you are affiliated with a large business or hospital, their public relations staff may help you. Television and newspaper reporters are interested in what is new at your center. If there is a new infant room opening, or you have a new custom-designed playground, reporters and cameramen will come to you. Other newsworthy items might be a new teacher who signs for deaf, installation of a ramp to accommodate children and adults with disabilities, or the use of senior citizen volunteers in the preschool classrooms.

Taking your message to the local lodge or church gathering, PTA groups, or community meetings where it will reach parents whose busy lives may limit the time spent reading publications or listening to radio or TV is still another way to publicize the program. Taking slides or videotapes to these meetings to show what children and teachers do in child care centers will enrich your presentation.

It is important to get your message out to companies in the community, as well as to individuals and community groups. The first wave of companies interested in addressing child care needs of their employees typically were attracted to setting up on-site child care centers. Recently, however, companies are more inclined to look to existing community child care centers where they can purchase slots, buy priority status, or negotiate for corporate group rates for their employees. Developing a professional presentation which is designed for use with corporate clients, and timely follow-up with appropriate contacts within the corporation, will enhance your chances of attracting corporate clients.[1]

Advertising Materials

The choice of words and the photographs used in the printed materials distributed by the

---

1 Sandy Duncan and D. Thornton, "Marketing Your Center's Services to Employers," *Child Care Information Exchange: The Director's Magazine,* January 1993, pp. 53–56.

DIRECTOR'S CORNER

"The thing we had the most success with when we opened our second center was the newspaper piece about using the "pod" concept for our infant program. It not only helped our infant enrollment, but it helped fill all the groups in that center. That notion about the "pod" bringing together the richness of group care and the individualized nurturance of home was very appealing—it seemed to give parents a solid idea to hold onto. It was the best public relations piece we ever had.

Director, independent not-for-profit center

center should reflect a subtle message of concern and appreciation for children, and should express the philosophy behind the center's program. These materials project the image of the center, and careful attention must be given, at all times, to enhancing and protecting that image.

The content and appearance of brochures or fliers make a statement to parents. The words should be informative and spell out the philosophy of the center's program; the photographs or some creative, clever artwork should convey, in less obvious ways, the fact that the staff of the center is professional and creative. The message for parents should be clear: any child who is sent to this center will share in that professionalism and creativity. When unsolicited letters from parents are available, using statements from those letters in brochures or publicity releases is an excellent way to get your message across. Every detail of any mailing piece to be used for initial advertising or in response to inquiries about the program should be carefully scrutinized.

Brochures. The director is responsible for the preparation and the mailing of brochures, but other staff members, as well as parents, can contribute to the effort by providing artistic talents, access to a printer they know about, or some

other expertise. When a brochure is prepared two major considerations are cost and content.

Costs vary depending on number, length, quality of paper, use of color and use of photographs. Therefore, it is wise to discuss ideas for the brochure with a printer as soon as possible. Costs increase when the professionally done brochure includes photos or a logo which requires art work, but it is these unique features which may be precisely what attracts the attention of prospective clients. Thus, money spent on an attractive brochure may be a good investment. Using a single color on heavy weight, standard size paper will give a look of high quality yet keep the costs down.

If the brochure is to be used over a long period of time, it is wise to avoid using items that are subject to change such as the school calendar or the fee schedule. These variable items can be detailed in a short insert. The brochure itself should contain information that remains constant from year to year. The following list includes some of the more stable items typically included in a brochure:

- name, address, and phone number of the center
- a map showing location of the program
- description of the program
- sponsorship of the program
- enrollment procedures and children served (ages, developmentally disabled, and so forth)
- licensing and/or accreditation status of the center

It is important to include the hours, days, and months for the program. The stability of the operational schedule will determine whether such information should go into the brochure itself or be part of the insert.

Public Relations

The center's image is an important consideration in all aspects of the public information and public relations efforts. The appearance of the physical setting and the behavior of personnel in that setting are fundamental factors in creating good public relations and sound relationships with the children and with their parents; these factors are what convey professionalism and concern about children and families. The director should serve as a model and encourage the staff to be mindful of their role as community advocates for children. Parents entering the building should see an interior prepared for use by children. Furthermore, parents should be greeted by a warm, caring person who expresses interest in them and in their children. When parents, or others, telephone the center, the person who answers must be pleasant, tactful, and knowledgeable.

An open house for parents who have made inquiries or have responded to your marketing efforts is a good way to expand the public relations program for the center. Remember to invite current parents, current staff members, and board members to these social events. An open house affords an opportunity for the staff to have an informal meeting with others who are interested in the center's activities. In the case of a new program, publicizing the open house can be part of the initial efforts at promotion. In the case of ongoing programs, staff and board members also will reap benefits from this kind of gathering since it provides a time for interaction and communication among adults who have common concerns and share an interest in the children attending the program.

When the center is opened for visitors, the environment should be prepared just as it would be for the children. In this way you can demonstrate how a well-planned environment should look and also provide an opportunity for parents actually to participate and use available materials. What better way to give parents a feeling for what happens each day than to have them use the materials in the classrooms! In addition, slides, a scrapbook of photos or a videotape of children actively participating in the classroom can give parents further insights into what a quality program can offer their children.

Planning for the open house should be done by people who understand the lifestyles and expectations of the clients who are likely to show interest in the event. Careful and sensitive planning regarding the time of the event and the level of informality communicates to members of the community that the people at the center understand and care about them and their children.

REFLECTIONS

Think about a center you have been in on a regular basis. You are sitting outside in the parking lot as parents arrive. Is the building inviting? Does it really *welcome* children and families? Now imagine yourself inside observing the way children are greeted. Do adults stoop down and extend a friendly welcome to the children? Are parents recognized and called by name? As you walk further into the building, how does it look? What sounds do you hear? How does it smell? The impressions you are reliving are the same parents and children experience each day they enter that center.

SELECTING THE CHILDREN

Ultimately, the director is responsible for the decisions about which children will be admitted to the program. The teachers are often called upon to assist in this decision, and sometimes a standing committee authorized by the board is asked to make policy or give advice. An Admissions and Recruitment Committee might be charged with policy-making decisions about the population to be served. There are also decisions about the admission of children who are atypical or developmentally disabled and about the grouping of children.

Other factors, such as readiness of the child, needs of the child and family, and age of the child, may enter into the final selection. Of course, there are pressures to admit all applicants when enrollment is not full. However, it is always important for the director to exercise good professional judgment about which children to admit, basing admission decisions on what is in the best interest of the child. The number of children to be served by the program will be determined by the size of the space, as well as the number of adults available for the children's programs. In many areas criteria set by licensing regulations must be satisfied (See Chapter 3).

Readiness of Children and Families

The Director or a member of the professional staff must assess the child's readiness to enter the program. It is essential that this assessment be made with the participation of the family. In some situations the age of the child is the only consideration, but that is clearly a tenuous criterion if it is the only one used in deciding whether or not a child can manage a group experience in a particular center. Indeed, it is analogous to the idea of judging a book by its cover. Chronological age is only one factor among many that will determine whether or not a child will be able to move into a program and profit from the experience. Other determinants are the emotional, social, and intellectual development of the child, and of course the child's health.

This is not to suggest that a child who does not meet some arbitrary standard or norm should be rejected on that basis alone, unless licensing regulations prohibit admission of children before a certain age. What it does mean is that the professionals at the center must decide if the available staff and the particular program offerings at the center can be adapted to provide the most enriching experience for a particular child. In other words, can *this* program provide what *this* child needs to develop to his or her fullest potential? If there is any doubt in the minds of either the members of the family or the director, careful consideration should be given to a number of questions. Can the program be adjusted to accommodate this child? Is there another program with a different focus that would provide a better match for this child and the lifestyle of this family? Is it better for the child and the family to consider waiting a while longer before placing the child in the center so that all will be more prepared for an initial separation, even though the family is seeking placement for the child so the parents can work? What other arrangements can be made for the care of the child?

What about the child who must be placed in full-day care to meet a family need that is both urgent and imminent? Perhaps there is some financial crisis or some tragedy or illness that makes it impossible to keep the child at home. Of course, that need must be heard. However, an experienced person with a strong sense of professional integrity would certainly avoid admitting a child to a program if the program, as it is currently set up, could be potentially damaging to the child. In special cases a child could be accepted on a trial basis, or alternatives such as a family child care home or a qualified baby sitter might be recommended for the child. In any case, as a director you must remember that your decisions are affecting the lives of children and families who are looking to you for help in the decision-making process. Your task is to provide help that is educationally and professionally sound.

There is also another side to the issue. Not only must the *child* be ready for the separation and the group environment, but the *family*, and most importantly the primary caregiver, must also be ready to leave the child. Members of the professional staff at the center may have excellent skills when it comes to adapting the learning environment to each child, regardless of the child's age or level of readiness. However, coping with the reluctant parent is another problem that may be much more difficult to manage. For this very reason, the assessment of readiness and the final decision on admission must be a cooperative effort between a member of the professional staff *and* the family. Interviews, visits to the home and to the center, and careful observation of the child in the context of the family are all helpful in making a final admission decision.

Admission of Children with Disabilities

The general question of readiness applies to *all* children and families seeking admission, whether the children are atypical or normal. The critical questions in each case are the same:

- Will the child's needs be met?
- Will the family's needs be met?
- Will the program meet the needs of both the child and the family without interfering with meeting the needs of all other children and families involved in the program?

In 1986, Congress enacted Public Law 99-457, amending the Education of Handicapped Act (EHA, PL 94-142). The reauthorization of both PL 94-142 and PL 99-457 came in 1990 with the passage of PL 101-479, Individuals with Disabilities Education Act, known by the acronym IDEA. The law requires that states provide a free *appropriate* public education to all children with disabilities, ages three to five years. States that fail to comply will no longer receive any EHA funding for preschoolers. The new law also mandates that states develop a state plan for expansion and improvement of early intervention programs for children with disabilities birth through age two, and there is a provision whereby funding is available to extend intervention programs to at-risk infants and toddlers as well. There is no doubt that, during the next decade, directors in early childhood education programs must be prepared to cope with the challenge of providing quality inclusion environments for increasing numbers of preschool children who are developmentally disabled.

Not only are directors faced with the issue of applying the critical question of readiness, as stated above, when considering admission of children with special needs, but they must also have knowledge of the law. It is helpful for them to know how the law applies to infants, toddlers, and preschoolers and to understand how preschools and child care centers are likely to fit into the scheme of services for atypical children. They should also know what role they and their staff can play as part of the interdisciplinary, interagency team effort to give these children the benefit of quality early childhood education experiences.

Provisions of PL 99-457.[2] PL 99-457 extends all rights and due process protection of PL 94-142 to children with disabilities ages three to five. Therefore, preschool children with special needs are assured free public education in a least restrictive environment based on an Individualized Education Program (IEP) developed by a team which includes the child's parents. The programs are to be administered through state or local education agencies (LEA) which may

contract with other service providers to offer a range of service models. The designated state agency is ultimately responsible for monitoring overall services and use of the federal funds. Other sources of funding such as Medicaid or Maternal and Child Health must also be utilized when the children are eligible, and the new funds are to supplement but not supplant these existing sources. Thus, the new funds may be used *in addition to* but not *instead of* existing sources of funding. States are not required to report number of children served by disability category, thus eliminating the necessity to categorically label these children because of data collection requirements.

PL 99-457 also establishes a state grant program for infants and toddlers with disabilities, ages birth to three years, for the purpose of providing early intervention for all eligible children. This part of the law, known as *discretionary legislation,* says that states *may* serve this age group, but are not required to do so. The exception is for those states which serve non-disabled infants and toddlers; they *must also* serve those disabled in that age group. The Governor of each state is to designate a lead agency in the state to administer the program. That agency will develop eligibility criteria, and the law *allows* but does not require extension of services to those babies viewed as "at-risk" for developmental delay based on medical or environmental factors, in addition to identified infants with disabilities. A case manager, sometimes called a service coordinator, must be designated for each child. That person, who is the liaison between agencies and services needed, is also responsible for the development of the Individualized Family Service Plan (IFSP) which must have evidence of multidisciplinary input and include information about the child's level of development, the family's strengths and needs as these relate to the child, the specific intervention services planned and the projected outcomes for the child and the family. Thus the IFSP is somewhat comparable to the IEP required for the three to five population.

Role of Child Care Centers. The law allows for variation in length of day as well as range and variety of programs, which means part-time or

---

2 Most of the information in this section is taken from *The Exceptional Child: Mainstreaming in Early Childhood Education* (2nd edition), K. Eileen Allen, Delmar, 1992.

full-time home-based or center-based services can be utilized. This is likely to lead to more inclusion models as state and local agencies contract with half-day and full-day child care programs in order to expand the continuum of services to include more center-based care in integrated settings. Now that the values of early childhood education programs are sufficiently high and demand public notice, state education agencies, which have almost unlimited discretion to choose program models, see that these programs offer viable alternatives to the current typical public school categorical model. In many public school models, children who are developmentally disabled may be in the same wing of the regular school building and the only time they share space with normal children is on the playground or at lunch. A major exception to this is where Head Start is in public schools because 10 percent of their classroom slots must be reserved for children with disabilities.

The vast majority of unserved atypical children who come into programs under the new law are mildly disabled because most severely disabled already receive services and are not likely to be included in preschools or child care centers. However, based on the Americans with Disabilities Act (ADA) which was signed into law in 1990, you must consider *each* applicant on a case-by-case basis, and may not exclude a child merely because of a severe disabling condition. If your program could include the child by making *reasonable accommodations* in the environment, you are expected to do that. You need not make changes that put an undue burden on the resources readily available at your center.[3]

The law requires that these identified special needs children be in a "least restrictive environment" (LRE). Legally this means that every effort must be made to maintain developmentally disabled children with their peers in a regular educational setting, and when placements are made away from normal peers, the state bears the burden of proof to demonstrate that the integrated setting is not appropriate.[4] In practice, the least restrictive environment is one which facilitates opportunities to function and grow optimally in all areas of development. Directors of centers with integrated classrooms are responsible for providing such an environment for children with disabilities who are admitted and funded under the new law. Children must share the pedgogical and social environment, and teachers must be specifically trained to facilitate

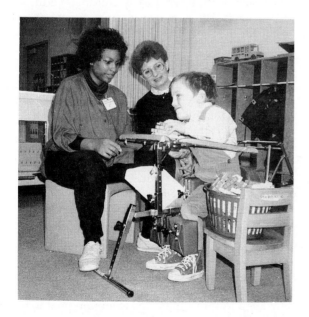

A disabled applicant's needs must be carefully assessed to insure that this is the best possible program for him or her. (Photo by Margaret Ruttle)

3 *Child Care Information Exchange: The Director's Magazine,* May 1992, pp. 43–46.
4 Barbara J. Smith and Phillip S. Strain, "Early Childhood Special Education in the Next Decade: Implementing and Expanding PL 99-457," *Topics in Early Childhood Special Education* (TECSE), Vol. 8(1), 1988, pp. 37–47.

interaction among and between normal children and those who are developmentally disabled.

Although there is evidence that significant benefits accrue to special needs children who participate in groups with normal peers, these benefits are not the result of merely being in the same classroom. The factors that determine how well children with special needs do in an inclusion environment depends both on the quality of the program and the presence of a teacher who has developed specific intervention plans which support interaction between and among the atypical and their normal peers.[5]

When available staff do not have sufficient time or background to provide the special support for children with special needs in the classroom, it may be possible to reach out into the community for additional help. Volunteers from parent groups, senior citizens or service organizations, or students from early childhood or special education programs can help in the classroom. Special training for the volunteers and the staff

can be arranged through special educators at the local school or university, or from other community agencies listed in Director's Resources.

Role of the Director in an Interdisciplinary/ Interagency Effort

"Cooperation among education agencies, social service agencies, Head Start, and private providers will be crucial, especially if much greater numbers of children are to be served in the least restrictive environment."[6] Directors conversant in the law and its implications for child care programs will be able to respond more knowledgeably to professionals from related agencies who make inquiries about placements for children with special needs. These directors may be called upon to make decisions about whether or not their programs can meet the needs of the selected special needs children, to serve on interdisciplinary teams where IEP's are developed and referral decisions are made, and to support their teachers, who will be working with special educators, therapists and the children's families. If the children are to benefit from what early childhood educators have to offer, turf-guarding must be set aside, yet they must assertively advocate developmentally appropriate practice which is the area of expertise they bring to the interdisciplinary and interagency team.

In order to facilitate communication between and among members of interdisciplinary teams and to support their work, directors must understand how and why inclusion works, and what makes it work or prevents it from working. That often means directors must learn more about children with special needs through additional training and reading, in order to prepare themselves for coaching classroom staff and for working with an interdisciplinary team. When members of the interdisciplinary team view each other as colleagues, all of whom bring special skills and training to the situation, and when they keep in mind that their common goal is to

DIRECTOR'S CORNER

"When I put a special needs child in a classroom I always talk at length with the teacher, telling her how I feel she can make it work—how I understand that it's important for all of us and for this child to really find ways to integrate this child into this group. It's very important for a staff member to tell me when she thinks it isn't working. I have to be able to confirm that it's not working both for the group and for the child, but I must also be able to tell her that there are ways to make it work, if that, indeed, is the case, and help her find those ways."

Director, independent not-for-profit center

---

5 Ibid., Allen, l992, pp. 63, 64.
6 "The Economies of Preschool Special Education Under Public Law 99-457," W. Steven Barrett, *Topics in Early Childhood Special Education*, Vol. 8(1), 1988, p. 22.

provide the best environment for the children, they can work together to that end.

SUMMARY

Publicity about the center must be drafted for and directed to the population that the program is designed to serve. Successful recruitment of children and families will depend on the content and dissemination of the publicity about the program, as well as on the total public relations effort. The written materials advertising the center must be carefully planned to attract the families to be served; any other efforts or activities to publicize the center deserve considerable thought and attention as well. After the families have indicated their interest, it is the responsibility of the professional staff to select children for the program, taking into account the readiness of the children and the capacity of the program to serve their needs and those of their families. The mandate to provide services for three- to five-year-old children with disabilities has far-reaching implications for early childhood programs and for responsibilities of directors of those programs during the decade of the 90s. It will influence the selection of children to be enrolled, and effect the dynamics within classrooms.

Class Assignments

1. Interview the director of a full-day or half-day program. Ask the questions listed on Working Paper 10-1.
2. Analyze the brochure, newsletters, or any advertisements you have seen about the program you inquired about in Class Assignment 1. Using Working Paper 10-2, evaluate the printed material as it relates to the information from your interview with the director of the program.

Class Exercises

1. Working in small groups (three to five students), discuss the questions and issues pertaining to inclusion of special needs children in early childhood education programs. Record the ideas of the group on Working Paper 10-3.
2. Using the information from the small group discussions, and other ideas generated from class discussion, summarize what your class views as the most critical issues and concerns facing early childhood educators during the next decade of PL 99-457.

Working Paper 10-1

Interview Questions

Interview questions for a director of an early childhood education program.

Indicate whether this is the director of a full-day program _____ half-day program _____

Who is enrolled in the program?

1. Tell me about your program.

   - How many children are enrolled? _____
   - What is the age range of the children? _____
   - How many groups of infants? _____ Toddlers? _____ Prekindergarteners? _____

2. Tell me about availability of service.

   - What are your hours? _____
   - What days do children come? _____
   - When are your holidays? _____

3. Can you give me an idea about the population you serve?

   - Are most of your parents working?

   - What is the racial and ethnic mix of your population?

   - How would you describe the socio-economic status of the families (i.e., upper class, middle class, impoverished)?

4. Could you give me an idea about the philosophy and the program goals?

5. Could I have copies of your brochure or any newsletters you distribute in the community or to your prospective clients?

Working Paper 10-2

Evaluation Form

Using the printed materials you collected from the director you interviewed (Class Assignment 1), describe and discuss how well these materials reflect what the director said about the program in each of the following areas.

1. Ages served and groupings of children.

2. Availability of service in terms of hours, days of the week, time of the year, etc.

3. Suitability of writing level, layout, and photos for the target population.

4. Clarity about what the program is like as philosophy and goals are mentioned in the printed material, and how these match what you were told.

Working Paper 10-3

Group Ideas

Discuss and record the responses of the group to the following issues related to PL 99-457.

1. How will an early childhood director determine if a program is indeed the least-restrictive environment for a specific developmentally disabled child?

   • What factors must be considered in the determination?
   • Where can the director go for help?

2. What are some of the strategies early childhood education professionals can use to communicate to other professionals, (i.e., special educators, physicians, psychologists, social workers, etc.) about "developmentally appropriate practice" and its importance for all children?

3. What are the major things early childhood educators need to learn from special educators?

4. What are some of the specific classroom strategies a director can share with the teaching staff that will facilitate interaction between and among the atypical children and their normal peers?

CHAPTER 11

Grouping and Enrolling the Children

Group 1

Andrew R.	Alex A.
Allison N.	Joey B.
Ned R.	Nadine C.
Dion J.	Sally Z.

Group 2

Sarita W.	Karen V.
Peter N.	Marcy S.
Sammy B.	Kenny L.
Brad A.	Tommy P.

Decisions about grouping the children must be reached before making the group assignments and pursuing all the subsequent steps in the enrollment procedure. Decisions about group size, ages of children and composition of the groups must be made before the children can be assigned. Once assignments have been made, teachers can contact families and initiate the enrollment process. Although the degree of flexibility around grouping in ongoing child care programs is more limited than in preschools, even there, the cyclical nature of demand usually follows the public school year, thus giving rise to numerous grouping decisions for newcomers in the fall.

Illustration above Grouping patterns must be determined before the enrollment process begins.

GROUPING THE CHILDREN

A number of factors are considered in dealing with the complex question of how children should be appropriately grouped. The size of groups is determined by a variety of factors, including the physical space available, the licensing requirements, the number of staff members, and the program philosophy. Appropriate group size is critical to achieving a quality environment.[1] Other factors that relate to the

---

1 Richard Ruopp, et al, Final Report of the National Day Care Study, *Children at the Center*, Abt Associates, 1977, p. 144.

grouping of the children are: the needs and skills of the staff, the needs of the children, the question of chronological age grouping versus vertical (sometimes called family) grouping, the number of special needs children to be enrolled and the nature of their disabilities.

Total Number of Children

To a large extent, the number of children available and the size of the physical space determine the total number of children in a center. If it is a new program, once the needs assessment in the community has been completed (Chapter 2) and the facility has been selected (Chapter 7), the final decision about the total number of children in the center must be made. Often this decision is simply to take all children available. However, when the requests for service are overwhelming or when the available space can accommodate large numbers of children, the director and/or the board may want to limit the enrollment.

Centers for young children must radiate a feeling of intimacy and warmth. Little children often feel frightened and uncomfortable about entering a large, forbidding building. The noise, the inevitable confusion, and the motion created by many people concentrated in one area can provoke anxiety in young children. It is difficult to maintain an inviting, comfortable atmosphere for small children when buildings are very large and when children are moved through crowded play yards, hallways, or receiving areas before they reach *their* room and *their* teacher.

Since the atmosphere in large public school buildings can be overwhelming for very young children, it is important for early childhood professionals and public school people to give special attention to the selection of the classroom and play yard space for the preschool children. Partnerships between early childhood educators and public school personnel can result in site selection for public school sponsored programs which may be in a separate wing of the building or in a facility completely separate from the school building. Greater stability and insulation from political attack, and protection from sudden economic shifts, may be some of the advantages of funneling preschool and day care services into public school sponsorship.[2] However, early childhood educators must guard the safety and well-being of the children when site selection for these programs is under discussion.

Space and Group Size

Group size varies according to the licensing regulations, and how the available space is organized. Licensing regulations often not only limit the number of children in a room but usually dictate the adult–child ratio for children of different ages as well. Since space requirements and adult–child ratio standards in the licensing regulations are, for the most part, based on the knowledge of experienced professionals, it is wise to follow a standard of small groups with low teacher–child ratios.[3]

DIRECTOR'S CORNER

"I had to go down the hall and upstairs when I wanted to take the children to the gym for large muscle activities. I always tried to avoid having them in the halls of the school building when the older children were moving in and out of the auditorium or the lunchroom. It was very confusing for the preschoolers to be taken through the long lines of older children—especially if remarks were made like, 'make room for the baby group' by the children or the elementary teachers."

Director, cooperative preschool in a public school building

2 Albert Shanker, President of American Federation of Teachers, "Public School Day Care," *Report on Preschool Programs*, Feb. 17, 1988.
3 Accreditation Criteria and Procedures of the National Academy of Early Childhood Programs, NAEYC, 1834 Connecticut Ave. N.W., Washington, D.C., 1991, p. 41.

REFLECTIONS

Can you recall how you felt as a first-year high school student when you initially entered your big high school building? Were you afraid and anxious? How did it feel to be the youngest or the smallest in the *whole* school? Did you feel that you might not be able to find your room or your locker? Did you ever have nightmares about forgetting your schedule or losing your most important notebook? If you can recall any of those feelings, perhaps you can begin to relate to the young child who leaves a familiar home environment and enters a large, strange crowded place called a child care center or school.

The organization or plan of the available space affects the size of the groups that can be accommodated. When bathrooms are two floors down or when outside areas are not directly adjacent to the classroom, groups must be smaller to be manageable during the transition periods when children move from one place to another. If fenced-in play areas outside can be reached directly from the classroom, the total space can be supervised more easily; which means a larger group could be assigned to the space.

When space is adequate to accommodate large numbers of young children, some directors and teachers find creative ways to use dividers, draperies, or movable partitions to break the space into smaller units. Even where available space would accommodate larger groups, smaller groups are viewed as optimal.[4]

Skills of Staff and Group Size

In deciding on the size of groups, the director must consider the skill level of the staff, and factor that into the decision about how many children should be assigned to each classroom. The staff for each group must be available to provide frequent personal contact, promote age-appropriate, meaningful learning experiences, create a nurturing environment using effective classroom management strategies, and respond immediately to all emergencies.

Needs of Children and Group Size

It is beyond the scope of this book to discuss the policy of making group size or placement decisions on the basis of differing individual family and child needs, even though every director must consider such needs carefully. However, some basic considerations apply to all children.

The needs of children will vary depending on their experiences, their level of development in all areas, and their ages. However, it is generally agreed that very young children in their first group experience find it most satisfying to relate to a constant adult. After the initial shift in attachment from the primary caregiver (usually the mother), to a constant adult at the center, the child begins to branch out and relate to other adults and to other children in the group. This

REFLECTIONS

Think about your first practicum experience in a classroom. Think about how many children you were able to manage at one time. Could you comfortably work with five children? If you were asked to work with ten children without a second person to help, did you still feel that you could practice effective management skills? What adult–child ratio and total group size is most comfortable for you, keeping in mind your philosophy of early childhood education?

4 Ibid., NAEYC, 1991, p. 41.

natural progression suggests that the child's first experience should be in a small, intimate group with a constant adult. The children in this group may be the same chronological age or they may range over a year or two in age. Volunteers, student teachers, or parent helpers may rotate through the classroom, but the one primary constant caregiver becomes the trusted adult figure to whom children can turn when they need caring and attention.

For young children spending the full day in a center, it is wise to consider small, intimate grouping patterns. Since children in full-day programs spend practically all of their waking hours in the center, it becomes a surrogate *home* for them. Young children who must deal with all the stimulation and the interpersonal relationships of a large group for an extended period of time may be exhausted by the end of their long day. Small groups in a carefully planned space provide both time and space for the child to be alone, to establish close relationships with just one or two children, or to spend time alone with just one adult. Quiet and intimacy in a comfortable setting with a few people more closely resembles the home environment and can soften the institutional atmosphere that prevails in most large centers.

Chronological versus Vertical Age Grouping. There is no consensus on the best grouping practice; therefore, unless licensing regulates how children should be grouped, the way children are organized within the program is left to the discretion of the director and the professional staff.[5]

Chronological Grouping. Grouping by age has recently been a more popular practice in early childhood programs than vertical grouping. It involves grouping based solely on the basis of age—three- and four-year-olds are in different groups and toddlers are separated from infants. When children are grouped chronologically, there is little discussion about which group a given child will join. The director's task is simplified, because in accepting the center program, parents accept the fact that their three-year-old

REFLECTIONS

Think about the progression of your feelings when you have spent an entire day in large, crowded classrooms, a busy, noisy cafeteria, community bathrooms, and noisy student centers. Consider those long days when you have found no privacy, no place to be alone and talk to a friend about a problem or listen to music either by yourself or with a special person. Your days on campus may be like this. If you can think through how you feel when following such a pattern, you will develop greater insight into how a child feels when placed in a large group for a full-day program. The lack of intimacy and warmth in an institutional setting creates both anxiety and fatigue.

will be in Group 1 and their four-year-old will be in Group 2. Of course, there will be ranges of ability and behavior within an age group due to individual differences, but the child's exposure to differences is inevitably lessened when chronological grouping is used. Thus, the child's opportunity to develop a broad appreciation for diversity is abated. On the other hand, there are advantages to age grouping, such as simplifying the planning of the learning environment and making classroom management less troublesome. The less experienced teacher may find both of these factors very helpful.

Chronological age grouping is based on the assumption that children of the same age are within the same range in ability and level of development. Because children of the same age are *not* homogeneous, many programs go to multi-age grouping where children advance at their own rate through individualized programming. Multi-age grouping allows for children's uneven development and provides an

5 Celia Decker and John R. Decker, *Planning and Administering Early Childhood Programs* (5th edition), Merrill, an imprint of Macmillan, 1992, p. 264.

environment in which younger children engage in more interactive and complex types of play with older children who are easily accessible.[6]

Vertical Grouping. Vertical grouping, or family grouping as it is sometimes called, involves placing children of different ages in the same group; the children in any one group may range in age as much as two to three years. This multi-age grouping more closely resembles one that would occur in a family; hence the label *family grouping.* Depending on licensing requirements, infants and sometimes even toddlers must be kept in separate groups. When vertical grouping is the pattern, decisions about the size and the composition of each group, as well as the number of adults needed for each one, become more complex. The broad age range also complicates managing the children and planning their learning environment.

Sometimes parents object to having their two-year-old with *older* children who may be viewed by the toddler's parents as being loud and rough. Not only are these parents concerned about the safety of their toddler, but sometimes they also fear that their young child will be unable to cope in a group covering a wide age range. However, many of these parents can be helped to see that a young child in a multi-age group has more opportunity to learn from older children in the group and that every child has a chance to teach the other group members. Peer teaching and learning has intrinsic value because it not only enhances a child's sense of mastery and worth, but also facilitates cooperation and appreciation of others. For example, two-year-olds may not be as efficient as five-year-olds about putting equipment back on the shelf, but the total concentration they give to an activity like water play and the sense of abandon they show in exploring this material may help their more controlled three- or five-year-old counterparts to try splashing in the water. The director must cope with the dubious parents and with the

teachers who are reaching out for support as they work with a broad age range. However, sometimes the advantages of multi-age grouping such as peer modeling and peer tutoring are outweighed by the challenges of planning for the age span, and equipping and managing the classroom. Directors become coaches and sources of support for staff as they try to meet these challenges.

Inclusion of Children with Special Needs

When children with special needs are included in the group, the size and composition of the group must be adjusted accordingly to ensure that enough adults will be available to respond to their needs. Consider which group can offer something to the child with a disability as well as where that child can offer something to the group. Unless the child is truly integrated into the group, each offering something to the other, there is a risk that the child with the disability will be ignored and become an isolate, thus *not* in the *least restrictive* environment. "The least restrictive ruling was never intended as an across-the-board mandate to enroll all children with a disability in regular programs."[7]

There is no ideal disabled/normal ratio, and recommendations range from at least two or more, to an even balance (50–50), to more disabled than non-disabled, sometimes called "reverse mainstreaming" where nondisabled make up no more than one-third of the enrollment.[8] "The best ratio of special needs to nonspecial needs children is the one with which teachers, administrators, and parents are most comfortable. Variables that must be considered carefully include the characteristics of the children without special needs, the number of teaching staff available, the extent of support services, and the types and severity of disabling conditions represented in the class."[9]

---

6 Lilian G. Katz, D. Evangelow, and J. A. Hartman, *The Case for Mixed-Age Grouping in Early Education,* National Association for the Education of Young Children, 1990, pp. 7, 15.
7 K. Eileen Allen, *The Exceptional Child: Mainstreaming in Early Childhood Education* (2nd edition), Delmar, 1992, p. 99.
8 Ibid., Allen, 1992, p. 99.
9 Samuel J. Meisels, "First Steps in Mainstreaming, Some Questions and Answers," in *Administration: Making Programs Work for Children and Families,* Dorothy W. Hewes (ed.), NAEYC, 1979, p. 64.

Multi-age groups are advantageous for children with special needs because they provide peer models with a broad range of skills and abilities. The atypical child is exposed to the peer model who has higher level skills or abilities, but will also have a chance to develop friendships with younger children who may be more compatible developmentally.

Decisions about group size or group patterns will affect program planning, child and teacher behaviors, group atmosphere, and ultimately, the experiences of both teacher and child in the learning environment. Poorly structured groups that are poorly staffed can have a negative effect on any child, from the most delayed to the most gifted.[10] Therefore, grouping the children is a complex issue that has far-reaching results.

ENROLLING THE CHILDREN

Filling out forms, interviewing parents, and visiting back and forth between home and school are the major components of the enrollment procedure. The director is responsible for developing forms that will provide the center staff members with the information they need about the families and the children. The director also manages the planning and timing of this procedure; however, these plans must be discussed with staff members who will be required to carry them out.

Information on Families and Children

The director must first determine what information is needed from each family, and then develop a plan for obtaining it. Forms and interviews can both be used for this purpose, and it is up to the director to design the forms and to develop the plan for interviews or conferences. The ultimate goal is to assemble the necessary information for each child and family and to make it available to selected adults at the center who will be responsible for the child and the family.

The following list includes the type of pre-enrollment information that is typically obtained from the family. Note that all the information is important to efficient business operation of the center, to the health and safety of the children, or to the better understanding of the child and the family:

- name of the child (including nickname)
- names of family members and ages of siblings
- names of other members of the household and their relationship to the child
- home address and phone number
- name, address, and telephone number of employer(s) of parent(s)
- arrangement for payment of fees
- transportation plans for the child (including how the child will be transported and by whom)
- medical history and record of a recent physical examination of the child by a physician
- social/emotional history of the child
- name, address, and telephone number of the child's physician or clinic
- emergency medical treatment authorization
- name, address, and telephone number of a person (outside the family) to contact in an emergency if a member of the family cannot be reached
- permission to participate in the total school program (field trips, photos, videotaping, research, and so on)

In order to ensure that you have all the information and signed releases required to satisfy licensing and to cover liability questions, contact your local licensing agent and also consult an attorney.

Forms

A number of sample forms included in Director's Resources demonstrate various ways in which the information listed above can be recorded. These are only sample forms and cannot be used in the exact format presented, but they *can* provide a basis for developing appropriate forms to meet the specific needs of each center. For

10 Ibid., Allen, 1992, p. 64.

example, the director of a small cooperative nursery school does not need all the data on family income that is required by Head Start or public funded programs, but needs details on family schedules to plan for parent participation.

Public-school-sponsored programs may or may not require family income information, but will require a Medicaid number for those children entitled to the benefits of that program, and may also need a birth certificate to validate the age of the child.

Because there is so much variation among programs about information required on children and families, directors must develop forms which meet the specific need of the program.

In the case of child care centers and preschools, applications for admission are mailed to interested families in response to their initial inquiry about the center. In fact, sometimes the application is enclosed in a brochure or is actually part of it. On receipt of the applications, the director can begin to arrange the groups, based on whatever guidelines have been adopted for grouping the children. If selection and grouping of the children requires more subjective data than can be gleaned from the application form or any other written information that has been collected prior to admission, the director can arrange to talk with the parent(s).

After most of the children have been admitted and assigned to groups, those who have not yet been placed are held for deferred enrollment, or, in the case of ongoing programs, put on a waiting list. If a child is rejected for reasons other than full enrollment, the reasons should be discussed with the family to avoid any misunderstandings which could quickly undermine the public relations efforts of the center staff and impair communication between the staff and potential clients from the community.

Confidentiality

Information on families and children that is recorded on forms or obtained by staff members during interviews or home visits is confidential and *must not* be released to unauthorized persons without parental consent. Furthermore, a federal law provides that any public or private educational institution which is the recipient of federal funds made available under any federal program administered by the United States Department of Education must give parents access to their children's educational records. Since all information in the files must remain available to parents, it is important that staff members use discretion when recording information to be placed in a child's permanent record. When parents review the records they have the right to request that inaccurate or misleading information be rewritten or deleted from the child's record.[11]

Records and other confidential information should not be disclosed to anyone other than center personnel without written consent of the parent or guardian, unless its disclosure is necessary to protect the health or safety of the child. Written parental consent is required in order to pass information on to the public school by any preschool or Head Start program. As a general rule, parental consent should be obtained except in emergency cases or where it appears that the parent is a threat to the child.[12] Centers that receive funds from government sources should be familiar with any regulations or guidelines on confidentiality and privacy that are tied to the funding source.

Intake Procedures

The director decides which staff members will be involved in each step of the intake procedure, but it is imperative that the child's teacher be actively involved throughout. The adult who will work directly with the child must interact with the child and the family to begin to establish feelings of mutual trust among the child, the family, and the teacher.

Parents often feel guilty and apprehensive about placing children in a child care program. A

---

11 Kristen Hildebrandt, "The Family Education and Privacy Act," *Apologist*, Ohio Legal Rights Service, Vol. 12, Issue 3, November 1992, p. 3.
12 III(B)(4) The Family Educational Rights and Privacy Act (Buckley Amendment), 1974 Education Amendments, sec. 513,88 Stat. 571,20 U.S.C.A. Sec. 1232g (Supp. 1875).

carefully planned intake process that provides frequent opportunities to talk with the teacher, the director, and the social services staff (if available) can help the parents cope with their feelings. At the same time, young children are upset when they are first separated from their parents and family. They feel frightened and lonely; therefore, their transition to a new physical and social environment must be made gradually and must be accompanied by continuous support from family members. Hence, for the mental health of both the parents and children, the sequences followed in the intake process should be arranged so that everyone involved will be able to cope successfully with the separation experience. Four steps are commonly employed in introducing the family and the child to the center program and to the teacher. They are discussed here because it is the director's responsibility to ensure that this careful intake procedure is implemented.

Initial Interview with Parents. The purpose of an initial interview is to get acquainted with the parent(s), answer their questions about the center program, communicate what will be expected of them, take them on a tour of the center, and familiarize them with the forms that must be filled in before their child can be admitted. It may be useful to go over the family information, the child's social history, the medical history, the emergency information record, and the various release and permission forms during the interview to answer questions about any confusing items on these forms. The sample forms in Director's Resources give some idea of the way these forms may look. The informality and friendliness of this first personal contact will set the tone for all future contacts. Since this is precisely the time to establish the foundation for mutual trust among director, teacher, parent, and child, it is important that these interviews be conducted in a non-threatening manner.

Scheduling the interview must be done at the convenience of the family. Even though the teacher or the office staff may do the interview scheduling, it is essential that the director monitor it to ensure that families are not unduly inconvenienced. Careful consideration of family needs indicates that the center staff is sensitive to individual lifestyles and family preferences. When parents work, evenings or weekends may be best for interviews. Center staff members must also consider the transportation problems for some families, the availability of baby-sitters, and the schedules of other children in the family.

Home Visit with the Family. A home visit may be the next step in the intake procedure. The director should describe the purpose of home visits to the staff and go over a home visit report with them before family appointments are made (Sample Home Visit Report, Working Paper 11-2). The purpose is not to *evaluate* the home, but rather to gather information which will enable the staff to have a better understanding of the child. Trust between the parent(s) and the staff will be destroyed and communication will be impaired if the family interprets the purpose of these home visits as evaluative. Observing a family at home will help the teacher understand the family lifestyle and the family attitudes toward the child.

Initial Visit to the Center. The scheduling of the initial visits to the center should be arranged by the director and the staff before home visits begin so that information about visiting the

DIRECTOR'S CORNER

"We are fairly firm with parents about spending some time here with their child because we know, from experience, that even a child who comes in with apparent ease may have a problem two months hence which harks back to skipping the gradual transition into the group. Even if a parent can spend only 15 minutes in the morning with a child for a week or two, we accept that and make it clear we *expect* it. My staff is *sold* on the importance of gradual separation and will even come in 15 or 30 minutes early—before we open—to give a new child time in the classroom with both the parent and the teacher present."

Director, independent not-for-profit center

The child's first visit to the classroom is made with a parent or some trusted caregiver who stays with the child throughout the visit and gives the child time to feel comfortable with the teacher. (Photo by Lisa Souders)

center can be given to parents during the home visit. The child's first visit to the classroom is made with a parent or some trusted caregiver who stays with the child throughout the visit.

This initial visit to the classroom must be planned to help the child make that first big step from home and its trusted caregiver to center and a new caring adult. The visit should last from thirty to forty-five minutes and should terminate before the child is tired or bored. Although the teacher is clearly responsible for working with the child and the accompanying adult during this visit, it is important for the director to be available to greet the newcomers and answer any questions that might arise. It provides a perfect opportunity for the director and the parent(s) to get to know each other better, and is a good time to give the parent a copy of the Parent Handbook. (See Chapter 15 for further discussion of Parent Handbook.)

Phasing-in the Children. The first three intake steps described (initial interview including a building tour, home visit, and initial center visit) can be implemented in all types of center-based programs. The scheduling of each step should be adjusted to individual family needs and obviously is much more difficult for working parents. In fact, the scheduling of these steps may seem to be somewhat unrealistic for full-day child care programs, but can be done through very creative planning. Implementing the intake procedures in child care programs could involve evenings, early mornings, or weekends. The director must, therefore, work out the scheduling with the staff, and may give comp time or extra compensation for overtime.

The phasing-in or staggered-entrance, which is the fourth and last step in the intake procedure, will of necessity be very different in ongoing child care programs than in programs that are just starting or those based on the typical school calendar.[13]

Arranging for the staggered entrance of a group of twelve to fifteen children at the beginning of the year poses a complex scheduling problem, but it is an essential step in the orientation process. Since scheduling is very involved, it is important for the director and staff to consult with parents about convenient times for

13 For discussion of staggered entrance, see Katherine Read, P. Gardner, and B. Mahler, *Early Childhood Programs: Human Relations and Learning* (9th edition), Harcourt, Brace Jovanovich, 1993.

them to come and stay with their child. Successful implementation of the plan depends upon staff and family commitment to it.

In public-school-sponsored programs, where there is no precedent for gradual intake of new children, early childhood staff will have to meet with administrators and building principals to explain the importance of this procedure for the well-being of children and families. Because early childhood programs in public schools are considered part of the elementary school, and are accredited with the elementary school in the local school district, they are usually expected to provide a given number of instructional days to maximize the amount of state funds they receive. Developmentally appropriate practice like phasing-in children is often one of the first issues which creates conflict between developmental early childhood educators and the academic/school readiness elementary educators.

In full-day child care programs, the major problem is to find a trusted adult to stay with the child until all persons involved feel comfortable about the child being at the center every day for the full day. When a family needs full-day care for a child, both parents are usually working or the child is a member of a one-parent family. In these special cases a grandparent or other member of the extended family may be the best person to provide the emotional support that is necessary for the child during the phasing-in period.

If there is any question among staff members about the importance of the gradual orientation program for the child, the family, and the success of the total program, it is up to the director to help everyone understand that this process represents the next logical step in developing mutual trust within the teacher–child–family unit. Orienting children is usually exciting and productive for the teacher, but it is also time-consuming and energy-draining. The process can only be successful if the entire staff understands its relevance to the total program and recognizes it as being consistent with developmentally appropriate practice.

SUMMARY

Most of the decisions about grouping the children appropriately are made by the director who must consider the unique needs of the children, space available, licensing regulations about ratios and group size. Policy decisions about chronological or multi-age grouping must be made before children are assigned to groups. Skills and experience of staff, ages of children, and the numbers and types of children with special needs selected for admission are all factors which will effect where children will be assigned.

Enrolling the children involves filling out forms, interviewing parents, making home visits, and gradually phasing-in the children. Although the staggered-enrollment procedure is complex and time-consuming, it is a critical step in the process of building trust between the school, the child, and the family.

Class Assignments

1. Using Working Paper 11-1, work out a staggered-enrollment schedule for 12 children.
2. Talk with at least two directors of child care programs in your community. Find out how children are grouped (chronologically or vertically), and how grouping decisions are made. Write a one-page paper, comparing and contrasting the grouping practices in each program, and the rationale for these.

Class Exercises

1. Working with another student, role play an initial interview with a young mother who is sending an only child, who is three, to your program. The Sample Personal History and the Permission Form in Director's Resources (11-5 and 11-8) are to be explained during this interview. At the close of the interview, discuss reactions to this role play with the entire group.
2. In groups of four, role play a home visit with a mother, father, and their three-year-old daughter. When you arrive, you see no evidence of toys in the home and you find the child dressed-up and sitting in a chair with her hands folded, apparently having been told to "be good and sit quietly while we talk to your teacher." The purpose of the visit is to explain the initial visit and the staggered-enrollment plan for the child.

   After the role play, stay in groups of four and evaluate your reaction to the child and to the family. Evaluate your reactions as you played teacher, mother, father, or child. Consider how successful the teacher was at developing a relationship with the child. Fill in the Home Visit Report, Working Paper 11-2, in sufficient detail so the director will have a clear picture of what transpired during the visit.

Working Paper 11-1

Develop a Staggered Enrollment Plan

- Enroll 12 children over a period of eight days.
- The plan is for a half-day preschool which meets from 9:00 A.M. to 11:30 A.M. daily.
- Remember to have children come for shorter hours, in small groups, and gradually move toward having all children together for the full 2½ hours on the ninth day of school.
- Fill in the time-slots with the child's number—1, 2, 3 . . . 12.
- Time slots can be adjusted to suit your plan.

Week 1	Monday—1	Tuesday—2	Wednesday—3	Thursday—4	Friday—5
9:00					
9:30					
10:00					
10:30					
11:00					
11:30					

Week 2	Monday—6	Tuesday—7	Wednesday—8	Thursday—9	Friday
9:00				Children 1–12	Children 1–12
9:30					
10:00					
10:30					
11:00					
11:30					

Working Paper 11-2

Sample Home Visit/Parent Contact Report

Center _____

Type of Program _____

1. Name of interviewer _____ Title _____

2. Child's name _____

3. Parent or guardian _____

4. Address _____

5. Date and time of visit or meeting _____

6. Purpose of visit or meeting _____

   _____

   _____

7. Specific action taken as result of visit or meeting _____

   _____

   _____

   _____

   _____

   _____

8. Observations and comments _____

   _____

   _____

   _____

   _____

   _____

   _____

Director's Resource 11-1

Sample Child Care Application Form (requesting income information)

For office use only

District Status: _____

Income Status: _____

Priority Status: _____

Date Application Received: _____

Date Eligible for Entrance: _____

Enrollment Age: _____

Child's Name: _____ Date of Birth: _____ Sex: _____

Race, Nationality, or Ethnic Group: _____

Address: _____ Phone: _____

Mother's Name: _____ Date of Birth: _____ SS # _____

Father's Name: _____ Date of Birth: _____ SS # _____

Child lives with _____

Children attend the center-based program four (4) half days per week; they eat lunch and snack at the center. Transportation is provided for handicapped or special needs children.

Do you wish to apply for center-based program?   Yes _____   No _____

     Session preferred   A.M. _____   8:45 – 11:45

                      P.M. _____   12:45 – 3:45

Children and families in the home-based program are visited once per week in the home and are transported to the center on Friday for a group experience. The home-based teacher will assist parents in creating a home environment to promote children's growth and development. This program is in the morning only.

Do you wish to apply for home-based program?   Yes _____   No _____

* *

Family Income   Family Size:

  $_____ per week $ _____ per month $ _____ per year

Source of Reimbursement or Services (Circle "Yes" or "No" for each source)

YES	NO	EPSDT/Medicaid (Latest certification #): _____
YES	NO	Federal, State or Local Agency: _____
YES	NO	In-kind Provider: _____
YES	NO	Insurance: _____
		I.D. #: _____
YES	NO	WIC
YES	NO	Food Stamps

Does this child or any of your family members have a disability or special need? Describe: _____

_____

How well does your child speak and understand English? _____

_____

How did you obtain information about this program? _____

_____

Director's Resource 11-2

Sample Application—No Income Information Requested

**walnut corner children's center
preregistration form**

CHILD'S FAMILY INFORMATION

Child's Name_____   Name Used_____

Date of Birth, or Expected Date of Birth _____

Child's Address_____

Father/Guardian Name_____   Mother/Guardian Name_____

Home Address_____   Home Address_____

_____   _____

Employer_____   Employer_____

Address_____   Address_____

_____   _____

Business Phone_____   Business Phone_____

REQUESTED DAYS OF ATTENDANCE

Days: M   T   W   TH   F   Hours: _____ AM _____ PM

Requested Start Date:_____

HOW DID YOU LEARN ABOUT WALNUT CORNER CHILDREN'S CENTER?

Personal Referral/If so, who? _____

Newspaper_____   Radio_____   Other _____

Thank you for this information

PLEASE INCLUDE THE NON-REFUNDABLE $25 REGISTRATION FEE WITH THIS FORM.

THIS FEE WILL SECURE YOUR CHILD'S NAME ON OUR WAITING LIST.

Reprinted by permission Walnut Corner Children's Center

Director's Resource 11-3

Sample Student Enrollment Form

SAMPLE STUDENT ENROLLMENT FORM
(Public School-Sponsored Program)
S T U D E N T   E N R O L L M E N T   F O R M
(MUST BE RETAINED IN STUDENT'S CUMULATIVE RECORD)

DO NOT WRITE IN THIS BOX
Assigned to: Gr____ Hr____
SDF sent to Census_____
Type a new CR_____
CR in office file_____
CR requested_____
Health Record Yes____ No____
Rec'd 4 part SDF_____

Name of school student is entering_____ Grade Entering*_____ Special Ed_____

Name _____
Student's Legal Name (as listed on Birth Certificate)

Circle
Sex: Male Female

Circle
Race: Black White Other

Address_____ Apt No._____ Zip Code_____ Phone No._____

Place of Birth_____ Date of Birth_____
          City   State   County   Mo   Da   Yr

Check one of the Birth Verifications listed below:

Birth
Certificate No._____

Baptismal
Certificate

Physician's Record

Passport

IMMUNIZATION DATA:	DPT	Polio	Measles	Rubella	Mumps

	Name		Place of Birth		Deceased (Date)
			State	County	
Father:					
Mother:					
Step-Parent:					
Guardian:					

SOCIAL RECORD

	Occupation	Place of Employment	Business Phone No.
Father's Occupation			
Mother's Occupation			

If Family Is Supported
By Another Source Indicate:_____

Names of Brothers & Sisters - School of Attendance	Still in School	
	Pre-School	

Circle one:
Family Status   Married   Single   Divorced   Separated   Remarried
of Parents: Student is living with_____ Relationship_____

LANGUAGE OTHER THAN ENGLISH SPOKEN IN HOME:_____

Did student attend this school   last year?

____YES

____NO   Name of school_____ Address_____

☐   YES - PRIVACY REQUESTED: If this box is checked no information pertaining to this student will be
           released to any person or institution (including colleges or universities) without your written
           approval.
☐   NO - PRIVACY IS NOT REQUESTED

                    Parent/Guardian's Signature_____

                              Date:_____

In case of emergency, call_____ _____ _____
                            Name   Relationship   Phone No.

NAME

Last

First

Middle

STUDENT NUMBER

SOCIAL SECURITY NO.

Director's Resource 11-4

Sample Developmental History

ARLITT CHILD DEVELOPMENT CENTER*

DEVELOPMENTAL HISTORY

Child's Name _____

How you want your child's name
written in the classroom _____

Address _____ Zip _____ Phone _____

Birth Date _____ Place of Birth _____ Race _____

Sex _____

I. THE CHILD'S FAMILY
   Parents or Guardians
   A. Name _____ Birthdate _____
      Education (include highest grade completed or degrees) _____

_____

      Occupation _____ Usual working hours _____
                                                             Work phone _____

   B. Name _____ Birthdate _____
      Education (include highest grade completed or degrees) _____

_____

      Occupation _____ Usual working hours _____
                                                             Work phone _____

Status of Parents (check):   Living together _____   Living apart _____
Child lives with _____
If parents work or are students, who keeps the child in their absence? Check one:
grandparent _____   other relative _____   friend _____   paid sitter _____   other _____

Other children in the family: (list in order of birth)

Name	Sex	Birthdate	What grade if in school

Sisters or brothers who attended Arlitt _____
Additional members of household (give number) _____
   Friends _____ Others _____
   Boarders _____ Relatives _____
                                        (indicate relationship)

What part do these other persons have in the care of your child? _____

_____

Has your child been separated from his parents for long periods of time and, if so why? _____

_____

*Reprinted by permission of Arlitt Child Development Center University of Cincinnati

Director's Resource 11-4 (*continued*)

Have you moved frequently? _____

What language is usually spoken at home? _____

(If more than one, what other language(s) are spoken? _____

II. DEVELOPMENT IN EARLY CHILDHOOD

Comment on the health of the mother during pregnancy _____

Comment on the health of your child during delivery and infancy _____

_____

When did your child walk? _____   When did your child talk? _____

Is your child adopted? _____   Does he/she know it? _____

Does your child have bladder control? _____   Child's terminology _____

Does your child have bowel control? _____   Child's terminology _____

_____   Does your child need reminding about going to the

bathroom? _____   Does your child usually take a nap? _____ At what time? _____ Describe any special

needs, handicaps, or health problems _____

_____

Does your child have any difficulty saying what he/she wants or do you have any trouble understanding

his/her speech? _____

III. HEALTH RECORD

Immunization Record. Enter month/day/year of each immunization.

DPT: 1 _____   2 _____   3 _____   4 _____   *5 _____

Polio: 1 _____   2 _____   3 _____   *4 _____

Measles, mumps, rubella—usually combined as MMR _____

If separate, measles _____   mumps _____   rubella _____

*The 5th DPT and 4th polio are normally administered just prior to kindergarten.

1. List all allergies and any special precautions and treatment indicated for these allergies:

    _____

    _____

2. List any medications (food supplements, modified diets or fluoride supplements currently being administered to the child):

    _____

    _____

3. List any chronic physical problems and any history of hospitalization:

    _____

    _____

4. List any diseases, serious illnesses, or operations the child has had:

    _____

    _____

5. List any accidents the child has had:

    _____

6. Has your child ever had ear/hearing examination or treatment? _____

    When? _____   By whom? _____

    Results: _____

Director's Resource 11-4 (*continued*)

7. Has your child ever had vision examination or treatment? _____

  When? _____ By whom? _____

  Results: _____

IV. EATING HABITS
  Dietary Habits
  1. What foods does your child especially like? _____
  _____
  2. Are there any foods your child dislikes? _____
  _____

	Yes	No	12. About how often does your child eat a food from each of the following groups?	Approximate Number of Times a Week (*circle the number(s) nearest to parent's answer*)								
3. Does your child take vitamins and mineral supplements? (a) If "yes," what kind are they? _____			(a) Milk, cheese, yogurt	0*	1*	2*	3	4	5	6	7	7+
(b) Do they contain iron?			(b) Meat, poultry, fish, eggs, or dried beans/peas, peanut butter	0*	1*	2*	3	4	5	6	7	7+
(c) Do they contain fluoride?												
(d) Were they prescribed?												
4. Is there any food your child should not eat for medical, religious, or personal reasons?	*		(c) Rice, grits, bread, cereal, tortillas	0*	1*	2*	3	4	5	6	7	7+
5. Is your child on a special diet? (a) What kind?_____	•		(d) Greens, carrots, broccoli, winter squash, pumpkin, sweet potatoes	0*	1*	2	3	4	5	6	7	7+
6. Has there been a big change in your child's appetite in the last month?	*											
7. Does your child take a bottle?	*		(e) Oranges, grapefruit, tomatoes (fruit/juice)	0*	1*	2*	3	4	5	6	7	7+
8. Does your child eat or chew things that aren't food?	*		(f) Other fruits and vegetables	0*	1*	2	3	4	5	6	7	7+
9. Does your child have trouble chewing or swallowing?	*		(g) Oil, butter, margarine, lard	0*	1*	2	3	4	5	6	7	7+*
10. Does your child often have: (a) Diarrhea?	*		(h) Cakes, cookies, sodas, fruit drinks, candy	0	1	2	3	4	5	6	7	7+*
(b) Constipation?	*											
11. Do you have any concerns about what your child eats?	*											

*Starred answers may require follow-up. Explain details or give additional comments here.

V. PLAY AND SOCIAL EXPERIENCES
  Has your child participated in any group experiences? _____
  Where? _____
  Did your child enjoy it? _____
  Do other playmates visit the child? _____
  Does your child visit other playmates in their homes? _____
  How does your child relate to other children? _____
  Does your child prefer to play alone? _____ With other children? _____
  Does your child have any imaginary playmates? _____ Explain. _____
  _____
  Does your child have any pets? _____
  What are your child's favorite toys and/or activities? _____
  _____
  What is your child's favorite TV program? _____

Director's Resource 11-4 (*continued*)

How long does your child watch TV each day? _____

What are your child's favorite books? _____

How many times a week is your child read to? _____

Is there anything else about your child's play or playmates that the school should know? _____

_____

VI. DISCIPLINE

In most circumstances, do you consider your child easily managed, fairly easy to manage, or difficult to manage? _____

What concerns do you presently have about your child? _____

_____

How are these concerns dealt with? _____

_____

VII. PARENTS' IMPRESSIONS AND ATTITUDES

From your point of view, what were the events that seemed to have had the greatest impact on your child (moving, births, deaths, severe illness of family members, divorce)? _____

_____

In what ways would you like to see your child develop during the school year? _____

_____

_____

_____

VIII. ADDITIONAL INFORMATION

_____

_____

_____

School Year	Date	Signature
_____	_____	_____
_____	_____	_____
_____	_____	_____
_____	_____	_____

Director's Resource 11-5

Sample Personal History—Your Child's Development

Date: _____

CHILD'S NAME: _____   NICKNAME: _____

ADDRESS: _____   ZIP: _____   PHONE: _____

DATE OF BIRTH: _____   PLACE OF BIRTH: _____   RACE: _____

I. THE CHILD'S FAMILY   SEX: _____
    Parents or Guardians
    A. Name: _____   BIRTHDATE: _____
        Education (Include highest grade completed or degrees): _____
        _____
        Occupation: _____   Usual working hours: _____
                                        Work phone: _____

    B. Name: _____   BIRTHDATE: _____
        Education (Include highest grade completed or degrees): _____
        _____
        Occupation: _____   Usual working hours: _____
                                        Work phone: _____

    Status of Parents (Check):   Living Together _____   Living Apart _____
    Child lives with _____
    If parents work or are students, who keeps the child in their absence?

    Circle one: Grandparent   Other Relative   Friend   Paid Sitter   Other

    Other children in the family: (List in order of birth)

Name	Sex	Birthdate	What Grade if in School

    Additional members of household (give number):
        Friends _____   Others _____
        Boarders _____   Relatives _____
                                          (Indicate relationships)

    What part do these other persons have in the care of your child? _____
    _____
    Has your child been separated from his parents for long periods of time, and, if so
    why? _____
    Have you moved frequently? _____
    What language is usually spoken at home? _____
    (If more than one, what other language(s) are spoken?) _____

    C. Income _____ (per month) _____ (per year)
    D. Medical card number _____ (parent)
            Child's number _____

Director's Resource 11-5 (*continued*)

II. DEVELOPMENT IN EARLY CHILDHOOD

Comment on the health of the mother during pregnancy. _____

Comment on the health of your child during delivery and infancy. _____

When did your child walk? _____   When did your child talk? _____

Is your child adopted? _____   Does he/she know it? _____

Does your child have bladder control? _____   Child's Terminology _____

Does your child have bowel control? _____   Child's Terminology _____

Does your child need help when going to the bathroom? _____

Does your child need reminding about going to the bathroom? _____

Does your child usually take a nap? _____   At what time? _____

Describe any special needs, handicaps, or health problems. _____

Does your child have any difficulty saying what he/she wants or do you have any trouble understanding his/her speech? _____

III. EATING HABITS

What is your child's general attitude towards eating? _____

What foods does your child especially like? _____

For which meal is your child most hungry? _____

Does the child feed himself entirely? _____

Does your child dislike any food in particular? _____

Is your child on a special diet? _____

Does your child take a bottle? _____

Does your child eat or chew things that are not food? Explain: _____

Do you have any concerns about your child's eating habits? Explain: _____

Is there any food your child should not eat for medical, religious, or personal reasons? _____

IV. PLAY AND SOCIAL EXPERIENCES

Has your child participated in any group experiences? _____

Where? _____

Did your child enjoy it? _____

Do other playmates visit the child? _____

Does your child visit other playmates in their homes? _____

How does your child relate to other children? _____

Does your child prefer to play alone? _____   With other children? _____

Does your child worry a lot or is he/she very afraid of anything? _____

What causes worry or fear? _____

Does your child have any imaginary playmates? _____   Explain: _____

Does your child have any pets? _____

What are your child's favorite toys and/or activities? _____

Director's Resource 11-5 (*continued*)

What is your child's favorite TV program? _____
How long does your child watch TV each day? _____
What are your child's favorite books? _____
How many times a week is your child read to? _____
Is there anything else about your child's play or playmates which the school should
know? _____
_____

V. DISCIPLINE

In most circumstances, do you consider your child easily managed, fairly easy to
manage, or difficult to manage? _____
What concerns do you presently have about your child? _____
_____
How are these concerns dealt with? _____
_____

VI. PARENT'S IMPRESSIONS AND ATTITUDES

From your point of view, what were the events which seemed to have had the greatest
impact on your child (moving, births, deaths, severe illness of family members,
divorce)? _____
_____
How would you describe your child at the present time? What changes have you seen
in your child during the past year? _____
_____
Does your child have any behavior characteristics which you hope will change?
Please describe. _____
_____
In what ways would you like to see your child develop during the school year? _____
_____
_____
_____
_____
_____
_____

_____
Signature(s) of person/persons filling out this
questionnaire

*Adapted from Arlitt Child Development Center form

Director's Resource 11-6

Sample Child's Medical Statement

Enrollment Date _____

DAY CARE CENTER/PRE-SCHOOL CERTIFICATE OF MEDICAL EXAMINATION
TO BE COMPLETED BY FAMILY PHYSICIAN OR CLINIC

This is to certify that _____   _____
                              Child's Name   Birthdate

Child of: _____   _____   _____
              Mother   Address   Phone

          _____   _____   _____
              Father   Address   Phone

was examined by me on _____, and based upon his/her medical
                          Date of Examination

history and physical condition at the time of this examination, is free from apparent communicable disease and is in suitable condition for enrollment in a child day care facility; and has had the immunizations required by Section 3313.671 of the Revised Code for admission to school, or has had the immunizations required by the State Department of Health for infants and toddlers, or is to be exempted from these requirements for medical reasons.

Tuberculin Test
(within last year
for new enrollee)   Date _____   Type of Test _____   Results _____

DPT Series and
Boosters Dates   1st _____ 2nd _____ 3rd _____ 4th _____ *5th _____

Oral Polio
Series Dates: 1st _____ 2nd _____ 3rd _____ *4th _____
                     *The 5th DPT and 4th polio are normally administered
                      just prior to kindergarten.

Measles (Rubeola,
10-day)   Date: _____

Rubella (3 day)   Date: _____

Mumps   Date: _____   (Hib vaccine is required
                                                  for children ages 2 yrs.
Haemophilus b Polysac-   through 4 yrs.)
charide (Hib)   Date: _____

Is able to participate in all regular activities except: _____

_____

REMARKS: _____

Physician's Signature: _____ Date _____

Clinic Name: _____ Phone _____

Office Location: _____

City, State, Zip:_____

PARENT SHOULD RETAIN THIS SHEET WHEN CHILD WITHDRAWS FROM CENTER

Director's Resource 11-7

Sample Emergency Information Record

EMERGENCY INFORMATION RECORD

Child's Name_____

Home Address_____ Home Phone_____

Father's name/Husband (or guardian)	Place of Employment	Bus. Phone

Mother's name/Wife (or guardian)	Place of Employment	Bus. Phone

Please fill in information below so that the school may act more effectively in event of illness or injury to the child.

EMERGENCY: Person to be called if parent (husband or wife) cannot be reached.

Name	Address	Phone

Date	Parent's Signature (or guardian)

Director's Resource 11-8

Sample Permission Form

While your child is enrolled in this program, he/she will be involved in a number of special activities for which we need your permission. Please read the following information carefully. You are encouraged to ask questions about anything which is unclear to you. You, of course, have the option of withdrawing permission at any time.

_____
(Child's Name)

(Please circle your choice)

A. I DO   DO NOT give my permission for my child to go on walks with the classroom teacher and class in the nearby neighborhood.

B. I DO   DO NOT give my permission for my child to be screened for speech and language.

C. I DO   DO NOT give my permission for my child to be screened for hearing.

D. I DO   DO NOT give my permission for my child to be screened for specific educational needs.

E. From time to time photographs of our preschool program will be made for educational and publicity purposes. These pictures will be representative of the enriching experiences offered your child during the year.

I DO   DO NOT give my permission for my child to be photographed for use in educational, nonprofit publications/presentations intended to further the cause of public education. This permission is applicable for current, as well as, future project use.

As part of this program, your child's records may be included in research which evaluates the value of the program. In all cases, the confidentiality of individual children's records is maintained.

_____
Parent's Signature

_____
Date

(Reprinted by permission of the Cincinnati Youth Collaborative.)

Director's Resource 11-9

Sample Transportation and Attendance Release Form

ESCORT FORM
TRANSPORTATION OF CHILDREN TO & FROM SCHOOL*

1. Child's Name: _____   Teacher: _____

    Parent Signature: _____   Date: _____

2. I authorize these people to assume responsibility for my child to and from school.

    _____

    _____

    _____

    _____

    _____

    If someone other than myself or these people are going to bring or pick up my child I will send a note or phone the school office 556-3802.

3. My child carpools with these children on these days.

    Child's Name   *Days*

    _____   _____

    _____   _____

    _____   _____

    _____   _____

    _____   _____

*It is our policy not to send a child home with anyone other than the parent without written permission.

Reprinted by permission Cincinnati Youth Collaborative

CHAPTER

12

Managing the Food and the Health and Safety Programs

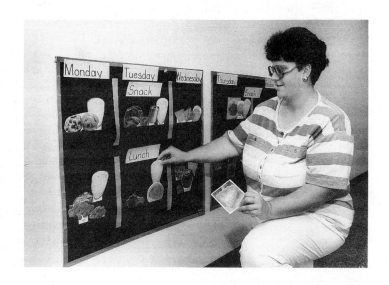

The director is ultimately responsible for the center's food service and health and safety programs, despite the fact that the components of these programs may be the immediate responsibility of assigned staff members. In large programs a nutritionist and/or food service coordinator and a cook may have full responsibility for the center's food service, but the director should be knowledgeable about the program and is accountable to the board, the funding agencies, and the center's families. Similarly, a social service or health coordinator may plan and implement the health and safety program, but again the accountability for the program is with the director. Directors of small programs often have full responsibility for both planning and

Photo above Weekly menus are posted where both parents and children can see what's for lunch. (Photo by Lisa Souders)

implementing the food service and the health and safety programs. Since you, as a director, will be expected to supervise and monitor these programs or, in small centers, to fully implement them, you must be informed about the elements of the food service and the health and safety programs and about the importance of these programs to the children and families in your center.

FOOD SERVICE PROGRAMS

The total food service program, whether it is limited to midmorning snack or consists of a two- or even a three-meal-a-day program, is important, not only because nutrition affects the mental functioning and the physical well-being of the child but also because nutritional habits and attitudes toward eating are established during the early years. Providing variety in food choices and in the style of serving the food and establishing an appropriate emotional atmosphere for mealtime are foremost considerations, whether the children's meals and snacks are catered, served from frozen, prepackaged dinners that are microwaved, come from public school or company cafeterias, or are completely prepared from start to finish in the center's kitchen. Nutritious foods selected appropriately from the Basic Four Food Groups should be offered daily, using variations in serving styles, such as self-help and group snacks, family-style and cafeteria-style meals, picnics, bag lunches, and more casual food service for special occasions.

It should be understood that the adults in the classroom sit down with the children when food is served, that the adults eat the same food that is served to the children, and that the adults take charge of creating pleasant conversation among the entire group during snack time or mealtime. Conversation can focus on food, on what children have been doing or expect to do later in the day, or on any topic that is of interest to most children. An accepting adult who avoids having children wait to be served, who encourages but doesn't demand tasting new foods, who uses utensils appropriately and suggests that children try to manipulate their own small forks or spoons, and who avoids associating unpleasantness or punishment with food, is demonstrating healthy habits and attitudes toward eating.

For the young infant, a caring familiar adult who is unrushed is important during feeding time. Infants should be held while taking a bottle but encouraged to begin to hold it for self-feeding, as voluntary control progresses. Staff must be reminded not to prop bottles for infants because of dangers of choking and the complications of falling asleep with milk or juice in the mouth which is detrimental to healthy gums and teeth. In addition, for their emotional and social well-being, it is critical that babies be held and cuddled while being fed.

Older infants benefit from sitting in adapted chairs, near the table with older toddlers and preschoolers, where that is possible. They can often enjoy finger foods with the toddlers, and participate in the pleasant atmosphere of eating time. Since choking may be a problem for babies who are beginning to feed themselves, a caregiver must be close by at all times. Foods should be cut in bite-sized pieces, be of proper consistency, and, at the very beginning, be offered one piece at a time. Make sure the cook and the caregivers in the program know that some foods are likely to cause choking in young children. It is wise to avoid serving peanuts, chunks of wieners, whole grapes, pieces of raw carrot, and hard candies.[1] It is also essential for children to sit down while eating or drinking to further avoid the dangers of choking.

Since directors are responsible for all aspects of the food service program, they must monitor and supervise the atmosphere and the health and safety features of mealtimes. They must also oversee the planning, buying and preparation of food, and provide opportunities for in-service training to the food service staff members and other adults who work with the children during snack and mealtime.

Menu Planning

The proportion of the total daily food requirement provided by the center depends on the total number of hours the child spends in the center. Licensing regulations vary but general guidelines are as follows:

- 3 to 4 hours: midmorning or afternoon snack timed no closer than two hours before the next scheduled meal

---

1 *Health in Day Care: A Manual for Health Professionals*, American Academy of Pediatrics (AAP), Selma R. Deitch, MD (ed.), 1987, p. 25.

REFLECTIONS

Think about your earliest recollections of eating with the family or with a teacher. Do you recall being pressured about table manners, finishing your main course before dessert, and tasting new foods that you disliked? Can you recall how you felt at those times? What emotions did you feel? How did you feel about the adults who made demands on you? How did you feel about eating and mealtime when you were put under pressure to eat too much or eat foods you disliked? What are your present attitudes about eating and about unfamiliar foods? Can you relate these present attitudes to your earlier experiences with eating and sampling new foods?

- 5 to 8 hours: one third to one half of the total daily food requirement given in one or more servings
- 9 hours or more: at least two thirds of the total daily requirement in the form of two meals and two snacks[2]

Of course, infants in group care have very different needs and must have individualized eating schedules with carefully prepared formulas and special diets.

Nutritious meals and snacks must be based on an appropriate selection from each of the following food groups:

- Milk and Milk Products Group (Milk, Yogurt and Cheese)

- Meat and Meat Alternates Group (Meat, Poultry, Fish, Dry Beans, Eggs, and Nuts)
- Fruit and Vegetable Group (Fruits, Vegetables)
- Bread and Cereal Group (Bread, Cereal, Rice and Pasta)[3]

In 1992, the United States Department of Agriculture (USDA) presented the Food Pyramid to replace the Basic Four as a guide for making daily food choices. The Food Pyramid includes the food groups listed above. Until the recommended quantities in the Food Pyramid are adjusted to amounts comfortably consumed by young children, nutrient needs for the young child are best done with the Basic Four guidelines.

It is important to check local licensing standards for additional details on nutrition requirements.

For centers involved in the USDA Child and Adult Care Food Program, nutritional standards for meal and snack serving sizes for children, birth through age 12 can be found in Figure 12-3. Headstart-funded programs must follow the Headstart nutrition guidelines which may vary somewhat from USDA serving size regulations.

Every precaution must be taken to ensure that children with food allergies or other conditions requiring a special diet will be served only those foods on their prescribed diet. Both the cook and all classroom staff must be alerted to these special dietary requirements, and both the director and the staff must know the emergency procedures to follow in the event a particular child should have an allergic reaction. For some special diet cases, parents may choose to send food for the child. It is important that these packed lunches be properly refrigerated until served.

Nutritional considerations in meal planning for young children are necessary but not sufficient to guarantee that children will be adequately nourished. Children's appetites and food preferences must also be taken into consideration

2 Ibid., AAP, p. 27.
3 Lynn Marotz, et al, *Health, Safety, and Nutrition for the Young Child* (3rd edition), Delmar, 1993, p. 293.

when meals are planned. Three- and four-year-old children tend to have small, unpredictable appetites and they are prone to food sprees. Their foods must be neither too hot nor too cold, not too spicy or gluey, and it is best if they are cut into bite-sized and manageable portions. Variation in texture, color, and flavor are also important considerations in planning children's meals. Every effort should be made to limit use of salt and sugar. Serving certain ethnic foods will provide wider variation for all the children and will make available familiar foods to the children from specific ethnic groups represented in the classroom. It is always a good idea to introduce a new food along with old familiar favorites.

Further considerations that affect menu planning are the availability of equipment and utensils and the preparation time for each menu item when all foods are prepared in the center kitchen. It is virtually impossible to prepare hot breads, an oven-cooked main dish, and a baked dessert for one meal if only one oven is available. Also, the number and sizes of pots and pans must be checked when menus are planned to ensure that there is an adequate supply of equipment of an appropriate size to prepare the foods for a particular meal. Preparation time is another factor that influences meal planning. Meals that require too much last-minute preparation create problems for the cook, which, in turn, could delay the serving time. Hungry children who are forced to wait for their food become impatient and restless, and teachers must then find ways to help them cope with these unnecessary delays.

Meal and menu planning can be systematized and simplified by using meal planning guides, standardized recipes, and sample menus. A number of government booklets and other menu planning guides are useful in planning four to six weeks of basic menus. Menu changes based on the availability of seasonal or plentiful foods can be made on a weekly basis, but, beyond those minor changes, basic menu patterns can be repeated every four to six weeks.

Teachers often have helpful suggestions about changes in the basic menu patterns. Some lunches include too many items which are difficult for children to manage or time-consuming to serve. For example, soup, banana sections which have to be peeled, and bread slices to be buttered is a menu both difficult to serve, and a problem for children to manage. If the cook has

a way to get input from the teachers, menu adjustments can be made easily.

Inviting the cook to lunch with the children provides an opportunity for him/her to hear comments from the children about the food, and to observe how well they manage the foods served. It also gives the cook a chance to feel more a part of the total center program rather than one who spends all day in the kitchen and away from the children.

Since parents are often interested in what children have been served for snacks and/or for breakfast and lunch, it is helpful to post weekly menus or publish them regularly in the parent newsletter. Posting menus not only helps the parents plan for a child's meals at home but also serves as a model for parents who may be inexperienced with planning balanced family meals.

An interesting feature to add to the menu posting area is a pictorial menu for the children. The cook, another staff member, or an interested parent may be willing to collect food pictures and post each day's snack and/or lunch on an eye-level bulletin board for children to "read." It creates interest among the children who then look forward to a dish they especially enjoy, and it becomes part of the center's nutrition program.

Food Buying

Careful menu planning reduces cost and waste and provides a clear-cut basis for setting up shopping lists for daily, weekly, and monthly food buying. Whether meals are catered, partially prepared from prepackaged meals especially designed for children, or fully prepared in the center kitchen, the food budget will affect both meal planning and food purchasing. Quantity buying and cooperative buying arrangements among a group of centers sometimes results in lower prices but might also limit choices, increase the pressure to purchase foods of lesser quality, and create storage problems when quantity purchases exceed the available storage space. Therefore, although price is an important consideration, quality, available storage space and, of course, food preferences of the children must be taken into consideration when food purchasing decisions are made.

Catered meal service requires practically no shopping time, no storage space, and very little time selecting foods and developing the shopping lists. It also eliminates the need for a complete meal preparation space and a full-time cook, but the service may be more expensive than when meals are prepared at the center. It could also turn out to be less satisfying to the children and is likely to give the director less control over the entire food service entity.

The prepackaged frozen meals that are prepared in conduction or microwave ovens are a very expensive convenience. This type of food service requires large freezers and special ovens, yet requires neither a full-time cook nor complete meal preparation space. The director must select carefully so the choices are appropriate for young children, and there is variety in the menu. Fresh foods and beverages must be bought daily or weekly as needed, if prepackaged meals are used.

Using company or public school cafeterias requires planning with the cafeteria manager and staff. Foods brought from cafeterias serving adults or older children are sometimes served in containers or in portions which are difficult for young children to manage. A whole hamburger, a large strip of dill pickle, catsup in a sealed foil container, and milk in a sealed carton are all difficult for young children to handle. But, since that is standard public school cafeteria fare, you may find no other choices for your children. Also, cafeteria service customarily means self-help and carrying trays, and that is out of the question for young children. It is important to develop clear-cut guidelines for portion sizes, family style service and alternative menus, so you can work with the cafeteria food service staff to find ways to make appropriate adjustments for young children.

Meals prepared at the center mean that the center must have not only a complete meal preparation space which meets all licensing requirements, but must also employ a full-time cook if it is a full-day child care program. Preferably, the cook will have planning and buying skills. If not, then a staff person (sometimes the director) will plan and purchase the foods in consultation with the cook. Planning purchases, doing the shopping, and checking deliveries are all time-consuming; however, total meal preparation at the center allows for greater variation in foods served and more involvement of the children in shopping, preparation, and serving. It also guarantees that items

on the menu will be prepared and served with young children in mind.

USDA Child and Adult Care Food Program. Some centers serve children who are eligible for free or reduced-price meals from United States Department of Agriculture (USDA), Child and Adult Care Food Program (CACFP). Although some programs may have a designated staff person or the cook do some of the paper work in order to receive the USDA reimbursement, in most cases the director does the necessary paper work, or, at least, is responsible for making sure it is done correctly.

Eligibility of children for free or reduced-price meals is based on family income. Income levels for family eligibility and reimbursement rates for providers is adjusted annually. Therefore, in order to determine which families in your center are eligible and what the reimbursement rate will be for those meals, contact your USDA Regional Director's Office. (See Figure 12-1.)

An Income Eligibility Form (IEF) (see Figure 12-2) must be on file for every child who receives meals under the USDA Child Care Food Program. These forms must be kept on file for at least three years to ensure that they will be available at the time your agency undergoes a Verification Review. It is essential that the information on these forms be complete and accurate

Figure 12-1   Regional Directors—USDA Food and Nutrition Service

	TELEPHONE
MID-ATLANTIC REGIONAL OFFICE	
Mr. Robert J. Freiler, Regional Director MARO, USDA, FNS, SNP Mercer Corporate Park 300 Corporate Boulevard Robbinsville, NJ 08691	COM (609) 259-5050 FTS 8-609-259-5050
MIDWEST REGIONAL OFFICE	
Ms. Theresa E. Bowman, Regional Director MWRO, USDA, FNS, SNP 77 West Jackson Boulevard, 20th Floor Chicago, IL 60604-3507	COM (312) 353-6673 FTS 8- 312-353-6673
MOUNTAIN PLAINS REGIONAL OFFICE	
Ms. Ann C. Hector, Regional Director MPRO, USDA, FNS, SNP 1244 Speer Boulevard, Suite 903 Denver, CO 80204	COM (303) 844-0354 FTS 8- 303-844-0354
NORTHEAST REGIONAL OFFICE	
Mr. John Magnarelli, Regional Director NERO, USDA, FNS, SNP 10 Causeway Street, Room 501 Boston, MA 02222-1065	COM (617) 565-6425 FTS 8- 617-565-6425
SOUTHEAST REGIONAL OFFICE	
Ms. Nena Bratianu, Regional Director SERO, USDA, FNS, SNP 77 Forsyth Street, SW, Suite 112 Atlanta, GA 30303	COM (404) 730-2612 FTS 8- 404-730-2612
SOUTHWEST REGIONAL OFFICE	
Mr. Ronald J. Rhodes, Regional Director SWRO, USDA, FNS, SNP 1100 Commerce Street, Room 5C30 Dallas, TX 75242	COM (214) 767-0214 FTS 8- 214-767-0214
WESTERN REGIONAL OFFICE	
Mr. Bob Kragh, Regional Director WRO, USDA, FNS, SNP 550 Kearny Street, Room 400 San Francisco, CA 94108-2518	COM (415) 705-2229 FTS 8- 415-705-2229 4/1/93 DRB

Figure 12-2 Sample Application for Free and Reduced Price Meals

If you receive food stamps or are on ADC for the children named below
COMPLETE ITEMS 1, 4, 7, AND 8

If you do not receive food stamps or ADC
COMPLETE ITEMS 1,2,3,5,6,7, AND 8

To apply for free or reduced price meals for your children, parents must carefull complete, *sign*, and return this application to the school. If you need help with this form, please call _____

1. Names of Children Applying (Are these foster children?) Yes No
Last Name _____ First Name _____ Birthdate _____

For School Use Only
Approved: Free ___ or Reduced Price ___
Denied ___ Reason_____
APPROVED BY   DATE NOTIFIED

How to figure income: *If you are paid:*
Weekly—multiply gross pay by 52 & divide by 12.
Each 2 wks, multiply gross by 26 & divide by 12.
Twice a month, multiply gross pay by 2.
Once a month, use total gross amount.
Every three months, divide total gross by 3.
Every six months, divide total gross by 6.
Yearly, divide total gross by 12.

(Attach sheet with additional children in order to have *all children* listed on the same application.)

4. Food Stamp or ADC Households: If your household receives food stamps or you receive ADC funds for the children named above, enter the
FOOD STAMP CASE NUMBER:_____

or the ADC CASE NUMBER:_____
and complete items *7 and 8*
OR

2. Household Members: List the names and indicate ages by a check mark in the appropriate box of everyone living in the household. Include yourself and the children listed above.

Also, enter the total number of household members

3. Social Security Numbers: Print the Social Security Number of each adult, age 21 or older. If an adult does not have a Social Security Number, print "None" next to their name. (See below)

5. Income: List ALL income received last month on the same line with the person who received it. List each amount under the correct title. **You must list the gross income before all deductions for taxes, Social Security, health benefits, union dues, etc. are made.** If you or a household member received higher/lower than ususal income last month, list the expected average monthly income in the space.

LIST ALL HOUSEHOLD MEMBERS

Name Last	First	Age Under 21	21 and up	Social Security #	TOTAL Earnings from work before Deductions include ALL jobs	Social Security Green/Gold Ck Pensions Retirement	Unemployment Workmens Compensation Strike Benefit	Welfare AFDC ADC Child Support Alimony	All Other Income Received Last Month

(Attach sheet with additional members if more reside at this location)   6. Total Household Monthly Income $_____
THE TOTAL MONTHLY INCOME MUST BE EQUAL TO THE SUM OF ALL INCOME FIGURES LISTED FOR EACH PERSON AND FROM EACH SOURCE
Race: Please check your children's racial or ethnic group. You are not required to answer this question. We need this information to be sure everyone receives benefits on a fair basis. ___White, not of Hispanic Origin ___Black, not of Hispanic Origin ___Hispanic ___Asian or Pacific Islander ___American Indian or Alaskan Native.
No child will be discriminated against because of race color, disability, national origin, sex or age.

8. Name and Address: Please print
Name _____
Address _____ Apt # _____
City _____ State _____ ZIP _____

7.SIGNATURE_____
Signature of Parent or adult family member   Date
I understand that all of the above information is true and correct and that all income is reported. I understand that this information is being given for the receipt of Federal Funds; that officials may verify the information on the application; and that deliberate misrepresentation of the information may subject me to prosecution under applicable state and federal laws.

to avoid the possibility of penalties should errors be discovered at the time of the review.

Providers who fit into one of the categories listed below may receive USDA reimbursement for eligible children enrolled.

Eligible providers are:

- public or private not-for profit child care centers

- profit making child care centers that receive Title XX compensation for at least 25 percent of the children attending
- Head Start programs
- settlement houses and recreation programs
- family child care homes (only if they participate in the CACFP under a sponsoring organization which has tax-exempt status)

Figure 12-3 Child and Adult Care Food Program—Meal Patterns

CHILD AND ADULT CARE FOOD PROGRAM MEAL PATTERN FOR INFANTS

BREAKFAST	Infants Birth through 3 months	Infants 4 through 7 months	Infants 8 through 11 months
	4-6 fl. oz. formula (1)	4-8 fl. oz. formula (1) or breast milk (5) 0-3 Tbsp. infant cereal (2) (optional)	6-8 fl. oz. formula (1) breast milk (5), or whole milk. 2-4 Tbsp. infant cereal (2) 1-4 Tbsp. fruit and/or vegetable.
LUNCH OR SUPPER			
	4-6 fl. oz. Formula (1)	4-8 fl. oz. formula (1) or breast milk (5) 03- Tbsp. infant cereal (2) (optional) 0-3 Tbsp. fruit and/or vegetable (optional)	6-8 fl. oz. formula (1) breask milk (5), or whole milk. 2-4 Tbsp. infant cereal (2) and/or 1-4 Tbsp. meat, fish, poultry, egg yolk, or cooked dry beans or peas or 1/2 to 2 oz. cheese or 1-4 oz. cottage cheese, cheese food or cheese spread 1-4 Tbsp. fruit and/or vegetable.
SUPPLEMENT			
	4-6 fl. oz. formula (1)	4-6 fl. oz. formula (1)	2-4 fl. oz. formula (1) breast milk (5), whole milk, or fruit juice (3). 0-1/2 slice bread or 0-2 crackers (optional) (4).

(1) Shall be iron-fortified infant formula.
(2) Shall be iron fortified dry infant cereal.
(3) Shall be full-strength fruit juice.
(4) Shall be from whole-grain or enriched meal or flour.
(5) Breast milk, provided by the infant's mother may be served in place of formula from birth through 11 months. Meals containing only breast milk or not reimbursable. Meals containing breast milk served to infants 4 months or older may be claimed when the other meal component(s) is supplied by the child care facility.

Figure 12-3   (*continued*)

CHILD AND ADULT CARE FOOD PROGRAM
MEAL PATTERN FOR CHILDREN

BREAKFAST	Children 1 and 2 years	Children 3 through 5 years	Children 6 through 12 years
Milk, fluid	1/2 cup	3/4 cup	1 cup
Juice or fruit or vegetable	1/4 cup	1/2 cup	1/2 cup
Bread and/or cereal, enriched or whole grain			
Bread or	1/2 slice	1/2 slice	1 slice
Cereal: Cold, dry or	1/4 cup(1)	1/3 cup (2)	3/4 cup(3)
Hot cooked	1/4 cup	1/4 cup	1/2 cup
MIDMORNING OR MIDAFTERNOON SNACK (SUPPLEMENT)			
(Select 2 of these 4 component(s)			
Milk, fluid	1/2 cup	1/2 cup	1 cup
Meat or meat alternate (4)	1/2 ounce	1/2 ounce	1 ounce
Juice or fruit or vegetable	1/2 cup	1/2 cup	3/4 cup
Bread and/or cereal, enriched or whole grain			
Bread or	1/2 slice	1/2 slice	1 slice
Cereal: Cold, dry or	1/4 cup (1)	1/3 cup (2)	3/4 cup (3)
Hot cooked	1/4 cup	1/4 cup	1/2 cup
LUNCH OR SUPPER			
Milk, fluid	1/2 cup	3/4 cup	1 cup
Meat or meat alternate			
Meat, poultry, or fish, cooked (lean meat without bone)	1 ounce	1 1/2 ounces	2 ounces
Cheese	1 ounce	1 1/2 ounces	2 ounces
Egg	1	1	1
Cooked dry beans and peas	1/4 cup	3/8 cup	1/2 cup
Peanut butter or other nut or seed butters	2 tablespoons	3 tablespoons	4 tablespoons
Nuts and/or seeds	1/2 ounce (5)	3/4 ounce (5)	1 ounce (5)
Vegetable and/or fruit (two or more to total	1/4 cup	1/2 cup	3/4 cup
Bread or bread alternate, enriched or whole grain	1/2 slice	1/2 slice	1 slice

(1)   1/4 cup (volume) or 1/3 ounce (weight), whichever is less.
(2)   1/3 cup (volume) or 1/2 ounce (weight), whichever is less.
(3)   3/4 cup (volume) or 1 ounce (weight), whichever is less.
(4)   Yogurt may be used as a meat/meat alternate in the snack only. You may serve 4 ounces (weight) or 1/2 cup (volume) of plain, or sweetened and flavored yogurt to fulfill the equivalent of 1 ounce of the meat/meat alternate component. For younger children, 2 ounces (weight) or 1/4 cup (volume) may fulfill the equivalent of 1/2 ounces of the meat/meat alternate requirement.
(5)   This portion can meet only one-half of the total serving of the meat/meat alternate requirement for lunch or supper. Nuts or seeds must be combined with another meat/meat alternate to fulfill the requirement. For determining combinations, 1 ounce of nuts or seeds is equal to 1 ounce of cooked lean meat, poultry or fish.

All participating agencies must serve meals that meet the standards for the Special Food Service Program for Infants, Preschool Age and School Age Children which are covered in Figure 12-3. Following these guidelines ensures well-balanced meals; however, some recommended serving sizes may be overwhelming for young children if put on the plate all at one time.

The USDA Child and Adult Care Food Program requires extensive paperwork which must be done accurately and on a regular basis. A Claim for Reimbursement form (see Sample Figure 12-4)

Figure 12-4   Child and Adult Care Food Program Claim for Reimbursement

CACFP 006 ■   Printed in U.S.A. ■■   Trans-Optic® by NCS MM90730:321   A1107

CHILD AND ADULT CARE FOOD PROGRAM CLAIM FOR REIMBURSEMENT
CHILD CARE COMPONENT

○ Original Claim

PLEASE READ INSTRUCTIONS ON REVERSE SIDE

PROGRAM TYPE: Fill in one
○ Day Care   ○ Head Start
○ Proprietary   ○ OSH

○ Revised Claim

* DO NOT FOLD OR STAPLE FORM

SPONSORING AGENCY

ADDRESS   CITY   ZIP

COUNTY   PHONE

I CERTIFY that to the best of my knowledge this claim is correct in all respects, that records are available to support this claim, that it is in accordance with the terms of existing agreement(s), and that payment, therefore, has not been received. I recognize that I will be fully responsible for any excess amounts which may result from erroneous or neglectful reporting.

SPONSOR IRN

A
Number of Operating Days

○ Oct.
○ Nov.
○ Dec.
○ Jan.
○ Feb.
○ March
○ April
○ May
○ June
○ July
○ Aug.
○ Sept.

Program Year

PERSON AUTHORIZED TO PREPARE REPORT   TITLE   PREPARATION DATE

B Average Daily Attendance	C Number of Sites	**Eligible Number of Meals Served**			**Eligible Supplements Served**		
		D Breakfasts	E Lunches	F Suppers	G AM	H PM	I Evening

PROGRAM ADULTS

Number of Meals Served			**Supplements**			**Enrollment by Income Category**		
J Breakfasts	K Lunches	L Suppers	M AM	N PM	O Evening	P Free	Q Reduced	R Paid

Figure 12-4 *(continued)*

Child Care Component
INSTRUCTIONS

General: In order to receive federal assistance for meal service, each program must report month-end counts on a claim for reimbursement. The claim covers operations for one calendar month only. Claims are due in the state agency office by the 10th of the month following the month being reported.

Original Claim: When this form is used, darken the bubble.

Revised Claim: When this form is used, darken the bubble and complete only the items needing changes; leave all other items blank.

Special Note: Claims or revised claims received more than 60 days after the end of a reporting month will not be processed for reimbursement.

To Fill Out The Form:

1. Use a No. 2 lead pencil. The identification data may be typed with care not to intrude into the reporting areas.
2. First write the numbers in the rectangles above the numbered bubbles. Pay attention to the commas.

   Second, darken the corresponding bubble below each number.

   Third, clearly erase any response that is changed. Completely darken the bubble for each number you mark.

3. Enter the IRN number of the program in the space provided & darken the bubbles that correspond to these digits. Darken the bubble of the month for which the report is being filed. Darken the bubble identifying this report as either the original submission or the revision for this claim month.

A Enter total number of days food service was provided to children for the claim month.

B Compute average daily attendance by adding daily attendance for the month and dividing the total by the number of days of operation during the same month.

C Enter the number of sites that were operating during the claim month.

D - Enter the total number of breakfasts, lunches, and suppers served to enrolled
E - children in attendance at child care centers and outside-school-hours care
F - centers during the claim month.

G - Enter the total number of a.m., p.m., and evening supplements served to enrolled
H - children in attendance at child care centers and outside-school-hours care centers
I - during the claim month.

J - Enter the total number of breakfasts, lunches, and suppers served in child care
K - centers and outside-school-hours care centers to adults who performed necessary
L - labor in support of the program: menu planning; preparing, serving, and clean-up, on-site recordkeeping; supervision of children at meals claimed for reimbursement.

M - Enter the total number of a.m., p.m., and evening supplements served in child care
N - centers and outside-school-hours care centers to adults who performed necessary
O - labor in support of the program.

P Enter the number of enrolled children classified as free. Each child so classified must have on file with the sponsor a correctly completed Income Eligibility Application.

Q Enter the number of enrolled children classified as reduced-price. Each child so classified must have on file with the sponsor a correct Income Eligibility Application.

R Enter the number of enrolled children classified as paid. This includes all children without Income Eligibility Applications or whose household incomes are above qualifying income eligibility guidelines.

The original and one copy of the claim for reimbursement shall be forwarded to the Ohio Department of Education, Division of School Food Service, Child and Adult Care Food Program, 65 South Front Street, Room 715, Columbus, Ohio 43266-0308, not later than the TENTH DAY OF THE MONTH following the calendar month being reported. A copy should be retained by the submitting agency for a permanent record.

must be filed monthly with the State Division of School Food Service reporting data on:

- attendance
- number of meals served
- cost of food which is calculated on the basis of information obtained from a monthly food inventory
- labor and purchased service costs
- income from reduced-lunch fees and other sources

To complete this claim form you must have accurate attendance records, invoices or cash tapes and receipts for all food purchases, and financial records on all cash received from those families who pay full or reduced-lunch costs.

Even when there is an extra person on staff to do the USDA paper work, data collection for the reports and preparation for the Verification Review involves the director, the cook, and the teaching staff.

Each program is subject to a Verification Review by the State agency every three years. The purpose of the review is to determine that all the income eligibility forms since the last review have been filled out correctly, that each family is properly classified as free, reduced or paid, and that the figures reported to the State on the monthly claim for reimbursement were accurate. When the CACFP consultant comes to the center to do the Verification Review, you must provide the following:

- all income eligibility forms
- attendance records
- enrollment forms (to confirm that children listed as eligible for reimbursement are enrolled)

In addition to reviewing records on children, the consultant will also review administrative records. For that review you must provide:

- record of meal counts
- menus
- monthly food inventories
- documentation of food and supply costs
- documentation of labor costs
- documentation of Title XX enrollments if it is a proprietary center

Complicated you say! Yes, indeed, very complicated. As a director, it is essential that you understand the USDA program so you can do the paperwork, if it is part of your job description, or delegate the responsibility and then coach those who are doing the detailed record keeping and reporting.

Food Storage

Storing food requires careful planning so that sufficient quantities of food items are conveniently accessible to the preparation area and storage areas and containers are sanitary and chilled. The available shelf space and containers must be appropriate to accommodate the packaged size of the food items as they are delivered from the supplier. All food items should be stored separately from nonfood items, and food storage rooms should be dry, relatively cool (60°F to 70°F), and free from insect or rodent infestation. Commodities should be stored in tightly covered, labeled metal or heavy plastic containers that are at least six inches above the floor level to permit air circulation and to protect them from dirt. Dating containers ensures food supplies will be used in the order received.

Perishable foods must be stored at temperatures that prevent spoilage. Refrigerator temperature must be 45°F or lower; freezer temperature should be at 0°F or lower. Shelf space should allow for air circulation around the refrigerated foods, and thermometers in the warmest sections of refrigerators and freezers should be checked daily.

Food Preparation

Cooks must follow recipes in meal preparation and must adhere to directions about cooking times and temperatures, proper techniques and temperatures for holding prepared foods, and proper methods for storing and using leftovers. Sanitation in the food preparation area is of utmost importance. The food service staff must follow sanitary food-handling practices and maintain good personal hygiene while handling foods and cleaning food preparation equipment and utensils. Even though there may be a nutritionist or other staff member responsible for the total food service program in the center, it is advisable for you, as director, to make periodic checks on the food preparation techniques and the sanitation practices of the cook as food is prepared and served to the children. It often becomes the director's responsibility to coach the cook when correct preparation procedures are not being followed.

Sanitation guidelines are available from your local health department or your state or local licensing agent. The licensing regulations at all levels include clearly stated sanitation requirements related to food preparation in child care centers. A local health department staff member or your center licensing agent are excellent resources for helping interpret and implement the sanitation regulations applicable in your area.

Resources

The list, "Sources of Child Health and Safety Information and Materials" in Director's Resources covers both public and private resources on the national, state, and local levels. These agencies can supply copies of laws, regulations, and guidelines in response to questions regarding nutrition and health. The following list includes additional places to go for printed material and for consultation on the center's nutrition component:

- public health nutritionists in state or local health department or the county extension agency
- nutritionists in local dairy councils or comprehensive health centers
- USDA extension home economists
- home economists in nearby high schools or universities
- members of local home economics associations
- dietitians in local hospitals

HEALTH AND SAFETY PROGRAM

The center staff members are responsible for the health and safety of the children while they are at the center; therefore, directors must be knowledgeable about health and safety regulations as stipulated in the licensing regulations, staff liability in cases of accidents at school, and procedures for protection from and reporting of communicable disease and child abuse. Although some large centers may have a health consultant on staff, in most places the director is the designated individual responsible for the health program.

The health services provided through the child care center may range from no service at all to comprehensive service, including regular physicals, dental check-ups and treatment, vision screening, hearing screening, and mental health services. The scope of the health services program depends on the program health policies set by the funding agent, the socioeconomic status of the families, the family expectations, and the licensing regulations. All centers should maintain up-to-date health and immunization records on the children whether or not direct health services are provided.

Health Records for Children and Staff

Children's health records should cover information up to the time of registration plus any new health or medical information received while the child is in the program. Formats for these records vary (see sample in Director's Resource 11-4, pg. 309, and Director's Resource 11-6, pg. 316) but the information provided, (in addition to the basic demographics like name, birth date, parents names, etc.) should include:[4]

---

4 Ibid., AAP, p. 19.

- results of standard screening (e.g. vision, hearing, measurements, dentition, and so forth)
- documentation of all immunizations and schedule for update
- health history from the parent and the physician or clinic
- description of level of functioning in motor, cognitive, communicative, social and emotional areas, noting areas which require special attention of the child care staff

Staff medical records which follow the licensing requirements must be on file at the center. Even when not required by licensing, there should be a medical record on every adult who has regular contact with the children including substitutes, volunteers, practicum students, cooks and van drivers. Not only should the staff records include a physical assessment but also an evaluation of the emotional fitness of those who are to care for the children. In designing the staff health form items to include are as follows:[5]

- freedom from contagious disease
- history of childhood infectious diseases (e.g., rubella, chicken pox, mumps, etc.)
- negative tuberculin test or follow-up on positive one
- immunization record, including tetanus booster within ten years
- hearing and visual acuity
- evidence of mental and emotional fitness

Unless licensing regulations require more frequent updating of staff health records, it is recommended this be done every two years.

Disaster Plan

Although licensing regulations do not always require disaster plans, it is important to plan for building evacuation in the event of fire and to detail additional measures to be taken during tornadoes, earthquakes, smog alerts, floods, or sudden loss of heat or air conditioning. The director must instruct all staff members on the best ways to evacuate the premises, and the safe places to shelter children in weather or civil defense emergencies. An evacuation plan should be posted in each classroom (see Figure 12-5). Fire emergency plans must include alternative exit routes, and evacuation drills should be held regularly so children become familiar with this routine. Parents must be informed, in advance, about alternative shelters, so they know the whereabouts of their children during emergencies.

Daily attendance records and information needed to reach parents must be maintained in a convenient location, and removed from the building by the designated adults as part of the evacuation procedure. The "chain of command" regarding who will call for emergency fire or police help, who will secure the building and make a final check that everyone is out, how the building will be secured, and who will contact the parents must all be arranged in advance and communicated to staff by the director. Fire alarms, fire extinguishers and emergency exit lights should be checked regularly to ensure they are in working order.

Supplies stored in emergency evacuation areas and to be taken to the alternative shelter include:

- first aid kit
- blankets
- food and water
- battery operated radio
- flashlight
- children's books, crayons, paper, etc.

To obtain more information on the best methods to provide protection in particular areas, directors can contact local health and fire department officials, building inspectors, the Environmental Protection Agency (EPA) or the Occupational Safety and Health Administration (OSHA).

Emergency Health and Accident Plan

An emergency health plan is usually developed by the director with input from board

5 Ibid., AAP, p. 21.

Figure 12-5 Sample Evacuation Plan

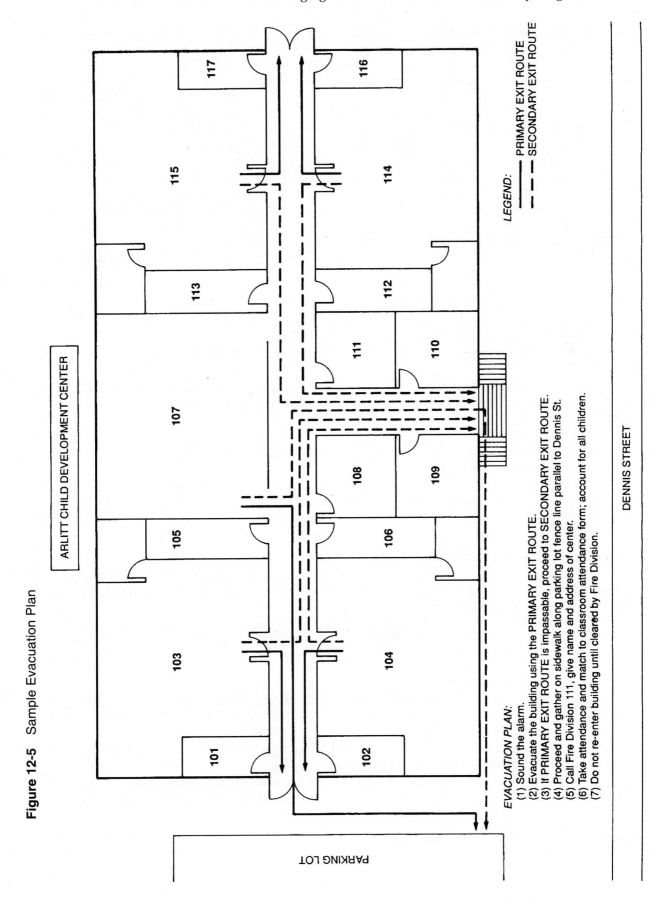

ARLITT CHILD DEVELOPMENT CENTER

LEGEND:
——— PRIMARY EXIT ROUTE
– – – SECONDARY EXIT ROUTE

EVACUATION PLAN:
(1) Sound the alarm.
(2) Evacuate the building using the PRIMARY EXIT ROUTE.
(3) If PRIMARY EXIT ROUTE is impassable, proceed to SECONDARY EXIT ROUTE.
(4) Proceed and gather on sidewalk along parking lot fence line parallel to Dennis St.
(5) Call Fire Division 111, give name and address of center.
(6) Take attendance and match to classroom attendance form; account for all children.
(7) Do not re-enter building until cleared by Fire Division.

DENNIS STREET

PARKING LOT

members, staff members, and families. It should include the step-by-step procedures to be followed when a child is injured at the center. The purpose of the plan is to provide the center staff with a detailed set of instructions to follow when giving an injured or sick child the best and quickest treatment, notifying the family, and filling out the necessary papers for maximum liability and insurance protection for both staff and family. (See Figure 12-6 for a sample emergency health and accident plan.)

If the child must be taken away from the center for emergency care, the caregiver must stay with that child until the parent arrives. Since the parent cannot give informed consent in advance for emergency treatment because the nature of the injury is not known, it is essential that parents understand that the center must know their whereabouts, or that of another responsible adult, at all times. It is suggested that the telephone numbers on the child's emergency record, including those for the child's usual source of health care, be updated several times a year.

The director as well as some members of the teaching staff should have first aid training, including cardiopulmonary resuscitation (CPR), so that preliminary emergency treatment can begin before professional help arrives, and minor injuries will be handled correctly. An injury report must be filled out any time a child

Figure 12-6 Sample Emergency Medical Plan

Procedures for Medical Emergencies

1. Each classroom teacher shall assume responsibility for care in any emergency which occurs on school property.

2. Assistant teachers or volunteers should contact the classroom teacher in case of emergency. If the teacher is not available, contact should be made with another classroom teacher in the building or the director.

3. If, in the judgement of the teacher, the injury needs medical attention, the director will call the parent of the child. If the parent cannot be reached, the director will call the emergency number on the Emergency Information Record.

4. If the injury requires immediate emergency treatment, call for medical assistance and transportation to the Emergency Room of the hospital authorized by the parent. Ambulance number is _____. The classroom teacher will accompany the child to the hospital and the director will call the parent.

Staff Instructions for Ill Children

1. If a child should become ill after arrival at school, contact the parent to come and take the child home. If parents cannot be reached, the director will call the emergency number on the Emergency Information Record.

2. If no transportation is available, provisions will be made for the child to remain at school until the regular departure time. The child will be removed from the classroom and will be cared for in the director's office.

Additional Instructions for Staff

1. An accident report must be filled out for any injury requiring medical attention. The report is to be filled out by the teacher and given to the director to be placed in the office health file with a copy in the child's file.

2. Any incident or injury occurring at school which appears to be upsetting or traumatic to the child shall be related to the parent by the teacher.

3. The center maintains a $25.00 deductible insurance policy on each child. If injuries sustained by a child incur costs above this amount, the parent should be told to contact the director for appropriate insurance forms for coverage.

(Adapted from Arlitt Child Development Center form).

is hurt, and it should be filed in a central location with a copy in the child's file (see Figure 12-7). It is essential to follow the accident plans, have staff properly trained to deal with injuries, and fill out injury reports, both for the safety and well-being of children and the protection of staff. Directors and board members must understand that taking all these precautions may not completely protect the staff from liability. Therefore, the center should carry accident insurance on the children and have liability coverage for the staff as an additional precautionary measure. It is wise to consult an attorney and your insurance agent about what constitutes adequate coverage.

Communicable Disease

Cases of communicable diseases at the child care center must be reported to all center families and to the local health authorities. The usual children's diseases, as well as cases of meningitis, scarlet fever, infectious hepatitis, and head lice, must be reported so that necessary precautions can be taken immediately. It is important that pregnant staff members consult their physician about precautions related to exposure to communicable diseases at the workplace.

Directors and some of the teaching staff should have training in communicable diseases, to enable them to recognize symptoms and make decisions about exclusion of children from the group. The most important measure in preventing spread of disease in child care centers is hand washing. Not only after toileting or diapering, but after nose blowing or helping a child with a runny nose or cough, and before handling dishes or serving food. Sanitizing surfaces after diapering or tables before using for eating will also help cut down on spread of disease. *Cleanliness* is the major contributing factor to effective disease control in child care environments.

Staff members responsible for giving first aid to children and those likely to come in contact with blood or body fluids should have special training in dealing with blood-borne pathogens like HIV or hepatitis B. These employees should also be offered hepatitis B vaccine and the director should maintain records of immunizations as well as exposure incidents.[6]

The spread of disease is also minimized through precautionary measures for handling situations where children become ill during the day and when children are ill upon arrival. A written policy regarding management of sick children must be conveyed to parents when children are enrolled. Since very few centers have facilities to care for a sick child who must be separated from the other children, the usual practice is to call the parent or a designated adult to come for the child. In the meantime, the child is usually removed from the classroom, and under adult supervision rests or plays quietly. Often the director is the only staff person who has a schedule which is flexible enough to allow for time to stay with the sick child. An extra cot and a few toys for use while waiting to be picked up by a parent is standard equipment in many directors' offices.

Exclusion Policy. Exclusion policies must be made clear to parents and to the child care staff. If the purpose of excluding an ill child is to prevent the spread of infection to others in the group, it is important to specify which types of illnesses require exclusion. This list should include infectious diarrhea and vomiting, untreated conjunctivitis, impetigo, ringworm, head lice, and scabies.[7] When the policy is clear it helps both parents and staff make decisions about when to exclude children from the group. Programs which have staffed facilities to care for mildly ill children can have more liberal exclusion policies than those with no staff or space for these children to receive the extra rest and supervision they require.

Although there is an ever-increasing amount of information on the risks posed by children with Acquired Immune Deficiency Syndrome (AIDS) attending child care programs, evidence is inconclusive at this time.[8] Despite the concerns among child care professionals about this question, few

6 Susan S. Aronson, MD, "OSHA Requires Employers to Give Hepatitis B Immunization and Protection to First Aiders," *Child Care Information Exchange, The Director's Magazine,* November 1992, p. 55.
7 Susan S. Aronson, MD, "Exclusion Criteria for Ill Children in Child Care," *Child Care Information Exchange: The Director's Magazine,* May 1986, p. 14.
8 Ibid., CCIE, 1986, p. 16.

Figure 12-7   Sample Injury Report Form

Name of Child_____Birth Date_____

Parent Name_____

Address_____Phone Number_____

Usual Source of Health Care_____

Date of Injury_____Time_____Age_____Sex_____

      Type of Injury (circle)   Bite,   Broken Bone,   Bruise,   Burn,   Choking,   Cut,   Eye Injury,   Foreign   Body,   Head   Injury,   Poisoning,   Scrape,   Sliver,   Sprain,   Sting, Other_____

Location Where Injury Occurred_____
      e.g., child care room, bathroom, hall, playground, large muscle room, bus, car, walk

Type of Equipment Involved_____

How Injury Happened (who, what, where, how, when)_____

_____

_____

_____

_____

Type of Treatment Required_____
      e.g., first aid only in day care, visit to doctor's office or clinic, emergency room, hospitalized/sutures, cast, bandage, medication given

Witnesses of Injury Incident_____

Signatures of Witnesses_____

Name of Medical Professional Consulted_____

Date_____Time_____Advice_____

_____

Retrospectively, what would have prevented this injury?

_____

_____

_____

_____

*American Academy of Pediatrics, "Health in Day Care: A Manual for Professionals," 1987, Appendix VI.7.

centers will face the issue due to the small numbers of young children with AIDS. "The primary risk of admitting children with AIDS is that these children run a greater risk of contracting illnesses and infections from the other children because their immune systems are not functioning properly. These infections pose a serious threat to the child's life."[9] The current information from the Center for Disease Control regarding the virus related to AIDS is that there are no known cases in the United States where this virus has been transmitted in school or child care environments, or through casual contact, such as touching, hugging, eating together or sharing bathrooms. However, many centers are choosing to have a written policy on AIDS in order to protect the rights of an infected child and the other children in the center.

The Centers for Disease Control (CDC) is recommending that children with AIDS be excluded from the group *only* if they have open sores or bleeding, which would put other children at risk from exposure to the infected child's body fluids.[10] To obtain updated information on this question or others involving infectious diseases contact Centers for Disease Control.[11]

Sick Child Care. As more children under five require some type of care outside the home, there is the consequent increase in the need for sick child care. The first alternative is to have the child at home with a caring parent whose employer allows time off for that purpose. Being at home may be the best alternative, but not always the most realistic. That means child care professionals, with the help of health professionals, are beginning to develop alternative sick child care models.

Sick children might be accommodated in:

- a sick bay at the center—a *Get Well Room*
- a center in a separate building which might be the cooperative venture of several child care programs
- a center in a wing of a hospital or on hospital grounds that is available to the general public

- a "satellite" system of family child care homes linked to a child care center
- the child's own home under the supervision of a trained person sent from the center or local health agency

"Deciding how to meet sick children's needs and parents' needs for child care is often difficult. Isolation and exclusion is not necessary for many illnesses. A balance must be struck between the needs of the child and the other children in the group and an arrangement made that does not strain the staffing resources of the day care program."[12] Since children with AIDS are extremely vulnerable to infection from other children, it is probably unwise to have them in a sick child care facility where they would be exposed to other sick children.

Child Abuse

Directors must be vigilant and take steps to prevent the possibility of abuse on the premises,

9 Ibid., Marotz, et al, p. 132.
10 Ibid., Marotz, et al, p. 132.
11 Center for Disease Control, Atlanta, Georgia 30333, (404)329-3091.
12 Ibid., AAP, p. 67.

recognize signs of abuse on children who come to the program, and make certain suspected cases of abuse are properly reported.

Prevention on the Premises. Precautions must be taken to prevent both physical and sexual abuse on the premises. Physical abuse occurs most often when adults are stressed; further, the abusive act is unplanned and explosive, and usually occurs when other adults are not around. Sexual abuse, on the other hand, although it also occurs when other adults are not around, is frequently planned ahead, and these pedophiles may even seek employment in child care centers to gain access to children. In the latter case, careful pre-employment screening, use of criminal record checks and fingerprinting may provide helpful information, but how effective these expensive measures really are is still unknown.[13]

Since abuse of all types usually occurs when other adults are not around, the preventive measures mentioned in connection with staffing patterns (Chapter 9), and developing the facility (Chapter 7), plus making it clear to everyone that parents may visit at any time, should help eliminate the possibility of abuse occurring in your center.

Recognizing and Reporting Abuse. All directors and members of the teaching staff in child care programs should have some training in recognizing the physical and behavioral signs of abuse whether or not licensing requires it. In most states, professionals involved with children are required to report suspected cases of abuse. When mandated to report suspicion of abuse, those reporting are not required to prove their allegations. Nonetheless, reports should be made carefully because much harm can come to children and families when the accusations are unfounded. The director should be notified of all suspected cases of abuse and review the case with the staff member who has found evidence of abuse before the case is reported to the authorities. In most states, information is given to law enforcement agencies or child protective agencies. Familiarity with state laws and local rules for reporting is essential for all child care directors.

SUMMARY

Directors are responsible for overseeing the food service and the health and safety programs in the child care center. Although a designated staff person and the center cook may plan menus, order food, and prepare meals, the director is accountable to both the center families and the sponsoring or funding agency for the quality of the food service program.

Monitoring the health program and implementing plans to care for children who are injured or sick is also part of the director's responsibility. It is important to have written policies and reporting procedures for injuries which occur during school hours. Plans for caring for sick children with specific exclusion guidelines are helpful. It is also important to take preventive precautions regarding child abuse in the center, and to make certain that suspected cases of abuse are detected and reported.

Class Assignments

1. Contact your regional USDA office (Figure 12-1), local child care center, or a Head Start program to obtain the current reimbursement rates for both free and reduced rate meals for eligible children.

13 Ibid., AAP, p. 48.

   a. Using Working Paper 12-1, record reimbursement allowances in the spaces provided.

   b. Using information from Working Paper 12-1 (Assignment 1-a) and the information given in the chart "Number of Meals Served" (Working Paper 12-2), complete Working Paper 12-2 by calculating the amount to be reimbursed for meals served during the month.

2. Using Working Paper 12-3, fill in the emergency numbers for the services listed. Include the name of the agency and a contact person where indicated.

Class Exercises

1. Work with another student and role play a conference between a director and a cook, assuming the two roles as follows:

   Director: As a director, you are responsible for monitoring food preparation and serving methods. You have carefully checked with the home economist at the local utilities company and you have read numerous government publications on the best way to prepare vegetables to retain nutrients. You know that cooking time should be short, that the amount of water used should be small, and that the vegetables should be prepared only minutes before eating. Furthermore, you know that children's foods should be cut in bite-sized portions; that is, stew meat in half-inch cubes, bread slices in quarters, and fish sticks halved, and so forth. Your cook prepares all vegetables early in the day and keeps them over low heat until serving time. Even though the recipes indicate that meat should be served in bite-sized pieces and portions should be small, the meat comes from the kitchen in the same sizes in which it was delivered from the meat market.

   Cook: You were hired for this job in the child care center after being an assistant cook in a restaurant for five years. You have looked forward to having your own kitchen and you are proud of your previous experience and what you know about preparation of food in quantity.

   As director, you must call the conference and deal with the problem. Keep in mind that you are committed to maintaining open communication and to promoting the personal and professional growth of your staff.

2. As a group, discuss the evacuation plan for the room in which you are now having class. Do you see exit signs or evacuation directions in this room or in the adjacent hallways?

   a. If you were responsible for this building, what steps would you take to develop a building evacuation plan and inform the staff about it?

   b. If you had to use this room for a children's classroom, how would you evacuate the children and how would you prepare the children for an emergency evacuation procedure without creating anxiety and fear?

Working Paper 12-1

Food Reimbursement Allowances

	Free	*Reduced*
Breakfast	_____ per child	_____ per child
Lunch/Dinner	_____ per child	_____ per child
Snack	_____ per child	_____ per child
(Supplements)		

Fill in the above grid with information from your regional USDA office, a local daycare center, or a Head Start program. Use this information to complete the assignment on Working Paper 12-2.

Working Paper 12-2

Number of Meals Served

Date	Breakfast		Lunch/Dinner		Snack	
	Free	Reduced	Free	Reduced	Free	Reduced
3	12	2	21	3	21	3
4	13	2	20	3	20	3
5	11	1	18	2	19	2
6	15	1	18	2	19	2
7	15	2	18	1	18	1
10	12	1	17	1	18	1
11	14	2	21	1	20	1
12	15	1	20	2	20	2
13	15	2	18	3	18	3
14	13	2	18	3	18	3
17	12	2	19	2	19	2
18	11	2	19	1	19	2
19	13	1	18	3	19	3
20	13	1	17	3	19	3
21	14	2	19	3	18	3
24	13	2	19	2	19	2
25	14	1	18	3	18	3
26	15	1	18	2	18	2
27	16	0	19	3	19	3
28	14	2	18	3	18	3
31	14	2	20	3	20	2
TOTAL						

Using the information from Working Paper 12-1 on reimbursement amounts for free and reduced meals, and the information from the chart Number of Meals Served, fill in the following table.

Breakfast	number of free meals X free rate =	_____
	number of reduced meals X reduced rate=	_____
Lunch/Dinner	number of free meals X free rate =	_____
	number of reduced meals X reduced rate=	_____
Snack	number of free meals X free rate =	_____
(Supplement)	number of reduced meals X reduced rate=	_____

Total claim for reimbursement   _____

Working Paper 12-3

Emergency Phone Numbers

Record the following emergency phone numbers and contact person, where that information is requested.

- General emergency number (e.g., 911)   _____
- Police   _____
- Fire   _____
- Ambulance   _____
- Poison Control Center   _____
- Health Department   _____

_____
Contact Person

- Report Child Abuse   _____

_____
Agency

_____
Contact Person

Director's Resource 12-1

Sources of Child Health and Safety Information and Materials

Federal

1. Head Start Health Service, Administration for Child, Youth and Families, P.O. Box 1182, Washington, DC 20013.
2. U.S. Department of Labor, Occupational Safety and Health Administration (OSHA), Washington, DC 20013.
3. U.S. Department of Agriculture, Food and Nutrition Information Center, National Agricultural Library Building, Room 304, Beltsville, MD 20705. 1-301-344-3719.
4. Clearinghouse on Child Abuse and Neglect Information, P.O. Box 1182, Washington, DC 20013. 1-202-755-0590.
5. Clearinghouse on the Handicapped, Room 338-D, Hubert H. Humphrey Building, 200 Independence Ave., SW, Washington, DC 20201. 1-202-245-1961.
6. Clearinghouse on Sudden Infant Death Syndrome (SIDS), 1555 Wilson Blvd., Suite 600, Rosslyn, VA 22209-2461. 1-703-522-0870.
7. National Information Center for Handicapped Children and Youth, 1555 Wilson Blvd., Rosslyn, VA 22209. 1-703-522-0870.
8. National Institute of Mental Health (NIMH), 5600 Fishers Lane, Rockville, MD 20857.
9. National Institute of Child Health and Human Development, Office of Research Reporting, 9600 Rockville Pike, Room 2A-32, Bethesda, MD 20205. 1-301-496-5133.
10. For anything developed by or procured through the Division of Maternal and Child Health, write to: Health Clearinghouse, 8201 Greensboro Drive, Suite 600, McLean, VA 22102.
11. Superintendent of Documents, Government Printing Office, Washington, DC 20402.
12. United States Consumer Product Safety Commission (USCPSC), Room 336B, 5401 Westband Ave., Bethesda, MD 20207. 1-800-638-2772.

National (private)

1. American Academy of Pediatrics, Division of Health Education, 141 Northwest Point Blvd., P.O. Box 927, Elk Grove Village, IL 60009. 1-800-433-0797. Resources: The Injury Prevention Program (TIPP): parent questionnaires and handouts with instructions for preventing injuries to children, child passenger safety pamphlets, the newsletter *Safe Ride News*, and the handbook Injury Prevention in Children and Youth (in press).
2. National Child Passenger Safety Association. Contact: Elaine Weinstein, 1705 DeSales Street, NW, Suite 300, Washington, DC 20036. 1-202-429-0515. Resources: pamphlet, quarterly newsletter, national networking child safety advocates, general information clearinghouse on child passenger safety.
3. Physicians for Automotive Safety. Contact: Annemarie Shelners, P.O. Box 430, Armonk, NY 10504. 1-914-173-6446. Resources: pamphlets, parent education films, slides, quarterly newsletter.
4. National Fire Protection Association, Batterymarch Park, Quincy, MA 02269. 1-800-344-3555.
5. American Society for Testing and Materials, 1916 Race Street, Philadelphia, PA 19103.
6. National Safety Council, 444 N. Michigan Ave., Chicago, Ill. 1-312-527-4800.
7. National Association for the Education of Young Children, 1834 Connecticut Ave., NW, Washington, DC 20009. 1-800-424-2460.
8. Child Care Information Exchange, P.O. Box 2890, Redmond, WA 98073. 1-206-882-1066.
9. American Red Cross National Headquarters, Health Services, 17th & D Street, NW, Washington, DC 20006.

(American Academy of Pediatrics, Selma R. Deitch, MD (ed.), "Health in Day Care: A Manual for Health Professionals," p. 190.)

Director's Resource 12-1 (*continued*)

10. American Home Economics Association, 2010 Massachusetts Ave., NW, Washington, DC 20036.
11. March of Dimes, Supply Division, 1275 Mamaroneck Ave., White Plains, NY 10605.
12. Society for Nutrition Education, 1736 Franklin Street, Oakland, CA 94612.
13. Metropolitan Life Insurance Company, Health and Welfare Film Library, c/o Association Films, Inc., 600 Aronid Ave., Ridgefreed, NJ 07657. 1-201-943-8200. Or One Madison Ave., New York, NY 10010. 1-212-578-5015.
14. Safety Now Company, Inc., P.O. Box 567, Jenkintown, PA 19046.
15. Preschool Enrichment Team, Inc., c/o Patricia Wise, R.N., 276 High St., Holyoke, MA 01040. A poster source for hand washing techniques and day care health training.
16. Child Welfare League of America, Inc., 67 Irving Place, New York, NY 10003.

State and Local (public)
1. "Safe Schools," a guide to creating safe environments for preschoolers, (A how-to manual for teachers). Department of Public Health, Division of Family Health Services, 150 Tremont St., Boston, MA 02111.
2. Cooperative Extension Service, located in different offices in each state.
3. Police departments, state and local.
4. Fire departments, local.
5. State and local injury prevention projects. These may be in local health departments, or in local hospitals, and in state health offices.
6. Child protective services. These may be located in different offices within the state and local welfare or human service agencies.
7. State and local health departments and within them their offices for environmental protection, maternal and child health, and health education.

State and local (private)
1. State and local medical societies.
2. State and local dental societies.
3. Association for the Blind, state and local chapters.
4. Lung Association, state and local chapters.
5. American Automobile Association, local office.

CHAPTER 13

Evaluating Center Components

Evaluation is an ongoing process. An evaluation can take the form of an analysis of a person's behavior, of an administrative procedure, or of some other component of an early childhood education program in terms of its usefulness or worth. Once an early childhood education program has been planned, the evaluation of that program should be designed immediately because continuation of an ineffective aspect of the program is fruitless and frequently expensive. Inappropriate staff behavior may be detrimental to children's development or to staff relations. Desirable behavior, on the other hand, should be recognized and encouraged as a result of the evaluation process.

Evaluation that is planned during the early stages of program development facilitates the assessment, and notifies everyone from the start how the evaluation process will be conducted. The evaluator uses the goals statement that was

Photo above Staff members participate in NAEYC Accreditation self-study by becoming familiar with accreditation materials and by discussing their program. (Photo by Lisa Souders)

prepared prior to the opening of the center as the basis for making judgments about what is valuable in the program. The objectives that grow from the goals are also helpful guidelines in assessing the center's program and the performance of individuals affiliated with that program.

EVALUATORS

A committee of the center's board or the director conducts evaluations. In some centers staff members evaluate other employees whom they supervise (for instance, teachers evaluate their aides) or employees evaluate all fellow employees whose jobs are related. Thus, teachers may evaluate each other, aides and teachers may evaluate each other, and everyone working under the director may evaluate and be evaluated by him or her. It is unlikely, however, to find auxiliary staff evaluating teaching staff, because the decision about who does the evaluating is based on how the assigned jobs relate to one another. In other words, the janitor would not evaluate the teaching staff even though teachers might be asked to evaluate the janitor's work in relation to their role; nor would the nurse evaluate the teachers.

Often parents are asked to give their opinions about the center, its personnel, and its operation to enable the center staff to understand how people directly affected by the program feel about it. In corporate systems a national or regional staff member may plan and conduct some or all of the evaluation; when funds are received from a governmental or private agency, an employee of that agency may be assigned to perform an evaluation. When public schools operate preschool or child care programs, the principal is usually responsible for evaluating the staff.

PURPOSE OF EVALUATION

Since the major purpose of evaluation is to determine whether the center's goals are being met, the evaluators need to know what these goals are before gathering data. In effect, the evaluators must know who the clients are, what their needs are, and which of these needs the center is attempting to meet. In a community where the local high school is expressing concern about the high number of dropouts due to pregnancy, a center director may decide to work with the school system to assess how many students could return to school if care were provided for their infants and toddlers. Together the center and the school may be able to obtain funding to provide this service. In such a situation, particularly if tax dollars are to be used, community education would be important since many taxpayers may believe that the program would cause teen pregnancy rather than prevent school dropouts.

A further purpose of evaluation is to determine how effective the program is in meeting the needs of clients and how efficient it is in terms of cost, time, and energy. Are needs met to the satisfaction of the center and of the clients? Are they partially met or not met at all? Even if needs are met, could the same job have been done for less money or by using less time or energy? Funding agencies, board members, and clients expect documentation that the center is doing what it has agreed to do. An evaluation provides the data for such documentation and possibly the basis for further funding.

A final reason for evaluation is the need to have a solid basis for future planning. The director uses the data from the current evaluation to determine the strengths and weaknesses of the program and to adapt the plan for the following year appropriately to correct any deficiencies or to respond to newly perceived needs. For example, if one of the goals of the center is to provide a parent education program for all parents, and the data show that only 10 percent of the parents participated, then the director needs to determine whether the goal is inappropriate or whether the method of achieving it is not meeting the needs of the clients. If a thorough evaluation has been done, the director will have information from parents regarding how they felt about the parent program and why they did or did not attend. The information can then be used to plan changes in next year's program or to ascertain that this community does not need parent education from this center.

It would be easy to arrive at the conclusion that parents in the preceding example do not want or need parent education. But the director has to consider other factors such as:

- Have parents been involved in the planning so that they feel as though they are part of the program?
- Is there another parent education program already established in the community that is meeting these parents' needs?
- Is the timing, format, or content inappropriate for these parents?
- Has there been a breakdown in communication so that parents do not feel welcome or comfortable about coming?

staff evaluation is to observe and analyze the work of a staff person, encourage the development of that person's strengths, and look for ways to promote growth in weaker areas. If the weak areas considerably outweigh the strong, then the director must terminate the employment of that individual because the director's role (except in special cases) is to promote growth rather than to provide total on-the-job training.

Some directors observe each teacher weekly, biweekly, or monthly and have a conference informally after making the observation. The director may take notes during the observation or write notes afterwards, but any notes should be shared with the teacher because they are useful in helping to fulfill the specific objectives that have been set. It is sometimes easy to pick out and focus on the weak spots in a teacher's style, which leaves the teacher feeling incompetent. Other directors concentrate only on the positive aspects and are unable to address problem areas. The teacher who is aware of a problem knows that the director is not providing appropriate guidance; the teacher who is unaware of a problem receives unofficial sanction of the behavior when the director ignores it. In either case, some of the center's objectives are not met and the observation and informal conference times are nonproductive.

When the agreed-upon observations have been completed and other assessments have been made, the director meets with the staff member for a comprehensive evaluation of the work that is based on the work plan set up earlier. The staff member may bring a self-evaluation, which can be in a form that is pre-selected by the director to be completed by the employee, in a narrative form that is written by the employee, or in an unwritten form, that is, thoughts the employee has planned to discuss with the director. During the conference, a work plan, including the objectives and an evaluation format, is drawn up again for the next evaluation cycle, and the director summarizes the staff person's evaluation for the previous cycle in a written form that is dated. The staff member may add written comments if desired, and then both the staff member and the director sign the evaluation form and the new work plan. Although this process is somewhat formal, the director's evaluation role becomes businesslike, as well as personal, if it is followed. (A sample staff evaluation form is included in Director's Resources.)

A similar evaluation process is followed for the director, and the board is usually responsible for its implementation. In a corporate system a regional representative may conduct the director's evaluation. Since the staff members in a well-run center may feel very close to one another and may consider the director as a personal friend, it is wise to maintain structure in the evaluation process to allow everyone to be as objective as possible. Parents' perspectives on the director's performance are significant and may be gathered via a survey.

Children's Evaluation

Because the major goals of an early childhood education center revolve around expectations about the development of children, the evaluation most commonly thought of and most frequently used is that of children's behavior. A number of techniques for conducting this process are available, but they must be examined carefully.

Since young children develop rapidly, it is important that the progress they make in their normal development is not attributed solely to the center's program. Many other conditions affect the child's development, including parental behavior, cultural background, nutrition, and general health. Any one of these variables or combinations of them can affect the child's development positively or negatively, just as the center's program may have a positive or negative

---

REFLECTIONS

Think about your own *feelings* about being evaluated. Are your feelings positive? negative? mixed? How does the evaluator influence these feelings? What is the behavior of an evaluator who helps you feel positive? Can you recall the behavior of an evaluator who left you feeling incompetent?

When teachers interact with individual children, their observations are important sources of data about the child's development. (Photo by Lisa Souders)

influence. The child's total development is a result of the interaction of many factors, which makes it almost impossible to evaluate the influence of one variable such as a specific child care or nursery school experience.

One way to obtain a measure of the effect of the center's program is to assess the children who participate in the program and a control group of children who do not. However, most centers do not have a control group available, nor do they have the time or funds for such assessment. Another way to evaluate children is to look at norms for similar children and compare the behaviors of the center children with those norms. However, as previously stated, the children's performances may or may not be the result of their attendance at the center.

Keeping in mind the preceding restrictions, the director, in consultation with teachers and sometimes with an educational testing consultant, organizes an evaluation plan for children to

assess whether or not the center's goals have been met for children. In general, the center's goal should be that each child develop in all areas. Therefore, information about the child at the beginning of the program is needed as a benchmark for assessing progress at future dates. There are several ways to collect these data.

Teacher Observations. Throughout the year the teacher may keep anecdotal and running records on each child. These notes, recorded on file cards or in a log book, are summarized by the teacher at the end of the year. The teacher notes the changes in developmental level and the specific objectives that the child has met. Using this method, the teacher is able to make statements about each child individually, placing emphasis on what the child's needs were, as based on initial observations, and how the needs were met. This method uses subjective data provided by the teacher and is valuable only if the teacher is a skilled observer and collects data regularly. In a center that is minimally staffed, use of this method may be difficult. However, NAEYC, in a brochure on testing of young children, states, "The systematic observations of trained teachers and other professionals, in conjunction with information obtained from parents and other family members, are the best sources of information."[1]

Checklist. The director may find or create a checklist that names the behaviors toward which the center's objectives are aimed. Then the teacher merely checks whether or not the child exhibits the listed behavior. A question arises when the child sometimes does the task and sometimes does not, either because the task is just being learned, because the child chooses not to do it, or because no opportunity is made available. For example, an item might be: "Buttons own coat." The child who does this occasionally may be in the process of learning and may not be ready to struggle with buttons on some days, or the child may be asking the teacher for help because he or she needs attention rather than help.

Rating Scales. The director may create or locate a rating scale that lists the behaviors aimed for in the center's objectives. The rating scale alleviates the problem created by a checklist by providing a way for teachers to qualify their answers. The teacher rates each child at least at the beginning and the end of the school year and perhaps more frequently. The rating may be based on numbers, for example,

Speaks clearly enough for a stranger to understand.
1   2   3   4   5

with an explanation of whether 1 or 5 is high.

The rating may involve descriptive words such as:

Participates in group activities:
never
seldom
occasionally
usually
always

(See Director's Resources for a sample rating scale.) The problems with rating scales are that each teacher may interpret the categories differently, and most teachers are reluctant to use the two ends of the scale (1 and 5, or *never* and *always*). Such scales, however, can be useful in pointing out general strengths and weaknesses in any child's development and in the functioning of the group. Rating scales are relatively quick to complete, and the teacher can do them when the children are not present.

Both checklists and rating scales are suitable for use if they are viewed as a particular teacher's assessment of an individual child rather than as a comparison of one child or class with another. In reporting data from checklists and rating scales, the director may comment on how many children recognize their name in print or play cooperatively in a group of two or more children; but this information must be placed in proper context by pointing out the children's ages and other factors that may influence the data. In any case, group data of this sort should be de-emphasized.

Standardized Tests. NAEYC has published an informative brochure entitled, *Testing of Young Children: Concerns and Cautions.* Because "(m)ass standardized testing of young children is potentially harmful to children educationally,"[2] it is important that directors become familiar with the issues. The NAEYC brochure describes types of standardized tests and appropriate uses and explains why standardized testing is inappropriate for young children. According to NAEYC, "Standardized testing seldom provides information beyond what teachers and parents already know."[3]

Other Observers. The director may observe a particular child when a teacher has concerns about that child. Sometimes an outside observer, such as the director or a consultant, brings a

1 National Association for the Education of Young Children, *Testing of Young Children: Concerns and Cautions,* Washington, D.C.: #582, 1988.
2 Ibid.
3 Ibid.

more objective analysis or may see factors in the environment or even in the teacher's behavior which appear to be influencing the chid's behavior. After collecting data, the observer confers with the teacher and together they design a plan for working with the child. When an individual child is being evaluated to an extent that is beyond the center's regularly scheduled observation plan, parental permission must be obtained and parental participation in planning is preferable and sometimes required by law.

When a child with identified special needs is enrolled, the director, with written parental permission, contacts agencies familiar with the case to obtain previous evaluations. The director and representatives of other agencies may also meet to share information which would be useful in working with the child and family.

Reporting a child's behavior to parents is usually handled in a conference (see Chapter 15). Written information may be provided, but the use of checklists and rating scales for this purpose is often misleading. Parents may misunderstand the significance of this type of written report and categorize their child as a success or a failure. A more appropriate written evaluation for parents is a narrative report that describes the child's strengths and progress at school and discusses areas in which the child has difficulty.[4] The teacher may also confer with parents about ways to help the child to continue progressing toward future educational goals.

Parents have the right to review information from their child's folder at any time. In some cases they feel that it is damaging to the child to have certain information passed along to the next teacher. In other cases they are eager for the new teacher to understand as much as possible about their child immediately so that the child does not have to endure a time period in which the teacher is discovering a hearing loss or some other condition for which an instructional plan should be designed. In any case, the teacher and parent discuss available information about the child and together determine which data should be sent forward to the next teacher.

REFLECTIONS

Think about *report card day* when you were in elementary school. Can you recall any of your feelings about receiving a report card? If the experience was not always a good one for you, who could have changed? you? the teacher? your parents? other children?

When you consider what you will include in a child's folder, try to remember your own grade school days. Think about the effects that the inclusion of data about your behavior may have had on your relationships with teachers and your parents.

Total Program Evaluation

The program goals of the center, and the program itself, are designed to meet the particular needs that the center was established to meet. Consequently, at evaluation time, the needs, the goals, and the program are evaluated.

At regular intervals, the community's needs must be assessed so that the center can plan for current and future populations. (The methodology for conducting a community needs assessment is discussed in Chapter 2.) Since goals are closely tied to the philosophy of the center program, they change slowly. Nonetheless, they should be examined periodically, perhaps every few years, to determine whether or not they are still applicable. Because the objectives are more directly related to the individuals served at a given time, they may change more rapidly than the goals; therefore, the objectives should be examined annually prior to the start of a new school year.

In addition, the director or the board may prepare checklists or rating scales for the evaluation of the program that can be distributed to

---

4 D. Horm-Wingerd, "Reporting Children's Development: The Narrative Report," *Dimensions of Early Childhood,* *21* (1), Fall 1992.

staff members, parents, and community representatives; or these people may be asked to provide evaluations in a written or oral form for the evaluation of the program. Board members and funding agency representatives may contribute to the evaluation by reviewing aspects of the overall program, such as the physical environment, curriculum, parent program, ancillary services, and board operations. They may also evaluate the staff performance in general, rather than individual, terms. Periodically, perhaps every few years, the policies and procedures manual, the job descriptions, and the board bylaws are reviewed. Even the evaluation plans and procedures are evaluated!

A widely used center-evaluation tool is the *Early Childhood Environment Rating Scale.*[5] Seven areas are covered in separate subscales. These are: personal care routines, furnishings and display for children, language-reasoning experiences, fine and gross motor activities, creative activities, social development, and adult needs. After observing, the rater circles the appropriate category from 1 (inadequate) to 7 (excellent). Each subscale total rating is plotted on a profile sheet. Center staff can then decide in which areas they wish to make improvements. Profiles produced at different points in time can be used to determine changes in the center's program during that time period. Similar scales have been produced for rating infant/toddler programs and family child care. Instructional guides for observers are available in print and on videocassette.

Perhaps the most important evaluation a director can conduct is to look at quality of work life. Jorde-Bloom points out that high staff turnover rate, stress, and burnout soon affect commitment to the profession. When staff experience these tensions, it becomes impossible for directors to maintain high quality programs.[6]

Jorde-Bloom recommends, therefore, that the director examine ten dimensions necessary to create a professional climate. Among these are supervisor support, opportunities for professional growth, and amount of staff autonomy in decision making. She further recommends surveying the staff and then using the resulting data to plan changes.[7] Another form of staff survey is included in the NAEYC center accreditation package.

Many center directors and staff members are aware that they need to check the quality of their relations with parents, children, and staff members from a variety of cultures. Although it was not designed specifically for child care centers, the *Cultural Competence Self-Assessment Instrument*[8] may help directors provide leadership in analyzing areas of strength and areas where improvement is needed. This publication includes sections entitled Valuing Diversity, Documents Checklist, Governance, Administration, Program and Policy Development, Service Delivery, Clients, and Interpreting Your Results.

Accreditation

The most professional way to evaluate the center is to use the National Academy of Early

---

DIRECTOR'S CORNER

"We decided as a staff to do more fun things together. This past year hasn't been much fun because everybody has been putting in overtime since we had two teachers on maternity leave. The steering committee gave us some money from a fundraiser and we're meeting next week to decide how to have fun together with it. It's a real morale booster."

Director, agency-sponsored child care center

---

5 T. Harms and R. M. Clifford, *Early Childhood Environment Rating Scale,* New York: Teachers College, 1980.
6 Paula Jorde-Bloom, *A Great Place to Work: Improving Conditions for Staff in Young Children's Programs,* Washington, DC: National Association for the Education of Young Children, 1988.
7 Ibid.
8 Child Welfare League of America, *Cultural Competence Self-Assessment Instrument,* Washington, D.C., 1993.

Center Accreditation as designed by NAEYC ...ousands of early child- ...m all over the United ...prove the quality of care ...d young children. Some ...they won't get involved because .... aren't perfect or because the process is too complicated. In many communities directors' support groups are springing up to encourage directors and to answer their questions. In some cases, these groups have obtained funding from community agencies or from business groups in order to provide technical assistance to centers which recognize the need to improve their programs.

Materials for the accreditation process may be obtained from NAEYC. Most directors find that when they take the time to read through the *Guide to Accreditation,* the steps they need to take are all laid out for them and the procedures no longer seem intimidating. The director's role then is to obtain the support of the Board and of the staff by letting them know what is expected and that they will be engaging in a worthwhile team effort. Sharing the accreditation materials with confidence and being open to addressing staff members' questions and concerns will help everyone get started willingly.

The next step is to begin a self study. Letting parents know that the center is engaging in this process and that their ideas and participation are essential contributes to the collaborative nature of the work.

NAEYC provides classroom observation booklets for each classroom. The lead teacher and the director, education coordinator or some other appropriate person observe in the classroom and respond to the items in the booklet. Some centers also ask that a parent observe each classroom and respond to each item. The advantage here is that many parents get involved, their ideas are recognized, and they learn a lot about the daily program. Every parent is asked to complete a questionnaire evaluating the program and each staff member evaluates the total program using the staff questionnaire.

Together the participants review the data and determine a plan of action. The director's role is to help staff and parents identify both strengths and weaknesses, to celebrate the strengths, and to determine how to rectify the weaknesses. The director must be cognizant of defensiveness on the part of some staff members and support them as they accept the fact that some changes will be needed. Everyone involved may feel stressed as change is discussed. Here again the director must listen to concerns and help the group decide about how to address them. Making changes is less stressful when the group feels ownership. Some changes may be out of the question, often because of the finances involved. This does not necessarily mean that the center cannot become accredited, but the program report will have to describe how the staff has designed an appropriate alternate approach. In many cases the staff will have to set priorities and create a schedule for working on various components within a certain time frame. Trying to tackle everything at once can be overwhelming and counterproductive.

NAEYC points out that in some cases the self-study is as far as a center wants to go. However, it is not necessary that a center be perfect. "Accreditation is awarded for substantial compliance with the Criteria."[9]

If the decision is to proceed toward accreditation, the director prepares the Program Description which includes:

1. the Center Profile (how the program is staffed and organized)
2. results of the Classroom Observations
3. information about administrative practices

This information is recorded on forms which NAEYC provides and the Guide provides help. The NAEYC 800 number is also a great support system. Once you mail the completed program description to the Academy, you can expect to

9 National Academy of Early Childhood Programs, *Guide to Accreditation by the National Academy of Early Childhood Programs: Self-study, Validation, Accreditation* (revised edition), Washington, D.C.: National Association for the Education of Young Children, 1991, pp. 81–98.

hear from them within 30 days in order to schedule a validation visit.

Your validator will be a volunteer early childhood professional. She or he will have participated in validator training, recognizes the importance of following the procedures carefully, and is committed to maintaining confidentiality. You and the Academy representative will agree on a date for her/his visit. You will have one or two validators for one or two days, based on the size of your program. The validator's role, as the name implies, is to validate the accuracy of the materials which have been submitted to the Academy. Validators work to ensure that everything they write is accurate. The director reviews the validator's work before it is submitted to the Academy and is encouraged to comment on any area where the program description and the validator's rating differ. Both the director and the validator sign the visit form and all materials are mailed immediately to the Academy.

Summarizing Data

The director is responsible for summarizing the data that is collected from all aspects of the evaluation process showing the progress (or regression) since the last evaluation rather than focusing solely on the present performance level. The summary should provide a clear data picture for the reader and should reflect accurately the facts, ideas, and opinions provided by those who participated. A comment or behavior that occurs frequently should receive more weight in the summary than an item that seldom appears in the data, no matter how striking or impressive that item appears. Furthermore, no new information should appear in the summary.

The summary is written, dated, and signed by the summarizer and should include a listing of sources used in its compilation. Some data may appear in graph or chart form, particularly if this format makes it easier to understand or more likely to be read.

Analyzing and Using the Data

The director or a designated committee uses the summary to cull out information. For example, in analyzing enrollment records, the dropout rate of children whose transportation is provided by the school may be compared with the dropout rate of those children who get to school by some other means.

In examining this information, it is necessary to keep other factors constant. For example, if all the children receiving transportation are from low-income families and if some, or all, of the other children are from middle-income families, the dropout rate might be more closely related to income level than to mode of transportation. To clarify the situation, additional data would be needed.

Once the data have been analyzed, the director prepares a report for the funding agency, the board, and the other people or groups to whom the center is responsible. This type of report is usually prepared annually, although interim reports may be compiled. The report should be clearly expressed, easily comprehensible, and professional in appearance. Using a word processor simplifies this task and enhances the results.

Each board member receives a copy of the annual report, one or more copies are submitted to each funding agency that is involved, and one or more copies are filed at the center. The narrative may be enhanced and clarified by the addition of appropriate graphs, charts, or tables. A pie chart showing the use of the director's time, for example, can be more effective than a lengthy narrative that contains the same information. Graphs and charts can be computer-generated and add an extra professional touch to a report. The fact that the report is read by people from a variety of backgrounds should be considered.

Usually, by the time the report for a given year is complete and is in the hands of board members, the planning process for the new year has been completed and put into operation. The annual report is then used primarily for future planning. The board looks at the report, which includes the director's recommendations, to determine the areas that need modification. For example, if there is a high rate of turnover among the teaching staff, the board looks further to see if the cause can be determined from the evaluation data. Perhaps the salaries at this center are much lower than those of other centers in the community, or perhaps the physical environment is poor. Decisions for change are based on available evidence that grows out of the total evaluation process.

SUMMARY

From the center's inception, an evaluation plan is an essential component of the total program. The purpose of the plan is to determine the value of the center's operation, to evaluate the individuals within it through an analysis of the progress and functioning of the staff, the children, and the overall program, and to provide a basis for future planning. The evaluation process is open and ongoing and relates to the goals and objectives of the center. The process includes collecting, summarizing, analyzing, and using data according to a prespecified plan that lets everyone involved know by whom, how, when, where, and why evaluation is being done.

Class Assignments

1. Ask the director of an early childhood center about the evaluation plan used in that center. Find out who conducts evaluations and why, when, where, and how they are conducted. Perhaps the director will share copies of the forms that are used with you. Be sure to ask about all three components of the plan (staff, child, and general program). Write your responses on Working Paper 13-1.
2. Create a rating scale by which the director of a center could be evaluated. You may want to use the sample director's job description in Director's Resources, Chapter 9. Write your responses on Working Paper 13-2.
3. Using Working Paper 13-3, assess two preschool children you know. This procedure should be carried out by recalling what the children have done and by observing them in the classroom or home. It should not be conducted as a test situation for the children. (Note that Working Paper 13-3 represents a small portion of a child assessment tool. This brief form is used to allow the student to complete the assignment within a reasonable amount of time.)

Class Exercises

1. Work with a partner and role play a conference in which a teacher and a director set up a work plan for the next six months. If you are assuming the role of teacher, try to use your own current classroom skills and areas in which you need improvement as a basis for the objectives in your work plan. If you are playing the director, use your communication skills to find out what help this teacher seems to need and where his or her strengths lie. After the role play, ask your classmates for a brief evaluation of the conference. Then have two other students repeat the role play. Is the second work plan different from the one formulated in the first role play?
2. You are a teacher responsible for evaluating your aide. The aide lives in the inner-city community in which the center is located and seems to be highly skilled at interacting with the children and at guiding them. The aide wants them to succeed in kindergarten and, as a consequence, frequently insists that they practice writing the alphabet and doing addition and subtraction problems. Role play with a classmate a midyear evaluation conference you might have with this aide.

Working Paper 13-1

Evaluation Response Form

Name of Center _____

1. Who conducts evaluations?

2. When is the evaluation done?

3. Where does the evaluation occur? (classrooms, director's office, parents' homes)

4. Describe the evaluation procedures for each of the components of the plan:
   • Staff

   • Children

   • General program

Working Paper 13-2

Rating Scale for Evaluating Director Form

(List at least five items on which a director could be evaluated. Include the format you would use to indicate the level of performance.)

Working Paper 13-3

Preschool Child Assessment Form

CHILD ASSESSMENT (1st child)

Child's Name_____Birth date_____

School_____Teacher_____

Form completed by_____Date_____

Note: These items are listed to give a sense of long-range goals. Preschool children are *not* expected to accomplish all of them.

	Consistent	Frequent	Beginning	Not yet
1. Comments on number and numerical relationships	_____	_____	_____	_____
2. Rote counts to _____	_____	_____	_____	_____
3. Counts sometimes using double counting or skipping items	_____	_____	_____	_____
4. Counts in 1 to 1 correspondence	_____	_____	_____	_____
5. Recognizes last number counted as total quantity	_____	_____	_____	_____
6. Compares quantities globally (more)	_____	_____	_____	_____
7. Compares quantities globally (less)	_____	_____	_____	_____

Working Paper 13-3 (*continued*)

CHILD ASSESSMENT (2nd child)

Child's Name_____Birth date_____

School_____Teacher_____

Form completed by_____Date_____

Note: These items are listed to give a sense of long-range goals. Preschool children are *not* expected to accomplish all of them.

	Consistent	Frequent	Beginning	Not yet
1. Comments on number and numerical relationships	_____	_____	_____	_____
2. Rote counts to _____	_____	_____	_____	_____
3. Counts sometimes using double counting or skipping items	_____	_____	_____	_____
4. Counts in 1 to 1 correspondence	_____	_____	_____	_____
5. Recognizes last number counted as total quantity	_____	_____	_____	_____
6 Compares quantities globally (more)	_____	_____	_____	_____
7. Compares quantities globally (less)	_____	_____	_____	_____

Director's Resource 13-1

Sample Child Evaluation Form for a Montessori Program

Name_____ Month/Year_____ Age_____

I. Personal Characteristics

Self Concept: Independence:

Order: Concentration:

Imagination/Creativity: Listening Skills:

II. Physical Characteristics

Height_____ Weight_____   Dominance: Right_____ Left_____ Not established_____

Body and Spatial Concepts: Large-motor Skills:

Small Muscle Skills: Hand–Eye Coordination:

III. Social Characteristics

Types of Social Interaction (individual,   Closest Friends and Type of Relationship:
small circle, universal, mixture, etc.):

Concern and Care for Others: Outdoor Environment Play:

Director's Resource 13-1 (*continued*)

IV. Activities, Skills, and Concepts

Everyday Living

Manipulative: Care of Self:

Care of Environment: Sequence of Activity:

Sensorial

Size Discrimination: Color:

Form: Auditory, Tactile, etc.:

Math

Number–Numeral Concept, 0–10:   Decimal System:

Teens/Tens: Operations:

Language

Vocabulary/ Self-expression: Visual Matching/Classification:

Story Comprehension: Letter Sounds/Phonetic Skills

Writing: Function of Words:

Science:

Art:

Geography:

V. Parent Contacts: Date and Topics Discussed

(Reprinted by permission of Xavier University Montessori Teacher Education Program.)

Director's Resource 13-2

Sample Teacher Evaluation Form

Xavier University Montessori Teacher Education Program

Evaluation Form

Evaluation of Xavier University Montessori Lab School Teachers

Name of Teacher_____ Position_____

Level of Teaching: _____Preprimary _____Elementary (Check one)

Director_____

Date_____   Scale: S = Satisfactory Performance
                                               NI = Needs Improvement

1. Maintains an aesthetically beautiful and intellectually stimulating environment. Includes daily
   clean up, repair of materials, making new materials, and clean personal appearance.
   1. S_____ NI_____   3. S_____ NI_____
   2. S_____ NI_____   4. S_____ NI_____

Comments:_____

_____

2. Develops each child's maximum potential in four areas: physical, emotional, intellectual, social
   a. Fosters warm, relaxed, non-threatening atmosphere in classroom   S____ NI____
   b. Develops warm relationship with each child   S____ NI____
   c. Acquires knowledge of background of each child   S____ NI____
   d. Continually evaluates each child in each area; introduces new
      activities to foster growth in all areas   S____ NI____
   e. Maintains record of child's progress   S____ NI____

Comments:_____

_____

3. Communicates as needed with parents for the purpose of fostering the development of the total
   child.
   a. Schedules conferences on regular basis   S____ NI____
   b. Holds unscheduled meetings, as needed, for exchanging
      pertinent information   S____ NI____
   c. Programs and participates in workshops and training sessions   S____ NI____

Comments:_____

Director's Resource 13-2 (*continued*)

4. Engages in frequent communication with staff for purpose of improving classroom operation and understanding of each child.

   a. Communicates frequently with appropriate staff to facilitate operation of classroom within above framework, including daily communication with assistants   S_____   NI_____

   b. Trains assistants and classroom volunteers, and interns, if present   S_____   NI_____

   c. Participates in staff meetings   S_____   NI_____

Comments:_____

_____

5. Assumes responsibility for furthering teaching skills.   S_____   NI_____

Comments:_____

_____

6. Constantly evaluates each of the above tasks to strengthen weak areas in order to improve development of each child.   S_____   NI_____

Comments:_____

_____

General Work Habits:

Responsibility and Dependability: Consider willingness to accept responsibility, time spent on assigned duties and follow-through on work.

S_____   NI_____   Comments:_____

_____

Stability and Adaptability: Consider ability to adjust to changes in job conditions, assignments, and schedules; receptiveness to constructive criticism; stability under pressure; calmness during crisis.

S_____   NI_____ Comments:_____

_____

Initiative: Consider how well teacher begins an assignment and recognizes the best way of doing it.

S_____   NI_____ Comments:_____

_____

Ability to analyze situation, develop options, form opinion and act: Consider ability to analyze facts and solve problems; estimate and foresee results of decisions, and ability to take action and make firm decisions.

S_____   NI_____ Comments:_____

_____

Director's Resource 13-2 (*continued*)

Proficiency: Consider effective use of time, quantity of acceptable work actually accomplished, necessity of follow-up.

S_____ NI_____ Comments:_____

_____

Cost Control: Consider ways to control costs without reducing efficiency.

S_____ NI_____ Comments:_____

_____

Has the teacher been counseled about his or her performance? _____Yes_____No

Date of Counseling since last appraisal:
(Attach signed written description of counseling)

APPRAISAL REVIEW

After teacher and Director have jointly reviewed this appraisal, each should sign below to acknowledge that appraisal has been reviewed and discussed.

Space is provided below each signature for comments.

Teacher's Signature_____Date_____
    Comments:

Director's Signature_____Date_____
    Comments:

(Reprinted by permission of Xavier University Montessori Teacher Education Program.)

Director's Resource 13-3

Child Evaluation Form

Use different color for each assessment. Record date in that color.

CHILD EVALUATION

Child's Name:_____ Birth Date:_____

School:_____ Teacher:_____

Form completed by:_____

Date:_____ Date:_____ Date:_____

General Autonomy

	consistent	frequent	beginning	not yet	comments
A. Initiative					
1. Develops and pursues own ideas in activities	____	____	____	____	____
2. Expands ideas of others	____	____	____	____	____
B. Self-confidence					
1. Assured in expressing ideas and convictions	____	____	____	____	____
2. Copes well with new experiences	____	____	____	____	____
3. Manifests general feeling of self-satisfaction	____	____	____	____	____
4. Verbalizes feelings	____	____	____	____	____
C. Independence					
1. Cares for self (bathroom, dressing)	____	____	____	____	____
2. Chooses activities	____	____	____	____	____
3. Separates comfortably from parent	____	____	____	____	____
4. Seeks attention, help and recognition when appropriate	____	____	____	____	____
D. Responsibility					
1. Cares for materials	____	____	____	____	____
2. Cleans up (with minimal prompting)	____	____	____	____	____
3. Keeps up with own belongings	____	____	____	____	____
E. Appears psychologically engaged in child-selected activity	____	____	____	____	____

Sociomoral Development

	consistent	frequent	beginning	not yet	comments
A. Responsibility					
1. Can verbalize classroom guidelines	____	____	____	____	____
2. Adheres to classroom guidelines	____	____	____	____	____
*3. Participates in setting classroom guidelines	____	____	____	____	____
*4. Participates in enforcing classroom guidelines	____	____	____	____	____
*5. Initiates or participates in a discussion of classroom problems	____	____	____	____	____
6. Facilitates and participates in classroom routine (by anticipating transitions, etc.)	____	____	____	____	____

*Asterisk indicates items that would not be expected until at least four years.

Director's Resource 13-3 (*continued*)

	consistent	frequent	beginning	not yet	comments
B. Cooperation					
*1. Uses appropriate assertive behavior and language to resolve conflicts	____	____	____	____	____
*2. Takes up for others' rights and attempts to help others in conflict situations	____	____	____	____	____
3. Channels feelings of anger, frustration, etc. in appropriate ways	____	____	____	____	____
4. Generates game rules	____	____	____	____	____
*5. Follows game rules agreed upon by players	____	____	____	____	____
*6. Considers others' point of view	____	____	____	____	____
*7. Discusses moral dilemmas (extra guests, enough cookies for class)	____	____	____	____	____
*8. Takes turns	____	____	____	____	____
9. Invites others to participate in activities	____	____	____	____	____
10. Responds to invitations to participate in activities	____	____	____	____	____
*11. Recognizes rights of others (may not act on)	____	____	____	____	____
*12. Channels competitive impulses in cooperative direction (enjoys the process and accepts the outcome)	____	____	____	____	____
C. Relating to Group					
1. Calls children and adults by name	____	____	____	____	____
2. Identifies which children are absent	____	____	____	____	____
3. Notices others' needs (such as getting tissue for another)	____	____	____	____	____
4. Interested in doing things for group (such as preparing snack)	____	____	____	____	____
5. Spontaneously expresses caring for others (solutions when another is hurt)	____	____	____	____	____
6. Shows interest in what others at grouptime say	____	____	____	____	____
7. Participates in voting process	____	____	____	____	____

Cognitive Development

	consistent	frequent	beginning	not yet	comments
A. Writing					
1. Writes using personal cursive	____	____	____	____	____
2. Writes pseudoletters	____	____	____	____	____
*3. Copies letter and numbers	____	____	____	____	____
*4. Writes own name	____	____	____	____	____
*5. Writes other words	____	____	____	____	____
*6. Writes from left to right	____	____	____	____	____
*7. Experiments with conventions of writing (such as writing from right to left)	____	____	____	____	____
*8. Asks for models (how to write a letter or word or how to spell a word)	____	____	____	____	____
9. Uses writing with intention of communicating	____	____	____	____	____
10. Asks to dictate messages	____	____	____	____	____
B. Reading					
1. Enjoys stories	____	____	____	____	____
2. Requests stories	____	____	____	____	____
3. Holds book properly and turns pages	____	____	____	____	____
4. Pretends to read	____	____	____	____	____
5. Distinguishes between print and picture	____	____	____	____	____
6. Recognizes first letter of own name	____	____	____	____	____
7. Recognizes own name in print	____	____	____	____	____

Director's Resource 13-3 (*continued*)

	consistent	frequent	beginning	not yet	comments
8. Recognizes printed names of other children	___	___	___	___	___
9. Recognizes meanings of signs	___	___	___	___	___
10. Matches words in print	___	___	___	___	___
*11. Knows what a word is	___	___	___	___	___
12. Recognizes letters	___	___	___	___	___
13. Reads own writing	___	___	___	___	___
14. Attempts voice print pairing	___	___	___	___	___
*15. Generates rhyming words	___	___	___	___	___
*16. Generates words that begin alike	___	___	___	___	___
17. Knows one reads from left to right, front to back, and top to bottom	___	___	___	___	___
*18. Reads predictable books	___	___	___	___	___

C. Language
  1. Spoken

	consistent	frequent	beginning	not yet	comments
a. Speaks clearly enough for a stranger to understand	___	___	___	___	___
b. Modulates tone of voice based on situation	___	___	___	___	___

  2. Understood Language

	consistent	frequent	beginning	not yet	comments
a. Responds appropriately to questions including who, what, when, and how	___	___	___	___	___
b. Responds appropriately to why questions	___	___	___	___	___
c. Carries on meaningful conversations	___	___	___	___	___
d. Stays on topic in group discussion	___	___	___	___	___

Cognitive Dispositions

A. Autonomy

	consistent	frequent	beginning	not yet	comments
1. Generates several alternatives in play situations	___	___	___	___	___
2. Has "wonderful ideas" (thinks of new ideas in relation to objects and activities)	___	___	___	___	___

B. Physical Knowledge

	consistent	frequent	beginning	not yet	comments
1. Experiments with objects (water, sand, art media, pendulum, and other mechanical apparatus)	___	___	___	___	___
2. Makes and verifies predictions (such as water will come out hole in side of container	___	___	___	___	___
3. Notices effects of actions on objects	___	___	___	___	___
4. Notices changes in objects	___	___	___	___	___

C. Logico-Mathematical Knowledge

	consistent	frequent	beginning	not yet	comments
1. Comments on number and numerical relationships	___	___	___	___	___
2. Rote counts to_____	___	___	___	___	___
3. Counts sometimes using double counting or skipping items	___	___	___	___	___
4. Counts in 1 to 1 correspondence	___	___	___	___	___
5. Recognizes last number counted as total quantity	___	___	___	___	___
6. Compares quantities globally (more)	___	___	___	___	___
7. Compares quantities globally (less)	___	___	___	___	___
8. Compares quantities globally (as much as, etc.)	___	___	___	___	___
9. Reasons about addition and subtraction in classroom situations	___	___	___	___	___
10. Compares quantities numerically (5 is more than 3)	___	___	___	___	___
*11. Identifies numerals	___	___	___	___	___

  12. Thinks about spatial relationships

	consistent	frequent	beginning	not yet	comments
a. Follows path on game board	___	___	___	___	___

Director's Resource 13-3 (*continued*)

	consistent	frequent	beginning	not yet	comments
1. Own path	___	___	___	___	___
2. Commmon path (straight)	___	___	___	___	___
3. Curved path	___	___	___	___	___
b. Reasons about spatial problems (as in aiming at target)	___	___	___	___	___
c. Reasons about body fitting in space	___	___	___	___	___
d. Uses prepositions such as in, on, over, etc. appropriately	___	___	___	___	___
*e. Uses "first" appropriately	___	___	___	___	___
*f. Uses "last" appropriately	___	___	___	___	___
*g. Uses "middle" appropriately	___	___	___	___	___
*h. Uses "second" appropriately	___	___	___	___	___
*i. Uses "in between" appropriately	___	___	___	___	___
3. Reasons about classes and relations					
a. Groups objects according to similarities and differences in games and other classroom situations	___	___	___	___	___
*b. Conceptualizes part/whole relations in sets of objects (as in card games with suits)	___	___	___	___	___
4. Temporal reasoning					
a. Knows order of classroom routine	___	___	___	___	___
b. Refers to clock to monitor routines	___	___	___	___	___
*c. Understands "today"	___	___	___	___	___
*d. Understands "tomorrow"	___	___	___	___	___
*e. Understands "yesterday"	___	___	___	___	___
*f. Global understanding of past and future ("a long time ago," "a long time from now," etc.)	___	___	___	___	___
g. Knows order of events in familiar stories	___	___	___	___	___
5. Patterns					
a. Recognizes patterns	___	___	___	___	___
b. Matches patterns	___	___	___	___	___
c. Creates patterns	___	___	___	___	___
d. Extends patterns	___	___	___	___	___
6. Constructs matching sets	___	___	___	___	___
a. 1–3	___	___	___	___	___
b. 4–6	___	___	___	___	___
*c. 7–12	___	___	___	___	___
7. Makes count–cardinal transitions	___	___	___	___	___

(This form was drawn from previous work of Rheta de Vries and of Brenda Hieronymus and Sally Moomaw.)

CHAPTER 14

Providing for Personal and Professional Staff Development

Agenda
Staff Meeting

12:30 Convene and present agenda
12:40 Present plan for self-study
for NAEYC accreditation - Joan
1:15 Discuss use of manipulative/
art storage room - Yvette
1:30 Plan a winter parent meeting - Sue
date? program? staff responsibilities
1:45 Report on meeting with carpenter
on new outdoor sandbox - Joan
2:00 Adjourn

The center director is responsible for the personal and professional development of the staff. In very large centers or in corporate systems, the business and fiscal maintenance functions may be separated from the educational program maintenance, in which case the education director is accountable for the educational program and the accompanying staff development programs.

Illustration above   The director is responsible for preparing the agenda for staff meetings.

However, in most centers, one person is responsible for both the business and educational program components.

373

A basic assumption underlying staff development programs is that adults have the capacity to change and grow; this capacity is, in a sense, similar to that manifested by children in their growth processes. Likewise, the director's responsibility as it relates to the center staff parallels that of the classroom teacher, namely, to create a favorable environment for optimum growth and development of all the people in the environment. Having the director serve as a model of professionalism in handling staff meetings, staff training programs, staff supervision, and assessing staff problems facilitates and enhances the personal and professional development of the center staff. The specific content or the specific strategy employed in any aspect of the staff development program depends on group composition. In the same way that classroom teachers assess the needs of children in planning appropriate learning environments, directors evaluate staff needs and plan staff development programs accordingly. In addition, just like teaching young children, where the responsible adult offers many opportunities to make decisions but there are times when children are expected to follow certain rules and expectations, so the director establishes expectations for teachers which represent the bottom line and are to be followed.[1]

STAFF MEETINGS

The director is responsible for planning and conducting staff meetings. Although conducting a staff meeting may seem to be a routine and relatively easy task, holding meetings which are satisfying and worthwhile for both the director and the staff require careful planning and preparation. Effective implementation of the planned agenda is largely dependent upon the director's ability to maintain open communication among those attending the meeting.

Purpose of Staff Meetings

Of course, communication is the main purpose of staff meetings. Although much can be communicated through memorandums and newsletters, posting bulletin board notices, and exchanging information on a casual, one-to-one basis, many issues and problems are resolved most effectively in a meeting.

Two-way communication in a meeting permits an interchange of ideas and feelings and provides a forum for thoughtful discussion and clarification of problems and issues. The final outcome, for each individual, should be a better understanding not only of problems and issues but also of self and others. When staff members are involved in discussing program issues or problems, when their opinions have been heard, and when they have had some voice in decision making, they feel a greater sense of self-worth and consider themselves to be a more integral part of the total center community. To be successful, staff meetings must provide a safe environment where staff members can ask questions, challenge others by presenting alternative ideas, and share feelings with the group.[2]

To prevent the meeting from deteriorating into a "gripe session," the director must take an active role in channeling the complaints and concerns toward improvement strategies. Open communication during staff meetings is one way to develop cooperation and harmony and to encourage the "we" feeling among staff members. As mentioned in Chapter 1, the sense of community is fundamental for the creation of a favorable environment for the personal growth of staff members, children, and families who participate in the center program.

Staff meeting discussions may involve specific questions such as which piece of outdoor equipment to buy or whether to buy tricycles or books with the equipment money available at the end of the year. Sometimes discussions focus on the use of available building or outdoor space or on the appropriateness of timing the meal service or the monthly fire drill. The director may decide to use staff meeting time to discuss more general philosophical or educational program issues, such as, What changes should

1 *Growing Teachers: Partnerships in Staff Development*, Elizabeth Jones (editor), National Association for the Education of Young Children, 1993, p. xv.
2 "Teamwork Terminators and Some Sure Cures by Hawaii Retreat Attendees," *Child Care Information Exchange: The Director's Magazine*, July 1992, p. 7.

we consider in our program planning in order to focus more attention on emerging literacy? A question that logically follows is, How do we, as a staff, learn more about the application of a whole language approach in the classroom? Discussions about both educational program and general program philosophy often lead to group decisions about the focus and content of future in-service training sessions. If the group makes decisions about the training needs of the teaching staff, there undoubtedly will be a greater commitment to the training program than if the director makes those decisions without group input.

Directors and teachers sometimes decide to use part of each staff meeting to discuss individual children and their needs. These discussions, which are confidential among those involved, are particularly productive for the total staff when the center program is open and free-flowing and the children regularly interact with different staff members. Although it may seem less productive to involve the total staff in a discussion of one child when that child is in a self-contained classroom, if others feel free to contribute, they can often lend a degree of objectivity to the discussion.

Nonetheless, when staff meeting discussions are not of particular relevance to those in attendance, boredom and restlessness become apparent and members feel that the time is wasted. To maintain interest and open communication, try to select agenda items that are of concern to most of the staff members who are expected to attend the regular staff meetings. The agenda items that pertain only to the work of a few can be reserved for special meetings or assigned to small committees for discussion and subsequent decision making.

Timing of Staff Meetings

The frequency and timing of staff meetings vary, depending on the amount of business typically transacted and the amount of time devoted to each meeting. Weekly or biweekly meetings that are well planned and brief may be more productive than long sessions that are held less frequently. Although staff members usually prefer daytime meetings because they need evenings and weekends to rest and take care of personal

---

DIRECTOR'S CORNER

"Our staff scheduling problems are so complex, there is no way I can plan a staff meeting during the day. We have evening meetings and everyone is expected to attend. Each new employee is advised of that expectation and assured that she will receive comp time or overtime pay."

Director, employer-sponsored child care center in hospital

---

matters, evenings may be the only time everyone can meet together.

In half-day programs staff meetings can be scheduled after the children leave at noon or, in centers with double sessions, either early in the morning or late in the afternoon. However, full-day child care programs present special problems because the centers are open from early morning until very late afternoon and the center staff usually works a staggered schedule. Naptime is often the time set aside for meetings because most staff members are present in the middle of the day; however, sleeping children must be supervised. Use of volunteers or parents for naptime supervision is an alternative, but one which licensing disallows in some places. In smaller centers, hiring substitutes to cover nap rooms may be a better solution.

The center staff and the director must decide which staff members, in addition to classroom staff, should be encouraged to attend staff meetings. It may be beneficial to have the bus driver, the cook, or the receptionist at staff meetings because the kind of contact these staff members have with the children and families enables them to make a unique contribution to staff meeting discussions. Directors may also find it useful to ask the consulting psychologist, the special education resource teacher, or other professionals who are involved in the program to attend staff meetings. Anyone who can profit from or contribute to the discussions should be encouraged to come to the meetings.

Preparation for Staff Meetings

Both the director and the staff members must prepare for a staff meeting so that the meeting will be productive for everyone. The director is responsible for preparing and posting the agenda and for distributing any material that should be read by the staff before the meeting. Even though the director holds final responsibility for planning the agenda, all staff members should be invited to suggest agenda items either before or after it is posted. The posted agenda should include a brief description of each item and the action to be taken. For example, if the agenda item about the use of outdoor space is to cover the timing for its use, the responsibility for setting up and cleaning up, and the equipment needs, then all these subjects for discussion should be listed. The agenda should also clearly state which items are open for discussion *and* group decision and which items are open only for discussion. In the latter case the director hears the discussion, considers the ideas and feelings of the staff, and subsequently makes the decision. In the case of the outdoor space questions, the classroom staff should probably decide about the timing for the use of outdoor space; the total staff including the janitor or housekeeper should be involved in the discussion and decision about setting up and cleaning up the space; and the final decision about equipment purchase should be made by the director after hearing the preferences of the entire staff. When all these expectations are clearly spelled out on the posted agenda, there is little room for confusion or misunderstanding about what will occur during the meeting.

Each item on the posted agenda should include the name of the person responsible for presenting the item and leading the discussion and a rough time estimate for adequate coverage of the item. This procedure notifies staff members about their responsibility during the meeting and ensures coverage of the entire agenda within a specified meeting time. Giving staff members responsibility for selected agenda items is an excellent way to encourage interest in center operations. Reserving part of each meeting to have a staff member present on a topic of interest also contributes to the feeling of collegiality.

The director should distribute copies of readings, minutes from previous staff or board meetings, and any other information that will

provide a common basis for discussion to enhance the quality of the dialogue during the meeting. For example, if there is to be a discussion about curriculum planning as it relates to emerging literacy, research studies and program ideas on this topic could be duplicated and given to staff members several days before the meeting. Individual staff members should also be encouraged to search out additional information on the topic so the time spent during the meeting is productive and informative for everyone. Occasionally, a specialist from the community can be invited to a staff meeting to contribute to a discussion that requires particular expertise, such as services provided by the local children's protective agency or new information on infectious diseases in child care centers. When the director prepares the agenda carefully and both the director and the staff members come well informed, the outcome can be more satisfying for everyone.

Staff Meeting Procedure

The director usually serves as the convener and assumes the responsibility for moving the group through the agenda by facilitating but not dominating the discussion, and helping the group maintain a balance between dealing with tasks and dealing with interpersonal processes.

At the outset, it is important that the meeting begin at the stated time and end on schedule. When the convener does not call the meeting to order on time and move immediately to the first agenda item, group members are inclined to come late because they assume the meeting will not start on time. When the discussion of an agenda item extends beyond the time assigned, the convener should call attention to that fact and have the group decide whether or not more time should be spent on that item.

Perhaps all this emphasis on time seems unimportant, but time management is important. Time is finite, and you and your staff must develop good time-management skills to accomplish as much as you can within a specified time frame. The staff meeting is an excellent place for you, as a director, to demonstrate good time-management.

Clearly, conducting an effective staff meeting takes careful planning and requires special skills on the part of the director. However, when meetings are satisfying and productive for the staff, they not only serve as a vehicle for communication but also promote cooperation and good feeling among staff. Furthermore, staff meetings give the director a chance to model good interpersonal communication skills that serve as the basis for all interactions with children, parents, and other staff members.

STAFF TRAINING

The staff training program begins with the orientation of new staff members and includes all aspects of in-service training. Planning the total staff training program depends on the composition of the center staff. Just as the classroom teacher individualizes approaches to children, so the director recognizes the development level of each teacher, and plans training accordingly. The training must be adjusted to the experiential level and career stage as well as to the specific concerns, capabilities and perspectives of each person, and should focus on long-term growth and change in individuals' thinking skills.[3]

Fully trained and qualified classroom teaching staff members should have basic child development information and should be able to plan curriculum and classroom management strategies with minimum additional training. However, they may be ready for some help on working with the special education resource teacher who comes to consult with them about the children with disabilities in the center. Because special classroom strategies must be employed in order to truly mainstream children with disabilities into a non-categorical classroom, training in techniques and strategies to accomplish that integration will also be helpful to the experienced teacher. The interdisciplinary classroom team of early childhood and special educators must work together to provide quality programming for all children in an inclusive environment. An interdisciplinary team building and staff development approach for both the special educators and the early childhood staff is to provide mutual training so these professionals together develop their own professional skills as well as come to appreciate more fully the knowledge and skills of other members of the team. As team members come to accept as well as extend the skills and knowledge of fellow professionals, mutual respect and camaraderie are reinforced. Further, with more preschools in public schools, where program expectations and philosophies

---

REFLECTIONS

Think about your class and study schedule and your other responsibilities. When a class is scheduled to convene at 4:00 P.M. and end at 5:30 P.M., you feel very frustrated if you rush to arrive on time only to find that the instructor is fifteen minutes late. Furthermore, you may have to get home to family or prepare dinner, and you become restless and inattentive if the class goes beyond 5:30 P.M. The only way that you are able to manage your time well is to have others with whom you must interact regularly maintain their time commitments to you. The same is true for you and your colleagues at the workplace.

---

3 Paula Jorde-Bloom, Marilyn Sheerer, and Joan Britz, *Blueprint for Action,* Horizons, 1991, p. 95.

are often incongruent with early childhood principles, team building and staff development programs for both preschool and public school personnel in these settings is clearly indicated.

On the other hand, paraprofessional classroom staff may need training in preparing classroom materials, in understanding growth and development, or in developing basic management skills. Custodians, food service staff, or clerical staff will need different levels and types of assistance. When planning a staff training program, the director will have to assess the training needs of everyone and then make decisions about time, content, and training methods for the sessions. An experienced director can assess training needs by observing staff as they carry out their job responsibilities and by having conferences with them to discover more about their own analysis of training needs and their interest in professional advancement. Assessment of training needs is an ongoing process, and, as personal and professional development proceeds, the director's task is to present more challenging training opportunities.

Time and Place for Training

Finding a suitable time for training meetings is even more difficult than finding a suitable time for staff meetings. In the case of regularly scheduled staff meetings, the staff can plan ahead for the full year and schedule their other duties and commitments around the meeting times. However, training sessions usually occur with less regularity, often require a larger block of time than a staff meeting, and have to be planned to coincide with the schedules of consultants or outside experts whose services are needed. If the director and center staff members are the only people involved in the training, scheduling difficulties are somewhat alleviated. Nonetheless, the problems of late afternoon or evening fatigue and the inability of the staff to leave the classroom during the day create special problems for the training of child care staff, unless the training can be planned for naptime or can be incorporated into the staff meetings. Since most training requires larger time blocks, it may be necessary to discuss the possibility of a Saturday meeting. Half-day preschool programs that usually meet during the public school academic year often have training meetings in the early autumn before school begins or in the spring after school closes. In any case, if in-service training attendance is mandatory, this point must be included in the employee's contract or job description.

Whether or not attendance at training sessions should be mandatory or optional is a question that must be decided by the director or by the group. In some places where licensing requires a given number of clock hours of training each year, the planned training could be mandatory for some staff and not for others. If attendance is mandatory, the feelings of resentment may negate the possible benefits. On the other hand, if attendance is not mandatory, those who attend may feel resentment toward those who have decided not to attend. As a director, you will have to work closely with your staff to get a feel for their commitment to the training program and their possible reactions to mandatory or voluntary attendance.

When there is a comfortable lounge or conference room at the center, the staff may prefer to stay in the building for the training sessions. The comfort and familiarity of the center will

REFLECTIONS

Think about your personal feelings when you were told that you had to attend some function, such as a meeting, a party, or a class, as opposed to the times when you were given a choice. When it was a matter of choice, what were the factors that motivated you to attend? Was it curiosity about who would be there or what would take place? Was it interest in what you expected would take place? Was it to please the person who requested you attend or who told you about the event? Can you analyze your feelings and reactions when you went someplace to please someone else as opposed to the times when you went because you were intrinsically motivated?

help create a feeling of openness, which could be very important if the success of the training is dependent on dialogue and exchange of ideas among staff members. If the training is a cooperative effort and several centers are involved, a space in a centrally located community building may be more convenient for the trainees.

Training Methods and Resources

The methods or strategies employed in the in-service training program will depend on the amount of time available, the resources available, and the nature of the content selected. For example, if one hour of a staff meeting is set aside for a refresher course in first aid, the best way to present that information may be in a lecture given by a representative from the health department, or with a film presentation. If, on the other hand, there is more time to spend on the topic of first aid, it may be desirable to plan a full day session with a Red Cross specialist. Enrolling some staff members who do not have first aid certificates in a Red Cross course that extends over several weeks and is available evenings or on Saturday is yet another alternative. First aid training can be expanded to include health, nutrition, and safety. The expansion of the program creates new training strategy possibilities. Group discussions led by the director would be an appropriate method to use in making the staff more aware of safety issues in the center. The program could include discussions about safety when using outdoor equipment, when planning cooking experiences, or when organizing field trips. The health or nutrition questions might be handled best by a nurse, physician, or a dietitian who would come for a seminar. A special educator might come to discuss health and safety issues as these relate to special needs children. When outside consultants are brought in, the director's role is to sit in on the training in order to be able to do follow-up with the staff, thus extending the new information to specific situations each teacher encounters in the classroom. There are any number of possible methods from which to choose—each one requiring different amounts of time and different resources, but, in this example, each one being adaptable to the content area of first aid, health, and safety.

On-site workshops are useful mechanisms for encouraging direct involvement of the staff in a special content area. Implicit in the workshop concept is the idea that those who attend participate actively in the program. Frequently, workshops are planned for a staff that expresses a need to know more about curriculum areas like developing writing centers, math or science experiences for young children, or music in the classroom. Other areas, such as building skills for more effective conferences with parents or for ways to interact with volunteers, can also be handled in a workshop format that involves participants in a series of role plays or simulation games. Workshops require active involvement from the participants, and therefore are more suitable for some training needs than are lectures, films, or seminars.

Visits to other centers are encouraged by some directors and certainly comprise part of the total staff training program. Watching other teachers and children is refreshing and interesting for some staff members. After such visits, they bring back program ideas, new and different ways to set up the physical environment, and sometimes a renewed interest in developing classroom materials such as math games or interactive charts. Some teachers who are able to

DIRECTOR'S CORNER

"One of the most helpful things we did in my administration class at college was role playing. I especially remember role playing a parent conference. Now I use that technique all the time with my staff. In staff training sessions, when we are discussing an issue like dealing with a difficult parent, I ask for a specific example, and immediately turn it into a role play. 'OK—now I'm the parent and here is my concern—you are the teacher,' and we play it out. Then we often reverse roles so I take the role of the teacher. It works very well for me as a director."

Director, YMCA-sponsored center

move beyond the more obvious things like equipment or curriculum ideas may begin to compare and contrast classroom environments and teaching strategies, relating these differences to the differences in the stated philosophies of the programs. Follow-up group discussions will help teachers refine their understanding of how theory relates to practice. Why are the children in one program encouraged to negotiate with one another about dividing up the play dough, while the teacher controls amounts for each child in another center? The two strategies clearly reflect different program goals. Group discussions may also encourage teachers to re-examine the theoretical basis for the center program in which they work and re-evaluate the curriculum to ascertain how closely it reflects the stated philosophy of the center, as well as their own philosophy of early childhood education.

Professional conferences and workshops provide excellent training opportunities for staff. Directors who commit to a personal program of professional development by attending professional meetings set a standard of excellence for their teachers to emulate. It is important to encourage staff to take advantage of these training opportunities and facilitate their attending conferences by allowing time off from work and subsidizing their travel and registration expenses if at all possible. Some child care programs not only subsidize conference attendance but also pay for teachers' memberships in professional organizations like National Association for the Education of Young Children (NAEYC) or Association for Childhood Education International (ACEI).

Staff members who express an interest in professional advancement are to be commended for their ambitious goals and encouraged to take courses toward a college degree in child development or early childhood education or the Child Development Associate (CDA) certificate in communities where these types of training programs are available. Some centers will help pay tuition for relevant courses as well as adjust work schedules to allow staff to attend daytime classes. Directors can lend further support to these part-time students by showing interest in what they are learning and guiding them to helpful resources available at the center.

In order to provide on-site materials to support and enhance all aspects of the staff training program, it is the job of the director to establish a professional library and also a teachers' resource center. The library books should cover information on child development, curriculum, classroom management, special needs children, and working with other professionals and with families. Books on specific curriculum areas like literacy, math, science, cooking or music will help the staff plan for the children. Recent copies of professional journals and newsletters should be available in the teachers' library along with a collection of audio-visual materials including tapes, slides, videotapes, and film strips which will provide a rich source of information on curriculum development and classroom management.

The teachers' resource center should be a space where teachers can make math games, charts, big books, and other teacher-made classroom materials. Supplies like paper, tag board, paper cutter, scissors, glue, tape, plain die, marking pens, and so forth must be available, plus a large working surface. It is a luxury to have things like a laminating machine or an Elison machine for stamping out letters and shapes for charts. When teachers have materials and space to work, they are more likely to develop individualized teacher-made classroom materials.

Training Content

A number of program ideas for the staff training program have already been mentioned in the previous discussions on methods of training. Training needs will vary according to the previous training and experience of the center staff. Many teachers are constantly seeking new curriculum ideas and resource materials for the classroom; consequently, training in curriculum areas is usually welcomed. There is always interest in strategies for dealing with the difficult, disruptive child or the withdrawn child. Furthermore, most teachers are interested in learning more about community resources where they can get advice about how to handle children with special needs or about where to refer children and families for additional help.

The director should determine if staff members need special coaching in conducting a home visit or a parent conference. These duties are taxing and anxiety producing and require very special communication skills which are suitable for the particular parent population being served. It is important to know that some families may be slow to accept a stranger and will draw back from a person whom they perceive as too intrusive. Attitudes about accepting newcomers, about education, and about child rearing vary among cultural, ethnic, and socioeconomic groups, and it is essential for staff to know what those differences are when they work with children and families. Staff members also find it helpful to have special guidance from the director in effective interpersonal communications.

There is a pressing need to assist staff with dealing with diversity in the classroom. Mainstreaming children with disabilities and children from diverse cultural and ethnic groups into early childhood education programs means there must be training programs that focus on providing information about ways to meet the individual needs of children from these groups. Other timely issues where teachers often need help include children of divorce, single parent families, hospitalization of a parent or the child, victims of child abuse, and so forth.

When the staff is experienced and fully capable of dealing with the day-to-day, here-and-now events in the classroom, training can move on to the question of early childhood education in the next century. What do children need to know to survive in the twenty-first century? How will life change in the next fifty years and what personality characteristics and thinking dispositions will be essential to function competently during those fifty years? The job of staff training is never completed because there are always new challenges.

STAFF SUPERVISION AND COACHING

The director, or the educational director in the case of large centers or corporate chains, is responsible for supervision of classroom staff. (The director will be referred to as *supervisor* for the purposes of this discussion.) By observing, doing one-to-one coaching, and working in the classroom with the children and the staff, the supervisor gives support and guidance to each staff member and establishes a trusting relationship with each one. The trust and mutual respect that develop provide the basis for building a teaching-learning relationship that parallels the relationship between adult and child. Then the supervisor is able to create a favorable environment in which each staff member can gain new understandings of children, of self, and of the supervisor's expectations.

An experienced supervisor knows that sometimes growth and change take place slowly. Working together, talking together, and planning together will promote personal and professional competence on the part of classroom staff members, provided the supervisor is supportive and encouraging, and is not perceived as being critical or threatening.

Principles of Supervision

A number of basic principles or assumptions should be kept in mind as you think about the director as staff supervisor. The same principles apply to the supervisory role whether you are working with a new, inexperienced staff member or a mature, qualified, experienced teacher, or are a new director moving into a fully staffed center.

- Supervision is a dynamic, evolutionary process that is based on trust.
- Supervision is individualized and adapted to the personality and teaching style of each staff member.
- Supervision provides a support system for each staff member.
- Supervision provides a framework within which the supervisor demonstrates professional skills for the entire staff.

However, an individualized model of staff development means you must use a developmental approach to supervision, and teachers who are at different stages in their careers will require qualitatively different supervisory strategies.[4]

4 Ibid., p. 98.

Supervisory Process

As classroom staff members grow and change, the thrust and focus of the supervisory process shifts accordingly. The process begins by providing support and guidance for a new staff member who is actively integrating past learning experiences into a personal teaching style that is compatible with the center philosophy. The process changes as the staff member adjusts and develops into an accomplished teacher who will in turn supervise assistants, aides, student teachers, or be paired with a new teacher and become a mentor. If you think of this supervisory process on a continuum, it moves from a very directive approach for new teachers where the control is in the hands of the supervisor, to a collaborative model where an accomplished teacher and the supervisor share control of the process.

One-to-one coaching is the essential ingredient of the supervisory process whether working with the beginning teacher or the accomplished professional who, in turn, will coach others in the center. Coaching includes modeling, observing, and the giving of specific feedback. Communicating with staff after an observation is usually handled in a conference, but, when time is short, a brief note with some specific feedback may have to suffice.

Supervising New Teachers. New teachers need daily or even hourly support; therefore, the supervisor must plan to spend some time each day not only observing but also teaching with the new teacher. If a new teacher is also recently trained, that teacher will be developing a personal teaching style and will profit from the example that is set by an experienced supervisor. It is very important for a supervisor to work beside a new teacher with the children in the classroom. This supervisory procedure creates a rich learning environment for the new teacher and often provides a more favorable transition for the children and families who know the supervisor but are not yet will acquainted with the new teacher. As a supervisor, you must make sure to remove yourself gradually so that the new teacher can build a relationship with the children and families and begin to manage the classroom without your constant support. What you are doing, in effect, is providing hourly or daily support during the initial trust-building

---

DIRECTOR'S CORNER

"Since I am new here I haven't developed a schedule for regular observations as yet, but I make the rounds at least twice a day, if only to let my teachers know I am available. Of course, I have a chance to catch things going on in each room—maybe a new chart or a teacher reading a book to a sleepy child. I make sure I leave a short note in each teacher's box, mentioning some little thing I noticed when I came by. If I see an activity or a procedure which concerns me, I mention it. 'I noticed you had the toddlers fingerpainting with chocolate pudding today. Drop by when you have a chance—I have some ideas about that which I would like to share with you.' It seems to work well for me."

Director, community-agency-sponsored center

---

period but stepping back when the new teacher is able to function autonomously. However, stay nearby because your ongoing support is still important when things do not go well.

Supervising Experienced Teachers. As teachers develop their skills and become more competent, they continue to profit from the supervisor's support. Positive reinforcement and constructive criticism from supervisors are excellent motivating factors, but experienced teachers are also ready for expansion and growth in new directions. They are still integrating and reorganizing what they have learned in the past, but they are now able to reach out for new learning opportunities. These teachers are now comfortable with their teaching style and can direct more attention to curriculum development. They are ready for the intellectual stimulation they can draw from taking course work, reading new publications, and attending professional meetings. Therefore, although the supervisor continues to observe these teachers and have conferences with them on a regular basis, emphasis is now placed on the supervisor as a resource person. The supervisor should supply new program ideas, new theoretical information, articles from professional journals, research materials, and as many opportunities as possible to participate actively in professional organizations and conferences.

While experienced teachers are perfecting their teaching skills under the guidance of the supervisor, they should also be developing self-evaluation skills. With encouragement and help from a supervisor, experienced teachers feel secure enough to step back and evaluate their teaching. They can begin to ask themselves some of the questions a supervisor has been asking them and engage in some self-searching about their methodology. For example, one teacher might make the inquiry, "How could I have better handled the situation between those two children who had a conflict over the sand bucket? What I did was really not productive. I *must* find alternative ways of handling those two children." Another teacher might ask, "How can I adjust my questioning techniques for all the children in order to help them become better problem solvers? I heard you mention Rheta deVries.

Maybe you could give me something she has written on that topic which will help me."

Supervising the Accomplished Teacher. The accomplished, long-term teacher is still perfecting teaching and self-evaluation skills and revising curriculum. However, having reached a new level of mastery, this teacher is ready to develop supervisory skills. While working with the teachers, the supervisor has not only exemplified teaching and self-evaluation skills but supervisory skill as well. In working with accomplished teachers, the supervisor now turns to coaching them in supervisory skills. This teacher is preparing to assume responsibility for the supervision of assistants, aides, and, in some situations, student teachers. To serve in this capacity, the teacher will need instruction and support to develop the necessary skills for fulfilling supervisory responsibilities. The supervisor is still observing and having conferences on a regular basis, giving attention to teaching strategies and self-evaluation. However, the new thrust is directed to this teacher's interaction with and supervision of other adults in the classroom.

Supervision is one of the most difficult and anxiety-producing aspects of the director's job. It draws upon every bit of professional skill the

By observing and holding conferences with individual teachers, the director gives support and guidance to each staff member. (Photo by Lisa Souders)

director has because it demands expertise in interpersonal communication, children's programming, teaching strategies, and self-evaluation.

ASSESSING STAFF PROBLEMS

Assessing what the staff members view as work-related problems provides the basis for designing the staff development program and focusing individualized supervision activities. Once you have identified what teachers feel to be their major problems you can take the first steps toward helping them solve those problems.[5] The expressed needs of staff can be addressed directly. If a teacher has problems handling the aggressive behaviors of a child, the director can respond in various direct ways, including offering relevant readings, observing or participating in the classroom and discussing various management strategies, calling in a consultant to observe and conference with the classroom staff, or discussing the general problem of dealing with aggression in a staff meeting. This direct response to an expressed need is certain to motivate the staff member to become involved in a training plan offered by the director. On the other hand, when the selection of staff development activities is based upon those issues the

director views as problems, motivating staff interest will be more difficult. For example, if a new director finds the long-term staff using punitive and age-inappropriate techniques in response to unacceptable classroom behaviors, but the teachers are comfortable with their management methods, those teachers will resist making a commitment to any training designed to encourage them to use more positive management strategies. The new director will have to spend time establishing a trusting working relationship with the professional staff before training related to the classroom management question will be accepted. Since the use of punitive management techniques can be hard on children, the new director may choose to bring in a consultant to work with individual staff members or may even consider making staff changes. A new director is well advised to design the initial staff development activities in response to the teachers' expressed needs.

Expressed Teacher Concerns

Expressed teacher concerns cluster around a number of problem areas.[6]

The director's task is to identify and then respond to these concerns. The areas of greatest concern are:

• *Dealing with Subordinate Staff.* Teachers have a problem getting their assistants to follow-through on assigned responsibilities and to work as a member of a cooperative team. In response to this problem, effective directing, evaluating and giving feedback to subordinate staff would be appropriate areas to address in the staff training program for the teachers. The best way for the director to help teachers with this problem is to model exemplary supervisory skills.

• *Managing the Classroom.* Teachers report problems with controlling children's unacceptable behaviors. Included in their list are things like aggression, not picking up, not sharing and not cooperating. In addressing this problem, the director might first focus on developmental

REFLECTIONS

Think about the cooperating teacher who supervised your practicum. Did you receive support and constructive criticism? Did that person serve as a model of good supervisory skills for you? Think about how your cooperating teacher might have been more helpful. What do you feel you need before you can become a supervisor of a center classroom staff?

5 Ibid., p. 250.
6 Ibid., p. 256.

expectations for the specific age group in question, followed by ways to encourage pro-social behaviors. This is a sensitive problem area because the perceived problem sometimes results from teachers' unrealistic expectations. Directors must model developmentally appropriate responses to children's behaviors whenever they have encounters with children in the center.

• *Helping Special Needs Children and Families.* Teachers report that they do not know enough about how to deal appropriately with atypical children. They want help on how to provide rich environments for these children as well as ways to work effectively with the family. Providing reading materials and planning special meetings on this topic will be helpful to teachers who are searching for better ways to help these special children. Directors must also watch for up-coming conferences and meetings on the topic, and encourage staff to attend.

• *Relating to Supervisors.* Directors must face the reality that they are often perceived as a major problem by staff members. Teachers complain about not being treated fairly and not being respected as professionals. The response to this problem is clearly in the director's hands. Directors must work on their own professional development to enable them to become better staff managers.

• *Maintaining Parent Cooperation.* Teachers have problems with parents who send a sick child, or are not prompt about picking up, and those who do not cooperate with the teachers' efforts with things like encouraging use of messy materials. Here, the director can reinforce center policies by reviewing the Parent Handbook material with the parent, as well as participating in parent conferences when necessary, to mediate

and to give support to both the teacher and the parent. In-service training focused on working with parents and becoming sensitive to their needs may help teachers feel more secure about handling difficult situations with parents.

• *Managing Time.* Time to deal with non-teaching tasks like cleaning, planning, making materials, or doing other paper work is a problem for teachers. Since time management is also a major problem for directors, it is something they have in common. Time-management seminars under the guidance of an experienced trainer can be part of the staff development program. It is especially important for the director to be a part of this training, and also to model good time management.

Although staff concerns are always situation specific, there is a common core of recurring problems which fall into the categories listed here. It can be reassuring to you, as a director, to know that your teachers' expressed needs are much like those of most teaching staffs.

SUMMARY

The staff development program contributes to both the personal and professional growth of the center staff. Through the planning and implementation of effective staff meetings, staff training programs, and staff supervision, the director creates an enriched learning environment for the staff. Given the benefits of an enriched environment and a director who demonstrates good interpersonal and professional skills, the staff members have the opportunity to enjoy the inevitable personal satisfaction and excitement that result from positive, individualized professional growth experiences.

Class Assignments

1. Contact a director in the community and request permission to attend a staff meeting. Answer the questions on Working Paper 14-1 after attending the meeting. (Do not take notes during the meeting!)
2. Use the list of expressed teacher problems on Working Paper 14-2, and complete a. and b. below.

   a. Based on your experience with children, rank order the list of teacher problems from most difficult (1) to least difficult (10).
   b. Select one from the first three in your ranking. Complete a staff training plan for that particular teacher concern by responding to the items listed on Working Paper 14-2.

Class Exercises

1. Role play a child care center staff meeting and discuss one agenda item, namely, "Timing for weekly staff meetings." It has been decided by the director that the entire staff (including the cook, the janitor, and the secretary) must meet every week. The question open for discussion is the day of the week on which the staff should meet plus when and how long the meetings should be. Assign the following roles to class members.

   a. Director: Works Monday through Friday 9:00 A.M. to 5:00 P.M.
   b. Teacher A: Works Monday through Friday 9:00 A.M. to 5:00 P.M.
   c. Teacher B: Works Monday through Friday 6:00 A.M. to 2:00 P.M.
   d. Assistant Teacher C: Works Monday through Friday 10:00 A.M. to 6:00 P.M.
   e. Assistant Teacher D: Works Monday through Friday 6:00 A.M. to 2:00 P.M.
   f. Part time Teacher E: Works Monday through Friday 10:00 A.M. to 2:00 P.M.
   g. Cook: Works Monday through Friday 9:00 A.M. to 3:00 P.M.
   h. Janitor: Works Monday through Friday 3:00 P.M. to 8:00 P.M.

   There are thirty-five children in the program who arrive on a staggered schedule between 6:15 A.M. and 9:30 A.M. and leave between 2:30 P.M. and 5:30 P.M. The children occupy two classrooms and two sleeping rooms. Sleeping rooms are adjacent to one another and to the outdoor area.

   The staff meeting discussion is to be led by the director and the group is to come to some decision about when the regular staff meeting will be held. Use the blackboard or newsprint for note taking if you need it. Practice good listening skills; make sure that everyone participates.

2. Role play a special staff meeting that has been called by the director to discuss and reach a decision about allocation of classroom space at the child

care center. There will be one additional classroom available beginning in September, and a new teacher, Mark, will be employed. The new classroom is larger than the others and opens directly to the playground.

Sandra presently has the best classroom, which has its own bathroom. (The other four rooms share a bathroom down the hall.) Jean will be working with a new pilot program and will have many parents participating in her classroom. She was responsible for getting the pilot program funded and it is a real asset for the center. Bob's classroom is far from the outside play area and from the storage room. Bob feels that this location is inconvenient. Sheila would like to keep her present classroom because she recently made curtains and painted the walls. Barbara feels that her ten years of teaching qualify her for the new classroom.

Name	Years at Center	Degree	Present Classroom
Sandra	6	M.S.	Excellent
Barbara	10	B.S.	Very good
Sheila	4	B.S.	Very good
Bob	6	A.S.	Good
Jean	1	A.S.	Poor
Mark	0	B.S.	

The staff has allocated thirty minutes for making this decision. After the group has arrived at a decision, individually rate your level of satisfaction with the decision from 1 (low) to 5 (high). Also rate your level of participation from 1 to 5. Tally the results on the chalkboard. As a group, discuss the factors that contributed to the level of satisfaction or dissatisfaction. Was the level of participation a factor?

Working Paper 14-1

Staff Meeting Questions

Based upon your experience at the staff meeting you attended, answer the following questions.

1. Did the director fulfill the role of keeping the group focused on the agenda items? How?

2. Was there any attempt to follow a time line? If not, what effect do you suspect that had on the feelings of the staff?

3. Were there any notable incidents where staff members seemed not to be heard? Describe them and indicate the behaviors that you observed in those staff members after the incidents.

Working Paper 14-2

Expressed Teacher Problems

1. Based on your experience up to this point in your professional career, rank order the expressed teacher problems listed below from most difficult (1) to least difficult (10).

   _____ Finding time to plan and do paper work.

   _____ Getting the supervisor to respect my opinion.

   _____ Knowing how to handle aggressive children.

   _____ Handling a physically disabled child.

   _____ Handling a demanding child without neglecting the other children.

   _____ Handling a parent who is very punitive with her child when she picks him up.

   _____ Getting the other adults in the room to do their share of cleanup and "dirty" work.

   _____ Keeping children's attention during group time.

   _____ Motivating myself to be involved with professional organizations.

   _____ Dealing with criticism from my supervisor.

2. Select problem 1, 2, or 3 from your rankings and complete a staff-training plan which addresses that problem. Address the following:

   What relevant material would you provide in the staff library for the staff to read?

   • Books

   • Journals (give name of articles and authors)

   • Audiovisuals

   Develop an agenda for a staff meeting addressing the problem. Include:

   • Format (panel, speaker, role-playing, etc.)

   • Outline of content

   • Discussion of the direct steps you would take, as a director, to support the staff as they deal with this problem on a day-to-day basis.

CHAPTER 15

Working with Parents, Volunteers, and the Community

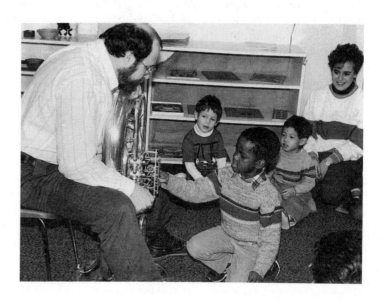

Photo above The community orchestra member who comes to play for the children must be prepared for the children's questions and their desire to handle the instrument. (Photo by Anne G. Dorsey)

"The job of the child care center director is one that calls for enormous skill, particularly in working with parents. It is being a professional who simultaneously creates a friendly atmosphere yet retains an appropriate distance; an expert who builds competence in others, who is understanding, empathetic, yet at times firm. Most important is the role of the model—whose words or way of handling a sad, tired or exuberant child are inspiring to parents."[1] Developing a first-class program for children is the primary goal of the child care center administrator, but many centers have a secondary focus on special programming for parents, which requires the director to assume an additional major role as leader of the parent program or as supervisor of the staff members that are responsible for the

1 Ellen Galinsky, "How to Work with Working Parents," *Child Care Information Exchange,* June 1984, p. 4.

parent program. Work with volunteers and community organizations or agencies is also an integral part of the total center program that falls within the director's purview in some centers.

PARENT PROGRAM

Although center directors are not always responsible for the total planning and implementation of all aspects of the parent program, they *are* held accountable for the program. Classroom staff members or someone designated as a parent coordinator may assume some responsibility for parts of the program, but directors monitor the work, train those who are working with the parents, supervise the program, and serve as a resource for both the staff and the parents.

A positive attitude toward parents and what they can contribute to the center program must be demonstrated by the director. There are a number of reasons why parents may be hesitant about coming to the child care center or preschool program. They may feel threatened by the idea that the teacher is very knowledgeable about children and fearful that their child-rearing practices will be criticized. Some parents, particularly from impoverished backgrounds, may feel inhibited around the school environment because of their limited or unsuccessful school experiences.[2] It is also difficult for parents who have other special problems such as having a child with a disability, being a potential abuser, or a single parent or one who is unable to read or write. Staff behavior and the atmosphere at the center must communicate to parents that each parent is valued as an individual and that each is highly regarded as the child's first teacher and as someone who knows a great deal about the child. All parents should be aware that they are welcome to come as frequently (or as infrequently) as they wish.

Any number of things can communicate this feeling of acceptance and trust to parents—although some are more tangible than others. A parent-receiving area is the place where parents establish their first impressions of the center. It

should be a well defined space where parents and center staff exchange information. It should be orderly and aesthetically attractive, with some adult chairs and evidence that it is an adult space, yet it should communicate the fact that the center is for children. Parent bulletin boards should contain information about the center and a calendar of coming events. Pamphlets and journals on child rearing, toy selection, nutrition, and how to make play dough or fingerpaint can be made available in the parent-receiving area. A parent and child book lending library or toy lending library might be located nearby. Sometimes interested parents are asked to manage the entire lending program.

The less tangible things that make parents feel welcome include the manner in which their calls are handled by the staff member who answers the phone or the greeting they receive from the van driver who picks up their child each day. Parents' feelings about the center program and staff are also substantially influenced by their first contacts with their child's teacher or the center director. Since it is very difficult to perceive what is having the most significant impact on the parents' reactions to a center program, directors have to be alert to any number of subtle factors that may be influencing parental attitudes and feelings.

The success of the entire parent program depends on the feelings of trust that must be built between the center staff and the children and families who use the center. Such trust begins to develop at the first contact and will continue to grow as it is nurtured by center staff.

The parent program can be divided into three major categories; (1) parent contacts, (2) parent education, and (3) parent involvement. Clearly, these three aspects of the parent program overlap; however, they are separated here for the purposes of discussion.

Parent Contacts

Parent contacts range from the most informal arrival or departure greetings to formalized interviews, regularly scheduled conferences, and

---

2 Celia Decker and John R. Decker, *Planning and Administering Early Childhood Programs* (5th edition), Merrill, an imprint of Macmillan, 1992, p. 362.

DIRECTOR'S CORNER

"I make it clear at my very first meeting with a prospective parent that we are open to parents visiting at any time. Our parents understand that even before admission to the program, they can come by to observe in our classrooms as they are weighing the pros and cons of sending their child to this center. It's the first step on the road to building a trusting relationship between all of us here at the center and the families that are with us."

Director, independent not-for-profit center

special conferences when problems are encountered. Whatever the occasion, contacts with parents can be useful channels for communication. It is through these contacts that the center staff members communicate to parents that they have important information to share with one another and that they have a very special mutual concern for a child whom they both value. Details of initial interviews and intake procedures were discussed in Chapter 11. When staff members are not fully prepared to handle initial contacts with parents, in-service training time should be devoted to discussion or role playing of parent interviews and intake procedures. (See Chapter 14 for the discussion of in-service training.)

It is important to plan regularly scheduled parent conferences where parents and teachers meet at a mutually agreed-upon time and place to discuss the child. It may take several scheduled conferences and unscheduled calls or casual contacts before a teacher can be successful in creating a totally relaxed environment in which both parent and teacher can comfortably discuss the child. When a good relationship exists, the scheduled conference is a time when parents and teachers can discuss the child's progress, present their concerns and their satisfaction about the child's progress, and develop a plan to follow both at home and at school that will stimulate the child to progress further. In the interval

between scheduled conferences, casual telephone calls and informal contacts at the center are both excellent ways to converse about how the plan for the child is working.

Pre-conference planning sheets can be a useful tool in planning parent conferences. Depending on the parent population being served, you, as a director, may have both the parents and the teachers complete a pre-conference planning sheet. (See sample in Figure 15-1.) Experienced teachers can plan the conference based on information from their notes and observations of the child, the information supplied by the parent and their knowledge of the characteristics of an effective parent conference. The director should provide some coaching for inexperienced staff before they conference with parents.

It is important that parent conferences start and end on a positive note, and that incidents or samples of work be used to make specific points about the child's progress. Parents must be given time to express concerns, while teachers practice their best listening skills. Just as early childhood professionals build trust with children by listening to concerns and reflecting those feelings, so they build trust with parents by practicing those same listening skills. Putting parents at ease and avoiding arousing anxiety will not only enhance the quality of the relationship during the conference, but will carry over to the daily interactions with parents as well.

Special conferences are sometimes necessary when either parents or teachers have a need to discuss particular concerns about a child or the center program. The special conferences are likely to produce anxiety for everyone because they are most often called when a problem arises. Sometimes the director is asked to sit in on a special conference to give support to both teacher and parent and to help clarify what is being said and heard. The teacher may have a conference with the director prior to a particularly difficult parent conference so that they both have a clear understanding of the problem to be discussed. The teacher may also ask the director to recommend the best way to present a problem and to offer some suggestions on how to handle the parents' questions and reactions during the conference. Sometimes these special conferences include other specialists or consultants from referral agencies, such as a mental health center or a speech and hearing center. Both the teacher

Figure 15-1   Sample Preconference Planning Sheet

Child's Name:_____

Parent(s) Name:_____

Date and Time of Conference:_____

Above is the date and time of your parent/teacher conference. Please call the office and reschedule if the assigned time is not convenient.

I look forward to talking with you about your child. Some of the things I have planned to share with you are:

I am specifically interested in finding out about the areas of interest or concern which you would like to discuss with me. Please use the space below to tell me what those things are.

Please return this to my box in the office at least a week before the scheduled conference. Thank you very much.

and the director should be well prepared for special conferences because they will be expected to make a knowledgeable contribution to the discussion about the child. In some cases they will have to provide support for the parent, who may feel tense and threatened.

Uninterrupted time and a comfortable space are essential for successful parent conferences. Timing is important; the time of day or evening that is chosen must suit both the staff members and the parents so that no one feels pressured or rushed. The time allotted must be long enough to discuss matters thoroughly, but not so long that the discussion becomes tedious. Both parents should be encouraged to attend conferences, and, in cases of divorce, teachers may be expected to arrange a conference with each parent. Both teacher and parents leave a successful conference feeling that they have accomplished their goals. In addition, parents should go away with an awareness that their child is valued and

appreciated. Finally, it is *critical* that parents have complete confidence that confidentiality will be maintained—the parent–teacher trust relationship will be seriously damaged if a parent should learn from some outside source that shared information about the family or the child was not kept confidential.

A post-conference review will help teachers evaluate the quality of their participation. The following checklist will help them focus on their responses during the conference. Directors may want to review the following questions with their teachers after their encounters with parents.[3]

- Did you give the parents a chance to talk about their concerns?
- Did you remain an acceptant listener?
- When you made comments, did you talk in terms of the parents' feelings rather than what they were doing?

3 Adapted from Dorothy Hewes and Barbara Hartman, *Early Childhood Education: A Workbook for Administrators,* 1988, p. 105.

- Were you able to restrain yourself from giving advice?
- Did you remember that suggestions are usually nothing more than advice under a different guise?
- If you did offer suggestions, did you give more than one so the parents have options?
- Did the parents do most of the talking?
- Were you able to restate to the parent the feelings just expressed?
- Did you *listen?* Furthermore, did you listen because you really cared?

Parent Education

Typically, the parent education program is designed to improve parenting skills or to interpret the center program to the parent group. In some centers there are more ambitious goals for the parent education program, including education on consumerism, nutrition, stress management, or time management. Some centers even provide vocational education programs or special remedial classes to help parents complete high school or take the General Education Development test (G.E.D.).[4]

Planning parent education programs is the responsibility of the director, but the planning group should include parent representatives. Format and content must reflect the needs and interests of the parents and be adjusted to the level of education and previous training of the parent population. Centers that serve families from diverse educational, cultural, and socioeconomic backgrounds should present a wide variety of choices from which the parents can select the programs that are best suited to their needs.

Activities in the parent education program may be as informal as casual classroom observations followed by one-to-one or small-group discussions with a staff member, or as formal as a planned lecture, workshop, panel discussion, or seminar. The planned activities should meet the parents' needs in terms of timing, content, and presentation strategy. Casual classroom observations are particularly helpful to parents who are curious about how their child's behavior compares with that of peers. For example, a mother who feels great concern about the explosive yelling and unacceptable language of her preschool son may feel reassured when she observes other four-year-olds who are also noisy and explosive. It is also helpful for that mother to discuss these erratic outbursts with a staff member who can interpret the behavior in terms of expected behaviors at this developmental stage. Group discussions, lectures, films, videotapes, or workshops that are offered by center staff members or by outside consultants are all useful tools for providing parents with information on child rearing, child development, or topics related to parental problems and concerns.

Topics of interest and concern to parents range from specific questions like, "What do I do about my child who awakens at 4:30 A.M. every day and wants to get up?" to broader issues facing employed parents who struggle with the stresses of job, home, and family. Programs should focus on building parents' sense of expertise. In planning parent education programs, consider emphasis on empowering parents to explore ways to cope with their concerns and issues around parenting.

Directors are responsible for ensuring that parent education programs and parent meetings are both timely and responsive to the parents' interests and concerns. A designated parent educator may select some of the topics for parent meetings, but when parents are involved in planning parent meetings, the topics are more likely to be relevant to parents' interests.[5]

Parent meetings are usually considered part of the total parent education program. The frequency of scheduled parent meetings varies widely from program to program. Some programs offer monthly meetings, while others have as few as one or two meetings a year. The first meeting of the year for a preschool on the typical public school calendar is often devoted to the parent groups, introducing the staff, and taking parents through a typical day at school by using slides or classroom visitation. The format for all parent meetings should include time for questions and for informal socialization.

4 A successful score on the General Education Development test leads to a High School Equivalency Certificate.
5 Verna Hildebrand, *Management of Child Development Centers* (3rd edition), Macmillan, 1993, p. 341.

Parent Involvement

Parent conferences and parent education are, indeed, parent involvement, but the parent involvement concept implies a more extensive parental commitment than participation in parent conferences or in selected parts of the parent education program. Although parents should be encouraged to become involved, they should also have the option to remain uninvolved. It is an imposition on the parents' right to choose if they are made to feel that they *must* become involved in the center program. Of course, if the program is a co-op, then by definition it requires full parent participation.

The purpose of a parent involvement program is to get parents active in planning, implementing, and evaluating the total program. In comprehensive child care programs, parents serve on advisory and policy boards, participate in all aspects of program planning and classroom activity, take part in the evaluation of staff and program, and participate in budget and personnel decisions.

Parents sometimes enjoy working regularly in the classroom or helping with children's parties or field trips, and some center programs depend on the help that parents can provide. Before parents participate in any aspect of the children's program they should know something about classroom ground rules, routines, and what to expect of the children. The mother who comes to read to the children may need some help on how to include children other than her own in a small, informal, shared reading experience. The father who takes a morning off to come and read to the children may be disappointed when only three or four children are interested enough to stay for more than one book. He must be helped to understand that children have choices and that they are free to choose not to participate. It is also helpful if he knows the ground rules about deciding who chooses books to be read, and techniques for helping children wait to have their choice read. Parents who work in the classroom on a regular basis should participate in a more extensive orientation program and should be assigned specific tasks when they

A parent who enjoys reading to the children will need some guidelines on how to include children other than her own in a small, informal group. (Photo by Lisa Souders)

come to the center. Both parents and volunteers can attend the same orientation sessions.

There are innumerable ways for parents to be involved in the center program other than direct classroom participation. They can do clerical work, repair or make equipment, take responsibility for the lending library, baby-sit during conference periods or committee meetings, or drive carpools. If they have special talents or interests in fund raising, they can serve as a resource for the center board or the director. If they have special language skills, they can provide priceless service in bilingual programs. There are also many opportunities for parents to serve in a variety of ways on the board, on advisory committees, or on any number of standing or ad hoc committees (see Chapter 4 for the discussion of the composition of the center board and of the committee structure).

Clearly, when the director is committed to a parent involvement program and that attitude prevails throughout the center, it is possible to find a special place for every parent to participate, provided that the parent has the time and interest to become involved. However, it is important for the director to be sensitive to individual family situations. Employed parents who are unable to be involved with center activities must be reassured that they are free to choose not to participate. A successful parent involvement program does require some management; thus, the center staff must feel a commitment to the program to give it the time and attention it requires.

PREPARING A PARENT HANDBOOK

A handbook for parents is a convenient way to communicate basic program information and should be distributed to all families at some point in the enrollment procedure. Since the contents may change from year to year and vary from program to program, directors will have to use some general guidelines for developing a handbook and then adapt those to their specific program. Some items, like program philosophy or grouping children, may or may not be part of the publicity brochure but could be repeated in the handbook. As a director, you will have to decide what information parents need to know and the best way to convey it to them. If a handbook seems too overwhelming for the particular parent population in your program, consider putting an item or two on colorful single sheets to be handed out over a period of several weeks after admission to the program.

The suggested list of items that follows is not exhaustive but provides useful guidelines for developing a parents' handbook (see Sample Parent Handbooks in Director's Resources).

- Names of center staff members and information about when and how to reach them
- Brief statement of the program philosophy
- Outline of the daily program and an explanation of how it fits the program philosophy
- Fees and arrangements for payment, including details about reimbursement possibilities and credit for absences
- Car-pool and/or transportation arrangements (if transportation is not provided, indicate that fact and state what information you need to have about the family's transportation arrangements for the child)
- Expected arrival and pick-up times and procedures
- Center policy on health and safety precautions to be taken by the family and the center staff to ensure the health and safety of children (state your policy about bringing medication to the center, children coming to the center when symptoms of illness are apparent and cover the procedures used by the center staff when a child becomes ill at school, and so on)
- Explanation of liability and medical insurance carried by and/or available through the center
- Sample menus for snacks and/or meals and any expectations the staff may have about eating
- Service the center staff will offer to children and families, such as opportunities for having conferences, special medical or psychological services or referrals, discussion groups, group meetings and so on
- Center discipline policy
- Requests for help from parents, whether it be for time spent in the classroom, help on

field trips, clerical help, making materials for the classroom and so on

- Summary of scheduled events at the center and what families may do at the center to celebrate holidays and birthdays, making the policies in this regard reflect the program philosophy (include what to send, what to expect the child to bring home, which holidays will be celebrated, and so on)
- Expectations about the child's use of transition objects while getting adjusted to the center and policies about bringing other items or food from home, making clear how these policies are developed to meet the needs of children and to reflect the program philosophy
- Description of the legal obligations of center staff to report any evidence of child abuse

This list provides guidelines for developing a handbook that ultimately must be fashioned to fit your program and your parent population. In writing material for a handbook, it is important to consider content, format, length, and, most importantly, style of writing. Should the style be scholarly or chatty, formal or informal, general or detailed? Answers to these questions can best be found by giving careful consideration to the families being served by the program.

The parent handbook is a useful tool to initially acquaint parents with the center program and to help them understand what to expect. However, it must be supplemented with other written and verbal communications to keep them abreast of center events and the progress of their children. Some directors send parents a chatty newsletter describing special events that are being planned for children or families. It is important for parents to know that one family brought their new baby to visit the classroom or that a symphony musician came to show the children a slide trombone. Such information will help parents understand a child's questions and any ideas that are expressed at home.

Other ways to communicate with parents include meetings, regularly scheduled parent conferences, and phone calls to tell parents about happy experiences that their children had at school. Center staff must take advantage of every opportunity to communicate with the family, to share ideas about the child, and to strengthen the basic trust in the relationship.

VOLUNTEER PROGRAM

Volunteers are welcomed in most early childhood education centers, and the volunteer program is usually managed by the center director. Occasionally a member of the center staff other than the director or a volunteer who is willing to undertake the coordinating responsibilities manages the volunteer activities. The coordinating function includes recruiting, orienting, and scheduling the volunteers. Other aspects of the volunteer program, such as planning activities for the volunteers and handling the supervision and the record-keeping responsibilities connected with a volunteer program, must either be delegated or performed by the director.

Volunteer Recruitment

Recruiting volunteers is time-consuming and often frustrating, but there are individuals in every community who are potential volunteers. Finding those people who have both the time and the interest in serving a child care center may present a problem at the outset; however, a program that provides both challenge and appropriate incentives will soon build up a roster of available volunteers who come regularly.

Available sources for recruiting volunteers will vary, depending on the size of the community and the demands of other agencies in the community. Larger cities have organized volunteer bureaus, Junior Leagues, universities with student volunteer programs, and any number of philanthropic groups that can supply volunteers. Church groups, high schools, senior citizen groups, and business groups are other sources that can be found and approached in both large, urban communities or small, rural areas. The volunteers must feel that they are welcome and needed; in addition, they must feel a sense of personal regard for their efforts.

Volunteer Orientation

Participation in the volunteer orientation program should be a requirement for every person who chooses to give time to the center program. Although it may seem presumptuous to insist that volunteers participate in an orientation, it is essential that they become completely familiar with the operation of the center and that they have a clear understanding of how their services fit into the total service offered by the center program. Furthermore, the volunteers usually recognize that a center staff that will take the time to plan and carry through a meaningful and helpful organizational program for them will also value their involvement in the center program.

Orientation meetings should provide volunteers with a staff directory and introduction to as many staff members as possible. The director should talk about the organizational structure of the agency, the goals and objectives of the center program, and the importance of volunteer help in meeting those goals and objectives. Further, licensing standards and health requirements for volunteers must be explained. That will not only clarify what is expected of them regarding immunizations, health examination, and classroom health and safety procedures, but also help them understand the rationale for restrictions on their participation. For example, in most places, a volunteer may not be alone at any time with a group of children because of licensing and insurance requirements. When the rationale for that ruling is understood, volunteers are less likely to be offended when told they may not take the children on a walk or drive them the few blocks to the park.

Confidentiality is an issue for everyone at the center, including the volunteers. It is wonderful to have volunteers who become ambassadors for the program in the community but it is essential that they adhere to a strict policy of absolute confidentiality. Volunteers who share their general enthusiasm about working with the children or doing other work for the center can be a great asset, but talking about specific children, families or teachers can be very damaging to your program.

Other details that should be covered at the orientation meeting include sign-in and sign-out procedures for volunteers and where they should call if they expect to be absent. The record keeping is necessary because many publicly-funded centers must report volunteer hours and some private agencies often choose to keep records and reward volunteers based on their hours of service.

Volunteer Activities

Volunteers can do most things that parents do in a center program, and they often have more free time than working parents or parents with young families. Volunteers, like parents, must be made to feel welcome; and like parents they must leave with a sense of satisfaction and a feeling that their services are needed and appreciated. Since they do not have the reward of seeing the joy their own children experience by having them participate in the program, it is doubly important for the center staff to make them feel welcome, to define their task for them, and to let them know how highly their service is regarded. Volunteers will continue to serve *only* in situations where they feel needed.

ORGANIZATIONS AND AGENCIES

In addition to working with parents and volunteers, the director is responsible for involvement with professional organizations, referral agencies, and the community in which the center is located. In each case the amount of time and degree of involvement varies according to the type of center and the director's individual style.

Professional Organizations

Directors frequently join one or more local, regional, and national professional organizations.

REFLECTIONS

Think about your own volunteer activities. Perhaps you tutor younger students or work in a program for children with disabilities. What motivates you to be there at the scheduled time? Do you look for excuses not to go? If not, why not? How do you feel about yourself after you spend time volunteering? What rewards do you receive?

Sometimes the board encourages and assists them by paying their dues. (A list of professional organizations is presented in Director's Resources.) Through these memberships directors can accomplish several goals.

First, directors can obtain information and make contacts that may be personally and professionally helpful. Therefore, they may select organizations that focus on development of administrative skills, presentation of research data, and provision of information about legislation and funding. Through contacts at group meetings, the director may meet potential staff members, although "pirating" staff from other centers should certainly be avoided. Directors may also see professional organizations as providing a forum for their ideas—a place where they can speak before a group and discuss their concerns with other professionals. They may volunteer to hold meetings at their centers, thus providing opportunities for others in the field to see different early childhood education facilities.

When directors join a professional organization, the organization is enhanced since the directors have had a number of years of education and experience and carry some influence in the community. As a result of their having belonged to these organizations or similar groups for a number of years, they have expertise that can help move the group forward, and they can give guidance to newer, less experienced members.

Directors may join professional organizations to become part of a group that effects change. Legislators who will not listen to an individual's recommendations on teacher–child ratios may be persuaded by an organization's stand, and directors can have input through their membership in the organization.

In some communities, directors form support groups because they need a forum to discuss problems unique to their particular position. They can share information and ideas, and work out cooperative plans for staff training. With the increased, widespread focus on child care, national support groups are forming to provide hotlines, consultation services, and management retreats.[6]

When they join organizations, directors serve as models for staff members. In some cases the staff profits more directly from the organization than the director, but staff members put off joining or may even be hesitant about attending meetings if they do not know other members. Directors can provide an incentive by offering to accompany teachers to the first meeting and by notifying staff members of upcoming meetings. Directors may work out a plan for released time from center duties that staff members can use for participation in the work of professional organizations. They may also provide staff meeting time for members who have attended sessions to share their information.

For similar reasons, directors should attend (and facilitate staff members' attending) lectures, courses, and conferences that are related to early childhood education. Directors also have the responsibility for reading current books and periodicals and for occasionally passing these materials on to staff members. (A list of periodicals appears in Appendix C.) Most staff members will respond positively to an article from the director that is marked to indicate a personal application, such as, "This article addresses an interest of yours, new ways of teaching math concepts." Or, "Have you seen the reviews of these new multiethnic books? Which ones should we order?" This personal touch encourages the staff member to read the article and perhaps discuss it further with the director. When the director has provided a model of this behavior, staff members may begin to circulate articles or books that they have found to be worthwhile.

Referral Agencies

Directors contact referral agencies and advise staff members to use special services when that is appropriate. Directors also help staff members delineate the boundaries of their own professional expertise and recognize those circumstances under which an opinion obtained from another type of professional could be useful.

---

6 An example of a national director's support system is the Director's Network. See *Child Care Information Exchange: The Director's Magazine,* March 1987, or call (206)883-9394.

The job of relating to referral agencies begins with the collection of a list of services that are available in the surrounding community. In some areas a booklet is published that contains the names of all the social service agencies, their addresses, telephone numbers, hours, charges, what services are provided and to whom, and whether or not a referral from a physician or caseworker is required. Some communities add other kinds of information, such as lists of recreation centers, churches, schools, and government agencies and officials. If this type of directory is not available, a center director can develop a referral list. Writing the data on file cards provides a convenient reference that can be updated easily.

After determining which agencies provide services related to the clients' needs, directors should attempt to make personal contact with as many of these agencies as possible. This contact can be accomplished by visiting the agency, by attending programs sponsored by the agency, and by meeting their staff members at professional meetings. Later, when the need for services from such an organization exists, it will be easier for the director to make contacts with the people who are already known. The director is also in a good position to explain the nature of the services provided by these agencies to the center staff and to parents, when that is necessary.

In addition to working with the staff in referring children and families for care and treatment, directors make use of agencies in other ways. For example, agencies usually have personnel and material resources available for in-service training or parent meetings. Some agencies in the community such as Community Coordinated Child Care (4C's) provide consultation and technical assistance. A range of services may be available from other types of agencies, such as the public library, which usually offers storytellers, films, and teachers' collections of books.

If the center's program includes the provision of medical, dental, and mental health services to children, the director may be able to provide these services, at low cost and with convenience in scheduling, through agency contacts. For example, arrangements can be made for a physician to come to the center to do routine physical checkups so that children do not have to endure long trips, boring waiting rooms, and frighteningly strange buildings. The director who is well acquainted with physicians, psychologists, speech therapists, and social workers is able to depend on their services but is sensitive to the needs and limitations under which they operate. It is important that directors establish reciprocal relationships with these professionals by being open to accepting children referred to the center by them and their agencies.

DIRECTOR'S CORNER

"When I first became a director one of the things I had trouble finding out about was the whole referral network, and I realize that takes time and comes with experience. You have to know the agencies, how they work, and the particular people to contact before you can help your teachers or your families with referrals. I always feel better when I can call a specific person whom I have already met."

Director, YMCA-sponsored center

WORK WITH THE COMMUNITY

The director explains the center to the community, and in turn, explains the community to the staff. This function requires familiarity with the community in which the center is located. If some or all of the children who attend the center live in other communities, the director should become informed about those areas as well.

In publicizing the center to the community, the director uses public relations and communications techniques, which were covered in Chapter 10. These include news releases, open houses, and tours of the center. The effective use of the interpersonal skills that were discussed in Chapter 1 is particularly appropriate when working with the community. Certainly the appearance and maintenance of the center's building and grounds also can have an influence on the relationship with the community.

Sometimes, individual members of the community become interested in the center and its work through the director's efforts. For example, the owner of a lumber yard may agree to provide scrap lumber for the children's woodworking projects or a printer will offer to save all the paper ends from print jobs for the children's use. If the director and staff have met the local grocer and other shopkeepers, these business people may be far more responsive to the children when they visit on field trips or when they walk by as they explore the area with classmates.

Directors help their staff members understand the community by encouraging involvement in community activity and by providing information about life in the community. Obtaining a knowledge of the historical background of the area and the cultural or ethnic groups that live there will increase staff awareness of the needs of families who come to the center. The director is responsible for making center staff members sensitive to the customs, language, and values of the people they serve. Frequently, staff members live in other communities and represent different cultural or ethnic groups. It is impossible for staff members to work effectively with children and parents from a culture about which they have no knowledge.

When the director has done a good job of understanding the community and when all the pertinent information is conveyed to the staff, everyone at the center gains an appreciation of the community from which a strong working relationship can emerge. The center's team of staff, parents, and children working together can be expanded to incorporate community members as well.

SUMMARY

The director works with or is accountable for the parent program. A major aspect of this role is helping staff members establish effective parent relationships. The parent program includes parent contacts, parent education, and parent involvement and places emphasis on the participation of the individual parent to the degree that is appropriate and comfortable for him or her. Directors are also involved in recruiting and orienting volunteers and in providing recognition for their services. In addition, they work closely with professional organizations, referral agencies, and members of the community. Part of their role involves setting an example for staff members of an appropriate amount of professional involvement, and training them in the techniques of working with a variety of resources. Directors also provide information to staff members and give them opportunities to make use of the services that professional organizations, referral agencies, and the community at large have to offer.

Class Assignments

1. Using Working Paper 15-1, develop a list of specific tasks a volunteer could do in the classroom areas specified.
2. Find out if you have a directory of social and health service agencies in your community. Use your directory to locate five agencies that an early childhood education director might use for referrals.

   If you do not have a directory, compile a list of five agencies that an early childhood center director might use for referrals. Include each agency's name, address, telephone number, type of services provided, and charges.

Class Exercise

1. Divide into groups of three for the purpose of role playing a parent conference. The situation is one in which a young mother has requested a conference about her three-year-old son who spends a great deal of time in the housekeeping area in the classroom. He also plays with dolls, washes dishes, and dresses up in a skirt and high heels at home. The father is very upset and annoyed by this behavior and has pressured the mother into calling for a conference but is unable to attend the conference. The roles are as follows:

   - male teacher
   - mother
   - female director

   Using the checklist in Working Paper 15-2, discuss each item listed. If you were director or mother in the role play, give your perception of how well the teacher handled the questions asked.

Working Paper 15-1

Volunteer Tasks Form

List specific tasks a volunteer could be assigned to do in each of the classroom areas or activities listed below. Think beyond supervising children—consider care and development of materials, enriching the area or making it more aesthetically pleasing, etc.

Dramatic play (expand beyond house-type play)

Carpentry

Literature/library area

Writing center

Lunchtime

Naptime

Working Paper 15-2

Role-Play Checklist

After the role-play in Class Exercise 1 is completed, discuss the items in this checklist. If your role was that of director or parent, respond to the questions in terms of your perception of how well the teacher handled the conference. You are expected to give more than yes or no answers. Document your answers with examples from the conference.

Did you give the parent time to talk about her concerns?

Were you a receptive listener?

When you made comments, did you talk in terms of the parents' feelings?

Were you able to restrain yourself from giving advice?

Did the parent do most of the talking?

What was accomplished during the conference?

Director's Resource 15-1

Sample Parent Handbook (Infant/Toddler)

Welcome to our Center! Parents are an integral part of a successful child-care program. Through parental involvement we are better able to meet the developmental and personal needs of children. As child-care professionals, we can serve as a valuable resource for parents and their children concerning most areas of child development. Therefore, we like to think that families and child-care centers can and should work together to provide an environment that facilitates the growth of a child into a physically and emotionally healthy individual.

This handbook has been developed to help facilitate the relationship between caregivers and parents by providing them with specific information about our Center, it includes descriptions of our policies and procedures, program's philosophy, role of the caregivers, goals for the children, and our expectations from parents. In addition, we have included a schedule of our program day and a listing of our curricular activities.

It is hoped that this booklet will reinforce the purposes that influence the activities and procedures that you, as parents, may observe at our Center. We hope you will find this booklet beneficial and informative and helpful in making you more familiar with the program and thereby more comfortable in our Center. We feel this is essential if we wish to work closely with parents in providing their children with the benefit of high quality child care.

I Background Information
The following is background information on our Center:

1. The Center is licensed by the State of Ohio Department of Human Services and the City of Cincinnati Department of Health. The number of children that we are authorized to serve is stated in the license and is posted in the entrance.
2. The laws and rules governing child day-care are available at the Center.
3. Cincinnati Learning Center accepts children from 3 months to 5 years of age.
4. The Center is open from 7:00 A.M. to 6:00 P.M., Monday through Friday.
5. We believe strongly that the ratio of children to adults directly affects the quality of the early learning experience. Due to this belief, we follow the standard listed below:

    Infant: 3 children to 1 adult
                   (Maximum size 9 infants)
    Toddler: 5 children to 1 adult
                   (Maximum size 10 toddlers)
    Preschool: 9 children to 1 adult
                   (Group size 18 maximum).

6. We at CLC do not discriminate against any race, creed, religion, and/or sex. This applies to hiring of our staff and applications of our students.

Cincinnati Learning Center promises to follow the rules and laws that have been written by the State of Ohio Department of Human Services. We feel that these laws have been written to insure that children are cared for in a safe environment. These laws ask very little of the day-care facility and we hope to go far beyond these standards to supply you and your child with quality day care.

Toll free complaint #_____ for parents to use if there are any complaints.

(Reprinted by permission of the Cincinnati Learning Center.)

Director's Resource 15-1 (*continued*)

II Philosophy of the Program

The philosophy of a child care center largely influences the types of activities, the curriculum and the kind of care that will be present in the center. Therefore, it is imperative that parents become familiar with the philosophy behind the center in order to understand the focus of the program.

Staff members at the Cincinnati Learning Center feel that the program should focus on the development of the whole child. In order to do this, we look at the cognitive, physical, emotional and social needs of each child. Our philosophy is largely based on the work of Erikson and Piaget; therefore, we feel that children develop sequentially from one stage of development to another. Because of this, we feel that children must be provided with opportunities that will challenge them and aid in their progression from one stage to the next. We also believe that children construct knowledge through experience; therefore, our program will provide children with a large variety of activities that will allow for success and encourage advancement in all areas of development. In addition, we feel that, in order for children to grow, they need to exist in a setting that meets their basic needs. Therefore, it is our utmost concern that our program provides a nurturing, comfortable environment that is specifically structured to meet the physical, emotional and developmental needs of each individual child. In order to do this, it is imperative that we individualize our program to meet each child's specific growth needs. Last, we feel it is most important that we work closely with the families in order to secure an environment that is most beneficial to the child.

III Discipline Policy

The goal at our center is to help children to develop a positive self image. We hope to encourage children to be self-directed and to exhibit self-control. In order to do this children need the opportunity to build self-esteem. Therefore, such practices that will humiliate or shame a child will not be used. Young children, due to their developmental age, are not capable of understanding the ramifications of many of their behaviors, therefore they need to be encouraged to make good choices and to be prevented from harming themselves and/or others. This can best be accomplished through close supervision, gentle guidance, and most importantly, redirection. Children need to learn to identify and express their feelings. However, often this requires the caregiver to verbalize these feelings for them. For example, if we see a child about to hit another child for taking a toy away, we will prevent that child from hitting the other saying, "That really made you angry when Billy took your toy, you wanted to hit him. Instead, tell him 'it's mine, I'm playing with it.'" This way, we hope to prevent one child from hurting another and at the same time help that child to learn to identify his feelings and verbalize his desires.

Another important disciplinary approach is to remember that small children are very egocentric and therefore are not yet capable of understanding the concept of sharing and taking turns. Therefore, it is our responsibility to lend guidance through redirection to other activities when conflict situations occur.

Caring for young children requires a lot of patience as they often need to be reminded about safety rules over and over again. Each ground rule will be stated clearly and precisely and then he will be helped to follow the rule by showing him other acceptable, safe activities. Last, we will try to always state directions in a positive manner as young children have a hard time comprehending the word "don't."

Through these disciplinary procedures it is hoped that we can help to encourage independence and self-control while promoting the development of a child's positive self-image.

IV Goals for Infants and Toddlers

Based on our philosophy, we believe that children develop naturally. However, in order for them to grow to their fullest potential, we feel that adults can aid children through providing an environment that will enhance, encourage and nurture their development. This can be accomplished in a large variety of ways by identifying a child's needs and matching these needs to materials and experiences that will stimulate his/her growth. With this in mind we have developed the following goals for the toddlers in our center.

Director's Resource 15-1 (*continued*)

1. Children will be cared for in a safe and nurturing environment.
2. The center will provide children with an enriched environment that will meet the physical and emotional needs of each individual child. Additionally, it will provide an appropriately stimulating environment that will further enhance his social, emotional, cognitive and physical development.
3. Children will be exposed to a wide variety of activities that will facilitate the construction of knowledge. Open-ended materials will be provided, whenever possible, to encourage continued growth in all areas of development.
4. Children will be encouraged to act independently in their explorations of materials and performance of activities, but gentle guidance will be provided to keep children safe and to facilitate essential successes in their new adventures.
5. Tasks and activities that are developmentally and age appropriate will be provided. This will be based on an assessment of each individual child's specific needs.
6. Children will be exposed to a language-rich environment that will facilitate their language development.
7. Children will be presented with challenging situations that encourage problem solving but minimize frustration.

V Role of the Caregiver in an Infant and Toddler Program

High quality caregivers are essential to a program that wishes to maintain high standards of care and education. Caregivers must be professionals who are willing to assume responsibility for establishing an educational program that meets the developmental and personal needs of a child. For these reasons, we have established some guidelines that we feel are imperative to the role of a caregiver.

1. Caregivers will provide a safe environment where toddlers can freely explore their surroundings without fear of harm.
2. Caregivers will assess each individual child's developmental needs. Based on this assessment, the caregiver will provide a personalized, individual program with activities and experiences that help to facilitate the child's continued growth.
3. Caregivers will be knowledgeable about infant and toddler development and use this knowledge to facilitate the toddler's learning.
4. Caregivers will provide a stable environment that maintains necessary routines but allows for flexibility in routines to most appropriately meet the growth needs of each child.
5. Caregivers will be a facilitator of communication between parents and the center. Caregivers will work with parents to provide an environment that is most beneficial to the child.
6. Caregivers will involve parents in planning a program for their child. The caregivers will arrange for parent conferences at least twice a year, more often if necessary to meet the child's needs.
7. Caregivers will be child advocates. They will look out for the child's best interest in the center, the family and the community. The will bring their concerns to the attention of the appropriate people.
8. Caregivers will maintain confidentiality about each child and his family.
9. Caregivers will act as a resource person for families and their children. They will bring information about child development and about other resources available in the community.
10. Caregivers will organize the setting to encourage open movement and involvement in activities.
11. Caregivers will keep accurate daily records on all the children. These records will include such things as the child's sleeping, eating and elimination habits during the day. In addition, records shall be kept regarding the child's social, emotional, physical and cognitive development. These records shall be used to keep the parents informed about their child's daily activities and chart observations about problems and progresses that the child may be encountering.
12. Caregivers will be responsible for attending in services and other conferences to keep them well informed about current topics in early child development.
13. Caregivers must always remember that a child-care program should be a supplemental service that can enrich a child and his family's lives. In order to do this, however, it is necessary to work closely with the child's parents to provide a program that is most beneficial to the child.

Director's Resource 15-1 (*continued*)

14. Caregivers must try to understand a parent's perspective on an issue and to provide support to parents during these often emotionally charged times.
15. Most important, caregivers must immediately see to the child's physical and emotional needs for food, clothing, cleanliness, safety, security, and nurturance. Above all, we want parents to feel that they have selected a center that they can trust.

VI Parental Participation Plan

Parents are always welcome to join in our program at the Center. We invite parents to participate in Board Meetings, parent groups, and fund-raisers. All parents are encouraged to share personal interests, including hobbies, talents, cultural backgrounds, favorite recipes, etc. Parents can volunteer in the classroom or repair equipment. If the center and parents are mutually able to work together to provide a setting that best meets the child's growth needs, then the child will most surely benefit. For this reason, we have included this section so that parents can fully understand our expectations from them.

1. *Parent Conferences.* Parents must be available for conference at least twice a year where caregivers and parents can mutually decide on program goals for their child. These conferences will be an information sharing session that allows each to express his/her feelings and concerns about progress or problems that the child might be experiencing. The parents and the caregiver, together, will then decide on goals for the child.

2. *Home/School.* We need for parents to realize that their home and our program should be continuous with each other. This means that parents must openly communicate with staff pertinent information about the child on a daily basis. This should include such things as illnesses, change in sleeping, eating or elimination habits, teething, and so forth.

3. *Center as a Resource.* Parents should use the Center as a resource. Staff members are trained professionals in the area of child development and can provide families with invaluable information about children.

4. *Parents are Welcome.* Parents are welcome to come to the Center at any time during program hours. Parental involvement is valued and therefore encouraged. Parents should feel free to come and spend lunch or other time with their child. We also want parents to feel welcome to bring special interest activities to the Center but please consult the director prior to doing so.

5. *Donations.* Donations to the Center are tax deductible. As your child develops mentally and physically, please consider whether books, toys, or outgrown clothes may be appropriate for use in our Center. A community resource directory is available upon request.

6. *Procedures for Resolving Parent Complaints or Problems:* (a) Complaints or problems must be resolved directly with the person(s) involved; (b)If the issue is not resolved, complaint or problem must be explained to that person's supervisor; (c) If the issue is not resolved, continue to follow the organizational chart until a solution is reached; (d) If the Complaints or Problems Procedure is not followed, person(s) submitting complaints or problems will be redirected to follow procedure; (e) Complaints or problems from the community-at-large will be channeled to appropriate staff person.

VII Agreement Between Parents and the Center

1. Parents will provide disposable diapers.
2. Parents of infants (not on table food) will provide formula and baby food.
3. Each child must be picked up *promptly* at the end of his/her program. A charge of $5.00 per each fifteen minutes will be made for the time the child remains in the Learning Center after the end of the session.
4. Each child will be accepted into a specific program (ex., Toddler class Monday, Wednesday, and Friday). Any change in the assigned program must be approved by the parents and by the director.
5. The Center will be closed nine days out of the year for holidays. They are: New Year's, Good Friday, Memorial Day, 4th of July, Labor Day, Thanksgiving, Friday after Thanksgiving, Christmas Eve, and Christmas. If any of these holidays occur during the work week, a full week's tuition must be paid to the Learning Center.

Director's Resource 15-1 (*continued*)

6. Each child must have a change of clothing that is left in the Center to be used for emergencies. All clothes must be marked. The Center cannot be responsible for unmarked clothing. Children should wear washable clothing in which they will be comfortable.
7. Parents are asked to see that children do not bring food to the Center. Adequate snacks are provided morning and afternoon, plus a hot lunch at noon. (Special arrangements for birthdays can be made.)
8. Food exceptions cannot be made for individual children, except in the case of allergies. Written statement from physician is required.
9. Weekly menus are posted in advance in the Center and parents may refer to these at any time.
10. Parents are asked to see that children do not bring toys to the Center.
11. Parents are expected to bring their child into the building and see that he is under supervision of his teacher before leaving the premises.
12. Children who become ill cannot remain at the Center. The parents will be called to pick up the child. Children absent from the Center with a contagious disease will not be re-admitted without a signed statement from a physician indicating that the child is no long contagious.
13. Routine visits to a doctor, clinic, or dentist are the responsibility of the parent.
14. Each preschool child in the Center will have the advantage of an afternoon nap.
15. Children will be permitted to play outside in the play yard daily, except in inclement weather. If you do not want your child to participate in outdoor activities, please bring a signed note from physician stating this to the director.
16. Parents must cooperate with the Center in carrying out all governmental laws, rules, and regulations affecting the operation of the Center.
17. This agreement may be changed at any time by the Learning Center to comply with governmental regulations or for any other reason.
18. The Center fund-raises in order to maintain fees. We will need your help.
19. The State of Ohio requires that all members of day-care institutions be on the lookout for, and report to the State, any and all cases of abuse to a child. The Center is, therefore, obligated to report to the State any suspected cases of child abuse and/or neglect.
20. Rosters of names and telephone numbers of parents, custodians, or guardians of children attending the Center are available upon request. This roster does not include the name and telephone numbers of parents, custodians, or guardians who request this information be excluded.
21. The Center's licensing record is available upon request from the department, including, but not limited to, evaluation forms from the health, building, and fire departments that inspected our Center.
22. An emergency transportation authorization form will be filled out upon enrollment for transportation of the child to the necessary medical or dental emergency care source. In the event emergency transportation consent is not granted, a non-consent form will be provided and must be filled out by parent or guardian. The Center is free from responsibility for children not granted emergency transportation authorization.
23. Parents and guardians are permitted access to all parts of the Center at the time of the pre-admission interview.
24. The Center will work to serve special needs children. A decision will be made by the director as to whether our Center can adequately provide for the needs of a handicapped child. A specific written policy will be designed for each special needs child by teacher and parent before enrollment.
25. RLC/CLC has liability insurance covering all persons on our property during business hours.
26. Orientation of new children: If a family's schedule permits, we ask that arrangements be made to allow children a gradual adjustment, i.e., Monday, Wednesday, Friday from 9:00 - noon. In order to foster a positive adjustment, we also believe it is beneficial for parents to spend a period of time with their child at our Center upon enrollment.
27. The Administrator and each employee of the child day-care center are required to report their suspicions of child abuse or child neglect.
28. If the child is to be picked up by someone other than the two names listed on the release form, the following steps will be followed: (a) the parent must tell the teacher in the morning at the time of drop-off who will be coming, or they must call to notify teacher in advance of pickup;

Director's Resource 15-1 (*continued*)

(b) if the teacher is called, identification will be requested of the adult picking up the child; (c) the child will not be released from the Center unless the above steps are taken.

29. I agree to have my name and telephone number included on my child's class roster which will be made available upon request to any parent whose child is enrolled in my child's class.

30. In order for the child's educational experience to broaden and enrich his life, we at the Center will attempt to enroll children from various diverse backgrounds. To provide a balanced population, we will base acceptance of applications on children who are representative of various racial, cultural and social-economic groups as well as those who are at different developmental stages in their lives.

31. The Center's philosophy concerning special occasions and holidays is that of simplicity. Parents are asked to consult the head teacher concerning wearing costumes or bringing Valentines. A child's birthday celebration should also be consulted about with the teacher first.

32. Events in the child's home and environment may markedly affect his behavior. Because of the child's ability to report accurately these events, we would appreciate communications between parents and staff concerning any unusual happenings or events, i.e., illness, death, changes in living situations, extra stimulations, etc.

33. Termination of a special needs child will be made only with staff recommendation, appropriate documentation and outside consultation, which would result in action to be in the best interest of the child. Particular care will be made to work closely with the child and family in any consideration of termination.

34. Upon entry to the Center, a child must be examined by his doctor and thereafter annually. Medical forms may be picked up in the office to be used by the child's physician.

35. A written emergency medical authorization must be on file at the Center for each child. This form is also provided from the office.

36. The Center's staff consults with specialized agencies as needed for your child. Speech and hearing exams are done regularly through Preschool Prevention Program (PPP) and any outside consultations involving your child will be discussed with you ahead of time.

37. Parents having any concerns about their child are encouraged to discuss these with the child's teacher. Any outside agency consultations will gladly be arranged.

38. The Center does not discriminate against any race, creed, religion, and/or sex. This applies to hiring of our staff and application of our students. In addition, the Center's staff has adopted the Ohio Association for the Education of Young Children (OAEYC) Code of Ethics. A copy of this code is attached.

39. Fund-raisers will be done periodically; we **must** have support from parents. This helps keep tuition down.

VIII—Policy on Communicable Disease Management

We feel that it is our duty to inform parents of the following precautions we take to help prevent the spread of communicable disease. Your cooperation in carrying these policies through is particularly appreciated.

1. A staff member trained in a Red Cross First Aid course to recognize the common signs of communicable disease observes each child daily before he or she enters a group. All staff are trained in hand washing and disinfection procedures through orientation and posted bathroom signs. The following are the signs the staff member will recognize as signals of a possible illness.
   - A fever of 100 degrees F. taken by the axillary method when in combination with any other sign of illness
   - Skin rash other than a localized diaper rash.
   - Diarrhea and/or vomiting two or more times in the same day.
   - Evidence of lice infestation.
   - Severe coughing, causing the child to become red or blue in the face or to make a whooping sound.
   - Difficult or rapid breathing.
   - Yellowish skin or eyes.
   - Conjunctivitis.
   - Unusually dark urine and/or grey or white stool.

Director's Resource 15-1 (*continued*)

- • Stiff neck.
- • Untreated infected skin patches.
2. A chart listing communicable diseases is posted in both the office and in the lobby.
3. We will not administer any medication or vitamins without both the physician and parental permission in writing (see medication sheets).
4. Any child who is suspected of having a communicable disease is isolated immediately in a room or a portion of a room not being used for child care but within sight and hearing of an adult. The child is given a cot/blanket for use. (When the child is discharged, these are sanitized.) The parents or emergency contacts are telephoned to pick the child up from the Center. If no signs of disease are present for 24 hours, the child will be re-admitted to the Center.
5. Any child who is suspected of being mildly ill (a child experiencing minor cold symptoms or does not feel well enough to participate in activities but does <u>not</u> exhibit any of the symptoms specified in #1) will be cared for within the child's group. The child will be observed carefully for signs and symptoms of worsening condition.
6. When a staff member exhibits any sign of a communicable disease, he/she leaves the Center and/or a substitute is called to replace the ill staff member.
7. Parents will be notified by staff if a child is exposed to a communicable disease on sign-in and -out sheets. It will also be posted on the Parent Bulletin Board as the Center is notified by parents or physicians of current exposure.

IX Safety of Children

A top priority of our center is to provide a safe place to leave your child. In order to assure that our center is a safe place, we have adopted the following policies:

1. A child-care staff member in charge of a child or a group of children is responsible for their safety.
2. When a parent or guardian brings a child to the Center, they must tell the staff member that the child is present at the Center.
3. No child is ever left alone or unsupervised.
4. In an emergency situation there are three working telephones. At Cincinnati Learning Center there is one in the director's office, the kitchen and in the first floor toddler classroom.
5. We have a monthly fire drill at varying times each month. A record of the fire drills is located in the director's office.
6. We have medical and fire emergency plans posted in each classroom.
7. When a field trip is taken, a person trained in first aid along with a first aid box is taken. The child also has identification attached to himself containing the child's name and the Center's name, address and telephone number.
8. A fire emergency and weather alert plan is posted in each classroom. The plans include diagrams showing evacuation routes.
9. In the event that a group of children would participate in swimming or other water activities in water two or more feet in depth, written permission must be granted by each parent or guardian. The group must be supervised by persons who are currently certified as lifeguards or water safety instructors by the American Red Cross or an equivalent water safety program.
10. The use of spray aerosols is prohibited when children are in attendance at our center.
11. An emergency transportation authorization form for each child and health records of children with allergies, handicapping conditions, or health conditions requiring special procedures or precautions will be available on field trips or special outings. Center classroom ratios will be upheld on field trips.
12. Any vehicle that is owned, leased, or hired by our center for the purpose of transporting children will be licensed and operated in accordance with the laws, including the Motor Vehicle Lighting Requirements and the Child Restraint Systems Requirements.
13. When a child is involved in an accident, injury occurs, syrup of ipecac administered, or emergency transportation is necessary, our center will fill out an incident report form. The report will be given to the parent or guardian on the day of the incident. Copies of the reports will be retained on file at our center for one year.
14. A child-care staff member shall immediately notify the local public children services agency (241–KIDS) when the child-care staff member suspects that a child has been abused or neglected.

Director's Resource 15-1 (*continued*)

X Policies and Procedures for Termination of Services to Clients
   The rights and responsibilities of the consumer was examined very closely when these termination policies and procedures were being developed.
   Your child may be terminated from the program based on abuse and neglect of the parent rules and guidelines. If you are found to be in violation of the rules and guidelines, the following procedures will be taken:
   1. Notice to bring the situation to your attention.
   2. Written warning of suspension.
   3. Suspension—three (3) days of child or children.
   4. Termination from the program if the situation continues. Written notice stating reason for termination.

   Major Reasons for Termination
   1. Attendance (infrequent).
   2. Fees (unpaid).
   3. Medical (not up-to-date as required).
   4. Behavioral (disruptive or abnormal).
   Each child is expected to attend daily and punctually. If absenteeism extends beyond five (5) days per month without a logical explanation, the above procedure applies.
   The Center door will open at 7:00 a.m. and close at 6:00 p.m. Each child is expected to arrive before 9:00 a.m. and depart no later than 6:00 p.m. For every quarter (1/4) hour beyond 6:00 p.m. there will be a $5.00 late fee. Payment should be paid to the staff person caring for the child.
   The following procedures apply:
   1. Written notice given at the time of enrollment.
   2. Written notice given at time of pick-up.
   3. Failure to pay in three (3) days result in suspension.
   The parent or guardian will be advised in writing of the effective date of termination.

XI Emergency Plan

		Hospitals	
Fire/Life Squad:	241-2525	Christ:	639-2235
Poison Control:	872-5111	Childrens:	559-4293
Police:	765-1212	Bethesda:	569-6464
Cinti. Health Dept.:	352-3100	University:	875-4571
Children's Protective Service:	721-7044	Good Sam.:	872-2536
		Jewish:	569-2111
		Deaconess:	559-2236

   1. The first aid kit is located in the director's office in the file cabinet.
   2. A list of the students with home and emergency numbers is in the index box on the director's desk. Each child's emergency medical release is in their file in the file cabinet. This must go with them if they are taken to the doctor or hospital.
   3. If there is a serious emergency, phone the life squad and parents immediately.
   4. If a child is involved in an accident, fill out an accident report form (in top drawer of the file cabinet). If a child becomes ill, fill out report on illness (located in top drawer of file cabinet).
   5. If a child exhibits any of the symptoms described in the Center's communicable disease policy, the child is isolated in the director's office. An adult must always be with the ill child.
   6. Fire extinguishers are located in each room for adult use.
   7. Doors are marked clearly for fire exit. Fire drills are held monthly involving children.
   8. Child restraint systems (car seats) are located in the tea room of basement.
   9. Staff will follow instructions for dental emergencies stated on the Dental First Aid chart located in classroom, bathroom and office.
   10. The staff trained in first aid is also listed next to the phone.

Director's Resource 15-1 (*continued*)

11. In case of a tornado or severe storm weather, take the children down front hall steps to tea room in basement. Look for tornado sign location against wall. Have the children lie flat against the floor. One teacher will be in charge of keeping in contact with weather station (phone in hallway of church).
12. Staff trained in first aid:

_____   _____

_____   _____

_____   _____

XII The Toddler Program
Daily Schedule

7:00– 9:00	Free play
9:00– 9:30	Breakfast
9:30–11:15	Free play/Activity Room/Outside
11:15–11:30	Transition to lunch
11:30–12:00	Lunch
12:00–12:30	Transition to Nap
12:30– 2:30	Nap (Activity Room when they wake up)
2:30– 3:00	Free play
3:00– 3:20	Snack
3:20– 6:00	Free play/Activity Room/Outside

The curriculum of a toddler program is based on providing the child with a large variety of activities and experiences to enable him to grow and to learn. According to Piaget's theory of cognitive development, children construct knowledge from their actions on the environment. Children also learn some things such as names through social transmission. For this reason, our toddler curriculum focuses on providing children with an environment that encourages their explorations and involvement in activities that help them to construct knowledge. In addition, toddlers will be exposed to a language-rich environment that will help to facilitate their developing language skills and encourages social interactions. The following is a listing of specific curriculum areas and how they relate to the developing toddler's growth needs.

Free Play

Free play is a period of time when a child is free to choose from a wide variety of games, toys, puzzles or gross motor activities. Toddlers are just gaining a newfound sense of independence through mobility and this freedom of choice allows them to further exercise this skill. Games, toys and puzzles are specifically selected to meet the child's development needs. Some of the free play activities include:

1. *Manipulatives.* This area includes puzzles, small building blocks, small vehicles, pegboard games, stringing beads, and so forth. These activities encourage the child's development of problem solving techniques and fine motor skills along with knowledge about how objects relate to each other.

2. *Water Table/Dry Pour Table.* Allows children to experience a large variety of textures such as water, sand, dirt, rice, oatmeal, beans, and so forth. Objects such as cylinders, measuring cups, bowls, and funnels are placed on the tables to enable children to experiment with pouring, dumping and scooping. This encourages fine motor skill development along with increasing their knowledge about various textures and materials and the characteristics of these objects.

3. *Dramatic Play Area.* For toddlers, the area is set up like a house with a kitchen and bedroom. It has familiar household items that children can use to imitate activities they see around the house. This encourages children to practice familiar activities such as cooking, sweeping, and talking on the telephone. This is important for their social, emotional and physical development. Because children at this age still participate in parallel play, most social interactions are between the adult and the child. Adults can use this time effectively to facilitate language about what the child is doing. This helps the child to put words to his actions and therefore encourage his language and social development.

4. *Book Area.* This area is established in a quiet corner of the room. It is set up with comfortable pillows and toddler sized chairs. Books are available for children to look at and to manipulate. They are made of sturdy cardboard that enable the child to learn to turn pages. Many contain simple story lines that adults can read to children. Books are a great language facilitator and a wonderful way to introduce children to the joy that can be found through reading.

5. *Play Doh, Silly Putty, Clay Table.* These materials are available for children to roll, squeeze, pat, pound and mold. Play Doh encourages fine motor strength and manipulation and also encourages the development of knowledge about another type of texture and material. This is another area where language should be used to describe actions, textures and characteristics.

6. *Gross Motor Area/Large Muscle Area.* Since toddlers are still practicing many newfound physical skills, large muscle areas are an essential part of their program. This area provides children with opportunities to climb, jump, crawl, run, walk, hop, and slide, all of which aid in mastery over gross motor skills.

7. *Crayons Corner.* Crayons are always available to encourage children to develop fine motor skills necessary for the eventual development of writing skills. In addition, it provides an open-ended activity that fosters expressions of creativity.

8. *Music Corner.* Musical instruments, records, and tape players are available for manipulation and for entertainment of children. Music helps children to begin to develop a sense of rhythm through dancing, swaying and clapping. However, music can also become a part of every activity, and adults are encouraged to sing to children many times during the day.

9. *Mirrors and Photographs.* Mirrors are a wonderful object the children can use to learn about themselves. This helps to encourage self-identity and increase self-esteem. Pictures of each child are hung low on classroom walls and further help children to identify self and others.

Special Activities

These include art and cooking experiences in which the child can actively participate. Art activities include painting, using various materials and on various textures, gluing a variety of items on paper, Styrofoam, etc., and drawing with pens, crayons, markers, and colored pencils on various materials. Cooking exercises include simple recipes that enable children to observe cause and effect relationships and to see how things are made. These special activities provide children with an additional learning experience through manipulation of materials. It further can be used, again, as an excellent language facilitator in talking to the children about what they are doing and the effects of their actions on the materials they are using.

Outdoor Play

Outdoor play allows the children more opportunities for freedom of choice. Children can choose from among a wide variety of activities such as climbers, sandbox, bikes, balls, etc. In addition, warm weather provides the opportunity to bring many other activities, such as art or the water table, outdoors. Outdoor activities enable children to further develop their gross motor skills and gives them the benefit of a change of scenery periodically throughout the day.

Naptime

Naptime is an essential part of a toddler's day. This gives them the opportunity to rest after a busy morning and refreshes them for the afternoon's activities. Many times toddlers don't know when they need to rest, therefore it is imperative to schedule a quiet time during the busy day to allow them the advantage of a few hours of sleep. Toddlers who are unable to sleep will be given quiet toys to play with while lying on their cots and a soothing, comforting staff person to rub their backs and encourage them to sleep.

Mealtimes

Mealtimes are a great time for toddlers to practice their independence in self help skills. Toddlers love to feed themselves and therefore are provided with bite size portions that can be easily manipulated with fingers or a spoon. Toddlers will be encouraged to use a spoon but using fingers is also acceptable. Mealtimes provide opportunities for social interactions between adults and child and therefore should be rich with language about morning events and types of food being eaten.

Arrival and Departure Times

This is the time for exchanges of information between the caregiver and the parent concerning the child's experiences at home and daily activities at the Center. It also provides the child with a rich learning experience regarding social interactions through greetings and farewells.

XIII   The Infant Program
Daily Schedule

Our program believes that each infant has his or her own schedule. The day will include napping, eating, quiet play, activity room and outside time.

The concept of the pod system was developed by Dr. Dorothy J. Sciarra of the early-childhood program, University of Cincinnati.

The infant room is divided into three small rooms or pods. In each pod three children will be cared for by one child-care provider. A trusted caregiver provides for changing, feeding, cuddling and nurturing. An early childhood professional will plan an educationally sound group experience in the attached activity room. By combining a family-type experience and a group experience the child will have the best of both worlds.

The curriculum of an infant program includes providing the infant with a wide variety of activities and experiences that will enable them to develop new skills and learn more about their world. In order to do this, you may observe the following activities at the Center.

1. *Rattle Corner.* Babies love rattles. They use long, round, shining, hard, squeezable, noisy or musical rattles for looking, listening, grasping, chewing, banging, shaking, and so on. This helps the infant to gain physical mastery with manipulative materials and also provides them with additional sensory stimulation and perceptual experiences.

2. *Reaching Center.* This area of the room might contain mobiles, objects suspended on yarn, and playthings attached to the wall. Through successful reaching, the infant can then bring some other aspects of the environment under control, expand his/her exploration of playthings, and spend small periods of time involved independently in play activities.

3. *Manipulative/Sensory Corner.* Babies are continually trying to figure out the working of toys and objects as they play with them and change them in some way. In addition, toys that are rich in a variety of textures, shapes, sizes, sounds, weights and colors can be an exciting experience for infants. For this reason, our center will provide a large variety of manipulative toys to help your child gain further knowledge through new experiences.

This parent handbook has provided a large amount of information regarding our Center. We hope that you, as parents, find it useful in helping you to feel more secure about your selection of our center and more comfortable and confident that you are a valuable and important part of our program.

Director's Resource 15-1 (*continued*)

The following references have been used to help us develop this handbook:

Cataldo, C.Z. *Infant and Toddler Programs: A Guide to Very Early Childhood Education.* Addison Wesley Publishing Company, 1983.

Honig, A.S. *Parent Involvement in Early Childhood Education.* National Association for the Education of Young Children, 1975.

Leavitt, R.L., and Ehert, B.K. *Toddler Day Care: A Guide to Responsive Caregiving.* D.C. Heath and Company, 1985.

Willemsen, Eleanor. *Understanding Infancy.* W.H. Freeman and Company, 1979.

Wilson, L.C. *Infants and Toddlers: Curriculum and Teaching.* Delmar Publishers, Inc., 1986.

Director's Resource 15-2

Sample Parent Handbook (Preschool)

The following is background information on our center:

1.   Our center is licensed by the State of Ohio Department of Human Services. The number of children that we are authorized to serve is stated in the license and is posted in the entrance to center.

2.   The laws and rules governing child care are available at the center.

3.   The center accepts children from 3 mths-5 years of age.

4.   The center is open from 7:00a.m. to 6:00 p.m. Monday through Friday.

5.   We believe strongly that the ratio of children to adults directly affects the quality of the early learning experience. Due to this belief, we follow the standards listed below.

Infant:	3 children to 1 adult	(group size 9)
Toddler:	5 children to 1 adult	(group size 10)
Preschool:	9 children to 1 adult	(group size 18)

6.   We do not discriminate against any race, creed, religion, sex, or national origin. This applies to hiring of staff and applications of our students.

The Center promises to follow the rules and laws that have been written by the State of Ohio Department of Human Services. We feel that those laws have been written to ensure that children are cared for in a safe environment. These laws ask very little of the child care facility and we hope to go far beyond these standards to supply you and your child with quality child care.

Toll free complaint # 1-800-282-1190 for parents to use for any complaints against the Center.

Reprinted by permission of Roark Learning Centers

Director's Resource 15-2 (*continued*)

PHILOSOPHY

We believe that a preschool day should reflect an interest in the whole child. Each child has physical, social, emotional, and cognitive needs that must be enhanced.

A good program includes stability and regularity, but must also be flexible. A familiar pattern enables the child to take part in routines more easily, and it allows for a sense of security. It is also necessary for the teacher to be in tune with the children's needs and desires, and to be willing to change when the child's needs change.

It is a necessity at this developmental level that learning be based on actual experience and participation. Talking without doing is largely meaningless at this young age.

At the Center, we attempt to fulfill these goals and meet the expectations of our children and parents. We are constantly striving to learn more and through this process, cannot only satisfy your child's needs, but also enrich his or her life.

Our beliefs concerning the education and growth of children exist due to many separate learning theories. Jean Piaget, Eric Erickson, and Tom Gordon are just a few of the people who formulated some of our basic concepts. Each specializes in a separate area, but when combined, set the stage for learning. In the broad sense, our approach can be labeled constructivist developmental. It emphasizes the identifiable patterns of growth, the child's interaction with the environment (both people and materials), and the interaction between the cognitive and effective spheres of development. One of the preschool's basic functions is to facilitate the transition from one stage to another. By consolidating knowledge of objects, time, and space, the child builds a foundation upon which he or she can build other concepts. The child gains the problem solving skills to take him or her through the later years in school. Our beliefs are also based upon a "consistent philosophy of education, comprising values, goals, and strategies congruent with a humanistic approach". Central to this philosophy are concepts of competence, individuality, and creativity.

Director's Resource 15-2 (*continued*)

CURRICULUM

Our activities and room structure reflect our philosophy. Just as the social, emotional and cognitive development of a child overlaps and intertwines, so do the activities and arrangement of the room. Lesson plans and areas of the room are arranged in a distinct pattern, but all parts carry over into the other parts. Both are created so the child may interact with the environment. Activities are constructed of concrete materials rather than presented in an abstract manner such as dittos and pictures. The room encourages independence and creativity. The children move freely throughout the room and may use the materials to meet their needs. Respect for each other and the environment is always stressed. We have stated that we believe in the whole child. From this perspective, it is apparent that by understanding the separate parts of the child we can better understand how these separate parts comprise the mechanics of the growing child.

Director's Resource 15-2 (*continued*)

DISCIPLINE POLICY

Our goal is to build a positive self concept. Future success in school and life depends on being able to handle various social situations and interactions. We believe that our attitude will be a great influence on the children. Mutual respect will always be respected.

Each head teacher will be responsible for handling problem situations within his or her classroom. If the problem persists, the administrator will be notified. The following steps are to be followed when trying to help a child handle a difficult situation:

* The children will be encouraged to settle disputes by expressing emotions (i.e. "I'm angry").

* A child will be reminded of the rules in the center in a positive manner ("You can walk inside and run outside").

* The child will have the situations explained ("After you pick up the blocks you may play with the puzzle").

* The child will be given a choice ("Keep the water in the water table or you will have to pick a different area").

* The child will be told to sit quietly with an adult in order to gain composure.

* If the child is endangering the safety of another child, he or she will have the situation explained with emotions expressed ("He really was scared--that hurt him") and will be told to sit quietly with an adult to gain composure.

Toddlers (non-verbal)

*If in danger, immediately stop behavior.

* Express emotions ("That really scared me--you can sit in the chair").

* Demonstrate correct behavior ("Tommy, be gentle" and pat his hand gently).

Director's Resource 15-2 (*continued*)

SAFETY OF CHILDREN

A top priority of our center is to provide a safe place to leave your child. In order to assure that our center is a safe place, we have adopted the following policies:

1. A child care staff member in charge of a child or a group of children is responsible for their safety.

2. When a parent or guardian brings a child to the center, they must tell the staff member that the child is present at the center.

3. No child is ever left alone or unsupervised.

4. In an emergency situation, there are six working telephones. At the center, there is one in the director's office, the kitchen, in each classroom, and in the muscle room.

5. We have a monthly fire drill at varying times each month. A record of the fire drills is located in the director's office.

6. We have medical, dental and fire emergency plans posted in each classroom.

7. When a field trip is taken, a person trained in first aid along with a first aid box is taken. The child also has identification attached to himself containing the child's name, and the center's name, address and phone number.

8. A fire emergency and weather alert plan is posted in each classroom. The plans include diagrams showing evacuation routes.

9. In the event that a group of children would participate in swimming or other water activities in water two or more feet in depth, written permission must be granted by each parent or guardian. The group must be supervised by persons who are currently certified as lifeguards or water safety instructors by the American Red Cross or equivalent water safety program.

10. The use of spray aerosols is prohibited when children are in attendance at our center.

11. An emergency transportation authorization form for each child, and health records of children with allergies, special needs, or health conditions requiring special procedure or precautions will be available on field trips or special outings. The center classroom ratio (at minimum) will be maintained on field trips.

Director's Resource 15-2 (*continued*)

12.   Any vehicle that is owned, leased, or hired by our center for the purpose of transporting children will be licensed and operated in accordance with the laws; including the Motor Vehicle Lighting Requirements and the Child Restraint Systems Requirements.

13.   When a child is involved in an accident, injury occurs, syrup of ipecac is administered, or emergency transportation is necessary, our center will fill out an incident report form.   The report will be given to the parent or guardian on the day of the incident.   Copies of the reports will be retained on fill at our center for one year.

Director's Resource 15-2 (*continued*)

AGREEMENT BETWEEN PARENT AND CENTER

1.   Each child must be picked up promptly at the end of his or her program. A charge of $5.00 per ten minutes will be made for the time the child remains at the center after the closing of the center. This fee doubles if not paid within one week.

2.   Each child will be accepted into a specific classroom. Any change in the assigned program must be approved by the parents and by the director.

3.   The center will be closed several days of the year for holidays.   They are: New Year's Day, 4th of July, Memorial Day, Labor Day, Thanksgiving Day, Christmas Eve and Christmas Day, Good Friday, and the day after Thanksgiving (the final two days are inservice training days for the teachers).

4.   Each child must have a change of clothing that is left at the center to be used in emergencies. All clothes must be marked. The center cannot be responsible for unmarked clothing. Children should wear washable clothing in which they can move freely.

5.   Parents are asked to see that children do not bring food to the Center. Adequate snacks are provided morning and afternoon, plus a hot lunch at noon. (Special arrangements for birthdays can be made).

6.   Food exceptions cannot be made for individual children except in the case of allergies and religious needs. A written statement from a physician is required for children with ANY allergies.

7.   Weekly menus are posted in advance in the center, and parents may refer to these at any time.

8.   Parents are asked to see that children do not bring toys to the center. A special stuffed animal or book for naptime is permitted.

9.   Parents are expected to bring their child into the building and see that he or she is under supervision of his or her teacher before leaving the premises. It is important that the parent or guardian sign in and out each day.

10.   Children who become ill cannot remain at the center. The parent will be called to pick up the child. Children absent from the center with a contagious disease will not be admitted without a signed statement from a physician indicating that the child is no longer contagious.

Director's Resource 15-2 (*continued*)

11.   Routine visits to a doctor, clinic, or dentist are the responsibility of the parent.

12.   Each preschool child in the center will have the advantage of an afternoon nap.

13.   Children will be permitted to play outside in the play yard daily, except in inclement weather. If you do not want your child to participate in outdoor activities, please bring a signed note from a physician stating this to the director.

14.   Parents must cooperate with the center in carrying out all governmental laws, rules, and regulations affecting the operation of the center.

15.   This agreement may be changed at any time by the Learning Center to comply with governmental regulations or for any other reason.

16.   Although we request cooperation in not disrupting our program, parents are permitted access to all parts of this center at any time their child is present.

17.   The State of Ohio requires that all members of day care institutions be on the lookout for, and report to the State, any and all cases of abuse of a child. The center is obligated to report to the State any suspected cases of child abuse an/or neglect.

18.   Rosters of names and telephone numbers of parents, custodians, or guardians of children attending the center are available upon request. This roster does not include the names and telephone numbers of parents, custodians, or guardians who request this information to be excluded.

19.   The center's licensing record is available upon request from the department. This information includes, but is not limited to, evaluation forms from the health, building, and fire departments that inspected our center.

20.   An emergency transportation authorization form will be filled out upon enrollment for transportation of the child to the necessary medical or dental emergency care source. In the event emergency transportation consent is not granted, a non-consent form will be provided and must be filled out by the parent or guardian. The center is free from responsibility for children not granted emergency transportation authorization.

21.   Parents and guardians are permitted access to all parts of the center at the time of the pre-admission interview.

22. The center will work to serve special needs children. A decision will be made by the director during the intake process as to whether our center can adequately provide for the needs of a special needs child. A specific written policy will be designed for each special needs child by the teacher and parent before enrollment.

23. The center has liability insurance covering all persons on our property during business hours.

24. Orientation of new children: We ask that arrangements be made to allow children a gradual adjustment to the center-- i.e. Monday, Wednesday, Friday from 9:00 to noon. In order to foster a positive adjustment, we also believe it is beneficial for parents to spend a period of time with their child at our center upon enrollment.

25. Children's bedding must be brought home and laundered weekly.

26. If the child is to be picked up by someone other than the two names listed on the release form, the following steps will be followed:

a.   The parent must tell the teacher in the morning
     at the time of drop off who will be coming to
     pick up the child, or they must call to notify
     the teacher in advance of the pick up.

b.   If the teacher is called, identification will be
     requested of the adult picking up the child.

c.   The child will not be released from the center
     unless the above steps are taken.

27. I agree to have my name and telephone number included on my child's class roster which will be made available upon request to any parent whose child is enrolled in my child's class.

28. In order for this child's educational experience to broaden and enrich his or her life, we will attempt to enroll children from various diverse backgrounds. To provide a balanced population, we will base acceptance of applications on children who are representative of various racial, cultural, and socio-economic backgrounds as well as those who are at various developmental stages in life.

29. The center's philosophy concerning special occasions and holidays is that of simplicity. Parents are asked to consult the head teacher concerning wearing costumes or bringing valentines. A child's birthday celebration should also be discussed with the head teacher first.

30.   Events in the child's home and environment may markedly affect his or her behavior.   Because of the child's ability to report accurately these events, we would appreciate communication between parents and staff concerning any unusual happenings or events such as illness, death, changes in living situations, extra stimulation, etc.

31.   Termination of a child will only be made with staff recommendation, appropriate documentation, and outside consultation, which would result in action to be in the best interest of the child.   Particular care will be made to work closely with the child and family in any consideration of termination.

32.   Upon entry to the center, a child must be examined by his doctor and thereafter annually.   Medical forms may be picked up in the office to be used by the child's physician.

33.   The center's staff consults with specialized agencies as needed for you child.   Speech and hearing exams are done regularly, and any outside consultation involving your child will be discussed with you ahead of time.

34.   Parent having any concerns about their child are encouraged to discuss these with the child's teacher.   Any outside agency consultations will gladly be arranged.

35.   The center does not discriminate against any race, creed, religion, or sex.   This applies to the hiring of staff and application of our students.   In addition, the center staff has adopted the Ohio Association for the Education of Young Children Code of Ethics.   A copy of this code is attached.

36.   Fundraisers will be done periodically.   We must have support from parents.

Director's Resource 15-2 (*continued*)

PARENTAL PARTICIPATION PLAN

Parents are always welcome to join in our program at the Center. We invite parents to participate in Board meetings, parent groups, and fund raisers. All parents are encouraged to share personal interests, including hobbies, talents, cultural backgrounds, favorite recipes, etc. Parents can volunteer in the classroom or repair equipment.

LUNCH WITH YOUR CHILD
We encourage parents to join us for lunch. Please try to notify your child's teacher a day ahead if you plan to have lunch with you child, so the cook can plan accordingly.

PARENT CONFERENCES
The teachers welcome requests for conferences at any time. Scheduled parent-teacher conferences are held twice a year.

DONATIONS
Donations to the center are tax deductible. As your child develops mentally and physically, please consider whether books, toys or outgrown clothes may be appropriate for use in our center.

A community resource directory is available upon request.

Procedures for resolving parent complaints or problems:

1. Complaints or problems must be resolved directly with the person(s) involved.

2. If the issue is not resolved, complaints or problems must be explained to that person's supervisor.

3. If the issue is not resolved, continue to follow the organizational chart until a solution is reached.

4. If complaints or problems procedure is not followed, persons submitting complaints or problems will be redirected to follow this procedure.

5. Complaints or problems from the community at large will be channeled to the appropriate staff person.

Director's Resource 15-2 (*continued*)

POLICIES AND PROCEDURES FOR TERMINATION OF SERVICES TO CLIENTS

The rights and responsibilities of the consumer were examined very closely when this termination policy was being developed.

Your child may be terminated from the program based on abuse and neglect of the parent rules and guidelines. If you are found to be in violation of the rules and guidelines, the following procedures will be taken.

1. Notice to bring the situation to your attention.

2. Written warning of suspension.

3. Suspension-three days (the child may not attend for three days).

4. Termination from the program if the situation continues. Written notice stating reason for termination.

MAJOR REASONS FOR TERMINATION:

1. Attendance (infrequent).

2. Fees (unpaid).

3. Medical (not up to date as required).

4. Behavioral (disruptive or abnormal).

Each child is expected to attend daily and punctually. If absenteeism extends beyond five days per month without a logical explanation, the procedure above applies.

The center door will open at 7:00 a.m. and close at 6:00 p.m. Each child is expected to arrive before 9:00 a.m. and depart no later than 6:00 p.m. For every ten minutes beyond 6:00 p.m. There will be a $5.00 late fee, payable directly to the staff members who stayed late. This fee doubles if not paid within one week.

Director's Resource 15-2 (*continued*)

POLICY ON COMMUNICABLE DISEASE MANAGEMENT

We feel that it is our duty to inform parents of the following precautions we take to help prevent the spread of communicable disease.   Your cooperation in carrying these policies through is particularly appreciated.

1.   A staff member trained in First Aid and Communicable Diseases observes each child daily before he or she enters a group.   The following are the signs the staff member will recognize as signals of a possible illness:

   a.   A fever of 100 F taken by the axillary method when in combination with any other sign of illness;

   b.   Skin rash other than a localized diaper rash;

   c.   Diarrhea and/or vomiting two or more times in the same day;

   d.   Evidence of lice infestation;

   e.   Severe coughing, causing the child to become red or blue in the face or to make a whooping sound;

   f.   Difficult or rapid breathing;

   g.   Yellowish skin or eyes;

   h.   Conjuctivitis;

   i.   Unusually dark urine and/or grey or white stool;

   j.   Stiff neck

2.   A chart listing communicable disease is posted both in the office and in the classrooms.

3. We will not administer any medication or vitamins without both the physician and parental permission in writing.   See Administration of Medication forms.

4.   Any child who is suspected of having a communicable disease is isolated immediately in a room or portion of a room not being used for child care but within sight and hearing of an adult. The child is given a cot and blanket for use.   (When the child is discharged, these are sanitized).   The parents or emergency contacts are telephoned to pick the child up from the center.   If no signs of disease are present for 24 hours, the child will be readmitted to the center.

5.   Any child who is suspected of being mildly ill (a child experiencing minor cold symptoms or who does not feel well enough

Director's Resource 15-2 (*continued*)

to participate in activities but does not exhibit any of the
symptoms specified in #1) will be cared for within the child's
group.   The child will be observed carefully for signs and
symptoms of worsening condition.

6.   When a staff member exhibits any sign of communicable
disease, he or she leaves the center and a substitute is called
to replace the ill staff member.

7.   Parents will be notified by staff if a child is exposed to a
communicable disease.

Director's Resource 15-2 (*continued*)

EMERGENCY PLAN

Emergency Numbers:

Fire/Life squad.......911
Poison Control........872-5111
Police................911
Cinti. Health Dept....532-3100
Children's Protective.721-7044

Hospitals:

Christ.......369-2235
Children's...559-4293
Bethesda.....569-6464
University...875-4571
Good Sam.....872-2536
Jewish.......569-2111
Deaconess....559-2236

1.   The first aid kit is located in the classrooms and the copying room.

2.   A list of the students with home and emergency numbers is in an index box on the director's desk.   Each child's emergency medical release is in his or her file in the front desk.

3. If there is a serious emergency, telephone life squad and parents.

4.   If a child is involved in an accident, fill out an incident report form.   If a child becomes ill, fill out report on illness.

5.   If a child exhibits any of the symptoms described in the center's communicable disease policy, the child is isolated in the director's office.   An adult must always be with the ill child.

6.   Fire extinguishers are located in each room for adult use.

7.   Doors are marked clearly for fire exit.   Fire drills are conducted monthly with the children.

8.   Staff will follow instructions for dental emergency as stated on the Dental First Aid chart located in the classrooms.

9.   The staff trained in first aid is also listed next to the phones.

10.   In case of a tornado or severe storm, the children will move to the basement.   One teacher will be in charge of keeping in contact with a weather station.

Director's Resource 15-3

Sample Handbook

Handbook

for
Families, Visitors, Volunteers
& Other Friends of Young Children

Children's for Children

The employer-sponsored child care center of
The Children's Hospital Medical Center

3255 Burnet Avenue
Cincinnati, Ohio 45229
(513) 559-4999

Reprinted by permission: Children's for Children
                        Children's Hospital Medical Center

Director's Resource 15-3 (*continued*)

CHILDREN´S FOR CHILDREN

the employer-sponsored child care center of
The Children´s Hospital Medical Center

HANDBOOK FOR
FAMILIES, VISITORS, VOLUNTEERS
AND
OTHER FRIENDS OF YOUNG CHILDREN

CHILDREN´S FOR CHILDREN
3255 Burnet Avenue
Cincinnati, Ohio   45229
(513) 559-4999
(513) 559-7193

Chris Stafford
Director

Mary Alice Callahan
Educational Coordinator

Accredited by the
National Academy of Early
Childhood Programs (NAEYC)

Director's Resource 15-3 (*continued*)

TABLE OF CONTENTS

Director's Resource 15-3 (*continued*)

Hello!

I bring you a warm welcome to **Children's for Children**, the child development center of the Children's Hospital Medical Center. Founded in 1987, the child care center is one of Cincinnati's largest, loveliest, and liveliest child care facilities. I like to think of **Children's for Children** as a place which children and adults consider their second home ... a place where they are accepted and loved ... a place where laughter and play are cherished ... a place where children's rhythms are caught and given warm response.

I hold special pride in the center's professional staff. Selected for their knowledge of child development as well as their strong interpersonal skills, they are the strength of our program. When visiting **Children's for Children**, please take time to listen, to watch, and to learn from this unique group. You will be enriched.

It is my role and the role of my staff to not only facilitate the learning of children, parents, and one another, but also to work as enablers to the important work of our outstanding hospital medical center. We are pleased to embrace these roles.

Sincerely,

Chris

Chris Stafford
Director

Director's Resource 15-3 (*continued*)

PHILOSOPHICALLY SPEAKING

Childhood is a time like no other. It's a time for exploring ... for creating ... for discovering about oneself ... for meeting the world ... for learning how to learn ... for being accepted "just the way I am". It's a time for blossoming and being cherished ... a time for being allowed the time to be a child.

Our child care center administrators and caregivers are committed to the belief that children have achieved ... that is, they CAN DO a lot.. It is the role of the caregivers to build upon those things that children are able to do. We believe that most of life's learning - including how to learn - occurs in the first five years of life. Since each child learns at her own pace, our staff will look to her to determine the next stage of development. This "can do" approach is the basis of our philosophy for the center. This "can do" viewpoint allows our society's precious future to become confident and to enjoy successes in an atmosphere of respect, warmth, and love.

Time and again, research is showing us that THE main component of sound, quality child care is the trained, sensitive adult who is the caregiver. Through careful selection of a staff trained in early childhood development who value, respect, and sensitively respond to the unique needs that children hold, we feel that children will best learn. The time that they are away from Mommy and Daddy must be a blossoming time.

We respect parents as the most significant providers of care and nurturance. We are pleased to serve as extended family members.

Director's Resource 15-3 (*continued*)

AN OVERVIEW OF OUR SERVICES

Child care centers are special places. A center becomes even more special when it is created to serve a unique population. So it is at Children's Hospital Medical Center (CHMC). Our on-site child care center, **Children's for Children**, provides services primarily to the children of hospital personnel in a convenient setting for the seven affiliated institutions of CHMC. Our center is the most comprehensive in Cincinnati. The hours extend beyond midnight, with weekday holiday care available. We offer full and partial day service for children over 3 months of age through preschool age.

Our center is accredited by the National Academy of Early Childhood Programs (NAEYC); we have also been successfully evaluated by Comprehensive Community Child Care on several occasions.

Research shows us that the most important component of quality child care is the choice of staff. We pride ourselves on our selection of caregivers whose special sensitivity to children is unmatched. Our caregivers are nurturing, positive in nature, understand children's needs, and are specially trained. The center's administrative team carefully evaluates staff performance to assure that the children are provided age-appropriate experiences in an accepting, warm environment.

Our services stretch beyond child care to support the whole family. Families using the center receive daily communications on their child's day, prompt attention to any concerns, and parent-teacher conferences at least twice a year. The parent group gathers periodically to hear speakers specializing in issues facing today's families or for social events. A Child Care Advisory Committee includes parents and lends important support to the center. A center newsletter offers classroom news, parenting tips, child legislation information, and a calendar of coming events.

The center does not discriminate in the enrollment of children or selection of staff or volunteers upon the basis of race, color, creed, age, religion, sex, national origin, handicap or status as a veteran.

Favoritism and nepotism are not practiced at the center. Persons desiring to be employees, to register their children, or to apply for tuition assistance must follow the established procedures.

Director's Resource 15-3 (*continued*)

COLLABORATING FOR CHILDREN

It is to the benefit of our children, families, and staff to collaborate with an extensive network of agencies and individuals.

Resources held by the affiliated institutions of Children's Hospital Medical Center are used by the professional staff of this center. All these groups focus on the healthy development of children, on providing the family ultimate support, and on advocating for safe environments for young ones.

The center is licensed to operate by both the Ohio Department of Human Services and by the City of Cincinnati. Licenses are posted in the first floor lobby. We are also licensed for food service operation with documentation displayed in the kitchen. Our compliance with all licensing requirements is monitored regularly. Licenses are renewed in a timely manner. To receive a copy of current state day care laws and rules, contact the Ohio Department of Human Services' local office, 852-3280. Our compliance reports/evaluations from the health, building, and fire departments are also available from ODHS. To report any suspected violation of the state law, please contact the Department of Human Services' toll-free number 1-800-686-1581. City regulations and compliance reports are available from the Cincinnati Department of Health, 352-3115. All state and city rules are also available at the center.

Administrators of **Children's for Children** have advocated and testified on numerous occasions to strengthen the city and state laws to their current level. We are pleased to cooperate in the important role of protecting children.

Director's Resource 15-3 (*continued*)

We are members of the Comprehensive Community Child Care (4C).   Individual staff members belong to various professional groups, such as the National Association for the Education of Young Children (NAEYC) and the National Association of Hospital Affiliated Child Care Programs (NAHACCP).   We uphold the Ohio AEYC Code of Ethics.

Students from the University of Cincinnati may be assigned to the center to complete their teaching internships.   In addition, student nurses come to observe healthy children at play.

Doctoral, corporate, or other research is conducted at the center with parental permission only.   On occasion, we have the opportunity to participate in consumer research (toy design firms, etc.). Sometimes we have assisted with research projects of CHMC.   No research is completed without the approval of the Center's Advisory Committee Research Review Committee.

Our staff also joins hands with hospital, community, and parent volunteers.   All volunteers are carefully screened and trained for their "jobs" by the center's administrators.   We request physical statements to be on file for volunteers who interact with our children.   Classroom or field trip volunteers are to support the staff but are never left in charge of the children.

Director's Resource 15-3 (*continued*)

DISCIPLINE

Children at our center will not receive physical punishment. Children who have conflicts or problems with others while at our center will be encouraged to verbalize their angers and concerns. Even infants without verbal skills will hear their caregivers describing problems, solutions and logical consequences. The role of the adult at school is to be a helper to positive problem solving. Our staff members guide rather than punish.

Children whose behavior endangers others will be supervised away from other children. The child then will process the problem with a staff member and any other concerned parties. Staff rarely use "time out" unless a child is emotionally out of control and needs a private time to regain composure. Verbal processing is our preferred technique.

Discipline, i.e., guidance, will always be positive, productive and immediate when behavior is inappropriate. Many of the staff members have had extensive course work in Dr. Thomas Gordon's Teacher Effectiveness Training (TET) and utilize TET techniques in assisting children with problems.

No child will be humiliated, shamed, frightened, or subjected to verbal or physical abuse by staff or by parents on the premises or during field trips.

Director's Resource 15-3 (*continued*)

OUR STAFF

We select our staff carefully in order to provide the best possible care and education for the children.   The Director has a minimum of a bachelor's degree in early childhood education and experience as a center administrator.   Our Educational Coordinator is a master teacher of children and adults. Lead teachers have degrees in early childhood education and experience as teachers of young children. Assistant teachers have special training as well as demonstrated competence with young children. They must have a high school diploma and most have graduated from vocational school programs or universities with degrees in early childhood.

We employ people who are warm and nurturing, who understand child development, who can apply their knowledge in the classroom, and who respect each child as an individual. We seek employees who value working as a team with parents, colleagues, and volunteers.

Each staff person has on file three written references from previous employers and/or supervisors. We require a police record check, a physical examination, and drug screening.

Continuing education is an important part of working at **Children's for Children**. Each staff person attends training in first aid, communicable disease recognition, child abuse prevention and recognition, child development, and teaching methods.

All staff are supervised by the center Director and Educational Coordinator who report to the Vice President of Human Resources.

Director's Resource 15-3 (*continued*)

PARENT INVOLVEMENT

Teachers meet with individual parents to review each child's progress throughout the year. A minimum of two parent/teacher dialogues are held each year. Additional conferences may be scheduled at any time. Parents of our children receive daily written information regarding their child.

Parents serve on the Center's Advisory Committee and its sub-committees to help guarantee a setting designed to reflect the needs of today's families.

If parents have concerns or need assistance with problems related to the child development center, they may discuss the issue, if applicable, with the teacher involved. If they are not satisfied, they may discuss their concerns with the Director or the Educational Coordinator.

Rosters of names and telephone numbers of parents, custodians, or guardians of children attending the center are available. The rosters will not include the name and telephone numbers of any parent, custodian, or guardian who requests that the Director not include that information.

Social and educational events are held throughout the year to encourage interactions between staff and families.

Director's Resource 15-3 (*continued*)

CENTER OPERATIONS

We are open for operation between the hours of 6:30 a.m. and 12:30 a.m., Monday through Friday. We ask that parents with fluctuating schedules inform us in a timely manner. Schedules are due the Wednesday prior to the week of service. To run a smooth operation, we appreciate cooperation in this regard. Our staff schedules will "go with the flow".

We are authorized to serve a licensed capacity of:

infants (3 months - 18 months) 35

toddlers (18 months - 36 months) 34

preschoolers (36 months - 60 months) . . . 59

schoolagers (60 months - 8 years) 3

We maintain these child/adult ratios and class sizes:

young infants	4:1 licensed for groups no larger than 12
older infants	4:1 licensed for groups no larger than 12
younger toddlers	5:1 licensed for groups no larger than 14
older toddlers	5:1 licensed for groups no larger than 14
preschoolers	10:1 licensed for groups no larger than 20
schoolagers	15:1 licensed for groups no larger than 20

Director's Resource 15-3 (*continued*)

The center may be open on CHMC holidays if parents must work. A survey to determine the need is taken a few weeks prior to the holiday.

Our financial policies are provided to parents enrolling their children. These policies are periodically reviewed and revised.

Director's Resource 15-3 (*continued*)

TYPICAL DAYTIME SCHEDULE

Although each classroom's daily schedule varies, activities alternate between quiet and active, free play, and total group experiences. Daily lesson plans are posted in classrooms of the five oldest groups of children. Infant schedules are at the baby's preference. An example of a daily schedule for older groups is:

6:30 - 8:00	arrival, warm greeting, play with parents, free play with friends
8:00 - 8:30	wash hands, breakfast
8:30 - 8:45	wash table space, brush teeth, transition to outdoors
8:45 - 9:30	outdoor play
9:30 - 9:50	language or music activities in whole group
9:50 - 10:00	transition to free play
10:00 - 11:15	self-selection in all learning areas
11:15 - 11:30	preparation for lunch, wash hands
11:30 - 12:15	lunch in small groups
12:15 - 12:30	wash hands, brush teeth, toileting
12:30 - 2:30	soft music, back rubs, naptime
2:30 - 3:00	toileting, wash hands, snack, some departures and second shift arrivals

Director's Resource 15-3 (*continued*)

3:00 – 3:45	self-selected activities
3:45 – 4:15	outdoor play
4:15 – 4:45	grouptime (songs, stories)
4:45 – 5:45	free choice of activities or muscle room
5:45	transition to evening program
6:00	dinner

Director's Resource 15-3 (*continued*)

TYPICAL NIGHT TIME SCHEDULE

The "Night Owls" are children who stay for dinner and beyond. Our staff plans special activities for these children who are in "family" groupings. An example of an evening schedule is:

6:00 - 6:30 p.m.	dinner is served
6:30 - 7:00	self selection of activities in all learning areas
7:00 - 8:00	muscle room or outdoors
8:00 - 8:30	quiet activities, story
8:30 - 8:50	handwashing, evening snack
8:50 - 9:10	preparation for bedtime (brush teeth, toileting, diaper change, hopping into p.j.'s)
9:10 - 9:30	soft music, back rubs, sleep
9:30 - 12:30 a.m.	evening sleep

Director's Resource 15-3 (*continued*)

WHAT TO BRING FROM HOME

Infants:
baby food, labeled with child's
name and dated
formula, labeled and dated
baby bottles, labeled and dated
pacifiers, labeled
favorite soft crib toy or crib
mobile
disposable diapers, labeled on box
or cloth diapers with pail
blankets
1 or 2 changes of clothes, labeled
security items
bumper guard (optional)
photo of family

Toddlers:
pacifiers, labeled
naptime toy
blanket and pillow, labeled
disposable diapers, labeled on box
or cloth diapers with pail
1 or 2 changes of clothes, labeled
sweater or jacket, labeled
security items
toothbrush, labeled
toothpaste, labeled
comb or pick
photo of family

Preschoolers:
naptime toy
blanket and pillow, labeled
1 change of clothes, labeled
sweater or jacket, labeled
toothbrush, labeled
toothpaste, labeled
comb or pick
security items, labeled
photo of family

Director's Resource 15-3 (*continued*)

Night Owls: all items above
                 pajamas, labeled

WHAT NOT TO BRING FROM HOME

                 toys of violence
                 candy
                 chewing gum
                 "jellies", sandals
                 anything unlabeled
                 a frown

                 (please check with classroom staff
                   as well)

Director's Resource 15-3 (*continued*)

THE INFANT PROGRAM

Our program for infants sets its pace around the needs and unique differences of each child. The teacher centers her day around the schedules of those for whom she cares. This care, while meeting basic needs for food, diapering and adequate rest, goes beyond that as this keen observer plans and enhances the interactions and activities the infant's behavior is identifying.

Routines are the curriculum for an infant's day. Every moment of a young child's day offers opportunities for learning. The skilled educator catches these moments and helps each baby establish trust, discover and feel good about herself, tackle a motor task, realize the power of language, and begin to understand this strange new world from many angles. This is accomplished as each teacher keys into the verbal and nonverbal messages the child is sending.

An infant teacher, with the education and understanding of early childhood development, knows that rich verbal interactions with children help them to understand that language is a tool for identifying and expressing their needs, ideas, and feelings in later life. Each of our caregivers accepts that infants developmentally need to explore the world through mouthing and touching and allows for this, viewing it as a valuable learning experience. This teacher is alert to the need for proper sanitation measures and follows them consistently and conscientiously. As the trained adult looks at the environment, she views it from the child's eye and creates a cozy, inviting, and stimulating place for children. She understands

Director's Resource 15-3 (*continued*)

that what is made available for children to use depends on who the' children are and what their needs are developmentally. This might necessitate frequent rotation of toys to "keep up" with a growing child, or prompt a teacher to make a toy that focuses on the child's interest or need.

Infants need to view the world from many angles and are allowed that experience. This includes crawling, being carried, stroller rides, outdoor play, climbing, and rocking so that various perspectives are gained. Diaper changing, feeding, and other routines are viewed as vital times for communication, self discovery, and socializing. They are encouraged to master feeding themselves despite the messiness that accompanies this activity. While being supportive of infants in their quest for competence, our teachers look to the parents as the best resource in working with their children. Early childhood educators view themselves as professionals with children and with parents.

Director's Resource 15-3 (*continued*)

THE TODDLER PROGRAM

In providing a program for toddlers, our teachers understand that these children learn with their whole bodies. They learn more by doing than by being told. Toddlers discover their world on a physical level, so it is expected that they will prefer walking, climbing, carrying objects, dumping, or dropping objects to sitting, picking up toys, or playing only in a designated space. These large muscle activities are the legitimate activity of toddlerhood.

In planning for toddlers, our educators are prepared to be flexible and spontaneous. Because they are active explorers, toddlers are eager to try new things and use materials in different ways. Our understanding teachers will go with the cues of the child and view that as learning, extending it even if it isn't part of the day's planned curriculum.

Toddlers are working on becoming autonomous. The educated teacher respects this and allows opportunities for the child to be responsible and to make choices. This teacher also understands why certain behaviors must be limited, and sets limits that are fair and consistent. Expectations for behaviors are developmentally appropriate and allow the child to be challenged yet to feel support from the teacher. Consequently, frustration is kept to a minimum and the child's dignity and self-concept remain intact.

Our teachers, with patience, warmth and respect, redirect toddlers to help guide them toward controlling their impulses and behaviors. The teacher draws more attention to a child's appropriate behavior than to the inappropriate

Director's Resource 15-3 (*continued*)

because she understands that toddlers will act in the way that draws the most attention. Constant testing and expressions of opposition are viewed as the child's development of a healthy sense of self. The teacher accepts this and offers positively worded directions to avoid getting into power struggles. The teacher views herself as a model for how she wants the children to develop. She does this in her verbal interactions because she understands that toddlers lack the skills to cope with frustrating situations and might act out in a physical way without her guidance.

The teacher recognizes that routine times are important moments to help children learn about themselves and others. An early childhood educator views play as valuable and facilitates this so that children stay interested and move from simple to more complex aspects of their play. The classroom includes materials for children to engage in imaginative play, appropriate art experiences for creative exploration, various manipulatives to develop cognitive and physical skills, as well as building blocks, music, and books. The environment allows for the children to choose activities and respects their need for ample time to use and reuse activities because repeated experiences foster competence. The setting is stimulating and inviting. It offers comfortable spaces for privacy and for interacting in small groups. Children's art is displayed proudly and respected for what it is. The little ones are encouraged by a knowing adult to care for the belongings and the environment in ways they can handle. The teacher creates and adapts the environment and activities to meet the children's changing needs from day to day.

Director's Resource 15-3 (*continued*)

THE PRESCHOOLER PROGRAM

Preschoolers are usually most responsive to activities in which they are involved in a "hands-on" manner. Our teachers accept that and design their classroom spaces with "learning stations" at which children can freely choose whether to participate or not and for how long. Our quality staff rotate and add materials frequently to maintain and extend the child's interest. Often our teachers create their own games and materials if commercial ones do not offer the challenge needed or do not reflect the interests of the children. Young children seem to learn best when trained teachers build on the interests and abilities of the children. This reflects the currently recognized theory which endorses non-pressured, child-centered activities guided by an adult with a solid child development base and strong problem-solving skills. In such a program, parents truly become partners with the professional staff. Information or discoveries about the child's development are mutually shared, resulting in a program tailored to the individual child.

The preschool curriculum includes activities centering on communication, science, math, social studies, music, art, large and small motor development. An enrichment program which includes field trips and visitors is offered. Dramatic play opportunities reinforce learning of practical life experiences.

LANGUAGE/COMMUNICATION - The whole language approach is our model. This is one in which children are exposed to print and language that is integrated into each activity center. Thomas Gordon's communication system is mastered by staff to facilitate problem solving.

Director's Resource 15-3 (*continued*)

SCIENCE - Open-ended questions by the trained teacher help the children learn how to question ... how to be thinkers. Hands-on activities include using simple machines, sensory table play, plant and animal life. Nutrition awareness and weekly cooking activities are offered.

MATH - Activities include concepts of introductory geometry, seriation, classification, sets, number, quantity, length, weight, use of simple graphs, simple addition/subtraction (more/less), and money.

SOCIAL STUDIES - Learning about the "world around us" is the focus of this curriculum area. Field trips and studies of occupations are included.

MUSIC - Exposure to and involvement with simple rhythm instruments and autoharps is part of our music program. Rhythms are also "practiced" by the learning of songs and finger plays. Guest musicians visit the children to give exposure to a variety of sounds and diverse musical styles. Tone, volume, and pitch awareness is part of the music curriculum.

ART - Exploratory, sensory art activities help the child experience a variety of media. Collages and creating mobiles are offered. Paints, chalk, pencils, paper, markers, glue, paste, and play dough are all available in a "free choice" activity center for the children to use as they wish.

LARGE MOTOR - Movement activities including free dance, parachute handling, climbing, crawling, running and balancing are just a small part of the large motor program.

Director's Resource 15-3 (*continued*)

SMALL MOTOR - From the handling of simple tools to completing pegboards, children are continually offered opportunities to develop their smaller muscles, an important prerequisite for writing.

FIELD TRIPS - Occasional trips are taken by the two oldest groups to nearby places such as the Art Museum, the Zoo, and the Museum of Natural History. Periodic walks to Levine Park, adjacent to the Medical College, are taken. Field trip fees are occasionally requested. Parents may ask the Director about field trip fee assistance. Our desire is to have all children participate in trips.

VISITORS - Classroom visitors might describe a career or hobby. They could include SPCA and zoo representatives with animals or parents describing hobbies.

DRAMATIC PLAY - From "playing house" to being a cashier in a pretend grocery store to repairing cardboard automobiles in a child-sized garage, the children are able to practice roles that productive adults hold.

Director's Resource 15-3 (*continued*)

HEALTH

Our center operates for well children and staff only. Children who are mildly ill (e.g. minor cold symptoms) may remain at the center only with the Director's approval. Children should be fully able to participate in all activities, including outdoor play. Parents should provide appropriate changes of clothing so children do not become either chilled or overheated. Snow pants and boots are needed for snowy days. Swimsuits are needed for toasty days. Light sweaters or jackets should be made available, as well. "Jellies", "flip-flops", and sandals are not appropriate for wear at school. Sun screens or diaper lotions may not be applied by staff except with the written permission of the parent and physician on a center-supplied form.

Children with symptoms of communicable disease are isolated immediately. A staff member remains with the child at all times, until the parent or designated representative arrives for the child. We will not serve children with:

- a fever of $100°$ F or above, axillary

- a skin rash that has not been identified by a phone call or in writing from a physician who has seen the rash

- diarrhea and/or vomiting two or more times in a day

- evidence of head lice or other parasites

- severe coughing

- rapid or difficult breathing

- yellowish skin or eyes

Director's Resource 15-3 (*continued*)

- conjunctivitis

- unusually dark urine and/or gray or white stool

- sore throat or difficulty swallowing

- stiff neck

- infected skin patches

- pain of which the child complains and interferes with normal activity

- evidence of infection

- excessive fatigue

Children may be readmitted:

A. With a physician's statement that the child is free from communicable disease and that returning poses no risk to the child or others.

or

B. If visibly free from communicable disease, fever free for 24 hours, and free of vomiting/diarrhea for 24 hours while on a normal diet.

The center retains the right to continue to exclude a child despite a physician's statement if that statement contradicts the center's policies. When any youngster in a child's class has a communicable disease, parents are informed in writing within 24 hours.

Staff with symptoms of illness will remain away from the center.

Director's Resource 15-3 (*continued*)

Our staff members have special training through the American Red Cross in recognizing communicable diseases. The staff rely on their training, as well as the disease chart posted in the Director and Office Coordinator offices to determine indicated diseases. We follow strict handwashing and disinfection procedures. The disinfectant policy is posted in the classroom and reviewed with any adult working in that space.

Medication is given only if parents sign a center-supplied permission form AND the medication has a prescription label with the child's name and date on it. Medical samples and over-the-counter medicines MUST have a written note from the doctor. This includes chap stick, supplemental fluoride, and modified diets.

Director's Resource 15-3 (*continued*)

NUTRITION

We provide nutritionally balanced snacks, meals, and cooking activities. Menus are posted in each classroom and copies are made available on Friday afternoons for the coming week. We encourage the children to have an "hello" bite, that is - to try a taste of everything. We limit sugars and prefer birthday celebrations sent by parents to be raisins or other fruits, yogurt-sicles or juice-sicles, or other nutritious alternatives to cake and ice cream.

Special diets required by a physician need to be described in writing and signed by the doctor. Families who are vegetarian or have cultural or religious limitations on certain foods must indicate same on the background information sheet and, if applicable, the infant information form. We make every effort to provide special diets but may ask a parent to provide certain items. Parents of infants need to supply any formula, strained or junior baby foods, and baby bottles.

We provide approximately two-thirds of the child's daily nutritional needs. Seconds are offered to the children. Adults eat seated with the children, except the infant staff. Mealtimes are to be relaxed times, rich with conversation and fellowship. Parents may join us for lunch or dinner if the Director is aware by 9:30 a.m. Cost of lunch or dinner is $2.00 per adult except staff, for whom meals are provided.

Director's Resource 15-3 (*continued*)

SAFETY

We ask that parents closely supervise their children in the driveway, lobbies and elsewhere in the center. It is recommended that children exit from cars on the curb side of the driveway and be offered a hand to hold. When departing from the center, please resist having the children run to the car while the parent signs them out. Sticking together seems to be a reasonable safety request. When going to the classroom, the family is asked to stay together. Sending the child on the elevator while the adult uses the stairs (or vice versa) is a safety concern. Likewise, older children should accompany parents to infant rooms and not be left in a lobby. So much could happen in a moment or two, and we request your cooperation.

Children must be signed in and out each day in the front lobby. This is extremely important since this list is used to check attendance during emergency drills or events. Children are released only to persons for whom the staff has written permission from the parents. Parents should provide us with the social security number of any person designated to pick up a child.

No child is ever left alone or unsupervised. At arrival, parents are expected to help the child settle into play, which may require ten minutes or so. Parents complete a portion of the daily report form before departing for work or training. Parents are permitted access to all parts of the center at any time, including nap times and pre-admission interview periods. Parents may request key cards, for building entry, from the Office Coordinator.

Director's Resource 15-3 (*continued*)

There is always immediate access to a phone at the center. Telephones are located in the entry, the Director's office, the Office Coordinator's office, and in most classrooms.

Aerosol sprays are not used when children are present. Smoking is not permitted in the building.

Maintenance is provided by the Children's Hospital Medical Center's Environmental Services department. Most cleaning is done after 6:00 p.m.

Admittance to the building is by a buzzer/doorbell at the driveway entrance. All doors are locked at all times for security. Doors are easily opened from the inside in case of emergency. Parents have keys (access cards) for immediate entry.

The building is monitored indoors and outdoors by camera surveillance.

All center employees are required under Section 2151.421 of the Ohio Revised Code to report any suspicion of child abuse or child neglect. All staff have training to recognize signs of neglect and abuse.

Children are well prepared for trips through classroom activities and conversations. Parents must sign a permission slip for each trip, which includes: child's name, destination, date of trip, and date of signature. The following ratios will be maintained on any trip, including walks on the hospital grounds:

Infants: 2/1   Toddlers: 3/1   Preschoolers: 6/1

Transportation for trips is provided by rented bus or van, or on public transit. A staff person trained in first aid goes on all trips, taking a complete first aid kit and emergency permission forms for each child. Children wear nametags which include the center's name, address, and phone number.

Monthly emergency drills are held at varying times and documented by the Security Office. The following procedures are rehearsed:

FIRE: Staff members remain calm and reassure the children. The person noting the fire sounds the alarm and calls the fire department, 8877. Staff members escort second floor children to the nearest safe exit and congregate on the grassy area near the Pavilion Building. First floor children walk to the Pavilion's back entrance (the "circle" drive). The infants are placed in a single crib and wheeled outdoors. The staff takes attendance which is compared to the daily sign-in sheets. The Director checks classrooms, bathrooms, kitchen, playground, and all other areas. Plans for evacuation are posted in each classroom. **Elevators are not used for evacuation.**

WEATHER ALERT: The staff members remain calm and reassure children. Children are escorted to the inner hallway near the first floor elevator, as free as possible from flying window glass. Staff may bring books or manipulative games for the children. Parents who arrive to take their children are strongly encouraged to remain at the center until the weather alert has been lifted.

Director's Resource 15-3 (*continued*)

ACCIDENT: The first aid boxes are kept in the offices of the Director, the Office Coordinator and in the preschool wing.   Emergency numbers for children, staff and volunteers are kept in the Director's office. All staff have first aid and CPR training.   In a serious emergency, the life squad is notified as well as the parents and the Director. When going for treatment, the child's complete file and injury report form (if applicable) is taken.   This contains a summary of the child's medical history as well as medical emergency permission forms.   Children not requiring treatment or observation remain supervised and reassured that their friend is being well cared for.   Any incident or accident, including the administration of Syrup of Ipecac or the emergency transportation of a child, that occurs on the center premises will be reported to the parent in written form.

Emergency closings occur when weather is so severe that the Mayor issues a travel ban, if there are problems with our physical plant, or if the Board of Health orders closure for disease control.   Each of these instances is highly unlikely.

Director's Resource 15-3 (*continued*)

EMERGENCY TRANSPORTATION

The center obtains written emergency transportation authorization from each parent or guardian before the child begins attending the program. We will not accept any children whose parents or guardians refuse to grant permission for emergency transportation.

If a child is injured and needs treatment immediately, the center will call the lifesquad or hospital security for assistance transporting the child. A staff member will go to the hospital with the child and will take the child's records. The parents will be called to meet the child and staff person at the hospital. The staff person remains at the hospital until the parent arrives or longer if possible.

Director's Resource 15-3 (*continued*)

FINANCIAL INFORMATION

Fees are determined by the Director and the Vice President of Human Resources. The rates are based on those charged by programs of similar quality and do not meet the actual cost of care that we provide. CHMC generously subsidizes our program.

We offer full day and partial day options. A full day is 5-11 hours in length and a partial day is 5 or less hours. A two week deposit is required by the child's first day. This is credited to the child's last two weeks at the center. Fees vary according to amount of time that children are scheduled and the ratio of the group the child enjoys. Tuition is due on the Friday prior to service.

No sick or vacation allowances are made.

Modest discounts are provided to families with more than one child using the center.

There are miscellaneous fees for late tuition, insufficient funds, use exceeding 11 hours, occasional field trips, and additional meals.

Parents receive the financial policies prior to enrollment. The Office Coordinator is available to clarify policies of a financial nature.

Director's Resource 15-3 (*continued*)

CLOSING STATEMENT

Children's for Children is designed for the unique needs of the Children's Hospital Medical Center. We hope that visitors and participants will sense that we have created a home away from home. We appreciate feedback from any visitor or family member. We are pleased to elaborate on any facets of our program. Tours are available by prior arrangement to small groups of persons wishing to see quality programming for children.

Thank you for your continuing interest in quality child care in our community.

CHAPTER 16

The Working Director

Any person who is doing a good job as the director of an early childhood education center is involved in all the jobs described in this text—from enrolling children to evaluating staff, from budgeting to taking inventory, and from maintaining a physical plant to bandaging a child's scraped knee. The director's job includes all aspects of program and people maintenance. To do any one of these tasks, a director must have skills and knowledge; to do all of them requires stamina, understanding, and organization; and to do all of them effectively demands exceptional interpersonal skills, as has been emphasized throughout this text. These skills enable the director to bring the best to several groups of people: parents, children, staff members, board members, and the community. In turn, serving as a model of these skills encourages those same people to give their best to the center. The effective director realizes that an early childhood education center can never be a one-person

Photo above Every director has a limited amount of time in which to do numerous tasks and develop many relationships. This work can be accomplished most effectively if the director is well organized. (Photo by Anne G. Dorsey)

operation. There is a network of caring that transcends the day-to-day chores and makes being a part of a center worthwhile.

ADMINISTRATIVE STYLES AND ROLES

Although all directors are responsible for administering a program, their administrative styles are unique, and therefore the outcomes of their programs are markedly different. Some of the differences are based on the roles that are assigned to the directors, while others are based on the personalities of the directors.

Roles

If all the directors of centers in one state or county were to gather and discuss their roles, the job descriptions would undoubtedly cover a very wide range of categories. Some directors teach, perhaps spending half of every day in their own classrooms. Others never teach but are responsible for several centers; they travel between the centers, keeping aware of two or more sets of circumstances, staff members, children, equipment lists, and so forth. Some may be responsible to an industry, to a corporate system, to a public school principal, or to a parent co-operative association, while others are proprietors and owners.

Some directors make all the policy and procedure decisions; others are in settings where some policy is set by a school system or corporate managing team. In other situations every procedural detail is administered by the board. A director in a large center may have an assistant director, secretary, receptionist, and a cook; however, a director of a small center often does all the record keeping, supervising, telephone answering, and meal preparation. Directors work with half-day programs, full-day programs, or perhaps even twenty-four-hour care programs. The programs may offer care for infants and toddlers or for older children, both before and after school. Sick child care or care of children with special needs may be provided.

The financial plan may involve proprietary or agency operation, and may or may not be organized to make a profit. Program goals range from providing a safe place where children are cared for to furnishing total developmental services for children, including medical and dental care, social services, screening and therapy, and activities that promote intellectual, motor, emotional, social, and moral development.

Both the expectations of the clients served by the program and the expectations of the community will affect the center director's role. Some communities appreciate a director who is active in participating in the affairs of their community council, in lobbying for legislative reform and in seeing that the cultural backgrounds of the children are preserved. Others prefer a director

DIRECTOR'S CORNER

"Wearing two hats (director and teacher) can be a challenge. Probably most people feel that there's never enough time to get things done. My relationship with the teachers is pretty good. When I came on as director, I did some things that were really positive for the program and maybe the teachers appreciated the changes they saw."

Director, parent co-op

who focuses strictly on center business or on preparing children to deal with the demands of the elementary school. Directors must blend their personal philosophies with those of the community to achieve a balance. This blending can occur only if a potential director and a board explore each others' philosophies before agreeing on the responsibility for administering a particular program. If the philosophies of the director and those of the center are truly incompatible, one or the other must be changed.

Sometimes the director is confronted with a conflict between the two roles. The job description and the expectations of the people connected with the center may dictate that the director be present to greet teachers, parents, and children each day and to bid them good-bye each evening. In between, the director may be expected to be present in case an emergency arises. Simultaneously, however, there are obligations to the profession and to the community that must be met. The director may be asked to speak to a luncheon meeting of a community group that is ready to make a contribution to the center, to attend a board meeting of a local professional association, or to provide information at a session called by the diagnostic clinic to plan for one of the children with special needs who attends the early childhood education center.

Directors, especially those with experience, also have a responsibility to serve as child advocates. Although the NAEYC Code of Ethical Conduct calls on all who work with young children to "acknowledge an obligation to serve as a voice for children everywhere,"[1] directors are more likely to have opportunities to see the broader picture of events in the community and beyond. They can keep informed about important legislative issues and about conditions affecting children and families by reading professional journals and newsletters and by being knowledgeable about local and national news. For example, NAEYC publishes *Alert*, an up-to-the-minute report of legislative proposals, etc. and a call to action. Because directors are leaders and models, not only in their own centers, but throughout the community, staff, parents, and others often look to them for information about advocacy issues. Some directors may post information for staff and parents, others may make a concerted effort to involve people in an action plan. Some may write letters to the editor or to legislators, while others may testify before various governmental groups. Each director needs to determine a level of involvement as an advocate, balancing that with their responsibilities to the center and with their personal needs.

Although most directors work more than a forty-hour week, it is unreasonable and unwise to expect them to devote evening and weekend hours to their jobs on a regular basis. Directors who spend too much time on the job may become physically and emotionally exhausted, leading to ineffectiveness. As models for staff members, directors must demonstrate that they balance meeting personal and center needs.

Personal Qualities

Directors may become enmeshed in unreasonable workloads because they have become personally involved in the center's work. An effective director should be closely involved with the activities of the center, while maintaining distance—a difficult combination to attain. The primary reason for the difficulty in achieving this balance is that good directors assume their role largely because they care about people, and yet at times they find that there are overwhelming numbers of people who require care. This caring is exemplified in their willingness to do the mundane, such as changing a diaper when a teacher is dealing with a crisis or mopping up the kitchen when the dishwasher overflows just before lunch. Caring is apparent when the director assumes the role of learner, as well as teacher, and keeps abreast of current research while providing this information to staff when it is relevant. Caring is demonstrated by paying attention to detail—spelling an unusual name correctly, ordering the special food a teacher would like for a project, seeing that each board and staff member is notified of an early childhood lecture that is being held in the community. Caring is regarding the operation of the center in a serious manner, yet maintaining a sense of humor.

For some people, caring is shown in an exuberant manner, with lots of enthusiastic conversation, hugging, and facial animation. Others, who are just as caring, are quiet, seem somewhat reserved, and perhaps move into a relationship more slowly. Directors may have other combinations of personal qualities, but the genuine and essential ability to care is the one that makes the difference.

An interesting aspect of caring is that it may be misunderstood. Because they are concerned for others, directors may sometimes have to adjust the style in which they relate to people. For example, some individuals may be uncomfortable about being touched; if the director unknowingly puts an arm around people who feel this way, they may be annoyed or insulted and be unable to accept the care and concern that is intended.

Being a caring person in the face of all the responsibilities of directing a center can be difficult. The caring director is constantly helping others by listening and providing emotional support for both children and adults and may well need people to respond in kind. Those individuals who become effective directors usually enjoy giving to others; they seem to thrive on it. However, because they are seen at the center as the source of so much giving, they must seek sustenance from either the caring network at the center or a relative or friend outside the center. Even those people who freely and happily give of themselves need, at times, to receive support and encouragement through recognition and understanding.

Directing can be stressful because the director, although surrounded by people, is in a very

1 S. Feeney and K. Kipnis, *Code of Ethical Conduct & Statement of Commitment: Guidelines for Responsible Behavior in Early Childhood Education,* Washington, D.C.: National Association for the Education of Young Children, 1990.

real sense an isolate. She has no peers in the center and no matter how loved and respected, is "the boss." It would be inappropriate for the director to confide in one particular staff member and some of the information with which she works cannot be shared with anyone at the center. Some directors have established a network of directors. They meet, perhaps monthly, for a relaxing lunch and conversation. There is reassurance in knowing that other directors have to report child abuse, experience staff turnover, have too many forms to fill out, and have considered quitting. As a group directors can create ways to solve problems, to support one another, and to heighten community awareness regarding the needs of young children and their caregivers.

In order to be effective leaders, directors must ensure that their own needs are met. Being a martyr, even a cheerful martyr, who never takes vacation or sick days, may in fact lead staff to feel somewhat guilty when they recognize and meet their own needs. Competent directors serve as models of balance.

PROGRAM MAINTENANCE

Although a broad range of roles may be assigned to directors and although they may bring a variety of personal qualities to these roles, every director is responsible for program maintenance. This task, whatever its parameters, is possible only when the director is skilled and knowledgeable. Throughout this text, the information essential to doing the work of a center director has been discussed. This information, when combined with some teaching and administrative experience, should help you perform the tasks that are necessary for efficient program maintenance. The tasks are:

1. Develop goals and objectives in relation to the center's philosophy, placing emphasis on the needs of clients
2. Work with staff to plan a curriculum to meet the objectives of the center
3. Develop a positive working relationship with the board of directors and its committees, placing emphasis on communicating the center's accomplishments and needs to the board

4. Establish policies for center operation or become familiar with policies established by the center board, parent corporation, board of education or other sponsor
5. Draw up procedures for implementation of policies
6. Prepare and maintain a manual for board and staff members
7. Work with licensing agents to meet applicable licensing regulations
8. Provide adequate insurance coverage
9. Comply with all local, state, and federal laws relating to the center's operation
10. Establish and operate within a workable budget
11. Keep accurate financial records
12. Pay bills and prepare payroll
13. Collect tuition
14. Write proposals and seek other funds for operation of the center
15. Locate and maintain suitable physical facilities for the center's program
16. Order and maintain equipment
17. Publicize the center
18. Enroll and group the children
19. Employ appropriate staff
20. Evaluate the program, the staff members, and the children's progress
21. Develop an effective communication system among staff members through regular staff meetings, conferences, and informal conversations
22. Provide in-service training for staff and volunteers
23. Fill roles of other staff members in emergency situations
24. Plan and implement a parent program that is responsive to parents' needs and interests
25. Explain the center's program to the community
26. Participate in professional organizations
27. Continue professional development through reading and attending pertinent courses, workshops, conferences, and lectures

PEOPLE MAINTENANCE

Directors sometimes acquire program-maintenance skills and stop there, failing to realize the importance of people-maintenance skills. Centers can and do run, at least for a while, without people maintenance; however, centers that lack program maintenance quickly close their doors. Yet people maintenance is at the very heart of a worthwhile early childhood education program.

Directors can enhance their people maintenance effectiveness by developing an understanding of their own interpersonal styles. They will also benefit from studying various approaches to management, analyzing their own managerial styles and determining their strengths and weaknesses in these areas. Most directors have had limited opportunities to acquire this information since directors often move into administrative roles because they have been effective as teachers.

Fortunately many seminars, books, and video and audio cassettes are available to enable directors to learn about interpersonal styles and management approaches. The center board of directors may be willing to fund some training opportunities for the director, particularly if board members themselves understand and use this type of information. Possibly a board member could furnish training or related materials.

Another option is to provide total staff or joint board/staff training in an approach such as Total Quality Management. This training, if well done, should lead to confirming the director's role as leader, while establishing the responsibility of each staff member for the success of the center's program and the responsibility of the director to see that staff are involved in decision making and that their ideas are valued and accepted.

The staff and board members who agree to commit to a total quality type of philosophy use as a starting point the concept that their customers (children and families) are their first priority. By extension, a priority of directors must be staff satisfaction and a priority of the board must be director and staff satisfaction. This approach works well when everyone understands it and accepts this basic principle.

Directors who are quite comfortable with a very authoritarian role may find it difficult or impossible to relinquish that role, just as teachers who are convinced that a teacher-directed approach is the only appropriate way to work with children may be unable to provide choices

for children. Directors who are willing to invest time and effort in learning about management will usually find that they are far more able to lead the staff and clients in ways that are more satisfying to everyone and that the responsibility for the smooth running of the center will no longer rest primarily with one person.

The staff-oriented director plans time each day to visit each classroom, to greet each staff member, and to acknowledge their efforts and successes. She coaches and supports them as they develop new understandings and skills and provides honest, sensitive feedback. The staff-oriented director remembers and relates to events and incidents that are significant to staff, children, and families. It may be commenting to a teacher about how well she managed a frightened child during a thunderstorm by describing specifically the effective approach the teacher used. Perhaps the director stops to greet a child who is proudly bringing his rabbit to school for a visit. Maybe the director phones a father to thank him for organizing a book fair to benefit the center.

Tending to the personal and professional development of the people associated with a center's program is seminal to the success of the program. The manner in which the director carries out people-maintenance tasks is a major contributing factor in program maintenance and vice versa. There is a delicate balance between successfully dealing with the mechanics of efficient program operation and simultaneously creating a caring environment for adults and children.

A director can have the human relations skills, care for others, ask for their ideas and opinions, encourage them to try new methods, and provide them with positive feedback. But if that same director does not have the skills and knowledge to accomplish the huge amount of work required of an administrator, the program cannot succeed. Similarly, the director who is task oriented, skilled, and knowledgeable may conduct a center that provides services but never really addresses or satisfies peoples' needs. Obviously, the director must combine work orientation skills with communication skills. If skills in either area are lacking, precious time will be wasted doing jobs or rebuilding relationships. Meanwhile, the children will not receive the excellent care they deserve.

MANAGEMENT TOOLS

Every director has a limited amount of time in which to do numerous tasks and develop many relationships. This work can be accomplished most effectively if the director is well organized. Then, when the inevitable unexpected event occurs, the director will be in a position that is stable enough to withstand the demands of the crisis. For example, the director whose financial records are in order may not have extra cash available to replace a broken water heater but at least is better prepared to adjust other budget categories to provide the funds. The disorganized director may not even know what funds and expenses will occur within the next few months in order to adjust the budget to meet the financial crisis. An efficient director can comfortably take time to listen to a group of excited children who burst into the office describing all the worms they found on the sidewalk, but a disorganized administrator may be too busy planning menus that are already overdue. It is obvious that administration will not always run smoothly for any director; however, the director who knows about appropriate techniques and uses them is certainly better prepared to cope effectively with the hubbub that is often evident in a child care center.

The use of several management tools can enable directors to administer programs effectively. These tools include policies and procedures manuals and time-use skills.

Policies and Procedures Manual

A manual containing all the center's policies and procedures facilitates the administrator's job. Generally, the board members make policies and the director develops procedures for implementation. For example, the board may establish a policy to admit any child between the ages of three and five who can profit from the center's program. The director then establishes the procedures that are necessary to accomplish the children's enrollment, such as plans for informing the community, distributing and receiving enrollment forms, and notifying parents that their child has been accepted or that the center is full. The director also designs the necessary forms and includes copies in the manual.

When procedures are overly detailed or cover self-explanatory material, they become burdensome and may even be neglected or circumvented by staff members. For example, teachers may be required to fill out a lengthy form to request permission to purchase something for which they will be reimbursed from petty cash; they might also be required to fill out another form after having purchased the item. At this point, some teachers may decide not to bother with purchasing needed items for their classrooms; they can carry their reaction one step further by disregarding the otherwise accepted procedures for using materials from the central storeroom. It is natural to anticipate that some established procedures will be unpopular with the staff, but if directors are open about why the procedures are important and if they are careful about limiting the number of procedures to be followed, they will find that staff members are willing to comply.

Staff input prior to the establishment of procedures is usual, although the director may still need to make some independent decisions. When directors focus on their own need for power rather than on the establishment of procedures that will ensure the smooth running of an operation, it becomes impossible for the staff to feel respected. Staff members for whom every procedure is spelled out have no freedom. How then can they be expected to offer freedom to the children with whom they work?

Other Contents. In addition to policies and procedures, the manual contains the center's bylaws, job descriptions, salary schedules, and information about the center, such as philosophy, goals, sponsorship, funding, and perhaps a brief history. If the manual is large, a table of contents and an index are helpful. Placing all materials in a loose-leaf binder enables staff members to add and delete pages as necessary. Each staff and board member receives a manual upon initial affiliation with the center, and it is the holder's responsibility to keep the manual up to date and to return it to the center when vacating the board or staff position.

Time-Use Skills

Some directors study time management as a tool to use in allocating available time wisely.

The board may provide tuition or released time for a director to attend a time-management course or seminar. Several time-management techniques can be acquired easily and put to immediate use.

Analyzing Use of Time. As a beginning, directors can analyze how they spend their time by writing down in detail everything they do for several days. The next step is to make a judgment about which of the activities have not been enjoyed, have not been done well, or have not been related either to the personal goals of the director or the goals of the center. When time is frittered away on such activities, less time is available to invest in other more productive activities. The individual alone can decide which activities should take priority. In some businesses listening to a client discuss an emotional problem would be considered a waste of the administrator's time. In early childhood education, with its focus on children and families, time that the director spends listening may be the most effective use of the available administrative time.

Although some of the director's tasks may not be appealing, they may need to be done. A director can, at least, recognize how much time must be devoted to undesirable tasks; then this amount of time can be put into perspective. Of course, if the majority of tasks seem undesirable, the director may choose to change jobs.

Grouping and Assigning Tasks. The director who needs to economize on time may also decide to make an effort to read and answer all mail, place outgoing phone calls, and record financial transactions at a specified time each day. Directors who allocate time for these types of chores and establish the policy that they are not to be disturbed during that time will probably have more time for meeting people's needs during the rest of the day.

Directors should also consider which jobs they must do and which jobs they can delegate to someone else. For example, could the janitor inform the director of supplies that are needed on a regularly scheduled basis rather than having the director do this checking? Perhaps the receptionist can be trained to respond to the general calls for information about the center rather than involving the director in a routine

REFLECTIONS

Imagine that you have planned to spend the evening writing a term paper that is due the following day. A friend phones. He is terribly upset about his wife's serious illness. Think about what you might do.

Now imagine that at 3:00 P.M. you, as an early childhood center director, are greeted by a teacher who is leaving for the day and who wants to talk about her husband, who has just lost his job. You had planned to spend the rest of the afternoon working on the major equipment order that is needed for a board committee report the following morning. You may choose:

1. to listen to the teacher
2. to tell the teacher that you do not have time to listen because of the report you must prepare
3. to schedule time the following afternoon to listen to the teacher
4. some other plan

Any of these choices could be appropriate; the director must make the best choice. But both the directors who always find themselves too busy to listen and those who always find themselves spending so much time listening that they must work all evening must analyze why their scheduling problems recur. Think about your own reaction to this situation.

conversation about when the center is open and the ages of children who are served.

Once the center's operation is reasonably under control, additional staff people can be trained to fill the director's role in his or her absence, thus allowing the director to move out into the wider community on occasion. It is not appropriate to insist that other staff people do the director's work, but it is appropriate to begin to train them to

—handling calls from prospective parents

—maintaining the physical plant

—checking in with teachers and children

—keeping up-to-date records

The director's job includes all aspects of the program and people maintenance.

assume the role of director temporarily. In this way both parties can benefit professionally.

Planning a Time Line. One of the ways a director develops efficiency is through the development of a time line. Jobs that must be done on a regular basis are scheduled, and then the director does them according to the schedule. This simple concept curtails procrastination by helping the director recognize that, when a job that is scheduled this week is postponed because it is distasteful, time and energy are going to be spent thinking about it anyway. Since the job must be completed eventually, no time is saved by waiting until next week; nor does the job become easier.

A suggested time line for a working director appears in Working Paper 16-5. Each director must develop a time line based on the personal responsibilities that are unique to the type of program and the client's needs. No matter which jobs and time frames are included, writing a time line gives the director and others a clear picture of the work to be done. The time line can be flexible when circumstances warrant, but, basically the goal is to adhere to the plan so that regularly scheduled tasks will be completed and time for working with people will be made available.

In Chapter 1, you learned about the importance of the director's interpersonal relationships and that they set the tone for the center. Now as you reach the last chapter of this text, the theme is again emphasized. It may seem impossible that a director really could focus on establishing a "we" feeling, when Chapters 2 through 15 have presented an almost overwhelming set of director responsibilities. Nonetheless, directors who know what is involved in the job, who work to acquire the necessary knowledge and skills and who use a managerial approach that reflects an understanding of the needs of staff and clients are found in nearly every community.

These competent and successful directors know that being a director is exhausting,
and frequently challenging,
sometimes, frightening,
never boring,
sometimes lonely,
many times hectic,
and, yes, even fun.
They know that being a director, a *really good director*,
a leader,
a manager,
a model,
a coach,
and a supporter
is hard work and time-consuming.
Being a director is just often enough
deeply satisfying,
even exhilarting,
and richly rewarding!

SUMMARY

An effective director is a person who combines skills, knowledge, and caring. Although directors fill a variety of roles in countless styles, no effective director can let either the management and operation of the center or the care of and communication with people occupy an inappropriate proportion of time. For each director in each situation, personal decisions must be made about the style of directing.

Two tools that enable the director to blend program maintenance and people maintenance are the policies and procedures manual and time-management techniques. Each director must develop an appropriate balance so that the program maintenance, which must be done, does not override the people maintenance. Because people maintenance can readily be overlooked by directors who find themselves in the throes of program maintenance, directors must develop skills that enable them to excel at program maintenance. Only then will they have the time and energy to devote to people maintenance, which is the very essence of a quality child care program.

Class Assignments

1. Keep a log of how you spend your time for two days. Be sure to write down everything you do and the amount of time each activity takes. Look at your list. Did you do all the things you wanted to do during those two days? If not, which activities could you have omitted or shortened to provide time for other interests?

   Directors use this same technique in evaluating their use of time on the job. You can use it periodically to check on how much time you actually spend doing what you want and need to do and how much time you devote to other activities.

2. Visit the director of an early childhood education center. Discuss approximately how much time is spent on various aspects of the job, such as keeping financial records, communicating with parents, staff members, children, and board members, and handling emergencies. Write your findings on Working Paper 16-1.

3. Read the policy statement on celebration of holidays (Working Paper 16-2) and the outdoor play policy and procedures (Working Paper 16-3). Using Working Paper 16-4, write a policy statement for an early childhood education center on any topic of your choice. Then write procedures for implementation of that policy.

Class Exercises

1. Compare your findings from Class Assignment 2 with those of your classmates.

2. Discuss with a classmate the activities on which each of you would like to spend more time. Were there any similarities between the activities you each mentioned? To what did each of you attribute your lack of time for your favorite activities?

3. Discuss with three members of your class the kind of director you would like to be. Read the Sample Director's Time Line (Working Paper 16-5). On which of the director's roles would you like to spend the most time? Put a check mark next to those tasks which you would enjoy doing. Put an X on those you would not like to do. Compare your ideas with those of your classmates.

Working Paper 16-1

Director's Time Form

Name of Center _____

Name of person interviewed _____

Title of person interviewed _____

How much time is spent on keeping financial records? _____

How much time is spent on communicating with parents, staff, board members, or children? _____

How much time is spent handling emergencies? _____

Other information: _____

_____

Working Paper 16-2

Policy on Holiday Celebrations

The staff of the Children's Center met to discuss developmentally appropriate ways to celebrate holidays with three-year-old classes. We agreed that our policies are as follows:

1. Meeting the child's needs appropriately will be our first priority.
2. We will be sensitive to the interests and wishes of other school staff, parents, and community.
3. We will inform parents, principals, and staff of our plans and of our rationale and welcome dialogue on these issues.

Before doing Class Assignment 3, you may want to practice by writing some procedures for the above policy. Use the space below.

Working Paper 16-3

Policy Statement for Outdoor Play

The NAEYC policy statement on Developmentally Appropriate Practice states that outdoor experiences should be provided for all young children through age eight, on a daily basis. Because their physical development is occurring so rapidly, young children should go outside daily to practice large muscle skills, learn about outdoor environments, and experience freedom not always possible indoors. Outdoor time is an integral part of the curriculum and should be planned.[1]

Procedures for Implementation of Outdoor Policy

1. All children will go outdoors daily for at least 20 minutes. This time may be spent on the playground and/or on a walk. The outside time is to be viewed as an integral part of the curriculum. Therefore, planning for and discussion of that experience will be included in the Friday processing and lesson planning.
2. Parents will be informed that all children will be going out each day. Children not well enough to go outdoors are probably not well enough to be in school.
3. Plans will be made to provide caps, mittens, sweaters, etc. if needed.
4. Circumstances which might preclude daily outdoor play are:

   a. chill factor below freezing (32°F) at the time the children go outdoors
   b. steady rain or downpour. Length of stay outdoors will be adjusted on drizzly or snowy days
   c. during tornado watch or tornado warning periods

5. On days when circumstances do preclude going outdoors, opportunity for large motor activity and/or walks within the building will be provided. Therefore, alternative plans will be discussed during the Friday processing and lesson planning.

1 Bredekamp, S. (ed.), *Developmentally Appropriate Practice in Early Childhood Programs Serving Children from Birth Through Age 8, Expanded Edition,* Washington, D.C.: National Association for the Education of Young Children, 1987.

Working Paper 16-4

Policy Statement Form

Policy on _____
(Write the policy or policies on the topic you have chosen.)

Procedures: _____
(Write the procedures for implementation of the above policy.)

Working Paper 16-5

Sample Director's Time Line

Annual Tasks

Early Spring

Prepare budget and get board approval.

Determine salaries for following year.

Get staff contracts for following year.

Make arrangements for special summer activities for children.

Late Spring

Advertise for, interview, and hire replacement or additional staff.

Conduct open house for families of potential students.

Enroll children for autumn.

Conduct election of parent advisory committee.

Participate in election of new board members (if director has voting rights).

Set up calendar for following year.

End of School Year

Evaluate all staff.

Hold staff conferences.

Do self-evaluation.

Evaluate operation of the program.

Hold final parent meeting.

Assist teachers in evaluating children's progress and in holding conferences with parents.

Recognize volunteers.

Evaluate the center's goals (may be done biannually).

Clean, repair, and inventory equipment.

Order equipment and supplies for Autumn.

Thoroughly check building for needed maintenance and arrange to have this work done.

Summer

Assign teachers and children to groups and classrooms for September.

Apply for license renewal.

Check insurance coverage.

Arrange for medical, dental, and social services.

Autumn

Orient new staff.

Recruit and orient volunteers.

Distribute keys and supplies.

Place new equipment and supplies.

Arrange with colleges for student teachers.

Orient new children.

Working Paper 16-5 (*continued*)

Conduct opening parent meeting.
Interview substitutes and draw up new substitute list.
Check on children's and staff medical records.
Establish individual work plans and evaluate procedures with staff.
Plan supervision schedule.

Winter
Write proposals for following year.
Evaluate policies, make suggestions for changes to board.
Evaluate procedures. Plan changes for following year.

Monthly Tasks
Prepare financial report.
Check budget; make report to board.
Attend and participate in board meetings.
Plan menus.
Order non-perishable food.
Order supplies.
Check building and grounds and equipment; provide for required
    maintenance.
Review teachers' classroom plans (may be done weekly).
Send bills.
Receive tuition.
Pay bills.
Complete forms for funding and governmental agencies.
Attend professional meetings.
Prepare parent newsletter.
Collect attendance records.
Conduct fire drill.

Weekly Tasks
Prepare payroll (may be bi-weekly or monthly).
Supervise teachers (observe and confer).
Order fresh food.
Conduct staff meetings (may be bi-weekly).
Maintain bulletin board.

Daily Tasks
Greet each staff member at least briefly.
Talk with children and parents.
Record financial transactions.
Answer mail and phone calls.
Deal with crises.
Deal with the mundane.
Teach, including planning, implementing, and cleaning up (if included in job
    description).

Working Paper 16-5 (*continued*)

Periodically

Fill roles of absent staff.

Participate in fund raising.

Attend fund-raising events.

Conduct visitors' tours.

Arrange for in-service training.

Confer with college supervisor about student teachers.

Conduct meetings to discuss individual child.

Contact other agencies to develop rapport.

Participate in community activities, such as the opening of a neighborhood recreation center.

Obtain and disseminate information on legislation.

Inform legislators of your opinion on issues related to early childhood education.

Attend courses, professional conferences, and workshops.

Give workshops.

Lead parent groups.

Attend parent advisory meetings.

Recommend termination of employment of staff member, as necessary.

Do any weekly, monthly, or annual job as need arises (for example, interview potential staff member or enroll new child as openings for staff or children occur.

APPENDIX A

Partial List: Sources of Early Childhood Materials, Equipment and Supplies

Afro-American Publishing Co.
407 E. 25th Street, Suite 600
Chicago, IL 60616   (312) 791-1611

Angeles Toys, Inc.
9 Capper Drive
Dailey Industrial Park
Pacific, MO 63069-3604
   (314) 257-0533

Caedmon Publishers
Division of Harper & Row,
   Publishers
1000 Keystone Industrial Park
Scranton, PA 18512 (800) 331-3761

Child Care Computer Systems
Child Plus
5883 Glenridge Drive
Steito, GA 30328

Childcraft Education Corp.
20 Kilmar Road
Edison, NJ 08817   (908) 572-6100
   (800) 631-5652

Child Life Play Specialities, Inc.
55 Whitney Street, P.O. Box 527
Holliston, MA 01746   (800) 462-4445

Children's Press
5440 N. Cumberland Avenue
Chicago, IL 60656   (312) 693-0800
   (800) 621-1115

Clarion Books
Division of Houghton-Mifflin
205 Park Avenue S.
New York, NY 10003
   (212) 420-5800

Community Playthings
Rt. 213
Rifton, NY 12471   (914) 658-3141
   (800) 777-4244

Concept Wood
P.O. Box 27
Eustis, FL 32727-0027   (904) 735-0661

Constructive Playthings
1227 E. 119th Street
Grandview, MO 64030-1117
   (800) 448-4115

Creative Educational Surplus
9801 James Circle, Suite C
Bloomington, MN 55431
   (612) 884-6427

Developmental Learning Materials
   (DLM)
One DLM Park
Allen, TX 75002

Delmar Publishers, Inc.
3 Columbia Circle, Box 15015
Albany, NY 12212-5015
   (518) 464-3500   (800) 998-7498

Didax Educational Resources, Inc.
One Centennial Drive
Peabody, MA 01960   (508) 532-9060
   (800) 458-0024
   FAX: (508) 532-9277

Diversified Management Services, Inc.
301 Sovereign Ct., Suite 101
St. Louis, MO 63011
   (314) 227-4855

Educational Teaching Aids (ETA)
620 Lakeview Parkway
Vernon Hills, IL 60061   (708) 816-5050
   FAX: (312) 520-7243

Edumate-Educational Materials
2231 Moreno Blvd.
San Diego, CA 92110-4134

Environments, Inc.
P.O. Box 1348
Beaufort Industrial Park
Beaufort, SC 29901-1348
    (803) 846-8155   (800) EI-CHILD

Four Winds Press
(Macmillan)
866 3rd Avenue
New York, NY 10022
    (212) 702-2180

Greenwillow Books-WH. Morrow Co.
1350 Avenue of Americas
New York, NY 10019   (212) 261-6500

Gryphon House, Inc.
Early Childhood Books
P.O. Box 275 W.
Mt. Ranier, MD 20712

John R. Green
411 W. 6th Street
Covington, KY 41011
    (800) 354-9737

Harcourt Brace Javanovich, Inc.
1250 6th Avenue
San Diego, CA 92101

Harper & Row Publishers
10 E. 53rd Street
New York, NY 10022   (212) 207-7000

Holcomb's Educational Materials
3205 Harvard Avenue
    P.O. Box 94636
Cleveland, OH 44105-4636
    (216) 341-3000
    Ohio (800) 362-9907 or other
    (800) 321-2543

Houghton-Mifflin Publishers
2 Park Avenue
Boston, MA 02107

Johnson & Johnson Consumer
    Products, Inc.
P.O. Box 71687
Chicago, IL 60694   (800) 526-3967

Kaplan School Supply, Corp.
1310 Lewisville-Clemens Road
Lewisville, NC 27023   (919) 766-7374
    (800) 334-2014

Lexington Books/MacMillan
    Publishing
100 Front Street
Riverside, NJ 08075   (800) 257-5755

Little, Brown & Co.
34 Beacon Street
Boston, MA 02108-1493   (617) 227-0730

Micro Revisions, Inc.
5301 Hollister, Suite 170
Houston, TX 77040   (713) 690-6676

Mulberry Park, Inc.
The Children's Story Hour Media
    Catalogue
P.O. Box 4096, Dept. B103
Englewood, CO 80155   (303) 694-3618

New Horizons
P.O. Box 863
Lake Forest, IL 60045
    FAX: (708) 295-2968

Penguin USA (Lodster Books)
375 Hudson Street
New York, NY 10014   (212) 366-2000

Personalized Software
15311 La Paloma Drive
Houston, TX 77083   (713) 561-5427

Picture Book Studio/Simon Shuster
200 Old Tappan
Old Tappan, NJ 07675   (800) 223-2348

Playtime Equipment and School
    Supply, Inc.
5437 N. 103rd Street
Omaha, NE 68134   (800) 28-TEACH

SofterWare, Inc.
200 Office Center
Fort Washington, PA 19034-3309
    (215) 628-0400   (800) 848-3279

The Little Tikes Co.
2180 Barlow Road
Hudson, OH 44236-9984
    (216) 650-3250

The Preschool Source (Division of
    ABC School Supply)
3312 N. Berkeley Lake Road
P.O. Box 100019
Duluth, GA 30136-9419

Private Advantage: Center
    Management Software for
    Macintosh Computer
Mt. Taylor Programs
1305 N Dutton Avenue
Santa Rosa, CA 95401
    (800) 238-7015

The Wright Group, Inc.
19201 120th Avenue N.E.
Both Ell, WA 98011-9512
    (800) 523-2371

Things From Bell, Inc.
230 Mechanic Street
P.O. Box 206
Princeton, WI 54968-0206
    (414) 642-7337   (800) 543-1458

Redleaf Press
450 N. Syndicate, Suite 5
St. Paul, MN 55104-4125
    (800) 423-8309

Toys to Grow On/Lakeshore
    Learning Materials
2695 E. Dominguez Street,
    P.O. Box 6251
Carson, CA 90749   (800) 421-5354

William Morrow and Company,
    Inc.
1350 Avenue of the Americas
New York, NY 10019

Woodlite Design and Manufacturing,
    Inc.
105 S. Street Louis, P.O. Box 385
Elwood, IL 60421   (800) 826-3273

APPENDIX B

Partial List: Early Childhood Professional Organizations and Information Sources

Administration for Children, Youth
  and Families (ACYF)
Division of Child Care
370 L'Enfant Promenade, S.W.
Washington, D.C. 20447
  (202) 401-9326

Administration for Children, Youth
  and Families (ACYF)
Head Start Division
P.O. Box 1182
Washington, D.C. 20013

American Academy of Pediatrics
P.O. Box 927, 141 Northwest Point
  Blvd.
Elk Grove Village, IL 60007
  (800) 433-9016

American Association for Gifted
  Children
1121 W. Main Street, Suite 100
Durham, NC 27701   (919) 683-1400

American Association of School
  Administrators
1801 N. Moore Street
Arlington, VA 22209   (703) 528-0700

American Council of Education (ACE)
1785 Massachusetts Avenue, N.W.
Washington, D.C. 20036

American Educational Research
  Association (AERA)
1230 17th Street N.W.
Washington, D.C. 20036-3078
  (202) 223-9485

American Federation of Teachers (AFT)
555 New Jersey Avenue, N.W.
Washington, D.C. 20001
  (202) 879-4400

American Home Economics
  Association
P.O. Box 603
Gainsville, VA 22065   (703) 349-4676

American Management Association
135 W. 50th Street
New York, NY 10020   (212) 586-8100

American Montessori Society (AMS)
150 5th Avenue, Suite #203
New York, NY 10011   (212) 924-3209

American Medical Association
535 N. Dearborn Street
Chicago, IL 60610

American Speech, Language and
  Hearing Association
10801 Rockville Pike
Rockville, MD 20852   (800) 638-8255

Appalachian Regional Commission
1666 Connecticut Avenue, N.W.
Washington, D.C. 20235
  (202) 673-7893

Association for the Care of Children's
  Health
3615 Wisconsin Avenue, N.W.
Washington, D.C. 20016   (301) 654-6540

Association for Childhood Education
  International (ACEI)
11501 Georgia Avenue, Suite 315
Wheaton, MD 20902   (800) 423-3563

Association for Library Service to
  Children
American Library Association
55 W. Huron Street
Chicago, IL 60611

Association Montessori
  Internationale
170 W. Scholfield Road
Rochester, NY 14617-4599
  (716) 544-6709

Association Montessori
  Internationale
Koninginneweg 161
1075 CN Amsterdam
Holland   Phone: 31-20-679-8932

Association for Supervision and
   Curriculum Development
   (ASCD)
1250 N. Pitt Street
Alexandria, VA 22314-1403
   (703) 549-9110

California Child Care Resource and
   Referral Network
111 New Montgomery, 7th Floor
San Francisco, CA 94105
   (415) 882-0234

Centers for Disease Control
   & Prevention
1600 Clifton Rd. N.E.
Atlanta, GA 30333   (404) 639-3534

Center for Parenting Studies
Wheelock College
200 The Riverway
Boston, MA 02215-4176
   (617) 734-5200

Center for Urban Education
33 W. 42nd Street
New York, NY 10036

Child Care Law Center
22 2nd Street, 5th Floor
San Francisco, CA 94105
   (415) 495-5498

BURUD Associates, Inc.
Child Care Benefits Planning
56 E. Holly Street, Suite 215
Pasadena, CA 91103
   (818) 796-8258

Child Development Service Bureau
400 6th Street S.W.
Washington, D.C. 20201

Child Welfare League of America
   (CWLA)
440 1st Street N.W., Suite 310
Washington, D.C. 20001-2085
   (202) 638-2952

Children's Defense Fund
25 E. Street N.W.
Washington, D.C. 20001
   (202) 628-8787

Council for Early Childhood
   Professional Recognition (CDA)
1341 G Street, N.W., Suite 400
Washington, D.C. 20005-3105
   (800) 424-4310 or (202) 265-9090

Council for Exceptional Children
   (CEC)
Division of Early Childhood (DEC)
1920 Association Drive
Reston, VA 22091-1589
   (703) 620-3660

Council on Interracial Books for
   Children
P.O. Box 1263
New York, NY 10023   (212) 757-5339

Directors' Network
Exchange Press, Inc.
P.O. Box 2890
Redmond, WA 98073-2890
   (206) 883-9394   (800) 221-2864

Ecumenical Child Care Network
1119 Daphine Street, #5
New Orleans, LA 70116
   (504) 524-2688

Education Development Center
   (EDC)
55 Chapel Street
Newton, MA 02160

ERIC Clearinghouse on Elementary
   and Early Childhood Education
(ERIC/EECE)
University of Illinois, College of
   Education
805 W. Pennsylvania Avenue
Urbana, IL 61801-4897
   (217) 333-1386

ERIC Clearinghouse on Handicapped
   and Gifted Children
Council for Exceptional Children
1920 Association Drive
Reston, VA 22091-1589
   (703) 264-9474

ERIC Clearinghouse on Teacher
   Education
One Dupont Circle, N.W., Suite 610
Washington, D.C. 20036-1186

Gesell Institute for Human
   Development
310 Prospect Street
New Haven, CT 06511
   (203) 777-3481

Government Information Services
Education Funding Research Council
1611 N. Kent Street, Suite 508
Arlington, VA 22209   (703) 528-1082

Handicapped Children's Early
   Education Program (HCEEP)
Office of Special Education and
   Rehabilitation Services
U.S. Department of Education
Donohue Building
400 Maryland Avenue S.W.
Washington, D.C. 20202

High/Scope Educational Research
   Foundation
600 N. River Street
Ypsilanti, MI 48198-2898   (313) 485-
2000

Institute for Childhood Resources
210 Columbus Avenue, Room 611
San Francisco, CA 94133   (415) 864-
1169

International Child Resource Institute
1810 Hopkins Street
Berkeley, CA 94707   (510) 644-1000

International Reading Association
800 Barksdale Road, P.O. Box 8139
Newark, DE 19714-8139   (302) 731-1600

Jewish Publication Society of America
60 E. 42nd Street
New York, NY 10165

League Against Child Abuse
3605 3rd Street, Suite 109
Columbus, OH 43215   (614) 464-1500

National Academy of Early
   Childhood Programs
NAEYC
1509 16th Street, N.W.
Washington, D.C. 20036
   (202) 236-8777   (800) 424-2460

National Association for Child Care
   Management (NACCM)
104 Sweetwater Hills Drive
Longwood, FL 32779   (305) 862-7825

National Association of Child Care
   Professionals
Rt. 1, Box 273CL1
Edwards, MO 65326   (314) 345-3131

National Association for the
   Education of Young Children
   (NAEYC)
1509 16th Street, N.W.
Washington, D.C. 20036
   (202) 232-8777   (800) 424-2460

National Association of Elementary
School Principals
1615 Duke Street
Alexandria, VA 22314-3483
(703) 684-3345

National Association for Family Day
Care (NAFDC)
725 15th Street N.W., Suite 505
Washington, D.C. 20005-2201
(202) 347-3356

National Association of Hospital
Affiliated Child Care Programs
ATTN: J. Disterhoft
Parkside Children's Services
Lutheran General Hospital
9375 Church Street
Des Plaines, IL 60016   (708) 824-5180

National Association of State Boards
of Education
1012 Cameron Street
Alexandria, VA 22314   (703) 684-4000

National Black Child Development
Institute (NBCDI)
1023 15th Street N.W., Suite 600
Washington, D.C. 20005   (202) 387-1281

National Center for Clinical Infant
Programs
2000 11th Street N., Suite 380
Arlington, OK 22201-2500
(703) 528-4300

National Child Care Association
(NCCA)
1029 Railroad Street
Conyers, GA 30207 (800) 543-7161

National Child Labor Committee
1501 Broadway, Room 1111
New York, NY 10036   (212) 840-1801

National Coalition for Campus Child
Care, Inc.
UMW - P.O. Box 258
Cascade, WI 53011   (414) 528-7080

National Council of Jewish Women
(NCJW)
Center for the Child
53 W. 23rd Street, 6th Floor
New York, NY 10010   (212) 645-4048

National Dairy Council
10255 W. Higgins Road, Suite 900
Rosemont, IL 60018

National Education Association
(NEA)
1201 16th Street, N.W.
Washington, D.C. 20036

National Head Start Association
201 N. Union Street, Suite 320
Alexandria, VA 22314-2928
(703) 739-0875
FAX: (703) 739-0878

National Indian Education Advisory
Council
College of Education
University of New Mexico, Dr. J. Suma
Albuquerque, NM 87131
(505) 277-7781

National Institute of Child Health
and Human Development
National Institute of Health
Public Health Service
U.S. Department of Health and
Human Services
Bethesda, Maryland 20014

Non-Sexist Child Development
Project
Women's Action Alliance, Inc.
370 Lexington Avenue, Room 603
New York, NY 10017

North American Montessori Teachers
Association (NAMTA)
11424 Bellflower Road N.E.
Cleveland, OH 44106   (216) 421-1905

Office of Human Development
Services
U.S. Department of Health and
Human Services
309F Hubert H. Humphrey Building
200 Independence Avenue S.W.
Washington, D.C. 20201

Parent Cooperative Preschools
International, U.S. Office
P.O. Box 90410
Indianapolis, IN 46290-0140
(317) 849-0992

Puerto Rican Association for
Community Affairs, Inc.
411 E. 10th Street
New York, NY 10009

Save the Children
1447 Peachtree Street N.E., Suite 700
Atlanta, GA 30309   (404) 885-1578

School-Age Child Care Project
Wellesley College
Center for Research on Women
Wellesley, MA 02181-8201
(617) 283-1000   (617) 283-2500

Society for Research in Child
Development (SRCD)
at the University of Chicago Press
5720 S. Woodlawn Avenue
Chicago, IL 60637   (312) 702-7470

Southern Early Childhood
Association (SECA)
P.O. Box 56130
Little Rock, AR 72215-6130
(501) 663-0353

SUMMA Associates, Inc.
735 E. Guadalupe
Tempe, AZ 85283   (602) 820-9844

Superintendent of Documents
Government Printing Office
Washington, D.C. 20402-9325
(202) 783-3238

The Children's Book Council, Inc.
568 Broadway, Suite 404
New York, NY 10012
(212) 966-1990

The Feminist Press
at The City University of New York
311 E. 94th Street
New York, NY 10128   (212) 360-5790

U.S. Consumer Product Safety
Commission
Washington, D.C. 20207
Att. Office of Information and Public
Affairs   (800) 638-2772

U.S. Department of Education
400 Maryland Avenue, S.W., Room 2017
Washington, D.C. 20202-6132

U.S. Department of Health and
Human Services
Administration for Children Youth
and Families (ACYF)
Washington, D.C. 20201

U.S. National Committee of OMEP
World Organization for Early
Childhood Education
1314 G Street N.W.
Washington, D.C. 20005-3105
(202) 265-9090   (800) 424-4310

Women's Action Alliance, Inc.
370 Lexington Avenue
New York, NY 10017

Work/Family Directions, Inc.
930 Commonwealth Avenue West
Boston, MA 02215   (617) 278-4000

Work and Family Life
    Studies\Research Division
Bank Street College
610 W. 112th Street
New York, NY 10025   (212) 875-4400

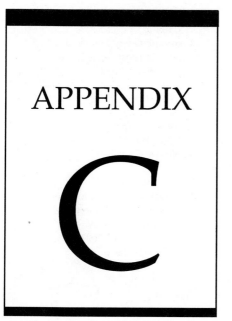

APPENDIX C

Partial List: Early Childhood Periodicals and Media

Periodicals

Access Child Care: News and Information on the Americans With Disabilities Act
Disability Resource Group, Inc.
8 East Long Street
Columbus, OH 43215-2914

Beginnings
Exchange Press, Inc.
P.O. Box 2890
Redmond, WA 98073-2890
 (206) 883-9394

Byte
Byte Publications, Inc.
70 Main Street
Peterborough, NH 03458
 (603) 924-9281

The Black Child Advocate
National Black Child Development Institute
1023 15th Street N.W., Suite 600
Washington, D.C. 20005
 (202) 387-1281

CCI&R Issues (Child Care Information and Referral)
Child Care Resource and Referral Network
2116 Campus Drive S.E.
Rochester, MN 55904

CDF Reports and *Child Watch Updates*
Children's Defense Fund
122 C Street N.W.
Washington, D.C. 20001

Campus Child Care News
National Coalition for Campus Child Care, Inc.
UMW - P.O. Box 255
Cascade, WI 53011 (414) 528-7080

Center for Parent Education Newsletter
55 Chapel Street
Newton, MA 02160 (617) 964-2442

Child Care Information Exchange
P.O. Box 2890
Redmond, WA 98073-2890
 (800) 221-2864

Child Care Quarterly
Day Care And Early Education
Human Sciences Press
233 Spring Street
New York, NY 10013 (212) 620-8000

Child Development
Society for Research in Child Development
5801 Ellis Avenue
Chicago, IL 60637

Child Health Alert
P.O. Box 338
New Highlands, MA 02161
 (617) 237-3310

Child Health Talk
National Black Child Development Institute, Inc.
1023 15th Street N.W., Suite 600
Washington, D.C. 20005

Child Welfare
Child Welfare League of America, Inc.
67 Irving Place
New York, NY 10003

Childhood Education
Association for Childhood Education
  International
11141 Georgia Avenue Suite 200
Wheaton, MD 20902

Children Today
Office of Human Development
  Services
Superintendent of Documents
U.S. Government Printing Office
Washington, D.C. 20402-9371

Children's Voice
Child Welfare League of America
440 First Street N.W., Suite 310
Washington, D.C. 20001-2085
  (202) 638-2952

Competence: News for CDA Community
Council for Early Childhood
  Professional Recognition
1341 G Street N.W., Suite 400
Washington, D.C. 20005   (800) 424-4310

Connections
Associates in Human Development,
  Inc.
P.O. Box 256
Palatine, IL 60078-0256   (312) 991-7740

Day Care and Early Education
Human Sciences Press, Inc.
233 Spring Street
New York, NY 10013   (212) 620-8000

Dimensions
SECA
P.O. Box 56130
Little Rock, AR 72215-6130
  (501) 663-0353

Early Childhood Research Quarterly
Ablex Publishing Corporation
355 Chestnut Street
Norwood, NJ 07648-2090
  (201) 767-8450 or 8455

Education Week
4301 Connecticut Avenue, N.W.
  Suite 250
Washington, D.C. 20077-6796

ERIC/EECE Newsletter
ERIC Clearinghouse on Elementary
  and Early Childhood Education
University of Illinois
805 W. Pennsylvania Avenue
Urbana, IL 61801-4897   (217) 333-1386

Exceptional Children
Council for Exceptional Children
920 Association Drive
Reston, VA 22091

Food and Nutrition
Superintendent of Documents
U.S. Government Printing Office
Washington, D.C. 20402-9325
  (202) 783-3238

Growing Child
22 North Second Street
P.O. Box 620
Lafayette, IN 47902-0620
  (317) 423-2624

Growing Child Research Review
22 N. Second Street
Lafayette, IN 47902-1100
  (317) 423-2624

InfoWorld (Intelligent Machine Journal)
InfoWorld
1060 Marsh Rd. Ste. C-200
Menlo Park, CA 94025
  (415) 328-4602

MacWorld
501 2nd Street, 5th Fl.
San Francisco, CA 94107
  (415) 243-0505

PC Magazine
Ziff-Davis Publishing Co.
25 W. 39th Street, 11th Floor
New York, NY 10018   (212) 503-5100

PC World
PCW Communications, Inc.
501 2nd Street
San Francisco, CA 94107
  (415) 243-0500

Report on Preschool Programs
951 Pershing Drive
Silver Springs, MD 20910-4464
  (301) 587-6300

Resource
High-Scope Educational Research
  Foundation
600 N. River Street
Ypsilanti, MI 48198-2890
  (313) 485-2000

School Age Notes
P.O. Box 120674
Nashville, TN 37212   (615) 292-4957

Software Digest Ratings Report
NSTL, Inc.
Plymouth Corp. Center, Box 1000
Plymouth Meeting, PA 19462
  (800) 328-2776

*Teaching Pre K–8: The Professional
  Magazine for Teachers*
Early Years, Inc.
325 Post Road W.
Westport, CT 06880

Young Children
National Association for the
  Education of Young Children
1509 16th Street, N.W.
Washington, D.C. 20036
  (800) 424-2460

Media

Associates In Human Development,
  Inc.
Rt. 1, Box 273CLI
Edwards, MO 65326   (314) 345-3600
Audio-cassettes:
The Person in Charge of Child Care
*Supervising Your Child Care Staff
  Effectively*
Success as an Effective Director
*How to Increase and Retain Your
  Center's Enrollment Through
  Marketing*

CRM/McGraw-Hill Films
P.O. Box 641
Del Mar, CA 92014   (619) 453-5000
Video-cassettes:
*Communicating Non-Defensively: Don't
  Take It Personally*
Communication: The Nonverbal Agenda
Decisions
A New Look at Motivation
*Performance Appraisal: The Human
  Dynamics*
Verbal Communication
Power of Listening

Teachers College Press
P.O. Box 2032
Colchester, VT 05449 (800) 488-2665
Video-Cassettes:
*Video Observations for Family Day Care
  Rating Scale*
*Video Observations for Early Childhood
  Environment Rating Scale*
*Video Observations for Infant/Toddler
  Environment Rating Scale*

DIRECTOR'S LIBRARY[1]

Leading People

Early Childhood Directors Association. *S.O.S. Kit for Directors.* St. Paul, MN: Resources for Child Caring (distributed by Toys'n Things Press), 1987.

Practical answers to directors' most frquently encountered problems in supervising, organizing, and supporting staff.

Gordon, Thomas. *Leadership Effectiveness Training (LET).* New York: G. P. Putnam, 1977.

The basic skills for effective interpersonal communication, including active listening, "I" messages, and no-lose problem solving are covered. These skills are analogues to those covered in Gordon's *Teacher Effectiveness Training* and *Parent Effectiveness Training.*

Jones, Elizabeth. *Teaching Adults.* Washington, DC, 1986.

Although this is a story based on the author's experience as a teacher of child development in a university setting, the notions about building trusting relationships, empowering learners, and trusting the learners' potential have implications for parent education, staff development and in-service training.

McGregor, Douglas. *The Human Side of Enterprise.* New York: McGraw-Hill, 1960.

A management classic. This book makes a persuasive case for abandoning traditional authoritarian leadership approaches and focusing instead on employees' abilities to direct their own performance.

Steinmetz, Lawrence L. *Managing the Marginal and Unsatisfactory Performer* (2nd ed.). Reading, MA: Addison-Wesley, 1985.

An in-depth look at the supervision of difficult workers. This book looks at the issue both from theoretical (motivational and personality theories) and practical (identification, appraisal, supervision, counseling, and severance) perspectives.

Working With Staff, Board, Community and Parents

Caruso, J. J. *Supervision in Early Childhood Education: A Developmental Perspective.* New York: Teachers College Press, 1986.

This book addresses supervisory issues pertinent to personnel in both public and private settings. The focus of this book is staff

1 Adapted with permission from Child Care Information Exchange, P.O. Box 2890, Redmond, WA 98073

...oth descriptive and

...J. Fuqua (eds). *Making*
...*ing, Evalauation and the*
...v York: Teachers College

...the current status of the
...d recommendations on how
to pro... ...ve changes. Issues dealt with
include envi... ...ments, caregivers, marketing,
evaluation, regulation, training, consultation,
and information and referral.

Jones, Elizabeth (ed.). *Growing Teachers: Partnerships in Staff Development.* NAEYC, 1993.

This book applies a constructivist model for staff development. It describes activities which are open in design; where philosophy and process are defined, but not outcomes. Using these approaches, teachers are expected to participate actively in the construction of knowledge about their work and about how they can grow professionally.

Jorde-Bloom, P., Marilyn Sheerer, and Joan Britz. *Blueprint for Action: Achieving Center-Based Change through Staff Development.* New Horizons Press (distributed by Gryphon House, Inc.), 1991.

This book does not offer "quick fixes" or prescriptions for improving relationships in a center. Rather it offers a comprehensive method for analyzing program components which will help with diagnosing organizational problems and selecting ways to implement and evaluate progress.

Jorde-Bloom, P. *A Great Place to Work: Improving Conditions for Staff in Young Children's Programs.* NAEYC, 1988.

Directors concerned about retaining qualified staff will find this book helpful. It provides information on the kind of environments that are conducive to professional and personal fulfillment.

National Directory of Children, Youth & Families Services (9th edition). P.O. Box 1837, Longmont, CO 80502-1837, 1993–94.

This is a current and up-to-date resource to State, County and Federal agencies and services for children, youth and families. It includes names, addresses, phone numbers and fax numbers for all agencies and services listed.

Warger, Cynthia (ed.). *A Resource Guide to Public School Early Childhood Programs.* Alexandria, VA: Association for Supervision and Curriculum Development (ASCD), 1988.

The purpose of this collection of articles is to address issues and concerns that surround decisions that administrators and teachers must make regarding preschools in public schools. Discussion of appropriate practice and concerns about pressures on young children is followed by descriptions of nineteen programs in public schools.

Watkins, Kathleen P. and Lucius Durant, Jr. *Preschool Directors Staff Development Handbook.* West Nyack, N.Y.: The Center for Applied Research in Education, 1987.

This guide provides practical techniques and materials for improving staff development and in-service training. It includes material on leadership styles, and also discusses the use of staff development as a means of motivating change.

Financial Management and Fund Raising

American Appraisal Associates, Inc. *Appraisal of an Operating Day-Care Center: Real Estate Valuation Guide.* 525 E. Michigan Street, P.O. Box 664, Milwaukee, WI 53201, 1986.

This booklet is designed to facilitate the appraisal of the real estate, equipment and the operation itself of a child care center. There is discussion of three valuation approaches—the cost approach, the income approach, and the market data approach.

Children's Defense Fund. *An Advocate's Guide to Fund Raising.* Children's Defense Fund Publications, 1990.

This booklet covers the basics of how to raise money from foundations, corporations, and individuals.

Finn, Matia. *Fundraising for Early Childhood Programs: Getting Started and Getting Results.* Washington, DC: NAEYC, 1982.

This booklet describes techniques used by nonprofit institutions to raise money by contacting sources of support including individual donors, corporations, foundations and government. It also includes a section on proposal writing and an updated bibliography.

Gross, Malvern, and William Warshauer. *Financial and Accounting Guide for Nonprofit Organizations.* New York: John Wiley and Sons, 1983.

Comprehensive, well-written resource. Detailed advice on cash, accrual, and fund accounting; financial statements; budgeting; internal control; tax requirements; and book-keeping.

Morgan, Gwen. *Managing the Day Care Dollars: A Financial Handbook.* Cambridge, MA.: Steam Press, 1982.

A practical guide to financial management in the child care setting. Addresses budgeting, accounting, financial statements, and meeting insurance needs.

National Governors' Association. *Taking Care: State Developments in Child Care.* Center for Policy Research, Washington, DC.

This report summarizes state funding resources for child care services as states begin to implement the federally mandated Family Support Act. Citing evidence from a recent survey, the report suggests that states will continue to expand their role as regulators, system builders, and employers in support of child care assistance for families.

Young, Joyce. *Fundraising for Non-Profit Groups.* Seattle, WA: Self-Counsel Press, 1981.

A practical fundraising guide with ideas on developing strategies, approaching corporations, foundations, and government agencies; direct mail solicitation; and fundraising in small communities.

Children With Special Needs

Allen, K. Eileen. *The Exceptional Child: Mainstreaming in Childhood Education* (2nd ed.). Delmar, 1992.

Although this book focuses on mainstreaming special needs children, emphasis is on teachers having a thorough knowledge of normal growth and development as a major avenue for creating developmentally appropriate programs for children who are "at risk" or have developmental problems.

Child Care Law Center. *Caring for Children with Special Needs: The American's With Disabilities Act and Child Care.* ADA Series, 1993.

A well-written booklet which discusses admitting and accommodating special needs children plus a discussion of liability and record-keeping issues when children with disabilities are enrolled. The booklet contains an extensive list of resources for center directors.

Meisels, Samuel J. and Sally Provence. *Screening and Assessment: Guidelines for Identifying Young Disabled and Developmentally Vulnerable Children and Their Families.* Zero To Three/National Center for Clinical Infant Programs, 1989.

These guidelines identify and assess children who should participate in programs related to the infant-toddler and preschool components of the Individuals with Disabilities Education Act. It focuses on the rationale, core components and guidelines for establishing a system of screening and assessing children with disabilities and those who are developmentally vulnerable, birth through age five.

Health, Safety, and Sick Child Care

American Academy of Pediatrics. *Report of the Committee on Infectious Diseases* (20th edition). 1986.

This manual and subsequent updated policies from AAP provide specific criteria for exclusion of children with infectious diseases from child care centers.

Child Welfare League of America. *Serving Children With HIV Infection in Child Day Care: A Guide for Center-Based and Family Day Care Providers.* 1991.

This book presents a straightforward and reassuring approach to working with HIV-infected children and their families. It provides information on how to safeguard children, families and staff while meeting the needs of HIV infected children.

Moratz, Lynn R., Jeanettia M. Rush, and Marie Z. Cross, *Health, Safety and Nutrition* (3rd ed.). Delmar, 1993.

This up-to-date, comprehensive text covers the essential aspects of health, safety, and nutrition for young children. It includes material on infant nutrition, AIDS, and sanitary procedures in group care facilities.

National Center for Prevention Services. *Immunization: National Resource Directory: Informational and Educational Materials for Health Care Professionals and the General Public.* U.S. Department of Health and Human Services, Centers for Disease Control, 1993.

This directory contains names, addresses and phone numbers for organizations which distribute informational and educational materials on immunizations.

National Association for the Education of Young Children. *Healthy Young Children: A Manual for Programs.* Abby Shapiro Kendrick, Roxanne Kaufman, & Katherine P. Messenger (eds.), 1988.

This excellent manual is a reference and resource guide to help you meet your health and safety responsibilities. The information reflects the current research and recommendations from experts in both health and early childhood education.

Work/Family Directions. *A Little Bit Under the Weather: A Look at Care for Mildly Ill Children.* 1986.

A comprehensive coverage of the need for sick child care and how it is viewed by child care professionals, families, employers, medical professionals and the child.

Infant/Toddler Care

Godwin, Annabelle and Lorraine Schrag. *Setting Up for Infant Care: Guidelines for Centers and Family Day Care Homes.* Washington, DC: NAEYC, 1988.

This collection of articles by practitioners describes quality care for infants and toddlers, and includes examples of kinds of equipment, personnel practices, uses of time and space, health and safety practices, and budget information for both center-based and family day care home infant/toddler care.

Greenberg, Polly. *Character Development: Encouraging Self-Esteem and Self-Discipline in Infants, Toddlers, and Two-Year-Olds.* NAEYC, 1991.

The twelve essays in this book examine what infants and toddlers need and how care can fill those needs in a high quality, respectful way.

Evaluation

Bredekamp, S. and T. Rosegrant (eds.). *Reaching Potentials: Appropriate Curriculum and Assessment for Young Children,* Vol.1. NAEYC, 1992.

This book presents guidelines for curriculum and assessment practices which will make it more likely for both teachers and children to reach their potentials.

Jorde-Bloom, Paula. *Improving the Quality of Work Life: A Guide for Enhancing Organizational Climate in the Early Childhood Setting.* Early Childhood Professional Development Project, National College of Education, 2840 Sheridan Road, Evanston IL 60201, 1986.

After an overview of the concept of organizational climate as it relates to the quality of work life in the early childhood setting, an assessment tool for measuring organizational climate is provided. Helpful suggestions for how a center director can improve the overall quality of work life are also included.

Planning Spaces

Greenman, Jim. *Caring Spaces, Learning Places: Children's Environments that Work.* Redmond, WA: Exchange Press, 1988.

This is a helpful guide to planning spaces for young children. It is full of ideas and observations as well as problems and solutions for those responsible for planning spaces for child care.

Vergeront, Jeanne. *Places and Spaces for Preschool and Primary (Indoors)* and *Places and Spaces for Preschool and Primary (Outdoors).* National Association for the Education of Young Children, 1987 and 1988.

These two booklets can be a handy reference on indoor and outdoor spaces for directors who need something to share with parents, boards members or funders.

Program Management

Child Welfare League of America. *Guide for Establishing and Operating Day Care Centers for Young Children.* Revised 1991.

This booklet provides a brief and concise overview of essential information in the areas of licensing, budgeting, housing and equiping, staffing, and dealing with health and safety issues for those who are responsible for operating a child care center.

Program Development and Curriculum

Boyer, E. L. *Ready to Learn: A Mandate for the Nation.* The Carnegie Foundation for the Advancement of Teaching, 1991.

This report is about all the nation's children and how we can be sure that all of them are ready for school.

Bredekamp, Sue (ed.). *Developmentally Appropriate Practice in Early Childhood Programs Serving Children from Birth through Age 8.* Washington, D.C.: NAEYC.

This book is intended to explain the position of NAEYC on what is developmentally appropriate practice birth through age eight. It will help teachers, directors, parents, and board members better understand sound practice which should reverse the current trend toward formal academics for young children.

Cohen, Dorothy H. and Virginia Stern, with Nancy Balaban. *Observing and Recording the Behavior of Young Children* (3rd ed.). New York: Teachers College Press, 1983.

A classic text for learning about children through observation. It includes material applicable to infants and toddlers and children with special needs.

Feeney, Stephanie, Doris Christensen, and Eva Moravcik. *Who Am I In the Lives of Children?* (4th ed.). Merrill (an imprint of Macmillan), 1991.

A particular strength of this book is the practical discussion of guidelines, strategies, and suggestions for coping with many of the troublesome parts of teaching. These authors are primarily concerned with the development of thoughtful teachers.

Gordon, Ann Miles and Kathryn Williams Browne. *Beginnings and Beyond: Foundations in Early Childhood Education* (3rd edition). Albany, N.Y.: Delmar, 1993.

A comprehensive text covering many of the traditional questions which are of interest to early childhood educators including: What Is The Field of Early Childhood? Who Is the Young Child? Who Are the Teachers of the Young Child? What Is the Setting? What Is Being Taught? and How Do We Teach for Tomorrow?

Hendrick, Joanne. *The Whole Child* (5th ed.). Merrill (an imprint of Macmillan), 1992.

This excellent book assumes that the function of education is to care for the whole child. Recommendations for curriculum are based on the assumption that children develop in stages, and that teachers can assist growth by offering age-appropriate and challenging classroom experiences.

Kamii, Constance, M. Manning, G. Manning (eds.). *Early Literacy: A Constructivist Foundation for Whole Language.* NAEYC, 1991.

The purpose of this book is to consider early literacy education and whole-language from the perspective of constructivist theory and research. It is meant to enable whole-language advocates to improve upon their beliefs and practices about how children acquire knowledge.

Phillips, D. A. (ed.). *Quality in Child Care: What Does Research Tell Us?* NAEYC, 1987.

The research reported in this volume reflects the full range of quality child care available. Together, the contributions to this monograph illustrate the value of pursuing answers to the question, "What is high quality child care?" if we are ever to make this goal a reality for children.

Read, Katherine, Pat Gardner, and Barbara Mahler. *Early Childhood Programs: Human Relations and Learning* (9th ed.). Harcourt, Brace, Jovanovich, 1993.

No director's library should be without this time tested book now in its ninth edition. Play is emphasized as the most important mode of learning for young children, and there is a major focus on understanding and guiding children's personality development. The authors point out the importance of a trusting, close relationship between the child and the teacher.

Rogers, C. S. and Janet K. Sawyers. *Play in the Lives of Children.* NAEYC, 1988.

This book reviews what is known about the intricacies of children's play. Based on that information, it offers suggestions for teachers and program directors to use to encourage children's playful living and learning at home and at school.

Diversity/Anti-Biased Curriculum

Child Welfare League of America. *Cultural Competence Self-Assessment Instrument.* 1993.

This self-assessment instrument will assist an agency in identifying strengths and weaknesses in its' response to a culturally diverse staff and client population, and will enable the agency to develop action steps for specific management and/or service delivery changes to progress toward the goal of cultural competence.

Derman-Sparks, L. and the A.B.C. Task Force. *Anti-Bias Curriculum: Tools for Empowering Young Children.* NAEYC, 1989.

Teachers can use principles and methodology from this book to create an anti-bias curriculum in relation to the specific groups of children and families in their settings.

Gonzalez-Mena, J. *Multicultural Issues in Child Care.* Mayfield, 1993.

This booklet is a companion to Louise Derman-Sparks' *Anti-Bias Curriculum* (see above). This author takes off from where Derman-Sparks stopped. Derman-Sparks' focus is on an anti-bias approach to preschool curriculum; the focus here is on an anti-bias approach to cultural information, adult relations, and conflicts in goals, values, expectations, and child-rearing practices.

Neugebauer, B. (ed.). *Alike and Different: Exploring Our Humanity with Young Children* (Revised Edition). NAEYC, 1992.

This is a collection of essays which will help teachers integrate children with special needs and children from diverse backgrounds, and make programs better for everyone.

Saracho, O. N. and B. Spodek (eds.). *Understanding the Multicultural Experience in Early Childhood Education*. NAEYC, 1983.

This book incorporates the contributions of professionals concerned with the education of children from various cultural and ethnic groups. It presents different interpretations of the functions and consequences of early childhood education and its impact upon people of different cultural groups.

Tobin, J. J., David Wu, and Dana Davidson. *Preschool in Three Cultures*. Yale University Press, 1989.

This book explains Japanese, Chinese and American preschools from both insiders' and outsiders' points of view. It ends with a comparative discussion of the ways people from each of the three countries conceptualize the purpose of preschools.

Funding

Annual Register of Grant Support. 1993.

A comprehensive guide to various types of grant support, both governmental and private.

It is arranged by broad subject areas and has subject, organizational, geographic, and personnel indexes.

Getting a Grant: How to Write Successful Proposals. 1990.

A general guide to writing proposals, chiefly aimed at gaining funding for programs.

Grants Thesaurus. 1986.

Listing of terms that can be searched by computer in the *Grants* database.

Grasty, William K. and Kenneth G. Steinkopf. *Successful Fundraising: A Handbook for Proven Strategies and Techniques.* 1982.

A guide to fundraising for organizations.

Lauffer, Armand. *Grantsmanship and FundRaising.* 1984.

How-to guide on finding funding and writing proposals.

National Databook, 7th edition, 2 volumes. 1983.

A listing of grantmaking foundations in the United States. Chiefly of use in seeking grants for groups or projects.

The Foundation Directory. 1993.

Nonprofit, non-governmental organizations with resources of one million or more, or those making grants of $500,000 or more per year. Covers both grants to individual grant seekers and grants to organizations. Excellent index by subject field.

The Foundation Grants Index. 1993.

Funding interests of major foundations by subject area, geographic focus, types of support, and types of organizations which received grants in the past.

INDEX